ALL THE PRESIDENTS' CHILDREN

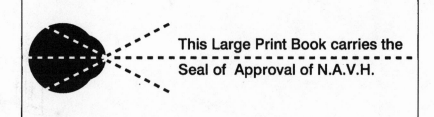

This Large Print Book carries the
Seal of Approval of N.A.V.H.

All the
Presidents'
Children

Triumph and Tragedy
in the Lives of
America's First Families

Doug Wead

Thorndike Press • Waterville, Maine

Thorndike Press® Large Print Nonfiction Series.

The tree indicium is a trademark of Thorndike Press.

The text of this Large Print edition is unabridged.
Other aspects of the book may vary from the original edition.

Set in 16 pt. Plantin by Al Chase.

Printed in the United States on permanent paper.

Library of Congress Cataloging-in-Publication Data

Wead, Doug.
   All the presidents' children : triumph and tragedy in the lives
of America's first families / Doug Wead.
      p. cm.
   Originally published: New York : Atria Books, 2003.
   Includes bibliographical references.
   ISBN 0-7862-5593-5 (lg. print : hc : alk. paper)
   1. Children of presidents — United States — History.
   2. Children of presidents — United States — Biography.
   3. Presidents — United States — Family relationships.
   4. Large type books.   I. Title.
E176.45.W43 2003
   973'.086'21—dc21   2003050983

To my children
Shannon, Scott, Joshua, Chloé, Camille

As the Founder/CEO of NAVH, the only national health agency solely devoted to those who, although not totally blind, have an eye disease which could lead to serious visual impairment, I am pleased to recognize Thorndike Press as one of the leading publishers in the large print field.

Founded in 1954 in San Francisco to prepare large print textbooks for partially seeing children, NAVH became the pioneer and standard setting agency in the preparation of large type.

Today, those publishers who meet our standards carry the prestigious "Seal of Approval" indicating high quality large print. We are delighted that Thorndike Press is one of the publishers whose titles meet these standards. We are also pleased to recognize the significant contribution Thorndike Press is making in this important and growing field.

Lorraine H. Marchi, L.H.D.
Founder/CEO
NAVH

CONTENTS

PREFACE

*"One of the worst things in the world
is being the child of a President.
It's a terrible life they lead."*
— FRANKLIN DELANO ROOSEVELT

Shortly after the 1988 election I sat with my
boss, George W. Bush, in his office at campaign
headquarters on Fourteenth Street only three
blocks from the White House. As a liaison to co-
alitions during the campaign I had learned to
read the various moods of George W. as we
called him. His father had just won the presidency and, in a few days, the whole tedious and
cumbersome business of a presidential transi-
tion would be charging into high gear.

"So what happens now?" he asked, leaning
back in his chair and kicking his feet up on the
desk. It was a rhetorical question, but it was
nonetheless an unusual moment for a man who
seldom took time for self-reflection. He was not
sticking around Washington; that much had been
settled. He was going back to Texas and a life of
his own.

"Want me to do a paper on presidential children?" I asked.

"Sure," he said. He later told me that he thought no more about it. He certainly did not "commission" a study on presidential children, as some news sources later claimed. I was offering a free memorandum, and he was accepting a free offer. That was all. As part of the campaign staff, I had churned out a thousand pages for his father, why not a few for him?

The forty-four page report was completed within three weeks and it was deeply troubling. Research showed that being related to a president brought more problems than opportunities. There seemed to be higher than average rates of divorce and alcoholism and even premature death. Some presidential children seemed bent on self-destruction.

Within days my 1988 report to George W. Bush, the son of the new president-elect, was secreted away in a confidential file, never intended to see the light of day, but the stories I had found continued to haunt me. The expectations set by the public for presidential children — and by the presidential children themselves — were murderously high. Eleven years after I put away my report, John F. Kennedy, Jr., and his wife disappeared while piloting a plane over the Atlantic. Yet another presidential child had died too soon.

On the bright side, one encountered an expansive oasis in this bleak landscape. Presidential children had written dozens of books, led armies, founded some of America's greatest corporations,

10

helped build some of her finest educational institutions, and worked tirelessly to correct social and political injustice. Lyon Tyler was the president of the College of William and Mary. James Garfield led Williams College in Massachusetts. Helen Taft Manning became dean of Bryn Mawr College when she was only twenty-five years old, and fought tirelessly for the rights of working women. James "Webb" Hayes and Robert Todd Lincoln were among the few exceptions to the curse of the presidential child in business. Both were hugely successful. Hayes founded what eventually became the Union Carbide Corporation. The daughters of Woodrow Wilson battled for woman suffrage and for safer working conditions for female factory workers. There were many great writers, especially in recent years, as evidenced by Margaret Truman's popular murder mysteries, John Eisenhower's critically acclaimed tome, *The Bitter Woods*, and Caroline Kennedy's scholarly, reader-friendly books on the Bill of Rights and the right to privacy.

If premature death took the lives of far too many presidents' children in early American history, that too was changing dramatically. Before the administration of Ulysses S. Grant, a presidential child could expect to die nine years before the general public, notwithstanding the educational and nutritional advantages a presidential child enjoyed. But after the Grant administration, a presidential child would actually outlive the public by six and a half years.

Some of the presidents' children's greatest achievements were in government and politics.

Eight were elected to Congress. Eleven presidents' sons served in cabinet or subcabinet positions in administrations other than their fathers'. Many served ably as ambassadors, such as Charles Francis Adams who, during the Civil War, skillfully negotiated behind the scenes in London to cut off British support to the Confederacy and keep them from entering the war. The poet James Russell Lowell said that not even Grant himself had done the Union a better service than the Adams son, toiling away in his isolation in London. Robert Taft was nominated for the presidency three times at Republican National Conventions. Of course, John Quincy Adams, son of the second president, was elected to the White House himself, as was Benjamin Harrison, the grandson of the ninth American president.

Still, the news was overwhelmingly dark, at least compared to the bright and sunny optimism that permeated the 1988 postelection world of George W. Bush, the new president's firstborn son. When I presented my report he was predictably unimpressed. And I was not surprised. Like Kipling's "man," he tended to be skeptical of news that was either too good or too bad; they were both imposters. I knew very well that my own amazement with the project would be a turnoff. The whole Bush family is understated. George W. cannot be stampeded into anything. The idea of a historical curse would not prompt the slightest curiosity or alarm. History could not easily threaten his life. This was particularly so because his self-esteem was inspired within and through his immediate family. Success was measured in terms of one's moral fiber and sense of duty, not by some material measurement of achievement, or money, or title. Fear normally relates to loss. And the only thing that George W. Bush feared losing was his integrity, and that was in his own hands.

For the most part, my study was irrelevant to him. What happened to other presidential children meant nothing. He was not in the least superstitious. He made only one personal comment during my presentation. It was when I spoke of the eerie similarity between the Franklin Roosevelts and the George Bushes. Both families had five children, four boys and a daughter. Both had an additional child that died young. One Roosevelt went west, just as Neil Bush had done, one went to Florida, like Jeb, where he was elected to office, and finally, FDR, Jr., the first-born and namesake, went home to New York where he ran for governor.

I took great pains to explain that it would all turn out very differently for the Bush family for many reasons. It was discreetly discussed among Bush friends that George W. was planning to return to the family base in Texas to run for governor someday, just as Jeb would run in Florida, and Neil would run in Colorado. Maybe one of them would win.

"What happened to FDR, Jr.?" George W. wanted to know.

"He lost," I said. "In fact, no presidential child has ever been elected governor of a state." He groaned. But six years later, George W. Bush was

13

indeed elected the governor of Texas and in 1998 was reelected, winning 69 percent of the vote in an historic landslide.

It may be that he did not entirely forget the study I submitted to him in 1988. Nine years later, when he was leading in the national presidential preference polls, I asked him what he was going to do. "I'm not going to run," he answered.

"And why not?" I asked, "You are at the head of the pack."

"Because of the girls," he said, referring to his twin daughters. "They would be in college then and it would ruin their lives."

"Did it ruin your life?" I asked.

"No," he paused, "It made my life."

When George W. Bush was finally, narrowly ratified the winner of the 2000 presidential election, he became the first child of a president to win that office since John Quincy Adams, the first "heir apparent" in American history. Remarkably, that was not all he had in common with Mr. John Quincy Adams. Both men were named after their fathers, but with different middle names or, in the case of Bush, differently configured names. And both lost their general election vote total to a candidate from Tennessee — George W. Bush losing to Al Gore but winning in the Electoral College, and John Quincy Adams losing to Andrew Jackson but winning the presidency in the U.S. House of Representatives.

There was a time when George W. Bush was the archetypal presidential son, the heir apparent, headed for disaster, scandal or an early grave, and moving with all the confidence of a sleep-

14

walker. Like many before him, he had the pre-requisite drinking problem. Cousins and family members generously dubbed him "a late bloomer." In 1988 I interviewed his younger brother, Marvin Bush, asking him if any of the new generation had a political future. "Jeb is the serious one," Marvin replied without hesitation. "We have always thought that he would have a public career."

"And what about George?" I asked. After all, he was the elder, the senior Bush of his generation.

"George?" Marvin laughed, "George is the family clown." Marvin was not being entirely disrespectful. It was a reference in part to the role George had assumed after the death of younger sister, Robin, of leukemia at age three. He had become the family cheerleader, his mother once remarked. He had taken on the responsibility of keeping the family's attention diverted.

Notwithstanding how history will eventually judge the presidency of the younger Bush, he is without doubt a renascent phenomenon among presidential children. What made the difference? Was the role of the presidential parents, George and Barbara Bush, significant?

There are some clear reasons why George W. was able to handle the stress that defeats so many other presidents' children, reasons which we will examine in later chapters, but certainly part of the formula was a trusty weapon that he had discovered early in life, and one that he consistently employs to this day. Keep the "expectations" low. Success is relative. It takes the pressure off if they

15

underestimate you. And if there is no pressure at all, well, who knows how far one can go?

On January 20, 2001, George W. Bush was inaugurated the forty-third president of the United States. The family "clown" was now the commander-in-chief, the most powerful man in the world. Even inside the family, brother Marvin had underestimated him, as had political rivals Governor Ann Richards and Vice President Al Gore and others before and after, even though in many cases they had been warned. Just as George W. had helped bring healing to the family in Texas after the tragic loss of Robin long ago, George W. was now bringing healing to the family after the father's national election loss in 1992 to Bill Clinton.

In 1988, while writing my report on presidents' children for George W. Bush, I struggled to find a positive slant to a very dark picture. Despite the cruel examples that preceded them, each new generation of presidents' children has been filled with hope and almost naïve ambition. And so I ended my paper with a number of upbeat stories and references to John Quincy Adams, the son who had become president himself. "Can lightning strike twice in the same place?" I asked, and I closed my forty-four-page paper with the rather smarmy conclusion that "anything is possible." That was 1988 and only twelve years later, indeed, the "impossible" had happened. Lightning had struck. George W. Bush, the president's son, had become the president himself.

ONE

THE CURSE OF THE
HEIRS APPARENT

"Don't you think that it handicaps a boy to be the son of a man like my father, and especially to have the same name? Don't you know there can never be another Theodore Roosevelt?"
— THEODORE ROOSEVELT, JR.

The first son born to an American president, John Quincy Adams, was a great figure in American history. He was one of our most effective secretaries of state, helping to conceive and write the enduring Monroe Doctrine. In 1825 he was inaugurated the sixth president of the United States. There was a sense that the sons of presidents were destined for great things. If they were not to be given power outright, as in the case of the sons of kings, they were certainly in a position to compete for it favorably. But it would be 176 years before another president's son, George W. Bush, would be sworn in as the nation's chief executive and the stories of the first-born sons between these two extraordinary bookends of history are dark indeed.

Many children of high achievers struggle with

17

feelings of abandonment and take more time in life to establish their own separate identity. But this seems especially true for the sons of presidents, particularly those sons who worked for their fathers in the White House, or who were the firstborn, or who bore the same name, sons who were in some way considered to be "in line" for the presidency themselves. It seems that the closer a male child was to the parent, the more likely he would be to self-destruct.

George Washington, who had no biological children, was stepfather to a notorious young man who tried to cheat him on a business deal. The young man died at twenty-seven.

Jefferson's only son died shortly after birth. He was not even given a name. Monroe's only son made it to age two. James Madison's stepson was an alcoholic, gambler, and womanizer, who tried to cheat his own mother after Madison died. Congress had to intervene to help the former first lady.

John Adams II died at thirty-one, William Henry Harrison, Jr., at thirty-five and Andrew Johnson, Jr., at twenty-six. All of them battled alcohol their whole lives.

Andrew Jackson, Jr., died after being shot in a freak hunting accident.

Martin Van Buren, Jr., died young of tuberculosis in a Parisian apartment, his father, the former president, sitting sadly at his bedside.

Marshall Polk, the nephew and ward of President and Mrs. James K. Polk "was thrown out of Georgetown and West Point, and ended his life in prison."

Calvin Coolidge, Jr., died at age sixteen from

septicemia, or blood poisoning. A foot blister had developed after a rigorous day of tennis without socks on the White House courts.

Even those who lived full lives seemed cursed. John Tyler, Jr., was an alcoholic for the last decades of his life. Ulysses S. Grant, Jr., was accused of bribery. Chester A. Arthur, Jr., was a disreputable playboy, whose antics were used by parents as object lessons on how *not* to live one's life. Journalists, suspicious about his endless source of "easy money," were hot on his trail when his father's presidency thankfully came to an end.

Franklin Roosevelt, Jr., the first of two sons to be named after the father, died shortly after his birth. The second namesake, colorful and spunky, married five times and finally was dropped from the New York Social Register. Meanwhile, he so infuriated the powerful Tammany Hall political machine that he was bounced out of political life as well.

Sometimes the heir apparent was just plain unlucky. Theodore Roosevelt, Jr., was a man of enormous integrity. While serving as governor of Puerto Rico he once used $100,000 of his own money to shore up the fragile banking system. He served for a time as the assistant secretary of the Navy, a post that had been a stepping-stone to the White House for his father and one that would later serve the same end for a distant cousin. But it so happened that on his watch the famous Teapot Dome scandal broke, involving Navy land leases, and his innocence in the affair offered little solace for his flagging political career.

Theodore Roosevelt, Jr., was so reckless that his father speculated whether he would ever reach the age of an adult. He was like a man with a death wish. Severely wounded twice in World War One, he was with the first wave of American forces to land in North Africa in World War Two, where he shot and killed a German with his own pistol in hand-to-hand combat on the beach. He was in the first wave to land in Sicily, and in the hardest fighting. He was the only general to land on the Normandy beaches in the first wave on D-Day. Roosevelt hobbled around the sand with his cane, directing forces while bullets whizzed about him. General Omar Bradley called it the single greatest act of bravery in the war. After winning every medal available to ground forces in the American Army, including the Medal of Honor, which was awarded in absentia, Theodore Roosevelt, Jr., died of a heart attack at the "old" age of fifty-six. It is about as good as it gets for a first-born presidential son.

There was another dark mystery woven insidiously throughout the biographies of far too many of these presidential children. When there was confusion over just who the heir apparent might be, the firstborn or the namesake, fate would often take them both. Thus firstborn presidential son George Washington Adams drowned at twenty-eight and his younger brother, John Adams II, namesake to two presidents, died of alcoholism at thirty-one. Likewise, firstborn John "Symmes" Harrison was accused of embezzlement and died in the middle of the scandal at the age of thirty-four and the namesake, William

Henry Harrison, Jr., died an alcoholic at thirty-five.

Remarkably, when this terrible process began, fate would sometimes, greedily, run the table. This happened to Franklin Pierce, who lost all three eldest sons in a row. It happened to Andrew Johnson, as well. Charles Johnson, firstborn presidential son was an alcoholic who died in a horse accident. Robert Johnson, who worked closely in the White House of his president father, died a likely suicide at the age of thirty-five. And younger brother, Andrew Johnson, Jr., the father's namesake, died at a youthful twenty-six. Fate was careful to make sure that the heir apparent, whoever it might be, was properly dispatched.

This is not likely a coincidence of history. Indeed, the research of Kevin Leman and others offer convincing proof that, far from being cursed, the firstborn sons in most families are themselves likely to be high achievers. And yet that dynamic is inverted in the lives of presidential sons. Something is at work here, something that drives these young men to escape through substance abuse or taking unnecessary risks. President George W. Bush, himself, admitted to fighting alcoholism for years. There is a burden that these firstborn, presidential namesakes carry that seems to disqualify many of them before they can even begin. With some exceptions their biographies reveal constant pressure to maintain the pace of the successful parent. They have "the name," or they are next in line and they have to perform. Sometimes the pressure comes from the presidential parent or the public and, when that is neutralized, for example, by an indulging parent and an inattentive public, it blossoms within the child.

Each son has handled this pressure differently. As many as three have opted out of the process altogether and are considered likely suicides. Some escaped through substance abuse. Others were risk takers. Some sought shortcuts to success such as firstborn Russell Benjamin Harrison, who was found to own $500,000 worth of railroad stocks, a suspicious achievement considering his many financial failings before his father's election. And for others the only shortcut was the grave. Considering the dozens of variables in the lives of these children, these early deaths may be the best evidence that on some deep level, beyond the glitter of instant and unearned national celebrity, there is a real and traumatic stress bearing down on presidential namesakes and firstborn sons. Indeed, in our own lifetime, we have seen John F. Kennedy, Jr., the foremost heir apparent of our generation, crash his Piper Saratoga II into the Atlantic and perish at the youthful age of thirty-eight.

There were a number of firstborn sons who defied the odds. Robert Todd Lincoln was the president of the Pullman Palace Car Corporation, the General Motors of its day. Civil War hero Richard Taylor was one of "Lee's generals," and the last Confederate general to surrender east of the Mississippi. Even after the war he became a sometime friend and counselor to presidents. John Eisenhower became a critically acclaimed historian. And of course there are John Quincy Adams and George W. Bush. But these are the few exceptions that only seem to prove the rule.

And then, what happened to John Quincy Adams's firstborn son, George Washington Adams? This young man with the promising name was both the son and grandson of a president. If there is indeed unique trauma experienced by these presidential children — and firstborn namesakes in particular — it would be multiplied in him exponentially. If there are lessons to be learned from the biographies of presidential children, a closer look at the life of George Washington Adams would be a good place to start.

George Washington Adams:
The Next in Line

George Washington Adams was born April 12, 1801, in Berlin, the capital of the Prussian state where his talented father, John Quincy Adams, was serving as the American minister to that country. His presidential grandfather, one of America's founding fathers and already a legend, had left the White House only the previous month. The family joyously welcomed reports of the new son's arrival, heralding yet another generation in a great family of statesmen.

From the beginning the pressure was on. You have not only your honor, little George was often reminded, but that of two preceding generations to sustain. As the head of his house, John Quincy

Adams demanded "perseverance, fortitude, temperance, resolution, industry." The path for his son's life was already neatly laid out for him. He would study and practice law, John Quincy decided, and then pursue a public career. George was simply expected to follow.

But while proud papa, John Quincy Adams, had big plans for his firstborn, he showed little inclination to help them along. From the beginning, his commitment to the good of the country took precedence over his wife and parenthood. Young George Washington Adams lived much of his life separated from his famous parents. The Adamses returned to America when George was only an infant and, soon afterward, his father launched a political career, eventually becoming a United States senator from Massachusetts. When the family was living at home the senator was usually in Washington, and when he moved them all to the infant American capital city, he often found compelling and urgent reasons to return to his constituent base in Massachusetts.

Notwithstanding long separations, the reunions were enthusiastic. Two more children were born to the family. John Adams II, named for his grandfather president, arrived on July 4, 1803, and little brother Charles Francis was born on August 18, 1807. Wife Louisa wrote a revealing letter during these years: "Oh this separation life is not worth having on such terms." According to Louisa, little George "talked of his father incessantly, though he has never forgiven you for your desertion. John calls everybody papa . . . poor little fellow he was too young when you left us to remember you."

The pattern of abandonment worsened in November 1805, when John Quincy and wife, Louisa, returned to Washington together, leaving sons George and John behind with family members. Then followed an even more traumatic separation. In 1809, John Quincy Adams was awarded the prestigious appointment as first minister to Russia. Eight-year-old eldest son, George Washington Adams and little brother John II, were left behind with family and teachers, while the baby, Charles Francis, was taken to Europe with his parents. In Russia, Louisa gave birth to another child, a daughter, who would die within the year and be buried in St. Petersburg.

Despite long and painful separations from their parents, George Washington Adams and his brother, John Adams II, were minutely managed by constant letters — often severe and chastising — from their absentee father. George, especially, was reminded of his educational deficiencies, urged to study Greek and Latin, and directed to prepare himself to be "most beneficial to your country and most useful to mankind." It was a tense atmosphere of high expectations, lonely abandonment, and sometimes a well-intentioned personal rejection, meant to provide motivation. Understandably, George Washington Adams began to develop interests outside the prescribed academic formula laid out by his ambitious and successful father, and dabbled in fiction, poetry, theater, and music, where he found a much-needed respite from the pressure. Occasionally young George showed signs of extraordinary brilliance, such as the time he entered and won a poetry contest; his closest competitor, the future great, Ralph Waldo Emerson.

In fact, young Adams may have been trying to satisfy one of his father's own unfulfilled fantasies. It was an instinct that would come to many presidential children. It was much easier than competing with the presidency itself, a back door device to win fatherly approval. John Quincy loved poetry and the theater and was an avid fan of Shakespeare, even publishing studies on the subject. When complimented on his works, Adams had once told a visitor that "this extension of my fame is more tickling to my vanity than it was to be elected president." But the grandfather, former president John Adams, saw it as an unhealthy diversion for his grandson George, and openly worried about it.

In 1815, with Napoleon Bonaparte's dramatic escape from Elba and his eventual defeat at Waterloo capturing the attention of the world, George W. and John II, were summoned to join their parents in London, where John Quincy would be serving as the new minister to the Court of St. James. They had not seen each other for more than six years and when the boys arrived in London neither John Quincy nor Louisa even recognized their sons. George was now a tall, awkward fourteen-year-old.

During the short time in England and even after the family returned to America, John Quincy grilled his teenage son on a whole range of subjects, hoping to expose any academic weaknesses and awaken the lad to the intellectual mettle he would need to excel. George W. was never able to reach his father's minimal expectations. His self-confidence flagged. He admitted to his mother that he was "shamefully ignorant."

Unsurprisingly, George W.'s most productive public years resulted from his father's immediate, if stern, intervention in his son's education. Convinced that only he could turn the lad around academically, John Quincy Adams himself supervised the tutoring of his firstborn son in preparation for his entrance into Harvard, and then pulled strings to make it happen. For the first time since childhood, George had his own room in the Adams's household. He graduated in 1821, studied law under Daniel Webster, practiced in Boston, and was elected to the Massachusetts State Legislature. Still, despite moments of promise, George was unable to sustain any level of success. According to younger brother Charles, correspondence from father John Quincy to firstborn George W. became increasingly caustic, and the older brother's fear of his ambitious father was "quivering." Having helped George stand, the father seemingly knocked him down again. By the time John Quincy Adams was the president of the United States he was treating his firstborn son, George Washington Adams, as an outcast.

During these troubling years, there were three loves, three slender threads that held together the fragile emotional fabric of the life of young George W. Adams. They were his mother; his beloved, retired presidential grandfather who had befriended him in his adolescence; and a girl, a cousin, by the name of Mary Catherine Hellen. In one way or another, all three threads would break in quick succession.

Louisa Catherine, George W.'s mother, was aware of the harsh demands her husband placed on her children. Concerned and guilty over the neglect of her son, she often exchanged poems and letters with young George. But the demands of her public and private life were overwhelming. In 1817, President Monroe appointed John Quincy Adams as secretary of state, and Louisa became an official state hostess. The following year she took in her sister's three orphaned children. All three cousins would later spell big trouble for the Adams White House. To the bitter disappointment of the first lady, one of the boys became involved with a chambermaid and would end up marrying her. The other boy would be dismissed from Harvard for "licentiousness," but it was the third orphaned cousin, a young beauty with ambition and cunning, who would cause the greatest conflict and pose the most immediate problem.

After moving into the Adams household, Mary Catherine Hellen, niece of John Quincy and Louisa Adams, wasted no time in testing her feminine wiles on her male cousins. Mary moved skillfully from one Adams boy to the next, eventually ensnaring them all. Charles was the first to be smitten. But in 1823, when George Washington Adams visited the family in Washington, spouting his artsy poetry, she dropped poor Charles and turned moonstruck eyes to the eldest Adams son. It was a singular triumph for the hapless George, who may have consistently failed to keep pace with his parents' career path for his life, but who had a charm with people that had eluded both his accomplished father and grandfather. In spite of reservations from his parents, the young couple publicly declared their eternal love and were formally engaged to be married. But it was not to be.

By 1825, John Quincy Adams had become the sixth president of the United States and, while young George W. was often the focus of his father's scorn and open disappointment, he was quite a catch for Mary Catherine Hellen. This was not lost on the president and first lady. She would be marrying the son and grandson of a U.S. president, a young man who was even then serving in the Massachusetts State Legislature. The public, if not the father, saw that the young man had possibilities. The first lady began to campaign actively against the idea of the marriage, whispering to George that his cousin was not worthy of him.

Right on cue, brother John Adams II was expelled from Harvard and came waltzing home to the White House. Cousin Mary Catherine transferred her affections to yet another of the Adams brothers. Watching the spectacle with disgust and no small amount of pain, young Charles pitied his brother John as the next "victim of her art." Meanwhile, George W. was humiliated. His best friend, his mother, had unwittingly helped set the betrayal into motion, pushing him away from his cousin only to see her eagerly captured by his younger brother. Within months, another blow would fall.

John Adams, the second American president, had expressed surprise and not a little disappointment when his son had named his own firstborn after George Washington. John Quincy tried to make up for the slight by naming his second son John Adams II. But in the end, it was not this innocuous decision that bothered grandfather John Adams. His greater concern lay with the stern parenting philosophy of John Quincy. He had come to regret his own harshness and neglect of his children. His first son, the ascendant, multitalented John Quincy Adams, now president, had surely lived up to any fatherly expectations. But another son had died an alcoholic. In his early years as an attorney in Boston, John Adams had "seen the ill effect of fathers who ignored their sons when a little help could have made all the difference." In 1818, perhaps feeling remorseful for his own mistakes, he had reminded John Quincy that "children must not be wholly forgotten in the midst of public duties." George Washington Adams, obviously longing for acceptance, took up the grandfather's extended hand and visited him often.

On Independence Day, July 4, 1826, with his son John Quincy Adams serving as president in the White House and his grandson George Washington Adams a Massachusetts state legislator at his side, John Adams died. It was a great moment for the history books, for Thomas Jefferson had died a few hours earlier on the same day. The whole country broke into celebration at the death of these two great founding fathers on the fiftieth birthday of the nation, seeing it as a clear sign of God's benediction. But George W. had no joy or appreciation for the historical irony. For the grandson longing for acceptance from a male family figure, John Adams was more than an historical icon. He had been a substitute father. The death was a deeply personal loss, a crushing and painful blow. For a long time he sat stunned and grieving at his grandfather's deathbed. He had lost his love, felt misled and betrayed by his mother, and now the last thread had been broken.

Disheartened and indifferent, George W. was voted off the Massachusetts State Legislature the following year. Only a few months later, on a Monday night, February 25, 1828, John Adams II and Mary Catherine Hellen were married in the Elliptical Saloon of the White House. It was a somber moment. Neither the jilted George W. nor the jilted Charles was in attendance.

During those months the life of George Washington Adams began to unravel. He neglected his law practice, acquired numerous debts and descended into an alcoholic stupor. On a surprise visit his mother was shocked to find "disgusting pictures of nature." An alarmed Louisa Adams warned her son that such indulgence would desensitize him to the more normal and "virtuous enjoyments" that one day awaited him in holy matrimony. But George W. was already beyond her reach. That fall his father was defeated in his reelection bid for the White House. The nation had turned to Andrew Jackson. Shortly after the inaugural ceremonies in 1829, with the attention of the nation finally diverted, Adams summoned his firstborn son to Washington for a talk. There were many reasons for George W. to be anxious. The retiring president was openly bitter over his children.

Meetings between father and son were always confrontational. It had become apparent that George "could not shoulder the demands, the cutting humiliations." But there was something even more sinister, more scandalous at stake. George Washington Adams had been living a secret, double life. He had fathered a child by a maid of the family's Boston doctor. It represented a serious social and moral failure for the family and, if made public, it was sure to be amplified by political enemies. Had his presidential father, with the power of the White House available to him, stumbled across this disastrous information? John Quincy, a stern and devout father who still prayed daily, would have been devastated by such news.

Historians have documented the bouts of depression common to the Adams kin. John Adams, the second president, battled depression much of his life, as did his sons Thomas, Charles, and John Quincy. Grandson Charles Francis, as well as his sons, Brooks and Henry, all suffered as well. Henry's wife, Marian Hooper Adams, committed suicide. Likewise, alcoholism ran rampant through the family, from First Lady Abigail Adams's brother, William Smith, to John Quincy's brothers, Charles and Thomas, and his own second son, John II. As he faced the upcoming confrontation with his angry father, George Washington Adams was at the lowest point in his life. "He had failed in every way." The depression so endemic to his family was in full bloom.

As he made plans for the trip from Boston to the nation's capital, George W. Adams began hearing voices and hallucinating. On the stagecoach journey to Provincetown and then on the steamboat trip to New York, which began on April 29, 1829, it was obvious to observers that George was troubled. By the evening, on board the *Benjamin Franklin*, he heard voices from the steamboat's engine room. After attempts to sleep, he got up and demanded to be set ashore. The captain refused, and George wandered away. Moments later, he either jumped or fell overboard. Historians often refer to his death as suicide, but no eyewitnesses actually saw his final, desperate actions. The body was found six weeks later drifting to shore. A coroner's discreet inquest concluded death by drowning.

There is a poignant scene from the diary of John Quincy Adams when, on an earlier Christmas Day, he had gathered his children around him to read aloud Pope's "Messiah." Adams wrote that he was testing the children, "an experiment on [their tastes.]" Not one of the children took the slightest interest except young George, who sat riveted. It is true that George W. Adams had a love for literature and poetry, and it is altogether possible that this alone accounted for his attention. But there is also no question that the little boy so patiently listening to the formal, tedious reading that Christmas Day was a child longing for acceptance and approval from his father.

Some would see the death of George Washington Adams as an obvious suicide message to a remote and severe John Quincy Adams. Suicide has become a more complex subject within the last generation, but "revenge, anger and punishment" directed at the living are still among recognized triggers. If so, it had some limited success. For a time, John Quincy and Louisa became closer than they had ever been. Filled with remorse and regret in their role as parents, they attempted to bond with remaining family members, invoking their faith to offer some solace and guidance.

The secret of George's illegitimate child eventually came to light and was used to blackmail the family. To their credit, the former president and his children refused to pay hush money, despite repeated threats. Eventually, a forty-four-page pamphlet was published; even so, the dignity and honor of the family held.

On October 23, 1834, John Adams II, the brother who had won the hand of the fair maiden, Mary Catherine Hellen, and the son who had worked closest to the father, serving as his personal secretary in the White House, died of alcoholism. He was thirty-one. A bitter Louisa Adams noted that yet another son had been sacrificed on the altar of politics. And so the first two sons of John Quincy Adams died. They were sons and grandsons of presidents, and namesakes of presidents, as well. There would be no third President Adams. The chain was broken, and no chief executive's offspring would ever again be elected president until the year 2000. The curse of the heirs apparent had begun.

The Death of the Harrison Boys:
Political Casualties

Understand that when we talk about the life of the presidential child we are not talking about the four or eight years that the family lives in the White House. William Henry Harrison would serve only thirty days, Zachary Taylor only fourteen months. Rather, we are talking about the *type* of person who seeks the office and gets elected. We are talking about a high achiever, an ambitious congressman, a successful businessman, or a commanding general, ordering armies in the field. Most presidential children are not born in the White House. They are born into the family of a man who is on his way there and a few are born into a family of a man who has already served.

The ninth American president, William Henry Harrison, was a hero to three generations. A great military talent, he defeated the Indians in the Northwest Territory, breaking up a dangerous alliance of tribes in a series of savagely fought pitched battles. It was in a fight along the Tippecanoe creek in the Northwest Territory that Harrison earned his popular and affectionate sobriquet, "Old Tippecanoe." But Harrison was more than a soldier. He was a man of sound judgment. More than once he saved the lives of both settlers and Indians through his patient ne-

35

gotiations. In the end, General Harrison was beloved by his soldiers and trusted by settlers and Indians, alike.

Though he publicly disdained politics, Harrison was able to navigate some pretty treacherous waters for a very long time. Appointed governor of the Northwest Territory under John Adams, he survived in place through the tumultuous change to Thomas Jefferson, continuing to serve in one role or another through numerous administrations that followed. In the War of 1812 jealous politicians in Washington promoted other commanders to key positions, but inevitably General Harrison was needed and called back. He drove the British out of Michigan and Ohio, finally defeating them at the battle of the Thames in Canada. The general, who would maintain a farm in North Bend, Ohio, would serve in Congress, the Senate and as the United States minister to Colombia before becoming the ninth American president.

John Cleves Symmes Harrison, the general's first son, was born on October 28, 1798, and lived most of his life in Vincennes, the capital of the new Indiana Territory. Symmes, as he was known by family and friends, married well, taking as his bride Clarissa Pike, the daughter of General Zebulon Pike, a Colorado politician and explorer, the man who discovered Pike's Peak. Harrison used his connections with the Monroe White House to arrange a job for Symmes in the government land office in Vincennes. It was all the start the young man needed. A man of integrity, with an engaging personality, Symmes became a popular and trusted local figure, elected at a young age as chairman of the borough board of trustees and appointed supervisor of the local library.

In 1819, during his service in the Fifteenth American Congress, General Harrison voted to censure his colleague, General Andrew Jackson, for hanging two British citizens during the Seminole Indian War in Spanish Florida. It was only a question of procedure for the meticulously honest, go-by-the-book Harrison, but it would have deadly political consequences for Symmes and the family. By 1828, the very same Andrew Jackson was president of the United States and arguably the most popular American personage since George Washington. Harrison, who was serving as the American minister to Colombia, was called home, and his son, working in the government land office in Vincennes, was abruptly fired and charged with embezzlement.

At the time, the senior Harrison was the subject of a smear campaign that would grow so fierce and so unreasonable that the backlash would eventually land him in the White House. But in 1829 that prospect would have seemed absurd to the embattled family circling their wagons at their farm in North Bend, Ohio. In his land office job, Symmes had cashed a $5,000 draft on the United States Treasury for a Captain William Prince. There was every reason to believe that it was valid. Prince was an attorney and an army colleague of his father's. But, after the fact, the draft was challenged as "unauthorized." Prince could not recover the funds, so the entire debt, with all its accrued interest, fell on Symmes and his father, who had pledged surety.

Harrison's enemies, including many pro-Jackson newspapers across the country, broadcast the scandal with delight, ignoring many of the facts. Investigations and audits found other smaller amounts of disputed land office claims, and all were laid at the feet of the fired and unfortunate Symmes. By the time the government took its case to court, the Harrisons owed more than $12,000. By all appearances, the family was ruined. On October 30, 1830, with his father at his bedside, thirty-four-year-old John Cleves Symmes Harrison died of typhoid fever.

The death of Symmes Harrison became a hotly debated subject, with anti-Jackson forces lashing out, describing Symmes as a casualty of Jackson's spoils system, and the huge Jackson newspaper machine answering back. Citizen groups in Vincennes, Indiana, voted to wear crepe armbands for thirty days. The *Indiana Gazette* wrote editorials about Symmes and "the goodness, simplicity and honesty of his heart." But none of that brought any solace to the General and his family. Symmes had left behind six "orphan children." Four of them were apparently ill, although there is no record of the nature of their illness or what eventually happened to them. We do know that Harrison was devastated and overwhelmed. In a letter to James Findlay, a close friend, he wrote that "never was a man taken away whose life was more necessary to his family . . ." Beyond the father's heartbreak at losing a firstborn son was the irony of Symmes's likely innocence. Harrison would write bitterly of the "supposed" amount of his son's "defalcation."

William Henry Harrison's own soldiers and their families, disgusted by political revisionist accounts of his battles, formed the base of his political comeback. No one in the country had fought harder for veterans' rights and the rights of their widows and orphans than the general. And so it was that, in 1836, William Henry Harrison found himself as one of several candidates running for the presidency as a member of the emerging Whig Party.

The idea was for the local Whig favorite sons to win their regions, thus denying the Republican-Democrat candidate a majority. It would throw the election into the House of Representatives. Candidates more prestigious than Harrison were vying for votes from their own various regions, including the venerable Daniel Webster and the powerful Henry Clay. But Harrison was popular in the states comprising the old Northwest Territory, and that popularity ran deep. Harrison was almost embarrassed by his candidacy, which was a long shot with no expectation of victory. Nevertheless, when the ballots came in, it was clear that the general had pulled off a bit of an upset, carrying seven states against an experienced, accomplished politician and sitting vice president, Martin Van Buren. There was a sense among many that given a second try General Harrison would win the White House without help from either Webster or Clay. Overnight, once more out of retirement, William Henry Harrison was the man of the hour.

It was during these heady times that all but one of the remaining sons of the general began dying off. William Henry Harrison, Jr., the general's namesake and the heir apparent after the death of Symmes, was the first to go. Born September 3, 1802, Junior had begrudgingly followed his father's career plan for his life, chafing under the long separations at boarding schools and colleges, writing plaintive letters asking to come home. He had eventually married Jane Findlay, daughter of a congressman and a close family friend. For a while, he practiced law in Cincinnati, while whispers about his growing addiction to alcohol spread, and the number of his clients declined.

During the time of Symmes's disaster, with the Harrison family financial crisis reaching critical mass and the general preoccupied with the political attacks raining down on himself and his eldest son, Junior was tapped to take on several family businesses, including the farm in North Bend. It must have provided some limited solace to a youth who had longed to spend more time with his famous father. But while the general wrestled with the Vincennes land office scandal, Junior proceeded to run the family Ohio farm into serious debt. It was the last Harrison asset. The young lawyer, battling alcoholism, maintained a cheerful bravado to the world that may have delayed discovery of the full extent of the damage, but nothing could hold back the flood. Every attempt to solve the problems failed. It was a dark period of family misfortunes. Morosely, Harrison senior openly pined about the failure of his two beloved sons, declaring the "destruction of my hopes."

On February 8, 1838, thirty-five-year-old William Henry Harrison, Jr., died of "alcoholism." A year later, he was followed to the grave by his brother Carter Bassett Harrison, age twenty-seven, and the following year by Benjamin Harrison, age thirty-three. A few months after that, William Henry Harrison was elected the ninth president of the United States. In the three consecutive years leading up to his victory he and his wife had lost three grown sons. First Lady Anna Harrison, in deep mourning, refused to attend the inauguration and would never in her life set foot in Washington, D.C. Thirty days after his inauguration, President Harrison died of pneumonia.

John Fitzgerald Kennedy, Jr.: *The Great Hope*

No firstborn son has captured the nation's attention more than John Fitzgerald Kennedy, Jr. Born weeks after his father's election, "John John," with his quick smile and dark eyes, shown scampering around the Oval Office with sister Caroline, endeared himself both to the fawning media and an obliging public. The scene of toddler John, standing at attention and saluting his father's grave, has become one of the most poignant signatures of American history and culture. In that moment he became one of the nation's most cherished of presidential children.

John F. Kennedy, Jr., was born to a family with a long history of power, money, and controversy.

41

His maternal great-grandfather, John F. "Honey Fitz" Fitzgerald, was a legendary Boston mayor. His colorful, millionaire grandfather, Joseph Kennedy, became ambassador to the United Kingdom and was the ambitious force behind the political success of the family. If the grandfather was not a president, he was certainly a contender from the wings, ready to step on stage if the slightest opportunity presented itself. Already, the deadly process seen in presidential families was under way.

The children, almost all of them, were risk takers on a breathtaking scale. Firstborn and namesake, Joe Kennedy, Jr., groomed for the presidency, was taken early, a casualty of war at the age of twenty-nine. John F. Kennedy, the second son, a consummate politician in public, nevertheless lived a private life that was on the razor's edge, leading to endless speculation and mystery regarding his assassination in 1963. As in the case of the Harrisons, the Pierces and the Andrew Johnsons, three sons were taken before fate was apparently sated. Robert Kennedy was assassinated in 1968, only hours after winning the California primary in his bid to be a second Kennedy president. After the death of three successive heirs apparent, the process stopped just short of the last son, Edward Kennedy, as if intentionally leaving a witness to its terrible power.

Elected in 1960, JFK was the first of many things. He was the first president to have been born after the turn of the twentieth century. He was the first Roman Catholic elected to the nation's highest office, no small feat at the time.

Opposition ran the gamut from fringe groups to the nation's top Protestant pulpits, including the renowned and respected pop ministerial icon, Norman Vincent Peale. Kennedy was the youngest man elected as chief executive, the first president of the space age, and the first to effectively use the powerful new medium of television.

His son, John Jr., born on November 25, 1960, three weeks after the election, was the first child born to a president-elect and the first infant to live in the White House since the administration of Grover Cleveland. JFK's world was ultimately dubbed "Camelot," romantic, youthful, strong, and vigorous, a land of boundless energy and possibilities. And the president, who privately led a scandalous and controversial life, appeared publicly to be devoted to his beautiful wife Jackie and their children.

Obviously, the quest for the presidency and its fulfillment meant enormous stress for the young Kennedy family. Jacqueline instinctively saw the danger. When the campaigning first began and she had to leave Caroline behind, she worried aloud, "I get this terrible feeling that when we leave, she might think that it's because we don't want to be with her."

At 12:30 p.m. on November 22, 1963, America was interrupted by news bulletins from Dallas, Texas. President John F. Kennedy had been assassinated. The American dream that was "Camelot" was gone forever. A grieving First Lady Jacqueline Kennedy reflected, "I should have guessed that it would be too much to ask to grow old with him and see our children grow up together. So now he is a legend when he would have preferred to be a man."

The first letter Lyndon B. Johnson wrote after becoming president was to young John: "It will be many years before you understand fully what a great man your father was. His loss is a deep personal tragedy for all of us."

In the years following the assassination, former First Lady Jacqueline Kennedy married Greek shipping magnate, Aristotle Onassis. John and sister Caroline traveled throughout the world at their mother's side. It was an exotic, freewheeling contrast to the stodgy life lived inside the Boston–Washington corridor but, even then, it was a life overshadowed by the legend of a father, a legend that was only growing with time.

John chafed under the constant protection and supervision of the Onassis-Kennedy public relations machine. When he finally left for private school he announced to friends that he was "Free at last!" But "freedom" in the sense of a normal life was an illusion. He was still followed by bodyguards and hounded by paparazzi. And the freedom to make significant and meaningful career choices was limited. As in the case of George Washington Adams, Francis Grover Cleveland, Steven Ford, and a surprising list of other presidential children, John, Jr., felt drawn to the stage. But when he announced his intention to study acting, Jackie "would have none of it." The theater was beneath him, she insisted, and "would besmirch the legacy his father had bequeathed." Arguments with his mother became heated. According to one story, John put "his fist through a wall." But in the end he seemed to begrudgingly accept the boundaries for his life and fall into line.

After attending Brown University, earning a bachelor's degree in history, and New York University Law School, JFK, Jr., famously flunked the state bar exam not once, but three times. Even in failure, the celebrated son of President Kennedy was cheered. "The hunk that flunked," the tabloids screamed, and *People* magazine put him on the cover, dubbing him the "Sexiest Man Alive." He dated glamorous women, from rock star Madonna to actress Daryl Hannah. But the failures, so publicly broadcast, took their toll.

True to the historical type of a presidential son and namesake, John, Jr., seemed to crave thrills and dangerous risks. His mother forced him to give up flying lessons while at Brown, but he persistently indulged his appetite for living on the edge. He paraglided, flew powered parachutes, kayaked in wilderness areas, and went deep-sea diving. Like both the Kennedys and Bouviers, he was an avid athlete, biking, swimming, rowing, water-skiing and playing football. He worked out nearly every day of his adult life, and it showed.

His name was golden in political circles. If anyone doubted his drawing power, the doubts were laid to rest when he stepped to the podium at the 1988 Democratic National Convention in Atlanta to introduce his "Uncle Ted," Senator Edward Kennedy of Massachusetts. *Time* magazine's Walter Isaacson worried that the roof of the Omni auditorium might collapse "from the sudden drop in air pressure caused by the simultaneous sharp intake of so many thousands of breaths."

Pundits everywhere speculated that John, Jr., was readying himself for a run for office. Instead, he went to work as a prosecutor for the Manhattan district attorney. And suddenly, after a 6–0 record from 1989 to 1993, he resigned. For months he remained coy about his political plans.

In 1995, John F. Kennedy, Jr. launched *George* magazine. Ironically, publishing and journalism had been the early dream of his father before the pull of history and the relentless, ambitious family patriarch Joe Kennedy had directed his life elsewhere. By entering the world of print, the young Kennedy was living out his father's own unfulfilled fantasy. During the many appearances to raise money and publicize the venture, he loved attacking head-on the question on everyone's mind. "I hope someday to be president," he would say slyly, waiting for the crowd to get past the initial shock. Then he would smile and add, "of a very successful publishing venture."

"He grew up with the notion that life has to be lived to the fullest," observed Frank Mankiewicz, a Kennedy family friend. "He didn't shrink or hang back from experience." A 1991 kayaking adventure turned into a near disaster. John, Jr. and several companions were in search of "manageable danger," kayaking in the frigid Baltic near the Aland Archipelago between Sweden and Finland. Early in the trip one of the friends' kayaks capsized. And at the end, confronted with high winds and rough seas, young Kennedy had his paddle blown from his hands as two more kayaks were capsized by a "huge wall of water." Said Kennedy, "We got what we came for: some laughs, some thrills and a few sea stories." But some saw a reckless streak. Veteran kayaker Ralph Diaz, watching John paddle on the Hudson River without a life jacket or any safety equipment, made the prescient observation that one day "this guy is going to get hurt."

On May 19, 1994, former First Lady Jacqueline Bouvier Kennedy Onassis died. With her passing much of the restraining influence on John, Jr., was gone. He almost immediately resumed flying lessons. His sister Caroline appealed to his sense of guilt, invoking their mother's warnings and urging him to honor her wishes, but John persisted and became a pilot. On September 21, 1996, he married Carolyn Bessette in a private ceremony on Cumberland Island, Georgia. She too had begged him to stop flying. He dismissed her admonitions as paranoia and superstition. "Don't worry, I won't take chances."

On the evening of Friday, July 16, 1999, John, Carolyn and her sister Lauren took off aboard his Piper Saratoga II airplane. They were headed to Martha's Vineyard for the wedding of Cousin Rory. At eight-thirty, the estimated arrival time, the plane was nowhere in sight at the small airport. By eleven, the family became very concerned. Ted Kennedy called John and Carolyn's TriBeCa loft to inquire about the flight. A friend whose air-conditioning was broken had been invited by the couple to stay at their place for the weekend. The friend confirmed their takeoff.

The news began spreading. Federal Aviation Administration officials alerted both the Coast Guard and the Air Force Rescuer Coordination Center at Virginia's Langley Air Force Base. Aircraft began searching the area between New York and Massachusetts. Rory's wedding was postponed, of course, as the family waited — along with the nation and the world — and prayed for a miracle. Television networks preempted regularly scheduled programs to cover the search for remains and the wreckage of the Kennedys' aircraft.

On July twenty-first, the plane was brought up from the waters off Martha's Vineyard, ironically within sight of Jackie's historic beachfront estate. The bodies of John, Carolyn, and Lauren were still inside the sunken craft. All three had died upon impact. After autopsies, the bodies were quickly cremated at the request of both the Kennedy and Bessette families.

The outpouring of grief over another fallen Kennedy reached across generational lines. Thousands of people left notes and flowers outside John and Carolyn's apartment. Someone even left a metal sculpture silhouette of a three-year-old John saluting his father's grave, an all-too-poignant reminder of the deaths that have touched the former first family. And in death, as in life, John Kennedy, Jr., was the subject of the same media frenzy that chronicled his every public move and speculated on his private affairs as well.

The National Transportation Safety Board (NTSB) concluded its lengthy investigation, suggesting that Kennedy suffered from spatial disorientation, a condition that arises from a loss of balance in the inner ear and causes confusion. Kennedy's problems were exacerbated by the hazy night sky and his resulting inability to see the horizon. The NTSB said investigators did not find any mechanical problems with Kennedy's plane.

Biographer Christopher Andersen wrote that "He held no high office, wrote no great books, created no masterpieces, performed no heroic feats. He cured nothing, discovered nothing. He didn't have to. From the very beginning, John was America's son."

In her final note to her son John, Jr., before her death, Jacqueline Bouvier Kennedy Onassis had written these words: "You, especially have a place in history." There is not much room for interpreting such a message. She certainly was not making Christopher Andersen's case that the accident of John's birth alone guaranteed him such a place. That was contrary to everything Jackie had taught her children. Nor is it likely that a former first lady, once married to one of the world's richest men, saw her son as finding a place in history as a publisher, even a great one, or even in a public career as a member of the House of Representatives, for example. It is more likely that she shared the same vision that the public so eagerly embraced, namely, that someday, somehow, he would make an attempt to reclaim the White House that had been so violently and unfairly ripped away from the family. Maybe she wanted her words to reassure him that she knew it could happen and that, if it were to happen, she herself had seen it and was there savoring the victory with him and so he would not be alone to sense the vindication, the full circle that life had taken.

Years before Abraham Lincoln's firstborn son, Robert T. Lincoln, faced the same expectations from an adoring public convinced that he could easily win any office he chose. But Lincoln hated politics and he had wisely learned that events which were guaranteed often evaporated when one reached out to take them. John F. Kennedy, Jr., who surely at some level felt the pressures of public expectations, and had his mother's word that he, "especially," had a place in history, knew that such a battle would mean the outing of every secret, every word and every deed, a process whose bitter taste he already knew well. And he knew just how dangerous it would be, far more risky than his kayaking adventures. Lincoln, who had also lost a father to an assassin's bullet, carried a similar concern and befriended the fledgling Pinkerton detective agency, employing them as bodyguards off and on throughout his life.

Shortly after penning her note to her son, Jacqueline Kennedy died. And five years after her passing, John F. Kennedy, Jr., finally an orphan, was gone himself. His place in history, unlike his mother's vision, would be alongside that of dozens of presidents' children before him, those who had been given great names like George Washington Adams, John Adams II, Andrew Johnson, Jr., Calvin Coolidge, Jr., and many others, all burdened by great expectations and all taken to early graves. Fate had not spared young Kennedy this common destiny but it had mercifully taken his mother before him, with her satisfying notions of her son's place in history still intact.

At a memorial service, John's sister Caroline eulogized his brief life with a speech from Shakespeare's *The Tempest*. It was a play that John knew well. He had played the role of Prospero in 1981 during his brief, hopeful foray into acting. "Our revels now are ended," Caroline quoted. "We are such stuff as dreams are made on, and our little life is rounded with a sleep."

TWO

DAUGHTERS SEEKING
FATHER'S APPROVAL

*"Keep my letters and read them at times,
that you may always have present in your mind
those things which will endear you to me . . .
The acquirements which I hope you will
make . . . will render you
more worthy of my love."*
— THOMAS JEFFERSON TO HIS DAUGHTER

If presidential namesakes and firstborn sons experience stress living up to the achievements of their fathers, the challenge for presidential daughters is different and has evolved along with the changing role of women in our society. In early America, there were certainly not the same public expectations for a presidential daughter as for a presidential son. Political ambition was not a consideration. Not only would a daughter be unable to serve in public office, she could not vote. For some time young women were not accepted at schools of higher learning. Many presidential daughters received no education at all. Others were privately tutored, even into the twentieth century. Women were not expected to pursue commercial interests. Initially, many female roles in the theater were played by men, as were many women's parts in early motion pictures. President Martin Van Buren failed to mention his wife's name in his own autobiography.

In earlier years the public expected a presidential daughter to comport herself with dignity and virtue. During the short window of time in the White House she was to serve as an assistant to the first lady and as a White House hostess, when necessary. She was to marry well and be a role model as a loyal wife and prolific mother. She was exempt from the great political discussions of her day, a respected neutral, thus a Letty Tyler could graciously entertain senators who despised the president and Martha Johnson could successfully raise money for White House refurbishment from congressmen who were viciously trying to impeach her father.

Today, public expectations are more complex. A presidential daughter must still be virtuous and marry well, but she must also achieve academically, show career talent, and do it all with a political balance that will not excessively anger women activists at either end of a shifting socio-philosophical debate about just what the role of a woman should be in our society.

All of this ignores what the presidential daughter wants for herself. Some would argue that she should strive for independence through her own personal achievements. But that assumes only a male-oriented view of the world, one that equates success with achieving independence and

53

power over others. Therapists and researchers at the Stone Center for Development Services and Studies at Wellesley College write about a "relational way of being." Many of today's writers suggest that women thrive in relationships and seek use of power "with others, rather than power over others." Thus a presidential son might seek to go his own way, inspired by his father's example, and live his life struggling to compare favorably. "Charles Strozier speculates that the bad blood between Lincoln and his eldest son may be ascribed in part to Oedipal tensions." A daughter, on the other hand, may feel no need to compete, but might rather seek to relate with her father and use whatever power and opportunity the relationship brings to achieve something worthwhile. At least that would be the ideal.

In one crucial respect presidential daughters of today share the same struggle that their predecessors faced, indeed that all daughters face, namely, how to relate to the father figure in her life and, just as importantly, how to obtain his approval. The relationship between a daughter and a father figure is crucial to the healthy psychological development of any young woman, and the need for affirmation continues into adulthood.

This ongoing process is deeply complicated by the White House experience. Everywhere the child turns she sees her father. His words and actions are on the lips of colleagues, teachers, employers, lovers, and spouses. Even after death he will still be there. In a sense he is not only a father figure, he is also a peer, part of the age that the child can never escape. His approval becomes critical to her self-esteem, not only as an infant and toddler when the role of a parent has its greatest impact, but also as an adult, when her life is more influenced by those outside the nuclear family.

Only this powerful dynamic explains the unique relationship between Anna Roosevelt and her father, Franklin Delano Roosevelt, in the last months of his life. Anna, who would eventually marry three times, came "home," helped run the White House, worked on a day-by-day basis with her president father and even accompanied him on his historic trip to Yalta. Incredibly, she carried the burden of dealing with some of the more intimate and painful decisions of her parents during their dysfunctional marriage, running interference for her father's infidelity, for example.

Surely this was not solely out of obligation to him, for she was close to her mother as well and had shared broken moments of terrible anguish with her over some of Franklin's earlier choices. This was more than Anna Roosevelt, the little girl, coming home to seek approval from her father, doing his dirty deeds, knowing how very human and flawed and different from the public image he really was. This was also Anna Roosevelt, the adult woman who had defended her father's administration over cups of coffee with journalist colleagues in editorial rooms across the country, seeking the approval of Franklin Roosevelt, the president, the public persona, an icon of her generation.

The stories of presidential daughters are replete with accounts of their sacrifices to gain fatherly approval and the daughters' anguish to find it unrequited by men who never understood their needs or appreciated their sacrifices. Most of these presidents were alpha male to the core. They saw the whole experience as a great adventure and one that required sacrifices all around, truly a family enterprise. After all, they all had benefited, all had become famous, all had unlimited opportunities. For the most part, these were fathers who never appreciated that, in the end, it was their personal approval and affection, not fame and advancement, that so many of their daughters sought.

Abigail "Nabby" Adams Smith: *A Woman of Silent Tears*

George Washington had no biological children. And so the first presidential child was born to John Adams, the second American president. Born July 14, 1765, Abigail "Nabby" Adams would experience a short life of great pain, lived at the mercy of the men she loved.

For practical reasons, many parents of white colonial America favored baby boys. Young men could grow up to work the fields and protect the family from Indians. One girl in a family was enough. She could sew, cook, and provide for a houseful of boys. A couple's only chance of retirement with dignity lay in producing enough boys to work the land and send back token help to parents growing too old and weak to provide for themselves.

Even beyond gender limits Nabby's life was overshadowed by her revered father John Adams and her mother Abigail, who together were living out an adventure of historic proportions. Abigail had been in her ninth month of pregnancy when the British had imposed the despised Stamp Act on the American colonies. Before the year was out, her father's career and name would be soaring into prominence in the New World. Of her first child, Nabby, Abigail Adams wrote that she was "the dear image of her still dearer Papa." John Adams, the hardworking husband, was, of course, the "dearer."

Compared to the long absences that would be endured by her brothers, Nabby was able to see her "dearer Papa" rather frequently in early childhood. But, when she was nine years old, he left for Philadelphia to serve in the Continental Congress. As father and daughter, they would never again be as close until the week that she died. His name would become a fixture in the thirteen colonies, he would debate and sign the Declaration of Independence, but she would rarely see him. No sooner did he return home, a hero to the family in Massachusetts, than he left for Paris, France, to serve on the reconfigured American Commission at the colorful Court of Louis XVI, taking her younger brother John Quincy Adams with him.

On the verge of becoming a teenager, Nabby was withdrawn, shy, easily dominated. "Much of her authentic personality was repressed by resentment and anxiety over the expectations placed upon her." Her mother's unrelenting demands for excellence "sometimes obscured her affection," and Nabby responded by becoming excessively "self-critical." Her father had always tried to see the positive in her personality, once bragging about her in a letter saying she had discovered a "remarkable modesty, discretion, and reserve." But words could not change the fact that he was often gone and, as much as she longed to hear from him, his well-meant letters almost always served to "put more pressure on her." The following year she broke out of the Adamses' bubble, leaving her mother for a joyous, extended stay with friends.

In the summer of 1779 her father surprised the family by returning to America with son John Quincy in tow. His assignment in Paris was at an end, he announced to a delighted Abigail; he hoped to stay at home, revive his law practice, and spend time with the children. Nabby was fourteen. She would finally have her father, a national hero to all her friends and neighbors, under the same roof. But it was not to be. Within days, a new assignment came from Congress, and Adams was back to Europe, this time with his indispensable son, John Quincy Adams, and the second son, Charles. Nabby, his firstborn, was left behind again.

Life on the farm in Braintree, Massachusetts, was a marathon in the summer. Work began at sunrise and did not stop until darkness. Not only was the man of the house gone, his two oldest sons were with him. There was work to be done. While hired hands likely ran the farm, Nabby and the youngest Adams, Thomas Boylston, had to carry their load. Winters were lonely and fierce, the farmstead often buried in snow and isolated for days on end. In a rare moment of frankness, the reticent girl wrote a cousin, expressing her longing for a life with her father.

Nabby was seventeen years old when the young Boston lawyer, Royall Tyler, came to town. Described by some historians as "classically tall, dark and handsome," Tyler was almost too good to be true. He was valedictorian of his Harvard class, "witty and well read." His father was wealthy. Tyler spent long hours with Nabby, talking by the Adams's fireplace. Mother Abigail was "nearly as charmed" as the daughter. But when gossip brought stories of scandal about the young man's earlier years, including a report of an illegitimate child, Abigail began to grow concerned. She passed her misgivings on to her husband, and he responded with characteristic decisiveness and possessiveness.

"I don't like the subject at all," he said of Royall Tyler. And then he added, with a note of jealousy, that he didn't appreciate Tyler's style of "courting mothers." It may have seemed invasive to Nabby. A father who was never there for her was now arbitrarily denying her happiness with anyone else. But Adams had high expectations for his daughter, and so great was her love and respect for her celebrated, absent father that simply upon his word the relationship with Royall Tyler cooled, for a time.

There soon followed a series of sad and ironic misunderstandings that were to leave Nabby in suspended emotional pain for the next years of her life. When John Adams's own investigations seemed to prove the young Royall Tyler quite acceptable and he realized how deeply his daughter loved the young lawyer, he proposed that the two give their love a test. Daughter and mother should join him in Europe. The Revolutionary War was at an end, and there was word that if the final negotiations in Paris went well, John Adams would be assigned to London, where he would serve as the first American minister to the Court of St. James. If the love survived a brief separation, he promised he would give his consent.

By this time, Royall and Nabby were informally engaged and privately inseparable. The panicked daughter, perhaps seeing her love slipping out of her grasp, broke with her uncharacteristic shyness to plead with her mother for the marriage. If the feelings were passed on to the father in France, there was no reply. In June 1784, a brokenhearted Miss Adams and her dashing fiancé, Royall Tyler, bid farewell. After tearful embraces, with both of them vowing eternal love and promising to endure John Adams's trial separation, Nabby obediently joined her mother, boarded the *Active*, and set sail for Europe. It would be a lonely voyage.

Only days later, Royall Tyler received a letter from an understanding and repentant John Adams, offering his permission for the marriage. It was dated April of that same year, two months before they sailed. A similar letter arrived at the Adams's homestead in Braintree, Massachusetts, addressed to his wife, Abigail. It was dated January but it too had arrived too late to influence events. Abigail and daughter were sailing to Europe.

Nabby surely experienced mixed emotions during her time away. Her letters to friends in Massachusetts reveal her joy at having her father, her hero, back in her life for the first time since childhood. Younger brother John Quincy, fluent in French, could show her the sights of Paris. There were glamorous dinners with Benjamin Franklin and Thomas Jefferson, both already world famous men and, of course, there was Versailles and the magical, if ill-fated, court of Louis XVI and Marie Antoinette. In 1793, the royal couple would be publicly beheaded at the spot of today's Place de la Concorde.

True to her promises, Nabby faithfully wrote to Royall Tyler almost daily, but after exchanging a few letters the correspondence began to dry up. Soon, none of her long letters were answered. By some accounts, the young woman was in anguish and, by others, she was relieved. Tyler would later insist that he had never stopped writing and had, in fact, received nothing in return. He had been stunned, he would declare, and his heart had been broken when she had broken off the engagement and asked for the return of her letters. Nabby would probably never know the truth about her suitor, whose efforts to win her hand had become famous in the little village and among the family. Had she lost Tyler through a misunderstanding? Or was he only dissembling, not wanting to offend the daughter of such a great man? For young Abigail, either alternative was painful.

An eighteenth-century painting of Nabby suggests a sophisticated beauty, but art from the time can be deceptive. For centuries, artists routinely favored their subjects. Four hundred years before, Henry VIII was fooled by a portrait of poor Anne of Cleves. The artist had brushed out her disfigurement from smallpox. This illustration is instructive, for as a young child the Adamses' firstborn suffered severely from the smallpox. Her mother, Abigail, had written John Adams, away at the Continental Congress, that every part of her body was covered, and that "Nabby has enough of the smallpox for all the family beside." The portrait by Mather Brown shows a beautiful girl with what appears to be heavy makeup — uncommon for the family — and soulful eyes.

On June 12, 1786, in a modest ceremony in London, England, Abigail "Nabby" Adams married Colonel William Stephens Smith, the handsome secretary of the American Legation. Smith had once served with distinction in George Washington's Continental Army, and John Adams, perhaps sensitive to the pain his daughter had endured over his earlier meddling, pronounced himself pleased. Wife Abigail was more philosophical. When writing to her son John Quincy about the relationship, she quoted Shakespeare, "A heart agitated with the remains of a former passion is most susceptible to a new one." And the night before the wedding, Abigail dreamed of Royall Tyler and "found herself feeling sorry for him." Royall Tyler would channel his pain into writing two popular plays that became huge national hits. *The Contrast*, produced in 1787, was the first theatrical work of "an American author to be performed in the United States." His law career would flourish, and he would eventually become the chief justice of the Vermont Supreme Court.

Nabby would have four children with husband William Smith, three sons before she would finally get the daughter for which she had longed. But John Adams's expectations notwithstanding, the gallant colonel turned out to be a disastrous disappointment. Smith was too fond of alcohol and was a spendthrift who pursued almost any get-rich-quick scheme. His sons were passed on to nearby relatives to keep them away from his corrupting influences. And so she, who had been abandoned by her father for much of her life, would find herself abandoned by her husband as well, with her own children unable to ease her loneliness.

In an earlier description of her daughter, Abigail had written that her difficulties "silently wear upon her spirits and produce many a silent tear." But twice, the shy and silent daughter reached out to her father, pouring out her shame and pain to him in letters that were intercepted by her mother Abigail. She feared the news would upset John Adams and scolded her daughter for adding further to her poor father's burdens.

After returning to America, William Smith would disappear for months on end, speculating in land in the West, or Europe, or involving himself in bizarre mercenary operations far from home, including a plot to overthrow the government of Venezuela. He tried his hand at running a farm, but the family was soon reduced to poverty. At the end of his life he traded on his famous, presidential father-in-law to get elected to one term in the U.S. Congress, but destroyed that great opportunity by his outrageous support of the British during the War of 1812. He is severely dismissed by historians as "having failed at nearly everything he tried."

Nabby Adams's three younger brothers would experience dramatically different lives. John Quincy would become the sixth president of the United States, arguably the greatest presidential child in American history. Thomas Boylston, the baby of the family, would be described by historians as "a very ordinary man." It is the middle brother, Charles, who would typify the tragedy of presidential children.

During the ongoing struggles of his life Charles befriended his discredited brother-in-law, Colonel Smith, and often sought out his stoic, suffering sister for emotional support. But by 1797 he had abandoned his own wife and children, sunk into poverty and severe alcoholism. For a time the family had remained in denial about the severity of the crisis. Charles had been entrusted with the life savings of his renowned brother, John Quincy, and asked to find investments, but the money was soon gone. His disgusted father eventually renounced him. Charles Adams died in the fall of 1800, the exact cause unknown, although some historians make the claim that he died of cirrhosis of the liver. He was thirty years old.

In October 1810, Nabby returned to the Adamses' household for help. She had discovered a "hardness" in her breast, and the doctors were insisting that she be operated on at once. Her father, now a former president and an ailing seventy-five-year-old, who had just suffered an accident, was in retirement at the old homestead. Wife Abigail was tending to his needs. As John Adams lay helplessly in the next bedroom, surgeons performed a mastectomy on his forty-six-year-old daughter. There was no anesthetic. The agony was intense. When Adams spoke of it later, he himself was the focus of the story, saying that he was "living in the Book of Job." The four attending doctors told him that they had never seen a patient show such courage. Nabby Adams knew how to suffer.

The family was pleasantly pleased by her apparent recovery and her subsequent announcement that she wished to stay with her parents to convalesce. But in July 1812, her husband, Colonel Smith, arrived suddenly to claim her. Nabby was promptly deposited in Smith's minimal accommodations in "a remote area" of New York and abandoned again as her husband parlayed his "patriotic" credentials into a run for the U.S. Congress.

Within a year cancer was spreading through Nabby's emaciated body. Abigail learned the news from Colonel Smith's sister, along with her daughter's plaintive, pitiful plea that her only wish was to die "in her father's house." She was rushed by carriage from upstate New York in what must have been an excruciatingly painful, fifteen-day, three hundred-mile trip back into the arms of her parents. Two of her children, John and Caroline, accompanied her. Her absent husband rushed back from Washington, D.C., to be at her deathbed. Dignified and circumspect to the end, Nabby suffered without complaint as her body, doubled up in agony, shrank to skin and bones. Her mother could not watch, but John Adams was there at her side every day and throughout the night, struggling to match his daughter's strength.

Just before sunrise on Sunday, August 15, 1813, Nabby alerted the family that she was dying. She called for a hymnal and with her last strength began to sing, "Longing for Heaven." The family gathered nearby, including Abigail, who had not been able to enter her daughter's room for any length of time. The whole family tried to sing but soon broke into sobbing. And so ended the life of Abigail "Nabby" Adams, the first child born to an American president. She passed without public notice or fanfare. Abandoned throughout much of her life, she died in a house filled with parents, children, husband, and friends. Longing for a relationship with her famous presidential father, he was there at her side almost every hour of the last four days of her life. She was forty-eight years old. Her mother Abigail remembered the moment as "the most trying affliction" she had ever been called upon to endure. A heartbroken father described her death "release" as the most "magnanimous" he had ever seen.

Letitia "Letty" Tyler Semple:
A Battle with a First Lady

John Tyler, the tenth American president, was the father of fifteen children, eight born to his first wife, Letitia Christian Tyler, and seven born to his second wife, Julia Gardiner Tyler. All fifteen children lived remarkable lives, some of which are told in later chapters. One was a soldier of fortune who fought in Germany; another was a United States congressman. There was the typical alcoholic son who died young, even a John Tyler, Jr., who was addicted to alcohol and who lived up to "the curse of the juniors" with his many frustrations in life. There was a farmer, a daughter married in a White House wedding, several soldiers, and a president of the College of William and Mary.

But the life of the fourth child, Letitia "Letty" Tyler Semple, illustrates well how the White House can transform the most private, elegant, and dignified person into an object of public curiosity, and how the failed expectations of that same public can destroy even the strongest personality.

Letty, named after her beautiful mother, was stunning in her own right. She was born May 11, 1821. Her father, John Tyler, had already served in Congress and was elected governor of Virginia when she was four. Tyler hailed from a proud, aristocratic Virginia family, and his first wife, Letitia Christian, brought even more social prominence and wealth to the union. Although

Tyler's political career often strained the family's finances, they managed to maintain several sprawling Virginia plantations and, for retirement, purchased yet another. Young Letitia grew up on one of these large estates, with servants and slaves to attend her every need. In February 1839, she married James A. Semple, "the nephew and heir" of a Williamsburg judge.

From the beginning, Letty sensed that something was wrong with her husband. Semple would eventually serve as "paymaster" in both "the United States and Confederate navies." But brief references to him in letters and diaries suggest that he suffered deep-seated emotional problems. Not until later in life did any of these manifest themselves openly. In any case, Letty was dealing with this mystery and its attendant frustration when she received yet another blow.

Letitia Christian Tyler, her mother, experienced a paralytic stroke. In addition to dealing with an unpredictable, unbalanced, troublesome husband, Letty would now have to assume more responsibility for the growing brood of younger brothers and sisters. Two years later, her father would be elected vice president of the United States. Thirty days after that, William Henry Harrison would die of pneumonia, and John Tyler would be president.

The Tylers were accustomed to being the center of attention, socially prominent and politically viable. Northern candidates had been making the pilgrimage to Virginia for years, seeking out Tyler as a potential running mate who could deliver rich Southern electoral votes.

But the family was momentarily shocked by their father's sudden rise, the blow to their mother's physical health, and the disrupting move to Washington. Letty and another married sister vowed to stay behind to live their own lives with their husbands in Virginia. And yet their invalid mother, the new first lady, could not possibly assume her duties. She was moved into a second floor White House apartment, and there she would stay, reading her Bible and knitting clothes for her children, coming downstairs only once before her death in 1842.

For the first two years the role of White House hostess and the job of running the cumbersome machinery of the executive mansion fell to Priscilla, the wife of firstborn Robert Tyler. This daughter-in-law had been a Shakespearean actress, which in this case served her well, for she would be stepping into one of the nation's leading female roles. A mere four years earlier she had been bathing in "the muddy Delaware" and eating "potatoes and bacon." Then Robert Tyler had seen her onstage and was smitten. But Priscilla could do more than put on a good act. She was judicious enough to seek out the incomparable former first lady, Dolley Madison, then in her seventies, but still experienced and wise enough to help guide a willing student. In time, the workload overwhelmed Priscilla, and the younger children in the family needed help, so the call went out to Letty.

It was probably with a sense of relief that Letty left her husband behind in Williamsburg and rushed to her beloved mother's side. Letty was invaluable at the White House, stepping in to help Priscilla until the work overwhelmed them both and demanded yet another daughter, eighteen-year-old Elizabeth "Lizzie" Tyler.

As it turned out, the eighteen-year-old Lizzie would be of little help. In fact, she would soon be adding immeasurably to the workload at the White House. The story of her wedding to a young man on her father's staff is told in a later chapter. It was the one event that roused the invalid mother, who was helped downstairs from her apartment where, according to Priscilla, "she was more attractive to me in her appearance and bearing than any other lady in the room." Eight months after Lizzie's wedding, Letitia Christian Tyler, wife of President John Tyler, was dead.

The president was "crushed by grief," and daughter Letty was heartbroken. In a sense, she had needed her mother as much as the invalid mother had needed her. For years Letty's marriage had been a torment. She had no children to comfort her. Mercifully, her father had arranged for her husband, James Semple, to be packed off to sea as a purser in the U.S. Navy. It had made life easier, but also lonelier. Now, she had lost her mother as well. Robert and Priscilla Tyler announced that they would soon be moving to Philadelphia to a life of their own. Thus, the entire workload of the family and the White House would soon fall on the shoulders of the family's new surrogate mother, Letitia Tyler Semple. There was but one consolation. She would have her father, the fifty-two-year-old president, to herself. They could console each other. He would be her anchor, for he had been the one and only constant in her life.

And so the stage was set for the arrival of Julia Gardiner, a flirtatious, twenty-two-year-old New York social butterfly, full of confidence, who, within weeks, would become the "undisputed darling of the capital." Although she hailed from a wealthy and socially prominent family, Julia was susceptible to flattery, especially when it came to questions of her own beauty. Only three years before, she had posed in an advertisement for a New York department store, Bogert and Mecamly, where she was referred to as "The Long Island Rose," and where she hawked their products. Her parents and their friends were mortified, but Julia, whose beautiful face was soon famous and brought smiles to the men of the city, was unrepentant.

In December 1842, only three months after the death of the first lady, the David Gardiner family arrived in Washington, D.C. for the annual fall social season. Julia had made an impression the year before and, by some accounts, could have had her pick of the eligible bachelors. "The Long Island Rose" obviously delighted in the game and often gave every impression that she wanted them all.

The White House was still in mourning and was not hosting great events, so the Gardiners entertained the city themselves from the parlor of their boardinghouse. Because of the money and social prominence of their name, a long queue of Washington's elite paid their respects. Daniel Webster, the sitting secretary of state, along with his wife, came on more than one occasion. Congressman James Roosevelt and many other colleagues from the Hill visited. Julia was enjoying herself immensely, "I had more than half the beaux in the room surrounding me all the while." And it was not only a delighted Julia who noticed the sensation she was causing. A flattering article in the *New York Herald* commented on the social scene, describing Julia as "one of the loveliest women in the United States."

The visit of Senator James Buchanan of Pennsylvania caused a stir, for he was a wealthy bachelor, rumored to be a future president. But when Julia learned he was an ancient fifty-year-old, she promptly lost interest. Congressman Richard Davis pursued her ardently and showed such deference that the twenty-two-year-old Julia became amused, commenting that "one would think he was addressing a Goddess." But he never had a chance. He, too, was an "ancient," weighing in at forty years of age. Julia referred to him behind his back as "Old Davis." Francis Pickens, a congressman from South Carolina, would formally ask for her hand in marriage and, by the following year, Julia Gardiner would find herself pursued by Supreme Court Justice John McLean.

It was inevitable that all the commotion about young Julia Gardiner would reach the ears of the White House. In December, both Robert Tyler and John Tyler, Jr., would stop by the Gardiner parlor to pay their respects. John, Jr., had lived with his wife, Martha Rochelle, only a few months after their wedding before temporarily separating, and so considered himself very much in the game. On Christmas Eve, the whole Gardiner family was invited to the White House for dinner, where John Tyler, Jr., ignoring the fact that he was still legally married, pursued Julia to the point of embarrassment.

At a White House reception weeks later Julia waited with her escort in the long receiving line, fretting over the fear that the president wouldn't remember her. As in the case of most people who meet a president, she had not at first seen the man, but rather felt the ambience of the White House and was instantly impressed by the office of the presidency, with all the power and glamour associated with it. But, as in the case of most people who had met Julia Gardiner, the president had indeed seen the woman. He remembered her well. Five months after the death of his wife, the courtship was on.

At a White House reception in February 1843, America's fifty-two-year-old President John Tyler launched his romantic campaign by pulling Julia Gardiner away from the crowd, giving her a private tour of the candlelit White House, and formally asking for her hand in marriage. A surprised Julia instinctively blurted out, "No, no, no," shaking her head so forcefully with each answer that her tasseled Greek cap slapped the president's face. But it didn't take long for Julia to see beyond their difference in ages. As word spread of the president's romance, Julia and her family were overwhelmed by the national attention. Before leaving the city, the Gardiners had an informal understanding with the president.

They were obviously flattered, but Julia would need a little time to sort out her feelings. Throughout the summer the president sent love letters to New York.

Later, an "official" version of the story suggested that John Tyler and Julia Gardiner had fallen in love through a tragic accident. The following February the Gardiners had been among three hundred guests of the president onboard the U.S.S. *Princeton* for a cruise down the Potomac. "The Peacemaker," the world's largest naval gun, was fired several times, but when the ship passed Mt. Vernon the guests suggested one more shot in tribute to George Washington. This time the big gun "exploded at the breech" and, in the process, killed eight persons, including David Gardiner, Julia's father. Julia supposedly fainted into the president's arms. So persuasive was this version of the story that it appears in some history books today.

David Gardiner was indeed killed in the accident and according to a newspaper account, Julia did indeed faint. If she did not immediately faint in John Tyler's arms, the president did gallantly carry her across the gangplank to shore. But the romance had been on for almost a year. The tragic events onboard the U.S.S. *Princeton* served only to crystallize the thoughts of a frightened young lady. John Tyler was already being called a lame-duck president. He had managed to anger both viable political parties, but he was still the most powerful and prominent man Julia Gardiner had ever known. There was still almost a year left to his presidency, and he had a new plantation in Virginia where she could raise a family and entertain with dignity. Tormented by the loss of her father, Julia Gardiner began to have feelings of fear and vulnerability. Marriage with fifty-four-year-old John Tyler offered the security she needed. Within a few weeks of the tragedy she signaled the president that she was ready.

On June 26, 1844, with a discretion and secretiveness that would be the envy of any modern presidency, John Tyler and Julia Gardiner were married at the Church of the Ascension on Fifth Avenue in New York City. The nation was at first stunned and then thrilled and delighted by the surprising news. Gossip about the event and their courtship spread from one drawing room to the next. On their slow return south to Washington, D.C., Julia bragged to her mother, "Wherever we stopped, wherever we went, crowds of people outstripping one another came to gaze at the President's bride."

Tyler's sons had no problem with their father's clandestine wedding. Indeed, since John Tyler, Jr., the president's secretary and the only family member to accompany his father on the secret trip to New York, had once attempted to woo Julia himself, he likely considered his father a lucky man. But Letty Tyler Semple and all the other Tyler daughters were "outraged" and felt openly betrayed. Of course, they had known of their father's infatuation for Julia Gardiner, but they were hoping that, as time passed, their father would see the folly of such a relationship. Mary Tyler Jones, the president's firstborn, was actually five years older than her new stepmother. Letty especially had felt confident that there would be ample warning before any marriage plans could be made. She had been through one White House wedding and knew what work was involved. But there was more. As acting White House hostess, Letty was making decisions and long-range plans that necessarily involved the president's approval. Keeping Letty in the dark required a deception on the president's part that must have wounded her deeply. Eventually, slowly, the other daughters came to accept their father's new wife, but Letty, who instantly despised her new stepmother, kept up a "quiet vendetta."

It must have been painful and puzzling for Letty to see the nation so obviously entranced by the new first lady. Her own ideas and plans for the remaining months of the Tyler presidency were thrown out the window. Julia used her own money to refurbish a run-down, shabby White House that brought raves from all who visited and who compared it to the previous year when Letty had presided. A helpful reporter volunteered himself as the first lady's new press agent, referring to Julia in print as "the Lovely Lady Presidentress." Her new style openly "mimicked the court of Louis Philippe of France," with Julia, herself, seated on an elevated platform with twelve ladies in waiting, dressed alike, surrounding her. She enjoyed picnics in Rock Creek with a beautiful Italian greyhound prancing about for ambience.

Actually, most in the media privately ridiculed

the first lady's outrageous pretensions and, at first, this spilled out onto their pages. John Quincy Adams wrote that "Tyler and his bride are the laughing stock of this city." But she was such good copy, and the Tylers were on their way out anyway, what harm could she do to the presidency in a few brief months? And the first lady was so energetic, so resourceful, that some of the most cynical critics were reluctantly seduced by her enthusiasm. It was Julia Gardiner who adapted the words of "Hail to the Chief" for her presidential husband. The words were taken from Sir Walter Scott's *The Lady of the Lake* and the music by James Sanderson from the popular musical *The Knight of Snowden.*

Nor did Julia easily give up on her intractable stepdaughter, Letty Tyler Semple. She made several efforts to be reconciled, but was rudely rebuffed. It didn't help that the first lady openly basked in the glory of her husband's worship. "The President says I am the best of diplomatists[sic]," she bragged. She introduced the polka at White House balls, a dance considered so outrageous that Tyler had given strict orders to Letty not to allow it.

When the White House magic came to an end, Tyler and his young bride retired to his new plantation in Virginia. He named it Sherwood Forest in a good-natured allusion to his independence and his political outlaw status. On July 12, 1846, David Gardiner Tyler was born to the former president and his bride, thirty years his junior. Six more children would follow. By the time the last child, Pearl Tyler, would be born, the former president would be seventy years old and all of the daughters by his first marriage would be dead, except for the one lone holdout, a still-embittered Letty Tyler Semple. Eventually, the "unreasonable hostility was reciprocated by Julia."

In 1860, momentous national events overwhelmed the feud always simmering between the former first lady and her stepdaughter. Abraham Lincoln was elected president and the South seceded from the nation. As a proud and loyal Virginian, and with great experience as a chief executive, John Tyler was being urged out of retirement to help the new Confederacy. Tyler made an effort to prevent hostilities by calling for a peace conference, but war fever was spreading rapidly.

Meanwhile, James Semple, Letty's husband, was home and had new status as well, his naval experience sorely needed for the Southern war effort. In the summer of 1861, John Tyler was elected to the Confederate Congress. Then, on January 18, 1862, with Lee's Army of Northern Virginia holding the Union at bay, seventy-one-year-old John Tyler, the tenth American president, died. It was an event that went unnoticed in Washington, but the newly formed Confederate government tendered him a state funeral.

Before the war's end, the plantation of John Tyler was virtually destroyed by advancing Union armies. Julia fled north to Long Island to take refuge with the Gardiner family. By 1864, much of the rest of the Tyler clan, including two of Julia's teenage sons, David "Gardie" Gardiner

Tyler and John Alexander "Alex" Tyler, were huddled in the besieged Confederate capital of Richmond where, in the last months of the war, an unlikely leader emerged to rally their spirits. James Semple, Letty's enigmatic husband, took up the challenge, shoring up the family and sending messages north to Julia that he was personally watching out for her rebel soldier sons. Notwithstanding his wife's bitter resentment of the former first lady, Semple arranged for her sons' room and board, helped with their finances and lobbied for their place in the Confederate war machine.

Much has been written about James Semple's activities after the Civil War. There has been the suggestion that he was deranged, that he was fantasizing a role for himself as a figure in a restored Confederate government. There was the suggestion that, in his own mind, he was still fighting the war. In fact, Semple was a conduit for information, traveling to Canada to carry messages to Confederate expatriates who had fled across the border rather than surrender, and who were awaiting orders from Confederate government officials who had likewise fled abroad. In the process of his clandestine work, he carried messages from former first lady, Julia, to Varina Davis, wife of Jefferson Davis, and helped lead a propaganda effort to get the former Confederate president released from prison. Meanwhile, from his isolation, Davis managed to commission Semple for special assignments. There was great risk in all of this. Hundreds of thousands had lost their lives during the great Civil War, and bitterness ran just as deep among many of the winners as it did among the losers. James Semple's errands represented a dangerous threat for the whole family. Men were being hung for much less. Semple had two severe nervous breakdowns during these stressful times with moments of irrationality before eventually accepting the Confederate defeat and giving up the cause.

In 1866, Letty Tyler Semple became suspicious of her husband's marathon campaign for the defeated South. When she learned that he was using Julia's New York apartment as a "safe house" on his clandestine trips to the North she was furious. For the final time in their troubled marriage, a disgusted Letty broke off the relationship. Within the year she moved to Baltimore where she eventually opened a private school named the Eclectic Institute.

Julia Gardiner Tyler, the beautiful former first lady, now forty-six years old, who had been Letty's rival for her presidential father's affection twenty-two years before, took in Letty's husband, James Semple. Julia "nursed him, worried about him and gave him shelter." For his part, James Semple professed his love to Julia, like so many others before him. Back on his feet in 1866 he wrote her a love letter, "You are good, I know, and beautiful to my eyes, but you are not mine!! My love you know you have taken, one day share my lot . . . my Sister darling."

Julia, never one to ignore a flirtation, answered back provocatively. "It is so sweet to be caressed when the heart finds little difficulty in responding that I will forgive you the mere expressions of a letter and reproach only myself for suffering their influence to be so agreeable and soothing." She later added suggestively that "if necessary Cestorus himself must be invoked to stand guard between us . . ." It was inevitable that private rumors about the two would become public.

Julia Gardiner Tyler and James A. Semple stoutly denied that the relationship had been consummated, but Letty was convinced that Julia had seduced her husband only to complete her triumph over a hated stepdaughter. The public could not decide what had happened and had no desire to probe further. Whatever the facts, one wonders at the lack of discretion of a former first lady who was well aware of how such rumors would hurt a still-embittered Letty. Years before, Julia had been deeply offended by Letty's refusal to stand when she came into a room at the Sherwood Forest plantation. She was, after all, her stepmother and the former first lady, even if they were practically the same age. How could one so proper and so sensitive to protocol have missed the obvious tawdriness that any kind of relationship with James A. Semple would represent? Regardless of what Semple had done for the Southern cause or for Julia's own sons, there were more acceptable opportunities to express gratitude.

Letty fought back, suing her stepmother over family portraits, including one of her father, John Tyler, taken from the Sherwood Forest plantation. If she could not get her father back while he was alive, then she would snatch his portrait from the first lady's wall. But she was no match for the

81

talented and wily Julia, still a darling of the media. Even President Grant invited her back to the White House for a state dinner, giving her the place of honor.

On July 10, 1889, in a hotel room only a few doors down the hall from where her husband had died almost thirty years before, the former first lady, Julia Gardiner Tyler, suffered a stroke. A few hours later "The Long Island Rose" was dead at the age of sixty-nine.

Letty Tyler Semple took little satisfaction in outliving her despised stepmother. She had no children and, to the very end, was convinced that her bitter enemy, Julia Gardiner Tyler, had stolen the affections of her father, her husband, and a naïve, gullible public. On December 28, 1907, at the age of eighty-six, Letitia "Letty" Tyler Semple finally died. She was a president's daughter who had once served as the White House hostess, but she passed from the scene without comment or notice.

Alice Lee Roosevelt Longworth: *"Washington's Other Monument"*

She founded no school, built no hospital, never ran for office, feared public speaking, her book was a great disappointment, and yet Alice Lee Roosevelt Longworth, the first child born to President Theodore Roosevelt, is one of the most popular of presidential children. Her cousin, columnist Joseph Alsop, referred to her as "Washington's other monument." A biographer described her as the "first female American celebrity of the twentieth century." She was the February 7, 1927 cover story for *Time* magazine. Not many people have had a color named after them, "Alice Blue," nor been the subject of a best-selling song. Her acid commentary on the rich and famous delighted and amused the public for four generations. Considered controversial, even borderline delinquent to conservatives of an earlier generation, she lived long enough to see society embrace her right to her own individuality and even somewhat to embrace her mores. But popular as she may have been, eventually a favorite of Washington society, Alice Roosevelt Longworth is viewed by many historians as a woman who lived in great pain with suppressed rage.

Unlike most presidential children, the fame of Alice Roosevelt Longworth had a long shelf life. If most public figures earned respect by what they accomplished, Alice captured the nation by her flagrant exhibitionism and by what she said. A journalist once described her as having "fearless eyes," but it was her fearless tongue that frightened powerful politicians and delighted the average citizen.

Alice was seventeen years old when reports came that William McKinley had been assassinated and her vice presidential father would be moving his family into the White House. She shrieked, let out a war whoop and started dancing on the front lawn. In an interview with journalist Sally Quinn, she described the moment as "utter rapture." Alice's candor and beauty were an irresistible combination to the

American press, who dutifully passed on their infatuation to the American people. The media dubbed her "Princess Alice." Within days, people all over the country were talking about her clothes, her antics and did you hear what she said today? On inauguration day, 1905, when she began exuberantly to wave to friends in the crowd, her father pouted, "Alice, this is MY inauguration."

She was a shameless flirt, smoked cigarettes in public (at a time when a lady didn't smoke), and scandalized conservative matrons when she was seen driving an automobile with Nicholas Longworth as a passenger, before their engagement and without a chaperone in sight. When her father laid down the law that no daughter of his would smoke under his roof, she climbed to the rooftop of the White House to smoke in defiance, *on top* of his roof. "I can either run the country or attend to Alice," he told author Owen Wister, "but I cannot possibly do both." And yet there was still a little girl in there somewhere. Alice carried a blue macaw named Eli Yale and a pet garter snake named Emily Spinach.

After her society debut in 1902, the newspapers constantly speculated on her romantic links with dozens of Washington's most eligible men. One enterprising journalist estimated that in two years she had attended 407 dances, 350 balls, and 680 teas. TR complained that his daughter slept in till "well after noon." She was the toast of the Vanderbilts and Harrimans at Newport, where her father was despised by many as a traitor to his class. One of her rumored suitors was Congressman Nicholas Longworth of Ohio. It was a suggestion that was confidently dismissed by her brothers and sisters; after all, he was fifteen years her senior. But if her siblings had been more observant, they would have already noticed that Alice had a distinct preference for older men. She had once rejected an offer to dance from one of her cousin Franklin's friends, telling him pointedly that she preferred "older men like Rough Riders." Much later, reflecting on her life, she acknowledged the lifelong preference. It was, she said, "a father complex coming out, presumably."

On February 17, 1906, Alice Roosevelt married Congressman Nicholas Longworth in one of the most celebrated and famous weddings in American history. The full story is told in Chapter 10, but suffice it to say that it was a huge event for the nation, with front-page coverage across the country. Alice concluded, almost immediately, that her marriage to Nick was a mistake. Within the small-town Washington community Longworth had a reputation as a notorious philanderer and alcoholic, tendencies that would not be curbed by marriage to the president's famous daughter. For the moment, divorce was out of the question, and within a few years her unstoppable father would be attempting a quixotic comeback attempt that she wouldn't spoil. When Alice was forty-one, the marriage produced a daughter, Paulina. She would be an only child and Nicholas would dote on her, but his relationship with Alice did not improve.

Within time, while divorce was always an ever-present possibility, their marriage took on a mutually acceptable openness. They arrived at parties together but left separately. A visitor to Nicholas Longworth's office reached out to take a cigarette from an ornate box, only to discover to his embarrassment that it was filled with condoms. William "Fishbait" Miller, famous doorkeeper of the House of Representatives, described Longworth as one "of the greatest womanizers in history on Capitol Hill."

Even during these gloomy years Alice sparkled. Her congressman husband was elected Speaker of the House, and Alice Longworth became a social leader in the capital, a role that would survive countless presidents. By one reckoning, she would average 2.7 White House dinners a year for more than sixty years, meeting with every American president from Benjamin Harrison to Jimmy Carter. Her father and husband both died, but her status continued remarkably unchanged. She was no longer the daughter of a president or the wife of a congressman, just Alice Lee Roosevelt Longworth, but that was enough to keep the media intrigued.

It was not what she did or even who she was that commanded center stage. Over her lifetime, the city began filling up with presidential sons and daughters. Rather it was *what* she said that made her feared and popular. There is one thing politicians fear more than bad polls, lack of name recognition, or even scandal, all of which can be overcome, and that is ridicule. It was Alice Roosevelt's most powerful weapon. Her needlepoint pillow, usually displayed prominently on a sofa in her lounge, became famous for the expression stitched boldly: "If you haven't anything good to say about anyone, come and sit by me."

She said that President Warren G. Harding "wasn't a bad man, just a slob." Calvin Coolidge, she observed, looked like he had been weaned on a pickle. Of Herbert Hoover she said, "The Hoover vacuum cleaner is more exciting than the president. But, of course, it's electric." Republican presidential nominee Wendell Willkie, whose spin doctors portrayed as "the common man," was one "who sprang from the grass roots of the country clubs of America." Thomas Dewey, with his black, slicked-back hair and thin mustache, reminded Alice of the little plastic groom on a wedding cake. Her cousin, Franklin Delano Roosevelt, was "one part Eleanor and three parts mush." When FDR sought a third term, Alice cracked, "I'd rather vote for Hitler." Her constant ridicule of Franklin and Eleanor finally prompted an angry president to blackball her from all White House events. But she would outlive them all and would continue to be invited back into those marble halls long after they had passed on.

Senator Joe McCarthy, before the fall, when his word struck terror in town, called her by her first name only to be rebuked. "You will not call me Alice," she told him. "The truckman, the trashman and the policeman on the block may call me Alice but you may not."

When Lyndon Johnson teased her, saying that he couldn't kiss her because her big hat got in the way, she shot back, "But that's why I wear it, Mr.

President." No one was immune, nothing was sacred, especially the high and mighty. "There's been nothing like the Kennedys since the Bonapartes," she suggested. And later, after Jackie Kennedy's second marriage, she told a reporter, "I like Jackie very much, but I've always wondered what on earth made her marry Onassis. He's a repulsive character. He reminds me of Mr. Punch . . . Jack was so attractive." When the public began to learn of Franklin Roosevelt's affair with Lucy Mercer, she supposedly remarked that Franklin "deserved a good time, he was married to Eleanor."

Behind the public bravado that was sometimes amusing, sometimes cruel, a bitter seam ran through the life of Alice Roosevelt Longworth. Two days after her birth on February 12, 1884, her grandmother, a mere forty-nine years old, died of typhoid fever. A few hours later, in another room in the same house, her twenty-two-year-old mother died of Bright's disease and childbirth complications. A stunned Theodore Roosevelt, who had raced home from meetings in Albany, rushed from one room to the other, declaring that there was a curse on the house. Alice was an infant in a crib, unable to participate in the gruesome events, and yet it would be the defining moment of her life for, in a sense, she would also be losing her father as well.

For Theodore Roosevelt, the grief was beyond endurance. He would give his baby, Alice, to his maiden sister and in the summer head out for the Dakota Badlands to mourn, to hunt, to struggle with the elements as he struggled with his soul.

Theodore Roosevelt would only see his newborn daughter sporadically for the next two years.

There is some disagreement about the extent of the childhood trauma to Alice Roosevelt, if any at all. John A. Gable, executive director at the Theodore Roosevelt Association, points out that no father in those times would raise a baby without a woman's help and that TR was famous for his attention to his children. One could further argue that it was a common practice for prominent families to send their children away to boarding schools, while in fact Alice was tutored at home. S. L. Carson, onetime chairman of the White House Conference on Presidential Children, suggested that Roosevelt's sister, who cared for baby Alice, "was so crippled as to be unable to pick up or really hug the child." But the Theodore Roosevelt Society denies this, saying that there are pictures of the aunt holding the baby. Still, if historians are divided about the extent of Alice's pain, psychologists are unanimous in saying Theodore Roosevelt's firstborn is the virtual poster child of an abandoned baby. One pointed out that laymen often misunderstand the meaning of "abandoned" as a psychological term. It certainly does not have to mean that the child was unloved or economically deprived or that the abandonment was unnatural for the times and circumstances. Nor does it mean that the child was unable to achieve greatness. Winston Churchill was a famous "abandoned child," raised by a succession of nannies. Alice would live longer than any other presidential child in American history, making it hard to prove that she was the victim of unreasonable emotional and mental stress.

Still, her early life experiences seem to offer clues to the bitter elements that make her such a fascinating study to historians. Staff members at the Theodore Roosevelt Association are quick to point to a letter from TR to his sister, written in 1884, revealing his deepest feelings for baby Alice. "I hope Mousiekins will be very cunning. I shall dearly love her." Although curiously, even this example raises questions, for the father was speaking of his love of Alice in a future tense, as if it were something he had yet to do.

When Theodore Roosevelt returned to New York in 1886, he reconnected with his childhood sweetheart, Edith Kermit Carow, and they were married that December. The following year the toddler Alice was brought home, but it was an awkward triad. The Roosevelt family soon grew, with brothers and one sister arriving almost annually but Alice Lee, named after her departed mother, may have felt outside the circle. Theodore Roosevelt could not bring himself to say his daughter's name. He referred to her as "baby Lee" and, after the children began to grow, as "Sister," because of "the unspeakable memories associated with her given name." Even nephews and nieces referred to her as "Auntie Sister." It was not an uncommon nickname for the times; FDR referred to his daughter Anna as "Sister." But, coupled with the fact that her mother's name was never mentioned, it is curious. Scrapbooks were plundered, with every picture of Alice Lee, the first wife, removed. Alice Roosevelt grew to imagine that her mother had done something terribly wrong. And her father, infuriatingly, offered no explanation.

Nor was this all an invention of self-pity on the part of a young girl seeking to outmaneuver a stepmother, a rival to her father's affections. From the very beginning the other children in the family recognized "Sister's" vulnerable status. As early as two, Ted, Jr., had picked up on the fact and was teasing her about having a "sweat nurse." Even outsiders noticed the stepmother's treatment of Alice, with Edith usually appearing "brusque, if not harsh." Not that Alice was such an innocent. Her famous pet snake was named after Edith's spinster sister. The snake was more famous than the sister. In Alice's greatest moment, when she was finally the center of attention at her own wedding in the East Room of the White House, with the whole nation watching, not a single bridesmaid with which to compete and with her father at her side, Edith still tried to hurt her. "I want you to know that I am glad to see you leave," she told her stepdaughter. "You have never been anything but trouble."

In his remarkable analysis of presidents' children, S. L. Carson finds a connection for many of Alice's famous, clever public statements. In a birthday interview with a newspaper she had said, "No one must ever touch me. I don't want to be touched. That's probably some psycho thing that I don't understand." Senator McCarthy had tried to put his arm around her before her curt rebuff. Lyndon Johnson had tried to offer her a kiss. The clever and contemptuous repartee of

Alice Roosevelt may have sometimes been less political than personally defensive. The best-selling author of *The Drama of the Gifted Child* writes that expressions of contempt are a "defense against unwanted feelings" and, above all, "against the rage that one's parents were not available."

Some have argued that the hedonism and outrageous behavior of Alice Lee Roosevelt Longworth was a cry for attention from her father. And others have thought that it was her way of identifying with a fantasy of her rejected mother, who must have been very bad indeed to deserve such treatment from Theodore. It is likely that her mother, the forgotten Alice Lee, was still often in her mind. "Sister" could relish some small revenge in the fact that she inherited money from the Lees, enough to keep her financially comfortable and, more importantly, independent, throughout a long period of her life. Most agree that there was unresolved anger.

Alice rejected her faith early in adolescence, after reading Darwin's *Evolution of the Species*. She declined confirmation and the family respected her wishes. Yet she clung to her own homemade version of the occult, perhaps picked up from close friendships in the Gypsy community. When her father's rival, President Woodrow Wilson, passed by in an open carriage she crossed her fingers, made the sign of the evil eye and called down an ancient curse, "A murrain on him, a murrain on him, a murrain on him!" When Wilson later suffered a paralytic stroke, Alice reportedly took full credit.

Her relationship with her own daughter was just as complex as any of her other relationships. For many years Alice made no secret of the fact that her president father's approval was beyond reach. "Father doesn't care for me, that is to say one eighth as much as he does for the other children," she once confessed to her diary. And even years later, on reflection, she ventured, "I don't think he had any special affection for me." She was just as sure that her daughter despised her as well. This, she reasoned, was behind Paulina's emotional problems, and the cause of her embarrassing stutter. Her siblings spoke quietly among themselves about Alice's cruel words and treatment of Paulina. It was a bitter point that her presidential father had patently refused to mention his first wife, Alice's mother, in his own autobiography, but then neither did he mention his second wife, Edith. For that matter, Alice didn't mention her own daughter's name in her own book. Slapped by her stepmother's mean-spirited remark at her wedding many years before, Alice could not seem to resist hurting her own daughter the night before her wedding, the abused becoming the abuser. While Paulina was happily making plans for the next day, Alice felt compelled to reveal that her much adored father, Nicholas Longworth, was not really her father after all. She offered no further explanation.

If pain had only made Alice tougher and stronger, it did not seem to provoke the same reaction within daughter Paulina. Alice would see elements of her own life recycled in the life of her child, but at dizzying speed. Paulina and her husband would have their own baby, which they, too, would often abandon for "late night parties" and "heavy drinking sprees." The husband, an alcoholic, would die of cirrhosis of the liver at twenty-eight, and Paulina would die at thirty-one, some in the family suspecting a suicidal mixture of alcohol and barbiturates.

When Joanna Sturm, her granddaughter, came to live with her, a very tentative but visible emotional side seemed to awaken within Alice Longworth. A friend once suggested that for much of her life she was capable of loving only one person, her father, but in later years her granddaughter would become the second. Alice Roosevelt Longworth died of pneumonia on February 20, 1980. If the psychologists are right and she experienced severe trauma as a child and stress as the daughter of a public figure, it had only done justice to Nietzsche and made her even stronger. At ninety-six, she had outlived every other president's child in history.

A Fitting Epilogue for a Grand Lady

Alice Roosevelt's elusive relationship with her father illustrates a theme running throughout the vast majority of these biographies of presidents' children. While all children from every family seek the approval of a father figure, and while that need seems only enhanced when the father happens to be a president, men and women tend to deal with it differently. Young men often seek approval through mimicry and even competition, while young women seek reassurance through a personal relationship. When that "father figure" relationship is missing and cannot even be constructed as a credible fantasy from memories and pieces of a life already lived, the children seem forever scarred.

As you will see in many of these stories, the presidential child seems best able to resolve this when the father is gone and not around to contradict what the child is constructing. It is very possible that this is the unfolding process in the remarkable life of Patti Davis, the daughter of President Ronald Reagan. Her story is filled with conflict and a desire for fatherly approval. As in the story of Alice Lee Roosevelt, there is an older man, although in this case only a brief seduction. In 2001, when the story of congressman Gary Condit and his liaison with a young intern became a major news story, Patti wrote about her own pain when, as a youth, she was lured into a relationship with a teacher at her boarding school, a man who was supposed to have been a trusted authority figure.

As a president's daughter, Patti authored revealing books about her family and took loud, public stands against her father's policies. Of course, any child is free to have his or her own political views, but one could argue that the daughter of a president would be a far better advocate for her cause on the inside. Anyone else could shout objections from the street corner. Perhaps her protests may have been about something more than issues, namely, the need for attention and the desire to be loved and pursued. Come after me, stop me, change my mind. As legitimate and healthy as such feelings may be, Patti Davis may now have some remorse about how this has played out. There is a poignant, very personal scene from these latter, private years in the former president's life that offers a glimpse of this process. Patti Davis tells of visiting his bedside and whispering into her father's ear, "I'm here now. I'm not leaving." When he turned ninety-one she wrote, "I've missed birthdays when 'happy' was still an appropriate word to toss around. I've missed many things; it's the knotted chain I sometimes hear clattering behind me."

As in the case of many presidents' children before her who wandered off the family reservation hoping to be pursued, sometimes becoming a critic, fighting back at the insidious dehumanizing power of a parent who is no longer real but only a legend, Patti Davis now seems to be finding her way back. And not surprisingly, she has begun returning at a moment and time when her father cannot contradict her by what he does or does not do. Patti is finding a sense of peace in the tormented sunset of Ronald Reagan's years with Alzheimer's disease. She writes of "a mysterious sense of contentment," and as she leans toward him, kissing his forehead, "a feeling that we are exactly where we are supposed to be."

In 1974, at the age of ninety, Alice Lee Roosevelt Longworth experienced a similar moment that may have given her a glimmer of such peace. President Richard M. Nixon was giving his emotional farewell to his White House staff. It was an awkward and embarrassing scene, with the whole nation eavesdropping on national television. Nixon had not slept. His face was swollen from weeping. He told his staff that he had been perusing the White House library during the night and that he had found an old volume written by Theodore Roosevelt. He went on to quote Roosevelt's brave poem about "the man in the arena," the man willing to risk failure by trying to do something that others would not even try.

While briefly establishing the context for the famous Roosevelt poem, Nixon alluded to the words the former president had written of his love for his first wife, Alice Lee, and his deep and terrible grief over her loss. Alice Lee Roosevelt Longworth, watching with the nation from her home on Dupont Circle, was at once disgusted and intrigued. Disgusted that a president resigning in scandal would invoke her hallowed father's name, but intrigued by the words her father had written about her mother. She later told friends that not until that moment had she realized how deeply her father had truly loved her mother. And presumably, one would hope, Alice could finally move toward some resolution of her own struggle, toward some small degree of acceptance that he had truly loved her as well.

THREE

UNFULFILLED PROMISES

"It is perhaps as well if not better not to make too favorable calculations in favor of our children in early life for should they fail to meet or come up to them the disappointment will be felt with double the effect it would under different circumstances."
— ZACHARY TAYLOR

Much of the disappointment with presidential sons and much of the controversy regarding their apparent underachievement can be laid at the feet of unrealistic expectations. The public at large, sometimes presidential parents, and often the media and historians drive this phenomenon. A career that would easily impress most people is not enough for a president's child. Thomas Adams, son of the second American president and a Harvard graduate, served as chargé d'affaires for the American legation in the Netherlands at a critical time in America's early history. He was a philosopher, distinguished writer, lawyer, and judge. Yet his achievements were ignored and historians referred to him as "an ordinary man." Two sons of Franklin D. Roosevelt, James and FDR, Jr., were both elected to Congress, but Pulitzer Prize–winner Michael Beschloss describes them as "flaming out at their father's calling," an observation universally shared among historians.

Abraham Van Buren is faulted for his slow advancement in the military, taking five years to move from second lieutenant to first lieutenant and four more years to reach captain, "a slow promotion rate — particularly given his father's political positions of the time." Meanwhile, another FDR son, Elliot Roosevelt, would receive scathing criticism for his quick promotions. Two things are unforgivable for the child of a president — success and failure.

Even a measured career with perfect timing and credibility can be dismissed as undeserved. Fred Grant, presidential son and graduate of West Point, followed in his father's footsteps, eventually earning his star as a general. At one point he would hold the second highest military position in the United States. Making the difficult climb to the top of one of the world's most cumbersome and treacherous bureaucracies is no small feat, and obviously requires patience and political savvy. Even so, when a later president nominated him for secretary of state there was a huge outcry in the national press, suggesting that the whole nation knew he was named only because his father had been president. The Senate agreed and refused to confirm the appointment.

It is likely that presidential children, as in the case of children of the wealthy and famous, experience *dysgradia,* "a syndrome where there is a complete lack of connection between doing and getting." Since money, awards and honors are coming anyway, effort sometimes only interferes with the process. There is no reason for the child to excel. The result may be an extremely talented child performing far below his or her capacity. This can be complicated by one or both of the parents, who try to compensate for neglect, real or imagined. It does not mean that the child necessarily becomes spoiled, although that is clearly the case with some children in the Lincoln and Grant families. Nor does it inevitably lead to arrogance, although that, too, is occasionally a criticism of some presidential children by friends or colleagues. It does mean that all motivation for achievement is muted. Why strive to get something that will come anyway?

This syndrome, as well as the whole crisis of excessive expectations, applies to modern daughters as well as sons. "Children of men in public life," says Lynda Bird Johnson, "somewhat like the children of preachers — learn early in life that people expect them to be adults before they are even adolescents." In 1992, the idea of undeserved rewards was raised when Jackie Kennedy and Hillary Clinton sat down to discuss the joys and challenges of raising children in the White House. Hillary Clinton, with a twelve-year-old daughter, had become the new first lady of the land. As she remembers it, they talked about adults ". . . who cater, or play up, protect or give them all sorts of benefits, whether they earned them or not."

Dysgradia may explain the academic underachievement that characterizes many young male presidential children, the sons of William Howard Taft being obvious exceptions. As the sons of high achievers presidential children tend to go to the finest schools and eventually graduate or go on to earn their law degrees, but not without a struggle. George Washington Adams needed special tutoring to get into Harvard. William Henry Harrison, Jr., earned terrible marks and was constantly urged by his father to do better. Robert Todd Lincoln failed fifteen of his first sixteen entrance exams at Harvard. Birchard Hayes's lack of scholarship embarrassed his father, who sent him to an uncle to help prepare him for college. Webb Hayes was "not a particularly good student." James Roosevelt's academic career was referred to by the *Los Angeles Times* as "unbrilliant." His brother Elliot saved himself the bother by flunking the Harvard entrance exams. It took John F. Kennedy, Jr., several tries to pass his bar exam. Michael Reagan quickly realized that his boarding school could be pushed to the limit because he was the son of celebrities, and they weren't about to let him fail. "I stored away the knowledge that no matter what I did I could get away with it because the school and my parents would clean up the mess after me." George W. Bush once observed, "I was never a great intellectual."

There is another side to dysgradia, perhaps even more demoralizing. Not only do rewards come for the presidential child regardless of effort, but when the child achieves something great, there is no corresponding increase in the flow of opportunities or recognition. Although deserving of military promotion and honors, Teddy Roosevelt, Jr., was often passed over, simply because he was a former president's son. The military brass didn't want to deal with the likely criticism and charges of favoritism.

Education is an even better example, since it has touched almost all presidential children. When the son or daughter of a president is accepted and attends the best academic institution, no one is impressed. It is dismissed as a perk from their successful parents. This even happens to presidential children who have achieved academically before their parent's successes in public life. While an ordinary daughter or son is lauded for "getting into Harvard or Yale or Stanford," it is a given for the presidential child. Indeed, it may add to the pressure as in, "Why are you throwing away your great education and all the opportunity you have had in life just to do what you are doing?" Those who struggle academically merely confirm the public's suspicion that they only got into Harvard in the first place because of their father's name.

No accomplishment is ever enough. George Washington Adams is not seen as a bright, young apprentice to Daniel Webster, newly elected to the Massachusetts legislature, but rather as an underachieving son of an American president. Ron Reagan is not seen as one of the rare talents who made the cut at the Joffrey Ballet, but is rather criticized and even ridiculed for even aspiring to such a goal.

Sometimes a presidential child will win this game of expectations. Robert Todd Lincoln was out of the White House and out of the newspapers while his father was making history, but he later became immensely successful on his own. Rutherford Platt Hayes "was considered unfit for future hard work or hard study," but defied expectations to become one of the founders of the American Library Association and one of the nation's most important figures in the development of its library system. "I will show all that my family's famous name is safe in my keeping," wrote Benjamin Harrison, grandson of a president, who went on to win the White House for himself. And in modern times, George W. Bush has mastered the art of expectations, both politically and internally, refusing to become defensive about political critics who attack his competency, for example. In fact, he uses the attacks to his advantage, ridiculing any invasive personality analysis as so much "psycho-babble."

So ingrained is the idea that presidential children underperform that presidents themselves have not been above fueling the perception. William Henry Harrison warned his namesake to avoid the examples of the sons of public figures in his day. Two were especially notorious — Henry Clay's son, and the controversial John Van Buren, son of the eighth president, whose reputation actually preceded his father's election. As we have seen, Harrison's admonition did little good. William Henry Harrison, Jr., died in poverty at the age of thirty-eight, a hopeless alcoholic. Harry Truman once declared his daughter Margaret "one nice girl and I'm so glad she hasn't turned out like Alice Roosevelt and a couple of the Wilson daughters."

From the earliest days of our republic, the children of presidents were marked by bad reputations, some quite unfairly, others with exaggerated harshness. James Flexner, distinguished authority on the life and times of the first president, describes George Washington's much maligned, scheming stepson as "a monster." So much is expected of a president's children by family and the public that the corresponding odds of disappointment are great, and the criticism tough. It began in George Washington's time, and it is with us today.

John Parke "Jacky" Custis:
George Washington's Stepson

Ironically, George Washington, the father of the nation, was not the father of any children of his own. He married the wealthy widow, Martha Dandridge Custis, who had four children, two of whom died before her later marriage to Washington. A year after the wedding, Martha contracted measles, and some historians, unwilling to fault Washington, have held that this was why the marriage was barren. A more recent theory suggests that Washington had all the signs of a "chromosomal abnormality," referred to as the XYZ syndrome, one of its manifestations being the loss of teeth, another being sterility.

With his marriage to Martha on January 6, 1759, George Washington became the stepfather to two children, Martha Parke "Patsy" Custis, who was almost three, and four-year-old John Parke "Jacky" Custis. Both children were in awe of their new stepfather. Even had he remained a simple tobacco farmer, he would have been a hard act to follow. At six feet two inches tall, he stood head and shoulders above the average Continental soldier, who measured in at an average of five feet five inches.

Jacky, the heir apparent, if Washington had one, is a bitter disappointment to most historians. Described as "indolent and prissy," and "uneducatable [sic]," he married at age eighteen and lived comfortably on his substantial Custis inheritance with no apparent ambition. One of his teachers wrote to Washington, "I must confess to you I never in my life knew a youth so exceedingly indolent, or so surprisingly voluptuous; one would suppose nature had intended him for some Asiatic Prince."

The year after Jacky's marriage, on June 19, 1773, tragedy struck the family. Seventeen-year-old Patsy Custis died in what is presumed to be an epileptic seizure. She had suffered seizures all her life, but on this particular day there was no hint of disaster. As Washington wrote to his mother-in-law, "She rose from dinner about four o'clock in better health and spirits than she appeared to have been in for some time; soon after which she was seized with one of her usual fits, and expired in it, in less than two minutes without uttering a word, a groan, or scarce a sign. . . ."

Washington was devastated. He had loved his stepdaughter as his own and frequently ordered from London wonderful things for her, "two fans; two masks; two bonnets; one stiffened coat of fashionable silk," and every Christmas "one fashionably dressed doll." Of Martha's four children, only her eighteen-year-old son, Jacky, now remained. Already spoiled by his mother, Flexner writes that he soon "ripened into the monster he would become."

In 1775, George Washington was given command of the Continental Army; the Revolutionary War was on. For the next eight years Martha Washington heroically spent her winters by her husband's side, stoically enduring the harsh, dangerous marathon, including the infamous season at Valley Forge, where starvation and death by freezing were all around. Washington's stepson, Jacky, watched the drama comfortably from afar, receiving blow-by-blow accounts in letters from his mother and seeing with his own eyes the transformation of his stepfather from gentleman tobacco farmer to warlord and the most famous and lionized man in the New World. He even named one of his own babies, George Washington Parke Custis. According to one account, a suddenly inspired Jacky was elected to the Virginia State Senate. But if Jacky had a newfound appreciation for the usefulness of his relationship with his stepfather, he showed little desire to emulate his character and integrity. After agreeing to purchase a herd of his stepfather's cattle, he cleverly cheated him on the price and even then delayed payment.

In 1781, with the Revolutionary War reaching its climax, with Washington racing to confront English General Cornwallis in Yorktown, Jacky decided to get in on the action, announcing to family and friends that he was going to be a soldier. He rode to his stepfather's side, was immediately assigned to the general's personal staff and, only days later, caught camp fever, a virulent form of dysentery raging through the ranks. Jacky was transferred away from the battlefield to a nearby aunt's home where he could be nursed back to health. It was to no avail. Writing military instructions in his diary when he received word, George Washington threw down his quill in the middle of a sentence to race to his stepson's side, and Martha and Jacky's wife arrived shortly. But within the hour, John Parke "Jacky" Custis was dead. He was twenty-seven. The nation hardly noticed, but Washington was disconsolate; his Yorktown triumph only mocked his grief.

If Jacky Custis was a conniving opportunist, and clearly a disappointment when compared to his legendary stepfather, it is hard to prove him to be "the monster" that Flexner suggests. It is the expectations we have for the children of great men, especially their firstborn sons, which lead us to judge so harshly.

There is a famous reprise to this story that is of particular note. Jacky Custis was survived by a wife and four small children. After an appropriate time, Jacky's wife remarried, taking her two oldest children with her. The two youngest, Eleanor "Nelly" Parke Custis and George Washington "Wash" Parke Custis, stayed at Mt. Vernon with George and Martha. This was apparently a common practice for the time, and the families remained close and visited often. The other two children may have looked on enviously as their siblings enjoyed the royal court of the first American president. Washington ran his administration, first from New York and later from Philadelphia, with blissful summers on the Potomac at Mount Vernon. By all accounts, the grandparents shamelessly spoiled their two charges, a precedent that would be repeated often by presidential parents, sometimes with disastrous results. Perhaps the busy president and first lady, limited by time, felt guilty and compensated accordingly. In this case, it apparently did neither any harm, for they both stayed at Mt. Vernon, caring for their grandparents until their deaths, both becoming solid citizens.

Nelly married a George Washington nephew, Lawrence Lewis. Their first child, daughter Frances, was born only days before Washington's death. A youthful Wash Custis horrified his grandparents when he began to emulate his irresponsible father. But Wash soon settled down, serving in the military as a commissioned officer and eventually writing *Recollection and Private Memoirs of Washington,* lauded as an "invaluable remembrance of his famous step-grandfather."

Some historians believe that George Washington adopted these step-grandchildren, an idea probably born out of the marketing hype for Wash's book after his death, but no adoption was ever legalized, nor was it apparently ever intended to be. Washington's will states: "And whereas it has always been my intention, since my expectation of having issue has ceased, to consider the grandchildren of my wife in the same light as I do my own relations and to act a friendly part by them, more specially by the two whom we have reared from their earliest infancy, namely, Eleanor Parke Custis and George Washington Parke Custis . . . I give and bequeath to George Washington Parke Custis, the Grandson of my wife and my ward, and to his heirs. . . ."

Wash inherited the bulk of Washington's estate. He built his own mansion on a hill overlooking the Potomac River, just across from the emerging capital city of Washington, D.C. His daughter would eventually marry Robert E. Lee, and the stunning property on Arlington Hill would be known ever after as "Lee's Mansion." At the end of the tumultuous Civil War, the property would be dedicated as the "Arlington National Cemetery."

Andrew Jackson, Jr.:
The Man Who Couldn't Keep His Money

When he toured the country, factory girls would crowd the streets, screaming when they saw him and rushing forward just to touch him. He was the most famous and popular man in Nashville. He lived in a famous Greek Revival Tennessee mansion that would become a museum and the object of pilgrimages by thousands, even years after his death. Its driveway was shaped like a guitar. He had numerous nicknames, one of them being "King." He was the antebellum Elvis — he was Andrew Jackson, "Old Hickory," the Hero of New Orleans, General Jackson, King Andrew the First. Andrew Jackson, Jr., was his very disappointing son.

Andrew Jackson, Jr., was actually a nephew of President Jackson's wife, Rachel, born on December 4, 1808, to Rachel's brother Severn Donelson and his wife, Elizabeth Rucker Donelson. One of a set of twins (his brother being Thomas Jefferson Donelson), Andrew, Jr., was apparently adopted by General Jackson and Rachel for reasons that are unclear. One biographer speculates that his natural mother was ill at the time of the birth, and the family believed that she would be unable to nurse both twins. There is some controversy about the legality of the adoption. According to family oral tradition, the Jacksons received the child three days after his birth, adopting him formally a few weeks later before the Tennessee legislature, but no confirming documentation has ever been found. The Jacksons had no natural children.

If modern historians have doubts, Andrew, Jr.'s, pedigree as a Jackson and as a Donelson was impeccable for early nineteenth-century Tennessee mountain society. Andrew Jackson was already famous by the time Junior was adopted, and the Donelsons were one of the pioneer founding families of what was then considered a "western" state. He was raised at the family plantation, the Hermitage, just outside of Nashville.

Junior's youthful "sibling" and early playmate was a Creek Indian orphan named Lincoya, an irony that is not lost on most historians. General Jackson was one of America's most fearsome Indian fighters, architect of the Indian Removal policy and widely regarded by Native Americans as the man responsible for the "Trail of Tears." The young Lincoya lost his entire family at the Battle of Tallushatchee in 1813, and General Jackson, who came out of the Revolutionary War an orphan, was touched by the plight of the young Creek Indian boy. "He is a Savage [but one] that fortune has thrown into my h[ands] when his own female matrons wanted to k[ill] him because the whole race & family of his [blood] was destroyed. . . ." Andrew Jackson loved the boy, describing an "unusual sympathy for him" and identifying completely with his circumstances, "so much like myself." Lincoya was raised as a son and sent to school with the other boys of the family. But Lincoya would never visit the White House or see his adoptive father elected president. He died, apparently of tuberculosis, on June 1, 1828, just months before Jackson won the presidency. He was sixteen.

If young Andrew was ignorant of his father's heroics, he was quickly initiated on his first trip away from home at the age of five. Accompanying his mother Rachel, Andrew joined General Jackson in New Orleans just after his famous defeat of the British on January 8, 1813. The trip home was one giant parade as town after town along the route, from Louisiana to Tennessee, turned out to fete the Hero of New Orleans. His father had earned the legendary name of Old Hickory on a previous campaign with the Tennessee militia; now he became the stuff of legends and was being promoted all over the nation as a future president. While strategically unimportant, the Battle of New Orleans restored America's honor after the British invasion of the city and the psychological humiliation of the burning of the White House in Washington. From that moment on, Andrew Jackson's travel would come to resemble that of a modern day rock star. If a town knew that he was passing through, it would turn out in force to greet him. This continued for three decades, through his presidency and beyond. While George Washington had generated deep reverence in the American people, Andrew Jackson was the first president to inspire outright hero worship.

Andrew Jackson's loss to John Quincy Adams at the hands of Congress in the election of 1824 — an event that he would declare "the corrupt bargain" — seemed to cause little interruption to Junior's life as a young, carefree Tennessee gentleman. While away at school, fifteen-year-old Andrew had his own horse, a body servant, new suits, a hat, silk hose, and imported kerchiefs. In less than seven months he would run up a tab at the Nashville establishment of a certain Josiah Nicol to the tune of $309, an amount that equaled a reasonable year's income for the average Tennessee family. Perhaps feeling guilty about neglecting his son, General Jackson was patient.

Old Hickory would be swept into the White House in 1828 in a landslide popular vote, but the triumph would be bittersweet. Not only did he lose his "Indian son" Lincoya in June, just months before the election, but the Hero of New Orleans would lose his beloved Rachel only days after his victory.

Rachel had become increasingly devout in her Presbyterian faith in her later years. She rarely left their Hermitage plantation. When the 1828 election results were known in early December, she ventured into Nashville to buy dresses for the White House. It was there that she finally read the sensational accusations of adultery and bigamy that had been leveled against her in the campaign. There had been some discrepancy between the dates of her divorce to a first husband who had disappeared and her later marriage to Jackson, and the political opposition had taken every opportunity to trumpet their own interpretation of events. Rachel went into a mental and physical decline that culminated in her collapse on December 18, 1828. She died four days later and was buried on Christmas Day. Her husband mourned her by gazing at her miniature and reading from her Bible every night for the next seventeen years.

An embittered but triumphant president-elect, Andrew Jackson arrived in Washington on February 11, 1829, refusing to meet with the departing president, John Quincy Adams, blaming him for the attacks on Rachel. Adams returned the favor by not attending the March inauguration. Less than two months later, Adams's son, George Washington Adams, would die of drowning or possible suicide. Arguably, the election of 1828 was the toughest ever for presidential families.

During the White House years, Andrew, Jr., joined his notorious cousin Andrew Jackson Hutchinson in pursuing various ladies about town. Hutchinson, who found himself expelled from one college after another, brought out the wild side in his cousin, and a busy President Jackson was sometimes needed to head off scandal, writing letters of apology to the parents of young ladies. But in 1831 the young playboy was stopped cold by Sarah Yorke, a Quaker beauty from Philadelphia. Andrew proposed, the father approved, and the young couple was married in Philadelphia that November. When Sarah came to the White House, she quickly became Old Hickory's favorite, reading to him from Rachel's Bible each night.

With the coming spring, the president's new daughter-in-law awakened in him a renewed interest in the Hermitage, the great family estate in Tennessee. Hopefully, it would be his joyful preoccupation in his retirement years. But since the death of his beloved Rachel, the Hermitage had fallen into disrepair. Eventually, Junior and Sarah were tapped to take on the assignment. They returned to Tennessee with complete authority to manage the plantation. President Jackson was relieved, convinced that the combination of a solid marriage and delegated responsibilities would have a maturing and refining influence on his only son. But with the increased opportunity, Junior's uncontrollable spending habits quickly manifested themselves on an even grander scale. There soon followed a repeated cycle of mismanagement and debt, followed still by repeated bail-outs from the president father. Within a few months, much of the president's salary was needed to cover the business dealings of the son. Time after time Jackson, Sr., would write letters, offering patient advice on business management principles, or solutions to the competing business deals with cotton and other crops. And time after time reports of mismanagement would come back, along with news of added debts incurred by the incompetence and extravagance of his son.

Even after the White House years, with Jackson on hand to personally take charge, the pattern continued. The father would cover old debts and Junior would incur yet newer ones. In 1840, Old Hickory was asked to return to New Orleans to commemorate the battle that made him famous. Already in his seventies and fatigued from two decades of living with bullets in his body, some from duels of honor over his beloved Rachel, the Old General at first declined. When another series of his son's huge debts came to light, he was assured that backers of the trip would help cover them. Old Hickory roused himself to take the long trip down the Mississippi, nearly dying from a hemorrhage along the way. By sheer will power, the old warrior braved the celebrations, the speeches, and the fireworks. Content with his effort, the failing former president concluded he had finally saved his wayward namesake.

"Recollect my son that I have taken this trip to endeavor to relieve you from present embarrassments, and if I live to realize it I will die contented in the hope that you will never again encumber yourself with debt that may result in the poverty of yourself and the little family I so much Love."

It was a vain hope. Jackson would bail out Junior several more times before his death in 1845. Even though some of the principle creditors were covered by his father's will, Andrew, Jr., inherited the family property. Without any fatherly restraint he only accelerated his reckless spendthrift ways. By 1856, his debt was over forty-eight hundred dollars, a huge sum for the time. The state of Tennessee finally came to his aid by purchasing the Hermitage, and in 1860 invited the younger Jackson and his family to live there, rent free. Andrew did so until his death in 1865. His wife Sarah lived on at the Hermitage until 1888.

The ironies in the life of Andrew Jackson, Jr., are many. His father was known as a brave soldier and general, while Junior had no military career at all. His father was a famed Indian fighter and author of Indian Removal, while Junior grew up with a Creek Indian sibling. The Hero of New Orleans's proudest achievement as president was eliminating the national debt — yet he could never purge his son's private obligations. Finally, Old Hickory was famous for surviving decades while suffering the pain of bullets lodged in his body, one very near his heart. Andrew, Jr., died of lockjaw a short time after accidentally shooting himself in the hand.

John Van Buren:
"Prince John," America's Loveable Rogue

Perhaps no other presidential son had more potential than John Van Buren, second child of America's eighth president. He was a direct, confrontational, and brilliant lawyer, a stirring orator who rose to the top of an emerging political movement, "the barnburners," advocating the greatest moral cause of his century, the absolute and immediate end to slavery. Nevertheless, John Van Buren's notorious gambling, drinking, and womanizing caused him to forfeit much of what should have been a triumphant career. His ability to work and earn large sums of money was surpassed by his reckless speculations and addiction to gambling, leaving him perennially near bankruptcy. Alcohol and long nights soon ravaged his powerful, handsome physique. His great powers of persuasion were wasted on nameless, temporary conquests of the opposite sex. Most tragic of all, his great cause was cheapened and the moral high ground lost by his personal lifestyle. John Van Buren, derisively labeled "Prince John" by hostile journalists for his hobnobbing with European royalty, was for many generations the poster boy for errant sons of great men.

His father, Martin Van Buren, was the New York attorney general when his wife died suddenly of tuberculosis. She was thirty-five. Devastated and in shock over the loss, Martin could scarcely speak of his wife afterward. He closed up the family home and farmed out his four sons to relatives and friends. In 1823, while his father served as United States senator from New York, John Van Buren was "a lively lad of thirteen," living in the Rufus King household while attending school in New York City. Older brother Abraham was at West Point, and the two younger sons were pursuing their education while living with an aunt and family friends.

The career of the father, Martin Van Buren, was an exercise in volatility. He was elected as governor of New York, but resigned to accept Andrew Jackson's appointment as secretary of state. Only two years later he resigned as secretary of state to give Jackson an excuse to reshuffle his divided cabinet and was promptly rewarded with an appointment as minister to Great Britain. Jackson's enemies fought the appointment in the Senate, so Van Buren was called home, only to find himself exalted as Andrew Jackson's running mate and soon as the newly elected vice president.

His sons, ever proud of their father's ascendant career, longed to be with him. Van Buren, knowing he had neglected his family, looked for ways to make amends. While serving as Andrew Jackson's secretary of state, Van Buren invited firstborn Abraham and namesake Martin, Jr., to move in with him in Washington. The youngest son, Smith Van Buren, named after his father's friend, visited frequently. John, too, was allowed to make the trek down from Yale and, later, from Albany, New York, when his father was convinced that the interruption would not impede his studies and preparation for the bar exam.

From the earliest years, the second son, John Van Buren, had been the father's favorite. Some have suggested that it began with a childhood illness, but it must have been much earlier, for Martin Van Buren was then already closer to John than his brothers, and was in a near panic over the possibility of losing him. History does not record the nature of the boy's illness, but the father spent hours at his bedside, watching helplessly as the boy fought for his life. John Van Buren recovered and, perhaps energized by his father's pride, grew to be the most self-confident and robust of all the sons.

By most accounts, John Van Buren outdid his father in every category. While Van Buren, Sr., was a connoisseur of fine liquors and spirits, his son John drank to excess. The father defied the religious convictions of his prudish Dutch Reform background, enjoying an occasional friendly bet on a horse race, while the son became an addicted gambler. The father gloried in his bachelorhood, enjoying the ladies' attention, while the son was labeled a womanizer. John Van Buren was considered a better lawyer, orator and writer than his president father. He was much more attractive to the ladies. In the end, it made him a less electable politician. Concerned by his son's excesses, Martin Van Buren sent him long missives reminding him in the strongest language that the reputation of the family must be upheld.

Rebukes from his father seem to have had little impact on the son. John Van Buren's disarming personality beguiled parent and friend alike. His brothers, who might have chafed living in his shadow, seemed only to be delighted and proud of his antics, and faithfully defended him in public and private. A story published in *The Saturday Evening Post* shortly after the Van Burens left Washington, offers a vignette of the life of the bachelor household and the personality of the roguish second son, John.

During the father's time as vice president, the Van Buren family began to party until daybreak, sleeping later and later into the following day. The vice president finally was publicly embarrassed when, one morning, he was late for his noon assignment to call the U.S. Senate to order. The father called a family meeting and demanded reform, whereupon John, with best intentions, proposed a solution. The one who rose the earliest had the right to pull any late sleeper out of his bed. The good-natured father chuckled at this idea and promptly agreed. A few days later old habits reasserted themselves. John Van Buren spent a typical night with his male friends, drinking and gambling at cards until the sun broke through the windows. Suddenly remembering the new family rule, John called the party to an end, casually walked into his father's bedroom, and announced that morning had come.

"Oh, John! Let me sleep a little longer!" the father begged.

"Not a minute! You remember the bargain!" He carefully rolled up the vice president in his sheets and blankets and pulled the whole bundle off onto the floor. He then headed for his own bedroom for his much needed sleep.

On Inauguration Day, March 4, 1837, on a large wooden platform erected near the east portico of the Capitol, Supreme Court Chief Justice Roger B. Taney administered the oath of office to Martin Van Buren. He had just become the eighth president of the United States. Thousands in the audience never forgot the inspiring ceremony, as tall, dignified President Andrew Jackson passed the baton to his loyal cabinet officer and vice president, Martin Van Buren.

Among the honored guests for the occasion was the irrepressible, sixty-eight-year-old former first lady, Dolley Madison, and she was riveted to a different drama. Immediately after the ceremony, Van Buren's four handsome bachelor sons gathered around the newly inaugurated bachelor president, congratulating each other and their father. And Dolley was watching.

The Van Buren sons had good reason to celebrate. While the presidency meant separation for most first families, it meant unity for the Van Burens, at least for a few precious weeks. For the first time in years the whole family would live together in one house. Firstborn Abraham was appointed to a position as second auditor in the Treasury Department, receiving a government salary while being "loaned" back to the White House to act as his father's secretary.

The White House years were the highlight in the life of Abraham Van Buren. A West Point graduate, Abraham was less ambitious than his outrageous but likable little brother, John. It had taken the West Pointer nine years to advance from lieutenant to captain and, when his father

121

won the presidency, Abe gladly resigned from the army.

John, whose instincts the father trusted, would be used frequently, especially for important diplomatic errands. Sent as the representative to the coronation of Queen Victoria, he carried critical messages to the English foreign secretary. Meanwhile, third son and namesake, Martin, Jr., would stay on to help copy and catalogue the president's private correspondence. At first, his father would pay his son's salary from his own purse, but soon Martin, Jr., would be appointed to a phantom post as clerk in a government land office. Smith Van Buren, who reportedly hated Washington, D.C., returned with John to Albany. But they would both be back often.

After watching the Van Buren sons for a year, Dolley Madison made her move. In 1838, Abraham fell for a matchmaking ploy, every bit as skillful as the Machiavellian political games that Washington politicians took such pride in executing. Dolley brought her charming and cleverly coached cousin, Angelica Singleton, to a White House dinner. Miss Singleton was classically beautiful, and her father was a wealthy South Carolina planter. The president's firstborn son was smitten. Abraham and Angelica were married at Colonel Singleton's lavish plantation in South Carolina. The president, unable to attend, was nonetheless delighted. A powerful family of men finally had a lady.

Abraham and his beautiful, wealthy bride sailed to London for their honeymoon, where, coincidentally, his younger brother, John, was just wrapping up some business of his own. Brash and sanguine as ever, John showed up at his brother's hotel bedroom. The two were both anxious for news, so John sat in a darkened hotel corridor for more than a hour talking through a slightly ajar door to Abe, who was still in bed with his bride.

To the delight of Dolley Madison, Angelica Van Buren returned home to become the official White House hostess, earning a reputation that made the Abraham Van Burens society favorites for the rest of their lives. Their first child, Rebecca, was born in March 1840, but died in the White House only months later. Eventually, they would have three children.

With the spectacular years of the White House behind him, Abraham returned to the military, serving for eighteen years and reaching the rank of lieutenant colonel. At the height of the Mexican War, he was an aide to General Zachary Taylor, who would become the twelfth president. In 1854 Abraham retired, spending his later years working with his brothers, promoting the legacy of their father.

Third son, Martin Van Buren, Jr., was a life in slow motion. While the intrigue and excitement of the political world swarmed around him, he kept his own counsel and found fulfillment in serving his father. On the magical night in 1838 when Dolley Madison brought Angelica Singleton to the White House for dinner with the president and his sons, she also brought her sister, Marion Singleton. There was a daughter to match each of the resident Van Buren sons, but

Martin, Jr., was too shy to have an interest. He left the White House and disappeared with his father into retirement, editing and copying his letters and helping his brothers with the cumbersome work of preparing their father's presidential papers.

At some point after his father's retirement, Martin, Jr., contracted tuberculosis. In 1854, alarmed by his son's declining health, the former president traveled with him to Europe, visiting some of the more glamorous spas and resorts. The father and his namesake spent their last days and hours together in a magnificent Parisian apartment, the charm of which mocked the sad moment of farewell. The son was stoic, showing no signs of self-pity or fear, maintaining to the end the quiet dignity that had marked his life. Except for an occasional tear rolling silently and without apparent emotion down his cheek, Martin, Jr., offered no evidence that he was in pain. On March 19, 1855, Martin Van Buren, Jr., the bachelor third son to the eighth American president, died.

Smith Van Buren, the youngest of the four sons, devoted much of his life to his father, writing his speeches and handling his correspondence. Some writers suggest that he had "lived so long under the shadow of his father's fame and his brother John's brilliance that he underrated his own abilities." He had waited until leaving the White House to marry the wealthy heiress, Ellen King James, working two years as a lawyer before dysgradia sank in, and Smith seemingly lost all ambition for life.

Hoping to inspire his son, the former president talked Smith and Ellen into moving their young family to his famous home, Lindenwald, in upper New York. It was a fitting estate for a former president. Apparently at some point before the senior Van Buren had purchased the property, the great American author Washington Irving had visited and, according to tradition, had walked the grounds, dreaming up the plot for *The Legend of Sleepy Hollow*. Smith and Ellen finally accepted Van Buren's offer, taking up residence at Lindenwald, their four children filling the halls with shouts and laughter. But in a tragic replay of what had happened to Martin Van Buren himself, Ellen died suddenly, leaving her children behind for her husband to raise. Smith would marry again five years later. Ironically, he would marry Henrietta Irving, the niece of the great author, and they would have three more children. With the ghost of Washington Irving, Smith would toil on at Lindenwald, striving to complete the literary projects that his father had started. He would be the last of the sons to die and there would be little note of his passing. Francis Preston Blair, a Kentucky editor-journalist and a friend of Smith Van Buren, once wrote the former president suggesting that Smith was "afraid to display himself lest he [might] disappoint expectations."

The Van Buren sons' devotion for and pride in their father forced the old man out of retirement twice. In 1844, the former president actually garnered the largest number of votes on the first ballot for the nomination at the Democrat National Convention. But it fell short of the needed majority and, on subsequent ballots, the party turned elsewhere. James K. Polk was eventually nominated and elected president. Four years later, over his strenuous protests, the Free Soil Party nominated Van Buren for president once more. As Van Buren had anticipated, he was soundly defeated.

Throughout most of the former president's retirement, the focus was on second son John and his seemingly more viable, promising career. John had received quite an education at the feet of his presidential father. He had helped to negotiate appointments for his father's cabinet, conducted diplomatic errands across Europe, and, in Albany, New York, established a firm political base from which to launch a career.

In the bitter campaign of 1840, with his presidential father going down in defeat to William Henry Harrison, the Whig candidate, son John Van Buren was winning election to the U.S. House of Representatives. While Martin Van Buren and his other sons were packing their bags for the move out of the White House and back to New York, John Van Buren was looking for a boardinghouse room in Washington, D.C. If the father was out, the game was on for the son.

Congressman John Van Buren joined an historic new class of congressmen, including former president John Quincy Adams, coming out of retirement to serve in the U.S. House, and Millard Fillmore, who would eventually be elected the thirteenth president. But the new congressman from Albany, New York, was not in the least intimidated. He was sitting with some of the men who had harassed his father and helped drive him out of office. Empowered by the fact that he was arguing for his father, not for himself, John Van Buren's righteous wrath often flared up on the floor of the House, as he fought old battles. "I will tell the gentleman that, after he and those who act with him shall have passed into that contempt which is their doom, the integrity of Martin Van Buren, and the wisdom of the measures for which he contended, will be fully established." In spite of his preoccupation with his father's legacy, a tendency that diminished his own chances of developing his own identity as a political leader, the man from Albany had no problem holding his own. Thanks to his colorful oratorical skills, his unassailable base of support in his home district, and his increasing voice as the champion of antislavery, John Van Buren represented a potent political threat.

There was one last piece of public relations work to be done. A month after taking his seat in Congress, John Van Buren married Elizabeth Van der Poel, the daughter of his old law professor and friend of his father. The stage was set.

Four years later, after Martin Van Buren's name was briefly floated and rejected as the presidential choice at the Democrat National Convention and James K. Polk was nominated, the former president immediately began working for the party ticket. There were no hard feelings and for good reasons. The elder Van Buren, whose political moves had earned him the sobriquet of "the little magician," had one last gambit to try.

A studied appraisal of the shifting electoral map showed that if Polk could carry New York State, the Democrats could win back the White House. If Van Buren and son could help make that happen, they would be rewarded, and the reward they had in mind might very well propel young John Van Buren on to the presidency.

Part of the former president's plan lay in the illusion that he and his son wanted nothing for themselves. After all, he had already served as the nation's chief executive and his son was just starting his congressional career. They would both loyally use whatever chits came their way to promote another, more viable New Yorker for the president's cabinet, thus enlisting the whole New York party machinery to get the job done. But if it worked, if Polk won and rewarded New York with a national appointment, it would create a critical vacancy somewhere in state government. In the reshuffle, Martin Van Buren would make a modest request for his own son. Van Buren would ask that Congressman John Van Buren be appointed as New York State attorney general. It was a position that the elder Van Buren coveted for his son, not only because it mimicked the path of his own political rise, but because he had concluded that it was the *only* step the son needed before launching a national campaign to the White House. The younger Van Buren need not be elected governor as the father had been. Nor did he need a national cabinet post. In the extensive spoils system of New York politics, the job as attorney general would be the only launching pad he would need.

It had happened before, a son of a president becoming president himself. John was, after all, serving in Congress with the man. With John Van Buren's marriage, a sure antidote to the rumors of his earlier wild life, and with the last pieces of their presidential plan falling into place, it had come to be the happiest year in the former president's life.

The little magician had not lost his touch. In 1844, the Democrat candidate James K. Polk may have lost his own home state, but he did win the national election. His victory in New York proved pivotal. A New Yorker was indeed rewarded with a cabinet appointment and, in the reshuffle, John Van Buren was named the New York attorney general. The plan had worked flawlessly. And yet, the victory was empty. Once more the Van Buren curse asserted itself. John's wife, Elizabeth, died suddenly. As in the case of his father and brother, John Van Buren was left a grieving widower with a child, his political ambition momentarily quenched by his emotional devastation.

John Van Buren's political career would not end with the death of his wife. Throughout the decade he was an articulate champion of abolition, electrifying audiences in the Northern states and in the process, becoming a hero to tens of thousands. Perceived as a national political threat by the opposition party, he became the target of numerous, incessant hate publications that revisited all of his earlier, riotous escapades. As another son of a president, George W. Bush, would observe years later, he inherited all of his father's enemies and only *half* of his friends.

There was a silver lining; the exaggeration and unfairness of the personal attacks provided a backlash of support in his home state. Some historians suggest that he "was repeatedly re-elected to the House of Representatives" but the official *Biographical Directory of the American Congress 1774–1996* indicates that he served only one term. Even his law career sputtered once more into prominence when he represented a defendant in a spectacular, headline-grabbing case, involving infidelities and a great American actor. But clearly the great prize had eluded him. With the death of his wife, bad habits returned, and John Van Buren's health began to fail.

By 1860, the momentous year of Abraham Lincoln's election and the opening salvos of the Civil War, former president Martin Van Buren and his politician son, John, were all but forgotten, lonely figures, public personages still, but supplanted by a parade of more viable and interesting personalities. Twice that year the former president was at his ailing son's bedside, just as he had been when John was a young boy, fighting for his life. This time, too, John Van Buren would recover, but he and his father were alone, with only their memories to comfort them. Both men knew that the dream was over. The opportunity had passed.

In July 1862, the three living sons of Martin Van Buren rushed to his dying bed at Lindenwald. At three a.m. on the morning of July 24, the former president passed away. John Van Buren lived another four years in poor health. Retracing the path taken by his brother, Martin, Jr., he convalesced in posh health resorts across Europe. Then, in the autumn of 1866, John and his only daughter took passage on *The Scotia* for a return voyage to America. He would not survive the trip.

On October 13, 1866, "Prince John" Van Buren died of kidney failure in the middle of the Atlantic Ocean. He was clearly a figure of history in his own right, but unrealistic expectations robbed him of any recognition. He is usually remembered for his "notorious" lifestyle or held up as a bad example by presidents wanting to warn their children. John Bigelow, editor of *The New York Evening Post*, cruelly dismissed John's writings and congressional career with the observation that "John Van Buren was the son of a President; from his youth therefore a pet of society."

Doing What Father Couldn't Do

As was pointed out in the earlier biographical sketches, some presidents' children solve the challenge of living up to the accomplishments of a president father by pursuing his unfulfilled vocation or dream.

Most presidents have such an option tailored and ready-made. If their presidency is suffering, they will point out that they had only wanted to be a haberdasher, or soldier, or farmer. Until recent years, when the demand for leadership became so central to the selection of a president, it was almost obligatory for a candidate to be perceived as *not* wanting the post. Candidates did

131

not actively campaign, at least overtly, but sat on their front porches to await the outcome. Americans wanted to be assured they were not promoting a tyrant, but rather a modest person of manageable ambition. A president expressing other desires and dreams served to disarm critics and provide an ego safety net for himself, in case he were to tumble from such a height. "I never wanted to do this in the first place," he could say. Jefferson was always "suffering" as a reluctant president, which John Adams saw as total hypocrisy. If presidents' children experience pressure from expectations, obviously, so too, do presidents. Claiming only to be a farmer or soldier, "just trying to do my best," helps lower expectations so that the president can surprise the public by doing better than anticipated.

Whatever its role for a president, this phantom second vocation or dream — the one for which presidents supposedly pine — has its own utility for the president's child. By accomplishing what the parent could not or would not do, the child hopes to win the expectations game, at least within the family. This is far better than competing with the presidency itself, an almost certain no-win situation. The child may see this as a back door to parental approval. It allows the child to establish his own personal, separate identity, without diminishing the parent and thus ruining the intimacy of the family, if there is any.

The ninth president, William Henry Harrison, was originally planning to be a medical doctor and was in school when the sudden death of his father and financial desperation diverted him into the army. His sixth child, one of many famous Americans to bear the name of Benjamin Harrison, took up his father's unfinished career and became the doctor his father had wanted to be. How did a daughter in early America find a husband who could compete with a president? By marrying a man who could do what the president father always wanted to do. Mary Symmes Harrison Thornton married a doctor.

Woodrow Wilson, an educator most of his life, was horrified by the pace of the presidency. "There is no time to think," he often complained. His daughter Margaret never married and spent much of her life meditating in an ashram in India.

FDR's son, John Roosevelt, devoted years of his life working for the Polio Foundation, a service that would have touched his polio-stricken president father, who was confined to a wheelchair.

For young Kennedy it was accomplished by pursuing a career in publishing. Friends of the family insisted that it had been his father's dream.

Luci Baines Johnson picked up where "Daddy" left off when his political career hijacked him. She and her husband now run the media empire that Lyndon Baines Johnson and Lady Bird first began in Texas.

All of this brings us to the remarkable stories of the sons of Ulysses S. Grant, for they strove furiously to do the one thing that President Grant could not seem to do for himself, namely, achieve financial security. They would have varying degrees of success in this game, sometimes impressing their father, until the end, when the retired president reluctantly wrote his autobiography and thus made his fortune through book royalties, wiping out any last vestige of comparative success for his struggling children.

The Sons of Ulysses S. Grant:
The Root of All Evil

In some respects the children of Ulysses S. Grant are a microcosm of all presidential offspring. The Grant sons outnumber the daughters three to one, just as male presidential children far outnumber their female counterparts. There is the oldest son who faithfully follows his father's career path into the army, a resilient president's daughter who succeeds where her male siblings fail, and even a "Junior" who works in his father's White House office and who, as in the case of Adams and Bush, may not have technically been a "Junior" after all. Indeed, there is even "the curse of the heirs apparent" in this story, for the fateful namesake would become embroiled in a national scandal, dragging his father with him onto the front pages of the nation's newspapers.

Ulysses S. Grant, Jr., "a rotund, cheerful young man," was well educated, attending Exeter, Harvard, and Columbia Law School. Named "Buck" after his birth in Ohio, the Buckeye State, he was not technically a junior. His famous father had been born Hiram Ulysses Grant. Thomas L. Hamer, the congressman who recommended him to West Point, mistakenly listed his name as Ulysses Simpson Grant and "Grant went along with the change." Buck was only sixteen when he joined his father as White House secretary and served several years without controversy.

On November 1, 1880, he married Fannie Josephine Chaffee. Most agreed that it was a good match. Jerome B. Chaffee, the father-in-law, was accomplished, wealthy, and politically astute. He had been in government and business from New York to Colorado. Chaffee gave young Ulysses $100,000, a fortune at the time, to allow him to open a New York banking-brokerage partnership with an up-and-coming Wall Street operator by the name of Ferdinand Ward.

At first, the new banking firm, Grant & Ward, riding the economic expansion of the post-Reconstruction Era, appeared to be the answer to the stubborn financial problems that plagued the Grant family. Junior was poised to make a fortune and carry the whole family clan along with him. By 1883, his investment had increased four times. "Ferdinand Ward," young Ulysses told his parents, "was a financial genius." Eventually, the former president invested his entire life savings and encouraged friends to do the same. The involvement of America's most famous Civil War hero did the project no harm, adding prestige and credibility. And there was no better assurance than the involvement of a former president. Investors poured in. But all was not well at Grant & Ward. The partners, seeing the opportunity to increase their wealth and anticipating an ongoing bull market, secured several loans, using the same securities for collateral. It was an investment ruse far older than Wall Street, but it was illegal nonetheless. When the market fell and the paperwork was eventually untangled, the operation was clearly exposed to the world. Ulysses S. Grant, senior and junior, found themselves in the headlines in the midst of a national scandal.

Humbly and contritely, the senior Grant sought to correct the mess, earnestly hoping to avoid the disgrace of prison for himself and his son. Newspapers were incredulous. An 1884 article in the *New York World* labeled Grant and his sons as either "swindlers" or "idiots." The nation and prosecutors decided it was the latter, and thus the scandal eventually passed. But Ferdinand Ward "fled the country," and another partner, James D. Fish, served time in prison. One year later, former war hero and U.S. president, Ulysses S. Grant, was dead of cancer.

In the weeks before his passing, the senior Grant had finished his memoirs and, upon his death, they were widely acclaimed a critical and commercial success, regaining for the former president a measure of credibility and respect lost in the scandals. But Buck Grant, remorseful for the damage he had inflicted on the family reputation, took his father's death especially hard.

After the passing of his first wife, Grant's namesake, now in his sixties, married a young lady and together they traveled the world, visiting some of the same capitals that his younger brother Jesse had visited and finding themselves entertained by some of the same royalty.

At home, bolstered by new friends and ambitious political cronies, Buck Grant made a sophisticated and earnest attempt to run for the

Senate in California, but the effort collapsed when his alleged involvement in "bribery schemes" came to light. He settled in San Diego where he built the U. S. Grant Hotel in memory of his father, becoming a leading citizen. Outside of his San Diego sanctuary, critics continued to pour ridicule on the president's son, suggesting that he had made a career out of trading on his father's name. For a while it appeared that he might indeed have beaten the specter of poverty that had so often pursued the Grant family. But when Ulysses S. "Buck" Grant, Jr., finally died in 1929, at the age of seventy-seven, his "fortune" was determined to be a paltry $10,000.

Jesse, the last son, was "by far the most personable and mischievous" of the Grant children. Always a clever, brash personality even as a child, he once put on his father's boots and tumbled down the stairs of their Galena, Illinois, home, breaking off his front teeth. He loved to wrestle with his famous father, taking the battle to him even when his father was busy at other tasks. The White House was his playground. Young Jesse was often rebuked by the servants for charging his tricycle into lines of office seekers, who had to scurry to safer places.

From the beginning of his public career, the children of Ulysses S. Grant were encouraged to embrace the limelight for themselves. Jesse, the baby, was especially responsive, doing so unashamedly, egged on by the "indulgent parenting" of his father. Since Grant had experienced a troubled relationship with his own father, he made an effort, in spite of the relentless intrusion of his public career, to make up for it. Sharing his emergent personal glory was apparently one aspect of his generosity to his children. On the trip back east, after his election to the presidency, his train rolled from town to town with enthusiastic crowds cheering their hero along the way. At one stop, when the people demanded a speech, "the two youngest Nellie and Jesse went out," to receive applause and bask in the acclaim.

After his father's retirement from the White House, Jesse joined his parents on a trip around the world, where the Grant family was entertained as royalty. Grant was a huge international figure. The whole world had followed the battles of the American Civil War, where the death rate transcended earlier European conflicts. New weapons had been tested, and new strategic methods employed. Not since Napoleon had there been such a military figure on the world scene. Jesse must have learned much from the trip, for he would spend many years of his life traveling the world, taking on freelance contracts as a mining engineer and making a career out of being a president's son.

In the nineteenth century the American democratic experience was still something of a new phenomenon for the rest of the world. Most nations were ruled by families, either monarchies or dictators or the nobility. Nepotism was a way of life in most societies. Dictators' sons and daughters enjoyed monopolies and special treatment. Even nations that had thrown off such structure in violent revolutions would irresistibly slip back into the old habits. It was hard for most Asians, for example, to grasp that a sitting president would pass his power on to another with its power and claims intact. Everywhere he traveled Jesse was feted. Often there were expectations that the friendship would pay off, that the Grant boy was still connected.

Entertained royally abroad, Jesse twice returned to the United States to seek a divorce from his American wife, eventually succeeding in obtaining the needed document in a Nevada court and immediately wedding a young lady, nineteen years younger. He would survive her by ten years.

By all accounts, Jesse lived a lonely life, and one of self-deception. The farther from Washington he traveled, the more viable his White House connection appeared. His hosts often wondered why Jesse himself was not seeking the presidency, a perfectly normal question in Asian, African and South American societies where families ruled. In 1908, following a speaking tour during which he was often asked about his own political future, a self-confident Jesse Grant announced his quest for the presidential nomination of the Democrat Party. His announcement and candidacy were virtually ignored by the press and the nation.

During his last years, Jesse finally returned to the family script. His father had succeeded financially at the end by writing his memoirs. Jesse would write *In The Days of My Father: General Grant*. It was received with great criticism, with many of its "facts" challenged by historians. Even as an old man, he was seen as one who could not quite fit into his father's boots. Jesse died June 8, 1934, at the age of seventy-six.

Four

Suffer the Little Children

"We must not create an atmosphere of sadness in the White House because this would not be good for anyone — not for the country."
— John F. Kennedy

There is no more remarkable common denominator among American presidents than their early encounters with the premature deaths of loved ones, particularly the deaths of their own children. Twenty-six children of presidents died before the age of five and dozens more before they reached thirty. Rutherford B. Hayes had seven children; three died before their second birthday. John Tyler lost three of his adult daughters within a six-year period. Several presidents, including William McKinley and Franklin Pierce, saw all of their children die. To be sure, much of this can be laid at the feet of childhood diseases that took the lives of so many children in earlier generations, but even with that phenomenon factored in, presidential children born before the Civil War died nine years earlier than the general public. The impact of these deaths on the lives of the presidents and first ladies was profound. On a more modest scale, the same phenomenon would persist even into modern times. Franklin Roosevelt, Dwight Eisenhower, John Kennedy, Ronald Reagan, and George H. W. Bush would all bury children.

Many presidents who had no children were impacted by a death experience early in life and usually in some quite dramatic way. James Buchanan, the bachelor president, for example, lost his fiancée in 1819 to a sedative overdose. He never married. James Madison had no children of his own, but his wife Dolley lost a child in a previous marriage the year before they wed. And many presidents who escaped the pain of the loss of a child had some "substitute experience" that impacted them just before they launched their public career. Woodrow Wilson, who was outlived by his own daughters, was devastated by a senseless, early death. Ellen Wilson, his wife, had a younger brother who had been brought into the Wilson family as a boy of ten and lived in the household as an adopted son. In the spring of 1905, that boy, now a fully grown man, was drowned in a boating accident along with his wife and child. Ellen was so traumatized by the deaths that she questioned her religious faith, wondering how a benevolent God could "allow such horrible things to happen." Nine years later, First Lady Ellen Wilson would herself die in the White House, with the president at her side. The stories are endless and touch almost every American president. George W. Bush still feels the loss of his younger sister, Robin, to leukemia. "Forty-six years later, those minutes remain the starkest memory of my childhood, a sharp pain in the midst of an otherwise happy blur."

One is tempted to speculate that these experiences are more than coincidental, that the loss of a child, for example, made for more empathetic campaigners and human beings or that it gave a different perspective, allowing the candidate to better endure the harsh criticisms and anger of American elective politics. How worrisome is a cruel editorial compared to the searing pain and guilt that accompanies the loss of a child? "If the good people, in their wisdom, shall see fit to keep me in the background," said Abraham Lincoln to an audience in New Salem, Illinois, "I have been too familiar with disappointments to be very much chagrined."

Perhaps, as the lives of Andrew Jackson and Abraham Lincoln illustrate, such tragic events helped propel some future presidents outside the family circle into public life where they could ironically be alone and escape the tenderness of their loss. Here again the idea of escape mechanisms is irresistible. While divorce, which is a common event after the death of a child, is often seen as an act of "regression," perhaps some of these presidential figures were able to "sublimate" the pain and use it as emotional fuel to do something otherwise considered undoable. Did the death of girlfriend Ann Rutledge trigger Lincoln's political activism, as his law partner William Herndon suggested? And did the death of his son Willie, in the midst of the Civil War, give Lincoln the pathos and depth of eloquence to identify with the suffering of the nation and express its pain? Is Willie's death a critical part of the mix in the secret to Lincoln's greatness?

Historians and writers suggest that childhood death was so common in earlier times that it did not impact the parents as it does today, that they braced themselves and did not allow themselves to become attached to their children knowing that there would be a certain amount of attrition. This theory raises many questions. How does one control an emotional attachment? Can love be turned on and off? And wouldn't a child be even dearer if there were the possibility that he or she might be lost forever? In my interviews with grief counselors and psychologists, the idea holds up remarkably well. They all insist that families eventually become dulled to the pain of so many deaths. "There is a time in human suffering," wrote Patsy Jefferson, "when succeeding sufferings are but like snow falling on an iceberg."

Still, one wonders how much worse it could have been for these presidential families? When one-year-old Susanna Adams died, her father "was so upset by the loss that he could not speak of it for years." Thomas Jefferson would bury five of his six children and lose his wife, Martha, in the process. After losing the first three children, Martha Jefferson descended into a deep "melancholy" and "continued in this emotional state for the next seventeen months, when yet another birth caused her death." Most historians pass over the loss of the first Lucy Elizabeth Jefferson as having only lived a few months, pointing out that another Lucy Elizabeth was born later, but

143

Jefferson would carry a lock of the baby's hair for the rest of his life. First Lady Anna Harrison, grieving over the death of three sons, was a no-show for her husband's inauguration. Likewise, after the death of her first child, a grieving first lady, Jane Pierce, would wear black for the rest of her life, and with the death of her third child, she too, would skip her husband's inauguration and swearing-in ceremony. She would make her first public appearance two years into the administration. Mary Lincoln was an emotional wreck after the death of her son Willie and held White House séances trying to speak to him. A grieving Eliza Johnson lived in seclusion on the second floor of the White House during her husband's term. Grover Cleveland found the death of his twelve-year-old Ruth "almost unbearable." Presidential daughter and historian Margaret Truman writes that "the ambition that drives a man or his wife to the presidency can do terrible things to them when tragedy strikes down one of their children." John F. Kennedy embraced his infant's coffin and openly wept.

The sad and wistful story of Zachary Taylor's daughters bears mention. General Taylor, the twelfth president, lived most of his life in the military. It was during an assignment in the Mississippi delta that the Taylors lost their three-year-old daughter to "bilious fever," an unknown regional malady that most historians believe to have been malaria. A few months later, one-year-old Margaret died as well. A third daughter, Sarah Knox Taylor, was violently ill but managed to survive. Understandably, the Taylors were relieved when the assignment was over and they could leave the delta, but the family was forever traumatized by the experience.

Fifteen years later, in June of 1835, against her father and mother's earnest wishes, a beautiful "Knox" Taylor married a young Southern officer named Jefferson Davis. They moved to the Deep South where they were planning to live with Davis's relatives in that very same Mississippi delta region that had been the scene of such pain for the family. Well aware of her parents' worries and how they feared that part of the South, Knox Taylor wrote a letter of reassurance, proclaiming that the "country is quite healthy." Only days later she and her new husband became desperately ill. Eventually, Jefferson Davis would ride out the fevers and twenty-five years later become the president of the Confederate States of America. But three months into her honeymoon, twenty-one-year-old Sarah Knox Taylor died of malaria, the same disease that had almost taken her along with her sisters as a child. What the Taylors had feared had come upon them.

A truly unique story is that of William and Ida McKinley, who suffered horribly after the deaths of their two daughters, their only children. Far from leading to a divorce, it became the bonding glue of their relationship, a defining moment in their lives that played its part in propelling the McKinleys into the White House. After the deaths, Ida suffered epileptic seizures and frail health, while William's doting and constant attendance to his invalid wife made him a popular and sympathetic public figure that endeared him to hundreds of thousands. Even after being hit by an assassin's bullet, as he lay dying, President McKinley cautioned his aides on how to break the news to his wife. "My wife — be careful how you tell her — oh, be careful."

Eliza Arabella "Trot" Garfield

In the fall of 1863, in the middle of the great Civil War, Congressman James A. Garfield and his wife finally moved into a home of their own. It was small and the roof had leaks but, for the first time in their young married lives, they were not living with parents. That November the congressman rushed home to Ohio to be at the side of his gravely ill, three-year-old daughter. His wife later wrote that "it surprised me and made me love you so tenderly to see you taking care of our little girl, and watching beside her so gently. . . ." But Eliza Arabella "Trot" Garfield died of diphtheria on December 3, 1863. His young wife, abandoned throughout most of their short marriage, was not entirely sure of her status, writing to her husband that she had "almost feared that you were so saddened by the loss of our darling that you would dread to return here, and that our house would have little attraction for you now: but I hope it is not so." James Garfield said of his loss that it was "as if the fabric of my life were torn to atoms and scattered to the winds."

When Congressman Garfield finally returned to his Washington office there was a letter from home awaiting him. It was dated November 6, written just after his previous visit home, a month before the loss of his three-year-old. His wife was recounting how his little daughter, "Trot," had cried because he had left home without kissing her. It was more than Garfield could take. "I find myself sitting alone calling her by her pet names," he wrote his wife, "and asking her if she loved me and almost hoping to hear an answer."

The marriage of James and Lucretia Garfield held and their lives healed. On March 4, 1881, James A. Garfield was inaugurated as the nation's twentieth president and Lucretia "Crete" Rudolph became first lady. They moved into the White House, the nicest residence they would ever call home. But it would not last long. On July 2, 1881, four months later, President James A. Garfield would be assassinated by a disgruntled office seeker. He would live another eighty days, dying on September 19, 1881.

President Calvin Coolidge was "a different person" after the passing of his teenage son, refusing to seek a second term. Many years later, First Lady Grace Coolidge died on July 8, only the day after the anniversary of her Calvin, Jr.'s, passing. First Lady Mary Todd Lincoln had the same experience. On July 15, 1882, the anniversary of the death of her beloved "Tad," she "collapsed in her bedroom," fell into a coma, and passed away the next morning. Such occurrences are quite common to presidential families and nonpresidential families alike. The Eisenhowers lost their firstborn son, Dwight "Ikky" Doud Eisenhower, at the age of three of scarlet fever. The child had died in Ike's arms. The couple chose to forget his death and concentrate on the short life he had lived, sending each other notes and flowers every year on the anniversary of his birth. On September 24, 1955, on Ikky's thirty-eighth birthday, President Dwight D. Eisenhower suffered his first heart attack. Years later, First Lady Mamie had her final stroke the day before that same anniversary. Relatives insisted that it was more than coincidental. Mamie told a journalist that "giving up a baby is the hardest trial a young couple may have to face."

In any case, if the loss of a child was considered less traumatic in an earlier age as psychologists suggest, it was nevertheless very traumatic in the lives of the presidents. In our time it is universally recognized as one of the most stressful and painful events a human being will ever endure and yet the profound impact of these deaths of presidents' children on American history is virtually ignored.

Survivors' Guilt and the Death of the Daughters of William Henry Harrison

In 1816 the famous general, William Henry Harrison, and his wife Anna lost a granddaughter. The baby had been born to their oldest child, Betsey Harrison, and her husband John Cleves Short. It was a devastating experience for the family, but in retrospect it was like a gentle summer rain compared to the deluge that was coming. The Harrisons had ten children, a fact that kept the general always scrambling to pay the bills. The year after the loss of their grandchild the Harrisons lost their youngest son, three-year-old James Findlay Harrison. For the general, who had known death on the battlefield, this was a new and crushing experience. For Anna, this was the beginning of a lifetime of mourning.

In 1830 there were embezzlement charges against firstborn son John Cleves Symmes Harrison. His sudden death came two years later at age thirty-four. There followed three consecutive deaths of children leading up to the election of William Henry Harrison. In 1838, William Henry Harrison, Jr., died an alcoholic at age thirty-five. In 1839, Carter Basset Harrison died at age twenty-seven. And in 1839, Benjamin Harrison, a young doctor who held much promise, died at age thirty-four.

In 1840, numbed by the sequence of tragedies within his own family, William Henry Harrison was elected to the presidency in a Whig landslide, becoming the oldest elected chief executive until Ronald Reagan's victory in 1980. When Harrison arrived in the nation's capital for his inauguration, he was sixty-eight. A heavy snowstorm blanketed the city; the Democrats playfully blamed the president-elect. Other omens followed. Upon his arrival at the Capitol, the Senate scroll with *E Pluribus Unum* fell off the wall. Then a rope, stretched across Pennsylvania Avenue, draped with flags from all the states, mysteriously broke as Harrison approached.

On Inauguration Day, March 4, 1841, a cold northeast wind chilled the thousands who listened as Harrison stood bareheaded, without gloves or overcoat, for one hour and forty minutes, delivering the Daniel Webster–written, Henry Clay–edited inaugural address. The 8500-word speech is still the longest inaugural address in history. Not surprisingly, Harrison came down with a heavy chest cold, then pneumonia.

The elder Harrison had not forgotten his sons' families. He had faithfully supported their widows and children. And as president-elect he had brought back Jane Findlay Harrison, Junior's wife, to help at the inauguration and later to serve as White House hostess. It was all for naught; the tragedy was not complete. One month to the day after taking the oath of office, Harrison died.

The brief presidency of William Henry Harrison is often ridiculed during modern day presidential inaugurations. The irony is always invoked that he gave the longest inaugural address and served the shortest time as president. Modern political spin doctors suggest that his famous walks across Washington's snow-filled streets without hat, boots, or coat and his inaugural performance were clumsy attempts to prove that the oldest president was still fit, an invention of some behind-the-scenes Michael Deaver-type within the bowels of the Harrison White House. But it is more likely that Harrison was a victim of what we have come to recognize as "survivor's syndrome," the common post–Vietnam War malady of those who have seen others, perhaps considered more worthy than themselves, die, while fate allowed them to live.

As an army general in the Indian wars, Harrison witnessed carnage and torture at close range and took some of the deaths personally. He knew many of his own soldiers by first name. In an early letter to one of his sons he spoke of a friend who died at the hands of Indians "with Utmost Agony [sic]" and how he cared for the younger brother who had survived. As governor of the Indiana Territory, he was apparently the target of an assassin, upset with his kindness and concessions to the Indians. One night, as Harrison walked the floor with his baby John Scott, a bullet came "crashing" through the window of his house. In the famous battle of Tippecanoe, when the general's beloved gray horse became uncontrollable, he grabbed a black horse from another officer and rode out into the thick of the fighting, completely unaware that one hundred enemy warriors had been assigned to "slay the white chief on the gray mare." When one of his close fellow officers and friends, riding a white horse, was swarmed and killed, Harrison realized too late what had happened. Before the battle ended, the general became reckless in his bravery. A bullet hit his horse in the neck, another passed through Harrison's hat, another "grazed the side of his head," still another felled the man sitting on a horse next to him. The dying request of the soldier was that Harrison watch over his young child. There are many similar stories from the War of 1812, as when the general was shot in the hip and a man standing nearby was killed by a sniper. Soldiers wrote in their journals about his battlefield audacity and constant exposure to almost certain death. It is likely that these battle-field scenes continued to haunt the general long after he became involved in national politics, and account for his long and unwavering advocacy of compensation to the widows and orphaned children of American veterans.

Surely, William Henry Harrison experienced the remorse and guilt that most soldiers feel for the long separations from their families. This would have been compounded by his unexpected service in the diplomatic corps to faraway places. Even the most hardened man would have wondered if his own neglect were somehow responsible for his son's egregious debts and the charges of embezzlement that his firstborn had probably wrongfully endured. As an old man he had promised himself and his children that he would settle down, that it was now their turn, only to find himself suddenly in a contest for the presidency.

If losing a child is one of life's most painful experiences and "recognition of peers" is one of life's most rewarding, then William Henry Harrison, who was elected president after losing three sons in three consecutive years, was surely experiencing a stress overload. His wife went into permanent mourning, refusing to return to Washington for her husband's inauguration. She would never set foot in the White House or see the city of Washington, D.C. And thus it is likely that William Henry Harrison, defying the elements and sloshing through the snow-covered streets of the capital that fateful month of 1841, may not only have been planning his presidency, he may have been working out his grief as well.

More than an act of political gamesmanship, the hatless, coatless old man may have been consciously or subconsciously experiencing the depths of survivor syndrome, nursing a death wish. And, if we need more to prove the point, there is the story of his remaining daughters.

Upon the death of the president, only thirty days after his swearing-in ceremony, a second chain reaction was set into motion. Having lost five of his sons, one by one, his surviving daughters now began dying off. Mary Symmes Harrison Thornton, a doctor's wife, died in 1842, Anna Tuthill Harrison Taylor in 1845 and Elizabeth Bassett Harrison Short in 1846. None of them had reached the age of thirty-five. Within five years of the passing of the president, most of his family had been wiped out. Nine of his ten children were dead.

There is a positive seed of life within this depressing family story, made all the more inspiring by stark contrast. The name of the single surviving child was John Scott Harrison, and his remarkable story would go a long way to balance the debt that fate had dealt the family. He would endure the emotional holocaust that wiped out his siblings, rise to be a congressman, and have a son of his own, named after his beloved doctor brother. In 1889, that son, Benjamin Harrison, would be inaugurated as the twenty-third president of the United States. Thus, John Scott Harrison, who, over a lifetime, would see his family's fortunes rise and fall with breathtaking speed, would be the only son of a president to have his own son elected president as well.

Benjamin Pierce:
The Last Child

It is instructive to read accounts of the presidency of Franklin Pierce, in which the historians debate the pros and cons of his administration, the Kansas-Nebraska Bill, the repeal of the Missouri Compromise, and how all those dramatic decisions affected his chances to seek a second term, while the same accounts totally ignore the life-changing experience with his son, Benjamin.

Jane Appleton Pierce was a deeply religious woman from an aristocratic and educated Congregationalist family in New Hampshire and yet, at twenty-eight, she married a reformed alcoholic, a handsome, dashing, New Hampshire congressman and brilliant lawyer by the name of Franklin Pierce. Understandably, many considered them an odd couple. Pierce was a close friend of the great American author Nathaniel Hawthorne, whose eloquent prose captured early New England Puritan life in the novel *The Scarlet Letter*. It did not take long for Jane Pierce to become scandalized by the malicious and apparently dishonest nature of Washington politics. She brooded on how one could be a part of such a community and still profess any degree of "Godliness" or sense of ethics. Equally distressing, she worried that the Washington social scene, with its endless receptions and parties, would lure her husband back into a world of alcoholism that had scarred his earlier years.

Before the beginning of the next session of Congress, Jane became pregnant. She stayed home in New Hampshire while Franklin made the trek to Washington alone. On February 2, 1836, Franklin Pierce, Jr., was born. The congressman was overjoyed, but the baby died within days, and it is believed that the lonely congressman returned to drinking. In the following months and years Jane speculated endlessly on how and why God had allowed them to lose their firstborn son. When Franklin was elected the youngest member of the U.S. Senate, she returned once more to Washington, but found the experience much the same as before. She soon began to theorize that her husband's political ambition was grieving a righteous God and might be the reason for their loss.

Returning to New Hampshire in the summer of 1839, she discovered that she was pregnant once again. Not long after, Jane began a lifelong campaign to urge her husband to retire from politics. This, she felt certain, held the key to their happiness and the benediction of a merciful God. Right on cue, Frank Robert was born on August 27, 1839, and, by all appearances, was a healthy boy. On April 13, 1841, a second son, Benjamin Pierce, followed. Surely, through humility and prayer, Jane Appleton Pierce had solved the mystery. Eventually, Franklin Pierce succumbed to his wife's pious urgings and retired from the U.S. Senate, returning to New Hampshire to live in peace with his family and seek his fortune in a law career.

But leaving Washington and retiring from political life seemed only to postpone the ongoing tragic fate of the Pierce children. In 1843, four-year-old Franklin Robert Pierce died of typhus fever. Now only one child remained, Benjamin Pierce, and that one child was jealously protected. When President James K. Polk offered former senator Pierce the position of attorney general in his new cabinet, the New Hampshire lawyer declined, citing his wife's health. But Pierce soon had regrets about his decision to pass on the offer. Jane "was not always easy to be with." At times she was able to shed her habitual melancholy, but she was "short-tempered" and unable to show affection, fearful that God would take away anyone that she loved too much.

When war with Mexico loomed, Franklin Pierce enlisted as a private. No amount of persuasion deterred him. He was soon promoted to colonel and then appointed a brigadier general, successfully leading his men to battle at Contreras and Churubusco. The senator-general's résumé was now set and fate would take the family into its own hands.

The Democrat Convention of 1852 was a raucous affair. Issues of slavery states versus free states were hotly debated. Sensing that the rival Whig party was in decline, many Democrat politicians saw the nomination of their party as tantamount to the presidency itself. Infighting was tough and intense. Ballot after ballot was cast without a clear trend. And then a dark horse was introduced — the retired Senator Pierce of New Hampshire. Having walked away from Washington and any personal ambitions, he had fewer enemies than most, and his war record would look strong against the Whig candidate, which was most likely to be the old general Winfield Scott. The unseen Pierce campaign came out of nowhere, winning on the forty-ninth ballot. Franklin and Jane Pierce were out for a leisurely carriage ride when the news reached them by courier. The senator appeared stunned. "Mrs. Pierce fainted away." A few days later, eleven-year-old Benjamin Pierce wrote his mother, "I hope he won't be elected for I should not like to be at Washington and I know you would not either." It was an understatement. Throughout the campaign Jane fervently prayed that her husband would lose the election. But her prayers were to no avail. Franklin Pierce won an electoral landslide, carrying all but four states.

Ultimately, Jane Pierce recognized what she saw as the hand of God in the elevation of her husband, especially since he had assured her that he had not campaigned or maneuvered for the nomination behind the scenes. His party had drafted him, and he had won the hearts of the nation. On January 6, 1853, President-elect Franklin Pierce escorted wife Jane and son Benjamin on a train trip home to Concord, New Hampshire. By one account, they had been in Boston, attending the funeral of Jane's uncle. Another report suggests that they had been celebrating the election and the Christmas season. Just north of Boston the coupling on their train car experienced a "sudden snap and jar." "The car whirled violently around," and plummeted down an embankment. Franklin reached out for his tumbling son, but just missed him. When the train came to a stop, Franklin and Jane were unharmed, but eleven-year-old Benjamin, their only child, the heir apparent, was lying lifeless on his side, his hair filled with splinters. According to one of the family members, Franklin saw that some object, perhaps a flying seat, "had taken off the back of Benny's head [and] killed him instantly." Jane apparently caught a glimpse before Franklin covered the boy with a shawl and "drew her away."

A few weeks later, a lonely, suffering Franklin Pierce was inaugurated president of the United States. In seclusion, his stunned wife, ever the devoted Calvinist, sought earnestly for the reason behind this "act of God." Her chilling conclusion would haunt Franklin for the rest of his life and sap the energy from his every project. An all-wise, benevolent, omnipotent God had taken young Benny, Jane reasoned, because his newly elected father could not bear any sentimental distractions from his new assignment. In Jane's mind, young Benny had been sacrificed for her husband's honor. When Jane eventually learned that Franklin had indeed been quite active in pursuing the presidential nomination of 1852, pulling strings and directing events from the distance of their peaceful home in New Hampshire, she was revolted. Now convinced that she had a clearer understanding of what had really happened, the new first lady refused to make more than a few public appearances for her "ambitious" husband. For much of the term her close friend and aunt, Abby Means, and Varina Davis, the wife of Jefferson Davis, the secretary of war and soon to be president of the Confederacy, served as White House hostesses in her place. Mrs. Davis occasionally found Jane alone in the White House, writing letters to her dead son, Benny, pleading for his forgiveness.

The president seemed to acquiesce to his wife's conclusion in the matter. "We are commanded to set up no idols in our hearts," he observed. "My prevailing feeling has been that we live for our children. In all my labors, plans and exertions, in them was the center of all my hopes . . . We should have lived for God and have left the dear ones to Him."

At the end of his first term, Franklin Pierce was finally finished with politics, but it was too late for his troubled wife. Six years later, with the Civil War racing to its bloody conclusion, Jane Appleton Pierce died of tuberculosis in a boardinghouse only a few miles from the spot where her beloved young Benjamin had been killed in the train accident. She was fifty-seven, and her passing went almost unnoticed by the public. Freed from his wife's righteous constraints, Franklin returned to the bottle with a vengeance and died in 1869.

More than one hundred years later, Barbara Bush, a fourth cousin to Franklin Pierce, would move into the White House, becoming one of the most popular first ladies in American history. Her spirited good nature and sharp wit would sweep away any lingering cobwebs of pain from the earlier White House years of her cousin's family.

Thomas "Tad" Lincoln:
"The Tyrant of the White House"

Abraham and Mary Lincoln, perhaps the world's most famous melancholics, were each touched by death at an early age. Abraham was nine when his mother died and Mary even younger when she lost her own mother. For six terrible months young Abraham Lincoln and his sister Sarah were totally abandoned in a remote log cabin far from civilization, while their father traveled for miles in search of a new wife. "Left to live in squalor, they became hungry, ragged and dirty."

Lincoln was just a teenager when his sister Sarah would die giving birth to a child. Abe wept at the news, but it was the one death that sparked anger rather than depression. Convinced that his brother-in-law's family, the Grigsbys, had waited too long to get help for his dying sister, he used his wit and cunning to extract a measure of revenge, giving us an unsettling example of what could have happened if such a talented mind had been bent to more sinister purposes. At a joyous double wedding of the Grigsby boys, Lincoln arranged for the bridegrooms to enter the darkened bedchambers of the wrong brides. Only an alert mother averted catastrophe but a feud was begun that would last years.

When Abraham Lincoln finally experienced young love and found Ann Rutledge, she too died, a likely victim of typhoid fever, leaving him insane with grief, not eating, sleeping, or working. His law partner, William H. Herndon, suggested that the death of Ann Rutledge was the great catalyst, that Lincoln "threw off his infinite sorrow by leaping wildly into the political arena."

On November 4, 1842, Abraham Lincoln married Mary Todd in a hastily arranged ceremony. They would have four boys. As in the case of so many other presidential families, the children would all die young except for one, who would survive to tell the story. In this case, uncharacteristically, the firstborn, Robert Todd Lincoln, would be that survivor. Born August 1, 1843, "just three days short of nine months after the wedding," Robert would see little of his father during his younger years and, when the momentous White House events would unfold, he would be tucked quietly away from the family, studying at Harvard University.

Second son Edward "Eddie" Baker Lincoln was born almost three years later, March 10, 1846. When Abraham Lincoln was first elected to Congress, the two boys, Robert and Eddie, accompanied their parents to Washington, where the whole family lived together in a boardinghouse. Lincoln rose early before the family even awakened and often returned past midnight. The arrangement did not last long. Mary and the boys soon returned to her family home in Kentucky, where she impatiently waited out the congressional session. Lincoln, who had complained about not getting his work done with the family around, now wrote all the appropriate things, bemoaning their separation and declaring how much he missed her and the boys. "I hate to stay in this old room by myself." He spent one afternoon shopping for a pair of socks for "Eddie's dear little feet."

As a young congressman, Abraham Lincoln failed to make much of an impression on Washington and fumbled the few political opportunities that came his way. He returned to his law practice in Illinois, having his appetite for elective office momentarily sated. And then tragedy struck once more. Before Christmas, 1849, young Eddie fell seriously ill. Mary was distraught and in a state of panic. Abraham, who knew very well the pain of losing a loved one, watched helplessly. In January 1850, Eddie Lincoln died. "We lost our little boy," Lincoln wrote to a family member. "He was sick fifty-two days & died the morning of the first day of this month. It was not our *first* but our second child. We miss him very much."

Lincoln's previous experiences with death were insufficient preparation for the loss of one of his own children. Within a year a third son, William Wallace "Willie" Lincoln, would be born and Abraham Lincoln's father, Thomas, would die, but Lincoln, still numb from the loss of Eddie, could hardly appreciate either momentous event. He did not immediately rejoice about "Willie," and would not take the time off work to journey to his own father's funeral. Mary, still grieving for Eddie and still given to occasional dramatic bouts of hysteria, was inconsolable.

Thomas "Tad" Lincoln, the last child in the family, was born April 4, 1853. He was named after Lincoln's harsh, rough-hewn, uneducated father, but Lincoln, perhaps still feeling a measure of bitterness about Thomas Lincoln, could never bring himself to call his boy "Tom." The baby's head was too large for his small frame and he squirmed like a tadpole, so the name "Tad" was initially used and it stuck for life.

Willie and Tad, the two youngest Lincolns, were notorious hellions whose antics were legendary in Springfield, Illinois. Each apparently fed off the other. Willie was a miniature Abe Lincoln, minus the severe upbringing, using all of his wit and manipulation to provoke merriment, while the younger Tad was the precocious, fearless instigator, always leading the way and counting on his disarming childishness to soften the heart of any angry adult disciplinarian or critic. A typical trick had Willie and Tad sitting behind an open window using a pole to surreptitiously knock off the hats of passersby, recruiting an audience of amused onlookers in the process. On Sundays they would pull all of the leather-bound law books off the shelves at Lincoln's law office, causing his partner to marvel at Abe Lincoln's parenting philosophy, or lack of one. There is genuine debate over the degree of discipline administered to the Lincoln boys. Some accounts describe Mary as unpredictable, sometimes whipping the boys and sometimes giving up in exasperation. Lincoln's friend and sometime bodyguard said that "when occasion required the sacrifice, he showed great firmness in teaching them the strictest obedience." But according to Lincoln's law partner, there never was the slightest correction or discipline. The children ran wild, and the Lincolns apparently tiptoed around their adored young tyrants, staying out of their way.

In the summer of 1860, with his father eyeing the presidency, seven-year-old Tad "was stricken with scarlet fever." Mary panicked; the memories of the loss of Eddie came back in a flood. When his favorite, Willie, caught the same fever Abraham Lincoln became worried as well. In a letter to a friend dated July 4, 1860, Lincoln wrote about Willie, "Our boy in his tenth year (the baby when you left) has just had a hard and tedious spell of scarlet fever; and he is not yet beyond all danger." The crisis passed, but the illness would forever leave its mark on Tad. Most historians would blame scarlet fever for a speech impediment that preserved his boyish personality even into his teen years.

In the White House, with the nation engaged in a great Civil War, the antics of Willie and Tad were obscured by more imposing headlines, but the boys nevertheless plowed on. Nothing had greatly changed; the playground had merely expanded. When a portrait painter arrived to paint the president, the boys sneaked into the room after hours and "squeezed his paint tubes all over the wall." They turned the rooftop into a circus, dragging White House servants up to see. On yet another occasion they declared the roof to be a ship, nailing up sheets as sails to catch the wind.

Willie, the older of the two, was unquestionably the favorite son of the president and the public. His father enjoyed reading to him and exchanging ideas, while the younger Tad had practically abandoned his education. And while Tad could be moody like his mother, Willie possessed a kindly courtesy reminiscent of his father. He delighted in interacting with visiting royalty and visiting children alike. Tad depended on Willie, not only to provide diversions when life became unbearably boring or depressing, but sometimes out of necessity to interpret his often indecipherable lisp. And if the two hellions were both rambunctious, at least Willie had moments of regret. When Tad smashed a new ball into a giant mirror, he only kicked at the shards saying, "Well, it's broke, I don't believe pa'll care." But Willie was more circumspect, "It's not pa's looking glass," he said. "It belonged to the United States government." Julia Taft, often called on to watch the children, described Willie as "the most loveable boy I ever knew."

On a cold afternoon in February 1862, with a "chilly rain" drenching the city, Willie Lincoln took a ride on his favorite pony. That night he lay sick in bed with a high fever and a cold. His worried parents were hosting a White House event in the East Room downstairs, but first lady Mary Lincoln made several visits to the boy's bedside. It was apparent to guests that the president was preoccupied with the boy's condition. Within hours, little brother Tad was in a sickbed in a nearby room. A deathly silence descended on the house. While a number of historians believe that the boys were suffering from pneumonia, most believe that they had contracted typhoid fever. On February 21, 1862, the *New York Times* offered a simple announcement lost among the terrible drama of the Civil War. The president's son, William Wallace Lincoln, had died the night before. The newspaper announcement didn't know the boy's exact age. He was eleven.

Abraham Lincoln visited his deathbed, "lifted the cover from the face of the child" and stared sadly. "It is hard, hard to have him die." A few weeks after Willie's death a fire broke out in the White House stables. Security guards saw a tall, lanky man race toward the burning building, calling for help to free the horses. When they realized that it was the president, a quick-thinking official called for assistance and pulled Lincoln away from the fire. Perhaps it had been deliberately set to lure the president into a trap, he suggested. It wasn't safe. Later, a guard saw a chastened president standing at a White House window, looking out at the fire, weeping softly. The staff was puzzled until Tad explained that Willie's favorite pony had been inside. The president had hoped to save it.

Mary Lincoln's grief became legendary. She refused ever again to enter the "guest room" where her son had died or the Green Room where his body had been embalmed. She sought to speak to him in White House séances, banned flowers that he had so loved, canceled the Marine Band summer concert on the South Lawn, and went into mourning for months, giving herself over to hysterical outbursts of sobbing and wailing. Mrs. Keckley, her mulatto maid, tells the famous story of President Lincoln gently leading his wife to a window and pointing to a nearby "lunatic asylum" and saying that she must control her grief or "we may have to send you there."

Tad recovered, and with the passing of his older brother Willie, his parents became even more indulgent, a feat that most who knew the family would have thought impossible. The president would leave important meetings, with generals sitting in his office, while he marched off with Tad on a shopping excursion or simply to take a ride. A morning walk downtown to the A. Stuntz toy store became a father-son ritual. Visiting cabinet officers were irritated that Tad would not be dismissed, even in the most sensitive and private meetings of state. The boy was playfully commissioned a colonel, complete with uniform and sword, and sometimes reviewed the troops with his father. Many officers, numb from the bloodiest war in American history, were not amused.

In one famous incident, Tad and his friends hitched two goats to a dining room chair and drove it into a sitting room where the first lady was giving a tour of the White House to distinguished guests from Boston. Eventually, the White House staff was able to get rid of the most troublesome pet in Tad's menagerie. During one of Mrs. Lincoln's famous shopping trips to New York, the president wrote, "Tell dear Tad, poor 'Nanny Goat,' is lost; and Mrs. Cuthbert & I are in distress about it. The day you left Nanny was found resting herself, and chewing her little cud, on the middle of Tad's bed. But now she's gone!"

On another occasion, young Tad Lincoln discovered the central controls of the elaborate but

167

rudimentary White House communications system. A series of cables and pulleys allowed bells to be rung to summon various servants and staff. Suddenly, simultaneously, all the bells broke into a pealing clamor, sending staffers tumbling into the hallways to deal with the unprecedented emergency. It was only Tad.

Sometimes the lad's mischief had purpose. Colonel William H. Crook, the White House guard, told the story of Tad being accosted by a desperate and tearful woman whose husband was in prison and whose children were starving and cold. Deeply troubled, Tad carried the story upstairs to the president's office. Lincoln indicated that he would look into it, but Tad would have none of his evasions. The situation demanded immediate attention. The president, not willing to say no to anything his son really wanted, relented and promised that the man would be freed. When Tad returned with the news the woman wept with joy, and Tad, overcome by the goodness of what he had done, openly wept with her.

On April 14, 1865, ten days after Tad's twelfth birthday, Abraham and Mary Lincoln visited Ford's Theater to see the popular comedy *Our American Cousin*, starring Laura Keene. Son Robert was home from the war, visiting with staff at the White House. Tad Lincoln was escorted to the Grover's National Theater production of *Aladdin and His Wonderful Lamp* near the junction of E Street and Pennsylvania Avenue. Thirty minutes into the children's show a theater spokesman interrupted the performance with the announcement that the president had been shot. There was a moment of stunned silence, shattered by the shrill cries of twelve-year-old Thomas "Tad" Lincoln, "They've killed him! They've killed him!"

After being shot in the presidential box at Ford's Theater, Lincoln was carried across the street to a private home only a few blocks from the theater where Tad had been. The boy's tutor had quickly escorted him out and back to the White House. Throughout the night, Mary Lincoln, hysterical with grief, called for her youngest son. "Bring Tad — he will speak to Tad — he loves him so." Again, hours later she begged the attending doctors and cabinet officers, "Oh! that my little Taddy might see his father before he died." But after she experienced another outburst and fainted, Secretary of War Edwin Stanton had her removed from the room and sternly ordered that she not be readmitted. It was too late. A fearful and frantic Tad had been taken back to the White House where late in the night he had been finally put to bed by one of the doormen. Abraham Lincoln no longer belonged to his family; he had already passed into legend.

A few days later Tad would finally see his father's embalmed body in a public East Room ceremony, the boy lost in a crowd of important attendees, including the new president, Andrew Johnson, General Grant and others. Observers noted that the boy's face was red and swollen from crying. Later, twelve-year-old Tad spoke sadly to his nurse: "Pa is dead. I can hardly believe that I shall never see him again. Yes, Pa is dead, and I am only Tad Lincoln now, little Tad, like other little boys. I am not a president's son now. I won't have many presents any more. Well, I will try and be a good boy, and will hope to go some day to Pa and brother Willie, in heaven."

Tad was more accurate than he might have imagined. President Johnson and his family had suffered countless humiliations at the hands of the erratic first lady. While Lincoln was dying she had barred the vice president's entry to the room, shouting loud accusations that he was likely behind the assassination. Johnson did not even pen a note of sympathy to Mary Lincoln or any of her children. Nor was any government official on hand to say good-bye to the family of America's greatest president when a few weeks later they left the White House for the last time.

Six days after the assassination, the body of Abraham Lincoln and the disinterred body of his favorite son, Willie, were loaded onto a special seven-car train that took them back to Illinois on a seventeen hundred mile journey, retracing the itinerary that the Lincoln family had taken to Washington only four years before. On that earlier trip Willie had carefully memorized the various stops and had enjoyed preempting the conductor by calling them out along the way. Now, oldest son Robert Lincoln, surrounded by many dignitaries, made that sad journey alone, listening to the roll call of cities that young Willie had remembered and quoted with delight only a few years before.

For the rest of Tad's life his mother clung to

him, taking him on a long journey throughout Europe where she enrolled him in private schools, only to pull him out on one pretext or another. It was after such a trip, upon returning to the United States, that an eighteen-year-old Tad Lincoln contracted tuberculosis. Mary was again hysterical, but nothing could prevent destiny from taking its course. On May 18, 1875, largely forgotten by the public, Thomas "Tad" Lincoln, "the tyrant of the White House," the child who had often fallen asleep on the floor at his father's feet while generals talked strategy late into the night, died at the age of eighteen. Only Robert remained.

Quentin Roosevelt:
The White House Gang

Over time, Quentin Roosevelt has become one of the more romantic and dashing figures among presidents' children. As a boy he played pirates and water pistols in the East Room until the chief usher declared it off-limits. He and his friends played "chase the president" with Teddy Roosevelt nearly every afternoon in the murky attic of the White House. Quentin spent most of his allowance on joke books, searching out the worst jokes he could find about his father, the more to amuse him. There was no question that he was bright. Once, when an errant snowball angered a passerby, he was chased down the street by a policeman. Seeking sanctuary in the British Embassy, he shouted back at the officer, "This is English ground! You cannot come here!"

By sending Quentin to the Force Public School on Massachusetts Avenue, President Theodore Roosevelt has been credited (or accused) of starting the famous White House Gang, which included Quentin and the son of the secretary of war, Charlie "Taffy" Taft, and an expanding list of others. Believing strongly in egalitarian ideals, Roosevelt wanted Quentin to grow up with no illusions of special treatment. The youngsters of the school expected the president's son to be a stuck-up snob. But Quentin had a gift that would never fail him. He could charm almost anyone he met.

Earle Looker, one of the original members of the notorious White House Gang, remembered Quentin as a "towhead" who was "always mussed, his tie coming untied, his clothes being torn, his stockings refusing to stay up. There was no holding him down or back." It was said that Quentin thought things up, and Charlie Taft figured out how to carry them out.

The gang has been described as having "terrorized" the White House. Adults entered at their own risk. Brilliant sons of brilliant fathers, their ideas translated into imaginative action that often pushed the envelope. On one occasion a massive 350-pound bust of Martin Van Buren nearly toppled over onto the giggling, jostling boys. It finally settled back on its base, narrowly averting disaster.

One of the more lasting and historic signatures of the gang happened when Quentin accidentally ran the tongue of his wagon right through the lower part of a full-length portrait of first lady

Mrs. Rutherford B. Hayes. He raced to his White House friend Eddie Norris, who worked in the boiler room. "Help me, Eddie!" Quentin yelled. "I'm in an *awful* mess." Norris took one look and groaned. The Women's National Temperance Union had gifted the portrait to the White House because of Mrs. Hayes's ban on liquor. It was a priceless national treasure. Quentin suggested a piece of board, some tacks and some brown paint. If they worked diligently, they could fix it up before his father found out. Of course, the portrait was repaired, but by experts and not by Quentin, and not with a rough board and brown paint. Visitors today have to look very closely to see the historic mark of the White House Gang. Earle Looker wrote, "I fully appreciate now — with so many beautiful and historic things stored in the White House — how miraculous were the accidents, *which never happened!*"

Reenacting the battle of San Juan Hill, a favorite pastime for the gang, Quentin raced after Charlie, who was playing the role of an enemy Spaniard. Quentin brandished his father's sword — the real sword from the battle, razor-sharp. The boys were absolutely proscribed from touching it. Charlie tripped on a chair and landed on the floor. As Quentin swung the sword, portraying his hero father, he accidentally nicked Charlie on the cheek. The terrified boys gathered around, watching Charlie's blood drip onto the rug. Their boyish reaction was to quickly put away the sword, but when they heard someone coming, Charlie said calmly, "Remember, I fell on a chair." It was a great idea.

They smeared Charlie's blood on one of the brass chair feet as evidence. The gang barely had time to put away the sword and gather around Charlie in a concerned circle when an usher entered the room. He rushed them all to Edith Roosevelt's room for first aid. Chastened and scared to death, the boys simply sat quietly, while the first lady bandaged Charlie's face.

Theodore Roosevelt showed remarkable restraint considering the dangerous games the boys sometimes played, allowing them to test their limits without interfering. Once, when the boys were vying for leadership of the gang, Quentin laid books edge to edge on the floor and stuck knitting needles between them, pointing straight up, like an Indian fakir's nail bed. He then proposed stretching out over the needles, with only head and toes touching the chairs at either end. Anyone who could maintain the position for thirty seconds, he offered, would win the leadership of the gang. Of course, anyone who fell would be pierced. Quentin proceeded to accomplish the death-defying feat. No one else in the gang followed. A trembling gang member, Earle Looker, grabbed a nearby screen for support, only to realize that President Theodore Roosevelt was standing behind it, watching every move. Quentin survived his thirty seconds and the relieved boys hurriedly knocked over the dangerous knitting needles so their leader could relax. When Earle glanced behind the screen again, the president was gone. He had never uttered a sound.

But if Quentin was the unquestioned hero of the White House Gang, he was sometimes found wanting on the rigorous scale of Roosevelt manliness. The president complained that Quentin didn't hold his own in the family pillow fights. His tactic was to fall on the pillows and gather them under his arms to prevent his enemies from using them. It was an outrageous ploy to TR, maybe even cowardly. The president wrote to the other children, away at schools, suggesting that older brother Archie was disgusted with Quentin. Later, when the sons had all become young men, TR continued to push Quentin, telling his eldest brother that he still seemed a little soft.

Anticipating the outbreak of World War One, Theodore Roosevelt's sons competed to get into position to fight. One brother joined the British forces even while America was still neutral. The others trained and were immediately in the fray when America declared war. Within months, only Quentin had not seen action, and his brothers were not above telling him that he was "a slacker, unworthy of the Roosevelt name." The criticism hurt, especially since he was pressing for his chance. Commenting on his older brothers, Ted and Archie, Quentin admitted, "I don't grit my teeth like they do."

Quentin had opted for the most adventurous and tenuous new military service, the army air corps. He had gone to Washington, staying with his sister, Alice Roosevelt Longworth, while getting put through the paces at the Walter Reed Hospital. It was part of the drill for the air combatants, all to help determine who could pilot a plane and who could not. Alice wrote that they had poured hot and cold water into his ears, filled his eyes with belladonna, and made him hop about while blindfolded. Quentin passed those tests with flying colors, though he considered them ridiculous. It would be the vision test that would give him trouble. With poor vision like his father, Quentin solved the problem by memorizing the eye chart.

Still, events conspired to block him. While his brothers' war stories thrilled and shocked the family, young Quentin seemed to be perpetually set in a frustrating holding pattern. With America entering the war so late and so unprepared, there were simply no planes, no machine guns to arm them, and no bullets to load. And then he got his "break." In late February 1918, Quentin's 95th Aero was the first to receive French *Nieuport 28*'s. The planes were already considered obsolete. Even so, American pilots finally took to the air, fighting "more like Indians than soldiers," said the Germans sarcastically. They "upset all our training by dashing in single-handedly against our formations."

By May 1918, Quentin Roosevelt's unit was finally at the front. Captain Eddie Rickenbacker spoke for the whole squadron when he revealed his initial doubts about the former president's youngest son. Rickenbacker and all the others expected to meet a spoiled boy, but once again Quentin's gift disarmed new colleagues. Rickenbacker described him as "hearty and absolutely square in everything he said or did." He wrote in his memoirs that "Quentin Roosevelt was one of the most popular fellows in the group. We loved him purely for his own natural self."

Quentin flew his first patrol on July 1, 1918. His fearless recklessness earned him pleas from his own fellow pilots and orders from his commanding officers to be more cautious. Quentin merely laughed. A few days later his squadron came home without him. Peering anxiously into the skies, his friends finally saw his *Nieuport* fly into view. When he landed, Quentin was grinning broadly. He had just shot down his first German plane.

The story was classic Roosevelt. He had once again recklessly peeled off from his squadron to check out some enemy planes in the distance. When he counted twenty of them against his one, he decided that this was a time to be prudent and find his own fellows. Lost for a while, he finally saw a squadron ahead and moved into his usual spot at the last position. About fifteen minutes later, when the planes ahead of him began veering off, Quentin, to his astonishment, discovered black Maltese crosses on every one. He had been flying in formation with a German squadron! He fired one long burst. The plane ahead of him burst into flames and fell. Quentin "put down his nose and streaked it for home." His "Indian" tactics so astonished the Germans that they didn't even pursue. It seemed that the good luck that hovered over Theodore Roosevelt and all his sons would protect Quentin, regardless of the circumstances. From Sagamore Hill, the family home in New York, his father cheered the news, exulting with pride that "the last of the lion's brood had been blooded."

On July 14, 1918, Bastille Day in France,

Quentin Roosevelt and his five-plane *Nieuport* unit engaged seven German Fokkers of the famous flying circus, now led by one Hermann Goering. This was the same Hermann Goering who would one day build and lead the German Luftwaffe for Adolf Hitler. It was a classic dogfight, World War One knights battling over the skies. But Quentin spotted another German squadron zooming in from behind. He turned to meet them and engaged with two enemy planes. After a fierce fight Quentin's fabled good luck abandoned him. Suddenly, the American formation leader, Lieutenant Buford, saw a *Nieuport* dropping out of control through the clouds. He didn't know whose plane it was, but the pilot had effectively saved the lives of his compatriots. Lieutenant Buford knew it meant there were more enemy planes closing in, more than his small unit could handle. He signaled his men to head back across the lines.

The plane that Buford had seen spiraling to earth belonged to Lt. Quentin Roosevelt. The president's son was dead before his plane hit the ground. German reports referred to him as "brave but inexperienced." The Germans buried him with honors, near his plane, where it crashed at Chamery, France, near the Swiss and Italian borders. In the battle-ravaged wasteland, they twisted together a cross for his grave from saplings and wire scavenged from the *Nieuport*. On the cross they hung his dog tags. After the Germans had been driven back from the position, Americans found the grave, ringed it lovingly with white stones, and made a wooden cross for it. For years the crude cross held a position of honor in the family museum at the old family home at Sagamore Hill. Another war later, Quentin's body would be exhumed and buried next to his older brother, Theodore Roosevelt, Jr., at the American Memorial at Omaha Beach in Normandy.

After the death of Quentin, former president Theodore Roosevelt, the hero who had charged up San Juan Hill, seemed less enamored of recklessness and grew to appreciate the terror and helplessness of loved ones left behind to await the outcome of such blustery adventures. In the weeks preceding Quentin's death, TR had written him, with uncanny prescience, urging him to be careful. When a tearful reporter from the Associated Press brought word that his son's fighter had been shot down behind enemy lines, the former president was in despair. After a brave public statement declaring that it would have been worse had the young man not gone, Roosevelt took long, lonely walks, his face puffy from weeping. The former president confided to a friend that "to feel that one has inspired a boy to conduct that has resulted in his death has a pretty serious side for a father."

Theodore Roosevelt never recovered from Quentin's death. Six months later he would die himself. On a cold, snowy day in January 1919, he was buried in a family cemetery overlooking his beloved Oyster Bay. A grieving former president, William Howard Taft, once his best friend, would be seen standing watch at Roosevelt's grave, long after other mourners had departed.

Calvin Coolidge, Jr.:
A Boy Forever

Vice President Calvin Coolidge assumed the presidency in a remarkably humble and understated moment that captured the imagination of the country. He was visiting at the remote family farm, near Plymouth Notch, Vermont, on the day that President Warren G. Harding died. There was neither telephone nor electricity. A personal messenger had to be dispatched. Early in the morning of August 3, 1923, Coolidge was roused from bed. The vice president's father, a notary public, administered the oath of office to his son by a kerosene lamp at 2:47 a.m., while his wife, "an ashen faced Grace Coolidge," looked on. The ceremony complete, Coolidge, the thirtieth president of the United States, went back to sleep.

He was called "silent Cal." America's humorist, Will Rogers, liked to tell jokes about his taciturnity and his "penny-pinching" efficiency at handling a budget. According to one story, he was seated next to a hostess at a dinner party who prevailed on him to defy his legend. "You must talk to me, Mr. Coolidge," she reportedly said, "I made a bet today that I can get more than two words out of you."

"You lose," was Calvin Coolidge's alleged reply.

There were two children in the Coolidge family. John, the elder, spent most of his father's presidency at Amherst College, where he was

180

trailed by the Secret Service wherever he went. It was a heady time, but there were relentless pressures, public and private. As in the case of most presidential fathers, the senior Coolidge "demanded excellence in scholastics." The Coolidge firstborn was allowed only one day off to attend his father's inauguration. Family expectations notwithstanding, John failed to earn the academic laurels envisioned by his father but succeeded in business, serving as president of the Connecticut Manifold Forms Company. Eventually, he married the daughter of the governor of Connecticut, had two lovely children of his own, and became a major preservationist in the state of Vermont.

Calvin Coolidge, Jr., the younger child in the family, was a delightful contrast to his beloved but remote father. Described as "rollicking" and "full of fun and vigor," he nevertheless managed to convey some of his father's famous dry irony and wit. While working one summer in a tobacco field near Hatfield, Massachusetts, his identity was discovered by a co-laborer. "Gee, if the president was my father, I wouldn't be working here," his new friend said. "You would if your father was *my* father," Calvin replied glumly.

At first, 1924 was turning out to be a spectacular year in the life of the Coolidge family. Some clever Republican Party operatives were maneuvering to find a new, more glamorous candidate for the fall election, but the underestimated Calvin Coolidge was making some savvy strategic moves of his own that would clinch him the nomination. Grace Coolidge was turning out to be a popular first lady. The stock market was soaring to unbelievable highs. The Roaring Twenties were under way.

Meanwhile, teenager Calvin Coolidge, Jr., discovered and grew to love the White House tennis courts. During a tennis game he developed a blister on his right toe. Later claiming that he couldn't find clean socks, he played several more matches, his bare feet chafing against his tennis shoes. Later in the day, young Calvin dosed the blistered toe with iodine and thought no more of it. However, within hours septicemia had developed and blood poisoning was coursing through the boy's body. By the time the doctors were made aware of the situation, it was too late to treat the president's son.

Grace and Calvin Coolidge were stunned by the news. The boy's room was turned into a makeshift hospital. The normally stoic Calvin Coolidge walked around in a daze. In a sentimental moment, knowing that his teenage son loved rabbits, he brought one to his bedside to try to cheer him up. "When he was suffering, he begged me to help him," the president later wrote, "but I could not."

July 4 was not only Independence Day in the Coolidge household; it was the president's birthday as well. While their son lay mortally ill in his White House bedroom, the president and first lady could hear the sound of workers preparing for celebration and fireworks just outside on the Ellipse. Late in the afternoon on the nation's birthday, Calvin Coolidge, Jr., was rushed to Walter Reed Hospital in the Maryland suburbs. His parents held vigil. Three days later, in spite of all the ministrations of the best doctors in the nation, the president's namesake died. He was sixteen.

"He must have had some premonition, some intimation," his father related later, "for suddenly his body seemed to relax and he murmured, 'We surrender.' "

In a remarkable interview with journalist John Lambert, President Coolidge sat in his White House office and openly sobbed, weeping unashamedly. "He was such a good boy," the president said pitifully. Coolidge later wrote about his namesake's death in his autobiography, "When he went, the power and the glory of the presidency went with him."

In the days that followed the passing of his son, Coolidge exclaimed to visitors, "I can't believe it has happened." It became a mantra, repeated over and over. The president told one visitor that when he looked out the window he could still see his son playing tennis. When an acquaintance lost a son of his own, President Coolidge penned a poignant line, "To my friend, in recollection of his son, and my son, who by the grace of God have the privilege of being boys throughout eternity."

The chief executive no longer seemed to have much desire for the office. Three years later, while on a summer vacation in the South Dakota Black Hills, Coolidge typed a ten-word sentence, "I do not choose to run for president in 1928." He typed the sentence over and over, cut the paper into strips, and then calmly handed the pieces of typewritten paper to attending reporters. The bombshell caught everyone by surprise, even his wife and closest friends. For Calvin Coolidge, "the glory of the presidency" was gone forever.

Many years later, still grieving the son who had died at sixteen, First Lady Grace Coolidge wrote a poem as a tribute to Calvin Coolidge, Jr. It appeared on front pages of newspapers across the country. The first stanza reads:

> *You, my son,*
> *Have shown me God.*
> *Your kiss upon my cheek*
> *Has made me feel the gentle touch*
> *Of Him who leads us on.*

Why Do They Die Young?

Why do so many presidential children die prematurely? There are many variables and the details of their lives are so purposely shrouded in mystery and redrawn by political necessity that such a question may never be absolutely answered. Gathering the hard facts and creating normal comparisons for the various decades and centuries is likewise cumbersome. Some relevant information is simply not available. And yet, even so, we can discern blurry images.

Neglect is sometimes suggested as a cause factor. Would Calvin Coolidge, Jr.'s, blistered toe have escaped notice in the 1920s if he had lived in a Brooklyn tenement where mother and son would have bumped into each other several times a day? Or if they had lived in a rural farmhouse

184

where brothers shared the same room? Certainly, in a mansion with servants and privacy and very busy parents, it was easier for a teenager to limp around with an infected toe until it was too late to discover blood poisoning. As cruel and as unfair as such a suggestion may be, it crossed the mind of the president. "We do not know what would have happened to him under other circumstances," he wrote in his autobiography, "but if I had not been President, he would not have raised a blister on his toe, which resulted in blood poisoning, playing lawn tennis on the South Grounds." Calvin's mother, Grace Coolidge, who publicly spoke of God's "peace which passeth all understanding," may have been tormented at some deeper level. Thirty-three years later she was still mourning the passing of her son. She died on July 8, 1957, the very day after the anniversary of his death.

In most cases, stress is the common answer for the early deaths of these presidential children and stress helps provoke the self-destructive streak seen in many others. Robert Gilbert, in his book *The Mortal Presidency*, studies the impact of the chief executive's job on the man who must perform it, concluding what so many people who have compared the annual presidential portraits of Abraham Lincoln have long assumed. The stress of the presidency is a killer. Certainly some of that stress is passed on like secondhand smoke to the children of the White House, who have added challenges of their own, including undeserved celebrity, sudden public criticism and analysis of their every move, and unrealistic expectations.

How does one explain the suicides among presidential children and their spouses? Why are they such risk takers? Why do so many sons and daughters seek escape in substance abuse? Jib Fowles, a professor of media studies at the University of Houston–Clear Lake, studied one hundred celebrities from all fields, concluding that they were four times as likely to commit suicide as the average American. Death was more likely to be stress-related. Celebrities were twice as likely to die from ulcers and cancer, for example, as the general public. They were two and a half times more likely to die from an accident. Fowles also discovered a striking difference in lifespan. The average age of death among celebrities was fifty-eight, compared to seventy-two for the average American.

Similar findings among celebrities may help explain increased dependency on drugs and alcohol among children of high achievers. David Wellisch, professor of psychiatry at UCLA's medical school, suggests that beyond the two risk factors for substance abuse, namely, "a genetic predisposition and an environmental influence from childhood," there may be yet another. Wellisch refers to the "crisis of mobility," when fame transports a person into a new and alien world where the rules have suddenly changed and the person no longer is certain how to act. Alcohol and drugs might be an escape, if only momentarily, a stabilizer. Fowles's study showed celebrities as two times more likely to die from kidney disease and cirrhosis as the average American. Both diseases are related to drugs and alcohol abuse.

Another critical part of the experience for a president's child points to the fact that the fame comes instantly and not through his or her own achievement. They may get an early taste of public attention as the son or daughter of a governor or congressman, but the attention focused on the child of a president is oppressive. Even if out of respect to the child, the media do not report everything; they often know much more than the child or presidential parents would wish and details concerning the child are glibly passed around editorial rooms of the nation's newspapers, the information hanging overhead, ready to be published if there is a legitimate excuse. Like water, the fame of a president's child reaches every little corner of the world. Home run champion Barry Bonds can walk through European streets and only be bothered by American tourists, but a president's child is loved or hated everywhere. Charles Figley, director of the Psychosocial Stress Research Program at Florida State University, suggests that, "There's embarrassment and guilt among those who become superstars quickly." Figley suspects that they may have feelings of unworthiness, that "they may have a self-destructive streak."

Finally, there are stories of premature death in these historical archives that simply cannot be explained. The deaths of the children of Franklin Pierce come to mind. Eleven-year-old Benjamin Pierce surely held no death wish. His parents were not neglectful. The stress of being a son of the new president-elect did not provoke the train wreck that took his life. If his mother's theory was correct, that God took him so that the father could execute his duties as president without a "sentimental distraction," then it backfired miserably. Both parents were indeed "distracted" by the tragedy until the day they died. The death of Benjamin Pierce only days before his father's inauguration, as in the case of many other tragic stories told in these pages, must be laid at the feet of the unknown.

Thomas Jefferson would spend his life studying biology and horticulture, theology and history, language and the arts. For a man of so many diverse interests and so many profound experiences, he would achieve a remarkable degree of integration and sense of peace about life in general. But in a letter to John Adams, written in his retirement, he admitted to one last, great frustration. "I can accept all of the economy of life," he said, "and all of the human activities, and human nature, except one thing. What is the use of grief?"

FIVE

THE SEARCH FOR IDENTITY

"He was no longer my father. These people, strangers, who had chosen him to be their leader, had claimed him. He belonged to them. I had no part in it. I felt deserted and alone."
— ELEANOR "NELLIE" WILSON

Presidential children, as in the case of all human beings, are in a constant search for personal "intimacy" and "identity." The former requires the one thing that a president with all his power can hardly afford, namely, time. The latter, the quest for personal identity, is often smothered by the president's power and celebrity. Steve Ford is reminded that he is the son of a president every time he meets a stranger. "It's funny," he says, "You can tell that they are looking through you to some image they have of your father, the president. You feel almost nonexistent, like you are standing in front of a symbol."

First Lady Eleanor Roosevelt told of the bitter occasion when one of her sons sought advice

189

from his president father. Unable to reach him, he finally resorted to making an official appointment through White House staff. But when the day and hour arrived, the president sat through the meeting, reading a document. A humiliated son told his mother, "Never again will I try to talk to Father about anything personal." Ron Reagan, Jr., son of the fortieth president, met one of the Roosevelt sons many years later. He is an old man, Ron observed, but he still thinks of himself as "Roosevelt's little kid." Psychologists agree that "intimacy" and "identity" are more than just *needs*, but rather psychological *necessities* of life. Our emotional health demands them.

Remember, when we talk about "the life of the presidential child" we are not talking about the four or eight years that the family actually lives in the White House. Rather, we are talking about living with the type of personality who seeks the office and gets elected. We are talking about being the son or daughter of a high achiever. In one sense, the seeds of this struggle are intrinsic to *all* families. All children seek intimacy and identity, and continue the search for the rest of their lives. And all children begin this process with their parents or the parental figures in their lives. Even the sense of parental power is a given. Psychologists point out that all children are initially intimidated by their parents. The physical difference in size alone humbles each succeeding generation, thus preparing it to accept the necessary lifesaving counsel needed for its survival. Sigmund Freud and others suggested that this "size" difference was at the root of all adult feel-

190

ings of inferiority, especially in relationships between fathers and sons.

The point is that this process takes on a further dimension when the parents are high achievers. It is not much of a leap to accept that such feelings of inferiority would be revisited on the child of a celebrated artist, businessman, entertainer, sports figure, or successful person in any field, from academics to the military. In a democratic land of opportunity, where the mantra is "anything is possible," the pressures would correspondingly rise.

And yet, as has been pointed out, the presidency is not the normal kind of power and celebrity. Most children can rationalize their parents' power and success and by choosing a different field of endeavor, they can tell themselves that they are pursuing a more noble or relevant mission. This is the way out for the son or daughter of a great movie star or public performer. They can choose education or medicine or science, and say that they are doing something less egocentric and more substantial for society. The reverse is often true. The child of a great educator or doctor turns to the arts to find public acclaim that seems to transcend the importance of the seemingly unobtainable professional role of the parent. But in the case of a president's child that option is not open. Because ultimately, all disciplines look to the White House for recognition. There is no greater quest for a Catholic cardinal than to be secreted away in the private quarters of the White House, offering the president strategies for ending the Cold War and liberating

Eastern Europe or taking secret messages back to His Holiness in Rome. There is no greater moment in the life of a baseball Hall of Famer than to stand with one's peers on a platform in the East Room, bantering good-naturedly with the president for fifteen seconds in view of the nation. A medical doctor can have no greater honor than to be appointed to the President's Commission on AIDS or some other similar urgent task. The ultimate trophy for an American businessman or educator is to be invited into the president's cabinet. And of course, to a soldier the president is the commander in chief. No matter what choice an American young person makes, if he or she is ultimately successful, the road will lead back to the White House. And that is just where a president's child begins.

Ultimately, the presidential child must live with the fact that he or she is not going to be able to rationalize away the success of the parent. There is even more in this equation, and it is worse. The same child will not be able to rationalize away the stain of shame from the failure of the presidential parent, and most presidents fail in some way or another. "No matter who is in the White House," says Steven Ford, "half the country isn't going to like him." Even successful presidents have millions of vocal and angry detractors, and every criticism, no matter how low the volume, is heard clearly and felt dearly by the child. On the one hand, they must define themselves independently from the parent and establish their own self-worth, which often demands some kind of diminishing of the mother and father. At the same time they must maintain intimacy and defend persons they love and with whom they are publicly inseparable from the onslaught of a ferocious and cruel public. When asked which is easier, being the candidate or the candidate's son, George W. Bush never hesitates. It is easier to be the candidate, he says.

Obviously, there is constant tension in this process. The presidential child, as in the case of all children, will never stop alternately pushing the parent away and then seeking the parent's reassurance. One is the quest of an identity of one's own, the other for intimacy with a caring parent maintaining the security of home base. Ironically, the needs of a presidential child rise correspondingly with the emergence of a new, confusing public personae, namely the president and first lady. This is not mom or dad; this is a person created in concert with the public and the media, and, in recent decades, the president's own image-makers. It is, nonetheless, the person to whom their colleagues and teachers and friends relate. What obligation does the child have toward this second set of parents? On the one hand, the child may feel an even greater need for his or her own identity, to get away, even a sudden urgency about it, while at the same time have the need to come home and find reassurance that the familiar parents are still there and have not morphed into those unrecognizable public personae to whom their friends relate.

It is a love-hate relationship. "It's not just that you get tired of people asking about them," says a relative of a celebrity. "It's also that, in comparison, you feel kind of like a failure." The outspoken Alice Roosevelt Longworth, eldest daughter to President Teddy Roosevelt, took over her own White House wedding ceremony, declaring to the press: "My father wants to be the corpse at every funeral, the bride at every wedding, and the baby at every christening." George W. Bush was fond of saying that the difference between himself and his father was that "he went to Greenwich Country Day and I went to San Jacinto Junior High." It was a double-entendre. On the one hand he was trying to preempt a successful strategy that had been used against him in an earlier, losing campaign for the Congress in which his opponent stressed the Bush Yale-Harvard elitist education. George W. was saying *I am a true Texan.* But it was also a healthy, normal, instinctive reaction for a son, establishing a separation, a distinct and different identity from his father, and somewhat at the father's expense.

After the death of his presidential father, Millard Powers Fillmore successfully sued his stepmother to obtain many of the family papers, and then ordered the executor of his will to have them all destroyed upon his own death. One historian described it as "legal vandalism." Historians puzzle over the order; was it an act of rage against his father? Robert Todd Lincoln complained of his absent father, saying that "any great intimacy between us became impossible." And yet he made it clear that after his own death he did not want to be buried with his parents and siblings in Springfield, Illinois, but separate from them in Arlington National Cemetery.

While presidential children use their energies to separate themselves from their fathers and seek their own identity, they simultaneously defeat that process by sporadically, impulsively embracing the presidential identity. Frances "Fanny" Hayes served her father till the day he died, postponing marriage until he was gone. Yet incredibly, after she married and outlived her husband, she changed her name back to Hayes again. Her brother, Webb Cook Hayes, became a great businessman and war hero, clearly establishing his own separate identity from that of his president father, but in retirement devoted his life to establishing the first presidential library, honoring his father's legacy. After World War One, Ted Roosevelt, Jr., insisted that he be called, "Colonel Roosevelt," the name his father had used after leaving the White House. Luci Johnson, LBJ's daughter, married twice and then retook her father's family name and returned to Texas to run her father's old business empire. Today Neil Bush, among many other projects, promotes his father's Points of Light Foundation and serves on its board.

Anna Eleanor "Sis" Roosevelt:
Caught Between the President and the First Lady

Franklin Delano Roosevelt served as president longer than any other American chief executive, twelve years and thirty-nine days. The trauma to his children is clear. He had four sons and a daughter, with another son who died as a toddler. The daughter would marry three times, and the four sons would marry so often that historians can't seem to agree on just how many marriages there actually were. The authoritative *Facts About the President* lists thirteen marriages among the four boys; *America's Royalty*, a study of presidential children published by Greenwood Press, lists fourteen; and a Pulitzer Prize–winning account of the Roosevelts says that "between the four of them there would be eighteen marriages." In its obituary for Franklin D. Roosevelt, Jr., the *New York Times* says that he "is survived by his fourth wife," when in fact it was his fifth. Michael R. Beschloss, another Pulitzer Prize winner, says there were nineteen marriages among all five children, including Anna. A careful list compiled by family members and the FDR Presidential Library shows that only Beschloss is correct, but one comes to that conclusion with great humility. One wonders how something as clear as a legal marriage contract could become so obscured within such a recent period of history. Such confusion is itself a reflection of the fast pace and conflicted relationships in the world of the Roosevelt children. Seven of the marriages and divorces would take place while FDR was president. Two of the spouses would attempt suicide, and one would be successful.

Eleanor Roosevelt, the mother of this brood, was in a constant rivalry with her strong-willed mother-in-law, Sara. That rivalry spilled over into the lives of the children. Intimidated by Sara, Eleanor began her parenting career with great insecurity, which seemed to feed on itself. Often, her own children were more comfortable with nannies and their confident grandmother. In one remarkable account, Eleanor Roosevelt put her eldest child, Anna, in a "wire contraption" and hung her outside to give her "fresh air." The incident prompted concerned neighbors to outrage, with threats to call the Society for the Prevention of Cruelty to Children. At the age of three, Eleanor "began tying her hands to the bedposts at night to keep her from masturbating." It was a painful memory that Anna would carry into adulthood.

As the children grew into their teens, Sara, the grandmother, used her money to compete for their affection with gifts and tours abroad. Eleanor, the mother, was alternately strict and permissive, which added to the confusion. Sometimes she would sleep on a couch, waiting for Anna and eldest son James to come back from parties, as they straggled in at four in the morning, sometimes at six. But Franklin, the father, consumed by his ongoing personal struggle with polio and the juggling of a national career, could not or would not get involved. At times Eleanor accepted this as the "inevitable consequences" of a public life; at other times she deeply resented that, for her husband, the children could never be first.

Anna Roosevelt, the oldest child, at the age of twenty married Curtis Dall, a stockbroker ten years her senior. "I got married when I did because I wanted to get out," she told journalist Joseph Lash. They had two children and divorced just in time for Anna to move into the White House with her parents. Encouraged by a charming reporter she had met during the campaign, Anna began to develop a writing career in Washington, authoring two children's books, *Scamper* and *Scamper's Christmas*. The reporter, John Boettiger, worked for the hostile *Chicago Tribune*, a paper that would be her father's nemesis throughout his career. Nevertheless, Anna Roosevelt and John Boettiger were married on January 18, 1935. Another Roosevelt enemy, newspaper tycoon William Randolph Hearst, hired the couple to edit and report for *The Seattle Post Intelligencer*, where, for a time, Anna and John became a force. Anna developed a following as the woman's page editor until the bitterness of politics and her White House connection finally poisoned the arrangement.

In 1944, with World War Two raging and her husband overseas in the army's military-government branch, Anna moved home to the White House, where she was soon ensconced as "her father's hostess," working with the president day to day. More and more, as the president's health declined, Anna became a combination chief of staff, personal assistant, and social secretary. It was during the last months of the president's life that Anna was put in the awkward position of running interference for her father's relationship with other women. On one special occasion when the first lady was away, the president directed Anna to host a White House dinner, inviting his old lover, Lucy Mercer Rutherford.

On April 12, 1945, Franklin Delano Roosevelt died in Warm Springs, Georgia, with Lucy Rutherford nearby. First Lady Eleanor Roosevelt was just about to make a speech, when she received the news and was rushed back to the White House. The vice president was called in to meet her. There, in Eleanor's sitting room, with Anna and her husband John Boettiger, back from overseas duty, Vice President Harry S. Truman was told that the president had died.

"Is there anything I can do for you?" he said.

"Is there anything *we* can do for *you?*" Eleanor Roosevelt replied, "For you are the one in trouble now."

For one year Anna cohosted an ABC radio network talk show with her mother, and then joined her husband to pursue the heady dream of launching their own daily newspaper. They moved to Phoenix, Arizona, where they purchased a shoppers' advertising paper, pouring every dime they had into the project of converting it into a viable newspaper. The effort drained them of every resource, but it ultimately failed. They divorced in 1949, four years after the president's death. The following year, Boettiger, who had remarried, jumped from the seventh floor of a New York hotel.

As the White House years began to recede from her life, Anna Roosevelt seemed to find a new sense of security. On November 11, 1952, in Malibu, California, she remarried for the third time. But this marriage would last twenty-three years until her death. James Addison Halsted, her new husband, was a physician, and Anna was soon serving as a public relations officer for hospitals in New York, Michigan, and Kentucky. In 1960, Anna and James culminated two years of work by helping to establish a new medical school in Iran. On December 1, 1975, Anna Eleanor Roosevelt Dall Boettiger Halsted died of cancer at the age of sixty-nine.

James "Jimmy" Roosevelt:
On the Front Pages

According to the White House legend, Jimmy Roosevelt was an ambitious, hardworking, twenty-five-year-old insurance salesman when his father was inaugurated president in 1933. In fact, he had been in the political trenches throughout his father's 1932 campaign and had little time to make money. It would change in a hurry. Jimmy, married to a Boston debutante, Betsy Cushing, was anxious to get his career going. He would be at the center of controversy from the very beginning.

Since James Roosevelt had been active in his father's campaign in Massachusetts, he didn't hesitate to get his friends into plum federal jobs, including some as receivers for failed banks. More qualified men with banking experience were scandalized. By the first summer of his dad's presidency, James had clearly established himself as the man to see in Massachusetts for federal jobs. Worse, he publicly boasted of the fact, saying that anyone seeking an appointment "would be wise to obtain his endorsement." "As you know, I am probably closest by blood and affection to the man who makes the appointment." There were rumors that the young man had his eye on the governor's mansion.

The Democratic political machine of Massachusetts was outraged. There was a ten-day print media firestorm, with stories in *The Boston Evening Transcript* spilling over onto the pages of the *New York Times.* He was called the "patronage dictator." The heat got so bad that James was finally packed off to Europe.

James Roosevelt's escape did little to diminish his ambitions. As in the case of his younger brother, Franklin, Jr., who had passed through the European capitals only weeks before, his every move was covered by the press. In England he was "entertained" by the British prime minister. In France he was ushered into a meeting with the French president at the Elysée Palace. In Rome he was received by the pope and invited to the palace of dictator Benito Mussolini. With time to reflect on his Massachusetts experience, James returned home more measured and circumspect, but also more confident than ever. There was talk about bringing him into the White House to serve on his father's senior staff, but "public reaction" killed the idea.

In 1935, at the age of twenty-seven, Jimmy Roosevelt was named president of the National Grain Yeast Corporation, a New Jersey company with plans "to manufacture industrial alcohol." Newspapers had a field day. Underworld connections were alleged. There were charges that the president's son was a front man only used to help obtain government permits. In November he resigned, with the directors of the company in an uproar, complaining that he wasn't doing his job, while Roosevelt countered contemptuously that he had more important things to do.

The following year James Roosevelt was commissioned a lieutenant colonel in the Marine Corps and assigned as his father's military aide. But public criticism followed him into the marines as well, with charges of favoritism. When it was learned that he had received active duty pay for a trip to Latin America with his father, there was a howl of protest and indignation. In 1937, bucking the likely criticism from media and public, Jimmy moved into the White House to serve as a personal secretary on his father's senior staff. To mitigate the criticism, he resigned from the marines.

If the early travails of Jimmy Roosevelt had been a nagging, incessant, political nuisance for FDR, they were nothing compared to the storm that would descend in the summer of 1938. For some time journalists had been nibbling at stories surrounding the young Roosevelt's commissions as a life insurance agent. As innuendos began appearing in magazines that summer, the president's son became ill and checked himself into the Mayo Clinic. And then the news broke. According to the charges, Jimmy Roosevelt was earning between $250,000 and a million dollars in annual income from insurance commissions. Some had been obtained immediately after his father won the Democratic nomination in 1932, some from big donors to the party, some from institutions doing business with the government.

Time magazine questioned how the president's son had suddenly become such an expert on every conceivable kind of insurance, declaring that the industry was "startled." A bank was threatened with a lawsuit for switching an $800,000 policy to the young Roosevelt, allegedly just to put the commission into his pocket. But the most powerful story broke in *The Saturday Evening Post*, featuring the story of a salesman who received a phone call shortly after the nomination of FDR. The caller warned the salesman not to count on his commission for a lucrative policy he had just landed. "Jimmy's got it." The policy was going to be switched to the president's son.

It is not likely that today's media would let go of such a story, especially when reports suggested that Jimmy was enlisting his father's help. But by 1938, America was emerging from the Great Depression and World War Two was looming. FDR was one of the most popular and powerful American presidents in history, and he had extensive allies in the media.

The president and his son hit back. The popular *Collier's* magazine featured an artfully contrived rebuttal, with Jimmy answering questions from his sickbed in a hospital room. Using the same *Collier's* formula, with some of the identical questions, a carefully rehearsed interview was conducted on national radio. Major newspapers sympathetic to the president were called in to debunk the story. Young Roosevelt produced tax returns to refute the stories of large income. Still, there had been one clumsy mistake in the *Collier's* piece. The author had admitted to Jimmy Roosevelt's earlier days as a student selling insurance, "wallowing in an income of from $200,000 to $2 million a year." It was a staggering sum, and no one doubted why it had happened. Even more troubling, the salient points of corruption, including stories that major companies had transferred their policies to him, were left unanswered.

On September 1, 1939, Hitler invaded Poland and World War Two began. It would be another two years before America would enter the fray, but the drama in Europe soon swept aside all other news. Stories of Jimmy Roosevelt's insurance policies continued to trickle out throughout the 1940s with new revelations of conflict of interest. Some called it the biggest political scandal in America since Teapot Dome, but young Roosevelt survived and kept his money.

There is no question that the public pressures on James Roosevelt contributed to his physical decline. In the midst of his insurance scandal he suffered from a perforated ulcer. A large portion of his stomach was removed in surgery, and he was forced to send word back to his father that he would not be returning to the White House. It was during the long hospital stay that he began a romance with his nurse, Romelle Theresa Schneider. By the fall of 1940, with his ten-year marriage to Betsy Cushing at an end, James Roosevelt moved to California to try starting his life all over again.

The world of the arts and entertainment, Hollywood in particular, has had an appreciation for the instant celebrity syndrome and since its earliest days has provided sanctuary for weary presidential children, most recently, Jenna Bush, one of the twin daughters of President George W. and Laura Bush, who spent several months working for a Hollywood production company. In the fall of 1940, James Roosevelt took on a position with Samuel Goldwyn Productions and served for a time as vice president of the company. The move offered an opportunity for a harried president's son to remake his life far from the Washington press corps. And it provided an easier environment for a second marriage, a spreading custom among the Roosevelt children that was still causing a bit of shock to the public. On April 14, 1941, in Beverly Hills, California, the president's son married the nurse, Romelle Schneider. But their honeymoon year would be interrupted. Before Christmas the Japanese would bomb Pearl Harbor, and America would enter World War Two.

Even before the attack on Pearl Harbor two of the Roosevelt sons had been reactivated for military service. By the time the war was on, all four would be involved. James, whose health problems ruled out any serious assignment, begged his superior officers to send him to the front. He knew full well the criticism that would come if he was not involved in heavy action. By the end of the war, he had earned respect fighting in Guadalcanal, Tarawa, and the Solomon Islands. He was an officer of Evan Carlson's famous Second Raider Battalion and later commanded the Fourth Raiders, an elite force "assigned the most dangerous missions," earning the Navy Cross and the Silver Star. In the process he wiped away much of the resentment and lingering suspicions about his earlier scandals.

The death of president Franklin Delano Roosevelt and the end of World War Two marked a significant change in the life of James Roosevelt. He returned to California a war hero. In 1946 he was elected California State Democratic chairman. In 1950 he ran for governor of California, losing to future Supreme Court chief justice, Earl Warren, but with his name back in the public eye some political opportunity was certain. In 1954 he won a seat in Congress, where he served six terms, rising to "prominence on the education and labor committee." Lyndon Johnson appointed him as a delegate to the United Nations, and he wrote two books about his parents.

For James Roosevelt, the move back into the messy world of politics meant an inevitable marriage crisis. On July 1, 1956, he married Gladys Irene Owens in Los Angeles. That marriage ended in September 1969. A month later he married Mary Lena Winskill. It would be his fourth and last wedding. He would break into the public eye again in 1972 when he announced as a Democrat for Nixon. And there was one last scandal when the story broke that he was knee-deep in the offshore financial shenanigans of Bernard Cornfeld and Robert Vesco. James Roosevelt died of complications from Parkinson's disease in Newport Beach, California, on August 13, 1991. He was eighty-three years old.

Elliott Roosevelt:
A Recurring Pattern

During his father's presidency Elliott Roosevelt was the biggest story of all the president's children. There was an import-export scandal involving German airplane builder, Anthony Fokker. There were gossipy reports about his multiple marriages, and outrage over his fast advancement in the U.S. Army. Elliott Roosevelt was a man in a hurry. As a youth, he willfully flunked his Harvard entrance exam. "Obsessed with getting rich quick," he had no interest in being delayed by further education. FDR's second son immediately pursued a career in advertising, watching for special opportunities in which his famous name might prove useful.

At age twenty-two he married Elizabeth Browning Donner, but within months his father was president and he had fallen in love with someone else. As of yet, there had been no divorce in the Roosevelt family. Firstborn daughter Anna was struggling in her own marriage, and Sara, the ever-involved grandmother, was concerned, fearing that Anna's troubles would spill out into the public. Divorce for either child was not even an option in the grandmother's mind. The president and first lady must have felt that Anna would be sensitive to the situation, so the "first daughter" was dispatched to a meeting with Elliott in Chicago. But Elliott wasn't budging. Weeks later, the first lady herself made a difficult journey to the West Coast, tracking down her second son and trying to salvage the situation, or, perhaps more realistically, talk him out of an early second marriage.

Nothing slowed the Elliott Roosevelt express. Ignoring pleas from the family, he divorced Elizabeth Donner and almost immediately married Texas heiress Ruth Josephine Googins. It was a huge story. The White House was bombarded with letters from outraged and scandalized citizens. But Ruth Googins, attractive and rich, seemed very much "a keeper." Elliott wasted no time in Texas, using his experience in advertising to leverage a job as director of a Hearst radio network. Never mind that William Randolph Hearst, fearsome media mogul, was one of his father's bitterest enemies. Following the example of older brother James, Elliott arranged federal appointments from his Texas base, raising speculation that he was paving the way for his own political rise. Benefiting from his brother's bitter experience, Elliott wisely backed down when the stories surfaced. Meanwhile, *Time* magazine revealed that a second Texas radio network, this one organized by Elliott, himself, was heavily financed by the *Chicago Tribune*, yet another enemy of the president.

In the fall of 1940, a year before the Japanese attack on Pearl Harbor, with the British holding out against Hitler in Europe, Elliott Roosevelt decided that one of the president's sons should join the ranks of the growing U.S. Army. It may have been intended as a noble gesture, but perceived favoritism caused the story to backfire badly and was the beginning of a crisis that would only grow with time. Elliott Roosevelt, with no military training or experience, was commissioned a captain in the U.S. Army Air Corps. There was some rationale for the appointment; the president's son had experience with the aircraft industry, but the political opposition — most of the press and the public — saw it as outright nepotism. There was a firestorm of indignation. For weeks Captain Elliott Roosevelt was the talk of radio, his name vilified on editorial pages across the country.

After America's entry into World War Two, what had been a firestorm turned explosive. Elliott Roosevelt was rapidly promoted, first to major, then lieutenant colonel, and finally colonel. Each promotion was greeted with another round of media fury. This issue was offensive to the working-class people that FDR had always championed. As telegrams were delivered to homes across the country announcing the deaths of America's sons, there was a growing cynicism and deep bitterness about the perceived advantages of FDR's own boys.

That perception, like many tainted by the competitive world of politics, was both false and unfair. As in the case of older brother James, Elliott was a courageous and effective warrior for his country, flying three hundred combat missions, wounded twice, and "decorated for valor by the United States, France, Morocco and England." Commanding the 325th Photographic Reconnaissance Wing, he played his part in the invasions of North Africa, Sicily, and the D-Day invasion of Normandy in the summer of 1944. Still, the perception simmered beneath the surface, the president's enemies fanning the embers.

In 1943, Elliott Roosevelt met actress Faye Emerson at a Hollywood party. The two hit it off immediately. Emerson, a blond bombshell, had starred opposite Sydney Greenstreet, Errol Flynn, Ronald Reagan, and some of Hollywood's biggest stars. It was only a temporary, flirtatious friendship. Roosevelt was soon sent packing back to the European theater of the war. But in March 1944, Texas heiress Ruth Googins Roosevelt sued her husband for divorce. They had been married eleven and a half years and had three children. Ironically, at the time, it was the longest surviving marriage of all the Roosevelt children. There was immediate speculation that Elliott had fallen in love again, this time with a captain in the Women's Army Corps in London. Elliott was compelled to publicly deny the story. Ever the man in a hurry, six months later he stunned the media by announcing his engagement to Faye Emerson. On December 3, 1944, only two weeks before the Germans would launch the Battle of the Bulge, Faye Margaret Emerson and Elliott Roosevelt were married at the Yavapai observation station overlooking the Grand Canyon in Arizona. It was a glamorous moment. Emerson was at the canyon filming *Hotel Berlin*, a story about the end of the Third Reich, with Peter Lorre and Raymond Massey. Washington and Hollywood had married, and the nation was fascinated.

The stage was now set for one of the biggest

stories involving a president's son in modern times. Elliott's name had been submitted, along with a list of others, for promotion to brigadier general. Given his meteoric rise in the Army Air Corps, it was bound to stir up latent controversies surrounding his fast promotions. Then the atmosphere was poisoned by a further development. Elliott had ordered his large mastiff dog crated up and sent out to his actress wife in California. A military officer had marked the crate "A." During a transfer at an air base in Memphis, three American servicemen coming home from the war were bumped off the plane to make room. The story spread across the country, picking up a head of steam as it moved. Within days it was all over the front pages, the main subject in barber shops, restaurants, homes, and Capitol Hill. The *New York Herald Tribune* suggested that the story had become so big it was swamping the Great Russian offensive that was in the process of ending World War Two. Eventually, the popular, powerful president and his political coattails proved to be enough. Elliott got his promotion, and the story faded.

After the death of Franklin Delano Roosevelt, Elliott was soon plunged into yet another controversy. Journalists revealed that the president's son had borrowed $200,000 before the war and had repaid only $4,000. Roosevelt countered that the loan had come from an ex-wife. A congressional inquiry was inconclusive. Equally controversial was a book he authored, offering his own historical interpretation of his father's views. Using unpublished, personal conversations with his father, *As He Saw It* appeared in 1946, and, like everything else Elliott Roosevelt touched, it was radioactive. The book portrayed FDR as even more sympathetic to the Soviets than was the general perception. It split the family, offered fuel to Roosevelt critics and, in the process, became a huge best-seller, launching Elliott into a profession that would occupy him till the end of his life.

On Christmas Day, 1948, Faye Emerson Roosevelt was rushed to a doctor's office. She had self-inflicted slash marks on her wrists. Transferred to a hospital in Poughkeepsie, New York, she was released within two days. The family said it was an accident. Four years before, the Hollywood actress had arrived for Christmas at the Roosevelt family compound at Hyde Park. She was on Elliott's arm, with three children in tow. Eleanor had pronounced her "pretty, quiet and hard but I don't think she is more than a passing house guest." Two years after the suicide attempt she announced she was divorcing Elliott. The following year, March 15, 1951, Elliott Roosevelt married wife number four, Minnewa Bell Gray Ross, in a ceremony in Miami, Florida. Nine years later he wed wife number five, Patricia Peabody Whitehead.

As in the case of his older brother, James, the last marriage would prove to be the most enduring. He would remain with Patricia Peabody Whitehead the last thirty years of his life, adopting four children, serving as mayor of

Miami Beach, Florida, and establishing his name as a best-selling author. An insider book about his mother and father was released in 1973, *An Untold Story: The Roosevelts of Hyde Park*. It was the first in a trilogy of revealing books written with coauthor James Brough, and typically they sparked great controversy, angering family members.

Like big brother James, number two son Elliott Roosevelt resurfaced in one last scandal when, in his later years, he served as a lobbyist for Portuguese dictator Antonio Salazar. But his last decades passed relatively peacefully and productively. He retired to Scottsdale, Arizona, where he teamed with coauthor William Harrington and began penning a series of murder mysteries, starring his mother in a fictitious role as an American First Lady Miss Marple, who solved crimes in the Red Room, the West Wing, and even Buckingham Palace. Before his death in 1990, he had published twenty best-selling mystery novels and developed a large reading audience awaiting each new work. Controversial businessman, rancher, soldier, politician, historian, Elliott Roosevelt eventually found a degree of peace, with a stable marriage and a productive career. In fact, his mystery series survived him. Using notes and ideas he had prepared for future novels, his estate teamed up with Elliott's coauthor William Harrington to publish another book after his death. *Murder at the President's Door* was released in February 2002.

Franklin Delano Roosevelt, Jr.:
Almost Governor

Franklin Delano Roosevelt, Jr., was born August 17, 1914. He was nineteen years old when his father became the thirty-second president of the United States. Junior had followed in the footsteps of his two older brothers, graduating from the famed Groton Preparatory School and winning kudos academically and in sports. After the inauguration he headed for Europe, where he captured headlines and was entertained by heads of state. It was a harbinger of things to come, for the press would relentlessly follow his every move, waiting to see how he would compare to his two, controversial older brothers. They did not have to wait long.

After a summer abroad, Junior returned to the United States, determined to avoid the mistakes of James and Elliott, ignoring the limelight and seriously pursuing his education at Harvard. But his reckless driving defied his best intentions. He was arrested in New Jersey, Connecticut, Rhode Island, and New Hampshire, and sued over automobile collisions in New York and Boston. It was enough, together with the scandals of his older brothers, to cast them all as talented young men, but flawed.

Even so, there was something different about Franklin, Jr. His good looks and quick repartee as a debater earned him the reputation as the "golden boy" in the family. And then, on June 30, 1937, after graduating from Harvard, FDR,

Jr., married society heiress Ethel DuPont in Wilmington, Delaware. It was a huge event that captured the imagination of the nation. Here was the son of the president, the head of the Democrat Party, marrying into perhaps the nation's top Republican family and one that used its fortune to fight Franklin Roosevelt election by election. It was hailed a Romeo and Juliet story, "the wedding of the decade." Three companies of soldiers were called in to assist the president's family. Army engineers set up a field kitchen on the DuPont property. While his sister and older brothers would continually marry and divorce throughout their father's term in office, Franklin, Jr.'s, marriage to Ethel DuPont would survive his presidency and beyond. FDR, Jr., would graduate from the University of Virginia Law School, enter the navy during the war, and win the Purple Heart, the Navy Cross, and the Legion of Merit. Before the end of World War Two, Franklin Delano Roosevelt, Jr., would be commander of the destroyer, *Ulvert M. Moore*. Great things had been accomplished. More great things were expected.

In 1949, the twentieth congressional seat in New York was vacated by the death of U.S. Representative Sol Bloom. A special election was called. FDR, Jr., made his move. There was little time for candidates to prepare, and the former president's son had the critically needed name recognition, as well as the contacts to raise funds in short order. But the powerful New York political machine that had run New York politics for generations, Tammany Hall, insisted that the young Roosevelt son wait his turn. In a gutsy move, Franklin, Jr., defied Democrat Party insiders and ran for the seat with Liberal Party backing. He won, but there would be a price to pay.

Launching his new congressional career, Franklin, Jr., married for the second time on August 31, 1949, to Suzanne Perrin. The following year, FDR, Jr., was overwhelmingly returned to office, this time with both Democrat and Liberal party support, with the National Democrat Party adding their pressure to the local New York political machine. And in 1952 he won by an even greater margin. FDR, Jr., established a liberal voting record and made important friends during his years in Washington, including an up-and-coming young Catholic senator from Massachusetts named John Kennedy.

In 1954, FDR, Jr., "reached his political peak." He was the acknowledged frontrunner for the Democrat nomination for governor of New York. It was from this very position that his father had launched his campaign for the presidency, and a number of pundits spoke of him as a possible presidential contender as well. It was not to be. Tammany Hall was lying in wait. W. Averell Harriman won the nomination. In a gesture for party unity, the state party nominated FDR, Jr., for New York State attorney general, but he was the only statewide Democratic candidate to lose in the general election. It was a bitter blow.

For a few years, FDR, Jr., eschewed the public and political arena, pursuing business interests with success. He established the Roosevelt Automobile Company, a major importer of luxury cars. In 1960, when his old friend John F. Kennedy decided to make a run for the presidency, FDR, Jr., could no longer stand on the sidelines. Working hard for the Kennedy-Johnson ticket, he was rewarded with several high-profile appointments and his name was once more back in the news.

In 1966, Roosevelt resigned as the first chairman of the Equal Opportunity Commission to seek the New York gubernatorial office for the second time. In a replay of his upset congressional victory in 1954, he bypassed a clique of hostile party leaders and ran as a candidate for the Liberal Party. But the old magic wasn't there. FDR, Jr.'s, candidacy went down in flames, the only consolation being that the Democrat party insiders lost as well, allowing Republican Governor Nelson Rockefeller yet another term.

There were three more marriages — in 1970 to Felicia Schiff Sarnoff Warburg of New York City, in 1977 to Patricia Luisa Oakes, and finally to Linda McKay Stevenson Weicker, who survived him. In his later years, FDR, Jr., returned to a number of successful business endeavors, including a stint as chairman of the board of the Park Avenue Bank. Franklin Delano Roosevelt, Jr., the "golden boy" of one of America's most famous and powerful families, died of lung cancer on August 17, 1988, at Vassar Brothers Hospital, Poughkeepsie, New York. It was his seventy-fourth birthday.

John Aspinwall Roosevelt:
Without Trauma

John Roosevelt, the fourth son of FDR, was an investment banker who joined the Republican Party, never ran for political office, and experienced only one divorce. He was the exception in a family of public controversy and unstable personal relationships.

Born March 13, 1916, John was only sixteen years old when his father was elected president. His older brothers' antics captured the notoriety, which was fine with John, who pursued his education at Groton and Harvard. There was one early headline-grabbing episode that varnished him with the same "bad boy" brush as the other Roosevelt boys. During a tour of France John was accused of insulting the very proper mayor of Cannes, squirting champagne in his face. John hotly denied the report and his mother backed him, but the media and the public had seen too much mischief from his brothers to believe his side of the story.

As the baby in the family and as one who refused to trade on his father's name, John Roosevelt's military career was less sensational than those of his brothers. Still, he was awarded the Bronze Star and served with distinction as a lieutenant onboard the aircraft carrier *Wasp* in the Pacific. After the war he served briefly as a lieutenant commander.

John Aspinwall very clearly established himself as a different sort of Roosevelt. He declined more ambitious opportunities to work as a humble clerk in a department store. Remarkably, he would remain on that career track for two decades, working himself to the top of the retail business world, eventually owning and operating his own Los Angeles department store. In later years he spent most of his life quietly, privately, pursuing a career as an investment banker and aggressively promoting a favorite list of charities. In 1968, after twenty-eight years of marriage, he divorced Anne Lindsay Clark and married Irene Boyd McAlpin.

Within time, as John continued to endorse Republican presidential candidates, his political views gained some notoriety. It began with his support of Dwight Eisenhower for president and continued with his involvement in state political contests, including the supporting of Republican Jacob Javits, who in 1954 had almost ended his brother's political career by beating him in the New York attorney general's race. The last to be born, John Aspinwall Roosevelt was the first of the four grown sons to die, succumbing to a heart attack on April 27, 1981. He was sixty-five.

Two Extremes

The ongoing struggle for intimacy and identity can be seen vividly in the relationships and careers of the five strong-willed and talented children of Franklin Delano Roosevelt. Some of them traded shamelessly on their father's name, even while they sought their own identity. Two sons worked for their father's bitterest enemies, and another married into a family that openly despised him. One lobbied against parts of his legislative program in Congress. Another endorsed his father's opponent when he ran for a third term. And John, the youngest, complained about the New Deal, becoming a committed Republican, supporting Eisenhower, Nixon, and Reagan.

This conflict can almost be charted geographically, as their lives swung on an emotional pendulum from the East Coast to the West Coast. They were either seeking acceptance or intimacy, at their father's side in the White House and traveling with him on historic missions to Casablanca or Yalta, or they were as far away as they could get in the continental United States, seeking to define themselves as individuals. All four sons lived for a time in California. Anna worked in Washington State and Arizona. Even after her father's death she married her last husband in Malibu, California, and lived there until her senior years when her husband inexplicably pursued a career in the Veterans Administration, thus drawing Anna to Washington, D.C., once more. James Roosevelt also moved to the West Coast but ended back in Washington in Congress. For a time Elliott moved to Miami Beach, but finally settled in Arizona where he began writing his mystery series. Only the two youngest, FDR, Jr., and John, maintained a base in the Roosevelt home state of New York.

Historian J. J. Perling writes that Franklin Roosevelt lacked the "comradeship and constant intimacy which characterized the relationship between earlier presidents and their sons." This cannot be laid solely at the feet of FDR's successful career. Eleanor suspected that his bout with polio, which had left him in a wheelchair for life, limited more meaningful interaction with his robust sons. Some writers agree, venturing the idea that his sons, especially, were painful reminders of his own physical limitations. If so, it was the president's choice and his own demons that ordered the relationships, for there is no clinical support for the notion that children of handicapped parents experience any emotional disadvantage. Eleanor worried aloud about the impact it was having, joking nervously about the lack of access. "We laugh about it a great deal when I formally make an appointment for the children to see their father. . . ."

Curiously, presidents who loved spending time with their children sometimes fared no better. The child could claim a sense of being loved and treasured by the parent, but suffer in establishing his or her own separate identity. Thomas Jefferson so smothered daughter Patsy that her life became almost indivisible from his. It was clearly not the president who hurt the child but the presidency itself, the office. The celebrity and clout of the presidency either made a father unobtainable or overpowering. As we have seen, William Henry Harrison's last three daughters started dying off when he died. Their problem was not a lack of intimacy with a loving father but a lack of their own separate identity. It was as if their life had passed with his.

Either a child is neglected because of the insatiable demands of the presidency and the process of getting there, or else the child is smothered by the blinding light of the successful parents, making it difficult to establish a sense of identity and a confident role for their own life.

"For my children I regard my retirement as a favor," John Adams wrote. "They will now have fair play. They never had an equal chance with their comrades." Eleanor Roosevelt, who often disparaged her own efforts at motherhood, could feel the frustration of her children and the stifling impact that her own celebrity was having on their search for an identity. "My children would be much better off if I were not alive," she once observed. "I'm overshadowing them." But even with the passing of a presidential parent the process does not end. The long shadows cast by marble monuments are more enduring than the shadows cast by living flesh and blood.

And yet, almost unanimously, there is no bitterness among presidential children toward the parents. In spite of all that happened to her, Alice Lee Roosevelt Longworth never thought of blaming her president father for anything. He was one of the few persons she allowed herself to love. The children of Franklin Delano Roosevelt had only pride and devotion for their father and his memory. James Roosevelt, who stood next to his crippled father while he took the oath of office as governor of New York in 1929, literally propping him up so that he could stand, once said that what his father and mother "could do for the world was far more important than anything they could do for us."

Six

Resilient Women

"We are always equal to what we undertake with resolution. It is part of the American character to consider nothing as desperate; to surmount every difficulty by resolution and contrivance."
— Thomas Jefferson
in a Letter to Daughter Patsy

"As a child, girl, and woman I loved and honored him above all earthly beings."
— Ellen Randolph Coolidge,
Thomas Jefferson's Granddaughter

There is no record of presidential daughters committing suicide or destroying their lives with alcohol, or wasting time on get-rich-quick schemes, or thinking that the world owed them a living, as in the case of too many presidential sons. Perhaps it is a reflection of the unique feminine nature, an ability to internalize and adapt rather than to combat the circumstances and command the environment. Ironically, this may have led to even greater frustration, explaining the higher rates of premature death among presidential daughters. Or perhaps it has only been the absence of opportunity and the corresponding pressure of expectations. If so, as one sees the rights and opportunities of women advanced, one might begin to see the same negative patterns in modern presidential daughters who will more and more come under pressure to achieve on a scale with their parents. Only time will tell.

For the first part of our nation's history, women were expected to produce as many children as possible to work the land — presidents' daughters or otherwise — and there were no birth control options to release them "from these relentless conceptions." When their bodies were worn out, many simply died from complications of childbirth. There were no sterile delivery rooms with physicians trained in the latest techniques for dealing with neonatal emergencies.

And, if the daughter made a bad marriage — if her husband was an alcoholic, or a batterer, or did not provide for his family — there were no career choices for her outside the home where she might provide for all those babies. Sometimes, she could go back to her family. But if that option was not open to her, the woman simply did whatever she needed to do to survive.

The daughters of presidents, or presidents in the making, had all of that and even more, a much heavier load to carry. The fatherly demands for companionship and ego reinforcement and loyal work were often unquenchable. In many cases the mother in the family was spent, even before the great drama began. She would be called first lady and her biography would fill the pages of history but, in our nation's earlier years, it all too often fell to one of her daughters to raise the remaining children in the family, feed the ego of the presidential father, run the White House, and help prepare a safe landing for her parents' retirement, all while juggling her own marriage and raising her own children. Many daughters were buried in the process. Sometimes a president would use up the energies of several daughters. But there were many resilient women who drank this poison from childhood and in so doing developed an astounding immunity. They survived with a strength that the presidents themselves often did not possess. Sometimes the presidency devoured the children's lives, draining from it all identity, demanding years of intensely emotional service. Often the daughter would willingly give, without recognition or reward. Some would eventually bury the presidential father and still muster a final reserve to let the presidential legend live on and feed on her for the rest of her life.

The story of Patsy Jefferson has all those elements and more. She sought the fatherly approval discussed in Chapter 2, struggled in her own life for intimacy and identity, as discussed in Chapter 5 and, in the end, freely gave to her father, giving everything she had until he could take no more and was finally gone. And after all of that, there she was, Martha "Patsy" Jefferson Randolph, still on her feet.

Martha "Patsy" Washington Jefferson Randolph: *A Solitary Witness*

Thomas Jefferson, author of the Declaration of Independence, America's third president, always strove for the utopian life — as he envisioned it. For him the center of that vision was a tightly knit family, living together in harmony, with himself as the loving father. Jefferson "took care of people," historian Forrest McDonald says, ". . . and managed their lives gently, kindly, tactfully, and totally." There was only one thing he asked in return and that was their absolute devotion.

Jefferson lost his father when he was barely in his teens, and throughout his life untimely deaths kept coming, taking his mother, his sister, his adored wife, and four of the six children she bore him. As much as Jefferson gave the country, the only thing he wanted for himself was to be surrounded by a houseful of loving family, whom he could spoil, coddle, and adore.

On New Year's Day, 1772, Thomas Jefferson married Martha Wayles Skelton in a great celebration that included a wedding cake made with twenty eggs and two pounds of butter. Thomas Jefferson thought it would be the beginning of a lifetime of joy with Martha. Although he wanted a son, he was thrilled when his first child, Martha Washington Jefferson, or "Patsy," as she was called, was born on September 27, 1772. In the short ten years of

Thomas and Martha Jefferson's marriage, Martha was to bear six children. Two survived — Patsy and her sister Mary (or "Polly," as she was called). The others died quickly, some too sickly from birth, others falling victim to forces of the times. The son that Jefferson so desperately wanted lived only two weeks. There hadn't even been time to give him a name. Lucy Elizabeth I was born during the Revolutionary War, with British soldiers advancing. Through snow and freezing temperatures of January, Martha Jefferson fled upriver to safety with Patsy, Polly, and the five-week-old newborn. The baby fell ill and never recovered, yet another innocent casualty of America's dream for independence.

With each pregnancy Martha Jefferson grew progressively weaker. During the last four months of her life her husband never left her side. On September 6, 1782, shortly after Lucy Elizabeth II was born, Martha Jefferson died. Thomas Jefferson fainted in grief. As the ten-year-old Patsy later recorded, he "remained so long insensible that they feared he never would revive." Later that night, Patsy crept into his room "almost by stealth," and watched her father pace. It continued, night and day, for three weeks, with Jefferson throwing himself down on a pallet only when he was utterly exhausted. During the entire ordeal Patsy was "never a moment from his side." When Jefferson finally emerged, he took to horseback, "rambling about the mountain . . . In those melancholy rambles I was his constant companion, a solitary witness to many a violent outburst of grief."

Thomas Jefferson, against all custom for the time, never remarried. He wrote to a friend, "A single event wiped away all my plans and left me a blank which I had not the spirits to fill up." Historian Joseph Ellis wrote that, "He was scarred in a place that never completely healed. God had seen fit to reach down into the domestic utopia that he had constructed so carefully and snatch away its centerpiece." To the eyes of a loving ten-year-old, the grief made an indelible impression. She would do everything within her power to make him happy. She would take her mother's place.

Two months later, Jefferson was appointed as "Minister Plenipotentiary" and ordered to Paris to help negotiate peace with England and further treaties with France. It came at a propitious time, forcing Jefferson out of his debilitating grief. Thomas Jefferson took a delighted Patsy with him to Philadelphia, leaving Polly and the new baby, Lucy Elizabeth II, with his wife's sister, Aunty Eppes. Eventually, in May 1784, Patsy and her father set sail for Europe. She would have her father all to herself.

France was a great adventure for both Patsy and her father. While Jefferson was absorbed in the critical work of securing the new alliances for the fledgling United States, Patsy was quickly learning her supporting role. For a time she was taken under the wing of Abigail Adams, whose husband, John Adams, was also in Paris as an important part of the American diplomatic mission. Abigail and Patsy bonded quickly, with Mrs.

Adams teaching the young Jefferson how to dress and speak and act in French society. But the Adamses would eventually be transferred to a diplomatic assignment in England, and Patsy would need a new source of support.

The wife of Lafayette, hero of America's Revolutionary War, sponsored Patsy's admission into the most exclusive school for girls in Paris, the Abbaye de Panthemont. Jefferson's decision to enroll Patsy in what was, after all, a Catholic convent boggled the mind of the staunch New England Protestant, Abigail Adams. But there were many Protestants in the school, Jefferson assured Abigail, and Patsy would be exempt from theology classes. And it *was* the best school in Paris.

Life at the Abbaye was spartan in spite of the fact that three princesses attended classes there. No fires were built until water froze over in the basins. Students would "awaken at 6:00 a.m." with "candles out" at 8:30 p.m. There were classes all day and no speaking aloud except for lessons or during recreation. But Patsy was not even allowed the short times of recreation. Her father wanted her to study more and, Patsy, who desired only to please him, acquiesced.

At first, Patsy, who knew no French, was very lonely. For the first couple of months, her father visited daily until she could get acclimated. Later, when his responsibilities overwhelmed him, he wrote every day advising her in every aspect of life.

Even while her academic work was strenuous and complicated by a new language, Jefferson insisted that his daughter outperform any expectation even of her teachers. "We are always equal to what we undertake with resolution," he intoned confidently. "If you always lean on your master, you will never be able to proceed without him." Besides, he lectured, "It is a part of the American character to consider nothing as desperate, to surmount every difficulty by resolution and contrivance." One could almost hear a sigh of exhaustion in Patsy's answers, but she continued to reach beyond herself to fulfill her father's fantasy of perfection.

In January 1785, Jefferson's friend Lafayette returned to Paris. He had bad news. He silently handed Jefferson a letter from the family doctor, James Currie. Baby Lucy Elizabeth II had died on October 13 of whooping cough. Now he had lost not only his wife, but four of his six children. Patsy, of course, was there to console him again.

Part of Patsy's effort included reuniting Jefferson's disintegrating family. She urged him to bring her seven-year-old sister, Polly, to France. Jefferson readily agreed. For over a year, he corresponded with Polly and her Aunt Eppes, trying to convince his younger daughter to come to Europe. Polly, being much less pliable than her older sister, wrote back, "Dear Papa — I want to see you and sister Patsy, but you must come to Uncle Eppes's house." Polly *had* a home. Her Aunt Eppes had drawn the little girl into her own family, and Polly wasn't about to leave it. Jefferson, moved to desperate action, arranged for the *Arundel* to moor on the James River near the Eppes's plantation. For several days, all the children went aboard to play. One day, as planned, a game of hide-and-seek went on longer than usual. When young Polly finally grew tired and fell asleep, the other children left, and the ship set sail with Polly and her maid, Sally Hemings.

Once in Paris, Polly had to become reacquainted with her father and sister. They had been separated for so long she had no childhood memories of them. When a dismayed Jefferson understood this, he became even more convinced of the rightness of his drastic plan to bring his younger daughter to his side. Patsy took her sister to the convent every day for short visits so she would become accustomed to the strangeness of it all. No one need have worried. Joyous, blithe-spirited Polly won over the sisters as she had everyone else.

Jefferson was a happy man. He had both his remaining children with him at last. Things were looking up. Then Patsy's next letter arrived from school. She was asking her father's formal permission to stay at the convent to become a nun. Days later, Jefferson arrived suddenly at the Abbaye. He was jovial, never making a reference to Patsy's letter, but he quickly bundled up his daughters and left. Without missing a beat, Patsy assumed her role as mistress of her father's house with the added assignment of tutoring her little sister, Polly.

Within the year, the bloody French Revolution would issue out of the back streets of Paris, introducing the age of the guillotine, with royal heads being lopped off at an alarming rate. The religious would also be victims, including some of Patsy's own nuns and teachers. The privileged girls studying at the Abbaye de Panthemont would be in grave danger. During the winter of 1788–89, many French people starved to death. Others froze. By the following July, the bloody French Revolution was in full bloom. For Jefferson, it was a great philosophical opera. He was in the middle of the political machinations of a nation trying to hold the lid on a roiling cauldron of injustice, writing position papers, offering his insights from the American experience. But he fretted for his daughters' safety. They dared not even be seen in the street. People were being murdered for appearing well fed or well dressed. Jefferson wrote home, asking to be temporarily recalled, only to escort his children to safety, but months later he had heard nothing.

The Jefferson home was robbed three times before the storming of the Bastille in July of 1789. There was little food. Finally, that August, Jefferson received President Washington's permission, and on October 23 the Jefferson family set sail for the United States. All three were aching with longing for the sight of Monticello.

Polly gleefully reunited with her cousins, including her favorite, Jack Eppes. There was another old family friend, Tom Randolph, as well. The young Randolph and Patsy had climbed trees as children, and family tradition holds that Tom had visited her in Paris on his way home from school at Edinburgh. Thomas Mann Randolph, Jr., well educated, tall, rangy and dark, proudly counted Pocahontas as one of his ancestors. His ambition was a career in politics. Thomas Jefferson approved. The country, he said, "has much for you to do."

After a "scandalously" short engagement of three months, Patsy and Tom were married on February 23, 1790. The honeymoon was cut short as well. Monticello would need their care and supervision. Thomas Jefferson was off again in service to his country. He had been named secretary of state.

Jefferson was confident that Patsy was in good hands. Neither he nor Patsy were yet to know that there was a dark seam running through Tom Randolph's mind that would eventually destroy him — and impact her life forever. He would be incapable of making a decision, vacillating until disaster struck or the moment for success had passed. His paranoid rages would alienate everyone in his world. And, as his life with Patsy began to take shape, he came to understand that he would always be a distant second to Thomas Jefferson.

By 1792, Tom and Patsy had children of their own — Anne, born in January, and Thomas Jefferson Randolph, born a mere nine months later. Jeff, as he would always be called, was to Jefferson "the greatest of godsends which heaven has granted me." Patsy, unlike her frail mother, came through the births just fine. She was "built" for giving birth — fortunately, as it turned out, for she would bear twelve children in her life, fulfilling one part of Jefferson's fantasy of the perfect woman. What was unusual for the time was that eleven of Patsy's children would live to adulthood.

On October 13, 1797, sister Polly married her

beloved cousin Jack Eppes. For a wedding gift, Jefferson gave them acreage called Pantops, as close to Monticello as was Edgehill, the plantation that Tom had bought. If Jack and Polly couldn't live at Monticello, Jefferson begged, then "it must be at Pantops." But there was no house on the property, and Jack decided not to build one. He considered the proximity to Polly's father and promptly took his bride back to his own family home. Jack Eppes, unlike Tom Randolph, would always remain "his own man," while living in perfect respect and admiration for his father-in-law.

Within a year of their wedding, Polly delivered a baby that lived for only a few days. She contracted a painful "milk fever" and was still frail when she became pregnant for the second time. Never again would Polly be strong. She eventually had one son, Francis Eppes, but every other pregnancy ended in death.

During Jefferson's presidency, word reached the White House that Polly was failing. An anxious Jefferson, bound to Washington until the congressional adjournment in March, insisted that Jack Eppes, now a congressman himself, leave early to reach his wife. Jack struggled through ice to reach her side, often being forced to dismount and lead his horse over nearly impassable routes. He finally arrived at Edgehill, where Polly was being nursed by her sister. Jack dispatched daily updates to his father-in-law in the White House.

When Congress adjourned, Thomas Jefferson hurried home. He was stunned by Polly's appearance. On April 4, he wrote James Madison describing her as weak, unable to keep food down, with a fever and an abscess in her breast. They carried Polly home to Monticello in a litter, hoping against hope that she would recuperate. There was nothing anyone could do. On April 17, 1804, at the age of twenty-five, Polly died.

Father and sister grieved separately at first. Then Jefferson sent word for Patsy to come to him. When he saw her he began weeping. Ashamed, he apologized for his "weakness." He wanted her just to comfort him with her presence. Once more, Thomas Jefferson and daughter Patsy were alone at Monticello, grieving together.

After two months of intense and very private suffering, Jefferson was finally able to talk about what had happened, "Others may lose of their abundance, but I, of my want, have lost even the half of all I had. My evening prospects now hang on the slender thread of a single life." That slender thread was Patsy Jefferson Randolph. All of the president's hopes were now laid on her alone.

Now, more than ever, Thomas Jefferson's letters to Patsy spoke of his yearning to be free of political life, to return to Monticello as a simple grandfather and farmer. But it would be a dream delayed. His popularity was higher than ever. Jefferson was unbeatable. In the fall of 1804 he was reelected president.

During the social season Patsy accompanied him to the White House as acting first lady. While there, her son, James Madison Randolph, was born on January 17, 1806, the first child to be born in the White House. It was a joyous time after so much grief. Patsy made everyone feel at home, and Jefferson's dining tables groaned. The White House sparkled with fascinating conversation and the clink of wineglasses. In fact, with some degree of skepticism, Patsy wondered at the cost of these dinners. "He could have used a judicious wife to look after his domestic concerns," she later wrote. Had she known it, Patsy was speaking words of foreboding, for Jefferson was to spend $10,000 more during his presidency than his salary brought in. It would be as nothing compared to what was coming.

By the time Jefferson's difficult and unlucky second term as president was over, with American commerce hurt by embargoes and Jefferson blamed by many for the mess, Patsy was waiting at Monticello to surround him with a houseful of loving family. It was the beginning of seventeen years of intense joy and wrenching heartache, which would end with his death and Patsy's exile.

Monticello rang with the laughter of twelve grandchildren (including Polly's son, Francis Eppes, who visited often). Visitors would arrive to find the old president crawling on the floor with the youngest ones, or running races with them on the terrace. His grandchildren adored him. "I cannot describe the feelings of veneration, admiration, and love that existed in my heart towards him," wrote one. They would later speak of his impulsive generosity. Ellen Randolph Coolidge wrote, "Our Grandfather seemed to read our hearts, to see our invisible wishes." Anticipating their greatest desires, he would gift one with a beautiful new saddle and bridle, another with a guitar, yet another with a silk dress. "My Bible came from him, my Shakespeare, my first writing table, my first Leghorn hat, my first silk dress. . . ." But it would be, in part, this same generosity of spirit that would lead to the family's greatest trials, and to the eventual financial ruin of the Jefferson family.

Ironically, when Patsy was at the convent in Paris, she had sent her father a letter, requesting an advance of five weeks' allowance to pay for something she had already ordered. Although he sent the money promptly, it arrived with a letter of warning. "Do you not see, my dear, how imprudent it is to lay out in one moment what should accommodate you for five weeks? . . . Be assured that it gives much more pain to the mind to be in debt, than to do without any article whatever which we may seem to want." But his life continued to contradict this homily.

Thomas Jefferson, brilliant in the management of the nation's finances, was incompetent in dealing with his own. Having just completed two terms as president of the United States and thirty-five years of service to his country, Jefferson was rapidly approaching financial disaster. To be sure, it was not just his innate generosity and love of fine living that undid Jefferson. The situation was more complex.

A landowner of thousands of acres, Jefferson saw himself as wealthy. He never understood that his land did not necessarily equate to wealth. He was soon to learn that land in Virginia "cannot now be sold for a year's rent." In truth, by this time the entire plantation system of Virginia was sliding toward ruin.

In the face of destruction, Thomas Jefferson had kept right on building. Reared as an aristocrat, he had always taken luxury for granted. He spent a fortune remodeling Monticello, and filled it with wonderful things. He built the exquisite house at Poplar Forest as a retreat from the hordes of people that descended on Monticello, and who would stay and stay and eat and eat. As a tireless advocate of education, he took on what he considered the crowning achievement of his life, the building of the University of Virginia, begun when he was seventy-four. To do so, he spent money he did not have. And, inexplicably, while borrowing extensively himself, he continued to co-sign notes for others who were in as desperate straits as he.

Meanwhile, crops kept failing. In choosing the little mountain for his home, Jefferson apparently failed to notice that the soil was clay-based. It made for wonderful bricks, but grew poor crops. Rain destroyed grain on its way to market. Hessian flies descended and ate what little was left.

And then there was the cost of caring for slaves. Whether or not the farms made money, "my people" had to be fed, clothed, sheltered. (Jefferson could not even bring himself to refer to them as slaves.) As much as Jefferson wanted to see slavery end, it had, for him, become an economic impossibility. He naïvely hoped that the next generation would be able to end it. It would not. Slavery would slowly, inexorably splinter the nation.

Adding to the financial disaster were Tom Randolph's debts, often paid by Thomas Jefferson. Astoundingly, during all of this turmoil, no one shared a word of it with Patsy. Had she known, she might have been able to exert a tempering influence on the extravagance. Jefferson thought women needed to be "protected" from finances and politics. They shouldn't have to "wrinkle their foreheads" about such matters.

But Patsy had long been exposed to her own husband's problems. Tom Randolph's depression had throughout the years grown increasingly severe. He served in Congress, but his terrible temper only made enemies. In one famous altercation, he grabbed a rock and threatened to hit a stonemason who had called him a liar. His brother went bankrupt, leaving Tom the entire debt on their father's estate. And through it all, he gave away money to anyone with a woeful tale.

Although Tom grew abundant crops, he would let them rot in the barns unable to decide on the best time to send them to market. This "fatal indecision" may have been the most difficult of flaws. Patsy had grown up with a father of "absolute concentration of purpose." He had taught her to determine what needed to be done, and to do it. But something always seemed to divert Tom. On the very verge of success, he would fail. He was like those of whom the poet William Lawrence wrote: "On the plains of hesitation bleach the bones of countless millions who, at the dawn of victory, sat down to wait and, waiting, died." Perhaps he had come to accept that he would never be able to adequately compete with his father-in-law.

During the War of 1812, Tom took it into his mind to become a soldier. He put all his affairs in order (as much as possible, given his abysmal financial condition), wrote his will and, amazingly, considering they still had young children at home, made Patsy promise not to remarry if he should die. He then headed off to battle. Almost certainly he wanted to die gloriously, a hero. Then he would no longer have to be "something extraneous," as he had written to Jefferson, "like the proverbially silly bird . . . in the company of swans." Tom did not die in battle. He went on to become a three-term governor of Virginia. But his debts and difficulties with people only burgeoned as he grew older and wandered in and out of insanity.

By the time Tom Randolph returned home, most of the management of Thomas Jefferson's properties had been turned over to his twenty-one-year-old son, Thomas Jefferson Randolph. It was to be a fateful decision in the life of the family. Jeff was as pragmatic as his grandfather was visionary. He would never allow his grandfather's expenses to exceed his income.

Jeff had never been the scholar he thought his mother and grandfather wanted. While Jefferson was in office, Patsy wrote her father long, frustrated letters, saying that her children did not seem to be keeping up. She especially worried that Anne and Jeff "excite serious anxiety with regard to their intellect." She knew she was worrying over her children as her father had worried over her, and admitted, "Surely if they turn out well with regard to morals I ought to be satisfied, though I feel that I never can sit down quietly under the idea of their being blockheads." Her father sought to ease her mind, "I set much less store by talents than good dispositions: and shall be perfectly happy to see Jefferson a good man, industrious farmer, and kind and beloved among all his neighbors."

Now, in taking the reins of management, Jeff was proving himself the good man, the industrious farmer. A natural manager, he also worked like a draft horse. When he was six years old, Patsy had worried because he was sickly, and devised a way to toughen him up. Drawing on her spartan experiences at the French convent, Patsy insisted that Jeff sleep throughout the winter in an unheated "outer closet" with only a blanket for his bed. Now, the importance of that toughness became apparent. Jeff wrote, "Fortunately through my mother's training I had a hardy temperament and indomitable will — could sleep anywhere, eating anything and never tiring." Over the course of his lifetime it was to take every bit of hardy temperament and indomitable will that Jeff possessed.

In the spring of 1824, his father, Tom Randolph, threw in the towel. He gave his son, Jeff, a deed of trust to both his plantations, including their home, Edgehill. In return, Jeff assumed all responsibility for the family's debts. They totaled over $23,000, an enormous amount for the time. What Tom Randolph might have thought would happen is anybody's guess. But he certainly did not reckon with the steel will of his son. As a point of honor, Jeff made up his mind to liquidate all his father's assets and pay off every creditor. That meant Edgehill would be put up for sale the following autumn. Jeff would sell his own property, too; he would raise tobacco and do whatever had to be done to pay off these debts — both his father's and his grandfather's. It was in the spirit of Jefferson's letter to Patsy so many years before in which he told her, "It is a part of the American character to consider nothing as desperate, to surmount every difficulty by resolution and contrivance."

Patsy agreed with her son, now that she understood the depths of the financial problems from which she had been shielded her entire life. In discussing the situation with her father, it was agreed that his estate should be left in the care of trustees for her benefit. Should it come to her directly, it would be devoured by her husband's creditors.

On January 2, 1826, Tom and Patsy's home, Edgehill, was sold. And the son, Thomas Jefferson Randolph, was the buyer. That was, for his father, the ultimate indignity and insult. Tom Randolph was enraged. The family had betrayed him. No longer would he come to Monticello during the day. He told everyone it was to avoid the "supercilious looks of Mr. Jefferson's various guests." But the irrational Tom always returned after dark to badger Patsy, and took every opportunity to abuse his son. Edmund Bacon, Jefferson's overseer, wrote, "I have seen him cane his son Jeff after he was a grown man." The younger, more physically powerful Jeff would take his punishment and merely walk away.

Time was running out. The eighty-three-year-old Thomas Jefferson was dying. But he came up with an idea that just might save Monticello, as well as give Patsy support for herself and the small children left at home. It was a lottery. At ten dollars a throw, the winner would receive all his real estate except Monticello. The state legislature would have to approve. Surely, in light of all he had given the country, they would have to agree. Jeff thought it a grand idea, and took the proposal to the legislature. It was received with less than wholehearted enthusiasm. Games of chance in the social climate of the day were condemned. Finally, in February 1826, the legislature relented. But one additional proviso was added. Monticello would have to be included in the deal. When Jeff told him about this new tragedy, his grandfather's face blanched. "I must have time," he said. "I must consult Mrs. Randolph." Only Patsy had been with him from the beginning; she had cared for him always; she had done everything in her power to make him happy. Only she would understand. He would have to ask her advice.

By July 1826, no tickets had been sold. But the word had gone out that Jefferson needed help, and states had begun to respond. Jefferson was thrilled at the response of love that the money, freely given, represented. He was also relieved that none of his "people" would have to be sold, and that Monticello would be saved for Patsy. It was not to be, but he would die content, unknowing.

The dramatic death of Thomas Jefferson was something that no Hollywood scriptwriter would dare write. The fiftieth anniversary of the signing of the Declaration of Independence was imminent. Thomas Jefferson fought to live until the Fourth of July, "that he might breathe the air of the fiftieth anniversary, when he would joyfully sing with old Simeon, *'Nunc dimittis, Domine'*" ("Lord, now lettest thou thy servant depart in peace").

Jefferson sank slowly each day, drifting in and out of consciousness. He called Patsy to his side and gave her a small morocco case, asking her to open it only after his death.

On July 3, he awoke to ask, "Is it the fourth yet?" Not yet, came the answer. Not yet. That night, at 8:00, the doctor told his family that Jefferson would probably die within the next quarter hour. "Yet he lived seventeen hours longer, without any evident pain or suffering or restlessness, but with sensibility, consciousness, and intelligence for much more than twelve hours of the time. . . ."

The next morning, Thomas Jefferson opened his eyes. With his family nearby he clearly said, "I have done for my country and for all mankind all that I could do, and I now resign my soul without fear to my God, my daughter to my country."

In Quincy, Massachusetts, at about the same time, John Adams, the old patriot and friend of Jefferson, spoke his last words, "Jefferson still survives." He was wrong. Jefferson had died peacefully at ten minutes before one o'clock, fifty years to the day and hour after the Declaration of Independence had received its final reading.

Five hours later Adams, too, was dead. When America heard the news, it was with a sense of awe. "There was not a heart which did not feel a mournful pleasure at the miraculous beauty of such a death."

When Patsy opened the little morocco case that her father had given her, she found a paper written in her father's elegant script. It was his poem to her, "on the virtues of a dutiful and incomparable daughter." It ends thus: "The last pang of life is parting from you! Two seraphs await me long shrouded in death; I will bear them your love on my last parting breath."

Patsy and Jeff were unable to save Monticello. Thomas Jefferson's estate bore debts of $107,273.63. Everything had to be sold, even the slaves that Jefferson had desperately wanted to free. Jeff vowed that every debt would be paid, "to the last copper." It would take him forty years to do it. But the Civil War would strip him of everything except his land and "one old, blind mule."

The states of Louisiana and South Carolina each sent Patsy $10,000 in gratitude for her father's service. To keep it from being absorbed into the great debts, the money was invested in her father's greatest achievement, the University of Virginia, but the interest from the fledgling institution was not enough to make her independent. The Senate of the United States voted

Patsy a grant of fifty thousand acres of land, but there is no record that she ever received it.

Immediately after her father's death, Patsy took her twelve-year-old daughter Septemia and her eight-year-old son George Wythe to Boston to live with her daughter Ellen Coolidge. For the rest of her life Patsy would live in penury with one or another of her children, not even having "a warm shawl." She would never, however, lose her strength of character.

As for Tom Randolph, during a terrible storm he met an old man on the road who had no cloak. Tom gave him his own. Chilled and soaked to the skin, Tom fell ill with pneumonia. He called Patsy, Jeff, and the rest of his family to his bedside and begged their forgiveness before he died. He received it.

On October 10, 1836, at the age of sixty-four, Patsy died of "apoplexy," most probably from a stroke. She was buried at Monticello, at the feet of her father.

Martha Johnson Patterson:
Tending Her Father's Flame

No story better captures the dark side of life as a president's child than the story of the Andrew Johnson family. His wife was practically a life-long invalid. Two alcoholic sons died early, one of them a suicide. A third son, the president's namesake, vowed to his mother that he would never "let any kind of intoxicating liquors" pass his lips and "promised to be a comfort to his parents in their old age." But, as in the case of many other presidential children, his identity was hopelessly entwined with that of his controversial father. He died of a cause unknown soon after the president at age twenty-six. A younger daughter, Mary, became a widow during the Civil War, remarried a man she didn't love, and was forced to stay with him for years until her revered president father passed from the scene and she could obtain a divorce. But it is the older daughter, Martha Johnson Patterson, whose story is the most compelling and the exception that unfortunately proves the rule.

She was born October 25, 1828, in Greenville, Tennessee. Her father, who would eventually rise to the highest office in the land, was a poor, illiterate tailor who had never attended a single day of school in his life. For a while they lived in a two-room building on Main Street in the isolated Eastern Tennessee mountain town. Johnson ran his tailor shop out of the front room, and his growing family lived in the back room. His wife, Eliza, would give birth to three more children in the next six years.

Andrew Johnson's political rise was remarkable. Full of confidence in spite of his humble origins, he boldly spoke out on community issues, soon becoming the champion of the Greenville working class. He was elected alderman and then mayor of the town, defeating "the more aristocratic party." He served in the Tennessee State legislature and was finally elected to the U.S. Congress. Eliza Johnson was too ill and too overwhelmed with the family to follow her husband back to Washington D.C., so it was arranged for daughter Martha to travel east with the new congressman. She was enrolled at the nearby Georgetown Female Seminary, run by a certain Miss English, who as her name promised, was credited for transforming young "girls" into young "ladies."

When her father made trips to the home district in Tennessee, Martha was looked after by fellow Tennessean James K. Polk and wife, who just happened to be the president and first lady of the land and who happened to have no children of their own. This was Martha's introduction to the White House social scene and an education that would have a surprising utility in the life of a humble, unassuming, mountain girl. There was more. These brief months provided a critical introduction to the cynical life of Washington-style politics. At first, Mrs. Polk was taken with this easily underestimated girl from the hollows of eastern Tennessee. Martha was clearly gifted and "with her energy and intelligence, seemed to resemble her father." But when the political storm clouds rose, and her father opposed some of the president's policies, the Polks dropped young Martha as a device to punish the father. Welcome to Washington. A precipitous fall from such social heights might have been emotionally devastating to a woman of less strength and bearing. Martha seems to have taken the whole experience in stride.

Meanwhile, the career of her father Andrew Johnson defied gravity. After ten years in Congress his enemies were finally able to bounce him out through redistricting, but before the year was over he was elected the governor of Tennessee. He served two full terms before returning to Washington, this time as a U.S. senator and right on cue to join the great debate on the future of the union. That year the yawning cultural and political divide between North and South had reached its climax, and although living in a slaveholding border state, and even owning slaves himself, Johnson weighed in heavily in favor of maintaining the union. Branded a traitor or worse by Southern sympathizers in eastern Tennessee, the whole Johnson family was soon imperiled.

Mary, Andrew Johnson's youngest daughter, wed Daniel Stover, a farmer turned union guerrilla, who burned bridges behind enemy lines and experienced imprisonment before going into hiding. His farm in eastern Tennessee became the center of the Johnson clan until Southern sympathizers drove them out. But Stover's brief and harsh imprisonment proved his undoing, for, if the rebel forces were unable to recapture him, a disease contracted in the crowded prison camp eventually found him out. He died of tuberculosis in 1863.

Charles Johnson, eldest son of Andrew and Eliza Johnson, and Martha's younger brother, died that same year. He had "long been a source of worry." He had studied medicine and co-owned a pharmacy before the outbreak of the Civil War, and in the process, while preparing for his career, had developed an addiction to alcohol. When the conflict began, he joined the First Middle Tennessee Infantry as a surgeon. But

Charles Johnson, as in the case of Charles Adams before him, was a chronic alcoholic, a problem complicated by his easy pharmaceutical access to whiskey, the most popular "medicine" of its day. His death, in April 1863, is controversial and confusing for historians. In the most recent version of their work on presidential children, Quinn-Musgrove and Kanter cling to the idea that this was a suicide. "Completely exhausted, addicted to stimulants," they write, he had "ended his own life." Yet the source they cite is in fact referring to the death of Robert Johnson, not older brother Charles. Most accounts acknowledge the alcoholism but describe his death as entirely accidental, saying that he was "thrown from a horse and died from his injuries." Charles was thirty-three.

On December 13, 1855, five years before the outbreak of the Civil War, Martha had married her father's friend and supporter, Judge David T. Patterson in Greenville, Tennessee. Although Martha was admittedly her father's favorite child, he was too busy to attend the wedding. Martha, always the loyal servant and source of morale for her father, never complained. Two years later she gave birth to Andrew Johnson Patterson.

During the war, President Abraham Lincoln appointed Johnson military governor of Tennessee. The border state was hotly contested by both sides. For a while his family was behind enemy lines. Martha made frequent visits to her now invalid mother, completing simple household chores and living there for weeks at a time, helping with the youngest child in the family, Andrew "Frank" Johnson, Jr. Meanwhile, her husband, Judge Patterson, was captured along with the other son-in-law, Daniel Stover. Patterson was able to negotiate with the Confederate government to secure his own release. Eventually, he and Johnson's second son, Robert, escorted the family across enemy lines to safety.

In June of 1864, anticipating an end to the war and looking toward the eventual healing of the nation, President Abraham Lincoln encouraged Republican delegates to nominate Andrew Johnson of Tennessee as his new running mate. The hope was that by naming a southerner who had supported the Union, Lincoln could appeal for unity after the conflict was won. The Lincoln-Johnson ticket was elected, and on March 4, 1865, Andrew Johnson was sworn in as vice president. One month later, on April 15, 1865, Abraham Lincoln was assassinated. The poor tailor from east Tennessee was president.

Upon hearing the news, first daughter Martha Johnson Patterson's immediate reaction was one of alarm. "Are you safe?" she wrote in a letter to her father. President Johnson called the whole clan back to Washington. His wife Eliza was growing steadily weaker, but Martha and her husband, Judge Patterson, could help. And they could all take care of Mary Stover, the younger daughter in the family, who was now a widow with three children. Then there was Robert.

Robert Johnson, the second son of Andrew and Eliza Johnson, had for a long time been touted as a man with a future. A lawyer in the 1850s, he had supported the Union and kept his congressman father informed from the family base in Tennessee. In 1860, Andrew Johnson had used some of his own political clout to help his son get elected to the state legislature. Robert had acquitted himself well and had become a colonel in the Union Army, leading daring raids behind enemy lines. But, as in the case of older brother Charles Johnson, the pharmacist, there was the nagging problem of alcohol. In 1862, Johnson was openly worried about Robert and Charles, "both of them now addicted to drink." It was generally accepted that "young Bob had wasted great opportunities." Nevertheless, the new president needed someone close who could be trusted. Hoping to revive a relationship that had worked back in his congressional days, Andrew Johnson named Robert as his new White House secretary. It turned out to be a tragic decision for both father and son.

Seeking to fulfill the publicly stated agenda of his predecessor Abraham Lincoln, Andrew Johnson began work on reconstruction and the tedious process of reuniting the nation, with charity toward the conquered South. Notwithstanding that this had been Lincoln's own plan, northern Republican radicals reacted. Andrew Johnson found himself in the middle of an impeachment proceeding. It was one of the most brutal political battles in American history, a bitter time for the Johnson family and, some would argue, a potential tragedy for the presidency. Some in Congress were prepared to limit the power of the White House to the point of rendering it irrelevant.

Presidential son, Colonel Robert Johnson, who without flinching had bravely endured the butchery of the Civil War, who had witnessed the stacks of amputated legs and arms filling his surgeon brother's hospital tent, did not have the stomach to see his family pilloried in public. He began to "drink heavily again." While the most frustrating game in town lay in tracking down the multiple false and scurrilous stories about his father, Robert clumsily provided fodder to his enemies with his own erratic behavior. Prostitutes were reportedly seen leaving his White House office in full view of guests waiting to see the president. His actions severely harmed his father's political reputation.

In March 1869, his one-term presidency at an end, Andrew Johnson and family enjoyed a grand processional home to Greenville, Tennessee. They were greeted in villages all along the way with rousing cheers from southerners who had once vilified them all as "traitors" and who had, on several occasions, tried to lynch them. But the bitterness of his experiences and perhaps the disappointment with his own personal mistakes were gnawing at presidential son Robert Johnson. He committed suicide a few weeks later on April 22, 1869, while his father was away on an extended speaking tour. Some obituaries generously stated his cause of death as "alcoholism." He was thirty-five.

If the bitter White House experience successfully conquered the spirit of Robert Johnson, it met its match in the resilient and patient first daughter, Martha Johnson Patterson. She had no illusions about political allies and friends in Washington. And she had some idea about how to use the fleeting power and opportunity that the White House offered. Her brief glimpses of the White House in the glamorous days of President James K. Polk gave her a vision of how to restore the shambles her father had inherited. During the Civil War the White House had practically become a Union hospital and barracks. With the assassination of Abraham Lincoln and the prolonged stay-over of his widow, Mary Todd Lincoln, cloistered in grief in the privacy of her upstairs room, the president's house had been overrun with curiosity seekers and soldiers. Curtains, furniture, and china had been hauled off. Corners were stained with tobacco juice.

First Lady Eliza Johnson was too weak to offer any help. She would make only two public appearances throughout the presidency, living as an invalid in a front room of the private, upstairs quarters of the White House. Andrew Johnson, who had leaned on first daughter Martha during his early lonely years as a congressman in Washington, now called on her and her widowed sister Mary for help. Martha was named the official White House hostess. It turned out to be an inspired choice.

Most historical accounts agree that Martha Johnson Patterson, the humble mountain girl from east Tennessee, ushered in a White House elegance and style that has continued unabated to this day. In the middle of bitter impeachment proceedings, she used her powers of persuasion to convince a hostile Congress to allocate funds for White House refurbishment. She then stretched the modest allocation with hard work and volunteer labor to astound visitors by her extensive renovations. There was nothing fancy or pretentious in her modus operandi. The same White House hostess, who renovated the president's mansion and managed a return to elegant receptions and state dinners, stretched the family budget by supervising dairy cows, grazing on the White House South Lawn. There was always plenty of milk for the president's large extended family. According to most observers, "Martha had become his mainstay."

It all came at a price. Martha confided to a reporter that she felt confined. "If I could only walk about a little with my children sometimes in the grounds without being stared at, and really enjoy the comfort of an old dress and a little privacy."

In the president's retirement, Martha continued to be a constant and critical source of support. While his public persona projected confidence, he openly revealed to her his inner frailty. They frequently corresponded, and she kept his spirits from flagging. In June 1873, suffering from cholera, he visited her farm, planning to die in her house. He embraced Martha and her husband Judge Patterson for what he imagined would be the last time, carefully penning a farewell message to the family. But with the help of Martha and family doctors, "he was nursed back to health."

The following year, against all odds and expectations, his remarkable political career revived once more. Former president Andrew Johnson ran for the United States Senate. It was a long shot; he had earned a surfeit of enemies. Martha nervously cushioned his ego, ready to catch him if he fell, but he astounded the nation once again and won the contest. An ecstatic Martha Johnson Patterson wrote her father that it was "the greatest victory of your life."

Meanwhile, Mary, the widowed younger sister, had married a Mr. William R. Brown. Soon realizing her mistake, she had sought a divorce. Such an act was then social suicide, and a proud Andrew Johnson forbade it. For months at a time Mary lived separated and miserable at her old farm outside Greenville, Tennessee, surrounded by the mementos of her brave departed first husband, Daniel Stover, biding her time until her father would die and she could get on with her life. One is tempted to speculate on the trouble in her marriage. As in the case of Jefferson and son-in-law Randolph, was the presidential father too much competition? The family was too discreet to leave any hints behind.

On a Friday evening, July 30, 1875, former president Andrew Johnson visited Mary's farm, suffered a stroke, and lost consciousness. Martha and brother Frank arrived shortly afterward. The former president recognized neither. At 2:30 a.m., July 31, Senator Andrew Johnson, the seventeenth president of the United States, died. His wife, Eliza, who had been an invalid for most of her years, followed him to the grave six months later. Only four years later, in March 1879, Andrew Johnson, Jr., "Frank," died at the youthful age of twenty-six. And finally, four years after that, Mary died at age fifty.

But Martha Johnson Patterson lived on, determined to tend the flame of her father's memory. When her mother's health failed early in life, Martha had stepped in to take care of her younger siblings. When her father was elected to Congress, she alone in the family was tapped to move back to Washington to help him. She cared for the family during their frightful time behind enemy lines. She ran the White House flawlessly for four years. She nursed her father's wounded pride after his fall from power and, finally, rejoiced in his last political victory. She had named her firstborn Andrew Johnson Patterson. And yet, it had always been a one-way street. Her father had missed her wedding day and the births of her children.

Martha lived to see Teddy Roosevelt inaugurated president, and to see her father's name very briefly exonerated by a fickle flame of history. As in the case of many other presidents' children, she never tired of promoting him, finding in his life both a sense of her own identity and a sense of intimacy, of being needed and thus being loved. She finally died of natural causes on July 10, 1901; she was seventy-two.

SEVEN

DAUGHTERS OF COURAGE

"I will feel equality has arrived when we can elect to office women who are as unqualified as some of the men who are already there."
— MAUREEN REAGAN

It is a paradox of Thomas Jefferson's reasoning that he educated daughter Patsy better than most men of the time, yet would not allow her to be involved in family finances or ever give over to her the ultimate management responsibility for his beloved Monticello. Given the complexities of his situation, perhaps she would not have salvaged the family estate. And, yet, Thomas Jefferson's inconsistent micromanagement assured its loss. Martha "Patsy" Jefferson Randolph was an astounding woman, brilliant, accomplished, secure in herself, strong and resilient. She was, after all, the one who had been dissatisfied with the cooking methods of the day, where cooks used a pinch of this and a handful of that, and conducted scientific experiments with weights and measures to determine the cheapest, most efficient way to cook. And she was present at

Monticello almost every moment, not off at the White House or the governor's mansion taking care of the country. Who is to say that she might not have prospered her family had she been allowed to try?

It was a situation common for the times. Thomas Jefferson, like most of his counterparts, believed that women should be "protected" from worrying about security and money so they could attend to their domestic chores. Even more than a century later, Calvin Coolidge would say, "Women can never escape the responsibility of home and children, and the working woman as a mother and potential mother challenges universal interest."

In 1824, when they were very old men, Jefferson was reunited with his friend, the Marquis de Lafayette. Observing that reunion, in another bizarre quirk of history, was a remarkable woman named Fanny Wright, a friend and traveling companion of Lafayette. Reared in Scotland to "question conventional ideas," she would become the trailblazing advocate for the abolition of slavery and for woman suffrage in the United States. Jefferson found her brilliant mind an enigma and her arguments sometimes troubled him weeks later.

Patsy herself had already made her feelings known about the evils of slavery. After her father's death, as slaves had to be sold to meet expenses of Jefferson's estate, a devastated Patsy wrote to her son Benjamin: "You are right in supposing the interests of my children the first and dearest object in *my own* life, and I would lay down my own life with joy to ensure prosperity and happiness to them, but I have no right to sacrifice the happiness of a fellow creature *black* or *white.*" The questions of freedom and suffrage would rip at the country's heart for a century.

During the nineteenth century's "cult of domesticity," women were expected to take a stereotypical role — at least in the eastern half of the country. Pioneer women, of course, were more "equal" and expected to bear as much as their husbands. It should come as no surprise that woman suffrage would come first in the western states.

By the turn of the twentieth century, American presidents were being forced to listen to a phalanx of women — gutsy reformers, wealthy socialites, and the burgeoning female academic community. Courageous women — white, black, Native American, Latina — began to organize and take the first tentative, unpopular, often dangerous steps to full citizenship — even at great cost to themselves.

It was education that would drive woman's suffrage, temperance, human rights, and social reform in its path. Schools had already been founded that were finally teaching women more than art and music and dancing — Vassar, Radcliffe, Mt. Holyoke. Smith College would one day educate First Daughter Julie Nixon Eisenhower and First Ladies Barbara Bush and Nancy Reagan. Radcliffe would educate First Daughter Caroline Kennedy, who would go on to write important books on the Bill of Rights.

In 1885, the doors of Bryn Mawr opened near

Philadelphia. A rigorous, Quaker women's college that was the first to offer women a Ph.D., it sent a "signal that its founders refused to accept the limitations imposed on women's intellectual achievement." While Alice Roosevelt was smoking cigarettes on the roof of the White House, young Helen Taft was on her way to Bryn Mawr.

Helen Taft Manning:
The Torchbearer

When Helen Taft was nine years old, she was on board a ship, steaming toward the Philippines. Her father, Judge William Howard Taft, had just been appointed civil governor of the islands "liberated" from Spain in the Spanish-American War. It was up to her father to administer the new government, suppress violent rebels, and eventually to turn over the reins of leadership to Filipinos. It was a job he did with excellence and compassion, earning him respect from the people he governed. It allowed young Helen and her two brothers to gain a sophistication and an experience of the world far beyond their years.

Born on August 1, 1891, Helen Taft was enrolled in a Catholic convent school in the Philippines by her Unitarian father. As with Patsy Jefferson's extended family in Paris, this caused raised-eyebrow discussion, with the same resigned conclusion. The convent school was the best place for young Helen to be educated until the Americans could open their own school. The family returned to Washington, D.C., when President Theodore Roosevelt named his trusted friend, William Howard Taft, as secretary of war. Helen was thirteen. By the time her father was inaugurated the twenty-seventh American president in March of 1909, Helen Taft was already deeply enmeshed in the tough academic environment of Bryn Mawr, with an *earned* academic scholarship that had nothing to do with a presidential father's political clout.

At the end of her sophomore year, Helen "dropped out" to serve for a time in the White House. Her mother had suffered a serious stroke and, like presidents' daughters before her, Helen stepped into the breach. Alice Roosevelt, whose colorful antics had whetted the media's appetite for stories about presidential children, had just passed through the White House halls as first daughter before her. So with much anticipation, a new president's daughter, Helen Taft, was presented to the capital. It was a grand, gala affair, with the president's daughter wearing a gown dubbed "Helen Pink." The dress never did rival her predecessor's "Alice Blue Gown." But if the Taft daughter could not compete with the Alice Roosevelt personality cult, she showed no signs of disappointment. With strong encouragement from her father, Helen had more scholarly pursuits in mind.

In 1915, Helen Taft graduated magna cum laude from Bryn Mawr with degrees in history, economics, and politics. She would later earn a master's degree and a doctorate in history from Yale. In 1917, at the tender age of twenty-five, Helen Taft was appointed dean of Bryn Mawr.

Millicent Carey McIntosh, later president of Barnard College, was in the first class to experience Helen Taft's youthful administration. "She cut her administrative teeth on us, and we were both dismayed and yet reluctantly admiring," she wrote. The Bryn Mawr academic staff was impressed with their new dean. Said McIntosh, "It was clearly understood that I should pattern myself on her."

In July of 1920, Helen Taft married Dr. Frederick J. Manning, professor of history at Swarthmore. At the time, as evidenced by her contemporaries, she assumed that marriage spelled the end of any career. Her working days were over. But two years later Helen became acting president of Bryn Mawr. By the time she finally retired in 1957 as a professor emeritus, Helen Taft Manning had served as dean for another sixteen years, interrupted by a second round in the president's office (1929–1930), tenure as professor of history and, after 1941, as chairman of the History Department. An authority on American, Canadian, and British colonial history, Helen Taft published *British Colonial Government After the American Revolution* in the 1930s, and *The Revolt of the French Canadians* in 1962.

In her exceptional educational career, Helen Taft Manning influenced the minds and lives of thousands of young women. She was honored by Bryn Mawr for "bringing to every phase of its life, enthusiasm, wit, wisdom, courage, integrity, and the determination to promote whatever she judged best for the development of intellect and

263

of freedom in thought and action." But her work in education was only half of the story.

Parallel to her career, Helen Taft Manning helped pioneer a generation of work for the advancement of women in American society. Bryn Mawr President Thomas introduced her to woman suffrage meetings where Helen labored tirelessly, speaking out in her brusque, forthright manner. It was an activity that dismayed her parents, and her mother "suffered" whenever she heard that her daughter was on the road yet again, campaigning for her cause. But by the time the Nineteenth Amendment was ratified in 1920, and American women were finally given access to the ballot box, her father, then a Supreme Court justice, urged his wife to vote. "You must not allow the ignorant women to exercise their right and neglect to do your duty yourself." Helen's mother, who had suffered through her daughter's controversial campaign for years, accepted the benefits and went to the polls to cast her ballot.

Helen Taft Manning served as the national treasurer for the Women's International League for Peace and Freedom, founded "to create an environment of political, economic, social and psychological freedom for all members of the human community, so that true peace can be enjoyed by all." Its first president, Jane Addams, was the first woman to win the Nobel Peace Prize. Their activities in the establishment of the United Nations International Women's Year led eventually to the 1985 Nairobi Conference to chart a "practical course for the future advance-

264

ment of women throughout the world." Another presidential daughter, Maureen Reagan, would chair that very Nairobi Conference.

Described by her children as stubborn and career obsessed, Helen Taft Manning championed a cause that contradicted the theology and philosophy of her times, not to mention the politics of her president father and first lady mother. And she did so without any bitter recrimination or family estrangement, a fact that served her cause well, for a hostile father, who was president and later Supreme Court justice, could have damaged her cause more than all her good work combined. And of course, she saw her cause succeed. No small point. For it is one thing to be right on an issue and something altogether different to see it win acceptance.

Dr. Helen Taft Manning was the torchbearer for a new generation of women, not only as an eloquent advocate of her cause but by the example of her own life. For many advocates of women's rights today, she still represents the ideal, the successful marriage of family, career, social conscience, and personal excellence.

Jessie Woodrow Wilson Sayre: *A Woman's Right to Vote*

When the Woodrow Wilson family arrived in Washington on March 3, 1913, the day before the inauguration, they found few people to welcome them. The whole city had turned out to watch the first "giant parade of women." It was not a grand demonstration by today's post-

Vietnam standards. Only about eight thousand marching women were able to mesmerize the capital and turn the eyes of the nation to the cause of woman suffrage. But it was done with imagination and flair. It was led by the Vassar-educated lawyer Inez Milholland, astride a white horse like some beautiful, medieval herald. There were bands and floats, with pageantry and tableaux along the route. Some women had hiked all the way from New York and marched, mud-spattered, beside beautifully garbed society women. For too many years they had worked and presented bills to Congress, been voted down, only to rise up and try again. Now, with this election, women had earned the right to vote in nine western states, and the movement was reaching critical mass.

Some watchers were sympathetic; many were not. "Their flags and banners were spat upon, lighted cigars and cigarettes were thrown upon them, and the crowding in on the line here and there caused more than a hundred persons to be so trampled and bruised as to require hospital treatment."

The effect was not lost on the Wilson daughters, Margaret, Jessie, and Eleanor (nicknamed Nellie). Jessie had already taken a firm stand against what she saw as injustice, attempting to reform the snobbish selection process of new members in her college sorority, resigning in protest when her efforts proved fruitless. All three sisters were solidly in favor of woman suffrage, and had called their father to task on the issue, even before his election to the presidency, warning him that he was far behind the times. Jessie had pointed out the obvious, that he would miss out on four votes in his own household alone, those of his wife and three daughters.

Born on August 28, 1887, Jessie Woodrow Wilson had been, as in the case of Helen Taft, educated far beyond most women of the day. She studied at Goucher College and at Princeton University, earning a Phi Beta Kappa key for her high academic accomplishments. After college, Jessie began work at the Lighthouse Settlement House for women millworkers, near Philadelphia, and her observations of downtrodden women there turned her into a passionate believer in suffrage and women's rights.

As the tedious, often disappointing work of getting legislation through Congress continued, all three Wilson sisters supported the cause. In 1915, Margaret would act as honorary hostess for the convention of the National American Woman Suffrage Association (later known as the League of Women Voters). In 1917, with the country in the throes of World War One, Eleanor would speak at the convention, along with members of her father's cabinet.

Woodrow Wilson became convinced of the necessity of woman suffrage — particularly as it affected the conduct of the war. Women were serving overseas as nurses. Indeed, Ethel Roosevelt Derby, daughter of former president Teddy Roosevelt, was driving ambulances with her husband in Paris. How, asked Wilson, could the rest of the world perceive America as a land of democracy if those women — and the rest — were serving and dying without being full members of American society? In a speech to Congress reported in the *New York Times* on October 1, 1918, Woodrow Wilson said, "I regard the extension of suffrage to women as vitally essential to the successful prosecution of the great war of humanity in which we are engaged." It would take two more grueling years before woman suffrage was ratified. Jessie and her sisters would work until the last signature was collected.

After the war, Jessie continued to support social issues. She worked diligently toward the ratification of her father's Versailles Treaty, as well as for American involvement in the League of Nations. She fought for the election of the first Catholic presidental nominee, Alfred E. Smith. She became a strong leader in Democratic party politics, and for a while there was a bandwagon rolling, with efforts to get her to run for office. Party officials, impressed by her energy and charisma, urged her to run for senator from Massachusetts. Jessie declined, concentrating instead on building the party, eventually becoming the secretary of the Massachusetts Democratic State Committee.

There has been much speculation about what might have been. With the election and long tenure of Democrat President Franklin D. Roosevelt, Jessie Wilson Sayre would most surely have been offered the opportunity of service in a long line of prominent government positions. The young Wilson daughter was even then a major political figure in her own right. But on January 15, 1933, Jessie Woodrow Wilson Sayre died at the age of forty-five, following complications from surgery for appendicitis. Cut down in her prime, she had nevertheless served her country with integrity, honor and intelligence and been a major figure in the effort to win women's voting rights.

Elizabeth Harrison Walker

Benjamin Harrison, the twenty-third American president, was inaugurated twenty years before William Howard Taft and twenty-four years before Woodrow Wilson, but his daughter, Elizabeth, was younger than either Helen Taft or Jessie Wilson. Born on February 21, 1897, Elizabeth Harrison came into the world four years after her father left the White House. The daughter of his second wife, Mary Scott Lord Dimmick, Elizabeth was never to know the "cold-blooded and unsympathetic" politician, as his enemies called him, who stood up for what he saw as right, but who never "wasted words in his politeness." She knew him only as a beloved father, who showered her and her older siblings with love.

In March 1901, her father struggled for breath in his last hours of life, his lungs congested with pneumonia. Little four-year-old Elizabeth came into his room, proudly bearing a small apple pie she had made just for him. The old general opened his eyes and smiled at her fondly, but he was too weak to acknowledge her gift. Hours later he was gone.

Like presidential daughters Helen Taft and

Jessie Wilson before her, Elizabeth Harrison was educated in the toughest schools. Indeed, her education exceeded that of most men. She earned a bachelor's degree in both science and law from Westover School, followed by a second law degree from New York University Law School. A year after she began her graduate studies, Elizabeth also enrolled in Washington Square College of New York University, where she earned a degree in liberal arts. She was admitted to the bar in both New York and Indiana. And remarkably, she achieved these goals by 1919, when she was a mere twenty-two years old, even before passage of the Nineteenth Amendment allowed her to vote.

In 1921, Elizabeth married James Blaine Walker, who was the great-nephew of her father's secretary of state. He was also an investment banker who was a Cornell Law School graduate. Elizabeth, unsatisfied to bask in the high society revels to which she was accustomed, soon began a monthly newsletter, *Cues on News,* directed specifically to women and containing advice on economics and investments. In the early 1950s, Elizabeth Harrison Walker began appearing on numerous television and radio shows, breaking ground by teaching women about economic issues important to them. She gained such national stature from her work that she was eventually named secretary to the Committee for Economic Development, a commission that, until her appointment, had consisted only of men. She was later tapped to serve on the Committee for United China Relief.

Elizabeth Harrison was, in essence, the bridge between the academic worlds of Helen Taft Manning and Jessie Wilson Sayre and today's new generation of presidential daughters. Today's young ladies have been born into a world where woman suffrage is taken for granted, and where women have been empowered to utilize their strength, courage, and intelligence in passionate causes to change the world for the better. They are, as Lady Bird Johnson describes them, "the doers."

Maureen Reagan:
"A Glorious Powerhouse of a Woman"

"If one could harness the energy of a Maureen Reagan," said former New Jersey governor, Christie Whitman, "I can assure you that California would never have another brownout." During Ronald Reagan's terms in the White House, her Secret Service code name had been "Radiant." It fit. Bombastic, controversial, even pushy, Senator John McCain referred to her as "almost a force of nature." Said Whitman, "She set new standards on how women could and should be involved in the political arena."

Maureen Reagan was born on January 4, 1941, to Ronald Reagan and Academy Award–winner Jane Wyman, first daughter to two Hollywood movie stars. She would have her picture, with sunny face and blond curls, in all the movie star magazines of the day. But she was no ordinary, pampered Hollywood child. Maureen would be taught self-reliance beginning at a very early age.

Her mother would say, "If I get hit by a Mack truck tomorrow, you'll have to take care of yourself." Maureen would later laugh and say she was the only four-year-old in the neighborhood who knew what a Mack truck was. Her father treated her as an individual, capable of having her own thoughts and making her own decisions. Of course, Maureen said, from as early as she could remember he would "guide me along masterfully until my decisions were pretty much in line with his own."

One day, trying to teach Maureen "the virtues of hanging things up," her mother lectured, "If you're going to live in this house, you're going to do as you're told." Maureen decided not to live in that house. She drew herself up to her full five-year-old height and announced, "Moween is leaving." She packed her doll and her clothes in a little suitcase and put on her coat. When she reached the door, her father gave her a dollar and said, "Write, Mermie, if you find work."

Maureen marched down the driveway and onto the street. It was only then that she realized just how dark it was getting. She sat on her suitcase in the middle of the street and thought things over. Finally, with a big sigh, she stood up and started back home. She didn't know until much later that her parents were hiding behind the fence, watching out for her safety. But when she reached home again, they were sitting in the front room, exactly where she had left them. "Moween is back," she announced, and went off upstairs to unpack. She kept the dollar and considered the whole episode a money-making triumph. It was an auspicious beginning for a very young, independent, self-reliant woman.

Much has been written about the travails of the Reagan family — including Maureen's wanting a brother so badly that she would "buy" her brother, Michael, with all the pennies in her piggy bank; about Ronald Reagan's divorce from Jane Wyman when Maureen was seven; his subsequent marriage to Nancy Davis; the births of her half-sister and half-brother, Patti and Ron, and about the children's feelings of emotional separation and struggles to attain their own identities.

Maureen Reagan's character was formed in a thousand different ways, from observing her father or listening to her grandmother's stories about him, stories that he was too private to share. She learned how her father wasn't allowed to see the early hit movie *Birth of a Nation* because the family believed it justified the Ku Klux Klan's persecution of black people. She learned about his resignation from a golf club that refused Jewish members. Close friends George Burns and Jack Benny, both of whom happened to be Jewish, later invited him to be part of their club; Ronald Reagan accepted. Maureen would never forget a weekend drive with her father and little brother Michael. Reagan stopped at a small, roadside store, bought a box of animal crackers for the children and tore out onto the road. Several miles later, glancing over his shoulder, Ronald Reagan saw his kids devouring two boxes of animal crackers. Reagan turned the car around, drove back fifteen miles to the general store to pay for the second box of cookies. It cost ten cents.

In 1952, Maureen experienced what she termed a "life-changing epiphany." It was the first live television coverage of the Democratic and Republican conventions, and she was enthralled. She was seeing history, and she was a part of it! She would postpone going to the bathroom for fear she would miss something. Her mother wanted her to go outside and play in the beautiful day. "Not now, Mother," Maureen would say, "I'm busy." It was difficult for an adult to understand how an eleven-year-old could be busy watching a political convention. But Maureen Reagan was no ordinary eleven-year-old. She felt swept away by something larger than herself. The conventions were, she said later, like a "lifeline to another world, to another way of being, to the person I might become." That summer, at eleven years of age, Maureen Reagan became a Republican. She wore an "I like Ike" button and tried to convince all the kids in the neighborhood to vote for Dwight Eisenhower.

It would be eight more years before Maureen discovered, to her consternation and amazement, that her father was a registered Democrat! She put in an unheard-of long distance phone call to him, just to learn if it were true. By this time, Richard Nixon had asked Ronald Reagan to head up the Democrats for Nixon campaign. But in the middle of one of his meetings, a deputy registrar came onstage and reregistered him on the spot. Maureen was delighted, and relieved.

During these years, Maureen was living in Washington, D.C., and working as a secretary. Her father, long since divorced from actress Jane Wyman, had remarried Nancy Davis and was pursuing his career in California. Maureen met a policeman, ten years older than she, who worked near her apartment building, and in time, they were married. When she called her father to tell him of her plans, she could hear the hesitancy in his voice. But she was, after all, a grown woman and entitled to make her own choices about life.

The marriage was a mistake. Her new husband turned out to be a batterer. For all of her intelligence and personal strength, Maureen's experience became a textbook example of the maddening cycle of spousal abuse. Her husband would fly into rages at the slightest excuse, or none at all. At first, the battering was verbal. One night it turned violent. A sudden Washington blizzard had halted all public transportation, and Maureen had to walk three miles home from work. Infuriated by the delay, her new husband suspected an extramarital affair and no explanation would suffice. Before Maureen could imagine what was happening, he was raining blows on her face and head. She later described an out-of-body experience, as if she were detached, watching the whole thing happening from a distance, feeling powerless to fight back. When he finally stopped, her face was swollen, blackened with bruises. She couldn't eat. It hurt to speak. That night, she lay in bed wondering what she had said and done to provoke the outburst and how she could have handled it differently.

Maureen confided in no one, dismissing the experience as an anomaly. But the outbursts began repeating themselves, eventually settling into a cycle of beatings and abuse, silently observed by coworkers who looked the other way. Shamed by events, she never even considered informing her parents.

Maureen's sense of helplessness was compounded by her husband's career as a police officer. In the summer, as the beatings continued, anonymous neighbors began calling the police. Her husband would simply lock her in the bathroom, explaining that he was moving furniture. Today, of course, it is standard procedure for police officers to examine the spouse on any domestic violence call. But it was a different time. No officer ever pushed the issue or asked to see her. The beatings continued, with threats of death if she ever tried to leave. It is hard to imagine Maureen Reagan, the strong, self-assured, bombastic figure of the Reagan years, as an intimidated and abused spouse. Indeed, eventually she was able to gather her wits about her and walk out of the marriage, but her husband was not finished.

The denouement came one night when she was working in her office, alone. Her husband got into the building, pushed open the mail slot and threatened her life. This time the police arrived quickly. The captain told her that in the past few weeks her husband had been caught twice staking out her apartment building. He had been warned to leave her alone. Yet, ever loyal to a fellow officer, the police never found it necessary to alert Maureen to the unfolding crisis. It would be the last time her husband would threaten her life. When she finally returned to their old apartment to clear out her things, she found her wedding picture shattered, slashed with a knife.

In 1962, Maureen Reagan obtained a divorce. But her world was forever changed. "Trust" would take on a new meaning. Within time she repressed her experiences, convinced that her silence would bury her emotional pain as well. When she finally wrote about this devastating part of her life in her autobiography, she did so with misgivings. Realizing that other women were living the same life, in exactly the same way, with the same feelings prompted her to speak up. She wanted to give them the courage to get out, as well.

Maureen's personal crisis gave her an intense compassion for others, and colored her ideas about the importance of the Equal Rights Amendment. Later, White House aides pressured her to "follow the party line," but Maureen argued that only an amendment to the Constitution would provide long-term protection for the rights of women. "If we don't get the laws changed," she said, "then the society as a whole loses. We can no longer allow this to continue." Politically, her views on the Equal Rights Amendment and abortion complicated any run for Congress or statewide office. While possibly improving her chances in a general election, her stands antagonized Republican activists and exempted her from any easy Republican primary victory. But Maureen Reagan, traumatized by her own personal experiences, stood fast for a principle she utterly believed.

The indefatigable Maureen Reagan campaigned relentlessly for her father and other Republican candidates — even when some of Ronald Reagan's aides wanted her to disappear. Spin doctors reasoned that she was living proof of Reagan's divorced status. Maureen, of course, ignored them and continued to work for candidates and issues that concerned her. And her tireless work won praise and created a following among party stalwarts. During her father's second presidential term, in spite of anonymous White House sniping and attempts to dislodge her, she was elected as cochairperson of the Republican National Committee, an unprecedented accomplishment for the child of a president.

Former Republican State Representative Colleen House of Michigan once said that Maureen Reagan "did more to encourage Republican women seeking office than anyone in the 1980s." Maureen created a political action committee that supported over one hundred women candidates between 1985 and 1992. She was a prolific fund-raiser for them. She served as founder and president of the International Women's Leadership Exchange, a nonprofit, educational organization formed to "further understanding among women in leadership positions around the world."

Maureen Reagan headed the U.S. delegation to the 1985 World Conference on the United Nations Decade for Women in Nairobi, Kenya.

After her return, Secretary of State George Schultz appointed her the United States Representative to the United Nations Commission on the Status of Women. At her funeral, Ugandan President H. E. Yoweri K. Museveni would praise Maureen for her interest in human rights in his country. On one of her trips to Africa, Maureen and her new husband, Dennis Revell, whom she married in 1981, met a girl from Uganda named Rita Mirembe. Eventually, she and Dennis brought Rita to the United States and adopted her in 1994.

It was a time of mixed blessings for Maureen Reagan Revell. In the fall of that same year, her father, former president Ronald Reagan, appeared on national television, announcing to the entire world that he had been diagnosed with Alzheimer's disease, the degenerative brain disease that afflicts four million Americans. "I now begin the journey that will lead me into the sunset of my life," he said. It was an act of courage that would stun the country. He made it all right to talk about a terrible disease, and thus to do something about it.

Maureen Reagan wrote about a conversation she had with her father about a year before the announcement. She recalled that she was talking with her father about *Prisoner of War*, a movie he had made in the 1950s. "Finally, he looked at me and said, 'Mermie, I have no recollection of making that movie,'" Maureen said. She called that moment the "first click of awareness" that something was terribly wrong. "No actor ever forgets a role," she said.

She reacted in typical Maureen Reagan fashion, throwing herself into the fight against Alzheimer's. Senator John McCain said, "She made Alzheimer's her enemy, and fought like hell to cure it." Before she was done, she would be credited for raising $60 million to fight the disease.

Two years after her father's announcement came another blow, when Maureen Reagan, herself, would be diagnosed with malignant melanoma, the deadliest form of skin cancer. It began as a brown spot on the back of her leg that would not go away. She may not even have noticed it until it began to catch on her nylons. By the time she saw a doctor, the melanoma was already in an advanced stage. She entered into an aggressive treatment that seemed to bring the cancer into remission. It was only a stopgap.

In the meantime, Maureen redoubled her efforts, educating people to watch for the telltale early warning signs, known as the ABCD's. A is for Asymmetry, meaning that the two sides of the mole do not match. B, for the border, refers to the irregular border of a melanoma. C is for Color. A melanoma has varied colors, not always brown or black. And finally, D is for Diameter, more than six millimeters, the size of a pencil eraser. The statistics are terrifying. In 1935, only one in 1,500 Americans developed melanoma. Currently, the rate is up to one in seventy-one. It is predicted that the rate will soar to one in fifty by the year 2010. Presently, it is the most frequent cancer in women aged twenty-five to twenty-nine.

Maureen Reagan continued her commitment to finding a cure for her father's disease, hoping against hope that science would "find a way to erase the fog of dead brain cells so he could speak with her again." She put her father's health ahead of her own, and often postponed medical care so she could continue a killing pace of public appearances to combat Alzheimer's, including frequent testimony before Congress and state legislatures for more funding for Alzheimer's research and caregiver support.

Once it has spread, malignant melanoma is incurable. For a time, Maureen's cancer was thought to be in remission, but it returned with a vengeance, spreading throughout her body and finally attacking her brain. By July 4, 2001, she was experiencing seizures. On August 8, 2001, her indomitable spirit was still fighting, but her body had no more to give. Maureen Reagan, once dismissed as an obnoxious, boisterous figure trading on her father's power, but who had risen as an unlikely champion of women's issues and a major national fund-raiser for medical research, was suddenly gone. David Hyde-Pierce of television's hit show, *Frasier*, described her well. "When she was given lemons, she did not make lemonade," said Hyde-Pierce. "She took the lemons, threw them back and said, 'Oh, no you don't.' "

Mary Margaret Truman Daniel:
What Makes Margaret Sing?

In modern times, when budget for staff and new congressional allowances for former presidents finally kicked in, presidential daughters were able to satisfy the emotional and ego demands of their fathers and still establish thriving careers of their own. Margaret Truman, whose father, along with Herbert Hoover, was the first to receive a presidential pension, chose a career that budded in the harsh light of media criticism. She would take some hard knocks, with cruel accusations of only advancing on her father's name. It was a charge that all presidential children have had to face in one way or another. Some described the fair-haired girl from Missouri as too naïve and open and innocent for the rarefied air of the national spotlight. But she would prove to have an inner core as tough as Harry Truman himself. And Margaret's own tenacity would bring her ultimate success, although in a discipline far different than anyone might have first imagined.

Born February 17, 1924, Margaret Truman grew up on a tree-shaded street in Independence, Missouri, in a perfect world of an only child, cherished, loved, and assured of her position at the center of her father's universe. Her mother's avowed role was to keep their only daughter from being irretrievably spoiled. She was ten years old when she took her first singing lesson but that same year, Harry S. Truman was elected senator from Missouri and Margaret's dreams were put on hold. She was passing into the unfamiliar, frightening world of Washington, D.C., with its political intrigue and unrelenting media attention. It might have destroyed a lesser child, but Margaret, kept on an even keel by her common-sense parents, maintained her blithe spirit.

The most immediate challenge was changing schools in the middle of the year, an excruciating business for any ten-year-old. Margaret Truman had no siblings and not a single friend in a strange city. Try as she would, no effort could win her entry into the clique of schoolgirls her own age. Scholarship was not a sufficient common denominator and Margaret was no athlete. One day, however, there was a contest to see who could scream the loudest, the highest, and the longest. Margaret grinned in anticipation. She knew something they did not. She could hit a perfect F above high C, and hold it forever. When she finally stopped to look around, all the other girls were staring at her in stunned admiration. "Whenever there was any singing or screeching to be done, I was invited," Margaret wrote. She was in.

By the time Franklin Delano Roosevelt died and plunged Vice President Harry S. Truman into the last year of a raging world war, Margaret Truman was already a twenty-one-year-old student of history and politics at George Washington University and deep into years of voice lessons in Kansas City, Washington, and New York. In the fall of 1945 Margaret went to a production of *Rigoletto* at the Metropolitan Opera in New York, starring the great baritone, Lawrence Tibbett. Afterward, she met him backstage. "Tibbett also listened to me sing — with considerable trepidation, I think," Margaret wrote. "When I finished he said, 'Thank God, you've got the voice. Now all you need is more work!' "

And work she did. Margaret was headed for a career as a concert soprano. It was all she had ever wanted to do.

In 1947, Margaret debuted with the Detroit Symphony Orchestra on a national radio program. That led to recitals and concert tours across the country and a recording contract with RCA Victor Records in February 1950. She received generally good receptions, but there was a nagging doubt. Was she truly performing well or were people only welcoming the daughter of the president of the United States?

A concert tour is a grueling test of endurance, regardless of the music style. On December 5, 1950, Margaret was to end her tour with a concert at Constitution Hall in Washington, D.C. She was exhausted, but excited her parents would be in the audience; it was the first time they had ever heard her sing live in concert.

When Margaret walked onstage, she sensed that something was terribly wrong. She wrote that she did not know how well she sang; she does not even remember. But she does recall that the atmosphere "was charged that night, not only with grief but with mystery. This can be a disconcerting thing to a performer." What Margaret did not know was that Charlie Ross, her father's press secretary, whose friendship stretched back to high school together, had collapsed and died at his desk earlier in the day. Her parents had decided not to tell her, thinking that the news would adversely affect her performance. She said later that had she known, she might have acknowledged the great loss. Perhaps she would have dedicated the concert to Charlie Ross, thereby defusing a sad, mystifying atmosphere.

What happened next is famous. The following day, Paul Hume, the music critic for the *Washington Post*, wrote a scathing review of Margaret's performance. "It is an extremely unpleasant duty to record such unhappy facts about so honestly appealing a person," he ended. "But as long as Miss Truman sings as she has for three years, and does today, we seem to have no recourse unless it is to omit comment on her programs altogether."

It was a devastating blow. Her singing voice was at the very heart of her self-esteem and sense of personal identity. It had been her acknowledged "gift" since childhood. It had won her distinction from other children. As an adolescent it had even been her magic door-opener during her difficult rite of passage into her new Washington school. A singing career had been her only ambition. There were no other options.

Presidential father Harry S. Truman, who rose almost every morning of his life at four a.m. to write his daughter a letter, and who had shared her dream since childhood, was furious. "A frustrated critic on the *Washington Post* wrote a lousy review," the president angrily wrote in his diary. "The only thing, General Marshall said, he didn't criticize was the varnish on the piano. He put my baby as low as he could." The president took the critic to task warning him that he would "need a new nose and plenty of beefsteak." The exchange made headlines, and the media howled. History records it as one of the more endearing stories of a president and his child. Parents across the United States applauded a father for defending his daughter, but none of it offered any solace to Margaret Truman.

For a concert soprano, the stresses are enormous. Its intricacies differ from the free-flowing style of a pop singer or Gospel performer or jazz vocalist. In a January 1951 magazine article in *Woman's Home Companion*, Margaret's manager, Joe Davidson, who also managed the career of opera legend Helen Traubel, explained that most performers take ten to fifteen years to reach their full development. "Margaret's been giving recitals for only two. Her voice has come a long way and it shows every sign of developing further." But as the daughter of a president, Margaret would not be given those years. "She had no choice but to begin at the top of the ladder and gradually earn her right to stay there." Margaret Truman was under the microscope from her first note.

When her father finally left office, reporters sneered that her career would be over as well. It was not. Margaret appeared on popular radio shows, acted in summer stock, sang on the top-rated, televised *Ed Sullivan Show*, and hosted *People to People*, interviewing her parents on national television. She was easy and natural, and when Edward R. Murrow returned to his show the following week, he quipped, "I'm here tonight, substituting for Margaret Truman."

Without elaboration, Margaret swore she would never marry while her father was in the White House. She didn't. When Harry and Bess finally announced her engagement to the man who would be her husband for the next forty-three years, it shocked the press. With the help of sympathetic friends, the couple had courted in complete secrecy. He was E. Clifton Daniel, Jr., a dashingly handsome, debonair, brilliant journalist for the *New York Times*, who had served as foreign correspondent in the danger zones of World War Two, covered the founding of Israel, was posted in Moscow, and later became managing editor of the nation's most prestigious newspaper.

Margaret Truman quit her concert career when she married Clifton Daniel, but for many months she had been pursuing another project, one that would eventually give her a national audience and critical acclaim. In 1956, she published her own autobiography, *Souvenir*. It had been a reluctant effort, spurred on to "smother the success" of an unauthorized biography. It bore the stamp of a young, still naïve, woman. But what struck music critics as hesitancy and weakness struck book reviewers as revealing and compelling reading. The *Chicago Sunday Tribune* said, "It projects the simple dignity, warmth, and genuine modesty of a plain, unaffected midwest girl." And the *New York Herald Tribune* Book Review's Ishbel Ross said that *Souvenir* was a "gracefully written tale of an average American girl drawn by chance into the White House." The American public found itself fascinated by the extraordinary and unique perspective of a presidential child, and Margaret Truman's honesty guaranteed an untainted view.

In 1972, Margaret published her father's biography, *Harry S. Truman*. It sold well over a million copies, and made the critical cut for the prestigious Book of the Month Club. After her mother's death, and upon the discovery of a massive amount of correspondence stored in the Independence home, she wrote *Bess W. Truman* in 1986. Her mother had been one of the most private of all first ladies, and critics quickly sensed the historic importance of the book. From the moment the first project began, Margaret Truman never stopped writing. By the year 2000, seven nonfiction books had been published. An insatiable reading public saw her name and instantly knew they would be reading an interesting and important book.

It was during the writing of her many historical works that Margaret Truman ventured into the art of fiction. Employing her intimate knowledge of the people and places surrounding a president, *Murder in the White House* was published by Arbor House in 1980. The popular mystery novel was quickly optioned for a television movie; the paperback rights alone earned the president's daughter six figures. No one could know at the time, but a whole new industry had been launched. The 1980 best-seller was followed the next year by *Murder on Capitol Hill*. Each year, each successive mystery novel seemed to improve on its predecessor, building a huge international audience. Her 1987 book, *Murder in the CIA*, was a fixture for three months on the *New York Times* Best-seller List, and earned rave reviews in *Publishers Weekly* as "a colorful, seething story."

In the year 2000, her annual novel, *Murder in Foggy Bottom*, featured three commercial aircraft shot out of the sky on the same day. The following year, the whole nation watched the horrifying events of September 11 unfold, with the crashing of three planes used as terrorist weapons targeted at American civilians. Margaret Truman Daniel was thrust back into the national discourse. Some critics and readers were stunned that the mystery writer had anticipated the potential of such acts and scandalized by the thought that their government had not.

At seventy-eight years of age, Margaret Truman Daniel continues to write. Her inventive talent with the pen and stubborn refusal to accept defeat in public life has earned her fans, fortune, and the grudging respect of critics who once drove her from the concert stage. Dubbed the "queen of mystery," Margaret Truman Daniel, a presidential daughter who was once accused of only trading on her father's name, has become in her own right one of the most beloved and popular authors of our generation.

EIGHT

TRIUMPHANT SONS

*"Honesty, good intentions, and industry,
you will have of course. Without these
your career would soon end with the loss
of your good name. But you must be
ambitious to be a good deal more."*
— RUTHERFORD B. HAYES TO HIS SON

If being the son of a high achiever means certain doom, then many of the nation's chief executives would never have been elected president in the first place. While most presidents from John Adams to Abraham Lincoln to Richard Nixon experienced very humble beginnings, quite a number were the sons of successful fathers. The father of James Madison was a commander of the King's Army, respected citizen leader, and a Revolutionary War hero. William Henry Harrison's father was a famous signer of the Declaration of Independence, a land baron, and a successful politician in his own right. John Tyler was the son of the governor of Virginia. The father of James K. Polk founded a newspaper and was a bank director and magistrate. The father of Franklin Pierce was a brigadier general and later the governor of New Hampshire. William Howard Taft was the son of an ambassador and cabinet officer. In more recent times, FDR's wealthy father owned a coal mine. Kennedy's father was an ambassador to the United Kingdom and a successful millionaire-businessman. George H. W. Bush was the son of a U.S. senator. And, of course, both John Quincy Adams and George W. Bush were sons of presidents. Obviously, being the son of a high-achieving, successful father does not guarantee failure.

Likewise, many American presidents hailed from some of the most difficult of circumstances and dysfunctional homes. Gerald R. Ford's birth father was abusive; he was renamed after his stepfather, who was the real father figure and male inspiration in his life. Meanwhile, Bill Clinton's stepfather was an alcoholic who "terrorized" his own family. And while we make a great point out of the fact that presidential sons are often neglected, many presidents had no father at all in their life. Augustine Washington, the father of the first president, was "distant and preoccupied." Washington was eleven when he died and hardly ever mentioned him. Thomas Jefferson's father died when he was fourteen, Andrew Johnson's when he was only five. The father of Rutherford B. Hayes died before his son was even born. Actually, there are those who argue that a father who has passed on is better than one who is alive and unavailable, that losing a father early can be a liberating process for a youth. Nevertheless, the point is made that presidents have risen to the top in any number of different and difficult circumstances. There is no reason why a presidential child could not do the same.

One can find this same dynamic at work in the lives of celebrities' children. While many are seen as troubled or neglected, quite a few of them have achieved success, even beyond the accomplishments of their parents. Actor Kirk Douglas saw his son Michael Douglas become a star. The two sons of Lloyd Bridges, Beau and Jeff, became successful. Martin Sheen's two sons, Charlie Sheen and Emilio Estevez, have both become famous actors in their own right. Motor racing, baseball, and many other sports see sons follow fathers to greatness. With the curse of neglect and higher expectations comes powerful inspiration, the knowledge that great things are possible.

Quite a number of the most successful presidential sons appeared during or just after the bloodiest war in American history, the Civil War. With the country ripped apart, the glamour of the presidency was diminished. It was no great thing to be the child of a president who was despised. For most of his presidency Lincoln could please no one, from slaveholders to abolitionists, and half the nation was in secession. The Civil War was so disruptive that many points of reference were no longer valid. One public figure was admired in one state and hated in another. After his death, Lincoln became a towering figure, an icon, but for much of the war both North and South followed the career paths of the generals, who held the fate of thousands of sons in their hands and who became powerful figures loved and hated for their exploits.

There is an interesting perspective that many successful presidential children have, a strategic overview that is missing for most of the rest of us. Presidents are by necessity generalists. They must know a little about a lot of things. They have no time to completely understand and appreciate a new weapon's system or explore every nuance of our country's relationship with a particular nation or ponder the ways of building a relationship with a given political constituency. Others must give their lives to think through these issues and advise the president. The chief executive must set the priorities and weigh the conflicting arguments. He cannot be drawn into minutiae. As specialization has been taken to new extremes, this process has become even more severe. The president's view is one that very few need to take and so, in a way, the generalist has also become a specialist. That is, the person who retains a strategic view of the nation and its people is just as much an expert by experience and practice as any professional in the Pentagon or State Department. The point is that presidential children, as in the case of all children, see the world through their parents' eyes and thus many of them also have this gift, this strategic perspective that most of us lack. We enjoy the luxury of promoting our cause, of complaining about the clear injustices we see in our own circle of society, without a need to place any of it in context.

Perhaps no other story incorporates all of these many factors as completely as the story of Richard Taylor, son of our twelfth president,

Zachary Taylor. The turmoil leading up to the Civil War had certainly tarnished the Taylor name in their native South. As president, Zachary Taylor had once opposed the extension of slavery to the new western states, making his son Richard Taylor suspect to some in his native Louisiana.

There can be no doubt that Richard Taylor possessed the strategic perspective that was so unique to the more successful presidential progeny. He saw the storm clouds gathering early and warned that there would be a great war. And he knew instinctively that his native South would be the loser. Still, his wise counsel was lost in the cacophony of fanaticism. When war finally broke out, he knew that New Orleans would be immediately taken from the sea if forces were not rushed in. He understood what its loss would mean for the South. At the time, Taylor's analysis was rejected out of hand and only slowly appreciated in hindsight, long after the loss of New Orleans began to take on its strategic significance, when the fall of Vicksburg effectively choked the Confederacy.

The president's son could read other men. It took him forty-eight hours to appreciate "Stonewall" Jackson's genius and less than that to discern General Kirby Smith's costly conservatism. Like Lee, he knew that time was on the side of the North and a conventional war was doomed. He immediately understood the good military judgment of turning General Nathan Bedford Forrest loose to fight at his own time and choosing. So reliable was his advice that Confederate President Jefferson Davis would reject the counsel of ten others if "Dick" Taylor believed it differently. He was one of the few ordinary soldiers, with no military training, in either army, to rise to lieutenant general. At the end of the war, finally recognized for his ability, he commanded all the Confederate armies in the Deep South. It was upon his surrender, not Robert E. Lee's, that the government of Jefferson Davis finally accepted defeat and that the great Civil War finally ended.

Richard Taylor:
The Last to Surrender

Richard Taylor, the only son of Margaret and Zachary Taylor, was born at the family home in "Springfields," near Louisville, Kentucky, on January 27, 1826. He was named for his grandfather, a Virginian who had served as a Revolutionary War officer. No West Pointer, Taylor was nevertheless superbly educated at Yale, Harvard, and Scotland's Edinburgh College — and while at Yale, he concentrated on reading widely in classical and military history. In the Mexican War, he served as his father's military secretary and picked up his lifelong habit of profanity.

As a young man, Richard Taylor agreed to manage the family cotton plantation in Jefferson County, Mississippi, and later, when his father was president, persuaded him to purchase a large sugar plantation in St. Charles Parish, Louisiana, known to the local residents as "Fashion." After President Zachary Taylor's untimely death in July

1850, Richard inherited the St. Charles plantation, steadily increasing the acreage, improving its sugar works at considerable expense, and expanding its labor force to two hundred slaves. Within a few years, Richard Taylor was one of the richest men in Louisiana.

In 1851, Richard completed the fairy tale with marriage to Miss Louise Marie Myrthe Bringier, of the "Hermitage" plantation, St. James Parish, Louisiana. Louise was the daughter of a wealthy, aristocratic, Southern belle by the name of Aglae Bringier. In 1856, when a freeze destroyed the crops at "Fashion," her generous funds staved off disaster.

Richard and Louise Taylor soon had a family of two sons and three daughters. For a time they lived the life of Southern gentry. Taylor was well known in the state for his Thoroughbred race-horses, always competitors at the famous Metairie Track, and for his frequent appearances at the gaming tables of the exclusive Boston Club in New Orleans. In 1855, he was elected to the Louisiana Senate but Taylor, a big-picture man, had little patience with the pettiness of local party politics. First affiliated with the Whigs, then the American (Know-Nothing) Party, he eventually folded into the Democratic Party, along with almost all Southerners, but veering cautiously toward a reluctant proslavery position. Taylor had a disdain both for the Southern extremists, who were loudly demanding disunion, and for the agitating abolitionists. Both of these volatile positions Taylor sensed represented ultimate tragedy for the nation.

In 1860, he was a diffident and suffering delegate from Louisiana to the National Democratic Convention in Charleston, South Carolina. There, Taylor witnessed the party's fatal splintering along sectional lines. Attempting — but failing — he argued for a less radical course for the South, encouraging compromise between stunned moderates and implacable secessionists. With his dependable prescience, seeing the imminent war and eventual defeat for his beloved South, Richard Taylor sadly served as a delegate to the Louisiana secession convention in January 1861, voting with the convention's majority to withdraw from the Union. His pleas to protect the state from military invasion went largely unheeded by overconfident secessionists. In disgust, Richard Taylor retired to his plantation, recognizing the Confederacy's lack of unity and awaiting the inevitable.

It was not likely that a man of Richard Taylor's worldly experience and high-powered connections would go untapped in the cause of Dixie. Seeing patriots all over the region volunteering selflessly, Taylor agreed to serve and was promptly elected colonel of the Ninth Louisiana infantry. After assuming command in July, he took the regiment to Virginia, drilling the soldiers on the way. Although lacking in formal military training or combat experience, Taylor quickly gained the respect of his brigade. He was known as a competent leader, a consummate student of military history, strategy, and tactics, and a practical organizer of men. Simple rituals turned his troops into superb marchers. They were ordered to bathe their feet in cold water at the end of each day's long march. Taylor taught them how to nurse the unavoidable blisters and foot sores and how to find the right-fitting boots.

Richard Taylor had lost three sisters to malaria. Knox, the last to die, was an early bride of the new Confederate president, Jefferson Davis. The young Davis had taken her south for their honeymoon. Both had become ill; Davis had recovered but his new wife had not. Davis went on to a great career in government, and eventual leadership in the new South. He had remarried and become the head of a new family, but he had not forgotten his brother-in-law. In late October, Richard Taylor was surprised with a promotion to brigadier general.

In the spring of 1862, when Taylor's Louisiana regiment, three thousand strong, came marching north on the Shenandoah Valley Turnpike, "their white gaiters flashing to the cadence of their march," their peculiar Pelican banners flapping in the breeze and their officers barking orders in Cajun French, the onlooking troops of the famous Major General Thomas "Stonewall" Jackson were not impressed. Taylor was viewed by many soldiers in the field as a pampered dandy who owed his appointment to his credentials as the son and the brother-in-law of presidents. If the Louisianan was already a brigadier general, there were two reasons, Zachary Taylor and Jefferson Davis. But the commanding officer, a disheveled, dusty Major General Stonewall Jackson, who was sucking on a lemon and watching the Louisianans promenade, saw something quite different. How far had the men marched that day? Jackson wanted to know. Twenty-six miles, Taylor responded proudly. And they had crossed the Massanutten Mountains.

"You seem to have no stragglers," said a puzzled Jackson. There were not too many things that impressed Stonewall Jackson more than a fast-marching regiment.

"Never allow straggling," answered Taylor.

"You must teach my people," Jackson said, "they straggle badly."

Before sunrise on the morning of May 21, 1862, the Louisiana regiment of Richard Taylor resumed their march north on the Valley Turnpike directly toward Union forces under Major General Nathaniel P. Banks in Strasburg, Virginia, this time at the head of Jackson's reinforced, 17,000-man army. It was the beginning of one of the most famous and celebrated military exercises in history, Stonewall Jackson's Valley Campaign.

After a long march to New Market, Virginia, within full view of Union spies in the nearby mountains, Jackson mysteriously signaled for Taylor's men to turn right, directing them on to a road hidden from view of any curious observers, leading them back across the difficult Massanutten mountain range. Taylor, like many of Jackson's subordinates before him, was dumbfounded. If this were his final destination, why had he marched to meet Jackson in the first place? He had already been camped on the other side of the mountains, farther south. It was an exhausting effort. He could have saved sixty miles by simply marching north to rendezvous with Jackson's army. "I began to think that Jackson was an unconscious poet," wrote an amused Taylor, "and as an ardent lover of nature, desired to give a stranger an opportunity to admire the beauties of his Valley."

On the following morning, May 22, 1862, Jackson directed his army north to within ten miles of the town of Front Royal and Richard Taylor could see the plan as if scales had fallen from his eyes. Banks and his outnumbered Union army were still waiting in Strasburg, building defensive earthworks, expecting Jackson's army to come marching north, down the pike. His Union scouts had taken it all in. That was why Taylor's men had to be seen marching northwest of the Massanutten. Instead, the whole army, all 17,000 of Jackson's men, were on the east side of the mountain range, within striking distance of Union forces in Front Royal, behind Banks, blocking his escape across the Blue Ridge to Washington, sitting "astride the Manassas Gap Railroad." If Banks rushed north to his supply base in Winchester, Jackson could strike him on the move. If he waited, he would be outnumbered two to one, with all chance of reinforcement or renewed supplies blocked. The numbing, marathon marches had already won the first round of the Valley Campaign, without a shot having been fired.

The battle for Front Royal, with its Union detachment of a thousand soldiers, was not a great battle by Civil War standards, but it sealed the fate of General Banks's army holed up in Strasburg, which in turn left the road wide open to Washington, D.C., the Union capital. President Lincoln would be forced to withdraw soldiers from the drive to Richmond, thus relieving the Southern capital. But all hinged on the quick and thorough fight to dislodge the dug-in defenders at Front Royal. Though comprising less than 20 percent of Jackson's forces, Richard Taylor's Louisianans were all over the battlefield that day. His Louisiana "Tigers," "a battalion of New Orleans wharf rats," who had earned the nickname during the Battle of Bull Run, were sent charging right down the middle of Jackson's line at the enemy's center. Taylor, meanwhile, brought the bulk of his forces storming into the enemy's left flank. The Union soldiers fought stubbornly, thinking they were only fighting off a small detachment. When they finally realized the danger, that Jackson's whole army was on them, they rushed for escape across a bridge, burning it behind them.

Jackson was bemoaning the lack of artillery when he suddenly realized that Taylor's hard-charging men had raced across the burning bridge, stamping out flames as they went. "It was rather a near thing," Taylor later reminisced. "My horse and clothing were scorched, and many men burned their hands severely while throwing brands into the river. Just as I emerged from flames and smoke, Jackson was by my side. How he got there was a mystery, as the bridge was thronged with my men going at full speed, but smoke and fire had decidedly freshened up his costume."

More than nine hundred Federals had been killed or captured at a cost of less than fifty casualties to Stonewall Jackson. Still, Union General Nathaniel Banks was baffled, sending a message to Washington that it was the work of a rebel force of five thousand troops that "had been gathering in the mountains," and giving his reasons for holding firm because "Jackson is still in our front." But Jackson was not "in his front"; he was holding forth with his whole army, between Banks and Washington. When the Northern general finally learned the truth, he sent his army racing north for Winchester, the wagons stretching out for miles along the Valley Turnpike, a tantalizing military target. And Jackson pounced, like a cat tearing at a mouse. The bounty from the Union Army was so great that the Southern commanders could hardly contain their men, who ravaged the wagons for new weapons, ammunition, food, liquor, and shoes. Jackson assembled much of the captured loot, turned the wagons around, and sent them rolling back south where they were desperately needed.

The Battle of Winchester, the showdown between Jackson and Banks, centered around a series of hills south and southwest of the town. The army that controlled the hills would command the battlefield. Banks arrived first, placed his skirmishers on the important high ground, and retired to a warm bath and bed. Jackson spent the night standing watch, waking his troops at four a.m. and marching them to Winchester through an early morning fog. The famous "Stonewall" brigade, Jackson's veteran troops, were ordered to take the high ground, but the hills on the south-west held firmly. "I will send you Taylor," Jackson said.

Richard Taylor's Louisianans, bearing much of the brunt of the last battle, were in a reserve position on the approach to Winchester, but hearing the booming guns, Taylor instinctively ordered his men toward the roar. Jackson found him at the front of his brigade, pointed to the troublesome hills and ordered, "You must carry it."

Taylor moved his brigade to flank the enemy positions. The Louisianans moved forward, slowly, steadily, and then in perfect unison. The enemy lines blazed with rifle shots and cannon; here and there Taylor's men fell like ten pins, but on they came, the general himself riding at the front, his sword drawn and held high in the air. At his instruction, not a man fired his weapon. Jackson's whole army watched the drama with awe. And then, when they were near the Yankee line, Taylor shouted, his voice carrying across the battlefield, "Charge!" The Confederates swept the Union soldiers off the hill and down into the streets of Winchester. An exultant Jackson shouted in frenzy, "The battle's won, the battle's won! Now let's holler!" His army chased Banks and his men all the way to the Potomac River. After the war, when men reminisced and wrote of the conflict, a Confederate private declared, "That charge of Taylor's was the grandest I saw during the war."

There were other battles in the Valley Campaign. Lincoln sent three superior armies, converging from different directions, to finally trap

Jackson. Near Strasburg, Confederate General Ewell was ordered to keep the turnpike open for Jackson's men to escape. Outnumbered by a huge army many times larger than his own modest brigade, Richard Taylor's ferocious Louisianans performed a flanking movement that panicked the forces of Union General John C. Fremont, sending an entire army fleeing for cover. And at Port Republic and Cross Keys, Taylor was always in the very heat of the battle, once barely escaping with his life. By the time the spectacular Valley Campaign had finally come to an end, Brigadier General Richard Taylor had earned the respect of the South. Said Richard Ewell, "To General Taylor and his brigade belongs the honor of deciding two battles."

There was a symbiosis in the relationship between the legendary Stonewall Jackson and the president's son. Taylor came away from the Valley Campaign with a clear understanding of the bold risks that must be taken if the South were to win the lopsided contest. And Jackson, too, learned from the Louisianan and his "model brigade." The night after the battle at Front Royal, he had joined Taylor's campfire where "for hours he sat silently and motionless." Taylor assumed he was "inwardly praying." The next morning Jackson ordered his men to march fifty minutes and then stack their weapons and rest for ten. It was a formula that would turn Jackson's army into the "foot cavalry" and make them famous, and it was a ritual likely inspired by Taylor's marching brigade that Jackson had just seen in action.

They were unlikely soul mates, Jackson and Taylor. Stonewall Jackson was a deeply religious Presbyterian, an eccentric schoolmaster at the Virginia Military Institute, the constant subject of pranks and ridicule. He was a silent, awkward man, with none of the grace or style of Robert E. Lee and his other generals. Richard Taylor was the consummate insider, a fixture at the most rarefied levels of society, and a profane, even cynical man of the world. When he had readied his men for the charge up the hills at Winchester, he had cursed at the laggards. Jackson touched him and said quietly, "I am afraid you are a wicked fellow." But both men were ultimate warriors. Stonewall Jackson would go down in history as one of America's greatest military strategists and tacticians and in the Valley Campaign Richard Taylor had clearly found his gift. Jefferson Davis would need such a man to command other armies in the field.

On July 25, 1862, at thirty-six years of age, Richard Taylor was promoted to major general, then the youngest Confederate officer to attain such a rank. He was sent back to Louisiana to help protect the vital overland connection to Texas. Ports in Mexico brought valuable Enfield rifles in exchange for bales of cotton, desperately needed in Europe. In 1863, Taylor directed an effective series of clashes with Union forces at Fort Bisland and Franklin, Brashear City, and Bayou Bourbeau. But his plans for retaking New Orleans and for defending the civilian population from destructive Federal forays were continually frustrated by his conservative superior officer,

General Edmund Kirby Smith. Time and again Smith would deny Taylor the troops that were needed.

In 1864, Taylor's old nemesis from the Virginia Valley Campaign, Union Major General Nathaniel P. Banks, organized a major campaign to shut down the Confederate overland route to East Texas. The war was winding down to its inevitable conclusion and all eyes were on the climactic battles in the East. But there were new, urgent concerns that prompted Abraham Lincoln to action in the West. For years Northern mill owners had demanded access to East Texas cotton. In an election year it made good sense for Lincoln to act. And on the international front, Napoleon III had invaded Mexico. There was concern that the Confederacy might tempt the French with a trade — land for recognition and military support. Finally, there was the persistent problem of those imported guns for exported Southern cotton. President Lincoln and his War Department had personally ordered the campaign.

Banks made three efforts to achieve Lincoln's goals, even occupying Brownsville, Texas, for a time but he was thwarted at every turn. In Louisiana, Richard Taylor's meager troops were everywhere, continuing to bedevil his army at every turn. Finally determined to take Louisiana out of the equation, the War Department promised Banks all the help necessary. Grant peeled off ten thousand additional soldiers from General Sherman's forces, the War Department assigned General Steele's fifteen thousand-man army in nearby Arkansas to Banks, and Rear Admiral David D. Porter, hero of numerous battles along the Mississippi, would add his fleet of ironclads and powerful gunboats. Banks, who had once been Speaker of the House, had presidential ambitions of his own. Seizing bales of cotton and shipping them back to his native Massachusetts would not hurt his prospects.

The first step in the campaign called for a march to Shreveport, Louisiana, the last strategic Confederate stronghold in the state. The warehouses there were said to be overflowing with cotton. Banks, with his forty-five thousand troops and one thousand wagons, moved in close coordination with Porter, who commanded sixty vessels with more than two hundred guns. It was a formidable force. By way of comparison, the perfectionist Union General McClellan had needed only eleven hundred wagons for his great Peninsular Campaign of 1862. And all of it was opposed by Richard Taylor with five thousand rebel soldiers, whose only advantage lay in their knowledge of the swamps and back roads of Louisiana. Taylor furiously demanded help from his commander, General Edmund Kirby Smith, but Smith, worried by other Union armies in the region, and unaware of the recent concentration of Union forces, told Taylor to stand down, not to engage the enemy.

The opening salvos of the Red River Campaign of 1864 appeared unstoppable. The Union Army, led by Banks and Porter, moved upriver, blowing away a series of small Confederate defensive works and the one fort on the river. Taylor's army, deep in the swamps and forests, bode their time, waiting for reinforcements, their commander furious over the idea of giving up his state without a fight. For two hundred miles Taylor was forced to retreat, when finally some small help began to arrive. By April, his numbers had swollen to eighty-eight hundred. Still outnumbered four to one, he watched and waited for Banks to make a mistake.

There was a difficult part of the river where Porter's fleet and Banks's army had to part ways. The army would march overland, reuniting with the gunboats and ironclads upriver, thirty miles shy of Shreveport. It was along this overland route that Richard Taylor, veteran of the Valley Campaign, would lay his ambush. Understandably overconfident, Banks's army, with its one thousand wagons, stretched out for forty miles along the narrow Louisiana trail. When Taylor's unexpected attack hit, the lead elements of Banks's army panicked. Greatly outnumbered, Taylor's army nevertheless overwhelmed its enemy. For the next few months, in a series of brilliantly led battles, including one decisive encounter in Mansfield, Louisiana, Banks's huge army was driven back to its starting point. For a few frightening days, Rear Admiral Porter nearly lost his entire fleet. Only the quick thinking of engineers and the construction of a dam raising the water level at a key point allowed Porter's ships to escape to safety.

In May 1864, General Banks's bloodied forces finally crossed the Atchafalaya River, ending their disastrous Red River campaign. Lincoln and his cabinet gave up their dreams of conquering East Texas or even wresting complete control of Louisiana. According to some historians, Taylor's battles with Banks may have "prolonged the war by several months."

The fact that Richard Taylor had been able to achieve such victories, when the war was almost lost, Southern morale low, ammunition and supplies almost gone, and Northern generals much more savvy, was a further testimony to his brilliance. If it had happened two years earlier, it would have made Taylor a legend. But with the South disintegrating and its doom certain, and the nation weary of war, the defeat of the Red River Campaign became only part of the blur of events preceding the end of the Confederacy.

On July 18, 1864, President Jefferson Davis promoted Richard Taylor to lieutenant general and placed him in command of the Department of Alabama, Mississippi, and East Louisiana. He would be one of only three non-West Pointers to achieve such high rank in the South. Frustrated for years by the restraints of his own commanding officer, Taylor immediately sent for Confederate cavalryman, Nathan Bedford Forrest, telling him that from this moment on he was free to use his imagination to harass the enemy and raid deep in his territory. Many of Forrest's most spectacular sorties happened in those last months of the war. "He's the biggest man in the lot," Forrest said of Taylor. "If we'd had more like him, we would have licked the Yankees long ago."

After the surrender of Robert E. Lee to Ulysses S. Grant at Appomattox Court House, the Confederate government fled south from Richmond. President Jefferson Davis spoke of reaching "Dick" Taylor in Alabama. But Taylor had only ten thousand troops left to defend Alabama, Mississippi, and East Louisiana and could not hold out long. On May 4, 1865, almost a month after Appomattox Court House, Lieutenant General Richard Taylor surrendered Confederate forces in the Deep South to Union General Edward R. S. Canby in Citronelle, Alabama. The work of the soldiers was over, Taylor said; it was a time for the statesmen. Although forces west of the Mississippi would fight on for another month, many histories refer to Taylor's surrender as the final end of the war. When Jefferson Davis heard that his brother-in-law had been unable to sustain the fight, his hopes of escape and a government in exile collapsed.

The great Civil War inflicted severe personal sacrifices on Taylor and his family. His plantation was destroyed and many of his father's personal presidential papers scattered to the wind by Federal soldiers. His two young sons died of scarlet fever as wartime refugees. His wife suffered so much that she lapsed into a slow decline that ended with her premature death in 1875. After leaving the service in May 1865, Taylor moved to New Orleans, trying to revive his finances by securing a lease of the New Basin Canal from the state. But with the loss of his wife, he gave up the effort, taking his three daughters and moving back to Winchester, Virginia, the scene of one of his early military victories.

Richard Taylor had not lost his strategic perspective. If he had foreseen the futility of the war, he now saw the futility of sectarianism and the extended punishment of the South. He argued that a political and economic recovery for the South benefited the North. It was a point shared by many Northern business interests. Both presidents Johnson and Grant counseled with him in the White House. Grant invited him to dine with his family. In 1876, Taylor became intimately involved in Samuel J. Tilden's Democratic campaign for the presidency. Tilden of New York won the popular vote but neither he nor his oppponent, Rutherford B. Hayes, had the electoral majority needed. Taylor was tapped to help influence congressional maneuverings after the disputed returns, but to no avail. A national crisis was ultimately diffused by the widespread breakdown of solidarity among Democratic leaders.

As in the case of all presidents' children, his special status as the son of a former national leader retained its glamour to some. Before leaving New Orleans, he was elected president of the reopened Boston Club, the local watering hole for the city's elite. After moving east he was named to the board of trustees of the Peabody Fund. In England, the Prince of Wales, the future King Edward VII, was smitten by Taylor's Southern charm and became a close personal friend, making him an honorary member of the Marlborough Club, "which is reserved for reigning princes and their sons." Henry Brooks

Adams, a retired Harvard professor who happened to be the son of Charles Francis Adams and grandson of President John Quincy Adams, became a close friend. The two debated history and life as well as shared the special joys and sorrows of having great fathers.

In April of 1879, Richard Taylor visited at the home of a friend and benefactor, New York City attorney, Samuel Latham Mitchell Barlow, one of the Democratic Party's most powerful brokers. Taylor's account of the war, *Destruction and Reconstruction*, considered among the more popular of military memoirs, had just been published to critical acclaim. Taylor had been suffering from what doctors of the time called severe internal congestion, resulting from a long battle with rheumatoid arthritis. On April 12, while still visiting with his powerful friend, Taylor died. He was buried in a family crypt in Metairie Cemetery, New Orleans. William M. Evarts, secretary of state in the Hayes administration, was one of the pallbearers.

And so passed the life of Lieutenant General Richard Taylor, a personal friend of three presidents, known in history as one of Lee's generals, as one of Stonewall Jackson's most able lieutenants, the man who defeated Nathaniel Banks at Mansfield, Louisiana, and the last of the great Southern generals to surrender in the Civil War. The fact that he was also the son of President Zachary Taylor is only a curious footnote to a life that eclipsed its lofty origins and established its own identity and hard-earned celebrity.

Robert Todd Lincoln:
A Man of Wealth and Power

If there is special trauma to presidential children, then surely Robert Todd Lincoln drank deep from its dregs. When one journalist too many insisted on an anecdote about his famous father, he snapped that he had no memory of his father at all, except that of a man packing his saddlebags to leave home again. When pushed to seek the presidency for himself, he lashed out at the office, perhaps with unconscious anger directed at his father, who had once been its occupant. "It seems difficult for the average American to understand that it is possible for anyone not to desire the Presidency but I most certainly do not." He sometimes manifested that surly contempt for life that pop psychologist, Alice Miller, suggests is an expression of "rage that one's parents were not available."

Yet, Robert Todd Lincoln loved his father and was throughout his lifetime a jealous guardian of his father's legacy. Many historians suggest that Robert Lincoln was the most successful of all the presidential children. He was one of the greatest businessmen of his generation, one of the most powerful and celebrated figures of society, and a public servant, acquitting himself with dispatch at the cabinet level in two different administrations and as a superb diplomat in another. When Congress granted its new charter to the Red Cross in 1905, he was an original member of the incorporating body. Always, there hovered about him the perception that he could be president if he only wanted it, a perception that he wisely distrusted but one that often empowered him nonetheless.

Robert Todd Lincoln was born August 1, 1843, the firstborn son of Abraham and Mary Lincoln. He was not his father's favorite son; they were never close. Willie, the third son, seemed to hold that special place. Friends of the family said the two shared the same personality, which Lincoln himself acknowledged. With Willie's passing, his younger brother and playmate Tad filled the void.

Lincoln never ventured a reason for any estrangement with his firstborn, nor did either acknowledge that anything was wrong, but their conversations were "stiff and awkward." While there is a certain amount of competition between all fathers and sons, historians see Lincoln as strangely intimidated. His mother Mary wrote a friend, "I have a boy studying latin and greek [sic] and will be ten years old in a few days." Lincoln spoke about Robert getting a better education than he ever had but "guessed that Bob would not do better than he."

At Mary's urging, Abraham Lincoln visited his son at Phillips Exeter Academy, hoping to motivate him to earn better grades. He later wrote a letter to Robert's roommate, with more warmth and wisdom than any letter ever penned to Robert. When Abraham Lincoln was elected president of the United States, his oldest son was seventeen and finally off to Harvard. He made periodic visits to the White House, but by his own account he never saw his father more than "ten uninterrupted minutes." And there was often a sense of "relief to everybody" when Robert left home to go back to school. And yet, the president's submission to the whims of his younger children was legendary. They interrupted cabinet meetings, demanding hours of his time, which he obligingly supplied.

There is a degree of mystery surrounding Robert's accomplishments as a lawyer and businessman. What motivated him? And how did he establish successful work habits? After the death of Eddie, Robert's younger brother, parental discipline was virtually absent, all in stark contrast to the harsh severity of Abraham Lincoln's own experience. And Robert, too, had been corrupted by such an atmosphere. As a child, he had demanded attention. If his father became engrossed in a game of chess, ignoring his son's questions or banter, Robert would tip over the whole chess board, announcing the end of the competition. Lincoln would only chuckle. On the president-elect's historic train ride to Washington, Robert was entrusted with his inaugural address, which he lost. It was the only time many ever saw Lincoln lash out in anger at one of his own children. And yet slowly, tediously, Robert Lincoln learned how to discipline himself. Something drove him. Anger? A desire for approval from a father whose version of love was seen only as indifference? In 1864 he graduated from Harvard, with plans to go on to law school until political realities began to intrude.

In April 1861, President Abraham Lincoln had

called for volunteers in the war against the South. Citizen soldiers had flocked to the Union cause from every trade and profession, including students and professors from Robert's own Harvard University. In the following months, many who had so eagerly responded lost their lives. Forty of his classmates had left school for the battlefields, many enlisting as lowly privates. Six were killed in action. But Robert Lincoln, urged on by his parents, persisted with his academic career. Even the Todd brothers from his mother's side of the family poured themselves into the conflict on the Confederate side. But the son who bore the family name demonstrated no "eagerness to risk life in an espoused cause." Criticism began to mount. His parents had lost two sons to illness, Edward and Willie, and were in no mood to offer up a third. "As long as you object to my joining the Army," Robert wrote his father, "I am going to study law." But his situation was embarrassing and he urged his parents to let him fight.

Mary Todd Lincoln expressed her fearful opinion to her husband. "I know that Robert's plea to go into the Army is manly and noble and I want him to go, but oh! I am so frightened he may never come back to us!" To which the president responded in the saddest of tones, "Many a poor mother, Mary, has had to make this sacrifice and has given up every son she had — and lost them all."

On January 19, 1865, with the war winding down to its conclusion and criticism of Lincoln's son at its peak, the president timidly wrote General Ulysses S. Grant, seeking to see if Robert could be placed "into your military family with some nominal rank." General Grant's response was quick and affirmative. Robert was welcomed as a member of Grant's own personal staff. He was standing on the porch of the home of Wilmer McLean in the small village of Appomattox Court House a few months later when Robert E. Lee surrendered. Colonel Orville Babcock called him inside to witness the moment. Young Lincoln would remain officially on the army rolls for four months.

On the morning of April 14, 1865, Good Friday, Ulysses S. Grant arrived in Washington with Robert in his entourage. There are conflicting accounts of his activities that evening. Apparently the president and first lady invited Robert to join them for a performance at Ford's Theater, but Robert was exhausted and declined. By some accounts, he was visiting with friends in the White House when the frantic news was announced that Abraham Lincoln had been shot. Still other accounts say that he was exhausted from the travel and had to be awakened from a deep sleep. Robert raced to the scene. His father had been carried across the street to a private home. There in the bedroom of a stranger, Robert and government officials held vigil as his father died. At 7:22 a.m. the following morning, the president was officially pronounced dead. Robert, who had comported himself throughout the night with quiet courage, leaned on nearby Senator Sumner and broke into open sobs. Early morning fog turned into a steady downpour as

Robert helped his mother into a carriage and accompanied her through the muddy Washington streets back to the White House.

Mary Todd Lincoln was much too bereaved to attend the funeral in the East Room, or to accompany the body back to Springfield, Illinois. Twenty-one-year-old Robert Lincoln performed both of those chores, and with a poise and dignity that endeared him to many in the nation. Mary stayed on in the White House for forty days before slipping quietly out of town. It was too painful to live on in Washington, where she had learned quickly that things would not be the same, that, without her husband protector, her enemies and detractors were multiplying. Nor could she return to Springfield, where she had too many memories of life with her husband and sons, Willie and Eddie. And so she planned to follow Robert to Chicago, where her firstborn was pursuing a career in law and where, perhaps, in a new place, she and Tad could escape the pain and "find peace and solitude."

The glorification of Abraham Lincoln to sainthood began within hours of his death. Even while his body was being transported back to Illinois, Congress offered to bring him back and bury him in a crypt under the Capitol, originally planned for the body of George Washington. And with the rising esteem, Robert's career flourished. He apprenticed in a law firm and was admitted to the Illinois bar in 1867. Within the year there was hardly a prominent corporation in Chicago that was not scrambling to enlist his name as one of their attorneys or as a director on their board.

Although he avoided publicity, newspaper accounts reported on his lucrative practice in the courts.

On September 24, 1868, Robert Lincoln married Mary Harlan, daughter of U.S. Senator James Harlan and a former cabinet officer, in a private and quiet Washington, D.C. wedding held in the senator's own home. The event had been planned for a later time but Mary Lincoln was insisting on a trip to Europe; if her son wanted her presence, then the wedding date would have to be advanced. Robert and Mary Harlan graciously complied.

Mary Lincoln's trip to Europe was the fulfillment of a lifelong dream. She and her husband had often spoken of a European trip together, following their White House years, and Mary made every effort to stretch her limited funds to make the most of her journey with Tad. Much of their time was spent in Germany, where she enrolled her youngest son in one boarding school after another. When she returned to Chicago, three years later, tragedy struck again when Tad, at the age of eighteen, died of pneumonia on July 15, 1871. Mary had been only forty-seven at her husband's death, now at fifty-three she was left with "only Robert of all her family."

The Robert Lincolns might have easily provided the home that the former first lady needed, a place in which to retire with dignity and comfort. Todd was Mary Lincoln's maiden name and most agreed that firstborn, Robert Todd Lincoln, had taken after her more socially prominent side of the family. Lincoln's law partner referred to

319

young Robert as "proud, aristocratic and haughty." He wore the finest clothes and moved with ease and grace in the highest social circles. When Mary Lincoln had hosted a reception for P. T. Barnum's famous midget, Tom Thumb, whose wedding was in the news, Robert had been scandalized. Home from Harvard, he nevertheless stayed in his rooms upstairs in the White House, telling his mother that "I do not propose to assist in entertaining Tom Thumb. My notions of duty are somewhat different from yours."

There was no question that Mary was proud of her first son. But Mary Lincoln had grown erratic and confused. The impact of the death of her three children and husband had been incalculable. For a time she joined a spiritualist commune, claiming to speak with her departed family. And her life in Chicago was punctuated with irrational outbursts. Twice she rushed into the corridor of her hotel screaming that someone was trying to murder her. She imagined poison in her food. She once mistook an elevator for a lavatory. Eventually, Robert's new wife declared their home off-limits to the former first lady.

In the spring of 1875, distraught and humiliated by her behavior, Robert Lincoln decided to have his mother committed to an insane asylum. Even the most charitable and benign account of Robert's actions paints a dark picture. Without her knowledge, Robert had his mother followed for several weeks by Pinkerton detective agents. Alarmed, she saw one of the men getting on a train in Florida and then later outside her elevator in a Chicago hotel. Incredibly, her complaints of being followed were used as evidence of her irrationality. Robert enlisted six of Chicago's finest doctors, put them on his own payroll, and had them testify at her trial. None of the said doctors examined her or even interviewed her before declaring that she was insane. As her closest relative, Robert arranged for her own attorney, Isaac Arnold, an old Lincoln friend, to be brought into meetings beforehand with the prosecutor and doctors and coached on his responsibilities in the affair. Leonard Swett, the prosecutor, one of the men who had nominated Lincoln for president in 1860, warned them all that "an unfavorable verdict would be disastrous in the extreme." They all would be revealed as "double villains who had tried to take advantage of a widow at the same time that they had dishonored the memory of Abraham Lincoln." And Robert Todd Lincoln had done all of this drawing on his mother's own diminishing resources. The doctors and lawyers and detectives and store clerks who testified against her had all been paid by Robert Lincoln, spending her money. What Robert lacked as a compassionate son was clearly compensated for by his talent as an attorney.

On May 19, 1875, Mary Lincoln was confronted with this cabal suddenly and without warning. She was told of the trial and then taken within the hour to a public courtroom where all awaited her. She sat at the defense table, as if in a dream, stunned by her son's betrayal. Her attorney, showing the pangs of a guilty conscience, tried to back out. Perhaps he remembered the recent book that he had received as a gift from Mary, signed "from your friend, Mrs. A. Lincoln." But Arnold's backbone was sufficiently strengthened and in the end he did his part, which in this case was nothing. Mary's attorney, Isaac Arnold, cross-examined no witnesses and called none of his own, nor did he have Mary testify. Robert Lincoln had his way. He himself had been the final witness for the prosecution and provided the coup de grâce. "I have no doubt my mother is insane," he told the court. "She has long been a source of great anxiety to me." Leaving nothing to chance, he arranged to have the warden of the assigned asylum at her trial to see his carefully staged presentation and then continued to build a special relationship with him so that he could be counted on to censor her mail and advise Robert of her attempts to get legal help on the outside.

Perhaps the best defense of Mary Lincoln's sanity was her enterprising escape from the Bellevue Asylum in Batavia, Illinois. Passing messages under the nose of the hospital warden and outwitting Robert to win her release had been no small feat. She lived with her sister in Springfield for a time before fleeing to Europe, fearful that Robert would strike again. Mary Todd Lincoln spent her last years in anonymity and loneliness in the trendy resort village of Pau, in France, near the Spanish border. While her husband's estate and a generous congressional allowance had finally kicked in, the money often encountered mysterious delays en route to France, leaving her destitute for months. Referring to her only living son, Robert, as a "wicked monster," she insisted in her letters to relatives that "even his father had always disliked him." Dismissed as "crazy" by the American public, she managed nonetheless for years, an exile in a foreign country, subsisting on her new presidential widow's pension and her fluent French. When a former president and first lady, Ulysses S. Grant and his wife, passed through the resort in 1879, the whole town turned out to greet them in a grand banquet. Mary Lincoln, whose husband had been Grant's commander in chief, sat alone in a nearby hotel, uninvited.

On March 11, 1881, at only thirty-seven years of age, Robert Lincoln became the secretary of war for President James A. Garfield. There had been some speculation that Robert would make a run at the White House himself and a Lincoln would be restored to power. In spite of all that had happened, Mary took some small pride in such speculation. In 1882, Mrs. Abraham Lincoln returned to the home of her sister in Springfield, Illinois. Her death, as her life, was not an easy affair. At the end she was covered with boils, almost completely paralyzed, and blind. It was the result — she believed — of "constant weeping." Almost to the end, Robert Lincoln and many others insisted that her suffering was only in her own mind. But on July 16, 1882, she died after a severe stroke. She was sixty-four. An autopsy revealed a cerebral disease, from which she had been suffering for years. Her entire estate was inherited by her surviving son, the "wicked monster," Robert T. Lincoln.

Robert Lincoln's appointment to Garfield's cabinet proved to be a popular and effective choice. Lincoln continued on throughout the administration of President Chester A. Arthur. When Benjamin Harrison was elected president in 1888, he appointed Lincoln as minister to the Court of St. James in London, where he served with distinction till the end of Harrison's term. Understandably there was again renewed speculation about a second Lincoln presidency and, in spite of his protests, four delegates actually voted for him at one of the Republican National Conventions. But newspaper editorials, led by no less a figure than the great Joseph Pulitzer, denounced the idea that a candidate would be nominated simply because of his name. The *New York World* fumed about how "rotten Republicanism has learned to revere things that savor of monarchy and aristocracy. It would transmit the Presidency as their fathers' successors to crowns."

Robert Lincoln's greatest success in life came in the business world where he moved with the most prominent corporate leaders of his generation. S. L. Carson, past chairman of the White House conference on presidential children, credits him as a founder and organizer of A.T.&T. and Chicago Commonwealth Edison, facts that spokesmen for both companies dispute. But no one questions his role as president of the Pullman Palace Car Company from 1897 to 1911. Almost every railroad carried his luxury cars, which in 1901 transported more than 9 million customers over 300,000 miles. Under Lincoln's leadership, the Pullman Company became the nation's largest employer of black Americans. Visiting heads of state sought him out, not as a former president's son, but as an American business giant.

The Robert T. Lincolns had three children, including a middle child, Abraham Lincoln II, who was called "Jack" by the family. A legend held that Robert insisted his son not use his famous name until his own accomplishments earned him that right. The other two children included a firstborn daughter named Mary and the baby of the family, Jessie. Middle son, Abraham Lincoln II, never did earn the right to use his illustrious name, suffering under the curse of so many other presidential namesakes, from John Adams II to John F. Kennedy, Jr.; he died at the age of seventeen during the family's time in London.

There is an ironic mystery attached to the life of Abraham Lincoln's firstborn that continues to fascinate and puzzle historians. On the Tuesday before his death, Abraham Lincoln shared a recurring dream with his wife and a few friends. He said that he heard sobs in the East Room. That there was a corpse "wrapped in funeral vestment." Soldiers were on guard and crowds of people were "weeping pitifully." When Lincoln asked the soldiers who had died, they answered sorrowfully that it had been the president. "He was killed by an assassin." The following day Lincoln opened his Bible at random to the story of Jacob's dream in Genesis and spent several hours turning through the pages of the book finding dream after dream. "If we believe in the Bible," Lincoln told his bodyguard, Ward Hill Lamon, "we must accept the fact that in the old days, God and His angels came to men in their sleep and made themselves known in dreams. [This dream] has haunted me. Somehow the thing has got possession of me, and like Banquo's ghost, it will not let go." Robert Lincoln read accounts of this story later and grieved over the possibilities, wondering why Lamon had not insisted on accompanying his father that night and wondering what might have happened differently if he, himself, had attended the theater. He would never completely shake his feeling of guilt.

In 1881, President James A. Garfield sent word to his secretary of war, Robert Lincoln, of a troubling dream he had of his own death. He remembered the bizarre historical account from the life of Lincoln and thought the president's son might offer some insight. Garfield was headed for Elberton, New Jersey, and then on to a reunion at Williams College, and so invited Robert to join him on the presidential train. They were to depart from the Baltimore and Potomac railroad station in Washington. Robert, who was running late, arrived at the station just as the assassination of President Garfield occurred.

Twenty years later, President William McKinley began to experience troubling dreams of his own impending death. As in the case of Garfield before him, he remembered Lincoln's experience and sought out the former president's living son, Robert. The president invited Lincoln to join him at the Pan American Exposition in

Buffalo, New York. On September 6, 1901, Robert arrived in time to see the president shaking hands with the crowd. The president's secretary pulled Robert aside, instructing him to join President McKinley later at his hotel suite. Before leaving, Robert moved to greet the president, but as he drew near, he witnessed the assassin firing the fatal shot.

Thus, Robert T. Lincoln had been nearby at the first three assassinations of American presidents and in circumstances that seem to defy all logic. The supreme irony in these encounters was the son's deep humiliation over his mother's lifelong flirtation with spiritualism. It was partly Robert's resentment of his mother's convictions and practices that lay behind his drive to have her committed to an insane asylum. Yet, Robert Lincoln, the agnostic of all things mystical, was a prominent figure in one of history's most intriguing and mysterious series of events.

Lincoln's son avoided events and anniversaries that honored his father and often used his intimidating prestige to block projects, most of which he found either crudely exploitive or offensive. He forced a publisher to change the title of a book, *Honest Abe*, because he thought it vulgar. For years he refused to allow scholars a look at trunks full of his father's correspondence and papers. He was especially outraged at a proposed statue planned near Parliament in London, which portrayed his father as ugly and ill-dressed. A member of the Taft family caught in the controversy wrote to a colleague, "RL will continue his rage." Lincoln waded into the frustrations surrounding the building of the Lincoln Memorial in Washington, D.C., sometimes spurring politicians along and sometimes frustrating their best attempts to get something done. Wise politicos consulted him about every part of the project, involving him, for example, in the dispute between using Colorado or Georgia marble.

In the later decades of his life, Robert Lincoln's aversion to public notoriety was seen by many Americans as eccentric. He retired from business and moved to Washington, dividing his time between the capital and a sprawling estate in Vermont where he enjoyed his passion for golf. He wrote a book about his life's experiences and devoted himself to organized and personal philanthropic endeavors, many of which became known only after his death and that contradicted the earlier portrayals of an aloof, indifferent businessman-lawyer. In 1922, when the Lincoln Memorial was finally completed, he joined President Warren G. Harding at the dedication in Washington, D.C.

Robert Lincoln died on July 25, 1926, only days before his eighty-third birthday. While Abraham Lincoln, his wife Mary, Eddie, Willie, and Tad are all buried together in Springfield, Illinois, Robert chose to be buried alone at Arlington National Cemetery. Former House Speaker, "Uncle Joe" Cannon, told journalists that "Mr. Lincoln's death removes one of the most misunderstood citizens of the country. . . . Able, well educated and trained for his life work, he was constantly under the shadow of the great immortal Lincoln." Alternately controversial, dark, benevolent, and even ruthless, history sees Robert T. Lincoln, son of America's greatest president, as one of its most successful presidential sons.

Frederick Dent Grant:
A Soldier to the End

Frederick Dent Grant, eldest child of President Ulysses S. Grant, was born May 30, 1850. He would follow his father to West Point and distinguish himself as the second "General Grant" in the family, reaching the highest levels of the military. His father was serving as a humble lieutenant in the United States Army at the time of Fred's birth. Often separated from the family, the elder Grant anguished over those separations, especially empathizing with the pain he imagined his children were experiencing.

For a while, U. S. Grant left the army but his career prospects were poor. With the Civil War looming, he saw his opportunity. On a fateful summer day in June 1861, Ulysses S. Grant rode into Mattoon, Illinois, "with eleven-year-old Fred in tow," to become the colonel of the Illinois Seventh District Regiment. As battle with the Southern Confederates neared, he sent Fred home. Within months Grant had leaped up the chain of command, acquiring more clout and the requisite personal prerogatives that come to men of rank. From then on Fred practically lived with his father on the battlefields of the Civil War. He was present at the investment of Fort Donelson, joined his father in reconnoitering the Vicksburg defenses, watched the fireworks as Porter's gunboats moved downstream past the bristling guns on Vicksburg Heights, and even "beat his father" into Jackson, Mississippi. He experienced typhoid fever, dysentery, and was shot in the thigh, but young Fred always came back. On March 8, 1864, President Abraham Lincoln called Major General Grant back east to take command of the entire Northern armies. Young, wide-eyed, thirteen-year-old Fred Grant was there, standing with his father in the Willard Hotel, in a famous moment when it seemed as if all of Washington suddenly recognized their hero and exploded in applause and cheers.

Fred entered West Point at age fourteen and took five years to graduate. Some writers make much of this extra year, suggesting that Fred was slow or lazy or both. It is more likely that his earlier "home school" education left much to be desired. By the time he graduated, his famous father was the president and it was this relationship that is credited for landing him a prestigious job as the personal aide to Lieutenant General Philip Sheridan.

President Benjamin Harrison, grandson of a president himself, may have had a special appreciation for both the struggles and abilities of presidential children. He appointed Frederick Dent Grant as minister to Austria and Robert Todd Lincoln as minister to the United Kingdom, where both men distinguished themselves, juggling the rivalries and political intrigue of their respective embassies during tumultuous times.

In 1887, following a four-year stint as a New York City police commissioner, Frederick Grant was appointed secretary of state by Democratic President Grover Cleveland. For one brief moment the family entertained the intoxicating idea of a family dynasty. But the newspapers were unmerciful. The appointment was trashed in Boston and Washington, where journalists pronounced Grant unqualified, charging that his appointment was a gimmick, an attempt by the Democrats to broaden their base by stealing some of the Republican glory from the Grant name. Old, totally unsubstantiated charges of his involvement in the famous Whiskey Ring scandal were raised. The appointment went down to defeat in the Senate and the auspicious political career of Frederick Grant was stopped dead.

In 1889, with the advent of the Spanish-American War, Fred Grant was back for active service in the U.S. Army and moved quickly up the ranks, deftly avoiding the political minefields in one of the world's most cumbersome bureaucracies. After a lifetime in the army, he would reach the very heights, outranked only by Major General Leonard Wood, chief of staff. He would die April 11, 1912, at the age of sixty-one with honors, his funeral almost a state event with President Taft and most of New York society in attendance. By most accounts, Frederick Dent Grant had fought hard to carve out one of America's most successful military careers, even while the shadow of his father and the excessive expectations for a presidential child often transcended his best efforts. He had the talent for organization and the consummate political skills of a Dwight Eisenhower. Had there been a great war in his lifetime, he would likely have become a renowned figure of history, the second Grant to achieve immortality.

Webb Cook Hayes:
Adventurer and Soldier of Fortune

Webb Cook Hayes, the second son of the nineteenth president, Rutherford B. Hayes, was a dashing, swashbuckling hero in his time, a millionaire-adventurer who got tired of making big money and risked everything in a classic middle-age crisis to pursue life as a soldier of fortune. He was born on March 20, 1856, in Cincinnati, Ohio, and was originally named James Webb Hayes, after the first lady's father, James Webb. To his mother, who worshiped a father who had died young, it was a wonderful name, but for reasons that still confuse historians he had it legally changed to "Webb Cook." Perhaps he was emboldened by his older brother, born Sardis Birchard Hayes, who had his awkward name changed to the slightly less awkward, Birchard Austin Hayes.

Childhood for the Hayes boys consisted of one Civil War military camp after another. From the age of five to nine, Webb spent his winters with his father's Union regiment, usually in Virginia. Growing up in this exciting — and often heartwrenching — environment likely affected Webb for years to come. A letter from Rutherford to his uncle, Sardis Birchard, gives a touch of the pathos. "Lucy is here," wrote the senior Hayes. "She visits the wounded and comes back in tears; then we take a little refreshment and get over it."

Rutherford B. Hayes returned from the war a decorated hero and a brigadier general. His proud Ohio community promptly elected him to Congress and in 1868 he was elected governor. By every account, Rutherford and Lucy Hayes were exemplary parents. Three of their sons died before they reached their second birthday. The four surviving sons and one daughter were treated lovingly but with direction. The father was a man of principle and integrity who wrote encouraging letters to his children; the mother was gentle, kind, sociable, and creative. Both were devout Christians, though without rigid denominational commitment, who began each day reading from the Bible, each member of the family taking a turn reading verses. "Lucy instilled in the boys her own deep convictions of ethics and modesty; and, when they became president's sons, they shunned the glare and glamour which came to occupants of the White House."

Birchard, the firstborn son in the family, was pursuing a law degree at Harvard when his father's name was being bandied about as a presidential possibility. Second son, Webb, was graduating from Cornell University. That summer Webb enthusiastically jumped on board his father's political bandwagon. Rutherford B. Hayes had experienced a rocky political career, serving one term as governor, then failing at a return try for Congress, as well as attempts to obtain a federal appointment. But in 1875 he had made a spectacular comeback to win the Ohio governor's mansion for the second time. The following year he was considered a dark horse, unlikely to win the Republican nomination, but because the convention would be held on his home turf in Cincinnati, there would be plenty of Hayes supporters in the gallery rooting for their favorite son. Webb Cook Hayes, his dark-haired, tall, clever, twenty-one-year-old son, was full of energy and hopeful that something good would happen. He worked the convention floor assiduously for his father. Even before the first session opened, an ebullient and enthusiastic Webb sent a message home to his father that "if you are not nom. for Pres., you will surely be for V.P."

Republican House Speaker, James G. Blaine, led on the first ballot, with Hayes receiving only sixty-one votes and ranked in lowly fifth place. But undaunted, young Webb was still optimistic. "If Blaine is not nominated by the 4th ballot your nomination is considered to be certain."

And so it was. On the seventh ballot, Rutherford B. Hayes won the nomination and months later found himself in the tightest and most controversial presidential elections in American history, at least until the year 2000. At one point, Richard Taylor, presidential son and former Confederate general, almost threw the election, working in Louisiana, South Carolina, and Florida on behalf of Samuel Tilden, the Democratic opponent. According to one scenario, which was a very real possibility and eerily similar to events in the year 2000, Tilden could lose all of the three disputed Southern states and still win the election if a judge upheld "the governor of Oregon in the matter of the one Tilden elector of that state." Hayes was finally resigned to defeat when his son Webb raced up with a telegram saying that all was not lost; there was a new plan.

Although Rutherford Hayes lost the popular vote of 1876 and came in second in the electoral college, a congressional commission decided in his favor on March 2, 1877, and three days later he was inaugurated the nineteenth American president. Twenty-one-year-old Webb Hayes was brought into the White House as the president's "unofficial private secretary," a role he had previously filled with competence during the elder Hayes's third term as governor of Ohio.

Lucy Hayes, the first president's wife to have a college degree, was a hit as first lady. Journalists applauded her as "friendly and lacking in ostentation." She was involved in a wide variety of social activities and in 1878 opened the White House grounds to neighboring children for the first Easter egg roll. Under Lucy Hayes, old family religious rituals ruled over informal White House gatherings. Mornings began with Bible reading at breakfast. Hymns and prayers were offered in the evenings. On Sunday mornings the first family walked to the Foundry Methodist Church near the White House. But she had her critics. As a leader in the Temperance Movement, she banned alcohol in the White House, earning her the derogatory title of "Lemonade Lucy."

The Rutherford Hayes family was the wealthiest of all the nineteenth-century occupants of the White House, using their resources to live well, but never extravagantly. It was the early practice of presidents to hire their own personal secretaries. President Hayes employed four, but his close son Webb soon became the most important.

Webb Cook Hayes was everywhere, on Capitol Hill and at important social events across the city. He could go where protocol excluded a president and first lady. He could ask questions that they could not. He was more than an aide; he was the president's alter ego, his eyes and ears, his foremost counselor. As a White House presidential assistant and secretary, Webb was with his father throughout the working day. As a personal bodyguard, who packed a weapon, he watched over him after-hours as well. The experience of Abraham Lincoln was fresh in everyone's mind and the close election had produced bitter feelings. There had been a number of threats and at least one assassination attempt. As his mother's son and a single young man, he was knee-deep in the social activities of the capital, frequently called upon to escort important single ladies to White House functions, sometimes assigned "as many as eight girls to look after at one time." When the president angered many in the nation by naming black leader Frederick Douglass as the District's United States marshal, the Hayes White House turned back the political fire by tactfully reworking the duties of the job, relieving Douglass of his role as the official greeter at state events. Webb Hayes, instead, was tapped as "greeter." He stood next to the president in receiving lines, making the introductions and following up with any decisions or points of action. He wrote personal letters for the president and handled all of his most sensitive issues. The president's son made the difficult look easy.

Even after leaving the White House, when Webb Hayes was pursuing a life of his own, the first couple continued to call on their son in a crisis. When the former president and first lady wanted to retrieve their favorite coach and team of horses, on loan to the new president, James Garfield, Webb was brought in to help with the delicate mission. Employing the charm that made him famous in the capital, Webb managed to complete the errand without offense.

The business career of Webb Cook Hayes is the stuff of legend. Right out of the White House, he moved to Cleveland, Ohio, where he began as a secretary and treasurer of the Whipple Lock Manufacturing Company. He was soon an officer of the Thomas-Houston Electric Company. Six years later, in association with Myron T. Herrick, James Parmelee, and W. H. Lawrence, he organized the National Carbon Company. Herrick would go on to service as the United States ambassador to France. And their business venture would become one of the world's great multinational enterprises, known today as the Union Carbide Corporation.

In 1889, the former first lady, Lucy Hayes, died after a stroke. Her husband was shattered. Daughter Fanny, then twenty-two, assumed the role as traveling companion and hostess for her revered father. Less than four years later, Webb was putting the former president on a train to his home in Spiegel Grove, Ohio, when the senior Hayes began complaining of sharp chest pains. It reminded him, he said, of his wounds at South Mountain during the Civil War. When Webb couldn't convince his father to cancel the trip, he decided to accompany him. A few days later, at home in his own bed, the nineteenth American president died at the age of seventy, his loyal son Webb Cook Hayes at his side. It was January 1893, and the newly elected Democrat president Grover Cleveland insisted on attending the funeral.

Neither Webb nor sister Fanny had married as long as their parents had been living. Only Birchard, the firstborn, a successful lawyer in Toledo, Ohio, had taken a wife. On September 1, 1897, Fanny Hayes married Harry Eaton Smith. They had one child.

Rutherford Platt Hayes, the third son of the president, was a cashier in a bank when his father died. He married the daughter of a family friend for whom he had been named, Lucy Platt. They had three children. Rutherford went on to become one of the leading figures in the American library movement. Rutherford helped cofound the American Library Association, conceived of reading rooms for children, and inaugurated the first "mobile libraries," taking books to isolated communities.

Scott Russell Hayes, who had been only five years old when his father had become president, became a successful businessman who married

Maude Anderson. He died at the young age of fifty-two. All of the Hayes children became high achievers by any standard and Webb Cook Hayes eventually became famous worldwide.

By the time of his father's death, the business acumen of the president's second son had only enhanced the legend of his earlier years as a young assistant in the White House. President William McKinley tapped Webb Hayes as an unofficial advisor, bringing him back to Washington. During the crisis with Spain, Hayes was continually at the president's side. When a formal document was signed in the Cabinet Room, launching the Spanish-American War, McKinley used two pens, one for signing his first name, the other for his last. Both pens were given to Webb Hayes.

When the Spanish-American War began, a patriotic young Hayes quickly volunteered and was assigned to the First Ohio Volunteer Cavalry. He and his older brother had grown up as "army brats" on the military encampments of the Civil War, and the routine and ritual of army life brought back a flood of memories. He was immediately commissioned a major in the army, and during the short conflict served with distinction fighting in the campaigns of Santiago de Cuba and the invasion of Puerto Rico of 1898. While crossing the San Juan River Hayes was wounded, but nothing could prevent him from taking part in the assault on San Juan Hill. Theodore Roosevelt, a fellow soldier and former assistant secretary of the navy, became famous, leading the assault.

It was in the Philippines that the daring of Webb Hayes captured the imagination of the nation. A unit of American solders was isolated in a garrison at Vigan with seemingly no chance of escape or communication to the outside world. Alone, during the night, Lieutenant Colonel Webb Hayes stole furtively through enemy lines to reach the garrison. He returned the following morning with a full report to the navy, securing assistance. The men were saved and Webb Hayes became the first presidential son to win the Medal of Honor.

Wealthy and renowned as a young man, Colonel Webb Hayes spent his middle years as a soldier of fortune, traveling the world, moving from one adventure to the next, risking his life for the thrill of combat. He was on the scene of the Boxer Rebellion, the China Relief Expedition, and the Russo-Japanese War. He was part of the relief force that rescued the trapped Westerners in Peking, including the future president and first lady Herbert and Lou Hoover.

Webb Hayes was fifty-six years old when he married Mary Otis Miller Brinkerhoff, an employee of the Red Cross. Within a year he was back in uniform fighting bandits on the Mexican border. As the crisis in Europe unfolded, he was sent to Paris, representing the State Department. But with a war on, the president's adventurous son could never stay content on the sidelines. Webb joined British and French forces in Italy during World War One where he was decorated for bravery. When the United States entered the conflict, his experience was needed in the field.

Immediately commissioned a full colonel, he was assigned the role of a regional commander of the American Expeditionary Force in Italy.

Hayes became a great philanthropist and patron in his later years, establishing memorials for long forgotten veterans of faraway conflicts, as well as memorials to the dead of World War One. His work in his later years in behalf of his father's legacy resulted in the Rutherford B. Hayes Presidential Center, "the first presidential library in the United States."

Webb Cook Hayes died on July 29, 1934, at the age of seventy-eight. He was one of the most powerful White House staffers in American history and surely one of the most powerful of presidential sons during his father's own administration. Successful businessman, philanthropist, Medal of Honor winner, and adventuring soldier of fortune, he was the man who helped begin the tradition of presidential libraries, which ironically established a fitting legacy for himself as well as his father.

NINE

MEN OF VALOR

"No man should go into politics if he's afraid to be defeated. Once he gets that fear he'll lose his courage."
— ROBERT A. TAFT

While many great presidential sons came out of the Civil War period, an equal number appeared during World War Two, most of them off the battlefield. Bluntly stated, a great war seems to trump the presidency. When the life of a son or brother or husband is at risk, all other interests are subordinated. The focus is shifted to the drama of combat and survival. There are a whole new set of heroes, some who become presidents themselves. Thus Ulysses S. Grant, Robert E. Lee, Douglas MacArthur, Dwight D. Eisenhower, George Patton, and dozens of other names become huge public figures. While history shakes them out and presidents tend to have a longer shelf life, for a while, these important military figures blaze like stars across the firmament. During these periods of great emergency the trauma to presidential children is apparently disrupted, the playing field is leveled; presidential children are accepted for what they can achieve without prejudice or unrealistic expectations.

In the 1930s, the once-respected politician and humanitarian, President Herbert Hoover, was blamed for the Great Depression. Unfair or not, it was certainly more difficult for his children to trade on their father's name to win laurels in politics or business, yet both Hoover sons became hugely successful. Perhaps their father's reduced status was a source of freedom for them. Herbert Hoover, Jr.'s, fascination with radio work became a lifetime passion. As an engineer in geophysics, he helped develop new technical procedures, including weapons systems that greatly impacted America's effort during World War Two. *Time* magazine called him a genius.

During the same war, several of Franklin Roosevelt's sons were saved from potentially ruinous controversy and scandal by heroics on the battlefield. John Eisenhower, son of the allied high commander, became a critically acclaimed historian.

The previous chapter refers to the "strategic perspective" of presidential sons, that is, their ability to see the world through their fathers' eyes. This characteristic has persisted into modern times and made a number of these young men indispensable advisors and resources to presidents other than their fathers. Even beyond having a strategic perspective, presidential children know the pain and the needs of the office better than anyone else. They know the physical arrangements of the White House itself, the juggling of social and family demands, the different struggles in dealing with staff and media. And then, they often know how to get their man elected.

Robert Tyler, the successful first son of the tenth president, became a leader in the Pennsylvania State Democratic Party. After his father left the White House, he devoted several years of his life to advancing the career of one Senator James Buchanan. Through Robert's tireless energies the campaign succeeded, but Buchanan succumbed to advice from new friends, including his own and Tyler's rivals. The new president failed to appoint his own champion to his new cabinet. Tyler passed on a much lesser position. History credits him for grace and humility, remaining loyal to Buchanan to the end, moving to Alabama where he again rose to the top, serving as the Democrat state party chairman and as editor for the *Montgomery Advisor*, the leading newspaper in the city.

Harry and James Garfield were personal confidants to two different American presidents, Republican and Democrat. James Garfield was a close friend to Theodore Roosevelt, and Harry Garfield to Woodrow Wilson. Both presidential sons served in the administrations of their prominent friends, Harry Garfield becoming President Woodrow Wilson's powerful "Fuel Czar" in the middle of World War One, and James Rudolph Garfield serving as secretary of the interior. Some historians rank James Garfield as one of America's greatest cabinet officers and Theodore

Roosevelt, himself, said that it was his best appointment.

Theodore Roosevelt, Jr.:
Greatness in Absentia

Theodore Roosevelt referred to his six children as his "little bunnies." He built a home on a hill at Oyster Bay on the northern side of Long Island and named it Sagamore Hill, after a famous regional Native American chief. At four o'clock each day he walked out of his office on the second floor to join in the fun. In the winter there were sleigh rides and snowball fights; in the summer there were organized sports and hunting.

Over the years, Sagamore Hill became filled with the souvenirs of a lifetime of adventure and triumph. There were the trophy heads of wild game adorning the walls, some killed by hand. There were animal skins of zebras and jaguars covering the floors. There was exotic homemade furniture from India and Africa. The bookshelves were overflowing with volumes covering every science and discipline, with huge sections on history, especially the adventurous accounts of sailors and soldiers. It was a house of heroes, and the man who built it was one of them.

His second child and firstborn son, Theodore Roosevelt, Jr., was born September 13, 1887, a year after his father had lost a bid to become the mayor of New York City. As in the case of so many other presidential "juniors," the name was a bit tricky. In fact, his grandfather had the same name and thus Junior was, technically, Theodore Roosevelt III. To the family he was "brother" or Ted.

Alice Roosevelt, Ted's older sister, was born to Theodore Roosevelt's first wife, Alice Lee, who died shortly after the birth. On December 2, 1886, in London, England, Roosevelt had married again, this time to his twenty-five-year-old childhood sweetheart, Edith Carow. After Ted, four more children would be born — Kermit, Ethel, Archie, and Quentin.

Raised on tales of romantic valor, Ted, Jr., was "rambunctious," even reckless. His mother, Edith, was "in constant anxiety about his life and limb." His fearless father wondered aloud if Ted would live to manhood. Not that he served as a great restraint on his son's exuberance. On Ted's tenth birthday TR presented him with a rifle of his own. When Ted questioned if it was real, Roosevelt loaded it and shot a bullet into the ceiling. "You mustn't tell Mother."

In 1889, Theodore Roosevelt received an appointment by the Harrison administration as a U.S. Civil Service commissioner and a few years later an appointment by the mayor of New York City as the president of the city police board. If his afternoons at play were interrupted by work, he still returned home each evening for dinner, where the children were encouraged to speak their minds and where their father listened to each opinion. When young Ted, Jr., announced to dinner guests that he would one day be a soldier, his father beamed with pride.

In 1897, fresh from his successes in New York,

Roosevelt was appointed by the newly elected president, William McKinley, as the assistant secretary of the navy. The family moved to Washington and almost immediately TR was involved in the contentious debate over Cuban independence from Spain. In April 1898, two months after the explosion aboard the battleship *Maine*, America declared war on Spain, pledging to drive them out of the Caribbean. Roosevelt walked into the president's office asking permission to resign from his post to raise a cavalry regiment for battle in Cuba. McKinley agreed and Roosevelt went home to Sagamore Hill to get ready. Ted watched as his father shot at life-size paper targets of men and the reality of what was happening must have begun to sink in. Theodore Roosevelt's Rough Riders trained in Texas. When he wrote home, warning that his chances of survival might be one in three, and that if he were to be a casualty, Ted and Kermit should have his sword and revolver, both boys openly wept.

On July 1, 1898, while his family was eating lunch on the porch at Sagamore Hill, Theodore Roosevelt was leading his Rough Riders on a charge up San Juan Hill in Santiago, Cuba. He would call the moment his "crowded hour," an expression that would become famous within the family and the title of a future book authored by Alice Roosevelt. Those who witnessed Roosevelt's bravery at Santiago were forever moved by the experience. One seasoned correspondent called it the "best moment in anybody's life." Twenty percent of the Rough Riders were casualties, but Roosevelt, who had openly led the charge on horseback, was untouched. He confessed to a close friend that "no hunting trip equaled it." The next day the newspapers were filled with the story and the little bunnies on Sagamore Hill eagerly read of their father's exploits with relief and pride. Within days the war was over.

What thrilled the nation made some others in Washington angry and jealous. When letters recommending the Medal of Honor for Theodore Roosevelt reached the war department, they were dismissed. Edith confided to Ted, Jr., that it was "one of the bitterest disappointments" in his father's life.

If Washington bureaucrats chose to ignore the charge up San Juan Hill, the public did not. That very fall, the man who had failed twelve years before to be elected mayor of New York City found himself governor of New York State. The Roosevelts moved to the state capital in Albany. And two years later he was nominated vice president of the United States on the ticket with incumbent president William McKinley. In 1900, after a McKinley-Roosevelt landslide victory, Theodore and Edith and all their little bunnies moved back to Washington, D.C. Events had happened at a dizzying pace and the adventure was only beginning.

Life for the children during these tumultuous times was a mixed blessing. When Roosevelt won the gubernatorial office in New York, Ted and Archie were packed off to the Albany Military Academy. Alice and Ethel were placed in the keeping of an English governess. When TR was nominated for vice president, Ted was sent to Groton, the exclusive preparatory school. Still, there were summers at Sagamore Hill. When reporters pursued the children there, Roosevelt erupted. "I am a public man and free game," he roared, "but my house is my castle. In my home I will be let alone."

On September 6, 1901, at the Pan American Exposition in Buffalo, New York, an anarchist shot President William McKinley. Ted, Jr., heard the stunning news at Groton Academy and was distracted for a day or so, but reports insisted that the president would recover and Ted resumed his studies. On September 14, 1901, the day after Ted's fourteenth birthday, the president took a turn for the worse and died. At three o'clock in the afternoon, Theodore Roosevelt was sworn in as the twenty-sixth president of the United States. The school headmaster arrived with a telegram from Edith, instructing Ted to depart immediately for Sagamore Hill to accompany his mother on a train trip to Washington, where they would attend the funeral of the assassinated president.

With the rest of the family ensconced in the White House, Ted returned to Groton to pursue his studies, relatively safe from the limelight. But daily he read of his brothers' and sisters' antics. The American public was fascinated. When Quentin was chastised for walking on stilts in a White House flower garden, he asked his father what good it was to be president anyway, if they couldn't do anything? When Archie became sick,

Quentin coaxed his brother's pony on an elevator and walked it to his room on the second floor to cheer him up. And "Princess Alice," Ted's older, colorful sister, was all over the newspapers. In February 1902, sick with pneumonia, Ted was on the front pages himself. Edith and sister Alice rushed to Groton to be with him and the whole nation held anxious vigil, but the crisis passed.

When Ted expressed an interest to attend West Point, TR was openly disappointed. He had always expected Ted would follow him to Harvard. He wrote letters urging the boy to reconsider. "I am not satisfied that this is really your feeling," said one. "I have actually known lieutenants in both the Army and Navy who were grandfathers," said another. And in another note he complained, "You have too much in you for me to be glad to see you go into the army." In the end, Ted's desire to please his father won out and he went to Harvard.

In 1908, fifty-year-old Theodore Roosevelt announced that he was keeping an earlier pledge not to run for reelection. He had served three years of the first McKinley term and won reelection for four more in 1904. Seven years in the White House, he asserted, was enough. After naming best friend William Howard Taft as his choice for president, he was off on a much publicized safari to the densest parts of tropical Africa to hunt and gather specimens for the Smithsonian Institution. Ted, just graduating from Harvard, was invited along, but he was on a different kind of a hunt and passed on the opportunity.

Theodore Roosevelt, Jr., was dating a young

coed named Eleanor Butler Alexander. They met on a platform of a railroad station. Both had been weekend guests at a dinner party hosted by a prominent family in a nearby community. Eleanor was from a well-known and successful family and Ted, son of the president, had taken a lowly job at the Hartford Carpet Company, earning seven dollars a week.

His father's famous safari lasted more than a year, so the couple had to restrain their ardor. On June 20, 1910, two days after TR's return from Africa, Theodore and Eleanor were married at the Fifth Avenue Presbyterian Church in Manhattan. Their honeymoon took them to San Francisco, where Ted would work for the Carpet company's West Coast office. But it involved dodging swarms of reporters all the way. They would eventually have four children, Grace Green, Theodore Roosevelt III, Cornelius, and, finally, Quentin. Two years later, the couple was back east where, in New York and Philadelphia, Ted slowly built a very successful career in investment banking.

In 1914, World War One erupted and while the United States stayed on the sidelines, Theodore Roosevelt and his sons were itching for an opportunity to get involved. When the following year the *Lusitania* was sunk by a German U-boat, with loss of American civilians, Ted helped organize training camps. When America entered the war, all four Roosevelt sons lobbied their father to pull every string to get them to the front and into the hottest action.

Ted continually impressed the army brass,

ending up as a major with troops on the front lines. His father wrote exultantly, "You have the fighting tradition! It's a great thing you have done; I am very pleased." And by the time all four were in the heat of battle, he wrote Ted of his pride, "I am overjoyed that you four have your chance, whatever the cost."

In January 1918, Kermit Roosevelt, serving with the British forces in the Middle East, burst into a house full of armed Turkish soldiers. He was all alone. Kermit improvised, confidently demanding their surrender. The startled Turks threw down their arms and surrendered. The amused English awarded Kermit the British Army Cross.

Archie Roosevelt was the first casualty. Early in 1918 he had picked up a *Paris Herald* to learn that he was a new father. A few months later he was hit with hot shrapnel from an exploding German shell. His kneecap was crushed, his left arm broken, and the main nerve severed. Barely avoiding the amputation of his leg, he healed well, but doctors pronounced him a cripple for life. The French awarded him the Croix de Guerre.

In May the Germans launched a great offensive; Ted's sector was hit especially hard but it held against attacks from three different sides. Ted was all over the battlefield retaining his command in spite of German gas attacks that blinded him for days and injured his lungs. In the aftermath he was cited for "high courage and leadership" and awarded the Silver Star, while the French gave him the Croix de Guerre.

On July 14, 1918, Bastille Day in France, the youngest brother in the family, Quentin, was shot down over Germany. The family was devastated. A mourning father asked his children that the next son born into any of their families be named Quentin.

Only a month later, Ted was hit in the leg by machine-gun fire. He was soon ensconced in the same Parisian hospital as brother Archie. Wife Eleanor, working with the YMCA in Europe to be near her husband, was at his side. But as soon as possible he was back at the front, promoted to lieutenant colonel, and placed in command of the 26th Infantry Regiment. Limping on a cane, he and his forces fought to the very last minute of the war, executing nightlong marches followed by days of engaging the enemy.

There is a bitter postscript to Ted Roosevelt, Jr.'s, World War One experience. A friend on the command staff confirmed the swirling rumors that Ted was being touted by many for promotion and for the French Legion of Honor, but it would not happen. "People might say that you were promoted or decorated because you're the son of your father, and might criticize us. Now we can't have that sort of thing, now, can we?"

In January 1919, Ted's wife, Eleanor, visited the failing former president in the hospital. "You know, Father," she told him, "Ted has always worried for fear that he would not be worthy of you."

"Worthy of me? Darling, I'm so very proud of him," the senior Roosevelt said. "He has won high honor not only for his children but, like the

Chinese, he has ennobled his ancestors. I walk with my head higher because of him." Three days later Theodore Roosevelt, the twenty-sixth American president, passed away in bed at his home on Sagamore Hill. Archie cabled his brothers still in the field in France, "The old lion is dead."

Following World War One, Ted Roosevelt worked tirelessly organizing veterans and demanding help for the orphans and widows of soldiers. By the first anniversary of Armistice Day, he had been the driving force in the founding of a new powerful social and political organization, the American Legion. At their May 1919 convention thousands of delegates tried to draft him as their chairman, thundering in unison, "We want Teddy, we want Teddy!" But Roosevelt steadfastly declined, confiding to friends that he was planning to pursue a political career and he did not want to compromise the work he had done for veterans.

The political career of Theodore Roosevelt, Jr., was a tumultuous affair. That November 1919, he was elected to the New York Assembly. In the presidential election the following year, he campaigned tirelessly for the Republican ticket of Warren G. Harding and Calvin Coolidge, which was pitted against Democrats James Middleton Cox and his own cousin Franklin Delano Roosevelt, who was the vice presidential nominee. Ted was assigned to trail his cousin and give speeches needling him and asserting the "correct" Roosevelt positions. The Harding-Coolidge ticket won in a landslide and Ted was promptly rewarded with his father's old office, the assistant secretary of the navy. The pattern of his rise was not lost on anyone and there was little surprise when rumors began that he would run for governor of New York before following his father's path back to Washington and the White House. But the pattern was interrupted by a terrible event.

The Harding administration was one of the most corrupt in American history and the biggest event of all was the infamous Teapot Dome scandal. The U.S. Navy oil reserves in Elk Hill, California, and Teapot Dome, Wyoming, had been leased by two oil tycoons who had bribed the secretary of the interior, Albert B. Fall. The secretary of the interior would eventually go to prison for his actions, but it had all happened on Ted Roosevelt's watch at the Navy Department. It took time for journalists to separate the guilty from the innocent and regardless of Ted's personal integrity, the fog of scandal never entirely lifted. When Theodore Roosevelt, Jr., ran for governor of New York in 1924, his cousin Eleanor, wife of Franklin Delano Roosevelt, followed him around in a truck spouting a teapot on its top and labeled "Teapot Dome." It was sweet revenge for Ted's political campaign against her husband four years before. Democrat Alfred Smith defeated Ted Roosevelt for governor of New York by a 51–48 percent margin. The dream of a presidency for Theodore Roosevelt, Jr., was over.

As in the case of his father, Ted nursed his defeat by writing books and embarking on adventures. *East of the Sun and West of the Moon,* coauthored with Kermit, appeared in 1926. *Rank and File: True Stories of the Great War* was published in 1928. *All in the Family* would be published in 1929. And two other books would eventually be written. Before heading off into the wilderness he consulted with his wife Eleanor and his sister Alice. While he fought big game in an exotic hunting trip to Asia in behalf of the Chicago Field Museum, they would be lobbying the new Hoover administration for the right appointment. Ted and Kermit became the first Westerners to confirm the existence of the giant panda, a fact that rocked the zoological world and many naturalists who had doubted its existence. Nineteen new species or subspecies were confirmed on this expedition, including a previously unknown deer named by scientists the *Muntiacus rooseveltorum*. He reached the civilized world in the summer of 1929 to learn that the women left behind had done their job; President Herbert Hoover had appointed him the new governor of Puerto Rico.

Ted and Eleanor were popular governors of the troubled island, using their fame to call attention to the poverty of its people and rooting out graft. When the stock market collapsed signaling the beginning of what would become the Great Depression, Ted used his personal money to prop up the island's banks. The *Baltimore Sun* described him as "perhaps the finest colonial governor in our history." But such heroics were purchased at a price. Jealous island leaders, used to exploiting the island for themselves, fought back, accusing Ted of using government funds for his own extravagant lifestyle. Roosevelt's integrity survived, but in a nation with a two-party political system, many Americans believed what they wanted to believe, and the old charges of the Teapot Dome scandal resurfaced. Pleased with his effective service in Puerto Rico, President Hoover appointed Ted governor of the Philippines. But in 1932, his rival cousin, Democrat Franklin D. Roosevelt, was elected president. A journalist asked the Philippines governor what his exact relationship was with the new president-elect. Ted replied, "Fifth cousin, about to be removed." FDR would serve for the next twelve years. Theodore Roosevelt, Jr.'s, diplomatic and governmental career was at an end.

Ted returned to New York to wide acclaim. He was named to the board of directors of dozens of the nation's most prestigious companies and civic organizations, from the Boy Scouts to the National Association for the Advancement of Colored People. He joined Doubleday, Doran as a vice president and became a leader in the publishing industry and a central society figure among a bevy of popular American writers. He was elected chairman of American Express.

When war broke out in Europe, Ted's older sister, Alice Roosevelt, wife of Congressman Nicholas Longworth, helped organize and found the America First Committee. Rallies were held across the country with Ted Roosevelt, second only to Charles Lindbergh, as a favorite speaker. Advocating neutrality was a paradoxical role for the children of Theodore Roosevelt and it would not last long. Kermit maintained the tradition of early involvement by joining British forces in 1939, already at war with Hitler, two years before the attack on Pearl Harbor. Ted asked to be reactivated and was assigned to his old 26th Infantry. Four days after the Japanese attack, FDR promoted him to brigadier general. By the time he left for war, he was second in command of the division and his own son Quentin would be serving with him. *Life* magazine featured the famous father and son, serving in the same division. Taking the initiative to heal the rift between the Roosevelts, Ted called on his presidential cousin at the White House and emerged to waiting reporters saying, "This is our country, our cause and our president." Before the war would end, all three of Ted's sons and six of his grandsons would be in uniform.

The year 1943 would prove to be a defining year for the Roosevelt family. Ted's son, Quentin, would be almost fatally wounded in North Africa and taken from the field of battle. His brother Archie, a lieutenant colonel fighting the Japanese in New Guinea, would labor in combat "continuously for seventy-six days." He would eventually be severely wounded in combat and sent home. His brother Kermit, who for years had descended into an alcoholic funk and embarrassed the family by his escapades with a mistress, would commit suicide at a lonely post in Alaska. And Ted, wounded himself, would leave the Italian front with a Bronze Star with Oak Leaf Cluster and his second French Croix de Guerre.

Ted had landed with the first wave in North Africa and had personally shot the first German soldier who had "loomed up in front of him." He was with the First Infantry Division in Africa early in the year when attacked by German General Irwin Rommel's legendary Afrika Corps at Kasserine Pass. There were three thousand American casualties and another three thousand seven hundred captured. Two hundred American tanks had been destroyed. American General George Patton was called in to turn things around.

On the night of March 13, 1943, according to plans laid out by Patton, Brigadier General Ted Roosevelt ordered his men through pouring rain to surprise the Germans with an early morning attack at Gafsa. They then marched ten miles to take El Guettar, where they defeated two full German panzer divisions that were sent racing off in retreat. Patton was elated. The momentum in North Africa had shifted. When the Americans landed on Sicily, quick thinking by Roosevelt, including the personal direction of an artillery company at a key moment in the fighting, preserved the beachhead and saved the landing forces from being driven back into the sea.

By 1944, Theodore Roosevelt, Jr., was a fifty-six-year-old grandfather, who had already lived a full life of adventure and accomplishment. He was arguably a better naturalist, a more prolific writer, a more successful businessman and a braver soldier than his father. Eventually he would be the most decorated soldier to serve in World War Two, winning every combat medal awarded ground forces. And he would do it all without acclaim. Someone, perhaps FDR himself, had issued the order to censor his and Quentin's name from all press reports. Ted, Jr., had served as assistant secretary of the navy and twice as governor. He had even followed the path of so many presidential children before him by achieving something his father had always wanted but never attained. While then serving as governor of New York, Theodore Roosevelt, Sr., had written his friend Henry Cabot Lodge declaring that he didn't want to be vice president because of his strong desire to be named governor general of the Philippines. His son Ted had fulfilled that dream, if only for a short time. But Theodore Roosevelt, Jr., had not become president. When he was only twenty-three he had said, "I will always be known as the son of Theodore Roosevelt and never as a person who means only himself."

His wife Eleanor would write, "The disadvantages of being a great man's son far outweigh the advantages. Ted's truly remarkable career was to be cloaked inevitably and perpetually by the shadow of his father's fame." Wrote Peter Collier, "He had been overshadowed by his father in the first half of his life and by his cousin in the second half. . . ."

It was very clear in 1944 that the Allies would soon be opening a second front in Europe. To relieve the Soviet Union and bring an end to the war, American, English, and French forces would be landing somewhere along the French coast and Hitler's "Fortress Europe." It would take a massive, historic invasion and it would involve tremendous casualties. Brigadier General Theodore Roosevelt, Jr., was determined to be in on the show.

Ted sent his wife Eleanor to Washington to lobby the War Department. He refused to be hospitalized for pneumonia until someone at command headquarters in England assured him that there was still time to recover. He told no one that he was experiencing sharp pains in his chest. And as D-Day approached, he begged, pleaded, and maneuvered, appealing above his own commanders that he be allowed to go in with the first landing force. "No general will be part of the first wave," he was told. Others pointed out that his son Quentin was back in action and taking part in the landing as well. His wife, Eleanor, would be the only American mother to have both a husband and son as part of such a dangerous mission. "You are a cripple," someone else pointed out. "You would only get in the way." Yes, he answered, but the sight of a general hobbling along on his cane on the beaches might be just what the young lads need to calm their nerves and go about their business.

On June 6, 1944, described by Cornelius Ryan as "the longest day," Brigadier General Theodore Roosevelt, Jr., landed with his command on the Normandy beaches as part of the first wave of forces attacking Hitler's Fortress Europe. He played his role exactly as he had envisioned it, standing out in the open with bullets whistling by him, waving his cane, calmly sending troops to their assignments. So conspicuous was his courage that it would become legendary within hours, traveling by word-of-mouth along the beaches. Ted Roosevelt, at fifty-seven the oldest soldier in the first wave, and the only general, wearing only his comfortable knit cap, hobbling on his World War One injuries, was exposed for hours in the toughest of fighting and was untouchable. Dozens of reports were filed. Almost every history of World War Two would retell the story. Screen legend Henry Fonda would play the role when it was made into a major motion picture.

Twenty-five days after the Normandy landing, General Ted Roosevelt's Fourth Division took the important port city of Cherbourg. On July 11, 1944, his son Quentin visited him with his troops in the field. The father confessed for the first time that he had been experiencing heart attacks. The son urged the father to seek medical help and they agreed on it. A few hours later, Theodore Roosevelt, Jr., died of cardiac arrest. His son sent the message to Eleanor at Sagamore Hill, "The lion is dead."

Six generals served as pallbearers at his funeral, including Omar Bradley and George S. Patton. Many years later, Bradley was asked to name the bravest act he had ever known. "Ted Roosevelt at Utah Beach," was his answer. Patton would write that Ted Roosevelt was the bravest soldier he ever knew. He was buried in Saint Mere Eglise on July 14, Bastille Day, twenty-six years to the day after his brother Quentin was shot down over Germany in World War One.

In 1897, when Ted, Jr., was only a ten-year-old and the war with Spain was just beginning, he had begun to experience severe headaches. The persistence of the symptoms eventually alarmed both parents, but every possible explanation resulted in a dead end. Could it be, Edith finally confided to a doctor friend, that Ted was feeling the pressure of "trying to measure up to his father's excessive expectations?" The doctor examined Ted, Jr., and agreed. A chastened and embarrassed Theodore Roosevelt promised not to push his firstborn son. "Hereafter I shall never press Ted either in body or mind. The fact is that the little fellow, who is particularly dear to me, has bidden fair to be all things I would like to have been and wasn't, and it has been a great temptation to push him."

In 1944, sitting on Allied Commander Dwight Eisenhower's desk were a number of strong recommendations that Ted Roosevelt be awarded the Medal of Honor. This time, a recommendation for a Roosevelt to win the medal sailed through the bureaucracy and was passed unanimously by Congress. On September 22, 1944, at the White House, President Franklin D. Roosevelt made the presentation to Ted's widow Eleanor. At San Juan Hill, future president Theodore Roosevelt had his "crowded hour," but failed to win for the family the coveted honor. It had been, his wife admitted, his most bitter disappointment. But his son, Theodore, Jr., after his "crowded lifetime," from the grave, had finally brought it home to Sagamore Hill. As Franklin Roosevelt presented the Medal of Honor, he said to Eleanor, "His father would have been proudest."

There is yet another layer of irony to add to

this story. In 1998, a hundred years after Theodore Roosevelt's charge up Kettle Hill to the San Juan Heights, the Roosevelt family reopened the case for a posthumous Medal of Honor for the former president. After reviewing the circumstances, the Pentagon finally approved and, on January 16, 2001, President Bill Clinton made the presentation. Theodore Roosevelt had won the prize after all. Even from the grave father and son continued the contest, striving to achieve greatness.

Robert Alphonso Taft:
"Mr. Republican"

William Howard Taft, the twenty-seventh president, the man who followed Theodore Roosevelt and the only president to also serve as chief justice of the Supreme Court, had three children. Robert Alphonso Taft was his firstborn son. Helen Taft Manning, whom we have already met in our sagas of courageous daughters, was his middle daughter. And Charles Phelps Taft was the little brother. They were already part of an old, famous Ohio dynasty of public servants noted for their tradition of excellence. In 1907, heading into his presidential campaign, Taft was tapped by his friend, President Theodore Roosevelt, to make a goodwill trip around the world. With his mother sick and close to death, he decided to cancel the trip. In a trembling, dying hand, his mother wrote the last words he would ever receive from her, a statement that reflected six generations of one of America's greatest families. "No Taft, to my knowledge, has ever yet neglected a public duty for the sake of gratifying a private desire."

Firstborn, Robert Taft, was a genius at mathematics. Born on September 8, 1889, he was learning long division and fractions by the time he was seven. A teacher would say that Bob "stored facts in his mind as if it were a filing cabinet." His sister Helen noted that "he would have been a star on a quiz show, for his answers came with lightning speed." Ever the scholar, Bob preferred books to sports.

Robert attended the academically rigorous Taft School, where the founder, his own Uncle Horace, urged him to expand his interests. He was especially encouraged to pursue the subjects in which he was the least gifted, such as music and debate. His uncle said he "grasped arguments easily but was apt to be tongue-tied." With dogged persistence, Bob threw himself into confronting his weakness, entering every debate he could find. It was crucial training for a man who would one day be touted as an eloquent U.S. senator, never at a loss "for an argument." He would, however, always sing off-key.

Bob's brother, Charles Phelps Taft, known throughout his life to one and all as "Charlie," was a blithe spirit. He raced through life with enthusiasm and with such an infectious grin that he was roundly accepted wherever he went. When he became an attorney, opposing counsel would often grouse, "Charlie smiled me out of court." Nearly twenty years after his death, *Cincinnati Enquirer* columnist Laura Pulfer would give

Charlie the ultimate compliment by referring to him in the present tense, saying, "I, too, am smitten with Mr. T."

On April 17, 1900, the Taft family boarded the army transport *Hancock*, bound for the Philippines. President McKinley had just appointed William Howard Taft, Sr., as the civil governor of the island nation. Eleven years old at the time, Robert had taught himself to play chess from a book. He promptly beat all the army officers on board. Two-year-old Charlie was the terror of the ship. His father was to remark, "He is very badly in the need of discipline, and yet I cannot very well administer it in a crowd."

The Philippines brought all sorts of new experiences for the Taft children. Charlie was soon playing with the neighborhood Filipinos, communicating in a language his father termed, "fearfully and wonderfully made of Tagalog, Spanish and English." In the afternoons, young Helen and Bob rode ponies to the Luneta, an area where children played and people promenaded to the sounds of band music. Helen Taft, their mother, so enjoyed the grace and community of the Luneta that she would later try to re-create it in Washington, D.C. Those years the Taft children traveled the world, experiencing the whole panorama of political leaders and systems, from a visit to the pope in the Vatican to the Japanese imperial court.

In the summer of 1903, fourteen-year-old Bob Taft sailed home alone to the States, to begin studies in his uncle's school in the fall. Traveling alone was no big deal to Bob, who spent the voyage with his nose in one book after the other. The long, solitary trip made him two weeks late, but by Thanksgiving, Uncle Horace was able to report to Will Taft that his son was the best of his class. It was typical Taft. While other presidential children would flounder at school, Bob would graduate first in his class at both Yale and Harvard Law School, and go on to earn the highest score in the Ohio bar exams. And all while the pressures were at their greatest, for in 1909 his father, William Howard Taft, assumed the presidency and served his term while Bob finished his education.

On April 2, 1917, President Woodrow Wilson announced to Congress that hard choices had to be made. The German government was sinking every ship trying to enter their enemy's ports. Even hospital ships were being "ruthlessly sent to the bottom." Four days later, the United States declared war on Germany. Bob twice tried to enlist, and twice was rejected, disqualified by his poor eyesight. Meanwhile, he went to work for Herbert Hoover, who had been assigned the cumbersome wartime task of running the Food Administration. Typical of Bob Taft, he worked night and day, and the family heard virtually nothing from him. Relentlessly, he pursued every opening to get into uniform and was consistently blocked until Hoover, tired of the game, told him flatly that his work at home was indispensable. He could not afford to let him go.

When World War One finally ended with an Armistice on November 11, 1918, Bob Taft was involved in two enormous logistic tasks, bringing the soldiers home, and feeding the desperate people of war-ravaged Europe. The war had been a devastating emotional experience for young Bob Taft, watching his brother Charlie's heroics serving in France, while he worked at a desk. His father had written to Charlie, "It takes as much moral courage for him to continue his work there, without compensation, and without being in uniform, as it would to get into uniform and never be where he could smell gunpowder."

Working side by side with Herbert Hoover, young Bob Taft and the U.S. Food Administration had been able to reduce domestic consumption by 15 percent without rationing. Hoover called it conservation; the country called it "Hooverizing." There were "wheatless Wednesdays" and "meatless Mondays." Patriotic housewives responded, and American food shipments tripled. The armies were fed and, like Joseph in Egypt, Hoover built up a surplus of food to prevent a postwar famine in Europe.

With the war at an end, Hoover asked Bob Taft to go with him to Europe. He would serve as a legal advisor to the new American Relief Administration, which would quickly become the major source of food for 300 million people in Europe and the Middle East. Bob traveled around the continent, viewing the devastation and overseeing the distribution of the food. Everywhere he was acknowledged for his efforts, receiving decorations from the governments of Poland and Belgium, and becoming the first American ever to receive the White Rose, Finland's highest award.

In Paris with Hoover, watching the political

machinations at the peace conferences, Bob Taft became profoundly disgusted. He watched European governments selfishly redrawing their borders without consideration for new and more dangerous consequences. He described it as "the greatest field for intrigue" since the Congress of Vienna, the infamous convention that had redrawn European borders after the Napoleonic Wars. Writing to his father, he complained that we should have "let them settle their own troubles when we had licked the Kaiser." Those fateful days in Paris would forever color his view of American relations, giving him a profound aversion to war, and making him distrustful and cynical of any foreign entanglements.

On October 17, 1914, Robert Taft married Martha Wheaton Bowers, the daughter of Lloyd Bowers, former solicitor general in his father's cabinet. True to Bob's reserved personality, he had pursued her doggedly, while never outwardly expressing his feelings. When Martha had a serious riding accident — her spirited horse running headlong into a streetcar, breaking its neck, and pitching her into the street — Bob was jolted to action. He proposed and she accepted. It was destined to be one of Washington's great political marriages. Martha was Bob's opposite in personality — bubbly and a perfect political campaigner. Later, she would delight the press with such delicious bons mots as "To err is Truman," and "The Torch of Liberty is like your husband or a furnace — if you don't do something about it, it will go out." She balanced his reserve, and the people loved her.

In 1920, Bob was elected to the Ohio State House of Representatives where he served until 1928, the last two years as Speaker of the House. When his brother Charlie earned his law degree, the two brothers worked together for a time, launching their own law firm. In 1938, having established himself financially and socially as a good son of Ohio, Bob Taft ran for the U.S. Senate and won. It was the beginning of an extraordinary career, some say the greatest Senate career of all time. Many would lionize him as "Mr. Republican" and "Mr. Integrity." Others would vilify him as "the best nineteenth-century mind in the twentieth century." He would serve in Washington from 1938 until his death in 1953.

Robert Taft was a hard man to get to know. Noncharismatic and stiff, some perceived him as cold. It was a reserve gleaned from too many years in the public eye. As in the case of presidential sons Theodore Roosevelt, Jr., before him and George W. Bush who would follow, Bob Taft had no use for anyone currying favor with flattery. He had no time to waste. And yet he exhibited a dry wit when he chose to use it. One journalist had harshly compared him to Marie Antoinette, hardened to the suffering of the starving French. When another journalist asked him about the jab, Bob queried with a straight face, "Is it because of my glamour?" Later, when the famous senator lived in a fancy house in Washington, his silent comment on pretentiousness was to place a cake of soap in the outstretched hand of a marble goddess in the stairwell.

Robert Taft's speeches lacked fire. They were usually dry recitations of facts. He admitted that, "while I have no difficulty talking, I don't know how to do any of the eloquence business which makes for enthusiasm or applause." He has been described as looking like an owlish storekeeper. But when Bob Taft entered the Senate chamber, he was armed to the teeth with every fact needed on the subject at hand. He had the largest research staff in the Senate, and was clearly one of the best-informed senators in history. His mathematical genius could untangle budgetary dilemmas and other thorny questions, a talent he used to hammer away for a balanced budget.

Convinced that Franklin Roosevelt's New Deal represented an assault on the Constitution and believing that it would lead to socialism and political tyranny, Bob Taft opposed Roosevelt at every turn. Harry Truman fared no better. The feisty old president always spoke of Bob as a "thorn in his side." Adamantly against war and foreign entanglements, Taft was an isolationist until the attack on Pearl Harbor, when it became clear that his reliance on the oceans to protect the United States no longer was viable. Three of his four sons fought in World War Two, and the fourth served in the Pentagon, doing intelligence work.

Surprisingly, Mr. Republican voted for federal aid to education, a plan for federal matching grants to states to improve health care, and even sponsored the Taft-Wagner-Ellender housing bill to build 810,000 homes. "If the free enterprise system does not do its best to prevent hardship

and poverty," Bob said, "it will find itself super-
seded by a less progressive system which does."

As always, he stood up for what he believed, no
matter what the consequences. President John F.
Kennedy honored Bob Taft in his book, *Profiles
in Courage*, saying that "when those fundamental
principles were at issue, not even the lure of the
White House, or the possibilities of injuring his
candidacy, could deter him from speaking out."
Those fundamental principles were forever tied
to constitutional freedoms and responsibilities.
Incredibly, he argued against the Nuremberg
Trials, warning that the Constitution forbids "ex
post facto laws." It was an unpopular stand. And
he was the only senator to speak out against "the
greatest violation of civil liberties since slavery,"
the internment of Japanese Americans during
World War Two, a stand that now wins him
praise from historians.

Robert Taft, a presidential son, was far too discreet and wise to reveal when and how his first
yearnings for the presidency began. It may have
started at his own father's inauguration, for years
later he could still recount every detail of the day.
It may have been born in his father's humiliating
defeat, an incumbent president, coming in third
to Wilson and Roosevelt in 1912. In three Republican conventions, he would come close but
not win his party's nomination. After the 1940
Republican Convention, when Wendell Willkie
was nominated on the sixth ballot, Bob Taft left
the hall, muttering, "Never again!" But it happened all over eight years later when he lost to
Thomas Dewey of New York. In 1952, it seemed

he had the nomination locked up. But the Republican Party had been out of power far too long; Republican leaders, including Dewey, felt Bob Taft would be unable to win a national election. The nomination went to the war hero with the infectious smile, Dwight D. Eisenhower.

Taft partisans were furious with the outcome. Whole delegations threatened to campaign against Ike. But Bob Taft had seen a split in the party before. Theodore Roosevelt had left the Republicans with his supporters, sending his own father down to defeat and electing a president from the other party. Taft knew that a split party meant another four years of Democrat power. He met with Eisenhower and agreements were reached about his issues. Bob Taft campaigned solidly for the man who beat him, and Eisenhower won a landslide in November.

Bob's beloved wife Martha was not with him while he campaigned that year. She had suffered a stroke and was confined to a wheelchair. Bob's interaction with his wife revealed a completely new side of the man to staffers and friends. Tenderly, he would lift her in and out of cars, and patiently care for her needs. With Eisenhower's election, Bob's duties multiplied. Now he was also Republican floor leader. One political observer noted that "Republican senators showed more unity on key role votes in 1953 than in any time in years." Often Eisenhower would call for Bob's advice on issues. But the senator never allowed his duties to interfere with his care for Martha.

In April 1953, President Eisenhower invited

Bob Taft to play golf with him in Augusta, Georgia. As they neared the seventh hole, Bob was suddenly aware of stiffness in his hip. He admitted to the president that he hadn't felt well in some time. Ike urged Bob to go immediately to Walter Reed Hospital for tests; the doctors there suspected a tumor or arthritis. Bob ran a persistent fever, and began having difficulty getting upstairs to his bedroom.

He continued his work at the Capitol, but it was getting harder for him to do so. In May, Bob tried to carry Martha up the steps of a train and collapsed as soon as she was safely seated. He finally had to admit to her that he was having "a bit of trouble with his hip." Flying to Cincinnati to deliver a speech, Bob took his medical records with him and reported in at Holmes Memorial Hospital. They would not let him leave. Eventually, doctors met with Bob in his room, telling him forthrightly that his body was full of cancer. As his health deteriorated, Bob Taft continued his work in the U.S. Senate, hobbling around on crutches, in excruciating pain, woefully thin. Herbert Hoover was anguished that the senator was not hospitalized. Bob simply smiled and then declared to his old boss, "I'm going to die with my boots on!"

On July 4, 1953, with the Senate in recess to enjoy the holiday, Bob returned to New York Hospital for surgery. As he recuperated, he continued to read policy papers, and commented, "I've got to snap out of this in a hurry now. Eisenhower needs me." But his health continued to fail. On the morning of July 31, 1953, only a few hours after Martha's final visit, Robert Alphonso Taft, son of the twenty-seventh president, died. When they told Martha, she refused to speak. Months later, she said simply, "I wish I had been with him to hold his hand."

In March 1958, five portraits were unveiled in the Capitol — the greatest senators in American history. They were Henry Clay, Daniel Webster, John C. Calhoun, Robert M. La Follette, and Robert A. Taft. The following year the Robert A. Taft Memorial and Carillon was dedicated just north of the Capitol. The twenty-seven bells in the tower are among the finest in the world, ringing with pure, rich, resonant tones. On April 14, 1959, former President Herbert Hoover said, "When these great bells ring out, it will be a summons to integrity and courage." The carillon rings every quarter hour. The bells will not keep silent — just like Bob Taft.

Charles Phelps Taft II: *"Everybody Knows Charlie"*

When Theodore Roosevelt appointed William Howard Taft secretary of war, Bob's family steamed home from the Philippines and took up residence in Washington, D.C. Young Charlie and Helen Taft were constantly at the White House to have supper and enjoy the rowdy play of President Theodore Roosevelt's younger children, Ethel, Archie, and Quentin. Ethel Roosevelt was only twelve days younger than Helen. Charlie was exactly two months older than Quentin. With Theodore Roosevelt's ebullient personality imprinted on his children, the White House was an exciting playground. Charlie was soon a core member of the infamous White House Gang. Stories of their outrageous antics spread by word of mouth across Washington.

During his final months in office, TR awakened Quentin and ordered him away from Charlie and his other sleepover buddies, into the Grand Hall to remove spitballs from the portrait of Andrew Jackson. Earlier in the day the White House Gang had artistically arranged them on Old Hickory's earlobes, in the middle of his forehead "like an Arabian dancer," one on his nose, "to scare the flies away," and a glob on each button of his coat. Needless to say, the boys were very proud of their work. But faced with an angry TR in the middle of the night, cleaning off the spitballs, Quentin wasn't so sure.

The next day, TR lined up the boys in front of the portrait and wanted to know who stuck on the first spitball. Both Charlie and Quentin admitted it at once. TR roared, "Impossible!" Quentin admitted sheepishly that he had done the first deed.

TR proceeded with a lecture about caring for the treasures that belong to the nation. They had acted like boors, the president told them, and "it would have been a disgrace to have behaved so in any gentleman's house." As punishment, Quentin was not allowed to have any of his friends visit for a full seven days. Quentin grumbled that it wasn't fair that Charlie couldn't come visit because he was "one of us" and it would soon be his house anyway.

In 1909, William Howard Taft began his own term as president and the family moved into the White House. Even with Quentin gone, eleven-year-old Charlie Taft continued the mischief. Once, Charlie took control of the famous White House switchboard when the staff was away for lunch, giving a stiff and formal statement to a member of the press. Toward the end of his father's term in office the relationship with the Roosevelt family became strained and for a time, the two old White House friends, Quentin and Charlie, drifted apart.

While Charlie was considered the better personality of the Taft boys, he was judged to be no match when it came to scholarship. The family was a bit surprised when the happy-go-lucky Charlie took the Latin prize in his Yale entrance examinations, finishing first in a class of 415. He won the Gordon Brown Prize, an award for the student who best exemplifies the highest in manhood, scholarship, and capacity for leadership. He finished first at Taft School, second at Yale, and first at Yale Law School, graduating *magna cum laude*. And big, handsome Charlie Taft still loved sports. He was captain of the Yale basketball team and played football, all while being president of the debating club and trying to reform the fraternities. His Uncle Horace was to remark that Charlie "liked to play every instrument in the band."

When the United States entered World War One, Charlie Taft enlisted immediately. A junior at Yale, he was slightly younger than officers' age level. With a word from his retired presidential father, Charlie might have had those regulations waived. But he would have none of it. He enlisted as a buck private, with plans to serve in the 12th Field Artillery of the Second Division, A.E.F. His proud father wrote to the secretary of war, "I am not ambitious for his military promotion but only for his usefulness."

In October 1917, before leaving for war, Charlie Taft married his perfect complement in the quiet Eleanor K. Chase. Her father was president of Ingersoll Waterbury Company, whose clocks and watches were well-known all over the world. Before he would return, their first child, "Nonie," would be born. His father would write him on the battlefield, saying that the newborn infant seemed to be "well trained."

Missing Christmas, Charlie's unit sailed for Europe in December 1917. His father sent him the last letter he was to receive before embarkation. "It is hard, my darling boy, to let you go," his father wrote. "You are the apple of our eye. But we would not have it different. If sacrifice is to be made who are we that we should escape it? . . . You are a knight *sans peur* and *sans reproche*. God bless and keep you." Soon, Charlie was in the thick of the fighting east of Verdun, near the German border. He was promoted to sergeant-major and eventually, in May 1918, transferred for three months of advanced studies at the famous artillery school at Saumur, France. So many officers had died, it was imperative to school the best noncommissioned officers to take their place.

Charlie Taft was in Saumur when the news

came that the leader of the old White House Gang, Quentin Roosevelt, had been shot down. The two men were serving their country together halfway across the world and Quentin had died a mere three hundred miles away.

In the United States, his father, former President William Howard Taft, immediately telegraphed a heartfelt message of grief and condolences to Theodore Roosevelt. The two men had once been close friends, Roosevelt tapping him as his successor to the presidency. But later he had regretted his decision, saying that Taft had betrayed his policies and the two had become bitter enemies. Roosevelt's decision to challenge him by running as a third party candidate in 1912 had split the vote and thrown the election to Woodrow Wilson. In a moment reminiscent of the renewed friendship between John Adams and Thomas Jefferson, it was the death of this beloved child and the love of his childhood friend that sealed the healing of an estranged friendship. Like Adams and Jefferson before them, the two presidents resumed correspondence. When they met by accident in the dining room of the Blackstone Hotel in Chicago, Taft strode directly over to Theodore Roosevelt's table. The former president leapt out of his chair and grasped Taft's hand. In a spontaneous explosion of joy, the watching crowd of diners stood and cheered.

At the end of World War One, the Taft family eventually reunited in Cincinnati. Charlie graduated from law school in June 1921, just a few days before his father attained his heart's desire, appointment as the chief justice of the Supreme Court. Both Bob and Charlie settled into a partnership in their own law firm.

On New Year's Eve, 1922, Bob was ready to leave for Columbus where he was to be sworn into the Ohio House of Representatives the following day. He called Charlie and, in a worried voice, asked his brother to cover for him in the "unlikely" event his pregnant wife would go into labor in his absence. That evening, Martha made the unlikely phone call. Charlie picked her up and raced off to Jewish Hospital. He was no sooner home than his own wife, Eleanor, made the same announcement. On the last night of 1922, Charlie had taken two very pregnant Taft wives to the hospital. Just before midnight, Charlie's son, Seth Chase Taft, was born — to be followed a few minutes later, on the other side of midnight and into the next year, by Bob's son, Lloyd Bowers Taft.

Notwithstanding their sense of family loyalty, it wasn't long before the Taft brothers' disparate personalities began to manifest themselves in public service. It is a classic example of how two people, raised in the same environment, committed to addressing the same issues, can envision almost opposite political solutions. Bob was the doggedly persistent conservative; Charlie's energy and enthusiasm sparked liberal reform at every level.

In 1924, with Bob serving in the Ohio State House of Representatives, Charlie suddenly burst on the local scene in Cincinnati, beginning a long struggle for civic reform. The city was in serious trouble. Taxes were exorbitant. Streets were potholed. The water system was in need of improvement. The entire infrastructure was in disastrous repair.

Charlie Taft was elected president of the Cincinnatus Association, a group of professionals who had organized a City Charter Committee, attempting to change the city government from having an elected mayor and large city council to a government run by a city manager. His brother Bob, committed to effecting change from within the system, was opposed to the Charter Committee. The disagreement gravely worried their father, who urged Charlie to resign from the Association, and avoid direct political conflict with Bob. But Charlie and associates persisted, eventually getting their charter. With a city manager and a smaller, more manageable council, and with Charlie Taft on the council for a total of twenty-nine years and mayor for three, utilizing his incredible energy, Cincinnati became one of the better governed cities in the country.

If Robert Taft became a national figure, Charles soon became a respected figure in local Ohio politics, his self-deprecating humor endearing him to constituents and colleagues alike. Arriving late one evening to a board of education meeting, Charlie Taft was stopped by a security guard. "You can't go in there," he said, pointing to Charlie's satchel with the words "Time Magazine" across the side. "You're not allowed to sell magazines in this building." It was a story Charlie laughingly told on himself when someone ventured the oft-repeated compliment that "everybody knows Charlie Taft." Unpretentious, smiling, and always courteous, Charlie was known virtually by every leader of influence across Ohio and the Midwest. A phone call from him would galvanize committees into action. Charlie Taft began his career intending to move mountains, and before he was finished he did just that.

Will Taft, his prominent father, constantly worried about his son's pace. In 1925, he wrote to Charlie to stick to the job at hand and not take on more than could be finished. But Charlie was never able to say no to a need and, with his vast energies, he juggled his time between committees and jobs in Cincinnati and Washington, D.C. For over fifty years, Charlie battled against intolerance and civic corruption, mediated peace agreements in labor, and worked with churches, and government agencies. Always he invoked his motto, "Democracy can only exist while we look at each man, woman and child as a person, a child of God who in some degree can make his contribution to the common good."

A deeply religious man, Charlie served for years as senior warden of Christ Church Episcopal Cathedral, a socially active church that pushed for the formation of the Cincinnati Charter Committee, instrumental in reforming the corrupt municipal politics of the 1920s and 1930s. Christ Church is the home to the Charles Phelps Taft Memorial Program, which works for social action. Every year, the Memorial Program's lecture series attracts renowned speakers, recently the Bishop Desmond Tutu. But Charlie was fond of reminding laypersons and clerics alike to quiet down and "hear God speak through unexpected people."

Seeing the need for churches to work together, Charlie was a cofounder of the World Council of Churches, and became its president in 1947, the first layman to hold the office. In 1925 he was president of the International YMCA. He worked for the formation of the League of Nations and, later, the United Nations.

During World War Two, Charlie spent much of his time in Washington, serving as director of Community War Services, director of Wartime Economic Affairs, and as a member of the War Relief Control Board and the U.S. Advisory Committee on Voluntary Foreign Aid. Senator Bob Taft disagreed with nearly everything he did. When Charlie had to testify before Senate hearings, Bob wisely and diplomatically stayed away.

As deeply religious and committed to social action as her husband, Eleanor was very much willing to put wheels on her quiet idealism. After World War Two she and Charlie opened their own home to refugees. From time to time, a total of sixty-five displaced persons were to find refuge in their large, comfortable house, including one family of ten from Latvia who stayed for five years before finally settling in Kentucky. Charlie merely arranged the house so that the Tafts — including their own seven children — could have some degree of privacy, while maintaining friendly contact with their flood of guests.

During his years of civic service, Charlie broadcast a five-minute daily radio commentary,

"Charles Taft Zeroes In." He wrote, "If any of you have seen my table at my apartment, it is occupied by a pile of clippings and magazine tearouts which are one foot thick and a damn nuisance." He was never at a loss for subject matter, claiming to be interested in every clipping in the stack.

A radical Cincinnati Reds fan, Charlie was especially proud of his leading role in the construction of Riverfront Stadium, home to the Reds and the Cincinnati Bengals football team. Charlie would sometimes take his radio to council meetings, plug in his earphones, and keep fellow council members apprised of the scores. Even after retirement, Charlie would show up at meetings, sit in the back row and pull out a can of soup for his perennially missed lunch. While he would appear to be preoccupied with food, he would interject his views whenever he felt like it, keeping present council members on their toes. Charlie Taft missed nothing.

In 1907, on one of his visits abroad with his father, a young Charlie had visited Shibo Palace in Tokyo. While Will Taft was taking care of business with the emperor, Charlie got to fish for "big, red carp" in the gardens of the Palace. He never lost his love of fishing. A famous sight in Cincinnati was Charlie's muddy Maverick with its "matching gold canoe strapped to the top." "Just in case," Charlie would say. Who knew when there might be a break in meetings and he could head out to the banks of the Little Miami River? In 1999, when Donna Shalala, secretary of health and human services, spoke for the Charles

Taft Memorial Lecture series, she conjectured about what kind of a president Charlie Taft might have been. "Although," she said laughing, "I have a hard time picturing Air Force One with his canoe strapped on top of it."

In later years, severe arthritis almost crippled the powerful former athlete, and several hip joint implants forced him to walk with crutches. In 1980, Charlie moved into the Marjorie P. Lee Home, which is affiliated with the Episcopal Church. Even from there, Charlie continued to go fishing. He died on June 24, 1983, after a full life of service. During his last years, he had never lost the impudent wit of his White House Gang days. In his obituary, he was described as "a dignified man of unquenchable intellectual curiosity, much beloved for his pungent sense of humor."

The sons of Charlie and Robert Taft, born within minutes of each other, would grow up to offer another generation of political dialogue, each defending his father's philosophy. At Yale, the cousins, Lloyd Bowers Taft and Seth Chase Taft, wrote alternating columns in the *Yale Daily News*, entitled "Two's a Crowd." So diverse were their opinions that their classmate Barney Conrad drew a cartoon for the column heading, showing one hand extending into the column with a smoking gun. On the other side lay two feet, in snappy saddle oxfords, toes curled up.

Amazingly, Charlie Taft continues to live on. When the Taft Education Center opened right next to the William Howard Taft birthplace, at 2038 Auburn Avenue in Mount Auburn, Ohio, the featured attraction was the animatronic figure of Charlie Taft, dressed in his old fishing vest, sitting on a stump beside the river. His Maverick is there, too, and his canoe. He'll tell you stories of the Taft family, and share its values, including the fact that no Taft has ever yet "neglected a public duty for the sake of gratifying a private desire."

John Sheldon Doud Eisenhower

When Mamie Eisenhower was pregnant with her second son, John, she sailed on a troop transport to Panama, where Ike had just been assigned as executive officer for the infantry brigade in the Canal Zone. It was a fearful place even for adults, where thousands had died of malaria and yellow fever. The anxiety must have been especially great for the Eisenhowers, who had lost their four-year-old son, Ikky, to scarlet fever. Their assigned home, built at the edge of the jungle, had been unoccupied for almost ten years, and the Eisenhower's lived where the "cockroaches were the size of mice" and the "legs of their bed stood in pans of kerosene to fend off the bedbugs."

On August 3, 1922, John S. D. Eisenhower was born in Denver, Colorado, "standing at attention." He grew up in the shadow of his father, who was world famous as a military legend before he ever considered the White House.

When John graduated from West Point on June 6, 1944, his father was unable to be present. He was, at that very moment, commanding the D-Day Invasion of Normandy. By that evening, a stunned John Eisenhower was rushed on board ship and on his way to his father's command in Normandy. There had been no warning whatsoever.

Soon he was in Europe striding at the left hand of his father. One day, he had an important question to ask about protocol. "If we should meet an officer who ranks above me but below you, how do we handle this?" he asked. The General snapped back, "John, there isn't an officer in this theater who doesn't rank above you and below me." Almost before he had a chance to digest this dressing down, John was eating breakfast with Harry Truman at the Potsdam Conference in Berlin. It was the beginning of what John termed his "double life," alternating "between ordinary citizen and public fixture."

Dwight Eisenhower was always a factor in John's military career. On a return trip to Europe, when World War Two was ready to enter the "pursuit phase," an officer took John aside and advised that he would not be allowed to be a rifle platoon leader. Some general had recently "disintegrated" when his son had been captured. The army simply could not jeopardize its supreme commander by sending John into the thick of things. Before landing at Le Havre, General Wyman took John aside and empathized with his disappointment. "However," he admonished, "there are some things more important to this war than your career." John must have realized at that moment that he would never be allowed to serve to his utmost capability. He walked over to the side of the ship "to stand alone for a while."

John Eisenhower had a full military career as a U.S. Army officer from 1944 until 1963, and then as brigadier general in the U.S. Army Reserves beginning in 1974. After serving with his father he joined the staff of General Omar Bradley. When Ike became president, John was fighting in Korea, but with the full awareness that he could never allow himself to be taken prisoner.

Commenting on his own military career, John Eisenhower wrote: "For my seventeen years active duty I did my best; but a large portion of the time was spent in rather routine assignments, which could have been filled by anyone." He concludes, philosophically, "Most career officers, I think, share the feeling that over the course of the years they have spent most of their time preparing. . . ."

If John Eisenhower spent most of his time preparing, he did it exceptionally well. Despite his military disappointment, it positioned him to be a firsthand observer of the Allied high command in World War Two, and of all the peace treaty conferences afterward. He was again witness to history when he served as a White House staff officer from 1958 to 1961, where aides would invariably give him all the bad news to take to his father. (John wrote that he felt his father always associated him in later years with work and bad news.) During the time when President Eisenhower's health was ever declining, John served as his trusted advisor and protector. After the White House, John spent years sorting out presidential papers and working with his father on the presidential memoirs, *Mandate for Change* and *Waging Peace*. John wrote of himself as a "worker in the vineyard."

John Eisenhower's turn finally came in 1965. He was approached by publisher G. P. Putnam's with the idea of doing a substantive history of World War Two's Battle of the Bulge. John came away with a book contract. He began work on *The Bitter Woods*, sifting meticulously through World War Two archives for valuable information about the battle and interviewing military leaders. After nearly a year of work, and with a first draft finished, John went to Europe, where he surveyed the battleground again and interviewed both Axis and Allied generals, including British General "Monty" Montgomery and German General Hasso von Manteuffel.

One hundred fifty thousand words later, on January 9, 1969, the book would come out to rave reviews. But on January 2, 1969, while John was pacing about in anticipation, he received an unexpected, startling call from General Andy Goodpaster, who was organizing the new administration. President-elect Richard Nixon wanted to appoint John as ambassador to Brussels, he said. Was John interested? After a brief shock, John said yes. In his hospital room, weak from yet another heart attack, former president Eisenhower was still alive to share in his son's triumph.

In February 1969, right after the official announcement of John's appointment as ambassador to Belgium and the release of *The Bitter Woods*, John and his wife, Barbara, took a short vacation to the Bahamas. In the middle of a well deserved holiday, he received a happy phone call. His secretary gleefully announced that *The Bitter Woods* had just hit the best-seller lists of both the *New York Times* and *Time* magazine.

The celebration did not last long. Immediately upon their return to the States, the doctors called, advising that Dwight Eisenhower needed major abdominal surgery. By that evening, John and Barbara were back in Washington, D.C.

It was the beginning of the end for the former president. John visited frequently between book appearances and his testimony at hearings for his ambassadorship appointment. Father and son talked about many things in the next three weeks. Mostly, John listened. Once, Ike looked up and said, "Be good to Mamie." After years of suffering from heart disease, Dwight David Eisenhower died at 12:35 p.m. on March 28, 1969. He was ready. John was there to see the last heartbeat on the monitor.

Shortly before he died, Dwight Eisenhower had asked if John would bring a dozen copies of *The Bitter Woods* to the hospital. The old president signed each one as gifts for the doctors and nurses who were caring for him. It was the ultimate tribute to the presidential son who had served him faithfully his entire life.

In the months that passed, there was little time for John Eisenhower to grieve. Hard on the heels of tremendous relief that his father was no longer suffering came a week of state funeral ceremonies and, after that, departure preparations for Belgium. In Brussels, spasms of grief were suppressed by the work of settling in as ambassador. Finally, as it does to us all, grief caught up. One evening that autumn, as John was reading a *National Geographic* just arrived from the States, he turned a page to find a political cartoon by famed war correspondent, Bill Mauldin. The picture showed a World War Two cemetery. The caption said simply, "Pass the word; it's Ike himself." It triggered the grief that had to be expressed. "On seeing that cartoon," John wrote, "I went to my bedroom and sobbed. Barbara stuck her head in, took a look, and closed the door."

In 1971, John Eisenhower returned from Belgium and began his true life's work. By coupling painstaking research with his singular military/political experiences and a skillful command of words, John S. D. Eisenhower has been able to re-create the interwoven causes and effects of history. His many military histories are popular with readers and considered "top-flight" by reviewers. *The Bitter Woods*, which John put into his father's hands shortly before he died, is considered by historians to be the definitive study on World War Two's Battle of the Bulge.

Other works include *Agent of Destiny: The Life and Times of General Winfield Scott* and *So Far from God*, which is a balanced view of the Mexican-American War. In 2001, when he was nearly seventy-nine years old, John Eisenhower published *Yanks: The Epic Story of the American Army in World War I*.

Today, still writing from his estate in Kimberton, Pennsylvania, John S. D. Eisenhower is the senior living presidential child. As a soldier, he earned the Legion of Merit, Combat Infantryman's Badge, Belgium Order of the Crown Grand Cross, and numerous civilian awards, but it is as a military historian, not a soldier, that John Eisenhower established himself apart from his father and achieved his own brilliant success.

TEN

WHITE HOUSE WEDDINGS

"My father wants to be the corpse at every funeral, the bride at every wedding and the baby at every christening."
— ALICE LEE ROOSEVELT LONGWORTH

Nineteen presidential children were married while their fathers served as the nation's chief executive. Nine were married in White House ceremonies. Many presidential children had spectacular weddings outside the White House. After the death of her father, when Fanny Hayes was married in Ohio, the sitting president William McKinley was in attendance, as well as his cabinet. Esther Cleveland married a member of British high society in a spectacular wedding held in Westminster Abbey. The wedding of Luci Baines Johnson was a national social event, even though it took place at the Shrine of the Immaculate Conception in Washington. And the small, private wedding of Julie Nixon, shortly after her own father had won the presidency, to Dwight David Eisenhower II, himself the grandson and namesake of a president, prompted widespread public interest and curiosity.

Finding the right husband or wife is not an easy task for a presidential child. Quite a few of the earlier presidential children, from Maria Hester Monroe to Betsy Harrison, married their own first cousins. It was a practice common to remote regions of the American frontier where cousins may have been the only choice. But it was also common among European royals. It is hard to trust newcomers into the power orbit. What are their motives? Theodore Roosevelt, Jr., was reportedly "suspicious about girls who showed interest in him." Cousins were already inside the presidential family circle, and this may partly explain the phenomenon. In today's United States there is approximately one marriage in a hundred between first cousins. Genetic scientists now downplay the long-held belief that such marriages are more likely to result in the birth of abnormal children.

Other sons and daughters of presidents have fallen in love with White House or congressional staffers and, in more recent times, military aides or secret service agents assigned to protect them. Eleanor "Nellie" Wilson married Secretary of the Treasury William McAdoo, thus overnight becoming a cabinet officer's wife in her father's own administration. Two presidential daughters fell in love on ocean cruises while their fathers served in office. Both had spectacular weddings and both husbands turned out to be womanizers. Dorothy Bush, who is a daughter and sister of a president, married a congressional aide of the opposing political party. When it comes to finding love, the children of presidents, as in the case of the rest of us, can only look nearby.

Maria Hester Monroe:
An Event Marred by Murder

The first White House wedding was a glittering candlelit affair of elegance and grace. On March 9, 1820, James Monroe, the fifth American president, and First Lady Elizabeth Kortright Monroe, gave away their accomplished, seventeen-year-old daughter, Maria Hester, to Samuel Lawrence Gouverneur, her own first cousin and one of her father's "junior" White House secretaries. But if the event inside was glowing in warm candlelight, a cold, Washington rain lashed violently against the windows outside, a harbinger of the dark events that would soon taint what should have been one of the nation's early, triumphal social events. It is a tale of diplomatic intrigue, petty arrogance, and murder.

There is still some question over exactly which room hosted the marriage ceremony, but most historians have settled comfortably on what was called the "Elliptical Saloon," today's "Blue Room," with its grand view of the ellipse and eventually the towering Washington Monument. The Reverend William Hawley, pastor of St. John's Episcopal Church, located just across from the White House at the opposite corner of Lafayette Square, officiated at the ceremony. Hawley, a controversial religious figure in his day with an access to presidents that the nation would not again see until the Reverend Billy Graham, was a friend of John Quincy Adams, Andrew Jackson, Martin Van Buren, William Henry Harrison, and John Tyler.

Following the ceremony, the company of forty-two close friends and relatives retired to the State Dining Room for a feast. Only six years before, at the height of the War of 1812, British soldiers had burned the White House to the ground, so the furniture, much of it designed by the president himself, had been made to order by Pierre-Antoine Bellange, "the finest cabinet maker in Paris." Either by French law or at the insistence of the craftsman, the imposing crown of Louis XVIII had marked each handmade piece and had to be "carefully removed and replaced with an American eagle, at considerable expense." The new magnificent gold French clocks, with their pendulums of nude ladies, had been refitted to better reflect sensitive, puritan American values. Imported crimson silk, with a 50 percent surcharge for the color, was used in a new design covering the chairs and draping some of the windows. Special French lamps lit the dining room, where new golden urns overflowed with fresh fruit. And of course, opposition members on Capitol Hill expressed outrage at the expense.

Congress, however, had to wait in line to complain about the wedding of Maria Hester Monroe, for the event had somehow stirred resentment across the whole spectrum of Washington society, and especially within the international diplomatic community. Supposedly, the great puppet master behind this turmoil was one of the most controversial and sometimes unfairly reviled of presidential children, Eliza Kortright Monroe Hay, Maria's older sister.

History does not have an exact birthdate for Eliza Monroe. Their father's diary, which bravely labors on about hundreds of irrelevant subjects, only tells us that she was born in Virginia, sometime in December 1786. She was seven years old when her father was appointed minister to France. It was in Paris that she would experience the defining moment of her forty-nine years, for Eliza would be enrolled in Madame Campan's prestigious seminary for women, Montagne de Bon-Air in St. Germain and, for the rest of her days, the press would never let the public forget it. When her father was returned to Paris on a second mission, namely, to help negotiate the Louisiana Purchase, Eliza was sent once again to Madame Campan's, this time gaining a lifelong friend, Hortense Beauharnais, the daughter of Josephine Bonaparte and a stepdaughter of the Emperor Napoleon. Eventually, Hortense would become the queen of Holland and mother to the enigmatic French emperor of the Second Empire, Napoleon III. The friendships and experiences of continental Europe were to have a profound impact on James Monroe's wife and Eliza, her eldest daughter.

In 1816, James Monroe was elected president, succeeding James Madison. By that time, Eliza was a thirty-year-old woman, married to George Hay, a socially prominent New York attorney, and her little sister, Maria Hester, was a precocious fourteen-year-old. Their mother, Elizabeth Monroe, claiming poor health, virtually opted out of her role as first lady, the awesome duties falling to Eliza, who was deemed eminently qualified, her Madame Campan's imprimatur finally finding its purpose. But there was a context to these events. Monroe was succeeding James Madison, whose wife, Dolley, was arguably the most popular and successful first lady in American history. Not only was she the bon vivant of Washington society and its temperamental diplomatic corps, she had captured the hearts of the nation as well. Dolley Madison, one must remember, introduced that tasty French novelty, the ice cream cone, to the nation as a dessert at a state dinner. She was a hard act to follow. And then the city of Washington already had a picture of what life might be like under the Monroes, and it was not pretty. They had lived in town for seven years and hardly entertained once. Said an observer, "Both Mr. and Mrs. Monroe are perfect strangers, not only to me but to all of Washington."

First Lady Elizabeth Monroe and her elder daughter, Eliza, closeted themselves to hammer out an arrangement for running the White House. The practice of a first lady calling on members of the diplomatic corps and Washington society was thrown out. Elizabeth was an invalid and would not have her daughter running all over town, trolling for social engagements. If someone had business with the White House they could call and, depending on the validity of the social inquiry, the White House would respond, just as would any court in Europe. Diplomats posted to America who loved to complain about their trials, living in such a backwater? Well, the Monroe White House would make them feel at home. Social informality was out.

What followed was a major war between Washington society and the Monroe White House. The first lady's receptions, hosted by the proper Eliza Monroe Hay, were boycotted by the Washington matrons, whose husbands stuttered disingenuous excuses for their suddenly "ill" wives. But the more serious problem was the outraged diplomatic corps. So troublesome did the issue become that it was often raised in cabinet meetings, with gentle, tentative feelers put out to the president to rein in his two stubborn women. But such approaches went nowhere.

And so, the scene was set for the wedding of an innocent, plain, big-boned, seventeen-year-old Maria Hester Monroe (her name was pronounced "Mariah," the old Welsh pronunciation) and the dashing, twenty-one-year-old White House staffer, Samuel Gouverneur. When older sister, Eliza Monroe Hay, learned that the young lovers were busily making plans and that a Russian diplomat had actually inquired when diplomats might "pay their respects," Eliza was roused to action. Claiming that affairs of state and protocol trumped any of the young couple's wedding ideas, she successfully took charge of the event. By the time Eliza was finished, "not even the cabinet was invited." Samuel Gouverneur would deeply resent this wound to his young bride.

Shouldn't she be allowed to make her own decisions and invite whom she wished? But with the reclusive first lady approving each move, Eliza prevailed. The wedding of Maria Hester Monroe became yet another casualty in their ongoing war with Washington.

Eventually, with the likely interference of the president himself, arrangements were finally made for two wedding receptions the week following the ceremony, but the senior Monroe women gleefully succeeded in bumping the despised diplomatic corps out of these as well. Louisa Adams, the cultured wife of then Secretary of State John Quincy Adams, would confide to her diary in frustration and sadness that Eliza Monroe, the relentless older sister, was "so proud and so mean I scarcely ever met such a compound."

Maria and Samuel's best chance at escaping the Washington social war and asserting their own personalities, putting their own stamp on their wedding, lay in a series of private celebrations that would occur after the White House events had run their course. Here, they could encourage their respective hosts to invite whomever they wished and, thus, all of American society and even some of "the hated" diplomats would be touched and welcomed.

Only nine days after the wedding ceremony the first ball in their honor was sponsored by Commodore Stephen Decatur, a choleric, hugely popular American naval hero whose home fronted the prestigious Lafayette Square, just across from the White House. On the night of the event, horse-drawn carriages backed up the street while

George Washington marries the widow Martha
Custis. He became stepfather to her two children.
The son later cheated Washington in a business
deal. The daughter died of epilepsy at age
seventeen, breaking Washington's heart.
Library of Congress

George and Martha Washington with her
grandchildren, Wash and Nellie, which they reared
as their own. *Library of Congress*

A youthful John Quincy Adams at age twenty-six.
He bonded with his father on an early trip to
France. It gave him a boost of self-confidence that
he drew on for a lifetime. *Library of Congress*

A banner featuring the national candidates of the
Grand Democratic Free Soil Party. Former
president Martin Van Buren and running mate,
Charles Francis Adams, John Quincy's son.
Library of Congress

The deathbed scene of President Andrew Jackson. His adopted son, Andrew, Jr., is at his side. The president thought he had finally erased his son's debts but Andrew, Jr. was in financial trouble again within months. *Library of Congress*

Presidential son John Van Buren out-spoke, out-drank, and out-lawyered his famous father. He made it to Congress but he squandered his political equity trying to refight battles his father had already lost. *Library of Congress*

The Long Island Rose, Julia Gardiner, scandalized New York society when she appeared in this public advertisement. She was a twenty-four-year-old beauty when she married the fifty-four-year-old President John Tyler. *Library of Congress*

First lady Julia Gardiner Tyler was the nemesis to presidential daughter Letty Tyler. The first lady would steal the affection of both Letty's father and husband. *Library of Congress*

Mrs. Franklin Pierce was morally offended by her husband's political ambition, and suggested God had taken their last son because the child would have been a "sentimental distraction" to his job as president. *Library of Congress*

Abraham Lincoln and Tad. The youngest Lincoln would often fall asleep on the floor in the president's office while important meetings were conducted. *Library of Congress*

Young Robert Todd Lincoln, firstborn son of the president. He was at Harvard during most of his father's presidency. *Library of Congress*

Lincoln's firstborn attending dedication exercise at the Lincoln Memorial, May 30, 1922. *Library of Congress*

Lt. General Richard Taylor was a brilliant confederate hero who fought with Stonewall Jackson in the Valley Campaign. The fact that he was a son of a president and brother-in-law to Jefferson Davis is often only a historical footnote.
Library of Congress

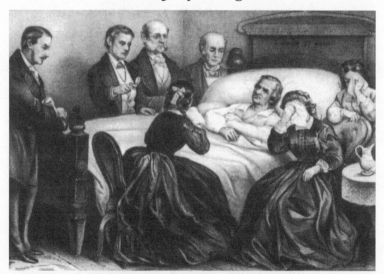

Deathbed scene of former President Andrew Johnson. At far right is daughter Martha Johnson Paterson, who was the president's greatest cheerleader. At the far left is Andrew Johnson, Jr., who died less than four years later.
Library of Congress

An illustrated newspaper features the White House wedding of Nellie Grant and A. C. F. Sartoris. After the wedding, President Grant went into Nellie's bedroom, collapsed on the bed, and sobbed. *Library of Congress*

Ulysses S. Grant, Jr., or "Buck," brought his father into an investment scheme that sent men to jail and prompted scandalous headlines. *Library of Congress*

Colonel Fred Grant eventually became the second
general in the family and reached the second
highest rank in the U.S. Army. But the Senate
refused to confirm his cabinet appointment, saying
he was only nominated because he was a
president's son. *Library of Congress*

President Grant seated on a porch with his
grandchildren gathered around him. Nellie Sartoris,
separated from her English husband, is seated at
the left. Colonel Fred Grant is at the far right. The
first lady is on the steps at the left. The man in
the white beard is the family physician.
Library of Congress

A journalist's drawing of President Garfield's assassination at the Baltimore and Potomac Railroad Depot. His son James was with him. Another presidential son, Robert T. Lincoln, was just arriving at the scene to meet him.
Library of Congress

President James Garfield and his family, left to right: Mary, James, the President and first lady, Harry, Irvin, and Abram. All the children were successful. Abram, shown here playing with building blocks, became a great architect.
Library of Congress

President William McKinley with first lady Ida. A portrait of one of their departed daughters looks down from the wall. After losing two children, William McKinley doted on his wife. The nation loved it and it became part of the chemistry for his political success. *Library of Congress*

Alice Roosevelt's outrageous and independent antics fascinated the nation. *Library of Congress*

Guests begin arriving at the East Wing of the White House on the morning of the Alice Roosevelt and Nicholas Longworth wedding. *Library of Congress*

Quentin Roosevelt with his black friend, Rosewell Flower Pinckney. Quentin was the leader of the famous White House gang. *Library of Congress.*

World War One aviator Quentin Roosevelt. All the sons of Theodore Roosevelt tried to live up to his heroic standards. Quentin was shot down over enemy territory. His brokenhearted father died six months later. *Theodore Roosevelt Collection, Harvard College Library*

Theodore Roosevelt watches his son TR, Jr., take his horse over a fence. The boy was so reckless Roosevelt wondered aloud if he would live to adulthood. *Library of Congress*

General Theodore Roosevelt, Jr. won every medal available to U.S. ground forces, including the Medal of Honor. *Library of Congress*

Theodore Roosevelt's home, Sagamore Hill, Long Island. *Library of Congress*

President William Howard Taft and family. Standing from left to right: Charlie, Helen, and Robert. Charlie served as mayor of Cincinnati, Helen became a college president, and Robert an outstanding U.S. senator. *Library of Congress*

Bob Taft and Republican nominee Thomas Dewey, conferring in the governor's suite at the Hotel Roosevelt in New York. Taft was nominated for president three times. *Library of Congress.*

Jessie and Nellie Wilson. Jessie was considered "angelic" by her family. Nellie was as close as any presidential daughter to become a first lady herself. Her husband, a cabinet officer and California senator, was a presidential favorite going into the 1924 election year. *Library of Congress*

Margaret Wilson never married. She eventually joined an ashram in India and spent the last years of her life in meditation. *Library of Congress*

President and Mrs. Calvin Coolidge flanked by sons John and Calvin, Jr. Within weeks of this picture, Calvin, Jr. developed a blister on his toe from playing tennis on the White House courts and died from septicemia. *Library of Congress*

Franklin D. Roosevelt and eldest son James. Reporters wanted to know how the son suddenly earned million-dollar commissions on insurance. Were they payoffs for access? FDR took telephone calls from some of James's clients, adding to the outrage. *Library of Congress*

Future First Lady Lou Henry Hoover reading to sons Allan and Herbert, Jr. Both Hoover sons became eminently successful. Did their success relate to their father's perceived failure as a president? *From the collection at the Herbert Hoover Presidential Library Museum*

Return of the Roosevelts. Back from a trip to Norway, Mrs. Eleanor Roosevelt and her son Elliott are greeted by Rep. FDR, Jr., and James Roosevelt with Elliott's two children. The five Roosevelt children had nineteen marriages between them. *Library of Congress*

Margaret Truman has become a mystery writer and historian. Her books appear regularly on the *New York Times* bestseller lists. Her father, President Harry Truman, often awakened each morning at 4:00 a.m. to write her a letter. *Library of Congress*

Mrs. Eisenhower arrives with her son, Maj. John Eisenhower, at Walter Reed Hospital to be near the convalescing president. John was urged to run for governor of Pennsylvania but declined. One presidential poll in 1960 had him leading the Republican field. He is an acclaimed historian and the dean of living presidential children.
Library of Congress

The youthful Kennedy clan fascinated the nation but first lady Jacqueline Kennedy sought to protect her children from the public eye.
Library of Congress

JFK, Jr., Caroline, and former first lady Jacqueline Kennedy. Her last note to her son said that you "especially" have a place in history. But five years later he was dead. *Wally McNamee/Corbis*

An anguished Luci Johnson watching a rerun of LBJ's speech to the nation, announcing he will not seek another term as president. When asked which is harder, being the candidate or the son of the candidate, George W. Bush declared without hesitation that it was tougher being the son.
LBJ Library: Photo by Yoichi Okamoto

Lynda Johnson marries Chuck Robb in the East Room. Robb was elected governor of Virginia and seriously considered for the presidency. While two presidential sons have won the White House, no presidential daughter has become first lady.
LBJ Library: Photo by Yoichi Okamoto

President Nixon with Tricia on the steps of the South Portico of the White House. The clouds broke and the sun shone through for the only Rose Garden wedding. *Library of Congress*

Alice Roosevelt Longworth and granddaughter Miss Joanna Sturm escorted by a White House social aide arriving at the East Gate of the White House for the wedding of Tricia Nixon and Ed Cox.
Library of Congress

The Fords in the Oval Office. Left to right: Mike and wife Gayle, Susan, the president and first lady, Steve, and Jack. Steve is an actor who was Meg Ryan's boyfriend in the pop classic *When Harry Met Sally. Courtesy Gerald R. Ford Library*

A teenage Susan Ford washing the family car outside the White House. She eventually pursued a career as a photographer before marrying attorney Vaden Bales. Today, she lives with her family in the Southwest. Her novel, *Double Exposure: A First Daughter Mystery,* was released in 2002. *Courtesy Gerald R. Ford Library*

President and Mrs. Carter with their family. James "Chip" Carter, standing left, is president of the Friendship Force. *Library of Congress*

Amy Carter with presidential father, shaking hands with Soviet leader Leonid Brezhnev. When her father mentioned a conversation with his daughter in the televised debates, she became an issue. *Courtesy Jimmy Carter Library*

President Ronald Reagan with grandkids and son Michael Reagan building a snowman in the Rose Garden. Michael hosts one of the nation's most popular nationally syndicated radio talk shows. *Courtesy Ronald Reagan Library*

A laughing Reagan with daughter Maureen. "I will feel equality has arrived," Maureen once said, "when we can elect to office women who are as unqualified as some of the men who are already there." Her father refused to endorse her bid for the Senate in 1982, but she was the only presidential child to be elected chairman of a major political party. *Courtesy Ronald Reagan Library*

Actress, author, and sometimes controversial public figure, Patti Davis, daughter of President Reagan, has reconciled with her family. Today, she travels the country, giving seminars and speeches about the process of forgiveness and her rediscovery of the power of family. *Courtesy Ronald Reagan Library*

George Bush on a toboggan with daughter Dorothy. She was the only presidential child to be married at Camp David. *George Bush Presidential Library*

Neil Bush with his fisherman father. Neil leads an
education program called Ignite! It has been
described as one of the most practical and
innovative uses of the Internet to date.
George Bush Presidential Library

George Bush, Sr., reading to his grandkids. Left to
right, sitting on the couch are: Pierce, Ashley,
Jenna, Sara, and Marshall. Standing behind the
couch are Barbara and Lauren. "I don't lecture my
family," Bush says.
Susan Biddle, White House/SIPA Press

George W. Bush and father, George H. W. Bush.
The only other presidential father-and-son team
was John Adams and John Quincy Adams.
George Bush Presidential Library

George Bush cooks up a storm for the family at
Kennebunkport. Son Jeb Bush looks on.
George Bush Presidential Library

Chelsea Clinton, daughter of Bill and Hillary Clinton, was protected from the limelight during her White House years and was called "the Garbo" of presidential children. A graduate of Stanford University, now pursuing further studies at Oxford, she has been called "scary bright."
Najlah Feanny/Corbis Saba

Jenna Bush, twin daughter of President George W. Bush and First Lady Laura Bush, shopping in Paris with a security detail keeping close watch. Jenna, a student at the University of Texas, was voted class president in high school. *Thomas Haley/SIPA Press*

Barbara Bush, twin daughter of President George W. Bush and First Lady Laura Bush. Now a student at Yale, Barbara was voted by her high school classmates as most likely to appear on the cover of *Vogue*. *Robert Trippett/SIPA Press*

inside, eager guests moved from room to room, twisting their heads to get a look at the now famous newlyweds. Some later remarked that Commodore Decatur was curiously preoccupied that night, and well he should have been. He had rashly accepted a duel with a navy rival whom he had been disparaging for years as a coward. His opponent, he believed, had avoided the War of 1812 by hiding in Europe. The following Wednesday, the two men lay on the ground next to each other, both wounded. A story made the rounds declaring that the rival had finally explained he could not afford passage home to fight in the war and that the whole feud had been a great misunderstanding.

The mortally wounded body of Stephen Decatur would be carried back to that very drawing room where the newlyweds celebrated and within hours he would die. The "murder" of Stephen Decatur shocked the country. Congress was adjourned, flags were lowered to half-mast, and all receptions and celebrations in honor of the newlyweds were duly canceled, thus ending abruptly the story of the first White House wedding. With no private occasions left to redress the hurt feelings of Washington, the exclusive nature of the original White House ceremony grew in infamy.

Ironically, the administration of President James Monroe would become distinctly famous and retain a resilient relevance even to our present generation by its declaration of "the Monroe Doctrine," which warned that any European or outside power interfering in the

Western Hemisphere represented a threat to the United States itself. This doctrine has been continually and usefully invoked by presidencies in each succeeding generation. Still, one wonders if First Lady Elizabeth Monroe and first daughter, Eliza, the obdurate twins in the social battle of Washington, relentlessly lobbying the president about the conniving diplomats, unintentionally played their part in helping it along.

After being in the White House for eight years, the reclusive, invalid First Lady Elizabeth Monroe would live another five, finally dying at age sixty-two. President James Monroe would die the following year on the Fourth of July, maintaining the tradition set by Thomas Jefferson and John Adams, who also passed away on the nation's birthday. After the White House, George Hay and first daughter Eliza Monroe Hay would retire to Virginia. Only after the death of her father and husband did she again feel free to visit her royal friend, Hortense, in Europe. If Eliza was impressed with Hortense and needed the friendship for her own validation, Hortense apparently reveled in the admiration. The two ladies, each intoxicated by the presence of the other, journeyed to Rome and, in a private ceremony with Pope Gregory XVI, Eliza officially converted to the Catholic faith. In the deadly pattern of many other presidential children before and after, Eliza did not last long after the passing of her father. Still a young woman, she entered a convent and soon died, only three and a half years after the death of the president. She was buried in Paris, France, not far from the Montagne de Bon-Air, the prestigious seminary for women, which had so profoundly marked her life and made her such an advocate for its own narrow and pompous version of social propriety.

There is a macabre footnote to this story. The famous Madame Campan, who headed the seminary, was none other than the lady in waiting for Marie Antoinette who, along with her husband, King Louis XVI, was beheaded during the French Revolution. The citizens of France were apparently no more impressed with this court's sense of propriety than were the American citizens who had been given only a small taste of it during the Monroe administration.

Finally, the newlyweds, Samuel and Maria Gouverneur, lived comfortably in New York City, thanks to President John Quincy Adams who, as a consummate politician and gentleman, repaid any political debt owed to the family by giving them all secure and lucrative government jobs. The controversial wedding, which for weeks galvanized the attention of Washington society and a number of European courts, would never quite be eclipsed. Maria spent the last years of her life as a plantation mistress, "safeguarding her family property in Virginia." Her first child was born in the White House and lived less than a year. Her second child, also born in the White House, was named after her father. She had two more children after her move to New York. She died at forty-seven.

John Adams II and
Mary Catherine Hellen:
A Quiet Affair

There is a curious thread linking the first White
House wedding to the second. Louisa Adams,
wife of then Secretary of State John Quincy
Adams, returned home from one of the Monroe
receptions in disgust and disappointment. "I
didn't get a bit of cake and Mary had none to
dream on." The Mary she referred to was her
niece, the same Mary Catherine Hellen who
would, one by one, win the hearts of each of the
Adams's sons. When her parents had died,
Mary, along with her siblings, was brought into
the Adamses' household. She was an impres-
sionable thirteen years old when her aunt came
home with stories of the biggest social event of
their day, the White House wedding of Maria
Monroe, and Louisa's excitement must have
been contagious.

Within two years, Mary Catherine Hellen was
a beauty in her own right and possessed of a flirtatious and beguiling instinct for seduction that
would reduce the three Adams brothers to sniv-
eling desperation. Charles was conquered first
and then dropped for older brother George
Washington Adams. A bitter, rejected Charles
described her as "one of the most capricious
women that were ever formed in a capricious
race." She became engaged to George, who
would postpone the wedding to please his parents and finish his education. It would prove to

be fatal for their relationship. Mary, whatever her best intentions may have been, was not one to wait.

Ironically, John Adams II, who was expelled from Harvard, would be the winner in this bachelor derby. Described as "arrogant" and "brusque" when compared to older brother George, the brilliant and sensitive poet, young John Adams, was brought back to the White House as his father's secretary, where day-to-day contact with Mary soon prompted whispers and mutterings that grew with each successive week. In 1827, alarmed that the relationship between Mary and her son was racing toward consummation, Louisa urged the president to have the couple get married immediately, but John Quincy would not consent.

They were finally married on February 25, 1828. True to the fantasies Mary Hellen must have held since age thirteen, the second White House wedding was almost a re-creation of the Maria Monroe experience. Once more they used the Elliptical Saloon, today's Blue Room. Much of the same furniture and candelabra were employed, and the same Reverend William Hawley officiated. With the sudden death and funeral of General Brown of the army, there was even an untimely passing of an American hero to force flags to half-mast and the cancellation of some receptions. Making one improvement on the Monroe affair, the Adamses' wedding provided lots of cake for everyone.

Still, the White House was once again denied a

truly grand wedding. The cloud surrounding the jilted brothers hovered over the affair. Neither Charles nor George W. attended, and the list of invited guests was kept short. Louisa wrote Charles the next day, suggesting that "Madame is cool easy and indifferent as ever" and that his brother John was not to be envied, for he "looks already as if he had all the cares in the world upon his shoulders and my heart tells me that here is much to fear." The first lady was sick for days after.

In the aftermath of the second White House wedding, George Washington Adams would begin his descent into alcoholism and depression, dying little more than a year later, by suicide or accidental drowning. He was twenty-eight. The groom, John Adams II, who would be the only presidential son ever married in the White House, would fail at business and die an alcoholic at age thirty-one. Heartbroken, rejected suitor Charles Francis would go on to a distinguished career that, with a little luck, might have produced a third Adams presidency. And, finally, the vivacious, carefree Mary Catherine Hellen would live with the former president and first lady to the end of their days, running their household and tending to their needs. She would even outlive her own two daughters, witnessing two more White House weddings before her death in 1870.

Elizabeth Tyler and William Waller:

Love Is Heaven

On January 31, 1842, at the White House, a beautiful eighteen-year-old Elizabeth "Lizzie" Tyler, was married to William N. Waller, a young attorney and old neighbor from Williamsburg, Virginia. And once more, circumstances conspired to deprive Washington of a truly grand affair.

When William Henry Harrison died in office only thirty days after his inauguration, John Tyler became the first vice president to ascend to the presidency. The country was not exactly sure what role a "substitute" chief executive should play. John Quincy Adams suggested that he should be called "Mr. Acting President." When Tyler assumed *all* presidential prerogatives and demonstrated a clear independent streak as chief executive, there was immediate and deep resentment. The Democratic Party saw him as a traitor to their values, a Southerner who had helped the Whigs to power. And the Whig party that had promoted "Tippecanoe and Tyler Too," putting him in office, was furious when he balked at many of their initiatives. They had won the election and, within thirty days, lost it again. It soon became very clear that the presidency of John Tyler was effectively over before it had begun. A hostile Congress threatened to allow no meaningful legislation.

Historians are often harsh on Tyler, ignoring the very critical role he played in defining the transfer of power and achieving statehood for Texas, an event that was quickly realized in the succeeding administration of James K. Polk. But the hostility on Capitol Hill meant a meager budget for running the executive mansion. Congress was intent on punishing the independent president, and the condition of the White House deteriorated rapidly. It would be a shabby setting for the wedding of a president's daughter.

Once more, Reverend William Hawley of St. John's Episcopal Church walked across Lafayette Square to officiate at a White House wedding. This time cabinet members, diplomats, and a long list of distinguished guests and their wives were invited as well. And this time the event was held in the much larger East Room. The occasion would mark the only public appearance for the invalid first lady, Letitia Tyler, who was helped down the stairs from her private apartments, "receiving in her sweet, gentle, self-possessed manner, all the people who were led up and presented to her."

Lizzie's sister-in-law and White House hostess, Priscilla Tyler, pronounced the bride as "covered with blushes and dimples." And the event inspired one of Daniel Webster's most famous and banal quotes. When asked how young Elizabeth had been able to give up the White House and the exciting life in Washington to return with her husband to the slow pace of rural Virginia, Webster supposedly replied, "Love rules the court, the camp, and the grove; and love is heaven and heaven is love."

Maria Monroe Gouverneur, the bride in the

first White House wedding twenty-two years before, sent the couple a poem in tribute to the occasion, offering a revealing insight into the role of a wife in those times, as well as her own feelings about power and fortune. Two instructive stanzas read:

> *Be to him all that woman ought,*
> *In joy and health and every sorrow;*
> *Let his true pleasures be only sought*
> *With you today, with you tomorrow.*
>
> *Believe not that palace walls*
> *'Tis only there that joy you'll find;*
> *At home with friends in your own halls*
> *There's more content and peace of mind.*

Beautiful, young Elizabeth Tyler would not have many years to know such content or peace of mind, for she would indeed let her husband's "true pleasures" reign. Only eight years after her spectacular White House wedding, where she had been "covered with blushes and dimples," she would die after giving birth to her sixth child. She was twenty-six years old. Her widower husband, William Waller, would later move to nearby Lynchburg, Virginia, and marry his cousin, Jane Meredith Waller.

Ellen Wrenshall "Nellie" Grant:

Not Happily Ever After

It was perhaps the greatest American social event of the nineteenth century. Finally, a White House wedding was bursting forth in full glory. The walls and staircases and chandeliers were covered in a mass of lilies, tuberoses, and spirea. Florida orange blossoms had been crated up and sent north.

The bride, Nellie Grant, was the eighteen-year-old daughter of an American icon, a war hero and the sitting president. One historian described her as "probably the most attractive of all the young women who have ever lived in the White House." The groom, Algernon Sartoris, was a twenty-three-year-old member of the English "minor gentry." They had met on a cruise across the Atlantic, courting in the moonlight and stealing "away to the darkened decks for kisses," while Nellie's chaperones lay moaning in their cabins with sea sickness. To the public, it was an irresistible, romantic story. One newspaper carried a twelve-page pictorial insert of the wedding, its presses running nonstop, unable to keep up with the insatiable public demand.

On May 21, 1874, "as the resplendent marine band played Mendelssohn's Wedding March," President Ulysses S. Grant escorted his daughter into the East Room. Nellie was radiant, wearing a white satin gown "trimmed in rare Brussels point lace" and reportedly worth thousands of dollars. The president "looked steadfastly at the floor" and wept. His new son-in-law would be taking Nellie to a life in England.

Nellie Grant, loved and doted on by her father for years, was the only daughter in a family with three sons. She had been a youthful thirteen when the Grants first moved into the White

House. And so the decision had been taken to send her to a proper finishing school. The president himself made arrangements for the trip, escorting his Nellie to Miss Porter's School in Connecticut, explaining that "Mrs. Grant will only cry and bring her back." But by the time the president had finally done the deed and returned to the White House, there were three telegrams awaiting him, each from his distraught daughter and each proclaiming her despair. The stubborn hero of Vicksburg immediately relented, sending an escort to bring her back.

Nellie Grant was the first teenage girl in the White House since Abby Fillmore, and the nation was fascinated. Washington society professed shock when she danced the night away at a society ball. Grant said not a word of rebuke but, as Nellie turned sixteen and found herself being pursued by "half-grown admirers" all over town, he and Mrs. Grant decided to get her out of the limelight, even out of the country. A quiet trip abroad, surrounded by trusted chaperones, seemed to offer the right formula. It would be educational, as well as buy time for a sixteen-year-old who was growing up much too quickly.

Nellie Grant's trip to England was triumphant. It was not what her parents and chaperones had intended or expected. America's first teen was received by Queen Victoria and feted at one garden party reception after the next. And on the voyage home, she had met Algernon Sartoris (pronounced *Sar-triss*).

According to some accounts, Sartoris was the heir to his family's estate, a considerable fortune.

The couple left the White House the afternoon of the wedding, boarding a special train for New York, pulling their private Pullman palace luxury car, made especially for the Vienna Exposition and covered with British and American flags. The next day they sailed for England.

Nellie Grant, who had once begged to come home after only hours at Miss Porter's School for Young Ladies in Connecticut, was brave throughout her experience in England. She had four children, who comforted her greatly. But, according to family tradition, her husband was "a womanizer and a heavy drinker." Nor did she ever really take to English society that from a distance had so impressed her parents. Adelaide Kemble Sartoris, the mother of the clan, who had for years held forth from her house in Park Place, London, entertaining Charles Dickens, Henry James, and other stars in the English literary galaxy, retired to the country in the south of England where she took the American Nellie under her wing. When Henry James visited the family, he described the dinner conversation as brilliant, but then added that "poor little Nellie Grant sits speechless on the sofa, understanding neither head nor tail."

By 1889, with Algernon's drinking problem out of control, his esteemed family finally agreed that the daughter of the American president had suffered enough. Clearly, the famous storybook marriage that had charmed the public on both sides of the Atlantic was over. Nellie, who longed for a return to America, was not faulted. She was granted a divorce, provided a large annual income, and finally allowed to take her children back to the United States, where a special act of Congress renewed her citizenship.

Her presidential father was gone now, having died of cancer in 1885. But her mother Julia, wealthy from his book royalties, welcomed her and her children back home. For a time, the public still attended her every move. Her wedding, whatever its outcome, had forever endeared her to the nation, who still thought of her as a young beauty. When Algernon Sartoris died at age forty-two, there was immediate speculation that Nellie would marry again. Prominent names were bandied about in news stories. But Nellie's children needed her, and her youthful romantic experience had left her wary.

Finally, on July 4, 1912, her fifty-seventh birthday, Nellie Grant Sartoris surprised the nation by marrying her childhood sweetheart, Franklin Hatch Jones of Chicago. He was not of English nobility or even a lion of Washington society. Nellie, thinking of herself for a change, was returning to her roots to find happiness. But it was not to be. Three months later she became quite ill, developing a paralysis. She would remain an invalid the rest of her life. She died ten years later on August 30, 1922.

On that famous wedding day in 1874, after Nellie and Algernon had left the White House, Ulysses S. Grant had walked into his daughter's empty bedroom, fallen on the bed and sobbed uncontrollably. They were surely the tears of a sentimental father, losing his only daughter and maybe something more. Grant may have wondered how the presidency and the demands on his time had impacted the life of his Nellie. Growing from thirteen to eighteen is quite a leap for any young lady in the best of times but, within the context of the White House, with its busy work and endless pressures, the months must have raced by. Grant may have been regretting what he had missed.

Then there were the demands on Nellie, herself. A girl of thirteen, only on the cusp of adolescence, had overnight become an adult public figure. Grant openly acknowledged his own inadequacy for the presidency; surely his children had some of the same feelings. If he was not ready, how could they be ready?

And finally, there were the nagging doubts about Algernon Sartoris. Grant couldn't know the future, but he knew that his new son-in-law had problems. While initially opposing the match, the Sartoris family had warned the president that their son was "a drinker." Grant must have feared that news as only one could who was intimately, personally familiar with such an addiction. A hundred years later an historian observed that "Nellie was sold at a low price."

Alice Lee Roosevelt
and Nicholas Longworth:
"America's Wedding"

In 1905, President Theodore Roosevelt was making a determined effort to end the Russo-Japanese War. He not only valued peace on the Pacific Rim, but also sought an ongoing, special relationship with the Japanese that would guarantee the security of America's new territorial acquisition, the Philippines. If he could help negotiate the end of the war, he would have it. As in all-important diplomatic efforts, its success depended greatly on discretion. He chose his closest ally, Secretary of War William Howard Taft, for the mission to Tokyo. And he cloaked the effort in secrecy by announcing an important fact-finding trip to the Philippines. Tokyo would be only one of several national capitals that would be quickly visited on the side. The Philippines, America's newly won territory, was the focus. And to offer one more diversionary factor, he decided to send along his famous daughter, Alice. It would turn out to be a stroke of genius.

During the first years of the Roosevelt administration, presidential daughter, Alice, mesmerized the American people. Conservative matrons were shocked by her public smoking, fast cars (which she herself drove), and open flirtations with the opposite sex, often in public, *sans chaperone.* And yet she was so popular that most preachers dared not rebuke her from their pulpits. Conventions and politicians clamored to have her in attendance. She was toasted at the Mardi Gras in New Orleans, the Chicago Horse Show, and the St. Louis World's Fair. The head usher of the White House later wrote that she had a party every night of her stay in the Executive Mansion. A French journalist predicted that if she kept up the pace, she would collapse.

445

The president's gambit worked. Alice Roosevelt was the number one story on the Taft diplomatic junket to the Far East. Alice stole the show so completely that even history has been fooled. Even if the true purpose of the mission had leaked, it is doubtful that it would have moved the president's daughter off the front pages. She jumped fully clothed into the ship's swimming pool, talked Hawaiian hula dancers into doing their real, more erotic, version of the dance, and smoked quaint pipes of Japanese tobacco. When she became bored at Philippine banquets, she furtively created paths of food, luring the insidious ants to the leg of the banquet table which was soon swarming with the invaders. Her encounter with the empress dowager of China was as frightening and colorful as a scene out of an Indiana Jones movie. Apparently growing jealous of her own interpreter's ability to talk freely to her famous guest and perhaps sensing in Alice another strong woman, the empress ordered her interpreter to prostrate himself on the pain of death and to keep his forehead touching the ground throughout the audience. Alice was duly impressed and amused.

Before the trip was over, Alice Roosevelt had successfully exported her brand to the world. So pressing were the crowds and so elaborate the growing entourage trailing her that falling behind Alice could mean getting shut out of the party altogether. Mrs. Taft, wife of the secretary of war and a future first lady, had to talk her way back into a hotel by saying her husband was traveling with Miss Roosevelt! It had long ceased being a diplomatic mission led by an American cabinet member. It was now the Alice Lee Roosevelt road show. A touring German prince gave her a bracelet, a South Pacific native king proposed that she join his harem, and everywhere she went she was feted and presented with beautiful gifts. Teasing relatives and friends back home referred to her as "Alice in plunderland."

There was another reason the president wanted his daughter on board the ship to the Philippines. He wanted to give her a "breathing spell," a chance to get away from the young men besieging the White House. It was an idea reminiscent of President and Mrs. Grant thirty years before, sending daughter Nellie to Europe, lest she fall for one of her Washington suitors and marry too young. And it would have the same result.

Thirty-five-year-old Ohio Congressman Nicholas Longworth had been one of the many Washington men pursuing Alice. He was older, bald, but rich and a saucy raconteur. As a member of the Foreign Affairs Committee, he wrangled a place on the Taft Philippines junket, giving him the chance to pursue Alice without competition. And Alice, restless as she was, fearful of even a moment of boredom, eventually found time on the long cruise for Nick Longworth. By the time the mission returned to America the romance was on.

When the couple announced a White House wedding for noon on February 17, 1906, the American newspapers went into a frenzy. Speculation over details and other nonnews items pushed the groundbreaking construction of the Panama Canal off the front pages. Reporters competed furiously for scraps of information, pursuing secretaries, caterers, florists, and seamstresses. There was a huge stampede for tickets and invitations. The president's announcement that it would be a small family affair did nothing to dampen the demand. Alice belonged to the people, and the people seemed to be driving the wedding plans as much as the family. After several rounds of invitations had gone out, great political battles developed for the remaining seats, with senators and diplomats weighing in with their arguments in behalf of key constituents or foreign representatives. Even those lucky enough to have an invitation could not settle down. Great questions of protocol arose. Should diplomats and veterans wear their uniforms? What about their medals? The local flower market was wiped out. One couldn't find an orchid in the city of Washington.

As wedding gifts began pouring in from foreign heads of state, the president was forced to declare an outright ban, but some got through early under the radar screen. The mikado of Japan sent silver vases, King Alfonso of Spain sent antique jewelry, and the Cuban government sent an exquisite string of sixty-two matched pearls with a diamond clasp worth almost half a million dollars in today's money. The president of France sent a rare Gobelin tapestry that was considered "priceless." The king of Italy offered a table so large that Alice could never use it. King Edward VII presented a blue-and-gold enameled snuffbox with diamonds on the lid. Pope Pius X presented "a mosaic representing the great paintings in the Vatican." The German Kaiser offered a bracelet of diamonds. The most exotic gift, and one of Alice's favorites, was a hand-carved teak chest from the empress dowager of China. Determined not to lose face in the international competition, the empress had secreted in the various compartments dozens of valuable gifts of jewelry, an ermine coat, a fox coat, valuable Chinese paintings, and jade carvings.

Common folk sent in gifts of their own and announced clever ploys to wrangle an invitation to the wedding, while the local press heralded the antics of its citizens as human interest stories. Telegrams arrived from new parents announcing that they had named their babies after Alice. When a group announced they were raising $800,000 so America's first daughter could live in style for the rest of her life, the president announced that Alice would not accept it. Most of the gifts Alice Roosevelt never saw and many were found still unopened at her death.

It was a foregone conclusion that the wedding of Alice Lee Roosevelt to Nicholas Longworth would be the greatest event of its kind in American history. There would be almost three times the number of guests that had seen Nellie Grant marry, and the scale of preparations and the level of anticipation were unprecedented. In the days just before the wedding the scramble for tickets became so desperate that the president publicly begged for true friends of the family to help ease the pressure by offering to stay home. Public announcements about the parking of carriages and dictating the protocol for the event were carried as major news items, even though they had no utility for the average reader. It was one great vicarious thrill for the whole nation.

The wedding day in the middle of February turned unseasonably sunny and warm. Thousands of people began gathering early outside the White House. Alice woke calmly and looked out her front window with amusement at the gathering throng, including inventive entrepreneurs hawking souvenirs of the wedding couple. Her stepmother nervously pushed her along, convinced that she would not be ready in time.

Since the East Room could not hold the crowd, the Grand Hallway and other state rooms had been cleverly employed to offer attendees a spot to witness the ceremony or at least witness the bride on the president's arm as she passed by. The anxiety of the guests, negotiating the cumbersome arrival and parking process and the crush to get into the White House amidst alarming rumors that they would be unable to honor all the invitations, led to bouts of near hysteria. One woman fainted, but was revived in time to see the ceremony. Another fainted and was carried out, missing the whole event.

Alice Roosevelt had served as a bridesmaid five times, including at the wedding of her own cousins, Franklin Delano and Eleanor Roosevelt. At such events she and her girlfriends loved upstaging the bride, which by her accounting had been an easy chore at Eleanor's wedding. Having learned such lessons all too well, Alice decided that there would be no bridesmaids and thus no competition at her own wedding. She would be the leading lady in this performance and no one else. There would be twelve military aides and eight ushers, among them U. S. Grant III, Theodore Roosevelt, Jr., and Douglas MacArthur.

Alice Lee Roosevelt was a beautiful young lady, as her pictures attest, and on her wedding day she was at her prime. But there was more. Alice was a personality who projected intimidating power and self-confidence. And this was her proudest moment. She would walk those few seconds on the arm of her father and no one else, no cantankerous stepmother, or sibling, or busy officeholder would share the limelight. There would be Alice and her father, alone, with the whole world watching, but alone. For those few moments Alice would accomplish what few presidential sons would ever do — for a brief moment in time, she would outshine her father right in the middle of his presidency.

Having anticipated the moment for weeks, the crowd was nevertheless not ready for what was coming and how it would make them feel. The Marine Band broke into a rousing rendition of the grand march from *Tannhäuser*, and Alice and the president suddenly appeared at the end of the Grand Hallway. They had taken the newly installed elevator from the second floor. At the sight of Alice, her poise, her twinkling eyes, her pompadour hairstyle with orange blossoms, her stunning wedding dress with its eighteen-foot-long train of silver brocade, there were audible gasps. She strode through the Hallway toward the

451

East Room on her father's arm, perfectly relaxed, her confident humor barely suppressed. Some women guests began to openly weep at the sight, overwhelmed by the pure beauty of the moment, saying later that they had never seen anything like it and knew that they would never do so again. There was no television or radio in those days and yet vicariously the whole world was watching from afar, a fact that seemed to register with many of the invitees who were privileged to see it all in person.

When the Reverend Henry Yates Satterlee asked, "Who will give the bride away?" an uncharacteristically subdued President Theodore Roosevelt answered so softly that it was hardly heard.

One of the most famous anecdotes to emerge from the wedding happened at one of the receptions that immediately followed the ceremony. The story has Alice grabbing a sword from Charlie McCawley, the president's military aide, and dramatically slicing her own wedding cake. Alice later referred to the incident as an exaggeration. One account says that McCawley actually offered her the sword. In any case, she did apparently use a sword to cut her cake, and the public insisted on believing that "their Alice" had done so in a typical act of fearless, good-natured bravado. And so the picture of Alice spontaneously grabbing a sword and attacking her cake has survived.

The next day, the wedding of Alice Lee Roosevelt and Nicholas Longworth dominated the entire front page of the *Washington Post*. Not a single other news item appeared on page one. And their names continued to be celebrated for years. Sightseeing stages and then buses brought tourists by their house. They were so frequently entertained that a local cleaner boasted in advertisements that he had cleaned "fifteen hundred pairs of Alice Roosevelt's gloves." When they traveled the world, royalty fell all over themselves to be seen in their company. At one point, Alice remarked that if she saw one more king she would have him stuffed.

Nick Longworth, his career boosted by his wife's popularity, went on to election as Speaker of the House. But the great wedding day with all its promise was mocked by events. Nick was a drinker and a philanderer. Alice could not bring herself to seek a divorce. After giving up the White House, her father was making a concerted effort to get back in, and she loved him too much to hurt his chances. But her granddaughter later described the Longworths as "not married in any real sense."

Almost all White House weddings have an interwoven link with the weddings that have gone on before them. On that sunny February 17, 1906, as Alice Roosevelt knelt at an improvised altar with Nick Longworth, watching back in the throng was Ellen "Nellie" Wrenshall Grant. At fifty, she was still a striking figure, looking elegant in gray chiffon velvet, a lace toque and gray furs. A wiser woman now than the eighteen-year-old bride she had been on her own wedding day, she was likely reliving that experience and comparing notes on how her expectations had compared to the reality of a painful marriage to Algernon Sartoris. It is likely that Nellie offered her best wishes to the couple, hoping that Alice Roosevelt would fare better. But history never tires of repeating itself. And we too often pay no attention. Thus, yet another great White House wedding would result in another disappointing marriage. Nick would die twenty-five years later. The legend spread that Alice burned his Stradivarius. She would live on to the age of ninety-six, never marrying again, dying in 1980, only a few days after the anniversary of her famous wedding day.

Jessie Woodrow Wilson:

"She Was Not of This Earth"

The American public was fascinated by Woodrow Wilson and his tight-knit family. He was the intellectual Princeton educator turned politician, and his family, devout Presbyterians, included three eligible daughters. They were a remarkable contrast to the Roosevelts, who had dominated the public stage for so many years. While the Wilsons were a distinguished family, they were not as wealthy as the Roosevelts, having given their lives to education. Nor was Wilson's résumé as complicated; he had served as president at Princeton and then governor of New Jersey. If Theodore Roosevelt was dynamic, Woodrow Wilson conveyed intellectual honesty. Historians would consider both men great presidents.

Woodrow Wilson was fiercely possessive of his daughters and protective of their privacy. Margaret was twenty-six, Jessie twenty-five, and Eleanor, or "Nellie" as she was called, twenty-three. While for years they had hosted an extended family of needy relatives, brothers and sisters and uncles and nieces, the Wilsons always managed to carve out time for themselves alone. For years they had spent their evenings reading together as a family, sometimes openly pining about the dreaded day when their little circle of five would be broken. Some historians saw Wilson as an American Disraeli in his dependency on the women in his life. Others ridiculed him for it. Wilson came alive when he assumed the role of the teacher, and his daughters, each with a questioning mind of her own, were willing pupils for him to instruct. Woodrow Wilson shocked Washington by declining an inaugural ball, spending his first evening as president alone with his family and retiring at a reasonable hour.

Of course, the presidency represented a great adventure for the family, but there were conflicted feelings. Even without the added pressure of the public spotlight, the tight family circle was beginning to crack. The two younger daughters, Jessie and Nellie, were secretly engaged. The White House would be adding its own unknown stresses on a family that was reaching a critical period of transformation. "Suddenly," recounted Nellie, "we became goldfish in a bowl."

Nellie's first impression of their rooms in the White House was that they were "terrifyingly large." The suite given to her and Jessie was complete with bedroom, dressing room, and bath. Nellie, the baby in the family, marched through the huge bedroom with its fancy gilt mirrors and marble mantel into the small dressing room beyond. It had cheerful, flowered curtains with a blue carpet, her favorite color. She dropped down onto the little white iron bed and announced, "This is where I live." The press, still savoring the excitement of the Alice Roosevelt wedding seven years before, was very curious about the Wilson daughters. At a tea, held early in the first weeks of the new administration, a reporter rushed up to them and gushed, "If any of you girls are engaged and I don't find out about it, I shall never, never get over it." Nellie just smiled, inwardly thrilled that the circle of five still had the will and the loyalty to hold off an intrusive press. Nellie and Jessie's rooms together were perfect, as they would be able to laugh and chat and plan their upcoming weddings.

The older sister Margaret, who was working on a career as a concert mezzo-soprano, had chosen a room some distance from the rest of the family. It was a bright place, and so large that her baby grand piano was nearly lost in one corner. Margaret loved solitude, as did her father. Woodrow Wilson would later complain about all the unnecessary social events and hand-shaking when he not only had to take care of his presidential duties, but desperately needed time alone to think. He said that in America it is considered odd if a person "requires time for concentrated thought."

When the sisters came to look at Margaret's room, one of them spied a small plaque under the mantel. "In this room Abraham Lincoln signed the Emancipation Proclamation of January 1st, 1863, whereby four million slaves were given their freedom and slavery forever prohibited in these United States." Nellie said that cold chills ran up and down her back. Their cousin, Helen Bones, who had come to live at the White House and be their mother's secretary, insisted the place was haunted, and the sisters all laughed at that, but none of them "ever quite lost the feeling that there was a special sort of light there." It was the perfect place for Margaret, who would spend her life a pilgrim, in a search for meaning.

The public fascination with the wedding of Jessie Woodrow Wilson and Francis Bowes Sayre is a testimony to the power of the presidency and the unique relationship president Woodrow Wilson had with his wife and three daughters. After the spectacular wedding of Alice Roosevelt, it could have been anticlimactic. But only the press fully remembered the details of the last White House wedding and, impressed with the understatement and angelic simplicity of Jessie Wilson, they passed on their fascination to the nation.

When the House of Representatives gave the president's daughter a necklace with a pear-shaped diamond pendant weighing more than six carats and surrounded by eighty-five smaller diamonds, "she suddenly collapsed in a chair and moaned in consternation." What could a poor professor's wife do with such a gift? The Peruvian minister and a Señora Pezet donated a rare white vicuña rug. The Andrew Carnegies sent a set of silver plates.

But Jessie and her mother delighted in a beaded bag from a four-year-old cousin, and a sack of potatoes and Bermuda onions, and a washtub with six boxes of soap. The gifts were not as ostentatious as those that crowned the Alice Roosevelt wedding, and the Wilsons seemed to triumph in that fact. The public, which had identified with the saucy Alice, grabbing for all the gusto she could get, now relaxed and enjoyed Jessie, the all-American girl next door.

Jessie Wilson and Francis Sayre had been introduced by his aunt, a Miss Blanche Nevin. The eccentric Auntie Blanche was an artist and world traveler who had met the Wilsons vacationing in Bermuda. Then governor of New Jersey, Wilson had posed for her as she sculptured a bust while peppering him with questions about his three daughters. In 1912, Blanche had hosted Jessie and Nellie Wilson at her country place in Pennsylvania, inviting her nephew, Francis Sayre, to help host the weekend. As she expected, Frank and Jessie hit it off immediately. Jessie had once hoped to serve as a missionary-teacher in some remote land, but her fragile health had prevented it. With similar dreams, young Frank had already served for some months at a mission post in Labrador. In October, with her father preoccupied in the last days of his presidential race, Jessie and Frank embraced under a "misty moon" and promised to marry.

When the White House announced the engagement in the summer of 1913, there was a frenzy in the press. Posing as a cousin and looking very much like a family member, Frank Sayre had managed to pass unnoticed in and out of the Executive Mansion, under the very noses of prying journalists. Now the press rushed to make up for lost time. It was learned that Sayre had attended Williams College and Harvard Law School. He had been involved in social work in Boston and was now working in the New York District Attorney's office. None of his colleagues, not even the district attorney himself, knew of the romance or that he was a friend of the Wilsons or that he had ever visited the White House. They read it all on the front pages, while their humble colleague in the next room went quietly about his work. The district attorney wisely praised the young Sayre, soon to be the president's son-in-law, describing him as conscientious and discreet.

With the wedding set for the fall of 1913, Sayre and the Wilsons spent most of July and August at the summer White House in New Hampshire. Meanwhile, the Executive Mansion in Washington was experiencing major and historic renovations. The roof was lifted to add five more bedrooms and two baths to the third floor. Throughout the summer as plans continued, the nation was riveted. The more they read about the young couple, the more they liked. Both avoided the limelight, which only aroused the press further; both were committed to settlement work and other social endeavors; and both were committed to their faith.

The Wilson daughters exhibited deep reservoirs of self-assurance. While creating and participating in the premier social event of the administration, they seemed singularly undaunted. Oldest sister Margaret, considering herself an authority on music, was adamant that the wedding ceremony include a piece composed by one of the bridegroom's cousins. Nellie fashioned headdresses "in the Russian manner" for the bride and each of the maids of honor, but they were almost a disaster. The two sisters enlisted help from the White House maids and spent most of the night before the wedding reworking them to perfection.

On November 25, 1913, the president escorted his second daughter, Jessie Woodrow Wilson, through the Grand Hall and into the East Room to the very spot that had witnessed the weddings of Nellie Grant and Alice Roosevelt. The ceremony itself was divided by Presbyterian and Episcopalian clergy, representing the Wilson and Sayre families, respectively. There was only a single awkward moment when matchmaker Auntie Blanche Nevin, overwhelmed by what she had wrought, began "shaking like a leaf," her arms full of jewelry, rattling like machine guns. The president did not weep, as Ulysses Grant had, yet he was not rejoicing either, as Theodore Roosevelt might have been. Wilson had taken the full day before the wedding to enjoy the rehearsal and perhaps prepare his emotions. Later, he would write that he felt bereaved by the loss, but the full effects would not hit until weeks after Jessie's European honeymoon. Once again, The *Washington Post* used every column of its front page to cover a royal American wedding.

Wilson could comfort himself in the knowledge that Jessie and Frank seemed perfectly suited. His daughter was marrying a man who looked very much like himself. He would be one of the more successful presidential sons-in-law, a Harvard professor, ambassador to Siam, assistant secretary of state for FDR and U.S. high commissioner for the Philippines. He and Jessie would remain true to their social calling and faith. Frank Sayre, Jr., would be born in the White House and become the dean of the National Cathedral. Writers of the time made much of the fact that it was the thirteenth wedding to be held in the White House, counting not only the presidential children but all the others as well. But if that implied a curse, it had little effect on the marriage of Francis Sayre and Jessie Wilson, who would remain happy and true to each other till death.

Eleanor "Nellie" Randolph Wilson:

Almost First Lady

Nellie first met William Gibbs McAdoo at the governor's mansion in New Jersey. He had been a guest of the Wilsons and was taking an early morning train home. Nellie was assigned to see him off. McAdoo was a leader in the Democratic Party who had greatly impressed Woodrow Wilson and, unknown to the governor, had prompted a bit of a reaction from his youngest daughter, as well. Nellie was so nervous at breakfast that morning that she spilled the cream and almost spilled his coffee.

By the time Wilson was president, William McAdoo was actively pursuing Nellie Wilson, not that anyone noticed. He was the new secretary of the treasury, a fifty-year-old grandfather, a widower with six children. She was twenty-three and secretly engaged to a mysterious young man she had met months before on a Mexican holiday. Nellie was often seen riding horses along the trails in Rock Creek Park and staying out at dances till three in the morning. The press, which had missed discovering Francis Sayre, was now on high alert. They speculated continually about each of Nellie's dancing partners, but understandably missed the significance of the treasury secretary's comings and goings at the White House.

One of the first times McAdoo had called late a servant had stepped into the Oval Room, interrupting the family with the imperious announcement, "The secretary of the treasury . . ." The president had almost stood until the servant added, ". . . for Miss Eleanor." On her sister's wedding day, Nellie had led Secretary McAdoo into the Blue Room, away from other guests, where she taught him the fox trot. In January 1914, McAdoo proposed to Nellie and was rejected. But after the idea had simmered awhile, and he had proposed a second time, she responded eagerly.

The weddings of Alice Roosevelt and Jessie Wilson had both been huge events involving widely contrasting personalities. It hardly seemed likely that another one, happening so soon, could further pique the public's interest or curiosity.

But this one did. Eleanor "Nellie" Wilson would be marrying a man who had a daughter her same age. She would instantly be a cabinet officer's wife and a major social figure in the nation's capital. McAdoo was often mentioned as a possible president himself. The press, including the new motion picture men, descended on the secretary of the treasury and his new fiancée until they could hardly function. But there was a great tragedy afoot.

For some time, Ellen Louise Axson Wilson, the first lady, had been in decline. She suffered from Bright's disease, a fatal and incurable disorder of the kidney. Doctors withheld their diagnosis from the president and his family, but within months they began to realize that she was failing fast. The wedding was announced for May 7, 1914, and under the circumstances it was to be a small, family event, held in the Blue Room where, on the night of Jessie's wedding, Nellie and Mac had briefly stolen away from the crowd.

The Blue Room was decorated with cherry blossoms and white lilies. Margaret and Jessie wore organdy gowns and carried shepherds' crooks garlanded with lilies. The first lady was seemingly experiencing a brief recovery that week and looked radiant. Nellie's gown was classic white, trimmed with an exquisite lace that was said to have once adorned the Empress Eugenie in the court of Napoleon III. Reverend Sylvester Beach, a Presbyterian minister who had presided at the earlier Wilson wedding, performed the ceremony for Mac and Nellie.

William McAdoo and Eleanor Randolph

Wilson would have two daughters and move to California, where he would two times make a run for the presidency. In 1924, the convention was deadlocked for ninety-nine ballots between William McAdoo and Al Smith, both of whom withdrew to let the nomination go to another. It was as close to the presidency as he would get. He was elected to the Senate in 1932, and he and Nellie were divorced two years later. Mac would remarry an even younger woman and fail in his bid for reelection. There was a move by some to promote him again as a presidential candidate. Nellie was ever loyal, defending his actions publicly but privately she poured out her grief over the failed marriage in letters to her sister Margaret. William McAdoo would die at seventy-seven, "a disappointed man, having lost his long fight for the Presidency." Nellie would write numerous short stories and two books, including an account of her family, *The Woodrow Wilsons*. She would become a frequent commentator on national radio and a popular public speaker, spending a number of years helping to establish the Woodrow Wilson Foundation.

Only three months after the famous Blue Room wedding, on August 3, 1914, the nations of Europe were plunged into what would soon become the Great World War. The news was kept from the first lady, Ellen Wilson. But nothing could stop the relentless disease that was racking her body. Three days later she died. For the following forty-eight hours a grieving Woodrow Wilson sat by her dead body. They had come to the White House a close-knit family of five, suspecting that the stress would change forever the dynamic of their happy circle, but hoping that they would survive it intact. None of them had envisioned how quickly their circle would be torn asunder.

Margaret Woodrow Wilson:

The Mysterious First Daughter

In an age before television, when the public might not instantly recognize a presidential child on the street, the Wilson girls took malicious delight in flitting about Washington, testing public opinion for themselves. Margaret, the firstborn, once instigated a sightseeing tour of Washington, with the sisters disguised as "hicks" from out of town. They patiently waited in line, bought tickets, and then proceeded to ratchet up the farce by asking inane questions of the tour guide. With a whiny, high-pitched voice, Margaret relentlessly implored the guide to let them go inside the White House itself. They wanted to see the family quarters, she said, where the Wilson girls actually slept. The exasperated guide patiently explained that it could not be done and then patronized them with his authority on the subject of the White House and his "authentic" stories of the first family. Neither he nor the other sightseers caught on to their true identities. Later, upstairs in the White House alone, the Wilson girls convulsed with laughter.

While Eleanor and Jessie were busy planning their weddings, Margaret continued her voice lessons. She had beaux of her own, but somehow never found the right one. One of them, Boyd Archer Fisher, was a graduate of Harvard, a writer, social worker, and efficiency expert from New York. Margaret's mother was impressed, describing him as "quick to take not only an idea but a point of view or an impression." But Margaret was not in love.

Boyd pursued the first daughter, trying to win her by writing a one-act play, using it to describe his jealousy over a singing career with which he couldn't compete. Aware of stories that suggested Margaret was the least attractive of the sisters, Boyd's protagonist in the play told her character, "When I think about you, you begin to radiate until I think you are the most beautiful girl in the world."

In one of his letters to her, Boyd described how he was attempting to make something of himself so she didn't have to be ashamed of him, just in case "you do decide to take me." He was her date at a party in Greenwich Village on February 14, 1914, after which Margaret was portrayed in a *New York Times* article as being the "chief factor in the evening's success." The article said that Boyd Fisher claimed Margaret for the first dance and "a share of the others," but he was not able to monopolize her evening. "Miss Wilson distributed her time among the two hundred men and women, boys and girls at the party so evenly that when it was over she had exchanged a few words with every one of them." Boyd and Margaret remained only friends for the rest of their lives.

When the first lady died, Margaret Wilson, the

only remaining daughter at the White House, stepped in as hostess, growing to hate the pressures as well as the role. In a note to her sister Jessie, she apologized for not writing sooner, saying she had to entertain houseguests and callers "every minute."

Margaret's musical career had long been the great love of her life. She had studied music at Goucher College, and continued her vocal training in New York. In 1915, with her father happily in love with Edith Bolling Galt, Margaret finally felt free to start her concert tours. The newspapers were filled with surprised praise, saying that her lyric soprano and personal charm would "command recognition quite independent of her distinguished parent." A piece in the *Baltimore Sun*, captured in one of her sister's scrapbooks, proclaims that "there are many voices that appear bigger, but hers is so clear, so pure, that it carries . . . just as a Stradivarius does." Her "Ave Maria," the newspaper said, was "an act of worship." After a sold-out concert for twelve thousand in Denver, a free concert was held the following day for the thirteen thousand who had been turned away the night before. Always, all proceeds after concert expenses were given to charities. During World War One the Red Cross was the benefactor.

From October 1915 to March 1918 Margaret and her accompanist traveled to every training camp in the country, giving concerts for the soldiers. Porter Oakes, a young journalist for the National War Committee of the YMCA, captured one such concert, held at twilight. He described a "sea of bronzed faces," ten thousand soldiers, waiting for Margaret to sing. The men had just received word that they were being shipped to the front. Her songs, favorite old melodies, made "a chain of musical memories to be carried away." Oakes described soldiers weeping, seeing through the music the love of a mother or sweetheart or father. The tears "loosened up and washed away that tight-around-the-heart feeling that came with the knowledge that there would be no furloughs home before the big movement began."

Margaret's tireless treks across the world for American servicemen were a constant worry to her father. She would travel twenty miles down artillery-blasted roads to sing for two or three wounded soldiers, often after much bigger performances. By the end of the war, her outdoor concerts had strained her voice beyond repair, and the sights and experiences of battlefield horror prompted a nervous breakdown. Recuperating some months after the war at Grove Oak Inn in North Carolina, Margaret was asked to sing by a convalescing General John J. Pershing and his staff. When she told them how she had lost her singing voice, General Pershing rose and lifted his glass. "To Miss Wilson," he said, "just as much a victim of war service as were the soldiers who filled this country's hospitals."

Less than a year and a half after Margaret's mother died, her father married Edith Bolling Galt on December 18, 1915. There was, of course, scandal in Washington because he married so soon. But Margaret and her sisters knew that Woodrow Wilson had been devastated by the loss of his wife, and was desperately lonely. They tried their best to be understanding and to welcome the new wife into the family.

After the war, with his postwar treaty in shambles, Wilson undertook a disastrous trip to urge ratification of the Treaty of Versailles and to try to gain support from the American public for the League of Nations. He traveled eight thousand miles in twenty-two days. He made thirty-two major speeches and eight minor ones. He collapsed on the trip, his health irretrievably broken, and was rushed back to the White House. He soon suffered a major stroke. His new wife, Edith Wilson, protected him. She was accused of being the Lady President, the Regent, the Iron Queen, "the Petticoat government" — and less complimentary terms. By this time, Margaret was living and working in New York, but she would come home on weekends to be with her father.

Finally, on Sunday, February 3, 1924, at 11:55 a.m., nearly three years after he left the White House, Woodrow Wilson died. His doctor stood on one side of his bed, taking his pulse, with Margaret and Edith Wilson on the other, as he breathed his last. At the time, Jessie and Frank Sayre were living in Siam and could not come. Eleanor and William McAdoo rushed home. Margaret moved about in a daze, and would not respond to conversation.

The Wilsons, who had always been so close, had lost the linchpin of the family. Their father left his modest estate to Edith Wilson, with the exception of $2,500 to be paid annually to Margaret as long as she remained unmarried. She was to remain unmarried for the rest of her life. Rent consumed half of her stipend, leaving her little to live on.

Margaret returned to New York. Her life there remains somewhat of a mystery. It is said that she worked as a consultant for advertising legend Milton Biow. Biow would later create wildly successful ad campaigns for Pepsi Cola and Philip Morris cigarettes, provide the advertising for *I Love Lucy* and Milton Berle, and conceptualize the television quiz show, *$64,000 Question.*

Later, she attempted some speculation in oil stocks that went sour. It is not known whether she actually sold the stock or just introduced people to brokers. However, a letter from Helen Bones, the cousin who had lived with the Wilsons in the White House, indicated that she had received repayment from Margaret. Helen Bones said she had entered the venture knowing it was a risk, and that it was not Margaret's fault. However, she kept the money, knowing also that it meant much to Margaret's sense of pride and honor to pay back every one of her friends.

Despite privation, Margaret finally had the space and "time for concentrated thought," as her father had once described it, reading philosophy and striving for a higher principled life. She served on the New York board for the League of Nations, and worked tirelessly for the passage of child welfare laws. In March 1926, Margaret appeared in court when two teen-agers were being arraigned for burglarizing her apartment. She refused to press charges. The magistrate said, "If they are not prosecuted now, they will not learn their lesson." Margaret smiled at the judge and said mildly, "The best lesson for them is the lesson of kindness." The following day the *Times* printed an editorial, stating that Miss Wilson was perhaps more kind than wise.

Margaret became interested in the religious classics of India and had begun reading about Indian mystics in the early 1930s. One day in the library she happened upon a book by Sri Aurobindo and sat down in the main reading room. She became lost in it, and an attendant had to tell her that the library was closing. Every day she returned to read until she finished the book.

Sri Aurobindo was a contemporary of Mahatma Gandhi. Indeed, both men had been educated in England, and both returned to India to seek freedom for their people from the English yoke. Gandhi, Aurobindo, and the Nobel Prize–winning poet Tagore were then considered the three great spiritual leaders of India, with powerful political influence. Educated at Cambridge, Aurobindo was a brilliant student, and would compose poetry for relaxation — in English, Latin, and ancient Greek. Convinced that "any political freedom must be imbued with spiritual elements," Aurobindo's philosophy was grounded in yoga and meditation.

Margaret's life would be altered forever. It was as if she had found the missing piece for which she had been searching all her life. She continued her studies in the States. In the 1930s, she and author Joseph Campbell edited Swami Nikhilananda's translation of *The Gospel of Sri Ramakrishna*. Joseph Campbell was even then famous for his work in comparative world mythologies, and would later fascinate the country with his public television series, *The Power of Myth*.

Margaret went to live at Pondicherry, India, where Aurobindo had his *ashram*, or spiritual community. There she spent her days in prayer and meditation, working at her assigned tasks in the flower garden, and helping to type and edit Sri Aurobindo's religious writings.

Her father's stipend went further there, and Margaret was able to contribute one hundred dollars a month to the ashram and still have a little money for fresh fruit, and for her favorite facial lotions sent by Eleanor from home. There were two servants to prepare her simple meals, although she reserved for herself what she perceived as the privilege of washing Aurobindo's dishes. "I am not homesick," she told a visiting reporter. "In fact, I never felt more at home anywhere any time in my life."

Her obituary as printed in the *New York Times*, called her a "recluse," as though she were some sad hermit, but such was not the case. Letters between Margaret and her sister, Eleanor, show a fully alive, happy soul, at peace with herself. "Do you remember those beautiful words in the Bible?" she wrote her sister. " 'And I shall keep him in perfect peace whose mind is stayed (or fixed) on me'? That is what we must do," she said, "learn to stay our minds on Him." In the same letter, Margaret told Eleanor of her new name, given by Aurobindo. It was *"Nishtha,"* she said, and it meant a "one-pointed fixed and steady concentration, devotion and faith in the single aim." Her intense times of prayer and meditation moved Margaret deeply. "Sometimes I feel as if the Divine were whispering to my soul, and I, in order to catch the faintest word, am listening as I have never listened before," she wrote to a friend in the States. "Sometimes it is as if the Beloved and I were telling each other secrets that none could share except in a wordless communion with 'Us.'"

At length Margaret's body, which had suffered ill health for much of her life, began to give way. In an ironic twist of fate, she suffered periodic occurrences of kidney problems that had eventually killed her mother, but she would beg the Indian doctor not to send her back to New York. For several days she hovered between life and death. On February 12, 1944, Margaret Woodrow Wilson, or *Nishtha,* died of uremia. She was buried in the Protestant section of the cemetery at the ashram in Pondicherry.

Risha Blackand, an Indian student at the ashram who had been assigned the task of escorting Margaret back to her apartment every evening after meditation, wrote of her death, "So lived *Nishtha* in her spacious apartment fanned by the fresh breeze from the sea and caressed by the palmy breath of her garden blossoms. So she thought and felt and dreamed: so she loved God and her fellow men. . . Suddenly, like a flower, she drooped and languished and faded away. But the unfading bloom and aroma of her soul still hovered over the atmosphere in which she aspired and prayed and adored her beloved Lord."

Lynda Bird Johnson Robb:

A Break in the Clouds

The decade of the 1960s was a tumultuous time in American history. The Vietnam War was provoking protests across the country. At times, the White House was virtually under siege. One of the most powerful presidents in American history would announce that he was not seeking reelection. Martin Luther King and then Robert Kennedy would be assassinated. Riots would erupt across the country, and tanks would be needed to restore order in the nation's capital. But in the middle of the decade there would be a break in the clouds, as the nation took in the first wedding of a presidential daughter in more than fifty-four years. Luci Baines Johnson would marry Patrick Nugent at the Shrine of the Immaculate Conception on August 6, 1966, and a year and a half later, Lynda Bird Johnson would marry a University of Wisconsin graduate, a marine and military aide named Charles Robb, in the East Room. Lynda's ceremony would mark the eighth White House wedding for a presidential son or daughter.

The White House had not been without weddings in the intervening years. Since the earliest times, close presidential staffers, as well as friends and relatives of the first family, had tied the knot in ceremonies within its hallowed walls. During World War Two, Harry Hopkins,

FDR's right-hand man, had been married there. But it had been a long time since the nation had experienced a truly national wedding event.

Luci Johnson, the president's younger daughter, had been a recent convert to the Catholic faith and at her request became the first person to be married at the Shrine but, for all practical purposes, it too was a White House wedding. Gifts were shown in the basement of the Executive Mansion, and the Lincoln Bedroom served as an improvised dressmaker's shop and dressing room for the bride and her maids. There was a display of previous White House weddings, including an invitation to Jessie Wilson's event signed by her father. The East Room was used for official photos. There were receptions and teas and many overnight guests.

The presidency had grown with time and with it the responsibilities of the first family. The president's daughters now had their own correspondence secretaries. The wedding of a president's daughter involved thousands of people. There were lists of guests for various functions, rated by a complex code, qualifying some for some events and not others. Some arrived in limousines, some escorted, some had to find their own way, and some would even be staying overnight in the White House. Relatives, friends, and gifts arrived long before the actual ceremony date. There were committees that thrashed out these details, including the extensive choreography for the hundreds of participants, detailing who should be where and at what time. All was compiled in a book called "the Bible," and the president's staff took it literally.

Lynda, the president's firstborn, was much in the gossip columns during this time, jet-setting around the country with actor George Hamilton, the man with the perpetual tan. After a party for Luci's bridesmaids, they had all trooped down to the theater in the East Wing of the White House where the first lady insisted that they see an old George Hamilton movie, *Home from the Hill*. Lady Bird's younger daughter would be leaving the nest the next morning, and she had a sudden urge to take another look at the man so often linked by gossip columnists to her older daughter.

Luci's wedding day, August 6, 1966, was a sweltering day in Washington, D.C. Bridesmaid Lynda Bird almost fainted in the middle of the ceremony. Eventually, a chair was rushed over for her and she was forced to sit through the last few minutes. But the bride was stunning and sailed through the event without incident. The design and delivery of her wedding dress had been a "carefully managed state secret," even protected from the eyes of maids and butlers. By all accounts, the grand, public, summer wedding of Luci Baines Johnson and Patrick Nugent was a success, socially and politically. When Luci tossed her bouquet from the Truman balcony, she placed it at the perfect spot below, delivering it up to her sister, Lynda, who needed only a few steps to take it in.

The following summer, Lynda Bird Johnson was indeed in love, with plans to get married, but the groom would not be actor George Hamilton. Lynda had met Charles S. Robb, a college graduate and handsome White House military aide, who was first in his Marine Corps Officer's Basic School at Quantico. The date was carefully negotiated. Robb would be leaving for the war in Vietnam, and there needed to be time for the couple to have at least a few weeks together. The date of December 9, 1967, was chosen.

Once again the White House lower level was used to store gifts, the second floor private quarters were invaded, with hairdressers setting up shop behind screens at the east end of the hall. A receiving line was planned for the Blue Room. The massive flower arrangements, featuring differing shades of pink and deepest red, would be more dazzling than ever. On December 4, master chef Clement Maggia was starting the finishing touches on the cake. Two days later he was dead of a heart attack. His staff, all in deepest mourning, struggled on to finish the job.

The ceremony itself began on time with the Marine Band breaking into strains of Lohengrin's famous march. On the arm of her president father, Lynda Bird Johnson descended the Grand Staircase from the private living quarters to the Grand Hall below and on into the East Room. An ecstatic first lady described her daughter as "queenly, radiant, stunningly beautiful." When Reverend Canon McAllister asked, "Who gives this woman in marriage?" the president answered, "Her mother and I do." It was a new era. With the band breaking into Mendelssohn's "Wedding March," the couple strode out of the East Room under a canopy of drawn swords.

Guests were served food, both in the State Dining Room and out on the South Lawn under a pink tent. "A Franco-Texan feast featured crabmeat bouchées and country ham with biscuits." The long Blue Room receiving line seemed to have no end. The vice president and the cabinet passed by, and then, right at the very front was Alice Roosevelt Longworth, who gave her approval for the whole affair to a relieved first lady.

Patricia Nixon:

The "Cover-Girl" Bride

By some accounts "Tricia" Nixon was the most beautiful of all White House brides. She was featured alone as the cover story for *Life* magazine, not once, but twice. By January 1971, the public was fascinated by her romance with Edward Finch Cox, a young Harvard law student who had once worked with consumer activist Ralph Nader, and had written for the liberal *New Republic*.

Tricia Nixon and Ed Cox seemed to come from opposite social and political poles. The young Mr. Cox could trace his lineage back to a signer of the Declaration of Independence. His parents were "society pedigrees" who spent their summers at a Long Island estate that had been in the family for six generations. Richard Nixon was already a lightning rod of the media. He had once defended himself from charges of using a private fund for personal reasons by showcasing his modest, politician's lifestyle, and saying that his wife could not boast a mink coat, but owned a "respectable Republican cloth coat."

Tricia and Ed had been seen together for years. Ed had been one of her escorts at the International Debutante Ball in 1964. And even after Nixon had won the presidency, Tricia would occasionally visit him on campus, the ubiquitous Secret Service painfully stirring up a cloud of dust and attention wherever she went. Actually, the two young people had much in common. Ed was described as "aloof and private." Tricia, who often avoided White House events, was described by her popular younger sister, Julie, as "the Howard Hughes of the White House."

A twenty-year-old Julie Nixon had married Dwight David Eisenhower II, grandson of the president, in a small, private ceremony in New York at the Marble Collegiate Presbyterian Church, the ceremony conducted by America's preacher, best-selling author Reverend Norman Vincent Peale. The event had taken place on December 22, 1968, only weeks after Nixon had won the presidency. The alliance of two political dynasties, Nixon and Eisenhower, fascinated the nation. It was assumed that should older sister Tricia marry, the event would reflect her more understated tastes, as well.

Surprisingly, the very private Tricia chose a large White House wedding with a guest list of four hundred. First Lady Pat Nixon suggested having the event in the Rose Garden, but the date had been set for June 12, 1971. Almost immediately, there were internal objections and concerns. Tricia and the first lady were told that there were very good reasons why no wedding had ever taken place in the beautiful and spacious Rose Garden. The summer weather in Washington was unpredictable, with rain one day out of three. White House servants and some staffers, aware of the history of such events, were convinced that the strain of such odds would be unbearable. It would require the planning of two weddings, not one, for the backup event could not be any less glorious than the Rose Garden ceremony Tricia desired.

Priscilla Kidder of Boston, "the doyenne of bridal outfitting," designed and made the dress as she had done for Luci Johnson and Julie Nixon. White House pastry chef Heinz Bender produced a 350-pound, cantilevered cake that was dismissed by some pompous food critics as a "lemony, sweetish nonentity."

There was intermittent rain the morning of the wedding. The president asked for the latest Air Force weather report, learning that there would be a break in the clouds around four-thirty. Tricia was asked to give the go-ahead or steer the guests to the East Room. She held to Plan A and the Rose Garden. Right on schedule, the sun obediently broke through the clouds, plastic coverings were removed from the chairs, and Tricia Nixon's Rose Garden wedding ceremony went forward as an unqualified triumph.

There was dancing in the East Room afterward, with the Marine Band breaking into "Lara's Theme" from *Dr. Zhivago*. The ongoing

Vietnam War left a number of ladies without husbands. Tricia's sister, Julie Nixon Eisenhower, was without her husband, David. Lynda Bird Johnson was seen standing alone.

Eighty-seven-year-old Alice Roosevelt was on hand, complaining that her seat had still been wet. In some respects her wedding continued to hover over all that had followed. Most subsequent White House weddings now called for a sword to cut the cake, as if reaching back to recapture what had been a spontaneous and magic moment of history. Talking about the Nixon girls, Alice would later offer one of her more biting comments. She said she liked "Julie better than Tricia. I've never been able to get on with Tricia. She seems rather pathetic, doesn't she? I wonder what's wrong with her?" The past chairman of the White House Conference on Presidential Children has pointed out that there were often deep reasons and issues behind the famous quips of Alice Roosevelt. Sitting in her damp seat in the Rose Garden, her glorious moment largely forgotten and her famous father now covered over by so many layers of important personalities and issues, Alice Roosevelt may have only been lashing out at the one White House bride whose beauty had transcended her own.

The day after the wedding, with Ed Cox and Tricia Nixon off to Camp David for their honeymoon, The *New York Times* broke a story on the Pentagon Papers. It would be the beginning of a long ordeal for the family and the Nixon White House, with the president resigning office three years later. The marriages of the two Nixon daughters have both endured and both women lived to see their father win back some measure of renewed respect as an author and retired American statesman before his death in 1994.

ELEVEN
WHERE HAVE YOU GONE,
AMY CARTER?

"Jack and I have a grand rapport and perfect understanding. I'm going to look after his mother and the White House, and he's going to look after the bears and tourists in Yellowstone."
— PRESIDENT GERALD R. FORD,
AFTER HIS PARK RANGER SON MISSPOKE

As of this writing, there are twenty-seven living presidential children, all with unique memories and feelings. My research team and I were able to reach nineteen of them. Most live very private lives. Many have already begun to repeat the same patterns of their predecessors. After her first marriage, Luci Nugent changed her name back to Johnson, just as a hundred years before her, the president's daughter Fanny Smith changed her name back to Hayes. Amy Carter's wedding to James Wentzel had a revealing moment, showing that endless conflict between intimacy and identity that has its own unique dynamic within the life of a presidential child. On the one hand, she refused to have her father give her away, since she "did not belong to anyone." But at the same time, she kept her name, "Carter."

Not many of these presidential children are very young. Elizabeth Ann Harding Blaesing, daughter of Warren G. Harding, is a great-grandmother. They manage banks, run businesses, teach in schools, and lecture in universities and for corporations around the world. Some live modestly in quiet neighborhoods, others are social icons, holding forth from their dining salons. Some are struggling to pay credit card bills. Some run million-dollar businesses, fly on corporate jets, and meet with heads of state. All carry with them the memories and feelings of their parents' short days and months of glory.

Caroline Kennedy Schlossberg:

All That's Left of Camelot

When Caroline Kennedy was a little girl growing up in the White House, she loved to have stories read aloud to her. It was not that she couldn't read them herself, young as she was. Caroline could "skim through a book almost as quickly as I could," remembers her English nannie, Maud Shaw, and retain all the details. If Miss Shaw was reading aloud and missed a word or mixed up a sentence, Caroline would stop her, saying, "Miss Shaw, you went wrong there."

Unknown to her parents, Caroline Kennedy had been reading since her father was a senator, running for president. One night as John Kennedy was relaxing in a hot bath after an exhausting day of campaigning, Caroline ran into the bathroom and gleefully "threw a copy of *Newsweek* with JFK on the cover into the tub, shouting 'Daddy!' " When it turned out that little Caroline had not only been finding her father's pictures but had actually been reading newspaper and magazine articles about the family, Jack and Jacqueline Kennedy grew "almost ferociously protective."

It would not be enough, as we all know. A thousand and seven days into John Kennedy's presidency, Miss Shaw would have to tell Caroline that her beloved father had been felled by an assassin's bullet in a far-off place called Texas. And with some preternatural gift of wisdom far beyond her years, Caroline apparently kept her own counsel, shielding her little brother John from the horror of the truth.

Today, Caroline Kennedy Schlossberg is the only living child of John F. Kennedy and Jacqueline Bouvier Kennedy, and she carries the burden of her family's considerable expectations of excellence on her capable shoulders. As the daughter of the president whose famous quote was, "Ask not what your country can do for you, ask what you can do for your country," she is lately finding herself ever more prompted to emerge from her guarded private life to become involved in public service.

Born on November 27, 1957, Caroline Kennedy was encouraged by her mother to have a strong sense of personal achievement. Earning a fine arts degree at Radcliffe and training at Sotheby's, Caroline worked from 1980 to 1985 in documentary film production for New York's Metropolitan Museum of Art. She currently serves as president of the John F. Kennedy Library board where she helps plan exhibitions, and works with the Kennedy Foundation, the American Ballet Theater, and the John F. Kennedy Profile in Courage Award.

In 1988, Caroline Kennedy graduated from Columbia Law School. During her studies, she and fellow law student Ellen Alderman read an astonishing newspaper poll showing that 59 percent of Americans could not identify the Bill of Rights. From this sprang the idea for what turned out to be their 1991 best-seller, *In Our Defense: The Bill of Rights in Action.* Written in a fascinating, almost fictional style, each chapter focuses on one of the Ten Amendments to the American Constitution that were demanded by our ancestors two hundred years ago, seeking to forestall abuses of liberty that they had suffered at the hands of the British monarchy. Caroline and Ellen Alderman explain the history of each Right, often invoking the eloquent language of the Founding Fathers. The two women traveled around the country, interviewing people whose cases corresponded with each Right. The stories are gripping, and her readers will never forget what the Bill of Rights means to each of us two hundred years later.

Caroline Kennedy and Ellen Alderman followed one best-seller with another. *The Right to Privacy,* praised by reviewers, "put a human face" on our constitutional rights, something many Americans studied in school and promptly forgot, taking them for granted unless some unexpected abuse brought them rudely and abruptly back to mind.

Laurence H. Tribe of Harvard University Law School remarked about the books, "If eternal vigilance is the price of liberty, Alderman and Kennedy have paid their dues." Caroline Kennedy has taken her place in the historic stream of many presidential daughters such as Helen Taft Manning and Elizabeth Harrison Walker, who were pivotal players in advancing the causes of civil rights and freedom.

On July 19, 1986, Caroline Kennedy married brilliant artist and interactive museum designer Edwin Schlossberg, who is intensely protective of his wife and family. They have three children, Rose Kennedy Schlossberg, Tatiana Celia Kennedy Schlossberg, and John Bouvier Kennedy Schlossberg (whom they call "Jack"). The Schlossberg family lives in New York.

In 2001, Caroline Kennedy edited and published *The Best-Loved Poems of Jacqueline Kennedy Onassis*, a volume of favorite poems that her mother had shared with her and her brother as they were growing up. The following year she became the chief executive for the Office for Strategic Partnerships for the New York City school system. Through her writings and work in education, Caroline is continuing the love of language and reading fostered in her by her parents and nanny, giving the gift not only to her own children, but to the children of America.

Lynda Bird Johnson Robb:

Daughter of the Pedernales

Born March 19, 1944, Lynda Bird Johnson is the elder daughter of the thirty-sixth president. Her husband, Charles S. Robb, a former White House military aide who was first in his Marine Corps Officer's Basic School at Quantico, served with distinction in Vietnam, earned a Bronze Star, and became a hero to his men. Robb went on to become the lieutenant governor, governor, and two-term senator for the state of Virginia. Along with Bill Clinton, he was a principal organizer and leader of a coalition of Southern moderate Democrats, and as such was seen as an almost certain future presidential candidate. Today he is a businessman and respected party statesman with an army of political supporters and contacts still urging him to make a comeback.

Lynda Johnson Robb has devoted her life and her considerable influence to energizing educational programs. She is chairman of the board of "Reading Is Fundamental," the nation's largest children's literacy organization. She is president of the National Home Library Foundation and vice chair of America's Promise, an organization to "build the character and competence of our nation's youth." Formerly, she was a member of the Selection Board of the President's Commission on White House Fellowships, member of the National Commission to Prevent Infant Mortality, chair of the President's Advisory Committee for Women, and a member of the boards of the Lady Bird Johnson Wildflower Research Center and of Ford's Theater. She graduated from the University of Texas and holds Honorary Doctorates of Humane Letters from Washington and Lee University and Norwich University, and has been honored with a plethora of civic awards for her public service.

"My children say sometimes a little adversity makes a better story," says Lynda Bird Johnson Robb, ". . . because, you see, nobody wants to hear how everything was so wonderful." From the outside it appears that Lynda Robb's life is wonderful. But there has been adversity.

In 1994, Chuck Robb faced the political fight of his life, running against Republican Oliver North. Chuck Robb eventually won the race, but not before news of his infidelity and stories of his presence at mid-1980s cocaine parties were smirking topics in Virginia newspapers and television. Robb sent a letter of confession to many of his followers, stating he had done things "not appropriate to a married man . . . For a period of time at Virginia Beach, I let my guard down, and when I did I also let Lynda down. But with Lynda's forgiveness and God's, I put that private chapter behind me many years ago."

Lynda politely told the *Washington Post* in November 2000 that essentially it was nobody's business but their own. "Chuck and I are in this for the long haul," she said, ". . . if anything happened, it's between the two of us."

Lynda's husband lost the 2000 election for senator. And with the defeat, Chuck Robb's chances of winning the White House were seemingly dashed. But considering Lynda Bird Johnson Robb's intense strength of will, inherited from her father and mother, the country can be certain this is not the end of her story. The couple has three daughters, Lucinda Desha Robb, born October 25, 1968; Catherine Lewis Robb, born June 5, 1970; and Jennifer Wickliffe Robb, born June 20, 1978.

Luci Baines Johnson:

"I Did It for Myself"

As a teenager living in the White House, Luci Baines Johnson was considered the "cute one" of the sisters. Lynda was supposed to have all the brains. It was an unfair comparison that caused a rift between them. The problem was exacerbated by their father, who once responded to a reporter's question, "Lynda Bird is so smart that she'll be able to make a living for herself. And Luci Baines is so appealing and feminine that there will always be some man around waiting to make a living for her." He *thought* he was complimenting them both, but the statements would discolor how each sister perceived herself.

Born July 2, 1947, Luci Johnson lived her whole life as the daughter of a politician. She hated living in the White House, struggling in every way possible to carve out her own identity. She converted to the Catholic faith and later changed the spelling of her name, a phenomenon common among presidential children. She married a National Guardsman named Patrick Nugent on August 6, 1966, at the Shrine of the Immaculate Conception in Washington. The wedding was criticized for taking place on the anniversary of the bombing of Hiroshima. Luci would later say, after the marriage failed, that "I was desperately looking to be normal. One way out of this fishbowl life was to marry." She changed her name back to Johnson after her divorce in 1979 and later, in 1983, when she married Ian Turpin, she agonized over her decision not to take his name. "I took my maiden name back once very reluctantly," Luci said, "and I just never wanted to go through anything like that again."

When Luci married Patrick Nugent in 1966, she had to drop out of Georgetown University's School of Nursing because of its rules against married students. For thirty years she never went back to school, the only woman in her family for three generations without a college degree. It seemed to give credence to her father's comment that she would need a man to make a living for her. And so, in 1995, Luci enrolled at St. Edwards University in Austin, Texas, graduating with honors in May 1977 with a degree in communications and a 4.0 grade point average. "I didn't need a university degree to be chairman of the board of the LBJ Holding Company," said the president's youngest daughter. "I did it so I could put a lifetime of feeling inferior behind me. I did it for myself."

Today, Luci Baines Johnson is chairman of the board of the LBJ Holding Company. In 1943, the Johnsons bought a small radio station with

$17,000 that Lady Bird Johnson had inherited from her mother's estate. While Lyndon lobbied Washington to allow his station to broadcast twenty-four hours a day, Lady Bird took on the day-to-day management of the enterprise, expanding and improving the station's format, and soliciting new, lucrative sponsors. By the 1950s, the station had been parlayed into the major piece in the Johnson's multimillion-dollar media empire. Luci today continues her mother's hands-on management, running the corporation with her husband, Canadian financier Ian Turpin.

Luci is also vice president of the BusinesSuites, and a member of the board of directors of LBJ Broadcasting. She received the 1997 Top 25 Women-Owned Businesses Award presented by the *Austin Business Journal* and K-EYE TV. She has received the Apollo Award, which is the highest award given a layperson by the American Optometric Association.

Luci Baines Johnson has endowed a number of nursing scholarships at the University of Texas School of Nursing. She is on the boards of directors of the Children's Hospital Foundation of Austin, PBS station KLRU, the Lady Bird Johnson Wildflower Center, and SafePlace Foundation. She is on the advisory boards of the University of Texas College of Communications, "Believe in Me," and the Texas Panhandle Heritage Foundation. In 1996, she received the Distinguished Service Award from Georgetown University School of Nursing. She also serves on multiple civic boards, raising funds for the American Heart Association, acting as trustee of Boston University and Life Trustee of the Seton Fund.

Luci and Ian live in Austin, Texas. She has four children by her first husband: Lyndon Nugent, now an attorney in San Antonio, and three daughters, Nicole Marie, Rebekah Johnson, and Claudia Taylor Nugent.

Patricia Nixon Cox:

"The Howard Hughes of the White House"

Born February 21, 1946, Tricia Nixon was seen by the public as inseparable from her younger sister, Julie. "They were attractive, engaging, stable young ladies," said Leonard Garment, special counsel to the president, "and that spoke well for Nixon as a parent and as a human being." Throughout the "long, national nightmare" that was the Vietnam–Watergate era, when political instability, and often violent protests against both Nixon and the Vietnam War scarred every day for a decade, there was one thing the country could depend on. That was the friendship, loyalty, and unswerving devotion of Tricia and Julie Nixon to their presidential parents — and to each other.

In fact, the sisters' personalities were diametrically opposite, even from childhood. Tricia was introverted and an extremely private person. She had often refused to attend White House functions, preferring instead to spend her time mentoring inner-city children. When reporters started to grumble about Tricia's frequent absences at White House functions, the outgoing Julie laughed and covered for her sister, "Oh, Tricia is the Howard Hughes of the White House." Tricia was a petite young woman, blessed with long, shining blond hair and blue eyes, a cover girl by anyone's standards.

In 1964, as a student at Chapin School, Tricia Nixon met a young Princeton student named Ed Cox. Both were very private about their relationship, but eventually the White House announced a wedding. Much was made at the time of the differences between the family backgrounds. One of Ed's ancestors was Revolutionary War patriot Robert Livingston, who had sworn in George Washington as the first president of the United States. The family is "old money." As an aide to consumer advocate Ralph Nader, Ed hadn't even supported Tricia's father in the election. Tricia went ahead with her plans to marry "Fast Eddie," the nickname, earned for his ability to get work done, not his talent in wooing the opposite sex. She took to her mother's suggestion of a Rose Garden wedding ceremony, an idea that surprised her friends who knew that her instincts were for a very private affair. Some suggested that she was only making her own shrewd political move, wanting to show her father to the wartorn nation in a warm, personal setting.

After the White House, characteristically, Tricia became a very private citizen and mother, staying home to care for their son, Christopher Nixon Cox, born in March 1979, now in law school. She lives a life of "chosen obscurity" as the wife of a corporate attorney, living off Fifth

Avenue in Manhattan. But neither is she idle; Tricia serves on the boards of many medical research institutions, as well as the Nixon Presidential Library and its adjunct, The Nixon Center in Washington, D.C. Surprisingly, considering her sister's public accomplishments, she has been called the more politically astute of the two.

Julie Nixon Eisenhower:

Power Couple

Born on July 5, 1948, the ebullient, sunny second daughter of Richard and Pat Nixon chose a wedding as private as her sister's was public. Julie Nixon's choice of husband was the stuff of political legend; he was Dwight David Eisenhower II, son of presidential son John S. D. Eisenhower, and grandson of President and First Lady Eisenhower. Julie and David met at the White House as children, when his Grandfather was president and her Daddy was vice president.

On January 20, 1957, in a private ceremony inside the White House, Dwight Eisenhower and Richard Nixon were sworn in for their second terms. Eight-year-old Julie was bored with the stuffy, grown-up affair. When it was time to leave, she began to cry. Mamie Eisenhower and Pat Nixon leaned down to listen as Julie tearfully told them that she had wanted to "play in the White House." The first lady graciously invited Julie and Tricia to stay and play with David and his sisters, Anne, age seven, and Susie, age five. It was a wonderful afternoon, until David got into serious trouble for leading the whole pack outside on the South Lawn, in January, with no coats. Young David had no way of knowing the horror that Mamie Eisenhower felt at any possibility of her children falling ill. It surely must have brought back a flood of memories of her son Ikky's death from scarlet fever so many years before. But even that flap couldn't spoil the visit, and the girls happily tromped upstairs to play with Anne and Susie's dollhouse.

The Republican Women's Club of Hadley, Massachusetts, can be credited with bringing Julie and David together again. Learning that David was a freshman at Amherst and Julie only seven miles away at Smith College, the club invited the two to be featured speakers. Julie and David discussed it over the phone, and both decided to opt out. They went for ice cream instead. A week later on election night, David came to visit again. They spent the evening "listening to returns and rejoicing."

Twenty-nine days before her father was sworn in as president, on December 22, 1968, Julie Nixon and David Eisenhower were married in a small, private ceremony at Dr. Norman Vincent Peale's famous Marble Collegiate Presbyterian Church. In a seeming "heretical" move, they did not invite the press, and were politely adamant in the face of media criticism that Margaret Truman, the Johnson girls, and even David's own mother had allowed media to come to *their* weddings. Both David and Julie were grateful that their parents "never questioned our decision, nor did they try to make the wedding a political thank-you party."

When Tricia and Julie Nixon arrived at the White House for their father's inauguration as president of the United States, they were met by Lynda and Luci Johnson, who made no effort "to conceal the tremendous sadness they felt." Later, while waiting at the Capitol for the ceremonies to begin, Luci took Julie aside and told her how much closer she and her sister had become during the past year, with their husbands both serving in Vietnam. Her advice to Julie was, "Don't let all the attention drive a wedge between you and Tricia." It was instructive advice and no doubt an unintentional revelation into the strain between the Johnson daughters. Publicly, at least, the Nixon sisters would abide by the dictum throughout their lives until the pressures of recent years intruded.

After the turbulent White House experience, David and Julie Eisenhower settled down to a more genteel life of their own. David studied law, and Julie wrote her first book, *Special People*, that featured fascinating stories of the world-famous people she had met, from Golda Meir to Mao Tse Tung. David Eisenhower spent ten years writing his grandfather's three-part biography — the first volume of which consisted of 1,600 typewritten pages — and lectured in political science at the University of Pennsylvania. Julie wrote a well-received biography of her mother, *Pat Nixon: The Untold Story.* They became featured speakers at events across the country and around the world, traveling to Beijing to meet Chairman Mao. Since that time, the couple has gained stature as writers, editors, educators, public speakers and historians — all while living a life-style of relaxed anonymity with their three children, Jennie, Alex, and Melanie, in suburban Philadelphia.

A Tale of Two Sisters

While the elder Nixons were still living, the former president focused his efforts on his political rehabilitation, writing book after book, slowly regaining stature as an American statesman, scrubbing away the stain of controversy from his presidency. He built his presidential library, and ordered its operation in great detail. This project was to be an essential part of his legacy and a means of speaking directly to future generations. His birthplace was restored and the Nixon Center was built, which now promotes principles of his foreign policy. His extensive will minutely detailed what portion of his estate was to be left to his beloved library and how it would be administered.

At the time Tricia and Julie spoke on the phone every day, helping to care for their parents' ever declining health. Each month, Julie and Tricia and their families would meet at the Nixons' home in New Jersey for a weekend with "Ba" and "Ma." It was a time of normalcy and happiness for a family that had been exposed to great public stress.

In 1976, Pat Nixon suffered a stroke, brought on, Julie stoutly maintained, because her mother read *The Final Days*, Bob Woodward and Carl

Bernstein's explicit account of the last days of Watergate and the self-destructed end of a presidential career. Pat Nixon would live another seventeen years, dying on June 22, 1993, of lung cancer. A mere ten months later, on April 22, 1994, their beloved father was dead as well. His funeral showed how effective his comeback had become. It was attended by the five living U.S. presidents, who heard Nixon eulogized as an "elder statesman," and a "hero."

With Richard Nixon's death came all the complex questions of his estate, including the Nixon Library and his presidential papers. Most presidential libraries are subsidized by tax dollars to maintain the papers and documents of their administration for researchers and the public. Such files were incredibly helpful in writing this book, for example. But Congress feared that Nixon or his associates would destroy incriminating White House documents. They decreed that all Nixon presidential papers be maintained by the National Archives, thus disqualifying the Nixon Presidential Library for the tax support enjoyed by other such institutions.

Something happened, media reports said, soon after the death of Julie and Tricia's father in 1994, causing a rift between the sisters. What the trauma of Watergate and the Vietnam War and dirty politics could not accomplish had apparently finally ensued. Details in newspaper accounts were murky and contradictory, and Julie and Tricia were much too experienced to be drawn into a public fight. But the contest centered around a large bequest to the library from

Bebe Rebozo, an old Nixon friend. Rebozo's will left 65 percent of his fortune to his friend's presidential library, with the proviso that all expenditures be approved by Julie Eisenhower, Tricia Cox, and Robert Abplanalp, another close family friend and a member of the Executive Committee of the library. When the bequest was made public, so was an ongoing contest between Julie and Tricia on how their father's legacy was to be preserved.

Tricia, who had seen her father and his policies betrayed by the best and most loyal people around him, had opted for closely held family control. Julie believed her father's legacy could best be served by giving other leaders a sense of involvement, allowing the library to be run by a professional board, empowered to do its job and thus motivated. Learning that *Time* magazine was closing in on the story, Julie and Tricia finally, privately, forged an understanding of how to resolve the issue.

The first week of August 2002, all parties involved met in a face-to-face, court-ordered mediation and, on August 8, 2002, reached agreement. An attorney for Tricia Cox assured the public that "everyone was happy." Walking together during a break in the mediation, Tricia Cox told reporters, "Julie and I have always loved each other for more than fifty years and we always will."

When Richard Nixon had sought refuge from the political wars in Washington he had flown south to his "Florida White House," a compound connected to Bebe Rebozo's estate.

"Nixon found on Key Biscayne," wrote the *Miami Herald*, "the one thing his public life denied him: unconditional friendship . . ." Nixon's quiet moments there, with the warm breezes, and a silent friend nearby who needed nothing from him, always had its restorative effect. There is no little irony that Bebe Rebozo's generous gift would cause such a storm in the family he had loved. But with the issues resolved, and an acceptable compromise in place, it is now likely that these two presidential daughters will be able to take on anew the task of tending the flame of their presidential parents. The public, irritated when its icons are slightly dislodged on their pedestals, can now rest at ease. Tricia and Julie, two sisters who came to embody the concept of loyalty for a whole generation, are at peace again.

Michael Gerald Ford:
A Lifetime of Service

On August 8, 1974, Michael Ford and his brand-new bride Gayle were on their way back to Boston after the wedding, pulling a U-Haul full of wedding gifts. It was time for the new semester to begin at the Gordon Conwell Theological Seminary in Massachusetts, where Michael was studying and preparing for the clergy. They no sooner reached Boston than Secret Service agents handed them plane tickets to fly back to Washington, D.C. Richard Nixon had just resigned, and Michael's father was preparing to be sworn in as president of the United States.

It was a first in American history. Gerald R. Ford had not even been elected as vice president. But Spiro Agnew, Nixon's duly-elected vice president, had gotten caught with his hand in the till. Both the U.S. Attorney's Office in Maryland and the Justice Department were investigating Agnew for allegedly receiving kickbacks. With the rising crescendo of indignation over the Watergate scandal, this was one more straw on the load. In October 1973, Spiro Agnew resigned as vice president.

And so a new vice president had to be appointed. And Richard Nixon needed "Mr. Clean." He needed Jerry Ford, the respected congressman from Michigan. Ford was a man of integrity, a man of decency. When President Nixon called to tell the family the news, Betty Ford couldn't decide "whether to say thank you or not." The president was going to name his choice before the television cameras that very evening. Nixon only made it through part of Gerald Ford's introduction when the applause started. Congress had guessed who it was, and wholeheartedly approved.

And now it had come to this. Gerald Ford, who had become an accidental vice president, was now an accidental president, replacing two leaders who had resigned in disgrace.

First son Michael Gerald Ford was born on March 14, 1950. He was followed by his brother Jack, almost exactly two years later on March 16, 1952. They were all-boy, a handful for their mother, who had to care for them while Jerry

Ford was away in Congress. Even so, they were personality opposites. Michael was neat. His brother was not. Betty Ford said, "You could have drawn a line down the middle of any room they shared, and one side would look like a picture out of a *Boys' Life* magazine, and the other side would look as if a bomb had gone off in a thrift shop." Michael was always a good student in school, and never seemed to feel the need to rebel. Even his adamant opposition to the war in Vietnam was subordinated to his sense of duty. At eighteen, he left for college at Wake Forest in North Carolina and made a point out of joining the campus R.O.T.C. (Reserve Officer Training Corps).

After four years at college preparing for a career in law, Michael seemed to experience a "divine discontent" that told him law was not for him. He worked six months for his national fraternity, Sigma Chi, his future life on hold, as he considered what he really wanted to do. That something turned out to be the ministry. He enrolled in Gordon Conwell Theological Seminary and began his studies. He was so seriously focused that Betty Ford began to worry about his girlfriend, Gayle Brumbaugh. Betty thought she was the perfect companion for her son. She was, after all, a very spiritual woman, and Michael would need one of those. Gayle had already gone to Switzerland to study with Dr. Francis Schaeffer at L'Abri. It was an intense place where many went to explore a deeper meaning for their Christianity. Michael wanted to wait until he was finished with school and could support a wife.

His mother was afraid Gayle would get tired of waiting. So she stepped in. "I told him I didn't think it was necessary for him to be graduated before he married," Betty Ford said. "He listened, but he didn't say much."

When Gayle returned to the States, Jerry Ford was already vice president. Months after his mother's little talk, Michael and Gayle came to her, with Gayle flashing the third finger of her left hand in the time-honored tradition of brides-to-be. They wanted to set a date, and suggested August 10, 1974, just before they had to return to school. Betty suggested they might like to get married earlier, in July, and enjoy the summer together. It seemed a good idea to Michael and Gayle. It turned out to be a fortuitous decision. Gerald Ford was sworn in as president on August 9, 1974.

Michael had been an outspoken critic of Nixon. Within the month of his father's inauguration he said that Nixon owed America "a total confession" for his role in Watergate. The media came running to President Ford for his comment. "All my children have spoken for themselves since they first learned to speak," President Ford said, "and not always with my advance approval. I expect that to continue."

Michael Ford graduated from divinity school and joined the ministerial staff of the Coalition for Christian Outreach at the University of Pittsburgh in 1977. He was appointed student affairs director at Wake Forest University in 1981. Today, Michael serves as director of student development. He and Gayle have three daughters,

Sarah Joyce, Rebekah Elizabeth, and Hannah Gayle Ford. Their daughter Sarah is married to Blake Goodfellow and has added yet another generation to the Ford clan by giving birth to Michael's first granddaughter, Riley.

John "Jack" Gardner Ford:
A Man Who Speaks His Mind

Jack Ford was riding horseback patrol as a park ranger in Yellowstone the summer Richard Nixon announced his resignation from office. The first inkling he had of the momentous events outside the federal park was when he reached a main road and was suddenly scooped up by Secret Service agents converging on all sides, taken to a helicopter, and raced to Washington.

Jack would finish out his summer stint as a park ranger, but would be ineligible for any permanent forestry position with the government. Even though he eventually earned a degree in forestry, by law he could not hold any federal job as long as his father was president.

About the time that Michael was announcing his opinion that Richard Nixon owed the country a confession for Watergate, Jack was telling reporters that his mother would be unhappy if his father ran for president in 1976. For the second time in a matter of days, Gerald Ford would be forced to comment on one of his children's colorful public statements. "Jack and I have a grand rapport, and perfect understanding," he told reporters. "I'm going to look after his mother (my wife) and the White House, and he's going to look after the bears and tourists in Yellowstone." One thing the country would love about Jerry Ford was his ability to laugh at himself and his family.

The White House was a heady time for a virile young man. Betty Ford said of him, "Jack, who is in my mind the best read and most intellectual of our children, has been the last to find himself. And he's looked in some funny places. . . ." He was invited to rock concerts, dated celebrities such as Bianca Jagger, invited former Beatle George Harrison to the White House to meet his father, and was interviewed and photographed wherever he went. He even confessed in an interview that he had smoked marijuana. Later, he explained why. "I said what I said because my father encourages the truth . . . I think it's a tremendous plus for him that he would encourage honesty at consequence to himself."

Years later, Jack would admit that his short years in the White House had been a fun time. "But it would be a shame if that was the highlight of my life. I sure didn't ever want that to be my crowning achievement."

Jack turned out to be the only member of the family to entertain the possibility of a political career. An excellent speaker and personality, he actively campaigned across the country for his father in the 1976 election. But no matter how hard he, or others, campaigned, it was not enough.

On September 8, 1974, less than a month after Gerald Ford was inaugurated president, he had announced that he was pardoning Richard Nixon. The country was enraged, sure that he'd struck a deal. Jerry Ford did what he thought was right. He had followed his own instincts. Those instincts told him that the country must put the agonies of Watergate behind it and get on with life. With the passing of time, Americans have come to see the truth of it, and to see that Gerald Ford sacrificed his political career for the good of the country. Indeed, in 2001, presidential daughter Caroline Kennedy Schlossberg presented Gerald Ford with the annual John F. Kennedy Profile in Courage Award, saying that he "placed his love of country ahead of his political future."

At the time, however, Jack was particularly hard hit by his father's defeat. "When you come so close, it's really hard to lose," he said. "But at the same time, if you can't lose as graciously as you had planned to win, then you shouldn't have been in the thing in the first place."

Since that time, Jack has cofounded a successful business, California Infotech, which supplies electronic information kiosks to malls. And in 1996, as a veteran of six Republican conventions, he was asked to serve as executive director of the host committee for the San Diego Republican Convention. Jack Ford married Juliann Felando in 1989. They have two sons, Christian Gerald and Jonathan August Ford, and live in California.

Steven Meigs Ford:
The Star

Born May 19, 1956, Steve has been described by his mother as the charmer of the family. When he was only four years old, he would visit his Grandma Ford and act as her escort, opening doors for her and sweet-talking her friends. But First Lady Betty Ford jokingly suggested he had always been a good actor. He could get angry and stubborn, the same as any other child. "Save it for Grandma," she would tell him wryly.

In 1968, when Steve was twelve years old, Gerald Ford went to Alaska to campaign for one of his colleagues, flying in and out of tiny towns in a bush plane. Steve went along and while there, met a family who ran a camp for hunters. With children near his own age, Steve found himself in perfect company. For the next two summers, he went to Alaska to work at the remote camp. It was a fascinating place, sixty miles from a telephone, which suited him just fine. Steve learned how to shoe horses, and how to stay out of their way when they kicked. He learned how to shoot a gun, and how to build camps in the boondocks for the hunters.

Steve Ford's path was pretty well set by the time his father was inaugurated. In fact, soon after Gerald Ford was sworn in, Steve headed west to put in a year as a wrangler on a ranch. Later, he enrolled in a Wyoming school for rodeo riders. Gerald Ford had to break the news to his mother, who was terrified that he would be hurt.

"He's too old [for us] to stop," his father commented. "And you know how well he's taken our advice on everything else."

Steve worked on the professional rodeo circuit as a team roper, studying under the famous Casey Tibbs. In 1975, he worked for the National Geographic Society, studying and radio tracking grizzly bears at 10,000 feet in the Rockies of Montana. Today, he owns his own ranch in San Luis Obispo, California, where he breeds Thoroughbred racehorses. He has served as associate vice president of Turfway Park Race Course in Kentucky and three years on the board of directors of The National Cowboy Hall of Fame.

But it hasn't just been on the back of a horse that Steve chose his own path in life. After his father left the White House, Steve was given a small role as Andy Richards on the Emmy award–winning daytime show, *The Young and the Restless*. He was so popular that his role was expanded, and he stayed with the production for six years.

Within a few years, Steve Ford was appearing in dozens of Hollywood films. He was Meg Ryan's boyfriend in the cult romantic classic, *When Harry Met Sally*, played in *Contact* with Jodie Foster, *Armageddon* with Bruce Willis, *Heat* with Al Pacino, and many others. He was a guest star on dozens of television shows and hosted the prime-time series, *Secret Service*, on NBC. It was a subject with which he was intimately acquainted. In 2002, Steve Ford appeared in the intense hit movie, *Black Hawk Down*.

Today Steve Ford juggles an acting career with his demand as a corporate motivational speaker. He serves on the board of directors for the President Gerald R. Ford Museum. He has never married and has no children.

Susan Elizabeth Ford Bales: *Writer-Photographer*

Born July 6, 1957, Susan is the only one of the Ford children to live for any length of time in the White House. After the Fords moved into the Executive Mansion, Susan received a letter from Alice Roosevelt Longworth, who advised her to "have a helluva good time." Remember Alice Roosevelt's green pet snake, Emily Spinach? When Susan Ford was a girl in Alexandria, Virginia, she kept a pet black snake in a hatbox under her bed. Nobody else in the family knew about it until it escaped one day and was found "slithering up the Venetian blind."

Like Alice Roosevelt, Susan Ford was famous for speaking her mind. When the family moved into the White House, staff escorted them around the family quarters to decide where each wanted to live. At first it was thought that the room across the hall from her parents would be a good place. Then Susan saw it. "I don't like pink," she said. Betty Ford laughed, saying that the disgusted look on her face was priceless. Susan finally chose the suite on the third floor that Julie and David Eisenhower had used when they came to visit the Nixons.

Susan admitted to being very, very scared

when they moved into the White House. "I was afraid of what was going to happen to our family, afraid Daddy's being President would tear us apart," she said. "I'd be the only kid left home, and I knew I would have to be very, very cautious because anything I did in the White House would reflect on my parents."

The Ford kids had had no time to adjust to the national spotlight. As children of a longtime legislator, they had lived in relative anonymity. Overnight, Gerald Ford, the "accidental vice president" became "an accidental President," thrusting his unacclimated family into the national spotlight.

As a young girl, Susan had felt the disappointment of a father being absent much of the time, although neither of her parents knew it at the time. It is a familiar pattern for presidential children. But it would be much later before Susan would openly discuss it. Her mother had known for years that her daughter had been jealous of her three older, very athletic brothers. As soon as her athlete father came home from Washington, he'd be in the backyard throwing balls around with his sons. Susan's athletic talents lay in modern dance, like her mother, and in ice skating, skiing, tennis, and horseback riding. Backyard football was not her forte. And by the time her father was appointed vice president, Susan was a junior in high school, stretching her wings, trying to "fly the coop," she says, with no interest in having her parents around.

When her father became president, with the

mobility of Air Force One, Susan oddly found herself seeing more of her father than ever before. Despite the intensity of White House meetings, the Fords felt their children more important, and others could just wait. Susan laughs that she was always able to interrupt a meeting to ask for money.

Susan Ford was the only first daughter to have her high school prom in the White House. But it was her eighteenth birthday party that she enjoyed most. It was smaller, more relaxed, with friends from Vail, Colorado, where the family loved to ski, including a Vail rock band, singing lyrics dedicated to Susan. There was dancing, barbecued hamburgers, and hot dogs on the South Lawn and beer in plastic cups. Just like any "regular" American teenager in any town across the country. They did, however, watch Fourth of July fireworks from the Truman balcony of the White House.

As other White House kids had already experienced, the Secret Service protection nearly drove Susan to distraction. She already had an appreciation of their necessity. While her father was still vice president, the Secret Service called and said, "Don't let Susan out this weekend; she's not to leave the house." Not until Monday did the family know what was going on. The Symbionese Liberation Army (SLA), a fanatical, terrorist group, was threatening violence. A piece of paper had been found with three names on it. The first man, a school superintendent, had already, for whatever reason, been shot and killed. The second person was Patty Hearst, whose kidnapping and psychological destruction made the front page for almost two years. The third name was "the vice president's daughter." From that point on, Susan had Secret Service protection, even before her father took the oath of office as president.

Later, however, she was to appreciate them for her father's sake, first when "Squeaky" Fromme, and then Sarah Jane Moore, tried to assassinate Gerald Ford. Still, appreciating the necessity for Secret Service protection made it no easier for a forthright, active young teenager to have her privacy disrupted so totally, twenty-four hours a day, seven days a week. In an ironic turn of events, Susan would eventually marry one of her father's Secret Servicemen, Charles Vance, on February 10, 1979. They would divorce in 1988.

While life in the White House required intense adjustments for Susan, there were, of course, benefits as well. When the Fords went to China, Susan went along. It has since been a standing family joke that when the ill and aging Mao Tse Tung saw blond Susan, he stood up straight and took on new life. Fit and fresh-faced American like her handsome brothers, Susan has a cover girl's beauty.

The White House opened up new vistas for Susan's future professional life. When Nixon was casting about for a new vice president, *Time* magazine sent photographer David Kennerly to photograph possible candidates. Later, in the White House, he was the day-by-day, documentary photographer of the Ford administration. In time, David Kennerly became like family.

As the young Susan watched Kennerly at his

job, he began to give her pointers. She signed up for a workshop with photographic legend Ansel Adams, and was gratified when he told her she had an eye for it. As an eighteen year old, Susan spent the summer working as a photographer on the *Capitol Journal*, a newspaper in Topeka, Kansas. Since then, her photo credits have included work with the Associated Press, *Newsweek*, *Ladies' Home Journal* and several film projects, including *Jaws 2*. Susan began her writing career during her White House years, penning a popular monthly column for *Seventeen* magazine. In 2002, Susan wrote a mystery novel called *Double Exposure: A First Daughter Mystery*, giving us an inside look at life in the White House from a "first daughter-photographer-detective" viewpoint.

When her mother was suffering with alcoholism, Susan Ford became the family catalyst, bringing them together for an intervention that put Betty Ford on the road to recovery. It was a healing that would lead to the establishment of the Betty Ford Center, where thousands of people have come to battle and overcome their addictions. Susan serves as board member of the center with her mother and has served as a national spokesperson for National Breast Cancer Awareness Month, a subject close to her heart because of her mother's mastectomy.

Today, Susan remembers her White House years as a fairy tale, a very special experience, meeting wonderful people and traveling to new places. "It was pretty hard to beat," she admits. But she doesn't expect people to treat her differently because of her experiences there, and no longer uses her birth name except for business. Today, Susan says, she is a "happily married wife with great kids." Susan lives in the Southwest with her husband, attorney Vaden Bales, and two daughters by her first marriage, Tyne Mary Vance and Heather Elizabeth Vance.

John William "Jack" Carter:
A Lawyer and a Banker with a Degree in Nuclear Physics

John William "Jack" Carter, firstborn son of the thirty-ninth president, was twenty years old when he "dropped a bomb" on his mother, telling her he was quitting college. Born on July 3, 1947, and then a child of the 1960s, he was disillusioned with school, with racist politics, and with the unfairness of men being drafted to go to Vietnam because they were too poor to go to college. No longer, Jack said, would he "take advantage of his privileged status as a student." Jack joined the U.S. Navy and soon found himself stationed on a buoy tender just off the coast of Vietnam. There, his mother said, he got to watch bombs being dropped in person, instead of on television.

First Lady Rosalynn Carter thought she had failed him somehow, but after Jack returned to the States, he enrolled at Georgia Tech and earned a degree in nuclear physics, went on to law school at the University of Georgia, and passed his state bar exams "with flying colors." She would later comment wryly, "So much for the guilt of motherhood."

Jack's idealistic stands on racism closely paralleled his father's. Once, Jimmy Carter cast the single vote against excluding blacks from the Plains Baptist Church and, in his gubernatorial inauguration address, he astonished his Georgian listeners by baldly stating, "The time for racial discrimination is over." His policies as governor and president, and later as leader of the Carter Center, fighting for human rights around the world, indicate that Jimmy Carter meant what he said.

After graduating from law school and passing the bar exam, Jack and his wife, Juliette "Judy" Langford, joined the presidential campaign for his father. He would later compare political campaigning to taking a bath as a boy. He never enjoyed it, he said, until his mother made him get in and then he didn't want out. "The campaign is like that." During the campaign, on August 7, 1975, their first child — and the Carters' first grandchild — was born. Jason James Carter would eventually become a Peace Corps volunteer in South Africa, following in the steps of his free-spirited great grandmother, Miss Lillian. His sister Sarah Rosemary Carter would arrive on December 19, 1978.

By the time Jimmy Carter finished his remarkable run for the presidency, Jack was practicing law in Calhoun, Georgia, with his father-in-law; he also owned and operated a grain elevator. While the other Carter children lived in the White House, Jack's life was moving on in its own direction.

In 1980, when First Lady Rosalynn Carter returned alone to Plains just five hours before the polls would open for the fateful election night, Jack was there, waiting for her. By that hour, the polling numbers were in, and the first lady finally had to face the facts: Ronald Reagan was going to win. "We're going to lose," she told Jack. "I know, Mom," he said. "I came back home tonight so you wouldn't be all by yourself." Mother and son talked until 3:30 in the morning. Jack resisted going to sleep wanting to put off Election Day as long as possible. By the next evening, however, it was all over, and the rest of the Carters began filtering back home to Georgia.

Eventually, Jack moved to Chicago with his family to work at the Chicago Board of Trade, running the floor operation for the Continental Bank. He specialized in financial futures and dealt primarily with U.S. bonds and futures contracts. He eventually divorced. Today, a banker, he is living in Bermuda with his second wife, Elizabeth Sawyer Carter. They have four children scattered across the United States.

James Earl "Chip" Carter III:
The Friendship Force

Growing up in the South during the civil rights movement of the 1960s brought its own particular challenges for Chip Carter. Born April 12, 1950, James Earl "Chip" Carter III was three years younger than his brother Jack. His first experiences grew out of school integration, not Vietnam. When he was a junior in high school in 1966, the people of Plains, Georgia, learned that their public schools would be integrated. On the first day of the first semester, state police cars patrolled the area with flashing lights, trying to anticipate and ward off trouble. People would come into the peanut warehouse and ask, "What's happening?" First Lady Rosalynn Carter wrote in her biography, *First Lady from Plains*, "by some sort of a miracle, nothing happened." Two black students arrived and simply walked into the school. There was no violence of any kind. Rosalynn, and indeed the entire town, was relieved that the day they had dreaded had passed peacefully. Of course, perhaps it was somewhat easier in Plains, she said, because everyone in town knew each other, black and white, and it wasn't as though strangers had come in. There was still racism, of course, and George Wallace swept Georgia in the presidential election that year. The only poster in town for Hubert Humphrey was on the Carter warehouse door. But integration had arrived in Plains, and it had come in peace.

Like many teenagers before him, when Chip went off to college, he started running with friends, some involved with drugs, who may not have had a positive influence on him. His parents were forced to deal with his extracurricular activities more than once. However, when Jimmy Carter announced his candidacy for governor of Georgia, Chip took time out to help campaign. He was an invaluable asset, Rosalynn said, and the experience matured him. When it was time to return to school, Chip "settled down and made the Dean's List."

James Earl Carter III turned out to be the

most politically adept of all the children. He threw himself headlong into each campaign. The team of Chip and Rosalynn became Jimmy Carter's most effective secret weapon. In 1975, before the family was known outside of Georgia, his father sent him to Texas to raise funds for the campaign, telling him not to come back until he had raised $5,000. Chip was so successful that his father sent him to other states, as well.

During the 1980 election cycle, President Carter refused to campaign because of his on-going commitment to the American hostages held in Iran. Chip and his mother traveled the country, giving important speeches and making political appearances on his behalf. Chip often introduced himself as "Amy's brother," a self-deprecating line that never failed to provoke laughter and charm his audience. He has since been actively engaged in politics in more than 150 campaigns, and served as special assistant to Democratic National Committee Chairman, Paul Kirk, and as deputy Southern regional coordinator for the Walter Mondale campaign against President Reagan. "I never have been as good a politician as Chip," former President Jimmy Carter says of his son. "He knows more people than I do; he understands the theory of politics better than I do; and he likes it better than I do."

Today, Chip Carter, who worked the family peanut business for years and then worked with his father in the White House, is vitally involved in the former president's post-presidential humanitarian works. He says he has no plans to jump back into politics, despite media speculation to the contrary. "We ran so many different campaigns . . . I kind of got that out of my system," he said. He has traveled extensively on humanitarian projects for the Carter Center, from trips overseeing foreign elections, to accompanying his parents to war-troubled Sudan to check progress on the eradication of parasites.

On May 1, 2000, Chip became president of Friendship Force, an international cultural exchange, where citizen diplomats stay two or three days in the homes of families in other countries, making friends and dispelling stereotypes. In 1992, the Friendship Force was a nominee for the Nobel Peace Prize. Chip was active during the founding years of the organization and served the two years prior to his presidency as vice president of international development. "I love representing my father when he can't go places," he told reporters during that time in his life. "That's fun, but it's my father's. This could be mine." And now it is.

He has one more enormous goal to meet in life. President Carter was in office when the Islamic Revolution ousted the U.S.-backed Shah government of Iran. In November 1979, Islamic militants stormed the U.S. Embassy and took fifty-two Americans hostage. Chip's father severed diplomatic relations with Iran. The hostages were held for 444 agonizing days and were not released until twenty minutes after Ronald Reagan was inaugurated as president, Iran's humiliating revenge on President Carter for a disastrous rescue attempt. Today, Chip Carter hopes to make friends with this country that many believe cost his father a second term as president. "It's more important for me to make friends in Iran than it is anywhere else in the world for those very reasons," he said. He would do it in his father's name.

While working for the Democratic National Committee, Chip and his first wife, Caron Griffin, lived in the White House. Their infant son, James Earl Carter IV, was born during this time on February 25, 1977. Chip was divorced during his father's presidency. He married Ginger Hodges, an accountant in Plains, Georgia, with whom he had his second child on September 23, 1987, daughter Margaret Alicia Carter, affectionately known as "Maggie." Chip is now married to third wife Becky Payne. They live in Atlanta, Georgia.

Grandson James has inherited the family love of politics, and has already worked on various campaigns in his young life. "Someone told me my grandfather is the only person who used the presidency as a steppingstone for something higher," said James. "He didn't do it for fame, didn't do it for glory. My grandfather is the best person, period, I've ever met." On October 12, 2002, former president Jimmy Carter was named the recipient of the 2002 Nobel Peace Prize. His son Chip still stands at the helm of the acclaimed Friendship Force where he works to advance the family's philosophy around the world.

Donnell Jeffrey "Jeff" Carter:
A Man of Computers

Jeff Carter's favorite place in the White House was the roof. He was not, however, pushing mammoth snowballs off onto the heads of hapless security officers like the White House Gang of Teddy Roosevelt's day. Jeff was intrigued with geography, whether on earth or in the skies. With his telescope on the White House roof, he had prime viewing space for the stars. The Smithsonian had a phone service called "Dial-a-Phenomenon," and he and his sister, Amy, would call to find out what special things were going on in the sky that night. If his telescope wasn't powerful enough to do the job, Jeff would simply borrow one from the Naval Observatory. And if he and Amy found comets or asteroid showers, they would call the entire family to come up and see.

Born on August 18, 1952, Donnell Jeffrey Carter was already grown and married to long-time sweetheart Annette Davis by the time his father won the presidency. Since Jeff would be attending George Washington University, he and Annette took one of the suites on the third floor of the White House, near his brother Chip and his wife Caron, and their soon-to-be-born son James. Most of his time was spent studying geography and computers, but there were times when he was of invaluable service to the country.

When President Jomo Kenyatta died, President Carter sent Jeff and Annette to the funeral as the representatives from the United States. The Kenyans were overwhelmed. In their country the son of the family is revered, Mrs. Carter said, and the fact that the president of the United States chose to send his son spoke words "that we could not have expressed in any other way." First Lady Rosalynn Carter wrote in her memoirs, "The countries of the Third World yearn for some contact with the United States, and we learned early how much it meant to them to have personal contact with the president through a member of his family."

Jeff graduated with honors from George Washington University in Washington, D.C., specializing in computer cartography. It was a fairly new science at the time, with computer-generated topographical and planimetric maps for city planners and demographers to use for determining utility locations, permits, civil engineering, surveying, property boundaries, and other engineering needs. As soon as Jeff graduated, he joined forces with one of his professors and founded Computer Mapping Consultants. It took a while to catch on; the first year didn't yield enough wages for two.

Then came a stroke of luck. In 1980, Imelda Marcos — she of shoe fame — wife of President Marcos of the Philippines, requested their help in her planned slum clearance project. Jeff, of course, first had to consult his father, who gave his approval, with the proviso that it would be sans presidential father's help. There was to be no appearance of impropriety. Computer Mapping Consultants received the contract, which paid over $200,000, and sent the company on its way to success.

Jeff is somewhat a cipher in this age of media coverage, remaining in the background and unavailable for contact. Some reports have him continuing to oversee Computer Mapping Consultants; others have him programming demographics at Rand McNally. He is, according to reports, living in Atlanta with Annette, his wife and teenage sweetheart. They have three children: Joshua Jeffrey, born May 8, 1984; Jeremy Davis, born June 25, 1987; and James Carlton, born April 24, 1991.

Amy Carter:
She Kept Her Own Name

Born in Plains, Georgia, on October 19, 1967, Amy Lynn Carter is the fourth child and first daughter of President and First Lady Carter. Her brothers were much older when she was born. Jack was already twenty, Chip was seventeen, and Jeff had just turned fifteen. She was unexpected, but she was wanted. Jimmy and Rosalynn Carter had wanted another child for many years, specifically a daughter to complete their family of sons. Rosalynn Carter worried about how her sons would take the news, but she needn't have worried. They immediately started scrambling for a baby name book. They couldn't agree on a single boy's name, but when they opened a book of girl's names, Amy was right at the top. After that, they stopped looking.

Rosalynn Carter said that if she had known

then about the dangers of older mothers giving birth, she would have been frightened. As it was, she was blissfully happy, "luxuriating in an indescribable feeling of satisfaction." When the campaign for governor took Rosalynn away for much of the year, Amy was only two. Rosalynn grieved after every trip, returning home to see the visible changes in her growing toddler.

Still, after Jimmy Carter won the election, life in the Georgia governor's mansion had to be fun for a little girl. Her big brother Jack was home from the navy; he had enlisted when she was just a baby. Chip and Jeff lived there, too. And her parents, ever occupied with state business, were not off somewhere on the campaign trail, leaving her behind. There was always someone around to love and coddle her.

In 1977 life in the White House, with its national spotlight, got hard fast. Amy was only nine years old when her father took office. Wanting her life to remain down-to-earth and egalitarian, President and First Lady Carter enrolled their daughter in public school. It was, of course, a circus. At first, all the children crowded around to peer at the nation's new first daughter. When the teacher kept Amy indoors during recess to "protect" her, Amy cried. Once the children got their fill of peering, however, it was no big deal and life went on. But the media never gets its fill, and Amy eventually had to be transferred to a private school.

The president and first lady included Amy in state dinners, a snoring bore to a child. She was allowed to bring a book and read at the table.

The press screamed, "Bad manners!"

Amy had duties. Once, when she was scheduled to unveil a poster for the new Department of Education, everyone waited and waited and looked at their watches. Amy had gone to her room to get ready, and should have returned in plenty of time. When she didn't come back, the first lady went to check. There was an exhausted Amy, sound asleep in the bathtub.

Traveling with her parents to an economic summit in Venice, the Secret Service became alarmed by the possibility of assassination attempts by the Red Brigade. They requested that the first lady and Amy wear bulletproof vests. They were hot and bulky, and both Mrs. Carter and Amy had to wear jackets to disguise them. Everyone around kept asking why they were wearing coats and the first lady made up lame excuses. During a visit to a glass-blowing plant, she nearly suffocated from the heat, but Amy took it all without complaint.

Worse was coming. Jimmy Carter's presidency was in crisis. In 1979, the Shah was forced to leave Iran, and the Ayatollah Khomeini returned. The American Embassy was overrun and hostages were taken. A disastrous rescue mission ended when one of the American helicopters collided with its fueling plane and burst into flames, killing eight soldiers. The Soviets invaded Afghanistan. Mt. St. Helens erupted. The economy soared into double-digit inflation. There were long gas lines at service stations. It was like the whole world had gone even crazier than usual. And Ronald Reagan was nominated for president on the Republican ticket.

On October 28, 1979, Jimmy Carter met Ronald Reagan in an infamous debate. It was a disaster — both for Jimmy Carter and for Amy. That night, the president told millions of Americans that he had asked his daughter, Amy, what the biggest problem in the world was, and she had told him that it was the nuclear bomb. Most people understood that the president was not implying that he routinely sought counsel from his own twelve-year-old daughter, that he was only illustrating that even a young person could see, strategically, the big issue facing the world was its own survivability in a nuclear age. But the frustrated media and a tough opposition went instinctively for the throat. Jimmy Carter and his young daughter, on the brink of puberty, were soundly ridiculed.

Amy would go off to college at Brown University. Her grades would suffer. She would actively protest apartheid in South Africa and CIA recruitment in colleges. Television news broadcast the scenes of passive resistance — just like the 1960s, except this time they starred the daughter of a former president, out of sync with her times. She was occasionally arrested while columnists and commentators endlessly dissected her motives and actions. Eventually, the little girl who read endlessly at state dinners, in her treehouse on the South Lawn, at an inaugural ball, and who earned a perfect four-point grade average in her college prep school, would be released from Brown University for scholastic reasons.

The Carter family's penchant for privacy has

led to numerous errors in Amy's public biography. For example, in 1994, national magazines and books reported with authority on her marriage and divorce to one Michael Antonucci. But according to family members, the wedding was canceled and never took place, making reports of the divorce problematic as well.

In time, Amy Carter found her love. She graduated from Tulane University in New Orleans with a master's degree in fine arts and art history. Her pastels, fresh and bright and cheerful, have illustrated some of her father's books, including *The Little Baby Snoogle-Fleejer*, a charming morality tale about not judging by appearances.

In New Orleans, she spent a summer working in a bookstore, cleverly named Chapter Eleven, and managed by a young man named James Wentzel. Amy was again engaged at the time but the Carter Center was forced to announce a "postponement" only a month before the date. There would be a wedding, but it would be with Jim Wentzel.

Their nuptials took place at Pond House, home of her late grandmother, Miss Lillian, on September 1, 1996. There on the banks of the pond, a favorite quiet place, a few family and friends — especially her big brothers — watched as Amy, wearing a 1920s-style, hand-embroidered dress, came down the path she had lined with magnolia leaves. She was not to be "given away," Amy decreed, as she "did not belong to anyone." Amy Carter kept her own name. After Jim and Amy took their vows under an arbor she created from her old swing set and wild vines, she served the wedding cake she and friends had baked, topped with a laid-back wedding couple. Amy and Jim went back to New Orleans where he served as computer consultant for the University of New Orleans.

Eventually, the couple moved to Atlanta, where they bought a house within jogging distance of the Carter Center. Her son, Hugo James Wentzel, was born July 29, 1999. She is on the board of the Carter Center, and has made trips to Russia with her brother Chip's Friendship Force, quietly living with ordinary Russian families and making friends. Amy Carter, so beloved by the American people during her White House years and so publicly savaged by her critics, declines all interviews.

Michael Edward Reagan:
America's Voice in the Night

When Maureen Reagan was about three years old, she began begging her parents for a brother. Her girlfriends all had brothers. Somewhere, she had picked up the idea that a brother could be purchased at a store — especially somewhere wonderful like Saks Fifth Avenue. She made regular trips to the toy counter, "to see if they had any in stock." Maureen's father would shrug at the clerks every time she asked. But privately he advised that if she truly wanted a brother she would have to save her money. So Maureen put pennies into her piggy bank for months.

On March 18, 1945, Michael Reagan was born and three days later, Maureen Reagan's parents told her that she was about to receive the thing she wanted most in her life. When she came down the steps that evening, there was baby Michael Reagan, wrapped in a receiving blanket. She was awestruck, although a bit puzzled. She had expected an older brother, one that talked. Ronald Reagan reminded her about the piggybank. Maureen ran upstairs and brought it back, where they broke it open and counted out the pennies. Ninety-seven cents — her entire life savings, and, Maureen said, "Michael Edward Reagan was worth every last one!"

After Maureen's difficult birth, it was thought that Ronald Reagan and actress wife Jane Wyman could have no more children. Maureen wanted a brother. Ronald Reagan wanted a son, so Michael was adopted when he was three days old.

During the 1940s and 1950s, it was the custom not to tell children they were adopted until they were "old enough to understand." Today, adoptive parents tell their children, immediately, that they were lovingly chosen especially for their family — not to make an issue of it, but to be honest, and to make certain the child doesn't find out hurtfully from a jealous sibling or some other way. In the case of the Reagans, the adoption was touted all over fan magazines, and the growing Michael was soon to find out about what he perceived as the "stigma" of being adopted. But he wasn't to know, until his father wrote the foreword to Michael's book, *On the Outside Looking In*, the depth of his father's love. "Traveling back in my mind to Michael's babyhood, seeing again his impish, angelic smile and recalling his unlimited energy," Ronald Reagan wrote, "I now realize that many adopted children do see themselves as different . . . But, as a parent then, I didn't know how Michael felt inside. To me, he was my adorable little son, and from the moment he first smiled at me, I never recalled he was adopted."

Michael Reagan often wondered why his parents chose to add another child to the family. The marriage was not the happy one pictured in the fan magazines. While Ronald Reagan was in the armed services, Jane Wyman's film career burgeoned. When he came back, she was a major star. He was considered the King of the B Movies, and his career was at a standstill. Perhaps the Reagans chose to adopt Michael because they thought another baby would help their struggling marriage. They would soon learn, like many other parents, that it doesn't work. In 1948, the Reagans were divorced, and Michael's adored father was suddenly and inexplicably gone from the home.

Three-year-old Michael and his older sister Maureen became shuttlecocks, shuffled between summer camps, boarding schools, and their parents' different homes, never really belonging anywhere. It was the poor little rich kid syndrome, except that Michael was adopted, and he wasn't sure if he even qualified for that.

If he was unsure of his own status, there was one thing Michael Reagan unquestionably loved and that was Saturdays. It was his one day a week with his father. Michael lived for Saturdays. He would park himself on the curb outside his mother's big circle driveway and peer down the street, waiting for Ronald Reagan's big red station wagon to come around the corner. Michael was always impatient with Maureen at such times, wanting her to hurry out and get into the car so they could get to the ranch. These were the best days of Michael's young life. He watched his father, "awestruck and admiring," as Ronald Reagan put up barns, cut horse trails, mended fences, or took his horses over difficult jumps. In the heat of the California afternoons Michael, Maureen, and their father would play impossible games in the swimming pool. Reagan, who had worked as a lifeguard at a dangerous river north of his hometown of Dixon, Illinois, had saved seventy-seven people from drowning between 1927 and 1932. Not only was he a powerful swimmer, he could hold his breath for, what seemed to young children, forever. Ronald Reagan would submerge in the water of the swimming pool and wait for his two youngsters to find him. "Maureen and I would thrash all over the pool, coming up for air three, four, five times, before he'd finally pop up in some other corner." That evening, going home, the three Reagans would stop by a cider stand for fresh, icy apple cider.

Then it was all over, and Michael would watch his father drive away until the following Saturday. And the shuttlecock life would begin again, with Michael being shunted for the week to Chadwick or St. John's Military Academy or Loyola High School, or whatever boarding school or camp he was attending at the time. And the fears of not belonging would come screaming back. It made Michael suspicious and argumentative, and he was often in trouble at school — and at home. When he became difficult, his mother would reach for a riding crop, bend him over and give him ten whacks on each leg. Even at the boarding schools, teachers showed no compunction about using a ruler on knuckles or bottoms. Michael said he found himself "acting up," knowing he would be punished, but doing it anyway so that he could get attention, "any attention — good or bad," from an adult.

In the early years, as a small child at a boarding school, he would often cry himself to sleep, drawing ridicule from other small children, but the pain was too great to be intimidated by peers. Michael often wept until the dorm mother came in to rub his back and then finally, he would find rest for another day. Before Ronald Reagan remarried, Nancy would come along on those revered Saturday outings, and Michael would get to sit on her lap, where she, too, would rub his back. It was such a comfort that he bonded strongly with the woman who would be his stepmother. He loved the trips to the ranch, but most of all, he loved having Nancy love him. "I never told her that, however, because I didn't want to be disloyal to my mom." And, of course, there were also the feelings of his sister, Maureen, sitting in the backseat.

Then Ron Reagan and Nancy Davis got married, and a new sister was on the way. Those Saturday drives became less joyous as Michael had grown too large for Nancy's lap. Once again, he was relegated to the backseat. In his mind he was outside of the circle.

Perhaps Michael could have dealt with the shifting dynamics of the family relationships had there not been another, deeply disturbing trauma. When Michael was at a day camp, a trusted counselor molested him and took photographs. For thirty-five years Michael felt dirty, ashamed, and terrified that if his father found out, he would hate and reject him. He had no way of knowing that his experience, however horrific, was not unusual. Thousands of children file reports of sexual abuse every year, but many thousands more live with feelings of personal degradation and disgust, holding it as a shameful secret, as did Michael, not understanding that it was not his fault that he had been exploited.

Thirty-five years later, it was obvious that, for Michael, healing could not happen until he was able to admit his terrible secret to his beloved father. But how could he do that? He knew it would shame him. On Palm Sunday 1987, Ronald and Nancy Reagan invited Michael and his family to the Santa Barbara ranch to celebrate the fourth birthday of Michael and wife Colleen's daughter, Ashley. As Colleen took their children Ashley and Cameron on a walk around the pond, Michael found himself alone with his father and stepmother. In an epiphany, Michael knew the time was at hand. He tried to talk, but only stammered. When he burst into tears, Nancy Reagan began to rub the back of his neck, just as she had so long ago when he was a child. "Tell us," she said softly.

Michael began slowly. His father was astounded and exploded with anger, threatening retaliation, "Who was this guy?" For an hour, maybe more, Michael spilled "all the scars of my childhood."

"Why didn't you tell us when all this happened?" Michael's father asked.

"Because I was afraid you would stop liking me," Michael answered. It was the true and honest answer from a small child's perspective.

"You should have known better," Ronald Reagan said quietly. But Michael didn't know better. No child does.

There by the horse corral, the Reagans experienced healing. Ron and Nancy Reagan embraced Michael in their arms. Nancy later whispered in his ear, "From this point on, it will be easier."

During this painful, healing time, Michael was already in the process of writing his book, *From the Outside Looking In*. It had obviously been on the elder Reagans' minds. Before Michael left the ranch that day, Nancy pulled him aside. "It would make us all feel better if we knew there were some positive things about your father in the book," she said softly. Michael smiled and reassured her there were, then said, "What I'm happy about is that there are also good things to write about you." Michael said that Nancy looked stunned, but she also knew what he was talking about.

In the foreword to Michael's book, Ronald Reagan wrote, "Being a father forty-five years ago was a much different role than it is today, and I sometimes envy the freedom Michael has to show affection to my grandchildren." He referred to parenting styles of the era. "Back then, a man went to work and left the child-rearing to the mother, much as it was when my mother raised me," he said. "Fathers didn't spend the amount of quality time with their children that today's fathers do, and they weren't always free to hug their sons or say I love you." And then, in an oblique reference to Michael's healing confession, Ronald Reagan wrote that parents must always let their children "know that there is nothing they cannot tell us, to let them know our love will always be with them." He ended the foreword with the words Michael had yearned for all his life, "Michael, whatever happens, always know I love you."

Aching for his father's touch, Michael realized he had never reached out, either. As they said good-bye after a television taping, Michael clasped his arms around his father's shoulders. He could feel his father stiffen. But the ice had been broken, and from then on, Michael always gave his father a hug when he visited.

In his later years, as former President Ronald Reagan descended into the cruel mental haze of Alzheimer's disease, he began to lose personal recognition of his family. But his face always split in a huge smile when Michael walked through the door. If he didn't know his name, or that he was his son, he knew instinctively that this was the guy who always gave him a hug.

Michael married Pamela Putnam in 1970, a marriage that failed. But in 1975 he married an incredibly strong and understanding woman named Colleen Sterns. This one "took." Colleen has supported him emotionally through the abuse issues, as well as his search for identity. Together, they have two children, Cameron and Ashley Marie, to whom Michael vowed always to be available. He wryly notes that maybe he's *too* "available," and wonders if parents always seem to swing too far the other way, like a pendulum carelessly released, with the next generation left to seek its own way, as well.

Like other firstborn sons of presidents, Michael has ambition and can be reckless. He soon learned that whatever he did would be belittled and ascribed to his father. Michael stretched the limits, the harder the better. He raced boats at eighty miles an hour in races called "Assaults." At one point, he would hold six world records. And he never quit, no matter how rough the water. After all, he was a Reagan.

In recent years Michael has thrived as a hugely successful national nighttime radio talk show host, now heard on more than 120 stations, and currently in his seventh year. He publishes *The Monthly Monitor* newsletter and maintains the Reagan Information Interchange (http://www.reagan.com). He serves on the board of the National Association of Radio Talk Show Hosts and was selected as a "Majority Maker" by the U.S. House of Representatives after the 1994 congressional election, an honor he shared with Rush Limbaugh. He delivered a keynote address to the Republican caucus of the 104th Congress, the first Republican congressional majority in forty years.

By learning to express his own opinions instead of his father's, Michael has managed to "out-Reagan Reagan." He is fiercely conservative. And he is thoroughly prepared on the issues discussed. He read all 1,342 pages of the Clinton health care plan and was one of its most effective critics. In 1994, a panel at the National Association of Editorial Writers Convention singled him out as one of the reasons the effort failed. Whether one agrees with Michael Reagan politically or not, there is no doubt that as much as any other presidential child, he has channeled the pain of early trauma into powerful expression. He has found his voice and clearly, effectively, carved out an identity that is all his own.

Patricia Ann "Patti Davis" Reagan: *Where Love Waits*

Her brother, Ron, would later say that the White House didn't change his family. "Our family is famously fractious, and it stayed fractious." Patti Davis may have been the most fractious Reagan of all and, assuredly, was the most rebellious. She also may be the one most changed in recent years.

Born October 22, 1952, seven months after her parents' wedding, Patti was delivered by cesarean section. Her mother, Nancy Reagan, would insist that Patti was holding on to her ribs. While that is, of course, anatomically impossible, it does show that the tempestuous battle between mother and daughter may have begun very early. According to Patti, there followed rage and slaps across the face in an escalating cycle of defiance and punishment. Patti says she was devastated by her father's seeming indifference to the conflict.

In fairness to the former first lady, Nancy Reagan has endured such public accounts with quiet dignity and grace, an attitude that belies Patti's story.

In any case, to escape home, the Reagan daughter turned to the bohemian life of the California subculture. As the Reagans' political career soared, so did her resistance. She wore tight jeans, black eyeliner and pale lipstick. She dropped out of school to become an actress, changing her name from Patti Reagan to Patti Davis, ironically enough, taking her mother's maiden name. She had guest roles in *The Love Boat* and *Fantasy Island*, and in the film, *The Curse of the Pink Panther*. She protested Vietnam. And slowly her energy and rage turned on itself. She took drugs, experienced severe bouts of anorexia, and subjected herself to a series of relationships that ultimately failed. She lived with Bernie Leadon, guitarist of the Eagles, writing a song that was recorded by the group. She was a featured celebrity of antinuclear rallies and, in 1983, married yoga instructor Paul Grilley. She posed nude for *Playboy* and wrote three erotic novels.

Eventually, Patti Davis began to recognize the self-destructive nature of her anger. She insisted that her mother "made me fear her, and fear that she may have passed along that rage to me in the mysterious linkage of chromosomes." Patti concluded that it was "usually the most wounded among us who inflict pain on others." And she had been angry at a father whose "presence felt like absence."

Patti began to take responsibility for her own part in the contretemps. She says that if she had really wanted to work for world peace, she would have stayed home from all those highly publicized rallies. All she did, she said, was to advertise to the world that she was at war with her father.

In 1992, Patti published her autobiography, *The Way I See It*. She had been on the search for self-discovery for some time, and had reached the point where it was important for her to confront the truth. This book was her attempt to do so. But the tone of the book held the hard edge of rancor. It was yet another wedge in the Reagan family.

Patti withdrew and for many years lived apart from her parents and siblings, pursuing doggedly her own internal path to reconciliation. She had come to a realization that she and her mother had shared some of the same realities and, in her "determination to be different from her, I have actually moved a little closer to her — not in personality traits, but in understanding." She says about her mother, "We have taken a tangled path to come finally into a clearing where love had been waiting for us all along."

Today, Patti Davis travels around the country giving seminars and speeches about the process of forgiveness, healing, reconciliation, and her rediscovery of the power of family. And as Patti's reconciliation with her father occurred, she not surprisingly experienced a renewal of faith. In an instructive moment, before the devastation of Alzheimer's took its toll, Patti was able to communicate with her father, to let him know that he was responsible for her belief in God. "The world knows much about Ronald Reagan," she says. "It should also be known that he passed along to his daughter a deep, resilient faith that God's love never wavers, and that no matter how harsh life seems, or how cruel the world is, that love is constant, unconditional and eternal."

Ronald Prescott "Skip" Reagan: *Dancing to His Own Drummer*

In the days when Patti Davis was living with Eagles' guitarist, Bernie Leadon, Ron Reagan looked her up. It wasn't as though it was a casual drop-in. The brother and sister had not seen each other in years, and Ron had no idea where she was. He went to the tax assessor's office in Los Angeles, found Bernie Leadon's name and address, and wandered around the hills of Topanga until he found her. Patti was so moved, she said, that she had to turn her face away so he would not see the tears.

They spent the precious time talking over their inexplicable childhood, attempting to make some sense of it. "I wasn't sure what they were about," Ron said, speaking of the fights between Patti and their mother, "but I didn't want that to happen to me."

Patti told him she didn't think he was ever in

danger of it. "Mom liked you."

"Yeah, I know," Ron answered matter-of-factly. "I had it a lot easier than you did."

Patti admired how Ron would never shy away from an admission like that. That was just the way it was. "He was the favored child — and we both knew it."

Born May 20, 1958, Ronald Prescott Reagan reacted to everything with a healthy sense of humor. Making people laugh was, apparently, a way of easing tension and staving off anger. He was closer to both his parents than the other siblings. Still, Ron told reporter Lou Cannon, "You know, there is something that [Dad] holds back. You get just so far, and then the curtain drops, and you don't go any farther."

Ron Reagan is another classic case of trying to discern his role in life either with or without his famous presidential parents. When he appeared on *Saturday Night Live*, he self-deprecatingly asked the audience, "How many people here think I was asked to host *Saturday Night Live* because I'm a contributing editor of *Playboy* magazine?" Some people applauded. "How many people here think I was asked to host the show because my father is President of the United States?" The crowd burst into laughter and loud applause. "That's what I thought," Ron laughed. "That's what I thought."

In 1976, Ron dropped out of Yale in his first semester, studied, and earned a scholarship to New York City's Joffrey School of Dance. He was eventually to become a regular member of the traveling troupe. Dancing had been his dream, he said, but it was a surprise to his parents. Political members of the Reagan entourage immediately began to ask the sensitive question. Was Ron Reagan, Jr., gay? And if so, what would it mean politically? There was a steady buzz in the editorial rooms of major newspapers: artists, especially male dancers, were stereotyped. But then and now Ron refused to play the game, neither admitting nor denying his sexuality, even though he has been married to fellow Joffrey Ballet dancer, Doria Palmieri, for more than two decades. He says his sexuality is nobody else's business. The gay community loved him for it and the media soon lost interest.

Because of Ron's dance career, he had many gay friends. As he started seeing them die from AIDS, he was spurred to action. He made a short film, attacking the sensitive subject head-on to educate the public about AIDS prevention. He also recorded a clever public-service announcement seeking more funds for AIDS research and more public awareness. "The U.S. government is not moving fast enough to stop the spread of AIDS," he said. "Write to your congressman," then, with a grin, "or write to someone higher up."

Eventually, Ron moved on to television journalism, proving himself a talented writer and host, interviewing Barbara Walters, George Burns, and other popular guests. He appeared on ABC's *Good Morning America*, and many other news shows. He produced documentaries. His controversial, entertaining, talk show was described by one reviewer as "part encounter group, part bear baiting." Today, Ron continues his television journalism career from his home in Seattle, where he and his psychologist wife, Doria, still live.

Washington news veteran Sam Donaldson met Ron Reagan in 1985 in Geneva, when his father was "locked in semi-mortal combat with Mikhail Gorbachev," and was impressed with the president's son. "I made the acquaintance of Ronald Prescott Reagan, age 27, who had been commissioned by *Playboy* to come along and write a story about the press corps. He is a good guy, intelligent, willing to listen and argue politics without being dogmatic or holier-than-thou, unpretentious despite the fact of who he is." More important than that, Donaldson wrote, he is "a young man who clearly loves and admires his parents."

John Ellis "Jeb" Bush:
The Serious One

Born in Midland, Texas, on February 11, 1953, Jeb Bush is the second son of George and Barbara Bush. He graduated magna cum laude from the University of Texas and became an executive with the Texas Commerce Bank in Houston. In August 1974, he converted to Catholicism before marrying the lovely, Mexican-born Columba Garnica. They moved to Florida in the early 1980s where Jeb founded a number of successful real estate development companies.

In 1987 he served as Florida's secretary of commerce. He ran for governor in 1994, losing in a close election, but he came back four years later to win. Florida prospered during the initial years of his administration, and Governor Jeb Bush was sometimes mentioned as a possible presidential contender. But in the election contest of 2000, it was his brother who found himself locked in a dead heat with Democrat nominee Al Gore. The state of Florida became the deciding factor in the election and Governor Jeb Bush's role during the months was closely scrutinized.

Governor and Mrs. Jeb Bush have three children. Firstborn, George Prescott Bush or "George P.," was treated like a rock star at the 2000 Republican National Convention and was named by *People* magazine as fourth in a list of the one hundred most eligible bachelors in the United States. He is a graduate of Rice University and studying law at the University of Texas. Daughter Noelle developed a dependency on prescription drugs but has been making a comeback in a drug rehab program. John Ellis, Jr., is the youngest in the family.

Neil Mallon Bush:
There's More Than One Way to Learn

Born January 22, 1955, in Midland, Texas, Neil Mallon Bush was dyslexic as a child. Perhaps because of his early struggles, he is today a passionate advocate of alternative educational methods. Neil has been described by some as the best public speaker in the family and has spoken to crowds as large as 35,000 in the United States and Europe. He was his brother, George W.'s, campaign manager in his failed bid for Congress and campaigned for his father's presidential efforts in 1980 and 1988. It was during his father's first run for the White House that he met Sharon Smith in New Hampshire. They were married on July 6, 1980.

Neil is the third son of President George Bush, Sr., and was named after Neil Mallon, a close friend of the family. He earned undergraduate and graduate degrees from Tulane University in international relations and business administration. He became president of a struggling Denver oil firm before joining forces with the Apex Energy Company. Neil and Sharon were an active part of the business and social scene in Denver, with Neil becoming an outside director of the Silverado Savings and Loan. When the S&L crisis swept the country and Silverado collapsed, Bush became a target of congressional and federal investigators looking into the demise of the financial institution. He was cleared of any wrongdoing, but his involvement created headlines during his father's presidential administration. According to historian Carl Sfezzarro Anthony, it was a controversy that might never have seen such attention had George Bush not been in the White House.

In the early 1990s, the Neil Bush family moved to Houston, Texas, where he worked as director of finance for Transmedia Communications, "before forming Interlink Management Corporation, a firm focused on education, high tech, and biomedical business development." Since the early

1990s, Neil has been planning and developing an Internet company devoted to alternative educational methods. The Austin-based company, Ignite!, which developed a reading program for children, has been heralded as "one of the most innovative and practical uses of the internet today."

While the Bush family is notoriously protective of its own, Neil's three children are already, sometimes, breaking into the limelight. Lauren Pierce is an international fashion model who has walked the runways in New York, Paris, and Milan, and graced magazine covers around the world from *Vogue* to *George*. Pierce Mallon Bush, young, personable and bright, wowed national television audiences during a brief appearance on the occasion of his uncle's nomination at the Republican National Convention in 2000. Ashley Walker Bush is the youngest.

Marvin Pierce Bush:
The Businessman in the Family

Born October 22, 1956, in Midland, Texas, Marvin Pierce Bush is the fourth son of George and Barbara Bush. He graduated from the University of Virginia and worked for Shearson, Lehman Brothers before becoming the new business development director at John Steward Darrel & Company in Charlottesville, Virginia. In the summer of 1981 he married Margaret Molster. They have two children, Marshall Lloyd Bush and Charles Walker Bush. In 1988, after developing intestinal ulcers, Marvin had his colon removed. Refusing to feel sorry for himself, he was soon spending hundreds of hours as a volunteer, encouraging children and adults slated for the same operation. Now living in Alexandria, Virginia, Marvin is the president of his own thriving investment firm, Winston Partners, L. P.

Dorothy Walker "Doro" Bush Koch: *The Only Daughter*

Described by her brothers as thoughtful, "always thinking of others," Dorothy Bush was born August 18, 1959, in Houston, Texas. She graduated from Boston University with a degree in sociology, and worked as a travel agent, caterer, bookkeeper, and tourism promoter before taking a job with the National Rehabilitation Hospital in Washington, D.C. Gifted with a great sense of humor, she has been one of the family's secret weapons on the campaign trail for both her father and brothers.

In 1976, Doro was with her parents in China while her father served as the first U.S. liaison to the People's Republic. The family, devout Episcopalians, realized that their daughter had not been baptized. On her sixteenth birthday, Doro became the first person to be publicly baptized in a Christian ceremony in China since the beginning of the communist regime. She married William Heekin LeBlond in September 1982, and served as the bookkeeper for his Cape Elizabeth, Maine, construction business, but the marriage ended in divorce. They had two children, Samuel

Bush, born August 26, 1984, and Nancy Ellis, born November 19, 1986.

In 1992, during her father's White House years, she married Robert Koch (pronounced "cook"), former aide to House Democratic leader Richard Gephardt, in a private summer ceremony at Camp David. They have two children, Robert Patrick Koch, born May 20, 1993, and Georgia Grace "Gigi" Koch, born January 11, 1996, and live outside of Washington, D.C.

Chelsea Victoria Clinton: *"Scary Bright"*

Born February 27, 1980, in Little Rock, Arkansas, Chelsea Clinton came into the world an adored daughter of politics, the only child of Governor and Mrs. Bill Clinton. All of Arkansas loved her. Even so, Chelsea was able to maintain the childhood of a normal "American kid," attending public elementary school, wearing braces and playing sports with her schoolmates. She was an extremely bright youngster — at the end of her second grade, she received a double promotion directly into the fourth grade.

Chelsea was twelve years old when her father was elected president of the United States, the first child to live in the White House since Amy Carter. Because of the woes of Amy and other presidential children, Bill and Hillary Clinton established a strict protocol for Chelsea's relationship with the public. She was to have as normal a childhood as possible. Interviews were strictly forbidden.

Chelsea attended Sidwell Friends High School, and achieved academic distinction when named a National Merit Scholar. She studied dance at the Washington School of Ballet and spent many hours a week in rehearsal, reprising her role as Favorite Aunt in the holiday classic, Tchaikovsky's *Nutcracker.*

After Chelsea graduated from high school, her parents helped her settle into a "normal" dorm room at Stanford University in Palo Alto, California. The room was normal except for one thing — the bulletproof glass in the windows. And there was the presence of Secret Service agents chasing her around campus on mountain bikes, wearing casual, college clothing.

In 2000, after Chelsea had completed three years of college, her mother was preparing to run for the Senate from New York. Chelsea dropped out of school to help her campaign. Hillary Clinton's approval rating spiked immediately. The press still didn't get to talk to her, but she became more and more visible in photographs with her family. After her mother was elected to the Senate, Chelsea returned to Stanford to complete her senior thesis, a 167-page history of her father's mediation of the 1998 Northern Ireland peace agreement, complete with interviews with Bill Clinton. "I've been doing honors theses at Stanford for more than twenty years," Chelsea's advisor, history professor Jack Rakove, said, "and I haven't seen too many which were as thoroughly researched as hers." Ken Burns, the noted filmmaker, described her as "scary bright." She graduated from Stanford, and was soon off to

Oxford University, where she began work on a master's degree in international relations. It was a path her father, Bill Clinton, had taken before her. Clinton was a Rhodes scholar at Oxford in the 1960s.

Chelsea substituted for the first lady at state dinners, and accompanied her parents on diplomatic trips overseas, where her poise and charm won accolades from people and presidents alike. In 2002, Chelsea began a summer internship with the World Health Organization in Geneva. Her set task was to "design strategies to reduce health dangers to children around the world." It may have been the beginning of her own political future. With her brilliant intellect and the political savvy that comes from growing up in a governor's mansion and the White House, she would be a natural.

Barbara Pierce Bush:
Coming to You on the Cover of Vogue

Barbara Pierce Bush, daughter of George and Laura Bush, was born November 25, 1981, the first of fraternal twin sisters. She and sister Jenna are the first recorded birth twins of any American president. (Andrew Jackson adopted one of his sister-in-law's twin sons and named him Andrew Jackson, Jr.) Barbara was named after her paternal grandmother, and Jenna after her maternal grandmother. Ironically, their personalities seemed to spring from the opposite sides of their respective families. Most say that Jenna Bush has the personality of her grandmother,

Barbara, the former first lady, and young Barbara Bush has the reserve of her mother, Laura Welch.

Barbara grew up in Texas and went to public school until the sixth grade, when the family moved to Austin and her father was elected governor. She was a student at St. Andrews Episcopal School until ninth grade, when she transferred to Austin's public high school. Barbara, a stunning brunette, was a high school homecoming queen and voted the "most likely to appear on the cover of *Vogue*" by her classmates. Described as the quieter of the twins, she physically resembles her mother, but has her father's competitive spirit. She has played softball and run cross-country. Barbara is currently studying at Yale University, representing the fourth generation of her family to attend the Ivy League school.

Jenna Welch Bush:
Class President

Jenna Welch Bush, daughter of George and Laura Bush, was born on November 25, 1981, just after her fraternal twin sister. She was named after her maternal grandmother, but otherwise experienced the same life as her sister, growing up in Texas, attending public school until the sixth grade and enrolling in St. Andrews Episcopal School when the family moved to the Texas capital.

In the ninth grade she joined her sister in switching to Stephen F. Austin High School, where the slogan was "Everybody is somebody at Austin High." While Barbara was voted most likely to appear on the cover of *Vogue*, Jenna was elected class president. Perhaps best known to the public for her emergency appendectomy on Christmas night 2000, and a publicity tabloid flap over trying to order a beer while still underage, Jenna is a freshman at the University of Texas. She is described as "bubbly" and "a blue-jeans-and-T-shirt kind of gal," admired and well liked by her friends.

Today's living presidential children represent three generations. Some of the old traumas are recycling, as well as some of the coping mechanisms of centuries past. But there is an evolutionary phenomenon, a social resiliency, developing as well. Many presidential children are living normal lives, showing less signs of stress. While the public still expects more from a presidential child, their rates of divorce and alcoholism are actually no higher than average and their incidents of premature death are now far lower, a marked change from earlier years.

The Bush twins, as in the case of Chelsea Clinton before them, have a loving family to provide support, and they manifest no apparent desire to exploit their station in life. It is much more than an even start. Each has a blank page to write on, a lifetime ahead, to create her own story for good or ill.

TWELVE

IN THE NAME OF THE FATHER

*"The first and deepest of all my wishes
is to give satisfaction to my parents."*
— JOHN QUINCY ADAMS

"I would run through a brick wall for my dad."
— GEORGE W. BUSH

Politics should be an easy profession for the children of elected officials. After all, they have early name recognition and fund-raising advantages over their opponents. And yet the public delights in seeing people in public life humiliated. Perhaps it comes from our nation's roots, where even the idea of privilege is anathema. When young Teddy Roosevelt, Jr., tried to win a lowly seat in the New York State Assembly, newspapers turned it into a marathon contest. When Roosevelt announced that "his hat was in the ring," his opponent, a humble tailor, told newspapers, "My hat's in the ring too and it isn't my father's."

Only two presidential sons became presidents themselves — John Quincy Adams and George

W. Bush. Only two presidential sons were ever elected governors — George W. Bush and Jeb Bush. It is an astounding feat, considering the number of presidential children who have fought for the honor. If a Roosevelt can lose in New York, a Stevenson lose in Illinois, a Humphrey lose in Minnesota, a Taft lose in Ohio, a Reagan lose in California, and a Kennedy be forced to back down from a race in Massachusetts, then perhaps the Adams-Bush presidencies and the double-Bush gubernatorial wins in Texas and Florida can be seen for the extraordinary historical events they really are.

Teddy Roosevelt, Jr., won the New York Republican primary and came within 108,000 votes of upsetting incumbent governor Al Smith, but that was about as close as any had come before the Bush family. FDR, Jr., actually announced for governor twice in New York but was never able to get the Democratic nomination. He finally ran on a third party Liberal ticket, splitting the vote and tilting the election to the Republicans. Meanwhile, his brother, James Roosevelt, ran for governor of California and lost.

Adlai Stevenson III, whose grandfather ran for vice president, whose father was twice the Democratic candidate for president, and who, himself, served in the United States Senate, was defeated for governor twice in his own home state of Illinois.

Even smiling Charlie Taft, son of the twenty-seventh president, ran for governor of Ohio and lost; his brother, Robert Taft, considered one of the five greatest senators in history, ran for president three times and never received his party's nomination.

Much was made of the political future of the son of Hubert Humphrey, presidential nominee and former vice president. In 1998, when the son won the Democrat nomination for governor in Minnesota, the general election seemed to be a certain victory. Minnesota was the safest Democrat state in the union, the only state they had carried against Ronald Reagan in 1984. But, the Humphrey son lost nevertheless, and to a third party independent candidate named Jesse Ventura.

Kathleen Kennedy Townsend, a presidential niece, was elected lieutenant governor of Maryland. In 1998, her younger brother, Joseph Kennedy II, was considering a run for the gubernatorial office in the Kennedy-safe state of Massachusetts, but after personal issues were raised, his poll numbers plummeted, and he withdrew. Townsend, meanwhile, finally ran for governor of Maryland in 2002. Registered Democrats overwhelmingly outnumbered Republicans, but she lost anyway.

And then there is Maureen Reagan, who failed in an attempt for the Senate in California. Her father refused to endorse her candidacy, which was even bigger news than her campaign.

The Role of the Presidential Parents

What happens when a presidential son becomes president himself? How is his perspective different from other presidents? How did it happen to John Quincy Adams and George W. Bush?

What role did the presidential parents play? And how does the relationship between George W. Bush and his father affect his decisions and impact the nation and the world?

The biographies of presidential children reveal the conundrum of the parents. How can they encourage productivity and excellence without destroying their child's spirit with unrealistic expectations? How can they help build their child's self-esteem and personal identity when the presidency overshadows everything they say and do? And how can they carve out a sense of family and personal intimacy for the child when the presidency and the quest to get it and hold on to it demand every waking moment for years on end?

Some psychologists suggest that modern parenting skills have had a positive impact on the lives of recent presidential children, and there seems to be some evidence to support this idea. Research shows that in recent years presidential children actually outlive the general public, which might indicate a lessening of the stress. This should be compared to earlier years when the occasions of premature death far exceeded those of the norm. Even divorce, seemingly rampant among presidential children, was more common in earlier years than recently, although this might be somewhat explained by the fact that, in earlier years, divorce was rarer and more easily obtained by the children of presidents than by the general public.

Perhaps the most obvious change in the relationship between presidential parents and their children is a new understanding and sensitivity to the pressures the whole family faces in the White House. Modern presidents, with some very notable exceptions, offer less personal criticism and more understanding for their children. Almost every day of his life, Harry Truman woke at four a.m. to write to his daughter Margaret, and virtually all of his words were supportive. Bill Clinton sometimes helped daughter Chelsea with her homework, an extravagant use of a president's time when the best of tutors are available. The children of George Bush, Sr., constantly tout their parents' declaration of unconditional love. "We are loved for who we are," says third son Neil Bush, "not for what we are accomplishing. And just as important, we are all loved equally." President George W. Bush often refers to this "gift" as his parents' greatest strength.

Of course, there is nothing profound about unconditional and equal love for one's children. It is an obvious attitude for any parent to embrace but, as these biographies show, it is certainly profound when put into action. Bright and capable as they may have been, until recently, few presidents and first ladies have manifested this "unconditional" quality in their own correspondence with their children.

As befit the times, John and Abigail Adams were severe and domineering in their parenting, dictating every aspect of their children's lives and setting impossible standards. "If you do not rise to the head of your country it will be owing to your own laziness and slovenliness," Adams wrote to his firstborn son. As we have seen, such admonitions wreaked havoc on his family.

The exception, the successful son, John Quincy Adams, who became the sixth American president, was a perfectionist and even more harsh with his own children. After all, it had seemed to work for him. Learning that his second son, John Adams II, was forty-fifth in his Harvard class of eighty-five, he refused to allow him to come home to the White House for Christmas. Desperate for his father's approval, John Adams II improved to twenty-fourth, whereupon his father announced that he would pass on coming to his son's graduation ceremony unless he was fifth or higher. "I had hoped that at least one of my sons would have been ambitious to excel," he wrote. "I find them all three coming to manhood with indolent minds." And toward the end of his presidency he commented wryly, "I am aware that no labor will turn a pebble into a diamond."

Not surprisingly, his children, the pebbles, responded appropriately. John Adams II was expelled from Harvard for misbehavior before the graduation ceremony. And the firstborn son, the heir apparent, was a likely suicide.

Historians tend to view President William Henry Harrison as "a devoted father," a much softer figure than the stern caricature we are often given of John Quincy Adams and other early presidents and first ladies. Nevertheless, subscribing to the "tough love" child-rearing philosophy of his generation, Harrison insisted that each of his children stay focused on a rigid career track. William, Jr., had been tagged for a career in law, and the stubborn father was not above employing guilt or any other weapon as a motivator. "If you have not the Perfect Education which I design for you," he wrote his son, "you shall in yr [sic] future life blame yourself for the misfortune." Even into adulthood Harrison could not resist lecturing his son. When William, Jr., was a twenty-six-year-old lawyer, he received a letter urging him to "abandon the lounging & procrastinating mode of life which for sometime you have followed." William Henry Harrison, Jr., died an alcoholic at thirty-five.

In more modern times, Theodore Roosevelt was keen to the problem of excessive expectations for his children and often, clumsily, tried to help out by adding his own analysis. Writing to Ted, Jr., he suggested that "each of my sons is doing and has done better than I was doing and had done at his age — and I had done well." Then, realizing that the presidency still towered over them all, he sought to diminish that achievement, to take it out of the equation. "I don't mean that any of you will be President," Teddy Roosevelt wrote, "as regards the extraordinary prizes the element of luck is the determining factor." But were his sons convinced?

Roosevelt was certainly well intentioned, "sometimes writing several letters a day" to his children. But the theme that kept constantly reappearing was to urge his children to excel, to achieve great things as he had done, with the added caveat that he, the former president, was joyously watching from the grandstand. In one letter he would try to reduce the pressure, and in the next he was practically demanding success.

"There is not leeway for the smallest short-coming on your part," he wrote Ted, Jr., before his exams at Harvard. As we have seen, in World War One, youngest son Quentin flew his plane into German territory where he was shot down, and Kermit became an alcoholic, taking his own life in 1943, a fact that mysteriously evaded historians until 1980.

All parents want their children to achieve something in life, to do their best, and to feel a sense of self-worth. But criticism coming from a high-achieving parent, one who is a public figure, can be devastating and crushing. Richard Nixon spoke of how relationships changed when he became president, how careful he had to be in offering criticism to a staff member who might brood over a mistake for days. President Grant once offered a quiet, offhand rebuke to son Buck saying, "That was careless." The moment haunted his son years afterward. "It hurt me. It nearly broke my heart." Correction from a parent is one thing, but when that parent happens to be an icon of the child's peer group — a famous sports, entertainment, or business celebrity or an admired ambassador, general, or senator — it can be something altogether different. It is as if the president is speaking for his age, his era. It is the voice of ten thousand peers.

At the other extreme, overaffectionate presidential parents seemed to diminish their children. Thomas Jefferson's relationship with daughter Patsy is described by historians as "suffocating." Her whole identity was smothered by his. Likewise, Martin Van Buren's bribery, offering his estate to son Smith Van Buren if he and his wife would move in and live with him, complicated the son's chances of achieving something significant on his own. Van Buren's sons spent their whole lives writing about and promoting their father. Even after he was gone they served as ghostwriters, finishing his autobiography and editing his presidential papers as if propping him up, keeping him alive a little longer so that they too would have an identity. "I will always be known as the son of Theodore Roosevelt," said the second child to the former president, "and never as a person who means only himself."

It is certainly not a case of excessive affection being bad for a child. How can one get too much love? Rather again, it is the power of the celebrity parent that comes into play. The same sunshine that brings life can scorch and kill. A child must not only be loved unconditionally, but must be appreciated for a specific reason as well. To be appreciated only because one is a son or daughter can leave a person empty, without self-esteem. Notwithstanding the self-defeating dangers of excessive expectations and criticism, a child must feel that he or she is doing something worthwhile on his or her own, something unrelated to the power of the parent.

The phenomenon of *dysgradia* again becomes a factor. The child needs to escape the limelight. "My Mother did not want us to grow up dwelling on the fact that we had been White House children," said Marion Cleveland. "She trained us for living on our own account." "Everyone knows that limelight is the worst thing for them," observed Jackie Kennedy.

This may explain why some of the more successful children often stayed away from the White House altogether. John Quincy Adams, Richard Taylor, Robert Todd Lincoln, Teddy Roosevelt, Jr., Caroline Kennedy Schlossberg, Margaret Truman, Jeb Bush, and George W. Bush are a few that come to mind. In the case of the Kennedys, where the children were young and had to be with the parents, the first lady spent as much time as possible at a second home in Virginia. Benjamin Harrison, the only grandson of a president to be elected to the highest office, spent his whole life distancing himself from the White House and his famous grandfather. "I want to avoid everything that is personal," he wrote to staffers. "And I want it understood I am grandson of nobody." Although, once again, there are exceptions to every rule, the Garfield sons thrived both at the White House, where their father insisted they come and live, and in their later careers.

One child-rearing rule that is continually being violated by presidential parents is favoring one child over another. This is seen almost from the beginning. George and Martha Washington took two of his step-grandchildren to live with them permanently, leaving two others with relatives. Andrew Jackson did the same with twin nephews, separating them at birth by taking one to be his son and leaving the other. When Patsy Jefferson alerted her father that her sister Polly was feeling excluded, an alarmed President Jefferson moved forcefully to redress the problem.

But even in this he conspired with Patsy, the obviously favored daughter.

A president has needs, too, and a dependable son or daughter is going to rise to the top when the unnatural pressures of power assert themselves. Martin Van Buren openly favored his son, John. Lincoln favored Willie. Teddy Roosevelt favored his namesake and wrote him letters telling him so. While this may have been empowering to the chosen child, it was usually devastating for the others.

Likewise, love without direction or discipline appears to be as crippling for presidential children as it is for children in any other family. This is especially true of presidents' sons. Some psychologists see a lack of discipline as just another form of neglect or abandonment. The disappointing stories of the sons of Ulysses S. Grant and Abraham Lincoln come to mind. Several of the young men in the Grant family had the talent and drive to prove themselves but, indulged since childhood, they had not the self-discipline to finish many of their best projects.

There is an interesting exception in both of these families. The firstborn sons of both Lincoln and Grant were great successes, suggesting, at least in the case of Fred Grant, that sometimes love is enough. Young Grant developed self-discipline in the army. And young Lincoln — well, his complicated psyche requires a book of its own. Feeling less loved and nurtured, firstborn Robert Lincoln nevertheless went on to become one of the nation's great businessmen and public figures, but he resented the lack of discipline and grew to see it as a failure in his parents. Visiting the White House during his father's presidency, he brought up the subject, but Lincoln ignored him. Young, rambunctious, brother Tad, a witness to the moment, pushed Robert away from his father with a taunt: "He likes me better than you." It was a barb that must have stung all the more because of its veracity.

Drawing on the best information available, a University of Minnesota research team concludes that "children who are high achievers generally have parents who are reasonable, who set high standards for behavior, and who are firm but gentle." In 1988, three years before the University of Minnesota published its report, George W. Bush was asked about life as the firstborn son to George and Barbara Bush. "Our home was one of discipline and love," he said. "Love first and discipline second. George Bush set standards. Respect your elders, be polite, be forgiving, be trustworthy, and above all, be honest. If any of us ever violated the basics of love he was quick to point it out to us, not in a mean way but in a loving and forgiving way."

It is a formula that has worked for other presidential children. The nineteenth American president, Rutherford B. Hayes, and wife Lucy, were loving and gentle, while simultaneously offering their children a steady stream of advice. To son Webb Hayes during his college years he wrote, "Thoroughness is a vital thing. More important than study, however, is honesty, trustfulness, and sincerity." Later, when Webb entered the business world, his father wrote, "Conceal nothing; be careful not to brag or talk too much — a common fault with beginners." Hayes, who read the Bible each morning with his family, urged his firstborn son Birch "always to do what you know is right. No matter what you lose by it, no matter what danger there is, always do right." All of the Hayes children are considered successful. William Howard and Helen Taft had this same sense of balance, demanding excellence and even invoking the family name, but in an atmosphere of unquestioned love and with a gentle nature.

Abandonment

One of the more curious features of the relationship between presidential parents and their children is the almost universal abandonment of the children. It is curious because so many of the children rise above it and lead successful lives. Robert Lincoln not only missed his father as a child but was virtually ignored throughout most of his college years, complaining that his father seldom wrote. The daughters of Woodrow Wilson and of George W. Bush may be extraordinary historic exceptions. The Wilson and Bush daughters had their parents at their side their whole lives, mostly because of their father's swift political rise and partly because of the parents' choices. Although, in the case of George W. Bush, it may be argued that the price had been paid in the previous generation, for name recognition was already a given. Chelsea Clinton has lived her young life close to her busy parents. The Clintons were criticized for an early family conversation that exposed their daughter to the ugliness of campaigns. They wanted her to know what it would be like to hear people criticize them. Reportedly, an upset Chelsea fled from the room in tears, but such preparation and inclusion in their lives no doubt cushioned the daughter to some of the traumatic public events that were to come.

Understandably, presidents are often preoccupied, even if physically nearby. Former president Jimmy Carter offers a revealing conversation with son Jack, who complained that while he was in the same house, his father was never really "there" for him. It was an eye-opening confrontation for Carter. The point is often made by psychologists that emotional abandonment can be worse than physical abandonment.

In earlier times, children of prominent families were often sent to schools or tutors far from the home. After a long separation, John and Abigail Adams didn't recognize their own son standing in front of them. Zachary Taylor once said, "I scarcely know my own children or they me." During childhood, Richard Taylor saw his father once in an eleven-year stretch. He was a student at Yale for a year and a half before writing his parents a letter and they didn't seem to mind. William Henry Harrison, Jr., was only a spectator to his father's military victories and almost never saw him as a youth. By the time he was seventeen, when a young man is often straining at the leash to get away from home, William, Jr., was still trying to find his place at the family hearth in Ohio. Soon after being sent to Transylvania College in Lexington, Kentucky, he petitioned his parents to allow him to return and find a college nearer home. The senior Harrison, who had meticulously planned each son's career, turned him down. When the boy earnestly begged to come back, only for a few days at Christmas, his uncompromising father still refused. "We certainly want to see you but I cannot consent for your return at Christmas."

George Washington Adams was separated from his famous parents for much of his life but was in utter rapture when his stern father finally decided to bring him home. Adams had decided to personally supervise his son's preparation for entrance into Harvard. For the first time since early childhood George was living with his parents and for the first time ever he was given his own room in his parents' house.

Robert T. Lincoln spent his whole life in an uphill battle to win fatherly approval. In a letter to a friend in 1846, Abraham Lincoln referred to his firstborn dismissively as "one of the little rare-ripe sort, that are smarter at about five than ever after." A few days after his father's assassination, a grieving Robert told a former professor that "in all my plans for the future, the chief object I had in view was the approbation of my Father, and now that he is gone . . . I feel utterly without spirit or courage." And then, of course, there is the story of Alice Roosevelt, given to her aunt to rear for the first two years of her life.

In more recent years, a fourteen-year-old Michael Reagan, an adopted son who was also the product of a divorced marriage, spent two years sleeping weekends on a couch in his father and stepmother's home. The future first lady, Nancy

Reagan, finally announced that this makeshift arrangement was over. Michael would be soon moving out of the living room. When construction workers began building a new room on the back of the house, he became overjoyed. "That room . . . was the symbol of acceptance." For the five weeks of construction Michael fantasized where he would put his things and how he would decorate the room. When the day arrived, he raced to the back of the house only to find his little brother's live-in nurse unpacking her boxes. "How do you like my new room?" she asked cheerfully. Michael was moved to the nurse's old station on the daybed in Ron, Jr.'s, playroom.

Ironically, separation was seen as a cure for alcoholism for some presidential sons. The Harrisons sought to send their son to a remote military post in the West to help him recover without temptation. Andrew Johnson was planning a trip for his son to the African nation of Liberia so that the young man could shake his alcoholism and find himself. As recently as World War Two, Kermit Roosevelt, son of TR, was urged by his wife to be transferred to a remote base in Alaska, thinking it might help him dry out. Lacking intimacy with spouses, parents and siblings, feeling rejection when compared to successful fathers, most of these sons *needed* family, not separation.

Even the most tragic stories of presidents' children show some signs of life when the powerful parents actually needed the child's help. The greatest months in the short life of William Henry Harrison, Jr., occurred when his father brought him into the inner circle. In 1824, Congressman Harrison assigned his young namesake to an important and delicate political mission. Harrison needed someone he could trust to visit Washington to discreetly promote his name as a prospective ambassador to Mexico. Within a week, young Harrison lined up support from "prominent politicians and influential newspaper editors." He had dinner with the consummate politician of the hour, Henry Clay, picked up a verbal pledge from General Winfield Scott and co-opted some of the support of his father's closest rivals. It was considered a masterful performance, executed with "the grace and skill of a political veteran." And while it failed to land the Mexican appointment immediately, an ambassadorship to Bolivia soon followed. The brief, successful lobbying effort of Harrison's son would be in stark contrast to the rest of his life.

Each presidential child reacted differently to his or her experiences of "abandonment." George Washington Adams, the reader will remember, ended his life. Harrison, Jr., died an alcoholic. Richard Taylor became a famous Civil War general. Robert Lincoln fought back, having his mother declared insane and institutionalized. Alice Roosevelt Longworth became a biting wit, offering years of irreverent commentary on the Washington scene. Michael Reagan channeled his pain into a career as a quick-witted, conservative political talk show radio host with a national following of millions. Some were devastated, and others transcended their trauma. And sometimes, events and fate itself seemed to turn capriciously on their own.

John Quincy Adams:
A Different Voyage

The formative years of John Quincy Adams and his siblings offer an illustration of how complex the parenting role can be and how very subtle differences in circumstances can lead to dramatically different results.

Nabby Adams, the first presidential child in American history, had three younger brothers: John Quincy, who would become the sixth president of the United States and is arguably the greatest of presidential children; Charles Francis; and finally, Thomas Boylston, the baby of the family, whom historians have described as "a very ordinary man."

John Quincy Adams, whose story is legendary, was born July 11, 1767. He would become the sixth president of the United States and, until, George W. Bush, the only presidential son to become president himself. His 1778 voyage to France with his father proved to be a defining moment in both of their lives. Not only was there an important bonding that would well serve the emotional needs of a growing adolescent boy, but John Quincy became practically indispensable to his famous father, a fact that undoubtedly contributed to his sense of self-confidence, a characteristic that would carry him to career heights. Fellow French commissioner and sometime political rival, Benjamin Franklin, could not be entirely trusted. Besides, Franklin was fluent in French and often busy. For many long days in a strange land, living with the stifling boredom that came from an ignorance of the native tongue, John Adams had only his son, John Quincy. There was an intellectual, emotional, and spiritual conversation begun in Paris that was evident in their ongoing correspondence to the end of their lives.

Writing his wife Abigail, Adams declared that their son, John Quincy, "is respected wherever he goes, for his vigor and veracity both of mind and body, for his constant good humor, and for his rapid progress in French as well as his general knowledge which, for one of his age, is uncommon." From what we now know of the science of learning a different language, it is altogether understandable that the young John Quincy mastered French with more ease than that of his harried, plodding, relentless older father, who was amazed at the boy's genius and natural talent. Nor could the father miss the positive tonic the trip was having on the son's sense of ambition and self-worth, a bonus attributed to the marvels of Parisian culture and the unique challenges of making one's way in a foreign land.

When the two returned to America, their work in France apparently done, the father was determined to make up for his neglect of second son, Charles Francis. As fate would have it, Congress dispatched John Adams back to France again, this time to head up an office authorized to negotiate an end to the Revolutionary War. After earnest discussions with wife Abigail, young Charles, who was only nine years old, was invited along with older brother John Quincy. Perhaps the return voyage and foreign experience would be the catalyst in Charles's life as well. It had worked its magic in the life of first son, John Quincy, why not for the second?

The middle brother, Charles Francis, typifies the tragedy of presidential children and helps to demonstrate how events and parental decisions play their part. Born May 29, 1770, in Boston, Massachusetts, he spent much of his formative years separated from his father. He was four years old when John Adams left for Philadelphia and the Continental Congress and six when his father signed the Declaration of Independence. The following year Adams returned home a hero but only months later was off to France, with the older brother.

As it turned out, the second Adams voyage across the Atlantic was a disappointment. The first trip had been a shared adventure between father and son. There had been a secret getaway by moonlight, avoiding the dangerous British warships; lightning had struck the main mast in the middle of the Atlantic; there was a chase at sea and an eventual victorious sea battle. In later years, John Adams would point to the trip in a letter to Thomas Jefferson as symbolic of his whole life. In contrast, young Charles's trip with his brother and father on the *Sensible* was hardly the stuff of romantic fiction. Two days out from shore, the ship sprang a leak. After a storm, the leak grew to such proportions that all hands spent the rest of the voyage manning the two pumps night and day. The ship came ashore at the first opportunity in El Ferrol, Spain.

Deciding against any further delays, John Adams and sons promptly set out by donkeys on a thousand-mile journey, crossing the Pyrenees in the dead of winter. Nearly two months later the party arrived, exhausted by sleepless nights with fleas, bedbugs, rain, fog, and snow. Both boys, Charles and John Quincy, were ill. This was hardly the spectacular introduction to Europe that father and son had experienced two years before.

Upon arrival in Paris, Charles and John Quincy were enrolled at the same school in the Parisian suburb of Passy. This, too, would be a departure from the John Quincy experience, when father and son had discovered France together. Then, they had shared accommodations with John's old Continental Congressional colleague, the redoubtable Benjamin Franklin. John Quincy saw his father every day after school, and the famous Franklin would often be there, bustling about in between appointments. They attended plays at the Comédie-Française, with the eighty-year-old playwright Voltaire sitting in the next box. It was a storybook introduction to Louis XVI's France, which held forth in glorious splendor from the world's greatest palace in Versailles.

By the time of John Adams's return to France, the relationship between himself and Benjamin Franklin, always wary, was openly strained. Adams chose lodgings in the center of Paris, several miles away from his sons' school in Passy. Nine-year-old Charles saw his father only occasionally on weekends, when they visited parks and museums. Both the father and elder brother were now well versed in French, so at social functions young Charles sat groping in the dark, trying to understand the language without the benefit of the constant translation that had once attended father and son.

There is no question that John Adams was making a serious effort to inspire his second son. And Charles Adams was struggling to meet his father's expectations. Both Adams boys appeared to possess remarkable linguistic ability. John Adams bragged to his wife Abigail that nine-year-old Charles, after less than six months in Paris, "speaks French like a hero." If he could have lived a little longer in France, he, too, would have mastered the language and gained all the career opportunities that came with speaking the requisite "language of diplomats." But circumstances were working against Charles.

Within less than half a year in Paris, the John Adams diplomatic mission moved on to the Netherlands. The change began with promise. Charles enjoyed a pleasant and educational overland trip with his father and brother, but soon after arriving, the two boys were enrolled in Amsterdam's famous but severe Latin school. It was a harsh and frightening experience that ended with John Adams coming to the rescue of his embattled sons. The Dutch schoolmasters are "mean-spirited wretches, punching, kicking and boxing the children upon every turn," Adams wrote to Abigail. Arrangements were made for a private tutor.

In the summer of 1781, with the Revolutionary

War at an end, Charles's accomplished older brother, John Quincy Adams, only fourteen years old, was asked to join a diplomatic mission to Russia. His fluency in the French language was now opening doors. John Adams decided to send eleven-year-old Charles back to the United States. He described him as "a delightful child," but with "too exquisite sensibility for Europe." Fearing danger or physical abuse, Abigail Adams begged that young Charles not be sent back across the Atlantic alone, and John Adams made an effort to arrange an escort. But events were moving too quickly and promises could not be kept. In the end, eleven-year-old Charles lost his escort en route and sailed on alone.

It turned out to be a frightening and mysterious journey. Charles's ship departed from England but was diverted to a Spanish port for repairs. There, he learned that his father was seriously ill, perhaps even dying. For several months Charles disappeared. Historians are tempted to speculate on what happened to a sensitive child, abandoned in a tough Spanish port city without any knowledge of the language. Nothing is known for certain and Charles never offered details. The family despaired, believed him lost at sea. Five months later, a shaken eleven-year-old Charles Francis Adams returned home to his mother and family in Braintree, Massachusetts. He refused ever after to speak of his trip.

Young Charles had little time to savor his mother's embrace — or to be healed by its warmth. Within days he and little brother Thomas were sent packing off to school in

Haverhill, Massachusetts, fifty miles away. No sooner had Charles settled in than he learned that his mother and older sister, Nabby, would be leaving for London. His esteemed father would be serving as the first United States representative to the mother country. There would be no joyous weekend reunions at the Braintree farmstead. Barely having seen his mother upon returning to America, Charles Francis was now losing her. He would not see his parents again for seven years.

Meanwhile, the adventures of the eldest son, John Quincy Adams, continued to astonish. At the age of sixteen he traveled alone throughout Sweden, Denmark, and the northern Germanic states, ending in France, where he was present at the signing of the Treaty of Paris. Once more, his father called. Serving as minister to the Court of St. James, John Adams needed John Quincy as his personal secretary. The son worked in Great Britain for a year and then returned to the States, where he enrolled as a junior at Harvard University, graduating early the following spring.

In the summer of 1788, younger siblings Charles and Thomas Adams were joyfully reunited with their parents in a grand family celebration at Braintree, Massachusetts. An eighteen-year-old Charles, a Harvard scholar, would tower over his mother. His father, favored to be elected as the first vice president of the newly formed United States of America, pronounced himself completely satisfied. And yet, always the constructive critic, he later expressed concern that his second son was not as "goal oriented" as firstborn John Quincy or he, himself, had been. "You have in your nature sociability, Charles, which is amiable but may mislead you . . ." the father warned. "Don't let companions, then, nor your amusements, take up too much of your time." As if on cue, Charles was involved in a Harvard "demonstration" that included naked students running through Harvard Yard. A number of students were expelled. Charles survived, graduating with a law degree and, in spite of the scandal, the promise of a great career.

After her husband won the vice presidency, Abigail insisted that Charles accompany them to the nation's new capital in New York City. Charles, deprived of his family for most of his life, cheerfully complied. The new vice president helped his son land a job at the Wall Street law office of the prestigious Alexander Hamilton, where he clerked until Hamilton became the first secretary of the treasury. When the nation's capital changed to Philadelphia, the largest city in the United States, the Adamses packed up and moved again. This time Charles stayed behind, determined to succeed on his own. He would remain in New York City throughout his father's tenure as vice president and later as president, pursuing his law career, but he was to fail miserably.

In early America, the New York political and business scene was dominated by two men, Alexander Hamilton and Aaron Burr. Before they decided to meet each other in the most famous duel in American history, they shared a common rivalry with John Adams. In this case, being the son of the vice president worked against Charles, as he struggled to build a law practice in New York. Hamilton and Burr were both superb political gamesmen, savvy and ruthless when they felt the situation so demanded, not above punishing their political rival John Adams by squeezing the son. At the time, New York City had a population of 18,000, still small enough for the power elites to control. Years later, when younger brother Thomas was put in charge of John Quincy's personal funds, he received a letter from the older brother referring to "the disastrous influence of New York upon everything in which our family is interested."

Charles's only New York family connection was with elder sister Nabby, who lived a poor and lonely existence not far from the city center. Her husband, Colonel Smith, was always away on some new and fanciful financial venture that promised much but in the end only hastened his downward spiral. Charles and Nabby consoled each other, both in their loneliness and in their material struggles. But it was another newly acquired friendship that most intrigues today's historians.

Somewhere during this time Charles struck up a friendship with Baron Freidrich von Steuben. The baron was a Revolutionary War general and the author of the "Blue Book," a manual that defined the duty of American army sergeants for decades to come. One of John Adams's distinguished biographers, John Ferling, suggests a possible homosexual liaison between the older Prussian and the middle Adams son, building his case on numerous references in the baron's biographies and pointing out that Charles actually lived with the general for a time. Ferling cites this friendship as a turning point in his relationship with the father, John Adams, and a possible reason for his sudden and severe rejection, as well as so many "lost" family letters to and from Charles Adams.

In line with this theory, Ferling suggests that the family was relieved when shortly thereafter Charles fell in love with Sally Smith, the younger sister of his controversial brother-in-law Colonel Smith. But Adams's biographer David McCullough takes a different view. In his best-selling *John Adams*, McCullough states that his parents actually objected to the romance. They had little confidence in the Smith family, especially after Nabby's experience with the colonel. In fact, the Senate had at first denied Smith an appointment to the general staff because Smith was a "bankrupt." When Charles and Sally Smith did eventually wed, in 1795, McCullough claims his parents were devastated. In any case, Nabby wrote her parents that Charles was now happy and he was "at last Safe Landed."

The more traditional view is that John Adams turned against his second son when he learned that he had squandered or lost his brother's investment money. Charles had been entrusted with $2,000 of John Quincy's life savings while his multilingual older brother was away on another diplomatic mission in Europe. Considering that in 1797, President John Adams earned a yearly salary of $25,000, the amount lost was considerable. Even worse, in the father's eyes, had been his son's attempt to cover up the affair.

On May 30, 1794, his twenty-five-year-old brother, John Quincy Adams, was appointed by President George Washington as the new American minister to the Netherlands. It was the beginning of a diplomatic career that would take him all the way to the White House. Sensing that his successor, President Adams, might be reluctant to push Quincy, Washington wrote to him: "If my wishes be of any avail they should go to you in a strong hope that you will not withhold merited promotion from Mr. John Adams because he is your son." At various times, John Quincy would serve as minister to Prussia, England and Russia. He would help negotiate the end of the War of 1812 and be dispatched all over Europe to negotiate commercial treaties to keep the fledgling United States afloat. He would still find time to squeeze in service as a U.S. senator from Massachusetts.

Parallel to the stellar career of his elder brother, Charles Adams would struggle. By 1798, he had two children, a failing law practice, a wife his parents had rejected, and a financial scandal on his hands. His uncle, Samuel Adams, was an elected official and a venerated Founding Father of the nation. His own father was now president of the United States. His older brother was a brilliant diplomat with a bright future, lauded by no less than George Washington. And his younger brother was working for his father as a personal secretary in the White House.

John Adams and son Charles began to send increasingly bitter letters to each other. Many of these missives have been curiously lost, even though it seems that the Adamses kept just about everything else on paper.

In the fall of 1799, in a surprise visit to his daughter Nabby's home in East Chester, New York, the president stumbled onto a scene that made him emotionally sick. Sally Smith was staying there with her two children. Charles had disappeared. His horrified father learned that his son was bankrupt, an alcoholic, and faithless. He declared his son "a mere rake, buck, blood and beast." Charles had become for his father "a madman possessed by the devil." The Founding Father, signer of the Declaration of Independence and second president of the Republic, could stand no more. He wrote to his wife Abigail, Charles's devastated mother, "I renounce him." Later in the year, Abigail paid a visit and found Charles sick and withering away.

On December 3, 1800, only hours after the presidential electors had assembled for the first time to decide the election of 1800, a messenger brought devastating news to President John Adams. Only days earlier his son Charles had died an impoverished alcoholic at the age of thirty. He left behind a widow and two children with no legacy of money, property, or professional success. An astute politician, President John Adams knew very well that he would lose the election to his own bitter rival, Vice President Thomas Jefferson. He was about to become the nation's first one-term president. Now, he had lost a son as well.

"The death of my brother affected me greatly," John Quincy Adams wrote. "Now there is no passion more deeply rooted in my bosom than the longing for posterity to support my father's name." Charles's older brother, John Quincy, would arguably become the nation's greatest secretary of state. He would successfully negotiate with England for the Oregon Territory, acquire Florida from Spain, and draft the Monroe Doctrine in 1823. Two years later, John Quincy Adams would be pitted against Andrew Jackson in one of the most controversial elections in American history. Although Jackson led in the general election and the electoral vote as well, neither man won a majority and thus the decision was passed on to the House of Representatives where the politically experienced Adams won over the politically unproven military leader.

The controversial election of 1824 was reversed in the next popular contest, when Andrew Jackson was overwhelmingly voted into the White House. John Quincy Adams spent the last years of his life in Washington, D.C., as a member of the House of Representatives from Massachusetts, where he became an outspoken opponent of slavery and a champion of woman suffrage. In 1848, he collapsed on the floor of the House from a stroke and was carried to the Speaker's Room. Two days later, on February 23, 1848, he died from a cerebral hemorrhage. Louisa died four years later. They were buried together, two presidents — father and son — and two first ladies, in the family gravesite at First Parish Church in Quincy, Massachusetts.

John Quincy Adams was convinced that the challenge of a foreign experience, the discipline of a rigorous academic regimen, and the stern discipline of a caring father had made him the success that he was. It was a formula that he strove earnestly to repeat with the next generation. But it didn't work, not for his siblings who had shared his environment, not for his own children.

If both he and his father were right, that the first voyage to France was a defining moment in their lives, then it is more probable that the intimacy and bonding that took place between father and son were one of the keys to John Quincy Adams's initial confidence and spectacular early rise. Bored in a country with a different language, they had only each other to entertain and trust. They were two men, father and son, both future presidents, living in the same room. It was a moment that would not be repeated. Adams, Sr., was convinced that his son was a genius with language. This genuine admiration, coming not only from a father but from a celebrated public figure of his generation, must have been intoxicating for a youth striving to establish his own identity and struggling with the insecurity of his adolescent years. It was probably the father's approval that allowed John Quincy to soar, not the father's stern, constantly interfering injunctions. It was this part of the formula that was missing for Charles and that hastened his despair and doom.

Many years later, when John Quincy Adams had become an old man, finally realizing the limits to his ability to solve problems, he would define genius as only a matter of concentration on a given subject. It was as if he were talking aloud to himself. Perhaps he was finally awakening to the fact that his "anointing" had been at least in part a self-deception, but even so it had taken him to the pinnacle. By then he was clearly established in the firmament of history as a man who had made a difference.

George W. Bush:
This One's for You, Dad

As we have learned, all sons and daughters seek the approval of the father figure in their lives and may spend many years well into adulthood trying to attain it. Studies show that young women tend to seek a relationship with this father figure and young men seek to mimic or even compete with it. This tendency occurs across the sociocultural gamut. For example, "the children of incarcerated parents are five times more likely to end up in jail themselves." The sons of high achievers, who are admired, not only by their children but by their peers, pose an additional challenge. How does one mimic or compete with a president? Especially in a democratic society where the father has been chosen to lead by many individuals from the son's own peer group?

As this study has shown, many presidential sons have been broken on the rocks in that attempt and others have reconstructed the whole résumé, only falling short of the presidency itself. While most of the sons of Martin Van Buren subordinated themselves to their father and spent their lives serving him behind the scenes, John Van Buren openly copied him. The elder Van Buren was known as a drinker, an orator, and consummate lawyer. John proceeded to out-drink, out-speak, and out-lawyer the father. He was no less devoted to Van Buren than his brothers, but gifted with a different personality, he sought to honor him in a different way. If Martin Van Buren coveted the presidency for his son, John coveted it for himself only to vindicate the father, to prove at the ballot box the arguments for his father's greatness that were even then pouring forth in his writings and speeches. In the end, John's own chances for political greatness were lost in his monomania.

Historically, George W. Bush is a remarkable exception, and whatever good or bad eventually befalls his presidency, the relationship between himself and his father will be a unique and compelling study, and not just for historians. Born in Midland, Texas, on July 6, 1946, George W. Bush is sometimes a remarkable copy of his father. The senior Bush went to Andover before Yale, and then joined the Skull and Bones Club. So did the son. Sometimes the father's accomplishments were beyond reach. George Sr., was the youngest aviator in the U.S. Navy, flying an Avenger over the Pacific in World War Two and getting shot down in a dramatic raid on an enemy island. The son flew an F-102 Interceptor jet back home in the Air National Guard during the Vietnam War. Father and son both started their own oil companies, but the times were right for the father. His business boomed. The son's company faltered. The father lost in a bid for the Senate but came back and won in a bid for Congress. In 1977, the son married Laura Welch, a Midland schoolteacher and librarian, and that same year launched a campaign for the U.S. Congress. Learning from the father's mistake, the son had bitten off a smaller piece, but he lost anyway. And for a long time any hope of pursuing a political career was shelved.

At other times, the son shot past the father's line in the sand. George, Sr., graduated from Yale with a degree in economics. The son graduated from Yale with a degree in history and then went on to gain an MBA at Harvard. The father, who had been an All-American first baseman at Yale, delighted in taking the family to see the New York Mets play baseball. He openly yearned for the fun his uncle must be having as a part owner of the team. As in the case of dozens of presidential children before him, George W. Bush clearly fulfilled his father's "other" dream, buying the Texas Rangers baseball team and helping to turn them into a contender.

As in the case of all father-son relationships, this process is ongoing. As president, the father ran a mile a day; the son now runs three. And it is reminiscent of so many other father-son political relationships. President Benjamin Harrison, grandson of a president, wanted it known that during the Civil War he had fought in more battles in six months than old President William Henry Harrison had fought in his lifetime.

People who first meet George W. Bush are

often struck by the great contrast with his father. George Bush, Sr., is methodical, careful, and cautious. The son is instinctive, decisive, and open with his personal staff. There are strengths and weaknesses to both styles, but the differences seem starkly clear. These two personalities were quite complementary when working in tandem during the 1988 presidential campaign. Many urged the son, George W., to go into the White House to help his father, as many presidential sons had done before him. Jack Ford had done it; Chip Carter and John Eisenhower had, too. For political convenience, he could have drawn a salary from the Republican National Committee. It was the accepted way to avoid restrictive laws about hiring blood relatives. Many wondered how the staff would work together without the son there to enforce loyalty as he had done in the campaign. But it was his father's decision; George Bush, Sr., wanted his kids to have their own life. No Bush kin would serve in the White House. John Quincy Adams had been one of the nation's most vigorous opponents of nepotism and the partisan spoils system; nevertheless, even principled, legalistic, old John Quincy had allowed for the necessity of a loyal son as a White House aide.

Later, a White House staffer remembered sitting in a meeting when a charity project proposed by son Marvin Bush was submitted. He wanted his dad, the president, to participate. Someone made a joke at Marvin's expense. The staffer was appalled. "As far as I was concerned, the White House belonged to the whole First

Family and each one should be treated with respect." Had the father inadvertently sent out the wrong signal, the staffer wondered, by saying that his own sons were not to be given special treatment?

Zachary Taylor had done just that with his own son. "I do not want him to locate at or near Washington," he said of Richard, "or to fill any office." As in the case of George W. Bush, Richard Taylor returned to the family's home state and, as in the case of Bush, he soon became an important public figure after his father passed from the stage.

While newcomers to the Bush orbit tend to see the different personalities between father and son, those who work with them for any length of time seem to be more impressed by how much they have in common. The differences, they argue, are only in personality, not character. Both men are understated, even humble. Throughout most of his political life, the father's heroic war record had remained buried. It was only finally brought out at the insistence of Pete Teeley, an old press secretary who found it in his research in the military archives. In 1997, when the son, then governor of Texas, was urged to get someone to write his biography before the project slipped out of his hands, he dismissed it with a laugh. "Nobody is going to write a book about me." Within two years there were three books. When friends of the son, George W., bought his Midland boyhood home to turn it into a museum, the younger Bush president was astounded. "Why would you want to do that?"

Both men are meticulously ethical. In 1988, when a campaign biography for George Bush, Sr., was compiled in a matter of two months, the tape-recorded interviews were transcribed, edited, and sent off to the publisher. Editors read about three hundred pages of Bush talking about his life, about his family, about the issues, and promptly gave it the title, "George Bush: Man of Integrity." Almost all who knew him agreed. The Bush son was just as straight. One aide witnessed him throwing a former congressman out of his office for suggesting a business deal with the sly suggestion that, "Of course, there is something in this for you, too."

In April and May of 2001, political pundits speculated about the proposed tax cut that had been relentlessly promoted by new president, George W. Bush. He had been pushing the idea from the beginning of his campaign for the presidency. Why was he still so insistent? The economy was humming along nicely, and incredibly polls showed that the American people didn't want it, while members of his own party weren't interested. Tax cuts had indeed been the voter mood of 1994. But what was the point now? Some speculated that it was about Bush family integrity.

In 1988, George Bush, the father, repeated a campaign mantra at every stop. "Read my lips, no new taxes." It was the one line that audiences insisted on hearing again and again, and it became deeply etched in the minds of the voting public. Two years later, when political realities demanded a compromise with a Democrat Congress and a Richard Darman–inspired tax plan resulted, it broke one of the most famous campaign pledges in recent political memory. Well aware that his father's integrity had been questioned by voters in his defeat at the polls in 1992, George W. Bush, the son, clung stubbornly to a tax cut for 2001 and eventually got it, or so the theory went. The issue may have been purely economic for Congress and the administration but, for the president, it was surely about unfinished family business, as well. In one fell swoop, Bush, the son, had restored the family honor and wiped "read my lips" off the pages of history.

In 2002, there was much speculation centered on an American invasion of Iraq and the defeat of Saddam Hussein. The circumstances were different from 1990 and the Gulf War, but the idea was nevertheless openly discussed that George W. Bush was finishing family business. Was he, as dozens of presidential children before him, trying to do something his father had not, namely, in this instance, get Saddam Hussein?

Likewise, both Bush men, father and son, are discreet and demand discretion from others. For Bush, Sr., a former CIA director, it comes naturally. Staffers speak of writing memoranda for him, suggesting options, with him responding with even more questions while never revealing his own opinions. For the son, who is gregarious and expressive and gives instant feedback, such discretion has apparently been an acquired trait, and involves some planning and staff discipline. Bush, Sr., was hotly criticized by CBS News anchor, Dan Rather, and others for the secrecy surrounding the Gulf War, but the restrictions pale compared to the son's handling of his war on terrorism and his confrontation with Iraq.

Says columnist Gloria Borger, "So how to explain this administration's grand obsession with secrecy? Simple: It's a business model." Former Reagan-Bush speechwriter, Peggy Noonan makes a convincing case that George W.'s preoccupation with discretion came from the hard lessons learned in seeing his father betrayed and weakened by untimely leaks. Staffers in his father's White House were warned not even to be seen in the presence of the crack *Washington Post* reporter who broke the story of an upcoming Bush-Gorbachev summit in Cyprus. Bush, the son, bridled at old memos leaked out of his father's presidential library during the 2000 campaign. Two years later, as president, he proposed new laws giving former presidents and their heirs greater power in keeping such documents secret longer.

Finally, both Bush men, father and son, have a great sense of the strategic. As has been pointed out, it is a trait of many presidential children. The two Bushes are both big thinkers, not allowing themselves to become the prisoners of minutiae. In 1989, Lithuanian Americans urged Bush, Sr., to take advantage of the confusion in the Soviet Union and help them gain independence for their homeland. "This is one chance in a hundred years for Lithuania," they said. But like a good chessman, George Bush was not going to waste a move on a pawn when the king was cornered and the whole game at an end. The entire Soviet empire was unraveling. If Bush did not disturb the process, provoking a counterrevolution, it would mean freedom, not only for Lithuania, but for millions more across Eastern Europe. The strategic planning leading up to the successful Gulf War of 1991 produced a world alliance almost unprecedented in history. It looked easy at the time, but it fell apart shortly after Bush, Sr., left office.

The dizzying speed of activity in the first months of the Bush son's administration and the corresponding favorable bump in the polls were the product of a disciplined adherence to a very clear, publicly announced strategy. Not distracted or reactive to the pressing and tempting events coming into the White House in-box, George W. Bush stayed on theme and stuck to his limited core campaign promises. If they failed and he was forced to compromise with the Democrats, well, that too was accounted for. One of his most frequent campaign promises held that he knew how to work with the political opposition and could get things done. If his programs passed, he won. If he was forced to compromise with the Democrats, he won anyway. Both had been promises. It was a no-lose situation.

In 2001, in the wake of terrorist attacks against America, George W. Bush, the son, suspended the rights of Taliban POWs, ordering them to be tried in military courts outside the continental United States. Pundits were alarmed, comparing his action to other notorious occasions of suspensions of rights and warning that "history has not looked kindly on some of these episodes, a lesson the president would do well to heed." But the examples cited were committed by George Washington, Abraham Lincoln, and FDR, a fact not lost on George W. Bush. The storm clouds quickly passed. A February cover story for *U.S. News & World Report* had pictures of Theodore Roosevelt and George W. Bush with the title "15 Presidents Who Changed the World."

The Great Difference

Most observers agree that if there is a difference between George the father, and George the son, it is in their decision-making style, a manifestation of their different personalities. As president, the father was methodical, and it served him well. He didn't invade Panama until he was ready. It saved lives and assured success. He carefully built his alliances against Iraq, with the skill of a true diplomatic craftsman. But his delayed reaction to the perceived economic downturn cost him reelection.

George W. Bush, the son, is direct, instinctive, and quick. The public and most reporters thought he had changed after the September 11, 2001, terrorist attacks on the United States. It was an observation that was baffling to his biographers and those who really knew him. "War and recession transformed the Bush presidency — and some say George W. Bush himself," read one account. "He went from an accidental president who was a *Saturday Night Live* joke to the commander in chief," said a Democratic political consultant in Los Angeles. A University of New Orleans historian declared that "Bush has grown into the role of commander in chief by scaling an exceptional learning curve." He is now "direct and to the point," suggested another report. When relations with the Saudis were deteriorating dangerously, the president sent a frank letter, spelling out with unprecedented clarity what the United States saw as the issues and the resolution. "Bush's letter transformed his reputation in the small circle of Saudis who run their country. His reputation went from rock bottom to sky high."

Likewise, junior White House staffers talked about how the president was shedding the William McKinley model in favor of the Teddy Roosevelt image, saying that the comparison had to "shock even Bush." Word leaked out that Roosevelt's biographer Edmund Morris "agrees that they're a lot alike." Indeed, First Lady Laura Bush was pronounced "new" by many observers as well. Democrat Senator Ted Kennedy, who watched her in the middle of the terrorist crisis, observed that "you take a measure of a person at a time like that. She is steady, assured, elegant."

If others saw him as a changed man, George W. Bush knew who he was all along, and so did his family and those who had known him for any length of time. "He's not changed," quipped his mother, the popular former first lady Barbara Bush. "I don't even see his hair growing any grayer." In an instructive interview, the new president referred to the European editorial cartoonists and writers, "They don't know what I'm like. Nor does the nation, by the way. . . ."

His friends and associates insisted that his decisiveness and leadership had always been his most pronounced characteristics. Indeed, they were the subject of an Associated Press article in 1989, long before he had run for governor of Texas. Staffers compared his possible presidency to that of Theodore Roosevelt as early as 1998, two years before he ran for president. If he didn't share Roosevelt's scholarship and championship of the environment, they declared, he was a similar dynamo of energy and had always resented the pompous elitists in American society. Roosevelt had once written that of all forms of tyranny, the least attractive and most vulgar was the tyranny of wealth.

Typically, George W. had no interest in proving anything to anybody. If members of the media who had rushed to judgment on him now wanted to imagine that he had been transformed by the crisis, he was not one to object to the good cards dealt him. He would let them think what they want. Who cares? If they want on board now, let them come on board.

In 2001, George W. Bush, "the leader," was becoming a known quantity. Mort Zuckerman, publisher and editor-in-chief of *U.S. News & World Report* described him as "a man on a mission." A *Washington Post* columnist suggested that "the president's reach could be monumental." A pundit observed that "the leitmotif of the Bush II administration is to avoid the mistakes of Bush I. The rules: Do not raise taxes, ever. Do not forget to translate war popularity into a domestic agenda. Do not lose touch with your conservative base." When asked by reporters what was the greatest presidential lesson he had learned from his father's experience, he answered, "Spend your political capital." When the economy stalled, he was out front, acting with alacrity, pledging to extend unemployment benefits and provide $3 billion in emergency aid to workers laid off because of the terror attack of September 11. "I am going to lead the Congress in a way that provides help and stimulus for growth," Bush declared during a visit to the Labor Department. A writer for *USA Today* suggested that the president was "avoiding the public perception that politically damaged his father."

And always George W. Bush pushed the effort against terrorism. He fumed about other national leaders who "lack the courage to stand up to states that may one day provide terrorists with nuclear or biological weapons." Into the summer of 2002, the nation was reassured by his strength of resolve: "I will not wait on events while dangers gather."

Sanctuary

Finally, there is one other pronounced quality that is shared by father and son, although manifested in a slightly different way in each. It is the same gift that Jackie Kennedy gave her children, Caroline and John. The Bush children, as the Kennedy children, have enjoyed a sense of perspective seldom seen in an ordinary life, not to mention in those so celebrated and powerful. They have an ability to become detached from the pain and pressure of public life, even to disdain it and diminish it and recoil neatly back into a ready-made tortoiseshell of family and love. On a conscious level, at least, they can look at the winning or losing of power with much less concern than the busy campaign workers who seemingly suffer in anguish around them.

Hours after the 2000 Michigan primary loss to John McCain, a low moment in a contest that was becoming alarmingly divisive, threatening chances for victory in the general election, Governor George W. Bush was joking with reporters. Wearing a sleeping mask over his eyes, a blinded Bush was "bumping his way down the plane aisle." That November, when the closest election in American history was up in the air, he told reporters that he would have no regrets either way because he had Laura and "I know she'll still love me. And that's more important than winning." Laura offered her own clever explanation of her role: "In politics you always have an opponent," she said. "It shouldn't be your spouse." Morphing that year into the most popular woman in America, Laura Bush told television talk show host, Larry King, "Since September 11, I've had the opportunity, or maybe I should say the responsibility, to be steady for our country — and for my husband." But the fact was, she had been steady for him long before.

The Bush family is famous for evading, even ridiculing, self-analysis, but ironically, their success and their style has helped promote what psychologists are calling "emotional intelligence," described as "the capacity to handle your own emotions and your relationships with others." Max Weber, a German sociologist, calls it "the firm taming of the soul." In a book on leadership,

Daniel Goleman says that emotional intelligence "is the primary factor that distinguishes great leaders from average ones." Jeffrey Birnbaum wrote that George W. Bush had been "forced to play two contradictory and probably irreconcilable roles simultaneously: Commander in chief and comforter in chief."

I Don't Lecture

To understand how the children of George and Barbara Bush and other very recent presidential children have managed to avoid so many of the traps that snared those who went before them, one need only visit the Library of Congress and compare presidential papers and letters. In 1983, six years before his presidency, George Bush sent a letter to all four boys, saying that he was getting older and that he was uncertain of the future, but "win or lose, older or younger, we have our family. " And then, describing his world after all the excitement of public life would pass, he wrote, "I'll be surrounded by love so what else counts?"

Marvin Bush was the only son not involved in his father's 1988 campaign, but the president bragged about him in his diary, saying what joy he and his family brought to his life in Washington. "It makes me feel that I haven't lost all sense of priority here," wrote Bush. In an interview in 1988, Marvin Bush said of his father, then a candidate for president, "I can talk to him about anything, at any time." It was a stark contrast to the humiliated son of FDR who had told his mother that he would never again "try to talk to Father about anything personal."

When third son, Neil Bush, nicknamed "Whit" by the family, offered his sympathy over a biting press attack on his vice presidential father, George Bush, Sr., answered by changing the subject to Neil's own newborn son, "None of this matters . . . compared to the joy that Pierce brings to our lives. We can't wait to see the lad. If he's as loving as his Ma, and as kind and as thoughtful and as decent as his Dad, then life will be great for him and he will give only happiness to his parents and his friends." Summing up his philosophy of life, Bush, Sr., added, "That's all that really matters, Whit — not politics — not public life but family, kids and now grandkids."

Before launching the Gulf War, George Bush, Sr., wrote his children a long letter offering his explanation of the crisis and ending with a familiar theme that runs through all his letters to his children. "And so I shall say a few more prayers, mainly for our kids in the Gulf. And I shall do what must be done, and I shall be strengthened every day by our family love which lifts me up; every single day of my life. . . . I am the luckiest Dad in the whole wide world." In an interview with *CNN*'s Paula Zahn, Bush said, "I don't lecture my kids."

President George Bush, Sr., always had a special sensitivity to the losing candidate in a race. He was famous for jotting off short letters of encouragement to the loser anywhere in the country, Democrat or Republican. "I know how it feels," he would always say, and "You still matter to me."

He had begun his political career by losing in a bid for the Senate in Texas in 1964. And in July 1992, his last year as president, he had a nagging feeling that he couldn't shake that it just might be how his career would end as well. Heading into the home stretch, in the last few hours of his campaign, George Bush, Sr., knew that what had been an intuitive fear was now a reality, and that he was losing. On Election Day, 1992, "the last day of campaigning of my entire life," the president invited sons George W. and Jeb on board Air Force One for one last trip across the Eastern seaboard. Jeb Bush was planning a run for governor of Florida in two years, a quest he would lose. And George W. was anticipating a run in Texas, but the odds were great and his incumbent opponent was openly ridiculing him, saying he wasn't even a Bush, "he was a shrub."

There, in the splendor of Air Force One, still president and the most powerful man in the world, Bush, Sr., and his family seemed strangely fragile and impotent. They gathered in the front cabin, in the president's airborne office, talking about the job of baseball commissioner, although even that hope was slipping away in the last hours of the political life of George Bush, Sr. They talked about the fallibility of pollsters — a hope that the father would occasionally hang on to until the headlines proclaimed it over. And the father talked about the fact that, win or lose, this was the sunset of his political career. There was no scenario in which he could ever imagine another campaign trip. This was it.

Somewhere over the Carolinas, the Oak Ridge Boys slipped into the front cabin and began to sing "Amazing Grace." Everyone had tears in their eyes. George Bush, Sr.'s, life must have been flashing by, for he leaned over to his strong first-born son to say how much his own dad would have loved to be with them now, "hearing these guys sing." Hurting for their father, angry, disappointed and helpless, George and Jeb Bush told him that he had run a great campaign, it was over, "there's nothing more you can do." Describing the deep hurt the morning after his loss, George Bush, Sr., admitted that "of course, it's impossible not to wonder why."

Jimmy and Rosalynn Carter had invited in their own Baptist pastor, Robert Maddox, shortly after their loss in 1980 to ask him the same question. Presumably every president not reelected, doing his best and believing that he was right on the issues, has puzzled over defeat. Jimmy Carter would find the answer for himself, pounding a thousand nails, building homes for the poor across the nation, building a reputation as a humanitarian and peacemaker, redefining the role of a former president, winning the Nobel Peace Prize in 2002. And George Bush, Sr., would get his answer nine years later on the frigid morning of January 20, 2001, standing on a wooden platform behind the Capitol steps, watching his son being sworn in as the forty-third president of the United States before a crowd of thousands.

There was some irony in the fact that, after the 1988 election, staffers had earnestly pushed George W. to work in his father's White House.

Had it happened, had he been brought into government as had many presidential children before him, serving his role as loyalty enforcer, the irreverent realist, his father might have been reelected in 1992. But then, if that had happened, it would not have come to this. He would not be standing before his country as its new leader. His father and mother had been right all along.

The story of the Bush family is not over. There are triumphs and tragedies ahead. Indeed the presidency of George W. Bush may yet flame out in some dramatic, humiliating fashion. Perhaps they will repeat the Adams phenomena and both be one-term presidents. Perhaps the son, with nothing to prove, will walk away from the White House anyway, and choose family time alone over a second term.

Whatever happens, the inauguration of the second Bush will likely remain for some time a singular moment in the history of America. One hundred seventy-six years before, presidential son John Quincy Adams had taken the oath of office only a few yards away in the nearby chamber of the House of Representatives. But his father, John Adams, the second American president, had been ninety years old, too frail to move from the family home in Massachusetts and come to Washington to see it happen. Four presidents would share Mount Rushmore, but only one would savor that moment. In more than two centuries of American presidents and their children, it was a rare story indeed. It was a story of triumph for the needs of a child over the demands of a career, the needs of a family over the demands of the nation. And it had been rewarded.

EPILOGUE

*"From my daughters I have learned what
every parent knows of himself —
that I do not know how to raise children."*
— WOODROW WILSON

Eventually, the pain and the glory of the White
House years fade. Indeed, the president and the
first lady themselves pass from the scene leaving
only their children behind to make a feeble effort to sort out the pieces for history and stop
the tide of infuriating inaccuracies, some more
blatant and ridiculous than others. It is not so
much the dates and facts of the past that need
pruning and care, for they are just as fluid and
untrustworthy in the memories of presidential
children as they are in the memories of the rest
of us, but rather it is the spirit, the emotions, the
feelings that these children carry with them,
feelings that no one else has, feelings that cannot
be recaptured. Even those children, such as
Robert Lincoln, who tell us that they have no
memories, that they were never close to their
parents, reveal much that no White House aide

or authorized biographer welcomed into the inner circle could ever discover.

The trauma of many of these children rules out any post-presidential role. They bury themselves in joyous obscurity. When we found Jack Carter, many of his own colleagues were unaware that he was the son of a president. Some such as Powers Fillmore even felt the need to fight back.

Elizabeth Ann Harding Blaesing, in her eighties, lives on Mt. Hood in Oregon, quite content to spend the rest of her remarkable life far from the limelight. Conceived on a couch in a Senate office, Elizabeth was the illegitimate offspring of Warren G. Harding's affair with Nan Britton, thirty years his junior. As president, Harding arranged for Secret Service agents to hand deliver child support payments to the mother, but he refused to meet his daughter. In one dramatic moment, Nan Britton wrote of visiting the president in the White House and surprising him with the announcement that their daughter was at that very moment sitting on a park bench in Lafayette Square, easily seen from a second floor window. Would the president come to the window to see his daughter? Harding declined.

Today, Elizabeth Ann, the little girl who was dangling her feet on a park bench outside the White House, refuses to look back at Harding. She lives quietly and privately, refusing all interviews and rejecting the urgings of her grandchildren to speak up about her life.

Other children, such as Webb Hayes and Alice Roosevelt Longworth, saw much unfinished business with the passing of their parents and seized on every opportunity to right a wrong. Hayes set into motion the presidential library system. Alice refined and honed her perfectly timed sound bites for history. Long before television, she learned that a presidential child is not allowed much time on the stage. Words have to be chosen with care.

Theodore Roosevelt's home, Sagamore Hill, was eventually purchased by the U.S. Park Service and opened to the public. Archie Roosevelt, who lived nearby, would often slip in among the tourists, silently passing through the sacred rooms that held such personal memories. As the only surviving son, he would stand behind the stanchions and ropes, staring at the tables that had once overflowed with sumptuous meals and thrilling conversation. He saw the carpets where he had burned his knees and romped and played with the man who now graces Mt. Rushmore.

After one such visit he found one of the rooms rearranged. Theodore Roosevelt's death mask and the axle from Quentin's downed fighter plane had been removed to the basement storage vault. The Park Service deemed them too disturbing for tourists. Time was passing and history was swallowing up whole the people and events he had known and loved. Archie Roosevelt stood alone as one more presidential child, taking to his grave the feelings and sights and sounds that others would never know except on the sterile pages of history books.

For us, these presidents and first ladies are figures of history to be debated and categorized and vilified and cheered. It is an easy game to rate them and second-guess their policies. But long after they are gone, their children must struggle with their words and deeds in a much more complicated way, in the same way that we process our own feelings for our own parents. Many of them can still feel their mother's embrace, or smell their father's aftershave, and feel his rough whiskers with a bedtime kiss. They hear real voices, sometimes raised in panic and anger and sometimes as soft and gentle as a warm breeze. For the children of these icons of Americana, as for the rest of us, there is the ongoing, usually unconscious, struggle to satisfy themselves with the fact that they were once really loved and wanted and important in their parents' busy world. And that if by some chance they weren't, they can still somehow find a way to break that cycle and find value and meaning in the lives of their own children.

APPENDIX A

A CHRONOLOGICAL LIST
OF THE PRESIDENTS' CHILDREN

1. President George Washington
(1789–1797)

The first president had no biological children, but acquired a family when he married the widow Martha Custis. Two of her children from her previous marriage died during infancy, leaving the two remaining children, Jacky and Patsy Custis, to be reared by the Washingtons.

John "Jacky" Parke Custis (Son of Martha Washington by a previous marriage. Born 1754, died of camp fever at Yorktown, 1781.) Jacky Custis lived off a generous inheritance from his natural father and became a bit of a rascal in the eyes of historians for attempting to cheat his revered step-father, George Washington, in a cattle deal. He served briefly as Washington's aide-de-camp in the Revolutionary War, but died of camp fever (probably dysentery) at Yorktown, within weeks of joining the army.

Martha "Patsy" Parke Custis (She was a daughter of Martha Washington by a previous marriage. Born 1756, died on June 19, 1773.) Some years after Martha's marriage to George

609

Washington, her daughter, Martha Parke "Patsy" Custis, died at seventeen after a lifetime of epileptic seizures. General Washington, who treated her as his own daughter, was devastated.

Children of Jacky Parke Custis:

At Jacky Custis's death at Yorktown, he left four small children to be reared. After an "appropriate" time, Jacky's wife remarried, taking her two oldest children with her. The two youngest, Nelly and Wash Custis, stayed at Mt. Vernon with George and Martha. This was apparently a common practice for the time, and the families remained close and visited often. Years later, biographers sometimes referred to Wash as Washington's adopted son, but the adoption was never legalized, nor was it apparently ever intended to be.

Eleanor "Nelly" Custis Lewis (Born c. 1779, died 1852.) As a girl, Nelly Custis attended Mrs. Graham's School for young ladies. Her grandmother, Martha Washington, insisted she take three piano lessons a week, whether she wanted to or not. Nelly learned from her grandmother how to run a large plantation. She spent her life caring for the elder Washingtons, even after she married, although she was always in respectful awe of her famous stepfather.

When Nelly was eighteen, George Washington invited one of his nephews, Lawrence Lewis, to move to Mt. Vernon and help with entertaining and other tasks. Nelly and Lawrence were soon married, and their first child, daughter Frances, was born only days before Washington's death.

After Martha's passing, Nelly bore seven more children, four of whom died before they reached the age of two. After her husband's death, Nelly lived with a son until her own passing at the age of seventy-three. They buried her at her beloved Mt. Vernon.

George "Wash" Washington Parke Custis (Born c. 1780, died 1857.) When he was a youngster, Wash Custis seemed to take after his irresponsible father, and both George and Martha despaired of him. However, Wash eventually settled down and became quite successful. He attended St. John's College and Princeton, then served in the military as a commissioned officer. He married at twenty-three, and after George Washington's death, built a home on Arlington Heights on the Potomac River and oversaw the land willed to him. He wrote *Recollection and Private Memoirs of Washington*, an "invaluable remembrance of his famous step-grandfather." Wash died before it was printed. Wash and his wife, Mary Lee Fitzhugh, had four children, but only one survived infancy. That daughter, Mary Anne Randolph Custis, married Robert E. Lee, commanding general of the Confederacy.

2. President John Adams
(1797–1801)

Abigail "Nabby" Adams Smith (Born July 14, 1765, died of breast cancer on August 15, 1813. She was forty-eight.) She was also nicknamed "Amelia," which some historians erroneously list as her middle name. Nabby was the

611

first of five children born to John and Abigail Adams. At seventeen, she was engaged to a young Boston lawyer named Royall Tyler. The young couple's plans were thwarted by a disapproving father who ordered her to join him in Paris, where he was a representative for the newly formed United States. Eventually, Nabby met and married William Stephens Smith, an aide to her father. That marriage produced four children and unhappy endings. Smith reportedly disappeared for months at a time, paid little attention to his wife or children's well-being, left them in devastating need, and wasted huge amounts of money on unsuccessful land speculations in the West.

John Quincy Adams (Born July 11, 1767. He died of a cerebral hemorrhage on February 3, 1848.) John Quincy became the first of only two presidential children to follow his father's footsteps into the White House. He graduated from Harvard and practiced law in Boston before being appointed by President Washington as minister to the Netherlands. In London, he met and married Louisa Catherine Johnson, the daughter of the United States minister to England. In 1802, John, with his family, moved back to the United States and the political scene, eventually winning election to the United States Senate. After an appointment as minister to Russia, he served as secretary of state under President James Monroe, where he helped to create the Monroe Doctrine.

In 1824, John Quincy Adams became the sixth American president, despite losing both the general election and electoral vote to General Andrew Jackson. Since neither candidate had achieved an electoral majority, the election was thrown into the House of Representatives, which selected the politically savvy Adams over the popular, yet unproven western military leader, Jackson. That election was reversed four years later when Jackson was elected in a landslide. Adams spent his last years in Washington, D.C., as a U.S. representative from Massachusetts, where he became an outspoken opponent of slavery and an advocate of woman suffrage.

Susanna Adams (Born December 28, 1768, she died in Boston on February 4, 1770.) She was the only child of John and Abigail not to survive infancy, dying shortly after her first birthday. "Adams was so upset by the loss he could not speak of it for years."

Charles Adams (Born on May 29, 1770. He died of cirrhosis of the liver on November 30, 1800. He was thirty years old.) As an eleven-year-old child, he was lost at sea for a period of months and presumed dead. The event seems to have cast a pall over his entire life. He attended Harvard, but never practiced law as planned. He married Sally Smith and they had two children, but by 1797 he was impoverished and floundering in depression and alcoholism.

Thomas Boylston Adams (Born on September 15, 1772, he died on March 12, 1832, at fifty-nine years of age.) Thomas graduated from Harvard in 1790, studied law and then joined his illustrious brother, John Quincy, at diplomatic posts on the Continent. He returned to the

United States when his father was elected president, and for several months lived with the first family in Philadelphia, then the capital of the new nation. Later, he returned to Massachusetts, married Ann Harold and began practicing law, eventually being named a state court judge. His great scholarship in literature and philosophy added to the Adams family reputation, but a propensity for luxurious living and hefty personal debts nagged him throughout his life. Overshadowed by the achievements of his presidential father and brother, Thomas was eventually lost to public life. It is as if he "failed by comparison."

3. President Thomas Jefferson (1801–1809)

Martha "Patsy" Washington Jefferson Randolph (Born on September 27, 1772, she died of apoplexy on October 10, 1836.) When her mother died, ten-year-old Martha quickly assumed the feminine head of the household. It was a position she would hold for life. Nicknamed "Patsy" by her father, she enjoyed a close bond with the third president, accompanying him to the first Continental Congress in Philadelphia, and witness to the most historic moments during the birth of our nation. At eighteen, she married Thomas Mann Randolph, Jr., and the couple became parents of twelve children. Her son, James Madison Randolph, was the first child born in the White House. Patsy served for a time as the White House hostess for her famous father while her husband Randolph served in Congress.

Randolph later was elected governor of Virginia (1819–1822), but also suffered several mental breakdowns and bankruptcies, as well as a growing, deep resentment of his legendary father-in-law. When Jefferson died in 1826, Martha inherited his debts. Her troubles mounted two years later when her husband died, also leaving a mountain of debt. She lived in penury with one or another of her children until her death.

Jane Randolph Jefferson (Born on April 3, 1774 and died seventeen months later, September 1775.)

The only **Jefferson son** was born May 28, 1777, and died within days, June 14, 1777. History has lost his name. During these momentous years, Jefferson was often away at the Continental Congress in Philadelphia. It was during these painful losses that Thomas Jefferson penned the Declaration of Independence.

Mary "Polly" "Maria" Jefferson Eppes (Born on August 1, 1778, she died from complications of childbirth on April 17, 1804. She was twenty-five.) Nicknamed "Polly" by her family, she was separated from her father for many years of her early life. It provoked in her a desperate need to secure his attention and approval. After her mother's death she traveled to Paris to join her father and older sister Martha, where she became known as Maria. It was the name she chose to keep the rest of her life. Accompanying Maria was a Jefferson household slave, the fourteen-year-old Sally Hemings, who later may have borne several illegitimate children with the man who would become the third president. Back in Virginia, Maria married her cousin, John Wayles Eppes, who became a member of the House of Representatives and the Senate.

Lucy Elizabeth I (Born on November 3, 1780, died a few months later on April 15, 1781.) At the time of Lucy's birth, Jefferson was Governor of Virginia. Little Lucy was born in Richmond, where the government had moved because of the Revolutionary War. With British soldiers closing in, Jefferson sent his family into the wilderness to safety. They fled through snow and wintry cold. The five-week-old baby Lucy fell ill and never recovered. For the rest of his life, Jefferson tenderly kept a private note from his wife and a lock of hair from the first Lucy.

Lucy Elizabeth II (Born May 8, 1782, died October 13, 1784.) Thomas Jefferson's wife Martha died shortly after the difficult birth of the second Lucy. Jefferson was in Paris when he received a letter from Dr. James Currie, stating that two-year-old Lucy had fallen "a martyr to the Complicated evils of teething, worms and Hooping Cough . . . [sic]." The grief-stricken Jefferson castigated himself for not having brought the baby with him to Paris.

Children of Sally Hemings:

Were the children born to Sally Hemings fathered by Thomas Jefferson? In the late 1990s, headlines and a television miniseries trumpeted the fact that DNA evidence confirmed the illegitimate liaison between Hemings and the third president of the United States. Closer inspection of the "evidence" has cast doubts on the conclusiveness of the DNA results, with other theories and explanations being proposed. My own research of the other Jefferson children leads me to believe that the president was indeed the father of Sally's children. **Tom** was born in 1790 in France during Jefferson's time as the U.S. representative, **Harriet I** on October 5, 1795, **Beverly** in 1798, **Harriet II** in May of 1801, **Madison** in January 1805 and **Eston** in May 1808.

4. President James Madison
(1809–1817)

John Payne Todd (Son of Dolley Madison, born 1792, died 1852.) The fourth president had no biological children, but married Dorothea "Dolley" Dandridge Payne Todd, a widow, who was the mother of two. One of her children died just before their marriage. The lifelong misconduct of her son, John Payne Todd, burdened both Dolley and the husband who loved her. The boy abused all privileges, refused to accept responsibility for his actions, and was an alcoholic, a gambler, and a thief. The president sent him to Russia on a peace commission, where the son embarrassed the delegation by carousing with "easy" women. James Madison had to pay for expensive art he contracted for in London, and for his female "indiscretions." After Todd returned to the United States, he often disappeared, drinking, for long periods of time. Only when he ran out of money and wrote his mother for more would she know that he was alive and where he was.

Madison prepared a packet that he gave to Dolley's brother, asking him to give it to Dolley after his death. In it were records of payments that he had made for John Payne Todd's debts, totaling about $20,000. These payments had been made without Dolley's knowledge, and were in addition to another $20,000 in payments of which she was already aware. Madison wrote that he did it "as evidence of the sacrifice he had made to insure her tranquillity by concealing from her the ruinous extravagance of her son."

After Madison's death, John attempted to cheat his mother by selling the former president's priceless personal papers. Congress eventually purchased a large portion of Madison's papers. An enraged John Todd threatened to sue the congressional trustees. It was the final blow. At eighty years of age, Dolley wrote him a bitter, disappointed letter, begging him to take back his threats. "Your mother would have no wish to live," she wrote, "after her son issued such threats . . ." She was never to receive an answer and died the following year.

5. President James Monroe (1817–1825)

Eliza Kortright Monroe Hay (Born December 1786, died in 1835, at the age of forty-nine.) Educated in Paris, Eliza grew to love the cultured life of Europe. She eventually married George Hay, a prominent American attorney. Eliza spent much of her time during her father's presidency as White House hostess, substituting for her invalid mother who was unable to entertain. Eliza became known, perhaps unfairly, as a domineering perfectionist who alienated much of Washington's social and diplomatic world with her pretensions. Following her father's death, she returned to France where she converted to the Catholic faith shortly before her death.

J. S. Monroe (Born in May 1799, he lived a little more than two years before dying on September 28, 1801.) He was the only son of James and Elizabeth Monroe.

Maria Hester Monroe Gouverneur (Born in 1803, she died in 1850, at the age of forty-seven.) She was the first *presidential* child to be married in the White House. "It was love at first sight" when she met Samuel Lawrence Gouverneur who worked as a junior secretary in the Monroe administration. In 1820, the couple married. They eventually moved to New York City, where Samuel was appointed postmaster. By the late 1820s, James Monroe, widowed and in dire financial straits, turned to Maria and her husband for help. He lived his final years with the Gouverneurs.

6. President John Quincy Adams (1825–1829)

George Washington Adams (Born April 12, 1801, his mysterious death on April 30, 1829, is considered by most historians as a suicide. He was twenty-eight years old.) Named for the father of our country, he was both a son and grandson of presidents. Unfortunately, despite early signs of brilliance, George was never able to aspire to the lofty plans his father had laid out for him. He graduated from Harvard, practiced law and was elected to the Massachusetts state legislature, but was unable to sustain any level of success. Beset by personal, secret scandals and mounting debts, he turned to alcohol before his death. He either fell or jumped from a passenger liner in New York Harbor.

John Adams II (Born on the Fourth of July in 1803, he died an alcoholic on October 23, 1834. He was only thirty-one.) John was an enthusiastic youngster, free from the pensive moodiness that afflicted his older brother. Educated at the best schools, he excelled in sports. But his perfectionist father greatly disapproved of his lackluster performance at Harvard and of the ribald antics that led to his embarrassing expulsion. John bested his brothers by winning the hand of his cousin, Mary Catherine Hellen. They were married in the second wedding ceremony to take place in the White House. Neither of the other brothers was in attendance.

John worked as a secretary in his father's White House, but a public humiliation by an enemy of the family derailed any political aspirations. For a while, he managed the family's business, but soon it began to lose money. Apparently his enthusiastic personality, always contrasted with his sensitive older brother George, was not enough to save him, for he likewise turned to alcohol for escape and died young.

Charles Francis Adams (Born on August 18, 1807, he died of a stroke on November 21, 1886, at the age of seventy-nine, beloved and respected by his peers.) The third child of the nation's sixth chief executive might possibly have become the third generation of his family to become president, but he insisted on championing causes ahead of their time. Charles was fluent in several languages, graduated from Harvard at seventeen and apprenticed in law under Daniel Webster. At twenty-two, he married Abigail Brown Brooks, daughter of a wealthy Bostonian, then turned to promoting the radical position of the abolition of slavery. He inherited his father-in-law's huge estate, enabling him to pursue politics without financial pressures, and by 1841 he entered the Massachusetts State legislature.

In 1858, Charles was elected to the House of Representatives. He was the third generation of Adamses to be appointed ambassador to the Court of St. James, where he gave his greatest service to America. During the Civil War, Charles arrived in England to find the Crown ready to step in militarily with support for the Confederacy. He negotiated, bullied, and reasoned behind the scenes, and eventually England stayed her hand. Historian John S. Cooper states that Charles Francis Adams's work was "arguably the greatest contribution to Union victory made by any individual in the war." In 1872 and again in 1876, Charles's name was placed in nomination for the presidency. By that time, however, he was leading the charge for civil service reform, another controversial idea years ahead of its time. Some historians, then and now, believe that Charles might possibly have been elected president had he been willing to do what was popular, rather than what was right.

Louisa Catherine Adams (Born in 1811, died in 1812.) The only daughter of John Quincy and Louisa Adams was born and died in St. Petersburg, Russia, far from the United States. The baby may have succumbed to the ferocious Russian winter.

7. *President Andrew Jackson (1829–1837)*

Andrew Jackson, Jr. (Born December 4, 1808. Many historic accounts mistakenly date his birth in 1809, this because he was adopted a few days into the new year. He died of lockjaw after being shot in a hunting accident in 1865.) He was one of a pair of twins, nephews of Andrew Jackson's wife, Rachel, but he was adopted by the Jacksons at birth and named after his new father. After Rachel's death, Andy, Jr., divided his time between Philadelphia (with his twin brother), the Hermitage in Tennessee, and the nation's capital. He married Sarah Yorke in 1831. The remainder of his life was spent accumulating debts through risky ventures and bad management. After Jackson, Sr., died in 1845, the adopted son sold the Hermitage, the family home.

8. *President Martin Van Buren (1837–1841)*

Abraham Van Buren (Born on November 27, 1807, he died March 15, 1873.) He was a West Point graduate who served two years on the frontier before resigning his commission to become his father's secretary in the White House. A year later he married Angelica Singleton, heir to a wealthy South Carolina family. After leaving the White House, Abe served in the Mexican War, retiring from the army in 1854. He spent much of his life in the shadow of his famous father, spending many years editing and publishing the Van Buren presidential papers and serving as an apologist for his father's legacy.

John Van Buren (Born February 18, 1810, he died at sea of kidney failure on October 13, 1866. He was fifty-six.) John Van Buren is one of the most colorful and notorious of presidential children. Graduating from Yale in his teens and admitted to the New York bar in his twenties, he was nevertheless able to squander this stellar head start on life. When his father was appointed minister to England, John tagged along, beginning a lifelong pursuit of drinking, gambling, and women. While American critics tagged him "Prince John" for his easy acceptance among European elites, he was still able to return stateside and build a career in law and as a U.S. congressman. Marriage to Elizabeth Van der Poel brought only a short-lived respite to his notorious partying. Incredibly talented, he had his moments of courage, standing boldly against slavery, but his personal life descended into further scandal, and his alcoholism left him an invalid.

Martin Van Buren, Jr. (Born December 20, 1812, he died of tuberculosis at age forty-two on March 19, 1855.) The third son of the eighth president never married and spent most of his life serving his father, first as a White House secretary and then as a personal assistant, helping to arrange the former president's papers for posterity. When "Mat" fell ill, his father sent him to Europe to find a cure, but the son died in Paris, his grieving father, the former president, at his side.

Smith Thompson Van Buren (Born January 16, 1817, he died in 1876 at fifty-nine years of age.) The last Van Buren son spent his adult life defending the reputation and historic profile of his father, while simultaneously covering for the notoriety of his brother, John. Little is known about his personal life, except that he married twice and fathered at least seven children. Clever and argumentative, he survived his father by fourteen years and eventually transcended his brothers as the chief apologist of the Van Buren presidency.

9. President William Henry Harrison (1841)

Elizabeth "Betsy" Bassett Harrison Short (Born September 29, 1796, she died on September 26, 1846, three days short of her fiftieth birthday.) First child of the seventh president and Anna Tuthill Symmes, Betsy's famous Indian-fighting father was often gone during her childhood. She married John Cleves Short, and the newlyweds were given farmland by General Harrison. Distraught over the deaths of so many of her brothers and sisters, she herself died five years after the untimely loss of her father, who served as president for only thirty days.

John Cleves Symmes Harrison (Born October 28, 1798, he died in controversy at thirty-four years of age on October 30, 1830.) "Symmes" lived his entire life in the Indiana Territory and was a popular and helpful figure to farmers and settlers in the region. He married Clarissa Pike, a daughter of the famous General Zebulon Pike, who had discovered Pike's Peak in Colorado. They had six children. Aided by his father, Symmes received an appointment to a position in the government land office in Vincennes, Indiana. After serving for years with a reputation for integrity, Symmes was caught in the political crosshairs of his father's political enemies, accused of embezzlement, and fired. There was an explanation for the events but, driven by a desire to hurt General Harrison, opposing politicians buried the facts. Disillusioned and stunned by his experience, Symmes died in the middle of the crisis.

Lucy Singleton Harrison Este (Born September 1800, she died April 7, 1826.) She married David Este, a judge of Ohio's Superior Court, and bore four children before her death at twenty-six.

William Henry Harrison, Jr. (Born September 3, 1802, died an alcoholic at age thirty-five on February 6, 1838.) He was not a high achiever in college and had a mediocre law career in Cincinnati before marrying Jane Findlay, daughter of a close family friend.

John Scott Harrison (Born October 4, 1804, he died May 25, 1878, at the age of seventy-three.) He was a two-term congressman who spent most of his life running the family's farm in

Ohio. He fathered three children with his first wife, Lucretia, and, after her death, six more children with his second wife, Elizabeth. Within five years of the death of his president father, nine of the ten children in the family were dead. Only John Scott survived. Ten years after his own passing, his son, Benjamin, was inaugurated as the twenty-third president of the United States, making John Scott the only presidential son to have his own son win the office. The greatest headlines he generated were after his passing, when his body was stolen by students at the Cincinnati Medical School and hidden in a dumbwaiter.

Benjamin Harrison (Born 1806, he died June 9, 1840, at the age of thirty-three.) He was taken prisoner during the Texas War of Independence, and his release drew heavy and inaccurate criticism of cowardice from the political enemies of the family. He had three children with his first wife, Louisa, and two with Mary, his second spouse. As a youth, his father had been forced to abandon his medical studies, but Benjamin picked up the baton and became a physician. He died only months before his father became president.

Mary Symmes Harrison Thornton (Born January 22, 1809, she died November 16, 1842, at the youthful age of thirty-three.) She married a physician when she was twenty, gave birth to six children, and died a year after the death of her presidential father.

Carter Bassett Harrison (Born October 26, 1811, died August 12, 1839 at twenty-seven.) By age twenty-five, Carter had finished his education and begun practicing law. He married Mary Anne Sutherland, fathered one child, and died slightly more than a year before his father was elected to the nation's top office.

Anna Tuthill Harrison Taylor (Born October 28, 1813, she died July 5, 1845.) As in the case of his other children, Anna lived in the shadow of her famous father. She married her cousin, named William Henry Harrison Taylor in honor of the general, and died at thirty-one years of age, less than two years after her father's tragic death in the White House. But another historic account dates her death at 1865, reporting that she had six children born after the 1845 date, which is often quoted as her official date of death.

James Findlay Harrison (Born in 1814, died in 1817.) He was the last Harrison to be born, but the first to die, setting off a chain reaction that would take nine out of the ten Harrison children to early graves.

10. President John Tyler
(1841–1845)

Mary Tyler Jones (Born April 15, 1815, died June 17, 1848.) Mary was the first of fifteen children born to John Tyler, eight with his first wife, Letitia Christian. Mary married Henry Lightfoot Jones, a "prosperous Tidewater planter." On a visit to the White House, Mary gave birth to her second son, Robert, who later served with honor in the Civil War. They had three children.

Robert Tyler (Born September 9, 1816, died

December 3, 1877.) He was an introverted child who overcame his handicap to become a powerful and effective lawyer and politician. In his twenties he married Priscilla Cooper and worked as a private secretary in his father's White House. The couple lived in the mansion, with Priscilla serving as White House hostess for an invalid first lady. Later, Robert rose to prominence in Pennsylvania politics, becoming a confidant and early supporter of President James Buchanan. During the Civil War he fled south, serving as registrar for the Confederate treasury. Time and again, Tyler refused opportunities to trade on his fame as a presidential son, maintaining a dignity and integrity that won deep friendships and wide respect. In later years he became the Alabama Democratic state chairman and editor of the Montgomery *Advisor*. He had nine children.

John Tyler, Jr. (Born April 27, 1819, died January 26, 1896.) Famous for defending his father in a much-publicized duel with a Richmond newspaper editor, John, Jr.'s, life is often seen as a frustrated struggle to live up to the esteem held for both his presidential father and his respected older brother. Junior was a writer, lawyer and politician who was not successful in any of these endeavors. He became an alcoholic. John, Jr., married Martha "Mattie" Rochelle, but lived with her only a few months before trying to get a divorce. Their on and off marriage produced three children.

Letitia (Letty) Tyler Semple (Born May 11, 1821, she died December 28, 1907.) A capable, highly self-motivated woman, Letitia stepped in as a substitute mother to the growing Tyler clan when her mother suffered a paralyzing stroke. When President Tyler's first wife eventually died, Letitia briefly succeeded her sister-in-law, Priscilla, as White House hostess. It all ended when the fifty-four-year-old president married twenty-four-year-old Julia Gardiner. The rivalry between the two women, first daughter and first lady, became a lifelong obsession.

Elizabeth "Lizzie" Tyler Waller (Born July 11, 1823, she died on June 1, 1850, from childbirth complications.) On January 31, 1842, she married William Waller in a White House wedding. They moved to Lynchburg, Virginia, where they had five children before her death at the youthful age of twenty-six.

Anne Contesse Tyler (Born April 1825, she died three months later in July 1825. Cause of death unknown.)

Alice Tyler Denison (Born March 23, 1827, "she died suddenly of colic" on June 8, 1854, at the age of twenty-seven.) She was just a teenager when her father became president. Alice was described as "tall and fat" by historians. She married Henry Mandeville Denison, the handsome Episcopalian rector of the Williamsburg parish. They had two children.

Tazewell Tyler (Born December 6, 1830, he died January 8, 1874.) The youngest of the eight children born to the tenth chief executive and first wife, Letitia, Taz was fourteen when his father married the second time. He became a physician, served during the Civil War, then moved to California, where his life ended in divorce and alcoholism. He had two children.

David Gardiner "Gardie" Tyler (Born July 12, 1846, he died September 5, 1927, at the age of eighty-one.) "Gardie" was the first of seven children born to Tyler's second wife, Julia. He left Washington College as a sixteen-year-old to serve in the Confederate Army. After the Civil War, he worked as a lawyer and in a number of elected offices, including the U.S. Congress. He and wife, Mary Morris Jones, had five children.

John Alexander "Alex" Tyler (Born April 7, 1848, he died at age thirty-five on September 1, 1883.) He ran away from home at fourteen to enlist in the Confederate Army. He was rejected as too young, then later joined the Confederate Navy. His wanderlust never quenched, Alex enlisted in the German Army at the outbreak of the Franco-Prussian War in 1870. He married a cousin but was often separated from her, working as an engineer and a surveyor in the American West. His death has spawned several mysterious theories, including murder, but most historians accept an account that he died of dysentery after drinking contaminated water in New Mexico in 1883. He had one child.

Julia Tyler Spencer (Born December 25, 1849, she died at twenty-one years of age on May 8, 1871, from childbirth complications.) She studied at a convent school in Nova Scotia, then married William Spencer, who ran up staggering debts, worked in the Colorado silver mines and California citrus groves. He eventually disappeared from the family's sight forever. She had one child.

Lachlan Tyler (Born December 2, 1851, he died January 26, 1902, at age fifty.) Though trained as a doctor, he lived much of his early married life in poverty. For years Lachlan unashamedly tried to use his credentials as a president's son to open doors but was persistently unsuccessful. Eventually, on his own merits, he obtained a position as a surgeon in the U.S. Navy, then achieved measured success in private practice. He and wife, Georgia Powell, had no children.

Lyon Gardiner Tyler (Born August 1853, he died February 12, 1935.) He practiced law for a time, but spent most of his life as an educator, serving as president of the College of William and Mary for thirty-one years. He was an author and respected historian. Married twice, he had three children by his first wife and two by his second. His last child was born in 1928, when Lyon Tyler was age seventy-five.

Robert Fitzwalter Tyler (Born March 12, 1856, he died December 30, 1927.) Forced by a lack of funds to drop out of Georgetown College, Robert turned to the life of a Virginia farmer. He fathered three children with wife, Fannie Glenn.

Pearl Tyler Ellis (Born June 20, 1860, she died June 30, 1947.) The last of the Tyler children, she was born before the Civil War and lived to see the end of World War Two. Pearl was a graduate of Sacred Heart in Washington, D.C. She married Major William Mumford Ellis and lived most of her life near Roanoke, Virginia, a homemaker and a mother, far removed from the traditional pressures of a presidential daughter. She had eight children.

11. President James K. Polk
(1845–1849)

Marshall Polk was the nephew and personal ward of President James K. Polk. The president was married to Sarah Childress when he was twenty-eight and she twenty. No children were born during their twenty-five years together, but the nephew provided plenty of stress. Dismissed from both Georgetown and West Point, Marshall was an alcoholic who "ended his life in prison."

12. President Zachary Taylor
(1849–1850)

Anne Margaret Mackall Taylor Wood (Born April 9, 1811, she died in Germany on December 2, 1875.) Anne married an army surgeon and gave birth to four children. During the Civil War, her husband, Robert C. Wood, fought for the Union, while two of her sons fought for the Confederacy. A widow by the war's end, she journeyed to Germany, where she lived with a daughter who had married a baron.

Sarah "Knox" Taylor Davis (Born March 6, 1814, she died of malaria at the age of twenty-one on September 15, 1835.) As a young girl she had survived a terrible bout of malaria in the Mississippi Delta. It had taken two of her sisters. As a young lady, over the objections of her parents, she married a military man, Jefferson Davis, who took her back to the same region. He would eventually become the president of the Confederate States of America, but she would not live to see it happen. She died three months after the wedding, still on her honeymoon, of the malaria that had almost taken her as a girl.

Octavia Pannel Taylor (Born August 16, 1816, she died of malaria on July 8, 1820. She was three years old.)

Margaret Smith Taylor (Born July 27, 1819, she died October 22, 1820.) Only three months after the death of her sister, one-year-old Margaret was taken by malaria as well.

Mary Elizabeth Taylor Bliss Dandridge (Born April 20, 1824, she died July 26, 1909.) "Betty," as she was called, served as White House hostess for her mother, who refused to entertain. She was immensely popular and was considered an elegant beauty. She married Major William Bliss, who died in 1853. She then married Philip Dandridge. Their home in Winchester, Virginia, became known as the "Salon of the Shenandoah Valley." She had no children.

Richard Taylor (Born January 27, 1826, he died on April 12, 1879.) Early education in Europe meant long separations from the family, but it seemed to do no harm to Richard Taylor. He later served as an aide-de-camp to his father during the Mexican campaign, and as his private secretary when the general became president.

During the Civil War he rose to fame as a Confederate general, fighting with Stonewall Jackson in the Valley Campaign. He was the last of the Southern generals to surrender east of the Mississippi. As in the case of a very few other respected presidential children, he refused to accept favors or promotion because of his name, earning even begrudging praise from Northern observers. A plantation manager, soldier, politician and author, Taylor has been hailed by many as a "successful" presidential son who earned his own reputation on its own merits. He died penniless but with dignity at fifty-three. Taylor had been suffering from severe internal congestion, resulting from a long battle with rheumatoid arthritis.

13. President Millard Fillmore (1850–1853)

Millard Powers Fillmore (Born April 25, 1828, he died November 15, 1889.) "Powers" served his father as a personal secretary during the latter's time as president. A student at Harvard, he later practiced law and was appointed as a federal court clerk, but much of the rest of his life is a mystery. He had no children, was never married, and before his death arranged for the destruction of all his private papers, including letters to and from his beloved mother and presidential father.

Mary Abigail "Abby" Fillmore (Born March 27, 1832, historians differ on the date of her death. It was July 26, 1854.) Ironically, the same year she was born, immigrants "landing in Quebec" brought with them the dreaded plague of cholera. It would kill her twenty-two years later. Abby lived a charmed life as a child and teenager. After the death of Zachary Taylor, her vice presidential father moved into the White

House where she often served as hostess, assisting her mother, Abigail. Fillmore was defeated in the election of 1852, but an ailing first lady insisted on proper protocol and attended the inauguration of their successor, Franklin Pierce. It was a wet, cold, and snowy morning; she died less than a month later of pneumonia. The following year, twenty-two-year-old Abby followed her to the grave. Like her brother, Abby never married.

14. President Franklin Pierce (1853–1857)

Franklin Pierce (Born February 2, 1836, he died three days later on February 5, 1836.) With each successive death of her children, Jane Appleton Pierce believed more strongly that God was displeased by her husband's political ambitions.

Frank Robert Pierce (Born August 27, 1839, he died of typhus fever on November 14, 1843.) By the time of the death of this much-loved four-year-old, Franklin Pierce himself had begun to wonder if God was taking his children. "It was doubtless needed," he conjectured, "a chastisement."

Benjamin Pierce (Born April 13, 1841, he died January 16, 1853.) With his wife convinced that retirement from politics was God's will, Franklin Pierce retired from the U.S. Senate to practice law in New Hampshire. But in 1852, in a fractured Democrat National Convention, he won the presidential nomination on the 49th ballot as a dark horse compromise solution. His wife fainted at the news and prayed fervently for his defeat. But her greatest fears were realized. Pierce won, and eleven-year-old Benny was killed in a train accident before his parents' eyes, only days before the inauguration.

15. President James Buchanan (1857–1861)

The only president never to marry, Buchanan was engaged at twenty-eight, but his fiancée died from a sedative overdose. Though successful in winning the highest elected office in the land, the fifteenth president remained a bachelor until his death.

16. President Abraham Lincoln (1861–1865)

Robert Todd Lincoln (Born August 1, 1843, he died July 25, 1926.) He served ably as secretary of war and as minister to Great Britain. He was an effective president of the Pullman Corporation, a giant American enterprise in its day. Considered by many historians as one of the most successful of presidential children, Robert married Mary Harlan, a cabinet secretary's daughter, had three children and lived into his eighties.

Edward Baker "Eddie" Lincoln (Born March 10, 1846, he is said to have died of tuberculosis at age three on February 1, 1850.)

William Wallace "Willie" Lincoln (Born December 21, 1850, he died of pneumonia or, according to some sources, typhoid fever, on February 20, 1862.) "Willy" and little brother

"Tad" were the terrors of the White House, whose childish antics disgusted and delighted staff and visitors. It was Willie's death at eleven years of age, in the middle of the Civil War, that pushed First Lady Mary Lincoln over the emotional edge and refined the president's ability to empathize with the nation's suffering.

Thomas "Tad" Lincoln (Born April 4, 1853, the best sources say he died of tuberculosis as a teenager on July 15, 1871.) Young Tad suffered from a speech impediment, which may have bought him some sympathy for his outrageous antics. Staff, observers, and even an older brother, Robert, were scandalized by Lincoln's indulgence of his youngest child. He was twelve when his father was assassinated. His distraught and emotionally disturbed mother hauled him off to Europe, where he was enrolled and withdrawn from a succession of private schools. He died shortly after their return to the States.

17. President Andrew Johnson (1865–1869)

Martha Johnson Patterson (Born October 25, 1828, she died on July 10, 1901.) Martha was another presidential daughter to serve as a White House hostess in place of an invalid or reluctant mother. But this first child of Andrew and Eliza Johnson transformed the executive mansion, helping to create the elegance that it enjoys to this day. It was a feat all the more remarkable, considering that it happened simultaneously with the impeachment of her father and a bitter relationship with Congress.

Charles Johnson (Born February 19, 1830, he died on April 4, 1863.) Before the outbreak of the Civil War, Charles studied medicine and co-owned a pharmacy. He soon plunged into severe alcoholism. He fought for the Union army and died at thirty-three in a horse accident.

Mary Johnson Stover Brown (Born May 8, 1832, she died on April 19, 1883.) Mary served with her sister as White House hostess during her father's administration but lived most of her life in Watauga Valley, Tennessee. Her first husband, Daniel Stover, was a Civil War hero for the Union. They had three children. She was soon estranged from her second husband, William Brown, but postponed divorce until her father died.

Robert Johnson (Born February 22, 1834, a likely suicide, died on April 22, 1869.) Robert became a colonel in the Union army, beloved by his men, but after the war his drinking problem descended into a full-blown crisis. He served briefly as a secretary to his father in the White House, where he caused a scandal when prostitutes were allegedly seen leaving his office. A highly eligible bachelor, he never married.

Andrew Johnson, Jr. (Born August 6, 1852, he died March 12, 1879.) After seeing his parents suffer over the alcoholism of his older brothers, Andy promised his parents that he would never touch "intoxicating liquors" and would live a long life and care for them in their old age. Married to Bessie May Kumbaugh, he tried to launch his own newspaper, but it was seen by critics as a propaganda sheet for his father, and soon failed. A faithful teetotaler to the end, it did not save him. He died a youthful twenty-six, a few years after the death of his parents.

18. President Ulysses S. Grant
(1869–1877)

Fredrick Dent Grant (Born May 30, 1850, he died of cancer on April 11, 1912.) As a child, he was with his father on the major battlefields of the Civil War and went on to graduate from West Point. He married a French daughter of wealth but struggled financially. He served as the New York City police commissioner, minister to Austria-Hungary and eventually advanced to the second highest rank in the U.S. Army, becoming the second General Grant. Nevertheless, the Senate turned him down for a cabinet position, with editorials claiming that he was being considered only because of his father's influence.

Ulysses Simpson "Buck" Grant, Jr. (Born July 22, 1852, he died September 25, 1929.) A lawyer, sometime politician and businessman, Buck studied at Harvard, the University of Göttingen in Germany, and Columbia Law School. He was briefly a White House secretary to his father, and much later made a bid for the U.S. Senate from California. It was a controversial campaign in which charges of bribery were unfairly leveled against him. It was Buck who talked his father into joining his new Grant and Ward brokerage firm. It eventually dissolved into scandal, sending some of the partners to prison.

Before his death, Buck Grant made a comeback of sorts, establishing himself in San Diego society and building the U. S. Grant Hotel.

Ellen Wrenshall "Nellie" Grant Sartoris Jones (Born July 4, 1855, she died August 30, 1922.) Nellie was thirteen years old when her father became president and only eighteen when she was married to the British diplomat Algernon Sartoris (pronounced "sartriss") in a spectacular White House wedding. The couple sailed for England, while a brokenhearted President Grant went to her empty bedroom and wept. The young couple had four children and became social elites, their every move chronicled by an insatiable and curious press. Her husband turned out to be an alcoholic and womanizer. She obtained a divorce, returning to the States a wealthy woman. Eventually, she remarried, but fell ill and was paralyzed during her last years.

Jesse Root Grant (Born February 6, 1858, he died June 8, 1934.) An author, engineer, and father of two, Jesse's defining moment may have been his around-the-world trip with his father following the White House years. Jesse never stopped traveling. He eventually divorced his first wife and remarried. At one point he made a bid for the presidency, but the press and the country ignored his candidacy.

19. President Rutherford B. Hayes
(1877–1881)

Birchard Austin Hayes (Born November 4, 1853, he died January 24, 1926.) A Harvard Law School graduate, Birchard spent thirty-six years in the legal profession as a successful tax and real estate attorney in Toledo, Ohio. He married Mary Sherman and had five children.

James Webb Cook Hayes (Born March 20, 1856, he died July 26, 1934.) Known all his life as "Webb," he later officially dropped the "James" from his name. He served as a secretary in his father's White House before launching a successful business career that spanned decades and made him rich. He reorganized one small enterprise, which would grow into the Union Carbide Corporation. Married to Mary Otis Miller, with no children, wealth allowed Webb the time to pursue his lifelong love of the military. He repeatedly risked his life as a soldier of fortune around the globe, but lived to see his seventy-eighth birthday.

Rutherford Platt Hayes (Born June 24, 1858, he died July 31, 1927.) Underestimated during his youth, he helped found the American Library Association and became one of the nation's most important figures in the development of a national library system. He married a cousin, Lucy Hayes Platt and had three children.

Joseph "Jody" Thompson Hayes (Born December 21, 1861, he died of dysentery on June 24, 1863.) With the Civil War interrupting his family life, General Rutherford B. Hayes finally arranged for his family to meet at a camp along the Kanawha River in the new state of West Virginia. He longed to see more of this new son, Jody, supposedly the very image of the general. But the baby died of dysentery, and what was meant to be a joyous reunion became a funeral instead.

George Crook Hayes (Born September 29, 1864, he died May 24, 1866.) A "sweet, bright boy," George died of scarlet fever before his second birthday.

Fanny Hayes Smith (Born September 2, 1867, she died March 18, 1950.) The only daughter in a family of seven brothers, she lived for her father. When they left the White House and her mother died, Fanny assumed the role of hostess and accompanied her father to speaking engagements. Only after her father's death did she marry navy ensign Harry Eaton Smith, who eventually became an instructor as the Naval Academy. She had one child and changed her name back to Hayes after the death of her husband.

Scott Russell Hayes (Born February 8, 1871, he died of cancer on May 6, 1923.) As a six-year-old, Scott joined other children on the South Lawn of the White House for the first Easter egg roll. It would become a messy, unruly, beloved White House tradition. He worked as an executive for a number of railroad service companies, and lived in New York. He married Maude Anderson but had no children.

Manning Force Hayes (Born August 1, 1873, he died shortly after his first birthday on August 28, 1874.)

20. President James A. Garfield (1881)

Eliza Arabella "Trot" Garfield (Born July 3, 1860, she died of diphtheria on December 3, 1863. She was three years old.)

Harry Augustus "Hal" Garfield (Born October 11, 1863, he died December 12, 1942.) A businessman and lawyer, Hal spent most of his life in education, teaching at Princeton University and Williams College, where he served as president. He married Belle Hartford Mason and had four children. While at Princeton, Hal befriended future president Woodrow Wilson, who, during World War One, tapped him to serve as the nation's fuel administrator. It was a position with almost dictatorial powers.

James Rudolf Garfield (Born October 17, 1865, he died March 24, 1950.) "Jimmy" was only fifteen when he saw his father gunned down before his eyes in the nation's second assassination of a president. A Columbia University graduate, he was a lawyer and politician who accepted a number of lesser government jobs before coming to the attention of President Theodore Roosevelt. The two became lifelong friends and, impressed with his work, Roosevelt appointed him secretary of the interior. James married Helen Newell and had four children.

Mary "Mollie" Garfield Stanley-Brown (Born January 16, 1867, died December 30, 1947.) A child at the time of her father's assassination, Mollie eventually married a man who had served him as a junior White House secretary. They had three children and lived for years in New York before moving to Pasadena, California, where he worked as an investment banker.

Irvin McDowell Garfield (Born August 3, 1870, he died on July 18, 1951.) As a youngster, he joined the ranks of Willie and Tad Lincoln as official "White House terrors," famous for bounding down the elegant staircases on his high-wheeled bicycle and racing through the East Room. He married Susan Emmons, had three children, and carved out a successful law and business career in Boston.

Abram Garfield (Born November 21, 1872, he died October 16, 1958.) After an education at Williams College and Massachusetts Institute of Technology, he built a career as one of the world's leading architects and was appointed to national commissions by two presidents. He married Sarah Granger and had two children. After the death of Sarah, at seventy-five, he married Helen Grannis Mathews, this second bride much younger than himself.

Edward Garfield (Born December 25, 1874, he died October 25, 1876.) The last child of James and Lucretia Rudolph Garfield died of the whooping cough before his second birthday.

21. President Chester Alan Arthur (1881–1885)

William Lewis Arthur (Born December 10, 1860, he died on July 7, 1863.) Chester Arthur and his wife, Ellen Lewis Herndon, were "prostrated with grief," at the loss of their first child, who died of convulsions at the age of two.

Chester Alan Arthur II (Born July 25, 1864, he died of a heart attack on July 17, 1937.) Known as a playboy who shamelessly traded on his father's fame and power, "Alan" Arthur married twice, had one child, and made a career out of hobnobbing with royalty and celebrities in Europe.

Ellen Herndon "Nell" Arthur Pinkerton
(Born November 21, 1871, she died on September 6, 1915.) President Arthur carefully protected the privacy of his only daughter, saying on one occasion, "I may be the president of the United States, but my private life is nobody's damn business." Nell was nine years old when her family moved into the White House. The press respected her father's wishes and left her alone. She married Charles Pinkerton, lived in upstate New York, and died at age forty-three from surgical complications.

22. & 24. President Grover Cleveland (1885–1889 and 1893–1897)

Oscar Folsom Cleveland (Born in 1874. Date of death unknown, although there were unsubstantiated reports that Oscar died in his late twenties of alcoholism.) Soon after Grover Cleveland received the Democratic nomination for president, the public learned that Cleveland had accepted responsibility as father of an illegitimate son born to a widow, Maria Crofts Halpin. The baby boy had been named after Cleveland's law partner, Oscar Folsom. It was soon learned that the woman in question had ongoing relations with a number of men. Cleveland, the only single man among them, had valiantly stepped forward to help with the child, even while uncertain if he was the father.

Battling an alcohol problem, Maria was institutionalized for a time. Cleveland arranged for Oscar to be adopted by a wealthy couple in Buffalo, New York. Oscar reportedly succeeded in an educational career or, by some accounts, as a medical doctor. Other reports have him dying of alcoholism before he turned thirty. Grover Cleveland was elected president in spite of the scandal, when his Republican opponent was himself implicated in various wrongdoings and was not as forthcoming.

Ruth Cleveland (Born October 3, 1891, she died of diphtheria on January 7, 1904. She was only twelve.) "Baby Ruth" had celebrated only one birthday when the Clevelands moved back into the White House for the second time. The nation immediately took to the frolicking infant, a fact that alarmed the president and first lady. With the dubious example of Alan Arthur before them, they tried desperately to keep their children out of the limelight, instinctively believing that this afforded them the best chance for a normal life. But even after leaving the White House, "Baby Ruth," as the public affectionately called her, fascinated the country. Her tragic death came as a surprise, and the whole nation mourned. In 1921, the Curtis Candy Company supposedly renamed one of its candy bars "Baby Ruth" in her honor.

Esther Cleveland Bosanquet (Born September 9, 1893, she died June 26, 1980.) Esther was actually born in the White House. Although overshadowed during the presidency by her baby sister, Ruth, Esther's later wedding to Captain William Sydney Bence Bosanquet, the son of Sir Albert Bosanquet, was held at Westminster Abbey, an important international social event. They had two children and lived most of their lives in Yorkshire. When the captain died in 1977, Esther returned to the United States and lived quietly in New Hampshire until her death.

Marion Cleveland Dell Amen (Born July 7, 1895, she died June 18, 1977.) Marion was twice married, first to William Stanley Dell, with whom she had a daughter, and, after his death, to John Harlan Amen. A sponsor of numerous charities, Marion used her time and skills extensively for the Girl Scouts of America, serving as community relations advisor, promoting empowering programs for girls until her retirement seventeen years later, in 1960. Marion's husband John Harlan Amen became famous as a special assistant to the U.S. attorney and a "racket buster." At the end of World War Two he served on the U.S. legal staff at the Nuremberg war crimes trials in Germany.

Richard Folsom "Dick" Cleveland (Born October 28, 1897, he died January 10, 1974.) Dick was a graduate of Princeton and Harvard Law School, a marine officer in World War One and a career lawyer at a large firm in Baltimore. Often mentioned as a possible candidate for office, Dick eschewed such suggestions. He was, however, active in Maryland politics, and at one time was mentioned as a possible vice presidential candidate.

Francis Grover Cleveland (Born July 18, 1903, he died November 8, 1995.) Francis was five when his presidential father passed away. Reared by his stepfather and the former first lady, he graduated from Harvard with a degree in drama, and married Alice Erdman. He unsuccessfully sought a career on stage and disappeared from public life.

23. President Benjamin Harrison
(1889–1893)

Russell Benjamin Harrison (Born August 12, 1854, he died on December 13, 1936.) In a refrain that has been repeated many times in American history, this son joined his father's White House staff, while his wife, Angeline Saunders, became official White House hostess for an ailing first lady. There was a scandal when Russell was found to own $500,000 worth of railroad stocks, an achievement made all the more suspicious by his many financial failings before his father's election. He had an army career, ran a streetcar company in Terre Haute, Indiana, and served in the state legislature.

Mary "Mamie" Scott Harrison McKee (Born April 3, 1858, she died of cancer on October 28, 1930.) She married James Robert McKee, had two children, but was a widow by the time her father became president. Considered a beautiful woman by her contemporaries, Mamie and her two sons lived in the White House during her father's first term and impressed a jaded Washington society as a glamorous hostess. When her mother finally died and her father married her cousin, a young woman her exact age, Mamie strongly protested. Despite her father's pleas, she remained estranged from her new stepmother and ignored her stepsister.

Elizabeth Harrison Walker (Born February

21, 1897, she died on December 26, 1955.) She was the only child of Harrison's second marriage. A graduate of New York University Law School, she married James Blaine Walker, a grand-nephew of a member of her father's cabinet. Far ahead of her time, Elizabeth was a member of the bar in two states, a leader in society, and active in public life. She published an investment newsletter for women, appearing on radio and later on television with tips for investors.

25. President William McKinley (1897–1901)

Katherine "Katie" McKinley (Born January 25, 1871, she died on July 25, 1875.) After her little sister Ida died within a few months of her birth, Katie's parents focused all of their attention on her, showering her with love, but it could not save her. The McKinley firstborn died of typhoid fever at the age of three.

Ida McKinley (Born March 31, 1873, she died that August 22, 1873.) After giving birth to her namesake, First Lady Ida McKinley was stricken with a litany of lifelong illnesses that included epileptic seizures and phlebitis. When she suffered seizures at state dinners, her husband would cover her face with a napkin until she recovered, keeping polite conversation all the while.

26. President Theodore Roosevelt (1901–1909)

Alice Lee Roosevelt Longworth (Born February 12, 1884, she died at age ninety-six on February 20, 1980.) She was the only child born to Theodore Roosevelt and his first wife, Alice Lee Hathaway. "Dubbed Princess Alice in the press," she was seventeen when her father became president. In 1906, she married Congressman Nicholas Longworth in a tradition-shattering, high-profile White House wedding. Her husband Nick Longworth went on to become Speaker of the House. In later years, a Washington socialite famous for her irreverent, sometimes cutting wit, Alice's most famous line was, "If you haven't got anything good to say about anybody, come sit next to me."

Theodore "Ted" Roosevelt, Jr. (Born September 13, 1887, he died on July 12, 1944.) The first of five children born to the president and his second wife, Edith Carow, Ted was a Harvard-educated military hero in both World Wars One and Two, winning every award available to ground forces, including the Medal of Honor. He was a governor of Puerto Rico, the Philippines, and served as the assistant secretary of the navy during the infamous Teapot Dome scandal. Although innocent of any wrongdoing, it doomed his political career. In later years, Ted returned to military service in World War Two, served as a brigadier general, and was part of the first wave to land on the Normandy beaches. General Omar Bradley called TR's fighting and leadership during the offensive the single bravest act he witnessed during the entire war. Actor Henry Fonda portrayed the Roosevelt son in the motion picture *The Longest Day.* Ted, Jr., died just five weeks after D-Day of a heart attack at age fifty-six.

Kermit Roosevelt (Born October 10, 1889, he died June 4, 1943.) Kermit, as was the case with all four sons of Teddy Roosevelt, graduated from Groton Preparatory School and was one of three to go on to Harvard. He married Belle Wyatt Willard and had four children, but lived the life of an adventurer, exploring the Amazon with his father, winning the British Military Cross as a soldier of fortune, and joining the U.S. Army just in time for World War One. He was back in action during World War Two, reaching the rank of major. According to official histories, he died in the middle of the war from amoebic dysentery contracted in the Middle East. But in 1980 it became public that he suffered from chronic alcoholism and had in fact shot himself with a Colt .45 automatic pistol.

Ethel Carow Roosevelt Derby (Born August 13, 1891, died December 10, 1977.) A rambunctious, playful child in the White House, Ethel was a favorite of the public. She married Richard Derby, a medical doctor, and had four children. She drove an ambulance in Paris during World War One. The nation saw her again briefly in 1960 when she made a seconding speech for the nomination of Richard Nixon at the Republican National Convention.

Archibald "Archie" Bulloch Roosevelt (Born April 9, 1894, he died of a stroke on October 13, 1979.) Businessman and war hero, Archie won the French Croix de Guerre as a captain in World War One, and the Silver Star and Oak Leaf Cluster as a lieutenant colonel in

World War Two. He married Grace Lockwood and had one son.

Quentin Roosevelt (Born November 19, 1897, he died at the age of twenty on July 14, 1918.) Suggesting to one of his older sons that Quentin "seems a little soft," presidential father Teddy Roosevelt was finally pleased when he received word of the boy's heroics at the front in World War One. Quentin, a fighter pilot in the new American Air Corps, had shot down an enemy plane. Only days later came the tragic report that Quentin's own plane had been caught in a dogfight between two German fighters and had crashed. The former president and first lady had to wait for days to receive the final confirmation of his death.

27. President William Howard Taft (1909–1913)

Robert Alphonso Taft (Born September 8, 1889, he died of cancer on July 31, 1953.) Educated at Yale and Harvard, he married Martha Wheaton Bowers and had four children. Bob Taft served in Congress where he was elected Speaker, and in the Senate where he was elected majority leader. Dubbed "Mr. Republican," Taft ran for president three times, and is considered by many as one of the fathers of the modern American conservative political movement.

Helen Herron Taft Manning (Born August 1, 1891, she died of pneumonia on February 21, 1987.) She was another presidential daughter who served as White House hostess for an ailing mother. Married to Yale professor Frederick Johnson Manning, Helen had two daughters and a remarkable career in education and public life. She served forty years as professor of history, chairman of the history department, and acting president of the prestigious women's college, Bryn Mawr, in Pennsylvania. A suffragist, she traveled the country, giving speeches in support of the vote for women and women's rights.

Charles Phelps Taft II (Born September 20, 1897, he died June 24, 1983.) Athlete, soldier, lawyer, author, politician, and civic reformer, he married Eleanor K. Chase and had seven children. A deeply religious man, he was a founder of the World Council of Churches, and he worked tirelessly to better his beloved Cincinnati, serving on the City Council for sixteen terms and one term as mayor. In 1925, he was the youngest president of the international YMCA.

28. President Woodrow Wilson (1913–1921)

Margaret Woodrow Wilson (Born April 30, 1886, she died on February 12, 1944.) Having studied music at Goucher College and in private lessons in New York, Margaret traveled across the United States and Europe during World War One giving concerts for soldiers and raising funds for the Red Cross. Devoted to social causes, she lobbied effectively for various programs. She studied the religious classics of India extensively, and later edited some English translations. She eventually traveled to Pondicherry, India, where she lived in the *ashram* of Sri Aurobindo, a contemporary of Gandhi. Never married, she died of uremia on February 12, 1944, and is buried in the Protestant cemetery at the *ashram* in Pondicherry.

Jessie Woodrow Wilson Sayre (Born August 28, 1887, died January 15, 1933.) A Princeton graduate, Jessie married Francis Sayre, a Harvard Law professor. They had three children. She worked vigorously for woman suffrage, social issues, and to promote her father's call for a League of Nations, and emerged as a force in the Massachusetts Democratic party. She died of surgical complications following an appendectomy at age forty-five.

Eleanor "Nellie" Randolph Wilson McAdoo (Born October 16, 1889, died April 5, 1967.) Educated at Princeton, twenty-four-year-old Eleanor was famous for her White House wedding to the fifty-two-year-old William Gibbs McAdoo, her father's secretary of the treasury. Overnight, they were a glamorous, powerful couple in the nation's capital. They had two children but divorced in 1934.

29. President Warren G. Harding (1921–1923)

Eugene Marshall "Pete" DeWolfe (Born September 22, 1880, died January 1, 1915 of "advanced tuberculosis of right lung aggravated by alcoholism.") Marshall DeWolfe was the son of a young teenage future first lady, Florence Kling, and a neighborhood boy, Henry "Petey" DeWolfe. Some say the couple eloped but no record of marriage has been found. Florence lived with DeWolfe while she was pregnant and for a time after Marshall was born, but the father was usually drunk and often absent. One night, just before Christmas, he left for good. A destitute Florence Kling made the humiliating journey back to the house of her abusive father, who gave her a cruel choice. He would pay for her son's food but she had to give him up forever. She did it, and apparently never looked back.

Marshall followed in his father's footsteps, drinking and gambling and running up debts, many of which were paid by the future president and first lady, Warren and Florence Harding. He contracted tuberculosis and went to Colorado to a "better" climate, where he married Esther Neely. They had two children. Petey DeWolfe, son of the first lady and stepson to the president, died of alcoholism and tuberculosis far from the glamour of the White House.

Elizabeth Ann Christian Blaesing, also called **Elizabeth Ann Harding,** and **Emma Eloise Britton** (Born October 22, 1919, at this writing she is still living.) Conceived on a couch in his Senate office, Elizabeth was the illegitimate offspring of Warren G. Harding's affair with Nan Britton, thirty years his junior. As president, Harding arranged for Secret Service agents to hand-deliver child support payments, but he refused to meet his daughter. When Harding's estate balked at continuing support for the child, her mother, Nan Britton, wrote a best-selling book called *The President's Daughter.* Royalties were used to establish the Elizabeth Ann League, which helped girls "in trouble." Many tried to discredit Nan

Britton, but their investigations seemed only to confirm her story.

In 1938, Elizabeth graduated from Sullivan High School in Evanston as "Elizabeth Ann Harding." She applied at Lake Forest College, giving her father's name as Warren G. Harding, but an educational career was interrupted by marriage to Henry Blaesing. They moved to California, where she bore three sons and lived quietly and privately. Refusing all interviews, she now lives in privacy near Mt. Hood, in Oregon. In 2002, at eighty-two years of age, a widowed Elizabeth Ann Blaesing is still a vibrant person, fondly looking after her family. "We were just normal people," she insists; "you won't be missing much by not knowing about us."

30. President Calvin Coolidge (1923–1929)

John Coolidge (Born September 7, 1906, he died at ninety-three on May 31, 2000, at that time the oldest living child of an American president.) A graduate of Amherst, John married Florence Trumbull, the daughter of the governor of Connecticut. They had two children. He worked for the New York, New Haven and Hartford Railroad for twelve years and then became president of the Connecticut Manifold Forms Co. in West Hartford in 1941. After selling that company in 1958, he revived the Plymouth Cheese Corporation in 1960. Preservation was important to John Coolidge. After his retirement, he began to buy buildings in the village of Plymouth. Sixteen buildings now serve as the basis of the President Calvin Coolidge State Historic Site in Plymouth, Vermont.

Calvin Coolidge, Jr. (Born April 13, 1908, died July 7, 1924.) He was a sixteen-year-old student, home at the White House for his summer vacation. After playing tennis all day he developed a blister on his foot and died of blood poisoning a few days later.

31. President Herbert Clark Hoover (1929–1933)

Herbert Hoover, Jr. (Born August 4, 1903, died of cancer on July 9, 1969.) He graduated from Stanford University and taught briefly at Harvard Business School. Junior married Margaret Watson and had three children. He is considered one of the more successful presidential children, respected not only for his career as a geologist, inventor, and diplomat, but because of his refusal to trade on his father's name.

Allan Henry Hoover (Born July 17, 1907, died November 8, 1993.) He married Margaret Coberly, had three children, and became wealthy as a California rancher. In later years he moved to Connecticut, where he promoted his father's legacy through the numerous Hoover foundations and nonprofit organizations.

32. President Franklin Delano Roosevelt (1933–1945)

Anna Eleanor Roosevelt Dall Boettiger Halsted (Born May 3, 1906, died of cancer December 1, 1975.) Caught in a triad of three strong-willed persons — her father, FDR; her mother Eleanor; and her domineering grand-mother, Sara — Anna had to grow up quickly. She would marry three times, have two children, and squeeze in a sometimes gutsy but ultimately doomed career as a journalist. Anna, who accompanied her father on the trip to Yalta, was a witness to many historic moments, but she also carried the burden of dealing with some of the most intimate and painful decisions of her parents during their dysfunctional marriage.

James "Jimmy" Roosevelt (Born December 23, 1907, died August 13, 1991.) A Harvard graduate, Jimmy Roosevelt was a war hero, author, White House secretary for his father, and a six-term U.S. congressman. Lifelong business scandals hampered his political ambitions. He ran for mayor of Los Angeles and lost, then ran for governor of California and lost. Married four times, James was the father of three children.

Franklin Roosevelt (Born March 18, 1909, died at eight months on November 8, 1909.)

Elliott Roosevelt (Born September 23, 1910, he died of congestive heart failure on October 27, 1990.) His heroics in World War Two earned him many medals; nevertheless, as in the case of his older brother, charges of exploiting his father's name for personal gain made him a controversial figure. He was the author of numerous books, including a famous, best-selling mystery series. Married five times, he was the father of four children.

Franklin Delano Roosevelt, Jr. (Born August 17, 1914, died on his seventy-fourth birthday, August 17, 1988.) Franklin Roosevelt,

Jr., was educated at Harvard and earned a law degree at the University of Virginia Law School. He served with honor in World War Two and was appointed by President Truman to the U.S. Civil Rights Commission. In 1965, President Johnson appointed him as chairman of the Equal Opportunity Commission. He served repeatedly as a New York representative in Congress. Two attempts to win the governor's office in New York ended in defeat. Democrat FDR, Jr., was married five times, including a marriage to Republican heiress Ethel DuPont, in an event that captured headlines. He had four children.

John Aspinwall Roosevelt (Born March 13, 1916 at Hyde Park, NY; died of a heart attack on April 27, 1981.) John lived his life quietly, although a "small" wedding to Boston debutante, Anne Lindsay Clark, drew 30,000 uninvited spectators along the wedding route. John served with distinction in the navy during World War Two and later developed a successful career as a retailer and an investment banker. In later years, the previously nonpolitical John Roosevelt surprisingly chose to support Republican causes, and campaigned openly for Eisenhower, Nixon, and Reagan. He was married twice and had three children.

33. President Harry S. Truman (1945–1953)

(Mary) Margaret Truman Daniel (Born February 17, 1924–) Margaret Truman was still studying voice at George Washington University when her father was thrust into the presidency in the middle of a world war. Her lifelong dream of becoming a concert singer was dampened by harsh critics who demanded a fully matured classical musician. Later in life, Margaret found a gift for writing, producing biographies of her parents, historical works, and a best-selling series of murder mysteries that earned her fame and a considerable fortune.

In 1956, Margaret married E. Clifton Daniel, Jr., a journalist who went on to become the managing editor of the *New York Times*. They had four sons. She continues to serve as honorary chair of the Harry S. Truman Library Institute board of directors, although her son, Clifton Truman Daniel, now serves on the board of the library and has begun to carry more of the load as spokesman for the family. Margaret lives in an apartment on Park Avenue in Manhattan.

34. Dwight David Eisenhower (1953–1961)

Doud Dwight (Ikky) Eisenhower (Born September 24, 1917; died January 2, 1921 at Camp Meade, Maryland, of scarlet fever.)

John Sheldon Doud Eisenhower (Born August 3, 1922–) Later a decorated hero in the Korean War, John Eisenhower had found his World War Two military career thwarted at every turn by fears for his safety and concern from the top brass that his capture would be a dangerous distraction to Ike, the Allied commander. He served as a White House aide to his father and as U.S. ambassador to Belgium in the Nixon administration. John's greatest achievements came as a military historian, his numerous books were popular with readers and reviewers alike. His most famous history, *The Bitter Woods*, is considered to be the definitive study on the Battle of the Bulge. *Yanks: The Epic Story of the American Army in World War I* was published in 2001 when John Eisenhower was nearly seventy-nine years of age.

John Eisenhower, the oldest living presidential child, lives in Kimberton, Pennsylvania. He married Barbara Jean Thompson on June 10, 1947, but they divorced in 1986. The Eisenhowers had four exceptional children, including Dwight David II, who married Julie Nixon, herself a presidential daughter.

35. John Fitzgerald Kennedy
(1961–1963)

Child, never named, stillborn in 1956.

Caroline Kennedy Schlossberg (Born November 27, 1957–) As the only living child of John F. Kennedy and Jacqueline Bouvier Kennedy, Caroline carries the burden of her family's considerable expectations on her capable shoulders. She earned a fine arts degree at Radcliffe and graduated from Columbia Law School in 1988. For a number of years she served as a member of the Office of Film and Television at New York's Metropolitan Museum of Art coordinating special productions, some of which have aired on Public Television. Reviewers have offered critical praise to two books focusing on the Bill of Rights and the right to privacy, coauthored with law classmate, Ellen Alderman. Caroline

Kennedy married brilliant artist and interactive museum designer Edwin Schlossberg in 1986. They have three children and live in New York.

John Fitzgerald Kennedy, Jr. (Born November 25, 1960, in Washington, D.C.; died July 16, 1999, in a plane crash off Martha's Vineyard.) John Fitzgerald Kennedy, Jr., was the founder and publisher of *George* magazine. He married elegant, blond Carolyn Bessette on September 21, 1996. John was a lawyer, an assistant district attorney, a Peace Corps volunteer in Guatemala after a severe earthquake, a tutor of underprivileged children, an amateur actor, an athlete, and an American icon. He had no children.

Patrick Bouvier Kennedy (Born August 7, 1963, at Otis Air Force Base, Massachusetts; died August 9, 1963, in Boston.)

36. *Lyndon Baines Johnson (1963–1969)*

Lynda Bird Robb (Born March 19, 1944–) Lynda Bird married Charles S. Robb in the East Room of the White House. A handsome White House military aide who was first in his Marine Corps Officer's Basic School at Quantico, he would serve with distinction in Vietnam, and go on to become lieutenant governor, governor and a two-term senator for the State of Virginia. Until a recent tough political race damaged him, he was seen as an almost certain future presidential candidate. Lynda Byrd Johnson Robb is chairman of the board of "Reading Is Fundamental," the nation's largest children's literacy organization. She graduated from the University of Texas and holds an Honorary Doctor of Humane Letters from Washington and Lee University and Norwich University, and has been honored with a plethora of civic awards for her public service. The couple has three daughters, Lucinda Desha Robb, Catherine Lewis Robb and Jennifer Wickliffe Robb.

Luci Baines Johnson Turpin (Born July 2, 1947–) As a teenager living in the White House, Luci Baines Johnson married Pat Nugent in a high-profile wedding. They had four children: Lyndon Nugent, now an attorney in San Antonio, Nicole, Rebekah, and Claudia. The Nugent marriage was annulled in 1979. Today, Luci is chairman of the board and "hands on" manager of the LBJ Holding Company, a multimillion-dollar media empire. She is married to Canadian financier Ian Turpin. She has served on multiple civic boards, raising funds for the American Heart Association, acting as trustee of Boston University, and as a member of the advisory board of the Center for Battered Women.

37. Richard Milhous Nixon
(1969–1974)

Tricia Nixon Cox (Born February 21, 1946–) Always an intensely private person, Tricia Nixon found tutoring inner-city children more substantive than White House functions. She married Ed Cox in a beautiful Rose Garden wedding on June 12, 1971. Characteristically, Tricia became a very private citizen and mother, staying home to care for their son, Christopher Nixon

Cox, born March 1979, now in law school. She lives a life of "chosen obscurity" as the wife of a corporate attorney, living just off Fifth Avenue in Manhattan. She serves on the boards of many medical research institutions, as well as the Nixon Presidential Library and its adjunct, The Nixon Center in Washington, D.C.

Julie Nixon Eisenhower (Born July 5, 1948–) Julie Nixon's choice of a husband was the stuff of political legend; he was Dwight David Eisenhower II, son of presidential son John Eisenhower, and grandson of President and First Lady Eisenhower. They had met at the White House as children. David and Julie Eisenhower were positive public figures during the turbulent Vietnam–Watergate era, but it was a difficult time for them to pursue their own lives. In subsequent years, David studied law, and Julie wrote her first book, *Special People*, featuring fascinating stories of famous people she had met, from Golda Meir to Mao Tse Tung.

In recent years, they have both gained stature as writers, editors, educators, public speakers, and historians. David spent ten years writing his grandfather's three-part biography, which won critical acclaim. He lectured in political science at the University of Pennsylvania. Julie wrote a well-received biography of her mother, *Pat Nixon: The Untold Story*. They became featured speakers at conventions across the country. Today, they enjoy a lifestyle of relaxed anonymity, living in suburban Philadelphia with their three children, Jennie, Alex, and Melanie.

38. *Gerald Rudolph Ford*
(1974–1977)

Michael Gerald Ford (Born March 14, 1950–) Michael studied at Wake Forest in North Carolina and then Gordon Conwell Theological Seminary in Massachusetts. In 1977, after ordination, he joined the ministerial staff of the Coalition for Christian Outreach at the University of Pittsburgh. In 1981, he was appointed student affairs director at Wake Forest University; today, he is director of student development at the university. He and his wife, Gayle, have three daughters, Sarah, Rebekah, and Hannah. Sarah is married to Blake Goodfellow, and has given birth to Michael and Gayle's first granddaughter, Riley.

John "Jack" Gardner Ford (Born March 16, 1952–) As a young man in the White House, Jack Ford was invited to concerts, dated celebrities, and was pursued by the media wherever he went. In later years he cofounded a successful business, California Infotech, which supplies electronic information kiosks to malls. And in 1996, as a veteran of six Republican conventions, he was asked to serve as executive director of the host committee for the San Diego Republican Convention. Jack Ford married Juliann Felando in 1989. They have two sons and live in California.

Steven Meigs Ford (Born May 19, 1956–) Steve Ford was seventeen when his father became president. He immediately went west, working on the professional rodeo circuit as a cowboy team roper and taking bit parts as an actor. As in the case of many successful presidential sons, the doors opened for him after his father left the White House. Steve parlayed a guest appearance on a television soap opera into a lifetime career. He played "Andy Richards" on the Emmy award–winning daytime show, *The Young and the Restless* and appeared in dozens of films with Hollywood's most famous stars, from Al Pacino to Arnold Schwarzenegger. Steve was Meg Ryan's boyfriend in the film *When Harry Met Sally* and recently a soldier in *Black Hawk Down*. He owns his own ranch in San Luis Obispo, California, and has owned and bred Thoroughbred racehorses. He is also in demand as a corporate motivational speaker and serves on the board of directors for the President Gerald R. Ford Museum. He has never married and has no children.

Susan Ford Vance Bales (Born July 6, 1957–) Susan Ford, the only presidential daughter to have her senior prom in the White House, wrote a monthly column for *Seventeen* magazine during her father's term in office. She became a professional photographer, studying with the great Ansel Adams. Her photo credits include work with Associated Press, *Newsweek*, *Ladies' Home Journal* and numerous film projects. She recently wrote and published a mystery novel entitled *Double Exposure: A First Daughter Mystery*, giving an inside look at life in the White House from a "first daughter-photographer-detective" viewpoint.

When her mother was suffering with alcoholism, Susan helped bring about a family catharsis that put First Lady Betty Ford on the road to recovery. It was a healing that would lead to the establishment of The Betty Ford Center, where hundreds of people have come to battle and overcome their addictions. Susan serves with her mother as a board member of the Center. She is a past national spokesperson for National Breast Cancer Awareness Month and now lives with her two daughters and husband Vaden Bales in the Southwest.

39. James Earl Carter, Jr. (1977–1981)

John William "Jack" Carter (Born July 3, 1947–) Jack earned a degree in nuclear physics from Georgia Tech and a law degree from the University of Georgia. He practiced law before taking a job with the Chicago Board of Trade. Today, he is an attorney-banker who lives in Bermuda with his wife Elizabeth Brasfield Carter. Jack and his former wife, Juliet "Judy" Langford Carter, had two children, Jason James Carter, who was a Peace Corps volunteer in South Africa, and Sarah Rosemary Carter.

James Earl "Chip" Carter III (Born April 12, 1950–) Chip worked in his father's peanut business, the Democratic National Committee and eventually cofounded a corporate consulting firm. In 2000, he became president of the Atlanta-based Friendship Force, a nonprofit international cultural exchange organization. He married Caron Griffin and had one son, James Earl Carter IV, but was divorced during the White House years. He married Ginger Hodges, an accountant in Plains, and had one daughter, Margaret Alicia Carter, before their divorce. He and new wife Becky Payne live near Atlanta.

Donnell Jeffrey "Jeff" Carter (Born August 18, 1952–) Jeff graduated with honors from George Washington University with a degree in geography. He cofounded Computer Mapping Consultants. He married Annette Jene Davis, and they have three children, Joshua Jeffrey Carter, Jeremy Davis Carter, and James Carlton Carter.

Amy Carter Wentzel (Born October 19, 1967–) Amy, who as a child melted the hearts of America when she walked beside her father during his inaugural parade, is now in her mid-thirties. A gutsy political activist, she was arrested for protesting apartheid outside the South African Embassy, and CIA recruitment at the University of Massachusetts. Today, she has a master's degree in fine arts and art history from Tulane University. Her pastels, fresh and bright and colorful, have illustrated some of her father's books. Amy married James Gregory Wentzel in 1996, a Website designer who works for the Southern Company in Atlanta. Their son, Hugo James Wentzel, was born July 29, 1999.

40. Ronald Wilson Reagan
(1981–1989)

Maureen Reagan Revell (Born January 4, 1941, and died August 8, 2001, of malignant melanoma, the deadliest form of skin cancer.) As a young actress, Maureen Reagan appeared in numerous movies. She was married to John

Filippone in 1961, David Sills in 1964, and finally to Dennis Revell in 1981. The indefatigable Maureen Reagan campaigned relentlessly for her father and other Republican candidates, eventually finding herself elected cochairperson of the Republican National Committee. It was a first for the child of a president. In 1985, Maureen headed the U.S. delegation to the World Conference on the United Nations Decade for Women in Nairobi, Kenya. After her return, Secretary of State George Shultz appointed her as the United States representative to the United Nations Commission on the Status of Women. At her funeral, Ugandan President Yoweri Museveni praised Maureen for her interest in human rights in his country. On one of their trips to his country, Maureen and husband, Dennis Revell, met a girl named Rita Mirembe. They adopted her in 1994. Before her death from skin cancer, Maureen Reagan fought to raise money and awareness of Alzheimer's, the disease that ravaged her father. She is credited for raising $60 million for Alzheimer's research.

Michael Reagan (Born March 18, 1946–) In recent years Michael has thrived as a hugely successful national nighttime radio talk show host, now heard on more than 120 stations, and is currently in his seventh year. He publishes *The Monthly Monitor* newsletter and maintains the Reagan Information Interchange (*http://www.reagan.com*). Michael married Pamela Putnam in 1970; they divorced soon after. In 1975, he married Colleen Sterns. They have two children, son Cameron and daughter Ashley Marie.

Patricia "Patti Davis" Ann Reagan (Born October 22, 1952–) First daughter of Ronald Reagan and Nancy Davis, Patti publicly fought against her father's politics and wrote books that exposed a dysfunctional Reagan family. Eventually, she resolved her ongoing conflicts with her parents and today travels the country giving seminars and speeches about the process of forgiveness, healing, reconciliation, and the power of family. Patti was married once and is now divorced. She has never had children.

Ronald Prescott Reagan (Born May 20, 1958–) Ron, Jr., as he is called, dropped out of Yale to pursue a dancing career with the Joffrey Ballet. When friends in the ballet began dying of AIDS, he helped produce a film about AIDS prevention, and spoke out for more funding. Ron has worked for years as a print and television journalist. He lives in Seattle with his psychologist wife, Doria. They have no children.

41. George Herbert Walker Bush (1989–1993)

George Walker Bush (Born July 6, 1946–) America's forty-third president, served as a pilot in the Texas National Guard, graduated from Yale University, and earned an MBA from Harvard Business School. He cofounded an oil firm in Midland, Texas, and was managing general partner of the Texas Rangers baseball team before being elected governor of Texas. In 2000, he became only the second presidential son to attain the nation's highest office. (John Quincy Adams was the first.) Married to Laura Welch, a former librarian, they have two daughters, Barbara and Jenna. The Bushes are the first presidential couple to have twins.

Pauline Robinson "Robin" Bush (Born December 20, 1949, and died October 11, 1953, of leukemia.) She was born in Compton, California, and was named after her maternal grandmother. She died in New York City and was buried at a family plot in Greenwich, Connecticut. But in May 2000, Robin Bush was reinterred at a gravesite on the grounds of the George Bush Presidential Library and Museum.

John Ellis "Jeb" Bush (Born February 11, 1953–) Jeb Bush graduated from the University of Texas, was an executive with the Texas Commerce Bank, and a successful real estate developer in Miami. He served as Florida's secretary of commerce and then governor. He converted to Catholicism when he married his Mexican-born wife, Columba. They have three children.

Neil Mallon Bush (Born January 22, 1955–) A graduate of Tulane University, Neil started his career in the oil business in Denver. When the S&L crisis swept the country he became a target of investigators looking into the demise of the Silverado Savings and Loan. "He was cleared of any wrongdoing." Today he is a Texas-based investment consultant who has helped arrange multimillion-dollar international contracts. His educational concept Ignite!, a reading program for youngsters, has been heralded as one of the most innovative and practical uses of the Internet to date. He and wife Sharon are separated, a divorce pending. They have three children.

Marvin Pierce Bush (Born October 22, 1956–) A graduate of the University of Virginia, Marvin worked for Shearson, Lehman Brothers and John Steward Darrel & Co. before founding his own successful investment firm. He lives with wife Margaret and their two children in Alexandria, Virginia.

Dorothy "Doro" Bush Koch (Born August 18, 1959–) A graduate of Boston College, Doro worked as travel agent, bookkeeper and tourism promoter, and finally with the National Rehabilitation Hospital in Washington. She is the mother of four children. In 1981 she married William "Billy" LeBlond, but the marriage ended in divorce. During her father's White House years, she married Robert Koch, former aide to House Democratic leader Richard Gephardt. She is the only presidential child to be married at Camp David. They currently live outside Washington, D.C.

42. *William Jefferson Clinton (1993–2001)*

Chelsea Victoria Clinton (Born February 27, 1980–) Chelsea was twelve years old when her father was elected president of the United States, the first child to live in the White House since Amy Carter. Because of the public pressures on Amy and other first children, Bill and Hillary Clinton maintained a strict separation between Chelsea and the press. Described as "scary bright," she graduated from Stanford University and is pursuing her graduate work at Oxford University in England. In 2002, Chelsea began a summer internship with the World Health Organization in Geneva.

43. George W. Bush
(2001–)

Barbara Pierce Bush (Born November 25, 1981–) She was born the first of fraternal twins. Named after her paternal grandmother, Barbara ironically takes after the Welch side of the family. Her Austin public high school voted her "most likely to appear on the cover of *Vogue*." She is the fourth generation of the Bush family to attend Yale University.

Jenna Welch Bush (Born November 25, 1981–) Jenna, twin sister to Barbara, is named after her *maternal* grandmother, but is said to have the famous "Barbara Bush" personality of her *paternal* grandmother. Her Austin public high school voted her class president. She is studying at the University of Texas.

APPENDIX B

I.) REALIZED LIFE SPAN OF PRESIDENTIAL CHILDREN

The following figures reflect the life expectancy of presidential children compared to the general public. Column one shows all presidential children. Included in this number are children born after the president has left office and is no longer in the spotlight or children who are grown adults when their father is elected.

Theoretically, presidential children should have longer than average life spans because they experience a better than average lifestyle and earn a better than average education, both factors that affect life expectancy.

The second column shows the life span of presidential children based on their age at the time of their father's inauguration. This shows the impact of stress associated with living a public life. To determine life expectancy for the various ages, I drew on data from the charts developed by Robert Gilbert in his work *The Mortal Presidency.*

These numbers exclude the childhood death factor. Such deaths are fairly random and introduce wide swings in the averages. For example, life expectancies in the eighteenth and nineteenth centuries were lowered drastically by childhood mortality rates. Once a person lived beyond the very early years, the expectancy more reasonably approximated a "normal" life. Example: Life expectancy at birth in 1800 was 35.2 but those surviving the teen years had an average life of 55.3 years.

Presidential Children Years lived beyond or less than the general public

	All Live Births	Based on their age at Inauguration
Males	+7.4	+0.9
Females	+1.5	−3.0
All Children	+0.5	−1.2

II.) THE DIFFERENCE BETWEEN EARLY AMERICAN AND MORE RECENT LIFE SPANS OF PRESIDENTIAL CHILDREN

The following chart shows stats for the pre- and post-Civil War Era, using the Grant administration as the dividing line. There are quite radical differences between the two eras that might bear further analysis. Modern presidential parenting is benefiting from new ideas and the children may be learning how to better cope. Modern presidential children are getting excellent educations and business opportunities. They are marrying well. First ladies are getting federal pensions. All these factors may have had some impact.

A. All Males:
    exceeded expected life span by . . .
    | | mean/average: | 0.9 years |
    | | median | 2.5 years |

    Pre-U. S. Grant: fell below expected life span by . . .
    | | mean/average: | 6.0 years |
    | | median: | 4.5 years |

    U. S. Grant administration and later: exceeded expected life span by . . .
    | | mean/average: | 7.3 years |
    | | median: | 13.4 years |

B. All Females: fell below expected life span by . . .
    | | mean/average: | 3.0 years |
    | | median: | 5.4 years |

    Pre-U. S. Grant: fell below expected life span by . . .
    | | mean/average: | 11.9 years |
    | | median: | 15.2 years |

    U. S. Grant administration and later: exceeded expected life span by . . .
    | | mean/average: | 5.3 years |
    | | median: | 10.0 years |

C. All Children: fell below expected life span by . . .
    | | mean/average: | 1.2 years |
    | | median: | 2.5 years |

Pre-U. S. Grant: fell below expected life span
by . . .

mean/average:	8.9 years
median:	11.5 years

U. S. Grant administration and later: exceeded
expected life span by . . .

mean/average:	6.8 years
median:	13.0 years

Note: If a child was below the age of 20 at
the father's inauguration, I used the life expectancy of that person at age 20 for two
reasons:

a. Tables for persons under age 20, except "at-birth" tables, do not exist before the twentieth century and would be highly speculative.
b. This figure gives a reasonable life expectancy for a person who has gotten past the pitfalls of childhood diseases that were so devastating in the eighteenth and nineteenth centuries.

Appendix C

Presidential Children Who Were Married While Their Fathers Were in Office

Those in bold type were married in the White House.

1.	**Maria Hester Monroe**	**March 9, 1820**	**Samuel L. Gouverneur**
2.	**John Adams**	**Feb. 25, 1828**	**Mary Catherine Hellen**
3.	Andrew Jackson, Jr.	Nov. 24, 1831	Sarah Yorke
4.	Abraham Van Buren	Nov. 27, 1838	Angelica Singleton
5.	**Elizabeth Tyler**	**Jan. 31, 1842**	**William Nevison Waller**
6.	**Nellie Grant**	**May 21, 1874**	**Algernon Charles Sartoris**
7.	Frederick Grant	Oct. 20, 1874	Ida Marie Honore
8.	**Alice Roosevelt**	**Feb. 17, 1906**	**Rep. Nicholas Longworth**
9.	**Jessie Wilson**	**Nov. 25, 1913**	**Frances Bowes Sayre**

	Eleanor Wilson	May 7, 1914	William Gibbs McAdoo
10.	Eleanor Wilson	May 7, 1914	William Gibbs McAdoo
11.	Anna Roosevelt	Jan. 1935	John Boettiger
12.	Elliot Roosevelt	July 22, 1933	Ruth Googins
13.	James Roosevelt	April 14, 1941	Romelle Schneider
14.	FDR, Jr.	June 30, 1937	Ethel DuPont
15.	John Roosevelt	June 18, 1938	Anne Lindsay Clark
16.	Luci Baines Johnson	Aug. 6, 1966	Patrick John Nugent
17.	Lynda Bird Johnson	Dec. 9, 1967	Charles Spittal Robb
18.	Tricia Nixon	June 12, 1971	Edward Ridley Finch Cox
19.	Dorothy Walker Bush	June 26, 1992	Robert Koch

Note: Julie Nixon married Dwight David Eisenhower II on December 22, 1968, after Richard Nixon was elected president but before his inauguration. Dorothy Bush was the only president's child to be married at the presidential retreat at Camp David.

Appendix D

Presidential Children Who Worked in the White House with Their Fathers

George Adams
John Adams II
Abraham Van Buren
Martin Van Buren, Jr.
Smith Van Buren
Robert Tyler, Jr.
Richard Taylor
Millard Powers Fillmore
Robert Johnson
Ulysses Grant, Jr.
James "Webb" Hayes
Russell Benjamin Harrison
Anna Roosevelt
James Roosevelt
John Eisenhower
Jack Ford
Susan Ford
James Carter

ACKNOWLEDGMENTS

My special thanks to Jillian Manus, agent *extraordinaire,* who gave me the chance to lose myself in history for several years and get paid for it. And to Emily Bestler, of Atria Books, who patiently lived up to her reputation as one of the tops. A special thanks to Mary Achor, my writing alter ego for more than twenty years, who researched, conducted interviews and even wrote many of the pages for this project. Former White House colleague Dan Godzich researched and wrote a first draft on Andrew Jackson, Jr. Mindy Herbert was an indispensable part of my team. She researched, interviewed, served as a liaison to dozens of museums, presidential libraries, associations, and many of the presidential children. Gay Kirsch could always be counted on to find an old manuscript when even the Internet failed. Roger Shaffer researched statistics and life spans. Scharee Zuccolotto helped check facts. Karla Strader, Dennis Scardilli, and Bob Proctor all read early drafts and provided critical advice. Best-selling authors Mark Victor Hansen, Bob Allen, Jim

Dornan, Hal Gooch, Bill Childers, Tim Foley and Charlie Jones were my cheerleaders when the project slowed.

I am indebted to several helpful employees at the Library of Congress, and librarians at Reston, Virginia; Scottsdale, Arizona; Sacramento, California; Fort Vancouver Regional Library, Washington; and George Washington University, among others. A special thanks to Frank Aucella, Woodrow Wilson House; Arianna Barrios, Richard Nixon Library; Cyndy Bittinger, The Calvin Coolidge Memorial Foundation; Selma Brittingham, Ulysses S. Grant Boyhood Home; Jennifer Capps, Anne Moore, and Phyllis Geeslin, President Benjamin Harrison Home; Nan Card, Rutherford B. Hayes Presidential Center; Debbie Carter, George Bush Presidential Library; Anne Cecere and Nicholas Graham, Massachusetts Historical Society; Elaine Clark, Andrew Johnson National Historic Site; John A. Gable and Linda Molano, Theodore Roosevelt Association; Robert E. Gilbert, author of *The Mortal Presidency*; Melinda Gilpin, Harding Home; Ray Henderson, William Howard Taft National Historic Site; Sheldon Hochheiser, AT&T; Florence Holden, Pierce Manse; Tina Houston, LBJ Library and Museum; Joan Kapsch, James Garfield National Historic Site; Bill McNitt, Gerald Ford Library; researcher Leslie Riggs, who provided excellent primary source material on Margaret Woodrow Wilson; Randy Sowell, Harry S. Truman Library; Tim Townsend, Lincoln Home National Historic Site; Kay Tyler, Harrison Tyler, and Christine

Crumlish Joyce, Sherwood Forest Plantation; David Voelkel, James Monroe Museum and Memorial Library; White McKenzie Wallenborn, authority on Thomas Jefferson; Tim Walsh, Hoover Presidential Library and Museum; and John Works, Thomas Jefferson Heritage Society.

There are a number of doctors and psychologists who offered opinions from their wealth of experience. Dale Pollard, Ed.D., Educational Psychology from Oklahoma State University, was especially helpful in plumbing the depths of the Robert Lincoln–Mary Lincoln relationship and did research on two other children, Webb Hayes and Richard Taylor. Dr. Patrick Reynolds of Sydney, Australia, offered insights into the conflicting needs of intimacy and identity and how that process can be interrupted by parents of high achievement. Mary Wong offered important counsel on how the loss of children impacts the parents.

Finally, I owe a very deep debt of love and gratitude to my wife Myriam and my children, Shannon, Scott, Joshua, Chloe, Camille and their spouses Janeen and Amy, who patiently allowed their father to be preoccupied for years, alternately depressed with Robert Lincoln, delighted and shocked by Alice Roosevelt, thrilled with John Eisenhower, and fascinated by Letitia Taylor.

A Word About Research

It was my privilege over the last few years to have conversations, correspondence, and to conduct interviews with five presidents and five first ladies, covering six different presidential families. In each case, I kept the notes, audiotapes, and — on one occasion — the videotape of these interviews. Quite often the subject of family and children was raised and the comments and attitudes elicited were of immense value in developing an understanding of this subject.

As of this writing, there are twenty-seven living presidential children, all with unique memories and feelings. My research team and I were able to reach nineteen of them. Most requested that their observations and comments be "nonattributable" and spoke only for purposes of helping me understand the subject or to correct factual details. This was because of a standing policy of not granting interviews and a fear that by doing one, the floodgates would open to others. Some presidential children were willing to answer questions and set the record straight but were concerned about parents or siblings who did not want them speaking publicly. Still others were quite open and willing to offer observations on their lives and were valuable ongoing sources. Out of respect to those who requested anonymity, we agreed not to list any of them in the bibliography. The exceptions were earlier interviews with some of the Bush family conducted in 1988 and already on the record, two conversations with then Governor George W. Bush in the 1990s, also on the record; and, finally, two approved quotes from Steven Ford.

Most presidential children live very private lives, but when news of this project spread by word of mouth, a great deal of unsolicited information came over the transom. Former spouses and lovers, hotel managers, agents, events coordinators, college professors, fashion models and celebrities, waiters, and maids all had stories to tell. One could get a feel for the lingering limelight and the pressures such a life represents. Stories came from Europe and as far away as Australia. One producer for a large American network offered to turn over his notes on a multimonthlong project that, in the end, his network, responsibly, decided to spike.

It was my feeling, and that of the writers and researchers who assisted me, that we should treat the living presidential children with respect and discretion. We had enough information from the past lives of other presidential children to get a feel for what happens to them and at the very least raise probing questions for psychologists and historians to pursue. In this case, the living children seemed more sacred to us than the departed.

An Editorial Note

In writing a book that sometimes spans centuries on a single page it was decided to use modern terms for places and things and modern spellings as well. For example, the White House was called the executive mansion until the time of Rutherford B. Hayes and only officially became the White House under Theodore Roosevelt, and yet I refer to it by its current name throughout the book. Likewise the term "first lady" was not in use till the 1870s. The Blue Room was once the Elliptical Saloon. The current spelling of Puerto Rico is used throughout, even though it was "Porto Rico" until 1932. I took such literary license to ease the narrative for the reader and only when it did not affect the major events and issues of history.

In recording more than 160 biographies of presidential children, including biological, adopted, illegitimate children, and wards, an abundance of contradictory details and opinions become evident. Every effort was made to determine the truth and to verify controversial events with multiple sources. One encounters remarkable carelessness in the recording of details of these lives, particularly the smaller elements on the periphery of the stories. Dates and events recorded are often flat-out wrong. Such misinformation is surely both a testimony to history's casual regard for minutiae and, perhaps, attests to the constant effort of presidents to protect the privacy of their children.

Errors and red herrings made the research slow and sometimes tedious. Up to the very end we continued to find correctable mistakes in this manuscript. Some discrepancies can be readily solved. Others continue to be mysteries until new information becomes available. Those errors that managed to pass through the last cut are my own responsibility.

BIBLIOGRAPHY

MANUSCRIPT COLLECTION & CORRESPONDENCE

Adams, Charles Francis. Diary entry, April 28, 1829. Adams Family Papers, Massachusetts Historical Society (MHS).

Adams, George Washington. Letter to Louisa Catherine Adams, September 30, 1817. Adams Family Papers, MHS.

Adams, John Quincy. Letter to George Washington Adams, September 3, 1810 and May 10, 1811. Adams Family Papers, MHS.

Adams, Louisa Catherine. Letter to John Quincy Adams, April 11, 1804. Adams Family Papers, MHS.

Adams, Louisa Catherine. Letter to John Quincy Adams, May 29, 1804. MHS. Also in Shepherd, *Adams Chronicles*.

Blackand, Risha. Library at the Sri Aurobindo Ashram, Pondicherry, India.

Blair, Francis Preston to former President Martin Van Buren, March 30, 1849.

Bush Presidential Library. College Station, Texas.

Carr, Hetty to Dabney S. Carr, March 13, 1826. Carr-Cary Papers, U. Va.

Coolidge, Grace. Letters, Coolidge Collection. Forbes Library. Northampton, MA.

Congress of the United States, *U.S. Statutes at Large*. Library of Congress.

Congressional Globe, 27th Congress, 1st session, Vol. 10, Appendix.

Cordery, Stacy Rozek. Alice Roosevelt Longworth: Life in a Public Crucible. Unpublished Ph.D. dissertation. University of Texas, Austin, 1992.

Fisher, Boyd to Margaret Woodrow Wilson, December 28, 1913. University of California, Santa Barbara, Wilson-McAdoo Collection. "Piggy Play," attached to letter.

Flick, Alexander C. History of the State of New York, New York Historical Society, Volume II.

Ford, Gerald R. Inaugural Speech.

Gardiner, Mary. "Helen Taft Manning, A Resolution," Annual Meeting of the Alumnae Association of Bryn Mawr College, June 1, 1957.

Harris, Gibson W. to Abraham Lincoln. Abraham Lincoln Papers, Library of Congress. November 7, 1860.

Harrison, General to Carter Bassett Harrison, November 27, 1794. Harrison Papers, 1: 21–22, Library of Congress.

Harrison, Jr., W. H. Letter to James Findlay, March 21, May 22, 1832. *Publications*. Historical and Philosophical Society.

Harrison, William to William Henry Harrison, Jr. Harrison Papers, 7:1145. The Library of Congress. November 7, 1828. Papers of William Henry Harrison, Library of Congress, Vol. 6. No. 1088.

Hayes, Rutherford B. *Diary and Letters of Rutherford B. Hayes*, Ohio Archeological and Historical Society, Vol. 4. p. 24, July 7, 1881.

Jackson, Andrew to Andrew Jackson, Jr., December 31, 1839. John Spencer Bassett, Ed. *Correspondence of Andrew Jackson*, Vol. VI. (1926–1935.)

Jackson, Andrew to Rachel Jackson, Fort Strother, December 29, 1813. Harold D. Moser, Ed.-in-Chief, *The Papers of Andrew Jackson*, Vol. II, 1804–1813.

Jackson, Andrew to John Coffee, April 24, 1815. Library of Congress.

Jackson, Andrew to A. J. Donelson, May 20, 1822. John Spencer Bassett, Ed. *Correspondence of Andrew Jackson*, Vol. III.

Jefferson, Thomas to John Adams, November 7, 1819. (Ford, 12:134, 135).

Jefferson, Thomas to Martha Jefferson Randolph. February 5, 1801.

Lincoln Address at New Salem, IL, March 9, 1832. Library of Congress.

Lincoln Library of Congress.

Lincoln, Robert T. to J. G. Holland. Chicago, June 6, 1865. Rufus Rockwell Wilson, ed., *Intimate Memories of Lincoln* (Elmira: Primavera Press, 1945).

McIntosh, Millicent Carey. "Helen Taft Manning . . . An Olympian Destiny," *Bryn Mawr Bulletin*, Summer, 1957.

Moser, Harold D. Ed.-in-Chief. *The Papers of Andrew Jackson*, Vol. II, 1804–1813. Knoxville: University of Tennessee Press, 1984.

Nichols, Josiah to Andrew Jackson, December

689

26, 1825. Jackson Papers.

Randolph, Martha Jefferson to Benjamin Franklin Randolph. Smith-Carter Papers, U. Va.

Randolph, Thomas Mann to Thomas Jefferson, March 20, 1802 (Massachusetts Historical Society).

Roberts, Elta to Margaret Woodrow Wilson, March 27, 1941. Library of Congress.

Roosevelt, Alice. Longworth Diary, entry for January 27, 1903. The papers of Alice Roosevelt Longworth, Library of Congress.

Roosevelt, Quentin to his fiancée, Flora Whitney. May 1918.

Roosevelt, Theodore to Kermit Roosevelt. July 13, 1918.

Royall, Anne. *Letters from Alabama* (1830).

Senate of the United States, 22nd Congress, 1st Session, March 20, 1832.

Tyler, Julia Gardiner to Juliana Gardiner, Washington, June 30, 1844. Tyler Family Papers.

Van Buren, John. *Biographical Directory of the American Congress.*

Van Buren, Martin to John Van Buren, *Van Buren Papers*, March 1830 and June 25, 1830. Library of Congress.

Wilson, Margaret Woodrow to Eleanor Wilson McAdoo, undated. University of California, Santa Barbara, Wilson-McAdoo Collection. Bernath mss. 18.

Wilson, Margaret Woodrow to Lois Kellog Roth, undated letter from India. University of California, Santa Barbara. Wilson-McAdoo Collection. Bernath mss. 18.

PERSONAL INTERVIEWS &
CONVERSATIONS

Aucella, Frank. Executive Director, Woodrow Wilson House. June 2002.

Barrios, Arianna. Press Attaché, Richard Nixon Library. June 2002.

Bittinger, Cyndy. Executive Director, The Calvin Coolidge Memorial Foundation. June 2002.

Blaesing, Andrea and Elizabeth Ann Blaesing. Interviews. April 18, 2002.

Brittingham, Selma. Ulysses S. Grant Boyhood Home. June 2002.

Bush, George W. Conversation. June 13, 1998.

Bush, George W. Conversation. December 21, 1998.

Bush, Marvin. Author's interview. January 1988.

Bush, Neil. Speech, 1998, Canyonville Symposium. CCA, Box 1100, Canyonville, OR.

Capps, Jennifer. Curator, President Benjamin Harrison Home. June 2002.

Card, Nan. Manuscript Curator, Rutherford B. Hayes Presidential Center. June 2002.

Carter, Debbie. Archivist, George Bush Presidential Library and Museum. June 2002.

Cecere, Anne. Curator, Massachusetts Historical Society. June 2002.

Clark, Elaine. Curator, Andrew Johnson National Historic Site. June 2002.

Cunningham, Caroline Manning. Interview with daughter of Helen Taft Manning. July 18, 2002.

Ford, Michael. Correspondence, September 4, 2002.

Ford, Steven. Author's interview. May 23, 2002.

Ford, Susan. Correspondence. August 2002.

Geeslin, Phyllis. Director, President Benjamin Harrison Home. June 2002.

Gable, Dr. John A. Executive Director, Theodore Roosevelt Association. June 2002.

Gilpin, Melinda. Site Manager, Harding Home. June 2002.

Graham, Nicholas. Reference Librarian, Massachusetts Historical Society. June 2002.

Henderson, Ray. Chief of Interpretations, William Howard Taft National Historic Site. June 2002.

Hochheiser, Sheldon. Corporate Historian, AT&T. July 2002.

Holden, Florence. Franklin Pierce, Pierce Manse. June 2002.

Houston, Tina. Chief Archivist, LBJ Library and Museum. August 2002.

Hunter, Helen Taft Manning. Interview. July 18, 2002.

Joyce, Christine Crumlish. Curator of Education, Sherwood Forest Plantation. June 2002.

Kapsch, Joan. Interpreter, James Garfield National Historic Site. August 2002.

McNitt, Bill. Archivist, Gerald Ford Library. June 27, 2002.

Molano, Linda. Theodore Roosevelt Association. June 2002.

Moore, Anne. Librarian, President Benjamin Harrison Home. June 2002.

Mullin, Marsha A., Chief Curator, Ladies

Hermitage Association, 2001.

Pitzer, K. *Guiding Children*. Children, Youth & Family Consortium. January 1991.

Pulfer, Laura, Correspondence, Columnist with *Cincinnati Enquirer*, August 2002.

Riggs, Leslie. Interviews with Margaret Woodrow Wilson's biographer. 2002.

Schaffnit, Wayne. So-called "wizard of the web pages" at the Canyonville symposium, 1998.

Shaffer, Roger. Canyonville Academy. June 2002.

Sowell, Randy. Archivist, Harry S. Truman Library. June 2002.

Taft, Seth. Interview with Charlie Taft's son. July 18, 2002.

Townsend, Tim. Historian, Lincoln Home National Historic Site. June 2002.

Tyler, Harrison. Presidential grandson, Director of Sherwood Forest and Tyler family historian. Interview. April 27, 2002.

Tyler, Kay. Managing Director, Sherwood Forest Plantation. June 2002.

Voelkel, David. Assistant Director and Curator, James Monroe Museum. July 2002.

Walsh, Tim. Director, Hoover Presidential Library and Museum. June 2002.

Works, John. President and CEO, Thomas Jefferson Heritage Society. June 2002.

BOOKS

Abels, Jules. *In the Time of Silent Cal.* (New York: G.P. Putnam, 1969).

Abrahamsen, David. *Nixon vs. Nixon: An Emotional Tragedy.* (New York: Signet Books, 1978).

Adams, John Quincy. *Diary.* (New York: Longmans, Green and Co., 1928).

Adams, Samuel Hopkins. *Incredible Era: The Life and Times of Warren Gamaliel Harding.* (Boston: Houghton Mifflin, 1939).

Adler, Bill, ed. *The Kennedy Wit.* (New York: Citadel, 1964).

Adler, Bill. *The Kennedy Children: Triumphs and Tragedies.* (New York: F. Watts, 1980).

Alderman, Ellen and Caroline Kennedy. *In Our Defense: The Bill of Rights in Action.* (New York: William Morrow and Company, Inc., 1991).

Aldrich, Gary. *Unlimited Access: An FBI Agent Inside the Clinton White House.* (Washington, DC: Regnery, 1996).

Allen, Charles F. and Jonathan Portis. *The Comeback Kid: The Life and Career of Bill Clinton.* (New York: Birch Lane Press, 1992).

Alsop, Joseph. *FDR, 1882–1945: A Centenary Remembrance.* (New York: Viking, 1982).

Alsop, Stewart. *Nixon and Rockefeller: A Double Portrait.* (Garden City, NY: Doubleday and Co. , 1960).

Ambrose, Stephen E. *Eisenhower.* 2 vols. (New York: Simon & Schuster, 1983, 1984).

Ambrose, Stephen E. *Nixon: The Education of a Politician 1913–1962.* (New York: Simon & Schuster, 1987).

Ammon, Harry. *James Monroe: The Quest for National Identity.* (New York: McGraw-Hill, 1971).

Andersen, Christopher. *The Day John Died.* (New York: William Morrow, 2000).

Anderson, Donald F. *William Howard Taft: A*

Conservative's Conception of the Presidency. (Ithaca, NY: Cornell University Press, 1973).

Anderson, Judith Icke. *William Howard Taft: An Intimate History.* (New York: W.W. Norton, 1981).

Anderson, Martin. *Revolution: The Reagan Legacy.* (Stanford, CA, Hoover Press, 1990).

Anderson, Patrick. *The President's Men: White House Assistants of FDR, HST, DDE, JFK, and LBJ.* (New York: Doubleday, 1968).

Angle, Paul M. and Miers, Earl Schenk, editors. *The Living Lincoln.* (New York: Barnes and Noble, 1992).

Anson, Robert Sam. *Exile: The Unquiet Oblivion of Richard M. Nixon.* (New York: Simon and Schuster, 1984).

Anthony, Carl Sferrazza. *America's First Families.* (New York: Touchstone Simon and Schuster, 2000).

Apple, R. W., Jr., et al. *The Watergate Hearings, Break-in and Cover-up: Proceedings at a Senate Select Committee on Presidential Campaign Activities as edited by the staff of* The New York Times. (New York: Viking Press, 1973).

Bailey, Thomas A. *Presidential Greatness: The Image and the Man from George Washington to the Present.* (New York: Appleton-Century, 1966).

Baker, Leonard. *The Johnson Eclipse.* (New York: Macmillan, 1966).

Baker, Ray Stannard. *Woodrow Wilson: Life and Letters.* 8 vols. (New York: Doubleday, Doran & Co. 1927–1939).

Barnard, Harry. *Rutherford B. Hayes and His*

America. (Indianapolis: Bobbs-Merrill, 1954).

Barzman, Sol. *The First Ladies*. (New York: Cowles Book Company, 1970).

Basler, Roy P., ed. *The Collected Works of Abraham Lincoln*, Vols. 1–3. (New Brunswick, NJ: Rutgers University Press, 1953).

Bauer, Karl Jack. *Zachary Taylor: Soldier, Planter, Statesman of the Old Southwest*. (Baton Rouge: Louisiana State University Press, 1985).

Bell, Jack. *The Johnson Treatment*. (New York: Harper & Row, 1965).

Bemis, Samuel Flagg. *John Quincy Adams and the Foundations of American Foreign Policy*. (New York: Knopf, 1949).

Bemis, Samuel Flagg. *John Quincy Adams and the Union*. (New York: Knopf, 1956).

Bennett, William J. *The Death of Outrage: Bill Clinton and the Assault on American Ideals*. (New York: Simon and Schuster, 1998).

Bergeron, Paul H. *The Presidency of James K. Polk*. (Lawrence, KS: University Press of Kansas, 1987).

Bernard, Harry. *Rutherford B. Hayes and His America*. (New York: Russell & Russell, 1967).

Berquist, Laura, and Stanley Tretick. *A Very Special President*. (New York: McGraw-Hill, 1965).

Beschloss, Michael R. *Kennedy and Roosevelt*. (New York: Norton, 1980).

Beveridge, Albert J. *Abraham Lincoln*, Vol. I (Boston: Houghton Mifflin, 1928).

Bishop, Jim. *FDR's Last Year*. (New York: Morrow, 1974).

Blue, Rose, and Corinne J. Nader. *The White House Kids*. (Juvenile). (Brookfield CT:

Milbrook Press, 1995).

Bonnell, John Sutherland. *Presidential Profiles: Religion in the Life of America's Presidents.* (Philadelphia: Westminster Press, 1971).

Bourne, Miriam Anne. *First Family: George Washington and His Intimate Relations.* (New York: Norton, 1982).

Bourne, Miriam Anne. *White House Children.* (New York: Random House, 1979).

Bowen, Catherine Drinker. *John Adams and the American Revolution.* (Boston: Little, Brown, 1950).

Bowers, Claude G. *The Young Jefferson, 1743–1789.* (Boston, Houghton Mifflin Company, 1945).

Boyarski, Bill. *Ronald Reagan: His Life and Rise to the Presidency.* (New York: Random House, 1981).

Bradlee, Benjamin C. *Conversations with Kennedy.* (New York: W.W. Norton & Company, Inc., 1975).

Brands, H. W. *TR, The Last Romantic.* (New York: Basic Books, 1997).

Brands, H. W., ed. *The Selected Letters of Theodore Roosevelt.* (New York: Cooper Square Press, 2001).

Brant, Irving. *James Madison.* 6 vols. (Indianapolis: Bobbs-Merrill, 1941–1961).

Breeden, Robert L., chief ed. *The Presidents of the United States of America.* (Washington, DC: The White House Historical Association, 1978).

Broder, David. *The Party's Over.* (New York: Harper & Row, 1972).

Brodie, Fawn. *Richard Nixon: The Shaping of His Character.* (New York: W.W. Norton, 1981).

Brodie, Fawn M. *Thomas Jefferson: An Intimate History.* (New York: Norton, 1974).

Brodsky, Alyn. *Grover Cleveland, a Study in Character.* (New York: St. Martin's Press, 2000).

Boetigger, Jr. John. *A Love in Shadow.* (New York: Norton, 1978).

Bromesamle, John J. *William Gibbs McAdoo: A Passion for Change.* (Port Washington, NY: Kennikat Press, 1974).

Brookhish, Richard. *Founding Father, Rediscovering G. Washington.* (New York: The Free Press, a division of Simon and Schuster, 1996).

Brooks, Stewart M. *Our Murdered Presidents: The Medical Story.* (New York: Frederick Fell, 1966).

Brough, James. *Princess Alice: A Biography of Alice Roosevelt Longworth.* (Boston: Little, Brown and Company, 1975).

Bruce, David K. *Sixteen American Presidents.* (New York: Bobbs-Merrill, 1962).

Bruni, Frank. *Ambling Into History: The Unlikely Odyssey of George W. Bush.* (New York: HarperCollins, 2002).

Bryant, Traphes, and Frances Spatz. *Dog Days at the White House: The Outrageous Memoirs of the Presidential Kennel Keeper.* (New York: Macmillan, 1975).

Burleigh, Ann Husted. *John Adams.* (New Rochelle, NY: Arlington House, 1969).

Burlingame, Michael. *The Inner World of Abraham Lincoln.* (Chicago: University of Illinois Press, 1994).

Burnham, Sophy. *The Landed Gentry: Passions and Personalities Inside America's Propertied Class.* (New York: Putnam, 1978).

Burner, David. *Herbert Hoover: A Public Life.* (New York: Alfred A. Knopf, 1979).

Burns, James MacGregor. *Roosevelt: The Lion and the Fox.* (New York: Harcourt, Brace and World, 1956).

Bush, Barbara. *Barbara Bush: A Memoir.* (New York: Scribner, 1994).

Bush, George H. W., with Victor Gold. *Looking Forward: An Autobiography.* (New York: Bantam, 1988).

Bush, George H. W. *All the Best: My Life in Letters & Other Writings.* (New York: Simon and Schuster, 1998).

Bush, George W., and Karen Hughes. *A Charge to Keep.* (New York: William Morrow, 1999).

Canfield, Cass. *The Iron Will of Jefferson Davis.* (New York: Harcourt, Brace Jovanovich, 1978).

Cannon, Lou. *President Reagan: The Role of a Lifetime.* (New York: Simon and Schuster, 1989.)

Cannon, Lou. *Reagan.* (New York: Putnam, 1982).

Caro, Robert A. *The Years of Lyndon Johnson: The Path to Power.* (New York: Knopf, 1982).

Caroli, Betty Boyd. *Inside the White House.* (New York: Canopy Books, 1992).

Carter, Jimmy. *Keeping Faith: Memoirs of a President.* (New York: Bantam Books, 1982).

Carter, Rosalynn. *First Lady from Plains.* (Boston: Houghton Mifflin, 1984).

Catton, Bruce. *U. S. Grant and the American*

Military Tradition. (Boston: Little, Brown, 1954).

Catton, Bruce. *Grant Moves South.* (Boston: Little, Brown, 1960).

Catton, Bruce. *Grant Takes Command.* (Boston: Little, Brown, 1969).

Charnwood, Lord. *Abraham Lincoln.* (Garden City, NY: Garden City Publishing Co., 1917).

Chessman, G. Wallace. *Theodore Roosevelt and the Politics of Power.* (Boston: Little, Brown, 1969).

Chidsey, Donald Barr. *And Tyler Too.* (New York: Thomas Nelson, 1978).

Chinard, Gilbert. *Honest John Adams.* (Boston: Little, Brown, 1933).

Chitwood, Oliver Perry. *John Tyler, Champion of the Old South.* (Newton, CT: American Political Biography Press, 1939 and 2000).

Churchill, Allen. *The Roosevelts: American Aristocrats.* (New York: Harper & Row, 1978).

Clark, Champ and the editors of Time-Life Books. *The Civil War: Decoying the Yanks.* (Alexandria, VA: Time-Life Books, 1984).

Clark, Harrison. *All Cloudless Glory: The Life of George Washington, From Youth to Yorktown.* (Washington, DC: Regnery Publishing, Inc., 1995).

Cleaves, Freeman. *Old Tippecanoe* (Newtown, CT.: American Political Biography Press, 1939).

Cochran, Bert. *Harry Truman and the Crisis Presidency.* (New York: Funk & Wagnalls, 1973).

Conwell, Russell H. *The Life, Speeches and Public Services of James A. Garfield.* (Portland, ME: Stinson & Co., 1881).

Coolidge, Calvin. *The Autobiography of Calvin*

Coolidge. (New York: Cosmopolitan Book Corp., 1929).

Cormier, Frank. *LBJ: The Way He Was.* (Garden City, NY: Doubleday & Company, 1977).

Cresson, William Penn. *James Monroe.* (New York: Archon Books, 1971).

Craven, Avery Odelle. *The Coming of the Civil War.* (New York: University of Chicago Press, 1942).

Cronkite, Walter. *A Reporter's Life.* (New York: Alfred A. Knopf, 1996).

Cross, Wilbur, and Ann Novotny. *White House Weddings.* (New York: David McKay and Co., 1967).

Cunliffe, Marcus. *George Washington: Man and Monument.* (Boston: Little, Brown, 1958).

Cunningham, Nobel E., Jr. *In Pursuit of Reason: The Life of Thomas Jefferson.* (Baton Rouge: Louisiana State University, 1987).

Curtis, George Ticknor. *Life of James Buchanan: Fifteenth President of the United States.* (New York: Harper & Bros., 1883).

Curtis, James C. *Andrew Jackson and the Search for Vindication.* (Boston: Little, Brown, 1976).

Curtis, James C. *The Fox at Bay. Martin Van Buren and the Presidency 1837–41.* (Lexington, KY: University of Kentucky Press, 1970).

Daniel, Clifton. *Lords, Ladies and Gentlemen: A Memoir.* (New York: Arbor House, 1984).

Davis, Burke. *To Appomattox.* (New York: Rhinehart, 1959).

Davis, Elizabeth Harbison. *I Played Their Accompaniments.* (New York, London: Appleton-Century Company, Inc. 1940).

Davis, John H. *The Kennedys.* (New York: McGraw-Hill, 1984).

Davis, Kenneth. *FDR: The Beckoning of Destiny.* (New York: Putnam, 1972).

Davis, Patti. *Angels Don't Die: My Father's Gift of Faith.* (New York: HarperCollins Publishers, 1995).

Davis, Patti. *The Way I See It.* (New York: G.P. Putnam's Sons, 1992).

Davison, Kenneth E. *The Presidency of Rutherford B. Hayes.* (Westport, CT: Greenwood Press, 1972).

Deaver, Michael. *A Different Drummer: My Thirty Years with Ronald Reagan.* (San Francisco: HarperCollins, 2001).

DeGregorio, William. *The Complete Book of U.S. Presidents.* (New York: Gramercy Books, 2001).

Doenecke, Justus. *Presidencies of James A. Garfield and Chester A. Arthur.* (Lawrence, KS: Regents Press of Kansas, 1998).

Donald, David Herbert. *Lincoln.* (New York: Simon and Schuster, 1995).

Donovan, Frank. *The Women in Their Lives: The Distaff Side of the Founding Fathers.* (New York: Dodd, Mead & Company, 1966).

Donovan, Robert J. *Tumultuous Years: The Presidency of Harry S. Truman.* (New York: Norton, 1982).

Druitt, Michael. *John F. Kennedy, Jr.: A Life in the Spotlight.* (Kansas City: Ariel Books, Andrews and McMeel, 1996).

Dublin, Louis J., Alfred Lofka, and Mortimer Spiegelman. *Length of Life.* (New York: Ronald Press, 1948).

Dumbauld, Edward. *"Jefferson and Adams' English Garden Tour,"* in *Jefferson and the Arts: An Extended View*, ed. William Howard Adams. (Washington DC: National Gallery of Art, 1976).

Dugger, Ronnie. *On Reagan: The Man and His Presidency.* (New York: McGraw-Hill, 1983).

Eckenrode, H. J. *Rutherford B. Hayes.* (New York: Kennikat Press, 1963).

Edwards, Anne. *Early Reagan: The Rise to Power.* (New York: William Morrow, 1990).

Edwards, Susan. *White House Kids.* (New York: Avon Books, 1999).

Eisenhower, Dwight D. *At Ease: Stories I Tell My Friends.* (New York: Doubleday, 1967).

Eisenhower, John S. D. *Strictly Personal: A Memoir.* (New York: Doubleday, 1974).

Eisenhower, Julie Nixon. *Pat Nixon: The Untold Story.* (New York: Simon and Schuster, 1986).

Eisenhower, Milton S. *The President Calling.* (New York: Doubleday, 1974).

Eisenhower, Susan. *Breaking Free: A Memoir of Love and Revolution.* (New York: Farrar, Straus, Giroux, 1995).

Eisenhower, Susan. *Mrs. Ike: Memories and Reflections on the Life of Mamie Eisenhower.* (New York: Farrar, Straus and Giroux, 1996).

Elium, Jeanne, and Don Elium. *Raising a Daughter.* (Berkeley, CA: Celestial Arts, 1994).

Ellis, Joseph J. *American Sphinx: The Character of Thomas Jefferson.* (New York, Alfred A. Knopf, 1996).

Evans, Rowland, and Robert Novak. *Lyndon B. Johnson: The Exercise of Power.* (New York: New

American Library, 1966).

Farley, James A. *Jim Farley's Story: The Roosevelt Years.* (New York: McGraw Hill, 1948).

Faulkner, Leonard. *The President Who Wouldn't Retire: John Quincy Adams, Congressman from Massachusetts.* (New York: Coward-McCann, 1967).

Felsenthal, Carol. *Alice Roosevelt Longworth.* (New York: G.P. Putnam & Sons, 1988).

Felsenthal, Carol. *Princess Alice: The Life and Times of Alice Roosevelt Longworth.* (New York: St. Martin's Press, 1988).

Ferling, John E. *The First of Men: A Life of George Washington.* (Knoxville: University of Tennessee Press, 1988).

Ferrell, Robert H., ed. *Off the Record: The Private Papers of Harry S. Truman.* (New York: Harper & Row, 1980).

Ferrell, Robert H. *Truman: A Centenary Remembrance.* (New York: Viking, 1984).

Flammonde, Paris. *The Kennedy Conspiracy.* (New York: Meredith Press, 1969).

Flexner, James T. *George Washington: A Biography.* 4 vols. (Boston: Little, Brown, 1965–1972).

Flexner, James Thomas. *Washington the Indispensable Man.* (Boston: Little, Brown & Co. 1974).

Foote, Shelby. *The Civil War, A Narrative, From Sumter to Perryville.* (New York: Random House, 1958).

Ford, Betty, with Chris Chase. *The Times of My Life.* (New York: Harper & Row, 1978).

Ford, Gerald R. *A Time to Heal.* (New York: Harper & Row, 1979).

Ford, Gerald R., and J. R. Stiles. *Portrait of the*

Assassin. (New York: Simon and Schuster, 1965).

Fowles, Jib. *Starstruck.* (Washington, DC: Smithsonian Institution Press, 1992).

Frantz, Joe. B. *Texas: A Bicentennial History.* (New York: W.W. Norton, 1976).

Frantz, Joe. B. *Thirty-Seven Years of Public Service: The Honorable Lyndon B. Johnson.* (Austin, TX: Shoal Creek Publishing Co., 1974).

Freeman, Cleaves. *Old Tippecanoe: William Henry Harrison and His Time.* (New York: Scribner and Sons, 1939).

Freeman, Douglas Southall. *Lee's Lieutenants,* Vol. I. (New York: Scribner and Sons, 1942).

Freidel, Frank. *Franklin D. Roosevelt.* 4 vols. (Boston: Little, Brown, 1952–1973).

Furman, Bess. *White House Profile: A Social History of the White House, Its Occupants and Its Festivities.* (Indianapolis and New York: The Bobbs-Merrill Company, Inc., 1951).

Garraty, John Arthur. *Woodrow Wilson: A Great Life in Brief.* (Westport, CT: Greenwood Press, 1977).

Garrison, Webb, and Beth Wieder. *A Treasury of White House Tales.* (Nashville, TN: Thomas Nelson, 2002).

Gerlinger, Irene. *Mistresses of the White House.* (Freeport, NY: Books for Libraries Press, 1950).

Gilbert, Robert. *The Mortal Presidency.* (New York: HarperCollins, 1992).

Glad, Betty. *Jimmy Carter: In Search of the Great White House.* (New York: Norton, 1980).

Goebel, Dr. Dorothy Burne. *William Henry*

Harrison: A Political Biography. (Indianapolis: Historical Bureau of the Indiana Library and Historical Department, 1926).

Goldhurst, Richard. *Many Are the Hearts: The Agony and the Triumph of Ulysses S. Grant.* (New York: Reader's Digest Press, 1975).

Goldman, Eric F. *The Tragedy of Lyndon Johnson.* (New York: Knopf, 1969).

Goodwin, Doris Kearns. *No Ordinary Time.* (New York: Simon and Schuster, 1994).

Gould, Lewis L. *American First Ladies: Their Lives and Their Legacy.* (New York and London: Garland Publishing, Inc., 1996).

Gould, Lewis L. *Presidency of William McKinley.* (Lawrence, KS: Regents Press of Kansas, 1980).

Graff, Henry F., ed., *The Presidents: A Reference History.* (New York: Simon and Schuster, 1997).

Grant, Major General Ulysses S., III. *Ulysses S. Grant: Warrior and Statesman.* (New York: Morrow, 1968).

Grayson, Benson Lee. *Unknown President: The Administration of Millard Fillmore.* (New York: University Press of America, 1981).

Green, Fitshugh. *George Bush: An Intimate Portrait.* (New York: Hippocrene Books, 1989).

Green, John Robert. *The Presidency of Gerald R. Ford.* (Lawrence, KS: University of Kansas Press, 1995).

Greenstein, Fred I. *The Hidden-Hand Presidency: Eisenhower as Leader.* (New York: Basic Books, 1982).

Hagdorn, Hermann. *The Roosevelt Family of*

Sagamore Hill. (New York: Macmillan, 1964).

Hall, Gordon Langley. *Mr. Jefferson's Ladies.* (Boston: Beacon Press, 1966).

Hamilton, Holman. *Three Kentucky Presidents: Lincoln, Taylor, Davis.* (Lexington, KY: University Press of Kentucky, 1978).

Hamilton, Holman. *Zachary Taylor: Soldier in the White House.* 2 vols. (Indianapolis: Bobbs-Merrill, 1941, 1951).

Harwood, Richard, and Haynes Johnson. *Lyndon.* (New York: Praeger, 1973).

Hatfield, J. H., and Mark Crispin Miller. *Fortunate Son: George W. Bush and the Making of an American President.* (New York: Soft Skull Press, 2001).

Hechler, Ken. *The Truman White House: The Administration of the Presidency 1945–1953.* (Lawrence, KS: University of Kansas Press, 1980).

Hecht, Marie B. *John Quincy Adams: A Personal History of an Independent Man.* (New York: Macmillan, 1972).

Hedley, John Hollister. *Harry S Truman: The Little Man from Missouri.* (Woodburn, NY: Barron's Educational Series, 1979).

Helm, Katherine. *The True Story of Mary, Wife of Lincoln.* (New York: Harper & Brothers, 1928).

Herndon, William H., and Jesse William Weik. *Herndon's Lincoln.* (Scituate, MA: Digital Scanning, Herndon Lincoln Publishing, 1999).

Hertz, Emanual. *Lincoln Talks: A Biography in Anecdote.* (New York: Viking Press, 1939).

Hess, Stephen. *America's Political Dynasties.* (New York: Doubleday, 1966).

Hinshaw, David. *Herbert Hoover: American*

Quaker. (New York: Farrar, Straus & Co., 1950).

Hoogenboom, Ari. *Rutherford B. Hayes, Warrior and President.* (Lawrence, KS: University of Kansas Press, 1995).

Howe, George F. *Chester A. Arthur, A Quarter-Century of Machine Politics.* (New York: Dodd, Mead, & Co., 1934).

Howar, Barbara. *Laughing All the Way.* (New York: Stein and Day, 1977).

Hugh, Russell Frazer. *Democracy in the Making: The Jackson-Tyler Era.* (Indianapolis: Bobbs-Merrill, 1938).

Hyams, Joe. *Fight of the Avenger: George Bush at War.* (New York: Harcourt, Brace Jovanovich, 1991).

Ide, Arthur Frederick. *The Father's Son: George W. Bush, Jr.* (New York: Minuteman Press, 1998).

James, Edward T., ed. *Notable American Women,* vol. 3. (Cambridge, MA: Harvard University Press, 1980).

James, Marquis. *The Life of Andrew Jackson.* (Indianapolis: Bobbs-Merrill Company, 1938).

Jeffers, H. Paul. *Theodore Roosevelt, Jr., The Life of a War Hero.* (Novato, CA.: Presidio, 2002).

Johnson, Lady Bird. *A White House Diary.* (New York: Holt, Rinehart and Winston, 1970).

Jordan, Judith V., Alexandra Kaplan, Jean Baker Miller, Irene P. Stiver and Janet L. Surrey. *Women's Growth in Connection: Writings from the Stone Center.* (New York: The Guilford Press, 1991).

Kane, Joseph Nathan. *Facts About the Presidents.* (New York: H.W. Wilson, 1981).

Kane, Joseph Nathan, Janet Podell, Steven Anzovin. *Facts About the Presidents.* (New York: H. W. Wilson, 2001).

Kaplan, David A. *The Accidental President: How 413 Lawyers, 9 Supreme Court Justices and 5,963,110 Floridians (give or take a few) Landed George W. Bush in the White House.* (New York: William Morrow, 2001).

Kearns, Doris. *Lyndon Johnson and the American Dream.* (New York: Harper & Row, 1976).

Keckley, Elizabeth. *Thirty Years a Slave, and Four Years in the White House.* (New York: G. W. Carleton, 1868).

Kelley, Brent P., and Arthur M. Schlesinger, Jr., ed. *James Monroe: American Statesman.* (New York: Library Binding, December 2000).

Kelly, Frank K. *The Martyred Presidents (And Their Successors).* (New York: Putnam, 1967).

Ketcham, Ralph. *James Madison: A Biography.* (New York: Macmillan, 1971).

King, Norman. *The Woman in the White House.* (New York: Birch Lane, 1996).

Kennedy, Rose Fitzgerald. *Times to Remember.* (New York: Doubleday, 1974).

Klapthor, Margaret Brown. *The First Ladies.* (Washington, DC: White House Historical Association, 1995).

Klein, Philip S. *President James Buchanan.* (University Park, PA: Pennsylvania State University Press, 1962).

Koch, Adrienne, and William Peden, eds. *Selected Writings of John and John Quincy Adams.* (New York: Knopf, 1946).

Kornitzer, Bela. *The Real Nixon: An Intimate*

Biography. (New York: Rand McNally, 1960).

Kucharsky, David. *The Man from Plains: The Mind and Spirit of Jimmy Carter.* (New York: Harper & Row, 1976).

Kunhardt, Jr., Philip B., Philip B. Kunhardt III, and Peter W. Kunhardt. *Lincoln.* (New York: Knopf, 1992).

Lamon, Ward Hill. *Recollections of Abraham Lincoln 1847–1865.* (Lincoln, NE: University of Nebraska Press, reprinted from the A. C. McClurg & Co., 1895).

Langhorne, Elizabeth. *Monticello: A Family Story.* (Chapel Hill, NC: Algonquin Books, 1987).

Lash, Joseph P. *A World of Love: Eleanor Roosevelt and Her Friends.* (Garden City, NY: Doubleday, 1984).

Lash, Joseph P. *Eleanor and Franklin.* (New York: Norton, 1971).

Lash, Joseph P. *Eleanor: The Years Alone.* (New York: Norton, 1972).

Lathem, Edward C., ed. *Meet Calvin Coolidge: The Man Behind the Myth.* (Brattleboro, VT: Stephen Greene Press, 1960).

Latner, Richard B. *The Presidency of Andrew Jackson: White House Politics 1829–1837.* (Athens, GA: The University of Georgia Press, 1979).

Lawson, Don. *Famous Presidential Scandals.* (Hillside, NJ: Enslow, 1990).

Leech, Margaret. *In the Days of McKinley.* (New York: Harper & Bros., 1959).

Leech, Margaret, and Harry Brown. *The Garfield Orbit.* (New York: Harper & Row, 1978).

Leigh, Wendy. *Prince Charming: The John F. Ken-*

nedy, Jr. Story. (New York: Dutton, 1993).

Leiner, Katherine. *First Children, Growing Up in the White House.* (New York: William Morrow, 1996).

Leman, Dr. Kevin. *The New Birth Order Book.* (Grand Rapids, MI: Fleming H. Revell, 1985).

Lewis, Dr. David, and Darryl Hicks. *The Presidential Zero-Year Mystery.* (Plainfield, NJ: Haven Books, 1980).

Limbaugh, David. *Absolute Power: The Legacy of Corruption in the Clinton-Reno Justice Department.* (Washington, DC: Regnery Publishing, 2001).

Link, Arthur S., et al. *The Papers of Woodrow Wilson.* (Princeton, NJ: Princeton University Press, 1966).

Link, Arthur S. *Wilson.* 5 vols. (Princeton, NJ: Princeton University Press, 1947–1965).

Lincoln Library of Social Studies. (Buffalo, NY: Frontier Press, 1968).

Lomask, Milton. *Andrew Johnson: President on Trial.* (New York: Farrar, Straus, 1960).

Longworth, Alice Roosevelt. *Crowded Hours: Reminiscences of Alice Roosevelt Longworth.* (New York: Scribners, 1933).

Looker, Earle. *The White House Gang.* (New York, Chicago, London and Edinburgh: Fleming H. Revell Company, 1929).

Lynch, Dennis Tilden. *An Epoch and a Man: Martin Van Buren and His Times.* (Port Washington NY: Kennikat Press, 1971. Originally published 1929).

Lynch, Dennis Tilden. *Grover Cleveland: A Man*

Four-Square. (New York: Horace Liveright, 1932).

Lyon, Peter. *Eisenhower: Portrait of a Hero.* (Boston: Little, Brown, 1974).

Lyons, Eugene. *Herbert Hoover: A Biography.* (New York: Doubleday, 1964).

Maddox, Bob. *A Preacher in the White House.* (Nashville, TN: Baptist Press, 1980).

Malone, Dumas. *Jefferson and His Time.* 6 vols. (Boston: Little, Brown, 1948–1981).

Manchester, William. *The Glory and the Dream,* Vols. I and II. (Boston: Little, Brown, 1974).

Marcus, Eric. *Why Suicide?* (New York: HarperCollins, 1996).

Mayo, Edith P., gen. ed. *The Smithsonian Book of the First Ladies.* (New York: Holt, 1996).

Mazlish, Bruce, and Edwin Diamond. *Jimmy Carter: An Interpretive Biography.* (New York: Simon and Schuster, 1979).

Mazo, Earl, and Stephen Hess. *Nixon: A Political Portrait.* (New York: Harper & Row, 1968).

McAdoo, Eleanor Wilson. *The Woodrow Wilsons.* (New York: The Macmillan Company, 1937).

McAdoo, William G. *Crowded Years: The Reminiscences of William G. McAdoo.* (1931. Reprint. Port Washington, NY: Kennikat Press, 1971).

McCormac, Eugene L. *James K. Polk: A Political Biography.* (New York: Russell, 1965, originally published 1922).

McCoy, Charles A. *Polk and the Presidency.* (Austin, TX: Haskell House Pub., 1977).

McCoy, Donald R. *Calvin Coolidge: The Quiet President.* (New York: Collier-Macmillan, 1967).

McCullough, David. *John Adams.* (New York: Simon and Schuster, 2001).

McCullough, David. *Mornings on Horseback.* (New York: Simon and Schuster, 1981).

McDonald, Forrest. *The Presidency of Thomas Jefferson.* (Lawrence, Manhattan, Wichita: University Press of Kansas, 1976).

McElroy, Robert. *Grover Cleveland: The Man and the Statesman: An Authorized Biography.* (New York: Harper and Bros. 1923).

McFeely, William S. *Grant: A Biography.* (New York: W. W. Norton & Sons, 1974, 1981).

McKinley, Silas Bent, and Silas Bent. *Old Rough and Ready: The Life and Times of Zachary Taylor.* (New York: Vanguard Press, 1946).

McNeese, Tim. *George W. Bush: First President of the New Century.* (Greensboro, NC: Morgan Reynolds, 2001).

McPherson, James M. *To the Best of My Ability: The American Presidents.* (London: Dorling Kindersley, 2000).

McReynolds, B.S. *Presidential Blips.* (University City, CA: B.S. Book Publishing, 1998).

Meyer, Bertrand. *Les Dames de L'Elysée.* (Paris: Librairie Academique Perrin, 1987).

Meyers, Joan, ed. *John Fitzgerald Kennedy . . . As We Remember Him.* (New York: Atheneum, 1965).

Miller, Alice. *The Drama of the Gifted Child.* (New York: Basic Books, 1997).

Miller, Hope Ridings. *Scandals in the Highest Office.* (New York: Random House, 1973).

Miller, Merle. *Lyndon, An Oral Biography.* (New York: G.P. Putnam's Sons, 1980).

Miller, Merle. *Plain Speaking: An Oral Biography of Harry S. Truman.* (New York: Berkley, 1973).

Miller, Richard Lawrence. *Truman: The Rise to Power.* (New York: McGraw-Hill, 1986).

Miller, William, and Frances Spatz Leighton. *Fishbate.* (Englewood Cliffs, NJ: Prentice Hall, 1977).

Mills, Judie. *John F. Kennedy.* (New York: Franklin Watts, 1988).

Minutaglio, Bill. *First Son: George W. Bush and the Bush Family Dynasty.* (New York: Three Rivers Press, 2001).

Mitchell, Elizabeth. *W: Revenge of the Bush Dynasty.* (New York: Hyperion, 2000).

Moore, Jim, and Rick Inde. *Clinton: Young Man in a Hurry.* (New York: Simon and Schuster, 1992).

Morgan, H. Wayne. *McKinley and His America.* (Syracuse, NY: Syracuse University Press, 1963).

Morgan, Robert J. *A Whig Embattled: The Presidency Under John Tyler.* (Lincoln: University of Nebraska Press, 1954).

Morgan, Ted. *FDR: A Biography.* (New York: Simon and Schuster, 1985).

Morrell, Martha McBride. *Young Hickory: The Life and Times of President James K. Polk.* (New York: Dutton, 1949).

Morris, Edmund. *Dutch, A Memoir of Ronald Reagan.* (New York: Random House, 1999).

Morris, Edmund. *Rise of Theodore Roosevelt.* (New York: Coward, McCann, 1979).

Morris, Roger. *Partners in Power.* (New York:

Henry Holt, 1996).

Nagel, Paul C. *John Quincy Adams: A Public Life, A Private Life* (New York: Knopf, 1998).

Nash, George H. *The Life of Herbert Hoover: The Engineer.* (New York: Norton, 1983).

Nathan, Richard P. *The Plot that Failed: Nixon and the Administrative Presidency.* (New York: Wiley, 1975).

Neal, Steve. *The Eisenhowers: Reluctant Dynasty.* (Garden City, NY: Doubleday, 1978).

Nevins, Allan. *Grover Cleveland: A Study in Courage.* (New York: Dodd, Mead, 1932).

Nevins, Allan, ed. *Polk: Diary of a President 1845–1849.* (New York: Capricorn, 1968).

Niven, John. *Martin Van Buren: The Romantic Age of American Politics.* (New York: Oxford University Press, 1959).

Nichols, Edward J. *Zach Taylor's Little Army.* (Garden City, NY: Doubleday, 1963).

Nichols, Roy Franklin. *Franklin Pierce, Young Hickory of the Granite Hills.* (Newtown, CT.: American Political Biography Press, 1931).

Nixon, Richard. *The Challenges We Face.* (New York: McGraw-Hill, 1960).

Nixon, Richard. *RN: The Memoirs of Richard Nixon.* (NY: Grosset and Dunlap, 1978).

Niven, John. *Martin Van Buren* (New York: Oxford University Press, 1983).

Noonan, Peggy. *What I Saw at the Revolution: A Political Life in the Reagan Era.* (New York: Random House, 1990).

Olcott, Charles S. *The Life of William McKinley,* 2 vols. (Boston: Houghton Mifflin, 1916).

Paletta, Lu Ann, and Fred L. Worth. *The World*

Almanac of Presidential Facts. (New York: World Almanac, 1988).

Parks, Lillian Rogers. *My Thirty Years Backstairs at the White House.* (New York: Fleet, 1953).

Parmet, Herbert S. *Jack: The Struggles of John F. Kennedy.* (New York: Dial, 1980).

Parmet, Herbert S. *Richard Nixon and His America.* (Boston: Little, Brown & Co., 1990).

Parrish, T. Michael. *Richard Taylor; Soldier, Prince of Dixie.* (Chapel Hill, NC: University of North Carolina Press, 1992).

Parry, Jay A., and Andrew M. Allison. *The Real George Washington.* (Washington, DC: The National Center for Constitutional Studies, 1991).

Patterson, James T. *Mr. Republican: A Biography of Robert A. Taft.* (Boston: Houghton Mifflin, 1972).

Perling, J. J. *Presidents' Sons.* (New York: Odyssey Press, 1947).

Peskin, Allan. *Garfield.* (Kent, OH: Kent State University Press, 1978).

Peterson, Merrill D. *Lincoln in American Memory.* (New York: Oxford University Press, 1994).

Peterson, Merrill D. *Thomas Jefferson and the New Nation: A Biography.* (New York: Oxford University Press, 1970).

Pittman, Mrs. H. D., ed. *Americans of Gentle Birth.* (Baltimore, MD: Genealogical Publishing, 1970).

Poen, Monte M. *Strictly Personal and Confidential: The Letters Harry Truman Never Mailed.* (Boston: Little, Brown, 1982).

Pringle, Henry F. *The Life and Times of William*

Howard Taft, Vols. I and II. (Hamden, CT: Archon Books, 1939).

Pringle, Henry F. *Theodore Roosevelt: A Biography.* (New York: Harcourt, Brace Jovanovich, 1956).

Quaife, Milo M., ed. *The Diary of James K. Polk During His Presidency, 1845–1849.* 4 vols. (Chicago: McClurg, 1910).

Quinn, Sandra L., and Sanford Kanter. *America's Royalty: All the Presidents' Children.* (Westport, CT and London, England: Greenwood Press, 1983, 1995).

Randolph, Sarah N. *The Domestic Life of Thomas Jefferson.* (1871; rpt. New York: Ungar, 1958).

Rayback, Robert J. *Millard Fillmore: Biography of a President.* (Buffalo, NY: Stewart, 1959).

Reagan, Michael. *Making Waves.* (Nashville, TN: Thomas Nelson Publishers, 1996).

Reagan, Michael. *On the Outside Looking In.* (New York: Zebra Books, Kensington Publishing Corp., 1988).

Reagan, Michael. *The City on a Hill: Fulfilling Ronald Reagan's Vision for America.* (Nashville: Thomas Nelson Publishers, 1997).

Reagan, Maureen. *First Father, First Daughter: A Memoir.* (New York: Little, Brown & Company, 1989).

Reagan, Nancy, with William Novak. *My Turn.* (New York: Random House, 1989).

Reagan, Ronald. *An American Life.* (New York: Simon and Schuster, 1990).

Reagan, Ronald. *Reagan: In His Own Hand.* (New York: Free Press, 2001).

Reagan, Ronald, with Richard G. Hubler. *Where's*

the Rest of Me? *The Autobiography of Ronald Reagan.* (New York: Karz Pub., 1965, 1981).

Reeves, Richard. *Running in Place. How Bill Clinton Disappointed America.* (Kansas City: Andrews and McMeel, 1996).

Reeves, Thomas C. *Gentleman Boss: The Life of Chester Alan Arthur.* (New York: Alfred A. Knopf, 1975).

Remini, Robert. *The Life of Andrew Jackson.* (New York: Harper & Row, 1988).

Remini, Robert V. *Andrew Jackson and the Course of American Empire 1767–1821.* (New York: Harper & Row, 1977.)

Remini, Robert V. *Martin Van Buren and the Making of the Democratic Party.* (New York: Columbia University Press, 1959).

Renehan, Jr. Edward J. *The Lion's Pride: Theodore Roosevelt and His Family in War and Peace.* (New York: Oxford Press, 1998).

Rice, Arnold S., ed. *Herbert Hoover: 1874–1964.* (Dobbs Ferry, NY: Oceana Publications, 1971).

Richardson, James D. *A Compilation of the Messages and Papers of the Presidents: 1789–1879,* Vol. 4. (Washington DC: n.p. 1897).

Roosevelt, Anna. *Scamper, the Bunny Who Went to the White House.* (New York: Macmillan, 1934).

Roosevelt, Eleanor. *This I Remember.* (New York: Harper, 1949).

Roosevelt, Elliott, and James Brough. *Mother: Eleanor Roosevelt's Untold Story.* (New York: Putnam, 1977).

Roosevelt, Elliott. *Murder in the Oval Office.*

(New York: Avon, 1990).

Roosevelt, Elliott. *Rendezvous with Destiny: The Roosevelts of the White House.* (New York: Putnam, 1975).

Roosevelt, Nicholas. *Theodore Roosevelt: The Man as I Knew Him.* (New York: Dodd, Mead, 1967).

Roosevelt, Jr., Mrs. Theodore. *Day Before Yesterday: The Reminiscences of Mrs. Theodore Roosevelt, Jr.* (Garden City, NY: Doubleday, 1959).

Ross, Ishbel. *An American Family: The Tafts — 1678 to 1964.* (Cleveland and New York: The World Publishing Company, 1964).

Ross, Ishbel. *Grace Coolidge and Her Era: The Story of a President's Wife.* (New York: Dodd, Mead, 1962).

Ross, Ishbel. *Power with Grace: The Life Story of Mrs. Woodrow Wilson.* (New York: G.P. Putnam's Sons, 1975).

Ross, Ishbel. *Sons of Adam, Daughters of Eve: The Role of Women in American History.* (New York: Harper & Row, 1969).

Ross, Ishbel. *The President's Wife: Mary Todd Lincoln.* (New York: G.P. Putnam's Sons, 1973).

Ross, Shelley. *Fall From Grace.* (New York: Ballantine, 1988).

Russell, Francis. *The Shadow of Blooming Grove: Warren G. Harding in His Times.* (New York and Toronto: McGraw-Hill Book Company, 1968).

Rutland, Robert A. *James Madison: The Founding Father.* (New York: Macmillan, 1987).

Rutland, Robert Allen. *The Presidency of James Madison.* (Lawrence, KS: University Press of Kansas, 1990).

Ryan, Patrick. *George W. Bush* (United States Presidents). (Edina, MN: Abdo Pub., 2001).

Sadler, Christine. *Children in the White House.* (New York: G.P. Putnam's Sons, 1967).

Sandburg, Carl. *Abraham Lincoln: The Prairie Years and the War Years.* 6 vols. (New York: Harcourt, Brace and World, 1926–1939).

Saunders, Frances Wright. *First Lady Between Two Worlds: Ellen Axson Wilson.* (Chapel Hill and London: University of North Carolina Press, 1985).

Schachner, Nathan. *Thomas Jefferson: A Biography.* (New York: Appleton-Century-Crofts, 1961).

Schlesinger, Arthur M., Jr., ed. *History of American Presidential Elections 1789–2001.* (Broomall, Chelsea House Pub., 2001.)

Schlesinger, Arthur M., Jr. *The Age of Jackson.* (Boston: Little, Brown, 1946).

Seager, Robert II. *And Tyler Too: A Biography of John and Julia Gardiner Tyler.* (New York: McGraw-Hill, 1963).

Seale, William. *The President's House.* (Washington, DC: White House Historical Association/ National Geographic/Harry Abrams, 1986).

Seigel, Beatrice. *George and Martha Washington at Home in New York.* (New York: Macmillan, Four Winds Press, 1989).

Sellers, Charles Grier, Jr. *James K. Polk, Jacksonian.* (Princeton, NJ: Princeton University Press, 1957).

Shaw, Maud. *White House Nannie: My Years with Caroline and John Kennedy, Jr.* (New York: The New American Library, 1965, 1966).

Shaw, Peter. *The Character of John Adams.* (Chapel Hill, NC: University of North Carolina Press, 1976).

Shepherd, Jack. *The Adams Chronicles* (Boston: Little, Brown, 1975).

Shepherd, Jack. *Cannibals of the Heart: A Personal Biography of Louisa Catherine and John Quincy Adams.* (New York: McGraw-Hill Book Company, 1980).

Sidey, Hugh, and Fred Ward. *Portrait of a President.* (New York: Harper & Row, 1975).

Sievers, Harry J. *Benjamin Harrison.* Vols. 1–2. (New York: University Publishers, 1952, 1959). Vol. 3 (Indianapolis: Bobbs-Merrill, 1968).

Silver, Thomas. *Coolidge and the Historians.* (Durham, NC: Carolina Academic Press, 1982).

Simpson, Brooks D. *Ulysses S. Grant: Triumph Over Adversity, 1822–1865.* (Boston, New York: Houghton Mifflin, 2000).

Sinclair, Andres. *The Available Man: Warren Gamaliel Harding.* (New York: Macmillan, 1965).

Smith, Elbert B. *The Presidencies of Zachary Taylor and Millard Fillmore.* (Lawrence, KS: University Press of Kansas, 1988).

Smith, Gene. *High Crimes and Misdemeanors: The Impeachment and Trial of Andrew Johnson.* (New York: Morrow, 1977).

Smith, Gene. *When the Cheering Stopped: The Last Years of Woodrow Wilson.* (New York: Morrow, 1964).

Smith, Jean Edward. *Grant.* (New York: Simon

and Schuster, 2001).

Smith, Merriman. *A White House Memoir.* (New York: Norton, 1972).

Smith, Page. *John Adams.* 2 vols. (Garden City, NY: Doubleday, 1962).

Smith, Richard Norton. *An Uncommon Man: The Triumph of Herbert Hoover.* (New York: Simon and Schuster, 1984).

Snyder, Charles M. *The Lady and the President: The Letters of Dorothea Dix and Millard Fillmore.* (New York: University Press of America, 1981).

Sobel, Robert. *An American Enigma.* (Washington, DC: Regnery, 1998).

Sorensen, Theodore C. *The Kennedy Legacy.* (New York: Macmillan, 1969).

Spade, James. *John and Caroline: Their Lives in Pictures.* (New York: St. Martin's Press, 2001).

Stefoff, Rebecca. *William Henry Harrison.* (Ada, OK: Garrett Educational, 1990).

Steinberg, Alfred. *Sam Johnson's Boy: A Close-Up of the President from Texas.* (New York: Macmillan, 1968).

Steinberg, Alfred. *The First Ten: The Founding Presidents and Their Administrations.* (Garden City, NY: Doubleday, 1967).

Steinberg, Alfred. *The Man from Missouri: Life and Times of Harry S. Truman.* (New York: Putnam's Sons, 1962).

Stewart, James B. *Blood Sport. The President and His Adversaries.* (New York: Simon and Schuster. 1996).

Stryker, Lloyd Paul. *Andrew Johnson: A Study in Courage.* (New York: Macmillan, 1929).

Styron, Arthur. *The Last of the Cocked Hats: James Monroe and the Virginia Dynasty.* (Norman: University of Oklahoma Press, 1945).

Spielman, William Carl. *William McKinley: Republican Stalwart.* (New York: Exposition Press, 1954).

Stinnett, Robert B. *George Bush: His World War II Years.* (Washington: Brassey's, 1992).

Strode, Hudson, ed. *Jefferson Davis Private Letters, 1823–1889.* (New York: Harcourt, Brace & World, 1966).

Stroud, Kandy. *How Jimmy Won. The Victory Campaign from Plains to the White House.* (New York: Morrow, 1977).

Sweetser, Kate Dickinson. *Famous Girls of the White House.* (New York: Thomas Y. Crowell Company, 1930).

Tanner, Robert. *Stonewall in the Valley.* (Garden City, NY: Doubleday, 1976).

Taylor, John M. *Garfield of Ohio: The Available Man.* (New York: Norton, 1970).

Taylor, Tim. *The Book of Presidents.* (New York: Arno Press, 1972).

Taylor, Richard. *Destruction and Reconstruction: Personal Experiences of the Late War.* Richard B. Harwell, ed. (New York: Longmans, Green and Company, 1955).

Teague, Michael. *Mrs. L: Conversations with Alice Roosevelt Longworth.* (Garden City, NY: Doubleday, 1981).

Teichmann, Howard. *Alice: The Life and Times of Alice Roosevelt Longworth.* (Englewood Cliffs, NJ: Prentice Hall, 1979).

terHorst, Jerald F. *Gerald Ford and the Future of the*

Presidency. (New York: Third Press, 1974).

Thomas, Benjamin P. *Abraham Lincoln.* (New York: Knopf, 1952).

Thompson, Josiah. *Six Seconds in Dallas.* (New York: Bernard Geis, 1967).

Thompson, Robert, ed. *A Collation and Co-Ordination of the Mental Processes and Reactions of Calvin Coolidge, as Expressed in His Address and Messages, and Constituting a Self-Delineation of His Character and Ideals.* (Chicago: Donahue, 1924).

Trefousse, Hans L. *Andrew Johnson: A Biography.* (New York: W.W. Norton, 1989).

Tribble, Edwin, ed. *A President in Love: The Courtship Letters of Woodrow Wilson and Edith Bolling Galt.* (Boston: Houghton Mifflin, 1981).

Truman, Harry S. *Memoirs: Years of Trial and Hope.* (Garden City, NY: Doubleday and Company, 1956).

Truman, Margaret. *Bess W. Truman.* (New York: Macmillan Publishing Company, 1986).

Truman, Margaret. *First Ladies, An Intimate Group Portrait of White House Wives.* (New York: Ballantine, 1995).

Truman, Margaret. *Harry S. Truman.* (New York: Morrow, 1973).

Truman, Margaret, with Margaret Cousins. *Margaret Truman's Own Story: Souvenir.* (New York, Toronto, London: McGraw-Hill, 1956).

Tugwell, Rexford G. *Grover Cleveland.* (New York: Macmillan, 1968).

Tyrell, R. Emmett. *The Impeachment of William Jefferson Clinton.* (Washington, DC: Regnery, 1997).

Vesta, Bud. *Jerry Ford: Up Close.* (New York: Coward, McCann & Geoghegan, 1974).

Vidal, Gore. *Great American Families.* (New York: Norton, 1977).

Washburn, Robert. *Calvin Coolidge, His First Biography.* (New York: Small Maynard, 1923.)

Walker, Jane C. *John Tyler, A President of Many Firsts.* (Blacksburg, VA: McDonald and Woodward, 2001).

Walker, Martin. *The President We Deserve.* (New York: Crown, 1996).

Walworth, Arthur. *Wilson and His Peacemakers: American Diplomacy at the Paris Peace Conference.* (New York: Norton, 1986).

Watson, Robert P. *The Presidents' Wives: Reassessing the Office of First Lady.* (Boulder, CO: Lynne Rienner, Publisher, 1999).

Wead, Doug, and Bill Wead. *Reagan: In Pursuit of the Presidency.* (Plainfield, NJ: Haven Books, 1980).

Wead, Doug. *George Bush: Man of Integrity.* (Eugene, OR: Harvest House, 1988).

Weatherford, Doris. *A History of the American Suffragist Movement.* (Santa Barbara, CA, Denver, CO, and Oxford, England: The Moschovitis Group, Inc., 1998).

Weisberger, Bernard A. *America Afire: Jefferson, Adams and the Revolutionary Election of 1800.* (New York: HarperCollins, 2000).

Welch, Richard E., Jr. *The Presidencies of Grover Cleveland.* (Lawrence, KS: University Press of Kansas, 1988).

Whitcomb, John and Claire. *Real Life in the White House.* (New York: Routledge, 2000).

White, Theodore. *Breach of Faith: The Fall of Richard Nixon.* (New York: Atheneum, 1975).

White, William Allen. *A Puritan in Babylon: The Story of Calvin Coolidge.* (New York: Macmillan, 1938).

Whitney, David C. *American Presidents.* (Garden City, NY: Doubleday, 1978).

Wicker, Tom. *Kennedy Without Tears.* (New York: Morrow, 1964).

Williams, Charles Richard. *The Life of Rutherford Birchard Hayes: Nineteenth President of the United States.* 2 vols. (Columbus: Ohio State Archaeological and Historical Society, 1928.)

Williams, T. Harry, ed. *Hayes: Diary of a President 1873–1881.* (New York: McKay, 1964).

Wills, Garry. *Nixon Agonistes.* (Boston: Houghton Mifflin, 1970).

Wills, Garry. *Reagan's America: Innocents at Home.* (Garden City, NY: Doubleday, 1987).

Wilson, James Grant. *Presidents of the United States 1789–1914.* (New York: Charles Scribner and Sons, 1914).

Wilson, Joan Hoff. *Herbert Hoover: Forgotten Progressive.* (Boston: Waveland Press, 1975, reprint 1992).

Winkler, H. Donald. *The Women in Lincoln's Life.* (Nashville, TN: Rutledge Press, 2001).

Winston, Robert W. *Andrew Johnson: Plebian and Patriot.* (New York: Henry Holt, 1928).

Wise, David. *The Politics of Lying, Government Deception, Secrecy and Power.* (New York: Random House, 1973).

Wister, Owen. *Roosevelt: The Story of a Friendship, 1880–1919.* (New York: Macmillan, 1930).

Witcover, Jules. *Marathon: The Pursuit of the Presidency 1972–1976.* (New York: Viking, 1977).

Wofford, Harris. *Of Kennedys and Kings.* (New York: Farrar, Straus, Giroux, 1980).

Woodward, Bob. *The Agenda: Inside the Clinton White House.* (New York: Simon and Schuster, 1994).

Woodward, W. E. *Meet General Grant.* (New York: Liveright, 1928).

Wooten, James. *Dasher: The Roots and Rising of Jimmy Carter.* (New York: Summit Books/ Simon and Schuster, 1979).

Wright, Mike. *What They Didn't Teach You About the American Revolution.* (Novato, CA: Presidio, 1999).

Young, Jeff C. *The Fathers of American Presidents: From Augustine Washington to William Blythe and Roger Clinton.* (Jefferson, NC: McFarland, 1997).

Zilg, Gerald Colby. *DuPont: Behind the Nylon Curtain.* (New York: Prentice Hall, 1974).

ARTICLES

Associated Press. "Anna Roosevelt dies at 69 in NY." December 2, 1975.

Associated Press. Newswire, May 16, 2001.

Barak, Barry. "Team Player Bush: A Yearning to Serve." *Los Angeles Times.* November 22, 1987.

Bedard, Paul. "George 'McKinley' trades up to a 'Theodore' Bush." *U.S. News & World Report.* January 14, 2002.

Benedetto, Richard. "Bush relays message from the heart." *USA Today.* June 21, 2002.

Newsweek. "Bush Down Home." June 18, 2001.

Berlier, Nancy. "Former First Kids: Where Are They Now." *Cincinnati Enquirer.* January 30, 2001.

Beschloss, Michael. "The Curse of the Famous Scion." *Newsweek.* August 14, 1995.

Birnbaum, Jeffrey H. "The Making of a President 2001." *Fortune.* November 12, 2001.

Blumenfeld, Amy, and Richard Jerome. "When Dad Is President." *People.* June 18, 2001.

Bly, Nellie. *New York World.* October 28, 1888.

Borger, Gloria. "A feuding first family." *U.S. News & World Report.* August 31, 1987.

Borger, Gloria. "Practicing the art of secrecy." *U.S. News & World Report.* March 18, 2001.

Borger, Gloria, "Same old, same old." *U.S. News & World Report.* January 21, 2002.

Carlson, Margaret. "A Pillow Away from the President." *Time.* December 31, 2001–January 7, 2002, double issue.

Carlson, Margaret. "Peace Is at Hand: The Nixon daughters, feuding over their father's library, finally patch things up." *Time.* May 13, 2002. (Time, Inc., 2002).

Carney, James, and John F. Dickerson. "A Work in Progress." *Time.* October 22, 2001.

Carroll County Independent. Center Ossippee, NY: November 9, 1995.

Carson, S. L. "Presidential Children: Abandonment, Hysteria and Suicide." *The Journal of Psychohistory.* New York: Spring, 1984, Vol. 11, No. 4.

Chicago Inter Ocean. May 20–21, 1875.

Cincinnati Daily Gazette. November 2, 1830.

Cleveland Plain Dealer. "Abram Garfield Rites Are Set for Tomorrow." October 17, 1958.

Collier's Weekly. August 20, 1938.

Corliss, Richard. "Ron Reagan Show." (Television program reviews.) *Time.* August 26, 1991.

Crowe, Cameron. "Why Jack Ford Still Lives with His Parents: A White House Portrait." *Rolling Stone.* July 29, 1976.

Dagostino, Mark. "Insider." *People Weekly.* July 22, 2002. (Time, Inc., 2002.)

Davis, Patti. "What We'll Do for Dad On His 91st." *Time.* February 4, 2002.

Davis, Patti. "A Chelsea Warning: A president's daughter should stay out of the spotlight, says Patti Davis. She learned the hard way." *Rosie* magazine. September 2002.

Dickerson, John F. "Meet the President as the Cutup in Chief." *Time.* February 18, 2002.

Dionne, Jr., E. J. "Conservatism Recast, Why This President's Reach Could Be Monumental." *Washington Post.* January 27, 2002.

Donaldson, Sam. "Home front" book reviews. *Washington Monthly.* April 1986.

Duffy, Michael, and Nancy Gibbs. "The Bush Dynasty." *Time.* August 7, 2000.

Elie, L. Eric. "Chip Carter working on the fringe of politics." *Atlanta Journal-Constitution.* May 16, 1988.

Eisenhower, Julie Nixon. "My College Diary." From *The Sixties* (1977), Journal Entry for April 17, 1968.

Ellis, Sam. "When George W. Bush Was the Stickball King." *Boston Globe.* June 20, 1999.

Fiore, Faye, and Geraldine Baum. "Column One: 2 Nixon Daughters, 1 Big Feud: The former president's daughters aren't speaking to each other in a dispute over the control of his library. The rift stalls talks on acquiring his papers and further threatens his legacy." *Los Angeles Times* (Los Angeles, CA: The Times Mirror Company; Los Angeles Times 2002). April 23, 2002.

Fitzgerald, Mark. "NNA Convention Celebrates First Amendment Rights" (National Newspapers Association). October 12, 1991.

Fournier, Ron. "Crises Transform Bush Presidency." Associated Press as reported in *The Orlando Sentinel*, January 20, 2002.

Friendship Force. Press Release. Atlanta, GA: May 1, 2000.

Gavrilovich, Peter, and Michele Lavey, "Getting It Straight: What Happened to Former First Kids." *Detroit Free Press.* November 7, 2000.

Heggie, Barbara. "What Makes Margaret Sing?" *Woman's Home Companion.* January 1951.

Hevesi, Dennis. "Elliott Roosevelt, General and Author, Dies at 80." *New York Times.* October 28, 1990.

Houston Post. December 15, 1980.

Hsu, Spencer S. "Campaigner Born, Wedded to Politics; Lynda Robb More Visible Than Ever." *Washington Post.* November 5, 2000.

Hume, Paul. "Postlude: Margaret Truman Sings Here Again with Light Program." *Washington Post.* December 6, 1950.

Illinois State Journal. June 30, 1936.

Illinois State Register. June 28, 1926.

Ingrassia, Robert. "Margaret Truman Sues Cab Company in Son's Death." Wilmington, NC: *Morning Star,* March 8, 2001.

Kaiser, Robert G., and David B. Ottaway. "Saudi Leader's Anger Revealed Shaky Ties." *Washington Post.* February 10, 2002.

Kennedy, Jr., John. "Laughs, Thrills and Stories." *New York Times.* August 1, 1999.

Kim, Lillian Lee. "Campaign aide, college student and grandson of a president, James Earl Carter IV is a politician in training." *Atlanta Journal-Constitution.* May 5, 1998.

Kleiner, Carolyn. "Breaking the Cycle." *U.S. News & World Report.* April 29, 2002.

Kulman, Linda. "Who owns history?" *U.S. News & World Report.* April 29, 2002.

Life magazine. "Nader's Raider among the Nixons: For Tricia and Ed it's no secret." January 22, 1971.

Life magazine. "Behind the Main Event." June 18, 1971.

Life magazine. October 30, 1992.

Loftus, Mary. "The Other Side of Fame." *Psychology Today.* May–June 1995, Vol. 28, Issue 3.

Los Angeles Times. August 13, 1938.

MacPherson, Myra. "Princess Alice Roosevelt Longworth." *Washington Post.* February 21, 1984.

Mayo, Linda. "Miss Adams in Love." *American Heritage.* February 1965.

McIntosh, Millicent Carey. "Helen Taft Manning . . . An Olympian Destiny." *Bryn Mawr Bulletin,* Summer, 1957.

McQuiston, John T. "Franklin D. Roosevelt, Jr.,

Is Dead; Ex-New York Congressman, 74."
New York Times. August 18, 1988.

Merzer, Martin, and Allison Klein. Herald Staff
Writers. "Nixon Pal Bebe Rebozo Dead at 85;
Key Biscayne Banker Loyal to the End."
Miami Herald. May 9, 1998.

Miami Herald. "Nixon Spoke of Break-In at Embassy, Newly Released Tapes Reveal." February 26, 1999.

The Mirror. (UK). "Chelsea Blue." May 18, 2001.

New York Herald. December 11, 1841.

New York Herald. May 22, 1874.

New York Herald Tribune. July 26, 1926.

New York Herald Tribune. January 19, 1945.

New York Times. Obituary, March 14, 1901.

New York Times. "Miss Wilson a Lobbyist: Tariff
Expert So Classifies Her in Jest Full of Praise."
June 4, 1913.

New York Times. "Miss Wilson Belle At Greenwich Party." February 15, 1914.

New York Times. "Freed by Mercy of Miss
Wilson." March 30, 1926, front page.

New York Times. September 13, 1933.

New York Times. July 13, 1935.

New York Times. Andrew Johnson's Obituary, August 1, 1875.

New York Times. January 19, 1889.

New York Times. Obituary, March 14, 1901.

New York Times. April 30, 1933.

New York Times. March 25, 1935; April 4, 1935;
November 20, 1935; December 23, 1935.

New York Times. "Wilson's Daughter Dies a Recluse at 57 in Religious Colony in India." February 14, 1944.

New York Times. "Mrs. Eleanor Wilson McAdoo, President's Daughter, 77, Dies." April 7, 1967.

New York Times. December 7, 1967.

New York Times. Marion Cleveland Amen Obituary. June 18, 1977.

New York Times. "Nixon Daughters Resolve Dispute." August 8, 2002.

New York World. May 10, 1884.

New York World. May 26, 1884.

Newsweek. July 10 and July 24, 1944.

Noonan, Peggy. "Loose Lips, Pink Slips," *Wall Street Journal.* January 22, 2002.

Palazzolo, Rose. "Born to the President: Living in the White House Spotlight Creates Unique Pressures for Children." *abcnews.com*, March 10, 2001.

People. "The president requests . . ." Time, Inc. July 25, 1994.

People. "Fords of a Feather: Gerald's son Jack gets (GOP) conventional." August 19, 1996. Time, Inc., 1996.

People. "What a Difference a Year Makes." January 21, 2002.

People. "The Graduate: With First Childhood and Now Stanford Behind Her, Chelsea Gets Ready for Life on Her Own." July 2, 2001.

Perlman, Jeffrey A. "James Roosevelt, Son of F.D.R. Dies at 83." *Los Angeles Times.* August 14, 1991.

Philadelphia Public Ledger. July 2, 1938.

Poughkeepsie Journal. "Elliott Roosevelt, author, dies at 80." October 28, 1990.

Pulfer, Laura. "Drag the kids to chat with

Charlie Taft." *Cincinnati Enquirer*. February 20, 2000.

Reed, Susan. *People*. November 28, 1983.

Reeves, Richard. "The Danger in the Limelight." *U.S. News & World Report*. July 26, 1999.

Quinn, Sally. "The Canny Candor of Alice Longworth." *Washington Post*. February 21, 1980.

Sanger, David. "Bush relishes reactions to his rallying cry." *New York Times*, as reported in the *International Herald Tribune*. February 18, 2002.

Saturday Evening Post. July 2, 1938.

Saturday Evening Post. August 26, 1848. "The Presidents" (Indianapolis: Curtis Publishing, 1989).

Scott, Walter. "Personality Parade." *Parade* magazine. April 22, 2001.

Smith, Evan. "George, Washington: What his first stint there taught him about loyalty." *Texas Monthly*. June 1999.

Steindorf, Sara. "Whatever Happened To . . . ?" *Christian Science Monitor*. February 17, 2000.

Baltimore Sun, undated. "An Intimate, Chatty Glimpse of Miss Margaret Wilson." University of California–Santa Barbara, Wilson-MacAdoo Collection.

Taylor, Stuart. "Before the Bar of History." *Newsweek*. December 10, 2001.

Texas Monthly. "Luci in the sky: Now firmly in control of her famous family's holding company, Luci Baines Johnson is flying high." March 1998.

Thompson, Bill. "Belated recognition of Gerald

Ford's courage." Knight-Ridder/Tribune News Service, May 25, 2001.

Time. August 29, 1938.

Time. July 4, 1938.

Time. December 31, 2001–January 7, 2002, double issue.

Time. Notebook. January 2002.

USA Today. "Offspring of artists make their own music." August 3, 2001.

U.S. News & World Report. "The Secret Skill of Leaders." January 14, 2002.

U.S. News & World Report. February 25–March 4, 2002, double issue.

Walsh, Ken. "All the President's Children," *U.S. News & World Report*. February 12, 1990.

Washington Post. "Anna Roosevelt Halsted, Only Daughter of FDR." December 2, 1975.

Washington Post. February 21, 1980.

Washington Post. "10 Days in September, Epilogue, There Is No Doubt In My Mind, Not One Doubt." February 3, 2002.

Washington Post. "10 Days in September, Epilogue, With World's Eyes on Him, Bush Stresses Results." February 3, 2002.

Washington Post. February 10, 2002.

Washington Evening Star. September 25, 1868.

Washington Star. April 28, 1981.

Washington Sunday Herald. *New York Times*. April 12, 1912.

Welch, William M. "Bush: Stimulus plan mostly tax cuts." *USA Today*. October 5, 2001.

Whitley, Glenna. "George & Laura, Love & Marriage." *Ladies Home Journal*. February 2002.

Willing, Richard. *USA Today*. "Research

downplays risk of cousin marriages." April 4, 2002.

Wilson, Jeff. Associated Press. Spoken by actress Shelly Fabares. "More than 1,000 attend Maureen Reagan's funeral." *The Californian North County Times, NC Times.net,* 2001.

Zakaria, Fareed. "Spend It Now, Mr. President." *Newsweek.* May 20, 2002.

Zuckerman, Mortimer B. "A Man on a Mission." *U.S. News & World Report.* March 18, 2002.

INTERNET SOURCES

American Civil War Overview, Chapter XII, The Trans-Mississippi: The Red River Campaign, *www.civilwarhome.com/redriver.*

www.toledo_bend.com/srala/area/mansfield

www.americanhi_story.si.edu/presidency/3a4.html

americanpresident.org/KoTrain/Courses/WHH/ WHH_Family_Life.htm

Anodea, Judith, "Sri Aurobindo: 1872–1950." *http://www.gaiamind.org/Aurobindo.html*

bioguide.congress.gov/scripts/biodisplay.pl?index= M000293

brynmawr.edu/about/history.shtml

Carter, Jimmy. A website quoting an informal book written by Jimmy Carter for a family reunion. *www.uftree.com/UFT/WebPages/jholcomb/ JECARTER/d0/i0000818.htm*

Contemporary Authors Online. The Gale Group, 2001. Reproduced in Biography Resource Center. Farmington Hills, MI: The Gale Group, 2001.

Cooper, John S. "Charles Francis Adams: Unsung Hero," Suite101.com. *www.suite101.com/article.cfm/presidents_and_first ladies/40724, June 2, 2000.*

Cooper, John S. *White House Heroes, Part II. www.suite101.com/article.cfm/presidents and first_ladies*

Fiore, Faye, and Geraldine Baum. *www.latimes. com/news/la-042302sisters.story*

Gizzi, John. "Maureen Reagan, 1941–2001," Online Human Events, *The National Conservative Weekly,* August 13, 2001. *http://www. humaneventsonline.com/articles/08-13-01/tgizzi. html*

Hayes, Lucy. *www2.worldbook.com www.rbhayes.orgmssfidn/hayes_coll/wchayes/ www.rbhayes.org/mssfind/HAYES_COLL/ hayesscttr.htm*

Hoover.nara.gov website

Infoplease.com website (almanac information about presidents, wives and children), 2001.

Learning Network Website (*http://www. infoplease.com/spot/kennedybio.html*).

Mays, Patricia J. "Former president's son following in dad's footsteps, From Wall Street to Main Street . . ." *www.onlineathens.com/stories/041899/new_ 0418990010.shtml*

McCain, "Eulogy Given by Senator John McCain at the Memorial Service for Maureen Reagan," *http://mccain.senate.gov/ maureenspch.htm*

Nichols, John. " 'Republican Feminist': Recalling a Better Reagan," *Common Dreams*

News Center, *http://www.commondreams.org/ views01/0809-03.htm*

Rayner, B. L. *Life of Thomas Jefferson* (On-line: edited by Eyler Robert Coates, Sr., 1997).

Reagan, Maureen. *http://womenshistory.about.com/ library/qu/blqureag.htm*

Reagan, Maureen. *http://europe.cnn.com/2000/US/ 01/24/reagan.health.01,* "Daughter: Ronald Reagan's health deteriorating," January 24, 2000.

www.skincarephysicians.com/melanomanet. For more information on malignant melanomas.

Reagan, Maureen. "Jane Wyman's Daughter, Maureen Reagan, 60, Dies of Cancer — August 8, 2001." *http://www.meredy.com/ janewyman/maureen.htm*

Roosevelt, Elliott. *Stopyourekillingme.com* website (dedicated to mystery novels; used specifically for information concerning Elliott Roosevelt).

Tapper, Jake. "Dead senator running?" *www.salon.com/newsfeature/1999/11/17obb/print. html*

Taft, Charlie. Quoted in the Taft Memorial Program of Christ Church Cincinnati, at *christchurchcincinnati.org/newweb1/programs_ organizations/taft_memorial_program.htm*

Taft.edu website

Texas Handbook, *www.angelfire.com/va3/ valleywar/people/taylor*

www.taylor-barry-roots.com/civilwar/RichardTaylor

Thefirsttwin.com website (historical and current information on the Bush Twins), 2001.

Twinstuff.com website (historical and current in-

formation on the Bush twins), 2001.
Whitehouse.gov website
Women's International League for Peace and
 Freedom; *www.wilpf.org/history*
www.multied.com/bio/cwcgens/csaTaylor
www.cyfc.unm.edu/Documents/H/N/HN1053.html
www.spartacus.schoolnet.co.uk/USAsuffrage.htm
www.suite101.com/article.cfm/4996/91157
*www.suite101.com/article.cfm/presidents_and_first_
 ladies/40724*
www.vassun.vssar.edu/-daniels/1905_1914.html
www.whitehouse.gov/history/firstladies/im25.html
www.whitehouse.gov/history/firstladies/mj3/html
www.worldwar1.com/dbc/roosev.ht

Public Television Sources

Burns, Ken. *Thomas Jefferson.* (The American
 Lives Film Project, 1996, PBS. Distributed
 by Warner Home Video, Burbank, CA).
Byker, Carl, and David Mrazek. *Woodrow
 Wilson, a Passionate Man.* (WGBH Educa-
 tional Foundation and Community Television
 of Southern California, 2002).
Grubin, David, and Geoffrey C. Ward. *Theo-
 dore Roosevelt,* a PBS Video. (WGBH Educa-
 tion Foundation, Boston, 1996).
Kunhardt, Jr., Philip B., Philip B. Kunhardt,
 III, Peter W. Kunhardt. *The American Presi-
 dent.* (Burbank, CA: Warner, a PBS film,
 2000).
Kunhardt, Jr., Philip B., Philip B. Kunhardt,
 III, and Peter W. Kunhardt. *Echoes from the
 White House.* (New York and Washington: A

Four Score Production, with WNET and WETA, distributed by PBS, 2001).

Ward, Geoffrey C. *Thomas Jefferson, A film by Ken Burns.* (Burbank, CA: PBS and AOL-Time Warner, 1996).

SOURCE NOTES

PROLOGUE

Peter Collier with David Horowitz, *The Roosevelts: An American Saga* (New York: Simon and Schuster, 1994), p. 341.

Michael Duffy and Nancy Gibbs, "The Bush Dynasty," *Time*, August 7, 2000, p. 41.

Evan Smith, "George, Washington: What his first stint there taught him about loyalty." *Texas Monthly*, June 1999, p. 111.

Ken Walsh, "All the Presidents' Children," *U.S. News & World Report*, February 12, 1990, pp. 28–29.

Ibid.

Amy Blumenfeld and Richard Jerome, "When Dad Is President," *People*, June 18, 2001, p. 56.

These are the author's figures. See the appendix for detailed analysis on the life expectancy of presidential children.

John S. Cooper, "Charles Francis Adams: Unsung Hero," *Suite101.com. www.suite101.com/article.cfm/presidents_and_first_ladies/40724*. June 2, 2000.

Evan Smith, p. 111.

From author's interview with Marvin Bush, 1/1988.

CHAPTER 1

H. Paul Jeffers, *Theodore Roosevelt, Jr., The Life of a War Hero* (Novato, CA: Presidio, 2002), p. 46.

John Niven, *Martin Van Buren* (New York: Oxford University Press, 1983), p. 604.

Carl Sferrazza Anthony, *America's First Families* (New York: Touchstone Simon and Schuster, 2000), p. 321.

Ishbel Ross, *Grace Coolidge and Her Era: The Story of a President's Wife* (New York: Dodd, Mead, 1962), p. 172.

J. J. Perling, *Presidents' Sons* (New York: Odyssey Press, 1947), p. 182.

Joseph Nathan Kane, Janet Podell, Steven Anzovin, *Facts About the Presidents* (New York: H. H. Wilson, 2001), p. 342.

Michael Beschloss, "The Curse of the Famous Scion," *Newsweek*, August 14, 1995, p. 59.

Peter Collier, p. 406.

Hans L. Trefousse, *Andrew Johnson; A Biography* (New York: W.W. Norton, 1989), p. 168.

In addition to George Washington Adams, the deaths of Robert Johnson and Kermit Roosevelt are considered suicides.

S. L. Carson, "Presidential Children: Abandonment, Hysteria and Suicide," *Journal of Psychohistory*, New York: Spring, 1984, Vol. 11, No. 4, p. 535.

There is some disagreement on the actual date of birth for George Adams due to an error in Perling's book *Presidents' Sons*. Perling writes that the birth date was July 4, 1801. J. J. Perling, *Presidents' Sons* (New York: Odyssey Press, 1947), p. 30. This is most certainly wrong and conflicts with family letters and documents. Quinn-Musgrove and Kanter place the date as April 13, 1801. Sandra L. Quinn-Musgrove and Sanford Kanter, *America's Royalty, All the Presidents' Children* (Westport, CT: Greenwood Press, 1995), p. 31. Meanwhile, McCullough says it was April 12, 1801. David McCullough, *John Adams* (New York: Simon and Schuster, 2001), p. 572.

Jack Shepherd, *The Adams Chronicles* (Boston: Little, Brown, 1975), p. 310.

Jack Shepherd, *Cannibals of the Heart: A Personal Biography of Louisa Catherine and John Quincy Adams* (New York: McGraw-Hill Book Company, 1980), p. 280.

Ibid.

Cross and Novotny and many other historians mistakenly refer to John Adams, II, as John Quincy Adams, II. But in fact he was named after his grandfather, John Adams, the second president, not his father John Quincy Adams, the sixth president. See Wilbur Cross and Ann Novotny, *White House Weddings* (New York: David McKay, 1967), p. 33.

Louisa Catherine Adams. Letter to John Quincy Adams, 11 April, 1804. Adams Family Papers, Massachusetts Historical Society (MHS).

Louisa Catherine Adams. Letter to John Quincy Adams, 29 May, 1804. MHS. Also in Shepherd, *Adams Chronicles*, p. 310.

David McCullough, *John Adams*, p. 599.

John Quincy Adams. Letter to George Washington Adams, 3 September, 1810 and 10 May, 1811. Adams Family Papers, MHS.

Wilbur Cross and Ann Novotny, *White House Weddings* (New York: David McKay, 1967), p. 33.

Carl Sferrazza Anthony, *America's First Families*, p. 245.

Paul C. Nagel, *John Quincy Adams: A Public Life, A Private Life* (New York: Knopf, 1998), p. 224.

George Washington Adams. Letter to Louisa Catherine Adams, 30 September, 1817, Adams Family Papers, MHS.

Jack Shepherd, *Cannibals of the Heart*, p. 188.

Jack Shepherd, *The Adams Chronicles*, p. 268.

Charles Frances Adams. Diary entry, 28 April, 1829, Adams Family Papers, MHS.

Even while tutoring his son for his Harvard entrance, John Q. had come to the private conclusion that his son was not destined for great things. Jack Shepherd, *Cannibals of the Heart*, p. 188.

Sol Barzman, p. 11.

John and Claire Whitcomb, *Real Life in the White House* (New York: Routledge, 2000), p. 52.

Historians sometimes incorrectly refer to Mary Catherine Hellen as Miss Helen, Helen Jackson, and Helen Johnson. Cross and Novotny, pp. 33–34.

Carl Sferrazza Anthony, *America's First Families*, pp. 192–193.

John and Claire Whitcomb, p. 52.

David McCullough, *John Adams*, p. 63.

Jack Shepherd, *Cannibals of the Heart*, p. 215.

The moment was dutifully recorded by John Quincy Adams, *Diary* (New York: Longmans, Green and Co., 1928), p. 360.

Carl Sferrazza Anthony, *America's First Families*, p. 88.

Ibid., p. 24.

Jack Shepherd, *Cannibals of the Heart*, p. 280.

Paul C. Nagel, *John Quincy Adams*, p. 329.

Jack Shepherd, *The Adams Chronicles*, pp. 310–314.

Jack Shepherd, *Cannibals of the Heart*, p. 96.

Ibid., p. 280.

Ibid., p. 318.

Ibid.

J. J. Perling, *Presidents' Sons*, p. 30.

Ibid.

Ibid.

Eric Marcus, *Why Suicide?* (New York: HarperCollins, 1996), p. 31.

Jack Shepherd, *Cannibals of the Heart*, p. 319.

Jack Shepherd, *The Adams Chronicles*, pp. 310–314.

Sandra L. Quinn-Musgrove and Sanford Kanter, *America's Royalty: All the Presidents' Children* (Westport, CT: Greenwood Press, 1995), p. 35.

Dr. Dorothy Burne Goebel, *William Henry Harrison: A Political Biography* (Indianapolis: Historical Bureau of the Indiana Library and Historical Department, 1926), pp. 20–42, 89–112.

The Lincoln Library of Social Studies. (Buffalo,

NY: Frontier Press, 1968) p. 1014.

Freeman Cleaves, *Old Tippecanoe* (Newtown, CT: American Political Biography Press, 1939), p. 27.

William DeGregorio, *The Complete Book of U.S. Presidents* (New York: Gramercy Books, 2001), p. 138.

Freeman Cleaves, pp. 247–249.

Ibid., p. 276.

J. J. Perling, p. 78.

Freeman Cleaves, p. 276.

Cincinnati Daily Gazette, November 2, 1830. Quinn-Musgrove and Kanter put his date of death as 1832. Almost all other sources confirm the date of 1830. Quinn-Musgrove and Kanter, p. 46. Joseph Nathan Kane, Janet Podell and Steven Anzovin, p. 102.

Freeman Cleaves, p. 279.

Ibid.

J. J. Perling, p. 78.

Ibid.

Ibid.

Different dates are sometimes given for his birth. Freeman Cleaves, Harrison's biographer, says it was September 6, 1802, but family correspondence and most histories confirm the September 3 date. Freeman Cleaves, *Old Tippecanoe,* p. 37. Joseph Nathan Kane, Janet Podell and Steven Anzovin, p. 102. Quinn-Musgrove and Kanter, p. 48.

W. H. Harrison, Jr., Letter to James Findlay, March 21, May 22, 1832, *Publications* (Historical and Philosophical Society); Dr. Dorothy Burne Goebel, *William Henry Harrison,* p. 294.

J. J. Perling, p. 78.

Ibid., p. 79.

Ibid.

Lincoln Library, pp. 1014–1015.

Different dates are given for his age at death. Quinn-Musgrove and Kanter write that he was thirty-four. Jennifer E. Capps, curator of the President Benjamin Harrison Home, put his age at thirty-three. See Dorothy W. Bowers, *The Irwins and the Harrisons*, December 17, 1999.

Theodore C. Sorensen, *The Kennedy Legacy* (New York: Macmillan, 1969), p. 65.

James Spade, *John and Caroline: Their Lives in Pictures* (New York: St. Martin's Press, 2001), p. 7.

Dr. David A. Lewis and Darryl Hicks, *The Presidential Zero-Year Mystery* (Plainfield, NJ: Haven Books, 1980), pp. 143–144.

James Spada, p. 42.

Ibid., p. 101.

Ibid.

Ibid.

Christopher Andersen, *The Day John Died* (New York: William Morrow, 2000), p. 186.

Richard Reeves, "The Danger in the Limelight," *U.S. News & World Report*, July 26, 1999, Vol. 127, issue 4, p. 28.

Christopher Andersen, p. 183.

John wrote about his kayaking adventure for the Travel section of the *New York Times*: "Laughs, Thrills and Stories," *New York Times*, August 1, 1999, Section 5, p. 25.

Christopher Andersen, p. 198.

James Spada, *John and Caroline*, p. 178.
Christopher Andersen, p. 260.
Learning Network Website (*http://www.infoplease. com/spot/kennedybio.html*).
Christopher Andersen, p. 280.
Ibid., p. 183.

CHAPTER 2

Carl Sferrazza Anthony, p. 88.
Alice Roosevelt Longworth was privately tutored.
Jeanne Elium and Don Elium, *Raising a Daughter* (Berkeley, CA.: Celestial Arts, 1994), p. 5.
See Judith V. Jordan, Alexandra Kaplan, Jean Baker Miller, Irene P. Stiver, and Janet L. Surrey, *Women's Growth in Connection: Writings from the Stone Center* (New York: The Guilford Press, 1991), p. 1.
Jeanne Elium and Don Elium, p. 6.
Michael Burlingame, *The Inner World of Abraham Lincoln* (Chicago: University of Illinois Press, 1994), p. 63.
Ibid., pp. 27 and 106.
Robert H. Ferrel, ed. *Off the Record: The Private Papers of Harry S. Truman* (New York: Harper & Row, 1980), p. 109. And yet later, Alice Roosevelt was considered "a favorite of Harry S. Truman." *Washington Post*, February 21, 1980, p. c4. The irony is that Theodore Roosevelt said something similar, comparing his daughter and son-in-law favorably with a notorious royal couple. Arthur H. Schlesinger, Jr., *Theodore Roosevelt* (New York: Chelsea House, 1985), p. 115.

Numerous history and reference books erroneously list "Amelia" as Nabby's middle name. Actually it was another nickname. Abigail was so fond of "Amelia" that she used the name for one of her own daughters. Kane, Podell, Anzovin, p. 26., *The Adams Papers*, The Massachusetts Historical Society and an interview with Anne Decker Cecere of the MHS.

David McCullough, *John Adams*, p. 58.

Paul Nagle writes that "after her tenth birthday, her father, John Adams, was rarely at home." Paul C. Nagel, *The Adams Women* (Cambridge, MA: Harvard University Press, 1987), p. 99.

Quinn-Musgrove and Kanter, p. 9.

Paul Nagel, *The Adams Women*, p. 99.

Ibid.

Ibid.

David McCullough, *John Adams*, p. 107.

Paul Nagel, *The Adams Women*, p. 99.

Ibid., p. 102.

Quinn-Musgrove and Kanter, *America's Royalty*, p. 9.

David McCullough, p. 288.

Ibid.

David McCullough, p. 289. Taken from the Adams Family Correspondence, V, pp. 74–75.

Ibid.

Drawing on Nabby's limited surviving correspondence, Paul Nagel questions whether Nabby really cared that much for Tyler, suggesting that Abigail was the force urging on the relationship. Paul C. Nagel, *The Adams Women*, p. 106.

David McCullough, p. 291.

Ibid., p. 299.

Ibid., p. 143.

Anne Cecere, Curator of the Massachusetts Historical Society points out that Adams once scolded his wife for using rouge. Correspondence with Anne Cecere, June 2002.

Ibid., p. 362.

Ibid., p. 363.

Paul C. Nagel, p. 117.

Linda Mayo, "Miss Adams in Love," *American Heritage*, 16 February 1965, pp. 35–47, 89. In fact, notwithstanding the legend of Tyler's great career, his financial security apparently evaporated at the end. Paul C. Nagel, p. 118.

Paul C. Nagel, p. 144.

Ibid., p. 130.

Ibid., pp. 126, 129. Anne Cecere, curator of the Massachusetts Historical Society, believes me to be excessively harsh on Abigail, pointing out that during this time of crisis she had also immediately dispatched son, John Quincy, to New York to bring Nabby home. Correspondence with Anne Cecere, June 2002.

Paul C. Nagel, p. 124.

David McCullough, p. 613.

Quinn-Musgrove and Kanter, *America's Royalty* (Westport, CT: Greenwood Press, 1983), p. 13.

Quinn-Musgrove and Kanter, p. 14.

David McCullough, p. 602.

Paul C. Nagel, p. 144.

David McCullough describes the moment as "before dawn." Paul Nagel tells the story of the singing of the hymn. David McCullough, *John*

Adams, p. 613. Paul C. Nagel, *The Adams Women*, p. 145.

Paul C. Nagel, p. 146.

David McCullough, p. 614.

Sol Barzman, p. 89.

Quinn-Musgrove and Kanter, p. 59.

From an interview with Harrison Tyler, presidential grandson, director of Sherwood Forest and Tyler family historian, April 27, 2002.

Ibid.

Oliver Perry Chitwood, *John Tyler, Champion of the Old South* (Newton, CT: American Political Biography Press, 1939 and 2000), p. 478.

Robert Watson, *The Presidents' Wives*, p. 59.

Robert Seager II, *And Tyler Too* (New York: McGraw-Hill, 1963), p. 173.

Many encyclopedias and books spell her name "Dolly." See *The Volume Library*. Editor and Chief Gorton Carruth, Mary R. Davidson, *Dolly Madison: Famous First Lady* (A Discovery Biography). She was in fact Dorothea Madison but used the spelling "Dolley" as her nickname. Joseph Nathan Kane, Janet Podell, Steven Anzovin, p. 50.

In a letter from Priscilla to her family, February 1842. Sol Barzman, p. 91.

Robert Seager II, *And Tyler Too*, p. 179.

Sol Barzman, p. 89.

Margaret Brown Klapthor, *The First Ladies* (Washington, DC: White House Historical Assoc., 1995), p. 28.

Sol Barzman, p. 93.

Robert Seager II, p. 181.

Ibid., p. 184.

Ibid., p. 180.

Ibid., p. 186.

Ibid.

Ibid., pp. 188–189.

Ibid., p. 192.

Ibid., p. 204.

William DeGregorio, p. 157.

Ibid., p. 205.

Some writers question whether the president carried Julia off the vessel. The story comes from an interview with the first lady written by journalist Nellie Bly, *New York World*, October 28, 1888. Cross and Novotny believe it to be an exaggeration. Wilbur Cross and Ann Novotny, *White House Weddings (New York: David McKay and Co., 1967), p. 76.*

Robert Seager II, p. 1.

Julia Tyler Gardiner to Juliana Gardiner, Washington, June 30, 1844, Tyler Family Papers.

Sol Barzman, p. 95.

B. S. McReynolds, *Presidential Blips* (University City, CA: B.S. Book Publishing, 1998), p. 50.

Ibid.

Margaret Truman, *First Ladies, An Intimate Group Portrait of White House Wives* (New York: Ballantine, 1995), p. 292.

Joseph Nathan Kane, Janet Podell, Steven Anzovin, p. 111.

Sol Barzman, p. 95.

From the John Quincy Adams Diary, Wilbur Cross and Ann Novotny, *White House Weddings* (New York: David McKay and Co., 1967), p. 77.

Lu Ann Paletta and Fred L. Worth, *The World Al-*

manac of Presidential Facts (New York: World Almanac, 1988), p. 53.

Robert Seager II, p. 8.

Julia Tyler Gardiner to Juliana Gardiner, Washington, June 30, 1844, Tyler Family Papers.

Margaret Truman, *First Ladies*, p. 293. Wilbur Cross and Ann Novotny write that Julia "enlarged the White House ball programs of quadrilles and polkas by adding the new dance, the waltz." Wilbur Cross and Ann Novotny, *White House Weddings*, p. 81. While Kane, Podell and Anzovin write that she was known for "dancing the polka in public in the White House." Joseph Nathan Kane, Janet Podell, Steven Anzovin, p. 111.

Margaret Truman, *First Ladies*, p. 293.

Sol Barzman, p. 19.

Robert Seager II, p. 8.

From an interview with Harrison Tyler, presidential grandson, director of Sherwood Forest and Tyler family historian, April 27, 2002.

Joseph Nathan Kane, Janet Podell, Steven Anzovin, p. 112.

Sol Barzman, p. 98.

Robert Seager II, p. 500.

Ibid.

Quinn-Musgrove and Kanter, p. 59.

Robert Seager II, p. 518.

Ibid., p. 519.

Ibid.

James A. Semple to Julia Gardiner Tyler, March 1866, Robert Seager II, p. 519.

Possibly a reference to "Cerberus," in Greek mythology the three-headed dog with mane and tail of snakes that guarded the entrance to Hades.

Julia Gardiner Tyler to James A. Semple, Robert Seager II, p. 519.

Quinn-Musgrove and Kanter, p. 59.

Robert Seager II, p. 352.

The portrait in question remained with Julia's side of the family and is today owned by the three children of David Gardiner Tyler, Jr., grandson of John Tyler. From an interview with Harrison Tyler, presidential grandson, director of Sherwood Forest and Tyler family historian, April 27, 2002.

J. J. Perling, p. 102.

Robert Seager II, p. 555.

Carol Felsenthal, *Princess Alice: The Life and Times of Alice Roosevelt Longworth* (New York: St. Martin's Press, 1988), p. 242.

Stacy Rozek Cordery, "Alice Roosevelt Longworth: Life in a Public Crucible," unpublished Ph. D. dissertation, University of Texas, Austin, 1992, p. 4.

When word came down, Alice was staying at a camp in the Adirondacks belonging to Mr. and Mrs. Robert Pruyns. From correspondence with Linda Molano, assistant director of the Theodore Roosevelt Association, June 2002. Also see Peter Collier, p. 117.

Sally Quinn, "The Canny Candor of Alice Longworth," *Washington Post*, February 21, 1980, p. d3.

Michael Teague, *Mrs. L: Conversations with Alice Roosevelt Longworth* (Garden City, NY: Doubleday, 1981), p. 72.

Owen Wister, *Roosevelt: The Story of a Friendship, 1880–1919* (New York: Macmillan, 1930), pp. 86–87.

Betty Boyd Caroli, *The Roosevelt Women* (New York: Basic Books, 1998), p. 400.

Peter Collier, p. 120.

Theodore Roosevelt to Ted, Jr. , January 8, 1903, *Letters of Theodore Roosevelt*, Vol. III, p. 402.

H. Paul Jeffers, *Theodore Roosevelt, Jr., The Life of a War Hero*, p. 60.

Peter Collier, p. 118.

Michael Teague, *Mrs. L: Conversations with Alice Roosevelt Longworth*, p. 76.

Betty Boyd Caroli, p. 406.

Ibid., p. 419.

William Miller and Frances Spatz Leighton, *Fishbait* (Englewood Cliffs, NJ: Prentice Hall, 1977), p. 103.

Most versions have the quote, "If you haven't anything *nice* to say about anyone . . ." Sally Quinn reported that the pillow with that very quote was visible during her interview with Alice. Sally Quinn, p. d3. The same quote is in *Time*, December 9, 1966. But *Britannica Online* has a slightly different quote . . . "If you can't say something *good* about someone . . ." And these are the exact words that Alice herself quotes in her autobiography *Crowded Hours* (New York: Scribners, 1933). Linda Molano, assistant director of the Theodore Roosevelt Association, insists that the correct quote was ". . . If you haven't anything *good* to say . . ." (from E-mail correspondence, June 2002). Which raises the question, was there more than one pillow?

Alice Roosevelt Longworth, *Crowded Hours: Reminiscences of Alice Roosevelt Longworth* (New York: Scribners, 1933), p. 325.

Barbara Hower, *Laughing All the Way* (New York: Stein and Day, 1973), p. 225.

Peter Collier with David Horowitz, *The Roosevelts: An American Saga* (New York: Simon and Schuster, 1994), p. 394.

Michael Teague, pp. 197–199.

S. L. Carson, "Presidential Children: Abandonment, Hysteria and Suicide," p. 538. And yet Lady Bird Johnson records an occasion where her husband kissed Alice, big hat and all. Lady Bird Johnson, *A White House Diary* (New York: Holt, Rinehart & Winston, 1970), p. 394. There is a claim that many of the stories of Alice Roosevelt are untrue.

S. L. Carson, p. 537.

Sally Quinn, p. d1.

Ted Morgan, *FDR: A Biography* (New York: Simon and Schuster, 1985), p. 206.

Linda Molano, assistant director of the Theodore Roosevelt Association, dismisses this analysis as "silly and untrue." From E-mail correspondence with Linda Molano, June 2002.

Molano at the Theodore Roosevelt Library points out that TR visited approximately every six weeks and stayed in the same house. Author Peter Collier talks of Alice "first meeting him at the age of almost three." From correspondence with Linda Molano, assistant director of the Theodore Roosevelt Association, June 2002, and Peter Collier, p. 118.

Interview with John A. Gable, executive director, Theodore Roosevelt Association, June 2002.

S. L. Carson, p. 533.

From E-mail correspondence with Linda Molano, June 2002.

Edmund Morris, *The Rise of Theodore Roosevelt* (New York: Ballantine Books, 1979), p. 288.

Edward J. Renehan, Jr. *The Lion's Pride: Theodore Roosevelt and His Family in Peace and War* (New York: Oxford University Press, 1998).

Molano points out that the pictures were later passed on to Alice. From E-mail correspondence with Linda Molano, assistant director of the Theodore Roosevelt Association, June 2002.

See Betty Boyd Caroli, p. 393.

Ibid., p. 399.

Peter Collier, p. 118.

Michael Teague, p. 128. Some point out that Alice, herself, wrote that her stepmother didn't mean what she said. Yet psychologists say this type of rationalization is critical for the child who must believe that the parent — or in this case the stepparent — really loves and respects them completely. It is significant that Alice was the only witness to this comment and yet chose to air it, perhaps seeking reassurance or feedback from others to help understand the relationship, a healthy sign.

S. L. Carson, p. 533. Carson attributes this quote to the *New York Times.*

Alice Miller, *The Drama of the Gifted Child* (New York: Basic Books, 1997), p. 106.

John A. Gable, respected expert on all things TR,

is nonetheless puzzled by the subject of Alice and the occult. Interview with John A. Gable, executive director, Theodore Roosevelt Association, June 2002. Peter Collier suggests that she may have pursued "white magic" during her period of private tutoring in the White House.

Sally Quinn, p. d3.

Alice Roosevelt Longworth Diary, entry for January 27, 1903. The papers of Alice Roosevelt Longworth, Library of Congress.

S. L. Carson, p. 541.

Betty Boyd Caroli, p. 427.

Peter Collier, p. 379.

Ibid., p. 426.

Myra MacPerson. "Princess Alice Roosevelt Longworth," *Washington Post*, February 21, 1984.

Patti Davis, "What We'll Do for Dad On his 91st Birthday," *Time*, February 4, 2002.

Ibid.

Ibid.

Ibid.

S. L. Carson, p. 539.

CHAPTER 3

Carl Sferrazza Anthony, *America's First Families* (New York: Simon and Schuster, 2000), p. 110.

Quinn-Musgrove and Kanter, *America's Royalty* (Westport, CT: Greenwood Press, 1983), p. 13. A later revised version of the same book dropped this description.

Michael Beschloss, "The Curse of the Famous Scion," *Newsweek*, August 14, 1995, p. 59.

Quinn-Musgrove and Kanter, p. 39.

Ibid., p. 105.

Attributed to the *Washington Sunday Herald*, *New York Times*, April 12, 1912.

Loftus, Mary, "The Other Side of Fame," *Psychology Today*, May–June 1995, Vol. 28, Issue 3, p. 48.

Carl Sferrazza Anthony, p. 307.

Ibid., p. 310.

H. Donald Winkler, *The Women in Lincoln's Life* (Nashville, TN.: Rutledge Hill Press, 2001), p. 139.

Quinn-Musgrove and Kanter, p. 99.

Ibid., p. 100.

Los Angeles Times, August 13, 1938. And yet others describe his academic career as "brilliant." Doris Kearns Goodwin, *No Ordinary Time*, p. 178.

Doris Kearns Goodwin, *No Ordinary Time*, p. 178.

Michael Reagan with Joe Hyam, *Michael Reagan: On the Outside Looking In* (New York: Zebra Books, 1988), pp. 82–83.

Doug Wead, *George Bush: Man of Integrity* (Eugene, OR: Harvest House, 1988), p. 132.

H. Paul Jeffers, *Theodore Roosevelt, Jr.: The Life of a War Hero* (Novato, CA: Presidio, 2002), p. 114.

Quinn-Musgrove and Kanter, p. 101.

Philip B. Kunhardt, Jr., Philip B. Kunhardt, III, Peter W. Kunhardt, *The American President* (Burbank, CA: Warner, A PBS film, 2000).

Cleaves, pp. 249–250.

Robert H. Ferrel, ed. *Off the Record: The Private Papers of Harry S. Truman* (New York: Harper & Row, 1980), p. 109.

James Thomas Flexner, *Washington: The Indispensable Man* (Boston: Little, Brown & Co, 1974), p. 43.

Sol Barzman, *The First Ladies*, p. 7.

Mike Wright, *What They Didn't Teach You About the American Revolution* (Novato, CA: Presidio, 1999), p. 173.

Barzman, p. 8.

Jay A. Parry and Andrew M. Allison, *The Real George Washington* (Washington, DC: The National Center for Constitutional Studies, 1991), p. 84.

Flexner, p. 43.

Frank Donovan, *The Women in Their Lives: The Distaff Side of the Founding Fathers* (New York, Dodd, Mead & Company, 1966), p. 123.

Parry and Allison, p. 84.

Alone among historians, Sandra Quinn-Musgrove and Sanford Kanter write that Patsy was actually thirteen years old at her death. Quinn-Musgrove and Kanter, *America's Royalty*, p. 3. Sol Barzman dates the birth of Patsy at 1756 and her death at 1773, age seventeen. Sol Barzman, *The First Ladies*, pp. 4 and 7. Flexner, a recognized authority on Washington, agrees. Parry and Allison place her date of death at June 19, 1773, again making her seventeen. Jay A. Parry and Andrew M. Allison, p. 84.

Donovan, pp. 124–125.

Ibid., pp. 122–123.

Flexner, p. 42, and Parry and Allison, p. 83.

Flexner, p. 43.

Barzman, p. 7.

Once again, there is a discrepancy in the telling of this story. According to Quinn-Musgrove and Kanter, Jacky "was with Washington in all of the War's battles." Quinn-Musgrove and Kanter, *America's Royalty*, p. 3. Perling makes the same claim. J. J. Perling, p. 350. James Flexner, the accepted authority on Washington, confirms the traditional account that Jacky opted out of the war until Yorktown. Parry and Allison state that Jacky "had sat out most of the war." Parry and Allison, p. 372.

Richard Brookhish, *Founding Father, Rediscovering G. Washington* (New York: The Free Press, 1996), p. 165.

Flexner, p. 359.

Ibid., p. 470.

Parry and Allison, p. 372.

Ferling, p. 511.

Perling, p. 356.

Robert Remini, *The Life of Andrew Jackson* (New York: Harper & Row, 1988), p. 61.

Harold D. Moser, Ed.-in-Chief, *The Papers of Andrew Jackson, Vol. II*, 1804–1813 (Knoxville: University of Tennessee Press, 1984), p. 218.

Letter from Andrew Jackson to Rachel Jackson, Fort Strother, December 29, 1813. Harold D. Moser, Ed.-in-Chief, *The Papers of Andrew Jackson, Vol. II*, 1804–1813 (Knoxville: University of Tennessee Press, 1984), p. 516.

Ibid.

Remini, p. 169.

Bill from Josiah Nichols to Andrew Jackson, December 26, 1825, Jackson Papers.

Marquis James, *The Life of Andrew Jackson* (Indianapolis: Bobbs-Merrill Company, 1938), p. 450.

Bill from Josiah Nichols to Andrew Jackson, December 26, 1825, Jackson Papers.

Ibid., p. 177.

Marquis James, *The Life of Andrew Jackson*, p. 546.

Ibid., p. 592.

Andrew Jackson to Andrew Jackson, Jr., December 31, 1839, John Spencer Bassett, Ed. *Correspondence of Andrew Jackson*, Vol. VI (1926–1935), p. 46.

James, p. 891.

Courtesy of the Ladies Hermitage Association, Marsha A. Mullin, chief curator, 2001.

Barzman, p. 75.

John Niven, *Martin Van Buren* (New York: Oxford University Press, 1983), p. 139.

Ibid., p. 272.

Ibid., p. 174.

While there is abundant evidence that John Van Buren had numerous public girlfriends before his short marriage, Perling insists that at this time in his life there was no evidence to confirm that his intentions or actions with the respective young ladies were ever less than honorable. J. J. Perling, p. 57. Even so, some of John's paramours became national stories, including Maria Ameriga Vespucci, a descendant of the great seventeenth-century explorer. *New*

York Herald, December 11, 1841.

Martin Van Buren to John Van Buren, Van Buren Papers, March 1830 and June 25, 1830, Library of Congress.

An excerpt from *The Saturday Evening Post*, August 26, 1848, *The Presidents* (Indianapolis: Curtis Publishing, 1989), p. 39.

Niven, p. 411.

Major L. Wilson, *The Presidency of Martin Van Buren* (Lawrence, KS: University of Kansas Press, 1984), p. 161.

Niven, p. 479.

Ibid., p. 480.

Ibid.

Robert P. Watson, *The Presidents' Wives*, p. 58.

DeGregorio, p. 124.

Niven, p. 479.

Ibid., p. 599.

Ibid., p. 604.

Ibid., p. 596.

Lu Ann Paletta and Fred L. Worth, *The World Almanac of Presidential Facts* (New York: World Almanac, 1988), p. 46.

Sources disagree on the number of children born to Smith by his first wife. Quinn-Musgrove and Kanter say four, Van Buren's biographer Niven suggests three. Quinn-Musgrove and Kanter, p. 43. Niven, p. 598.

Correspondence from Blair to former President Martin Van Buren, March 30, 1849, Van Buren papers, the Library of Congress. Francis Preston Blair was a Kentucky editor-journalist and a friend of Smith Van Buren, the president's youngest son.

Niven, p. 405.

Ibid., pp. 439–440.

Congressional Globe, Twenty-seventh Congress, 1st Session, Vol. 10, Appendix, pp. 145–146.

Niven, p. 481.

Ibid., p. 544.

Ibid., pp. 486–487.

Ibid., p. 548.

Ibid., p. 551.

Ibid., p. 592. And yet, because he opposed abolition of slavery by proclamation on constitutional grounds, he earned charges of inconsistency on the issue. J. J. Perling, p. 66.

From conversation with George W. Bush, June 13, 1998.

Quinn-Musgrove and Kanter, p. 42.

See John Van Buren, *Biographical Directory of the American Congress.*

Niven, p. 603.

Perling, p. 65.

Richard Reeves, "The Danger in the Limelight," *U.S. News & World Report*, July 26, 1999, Vol. 127, issue 4, p. 28.

There are eighty-nine sons and sixty-three daughters. Joseph Nathan Kane, Janet Podell, Steven Anzovin, *Facts About the Presidents*, p. 575. This count does not include stepchildren who were not formally adopted, or illegitimate children.

William S. McFeely, *Grant, A Biography* (New York: W.W. Norton Co., 1981), p. 489.

DeGregorio, p. 269. See Lu Ann Paletta and Fred L. Worth, *The World Almanac of Presidential Facts*, p. 84.

Lawson, Don, *Famous Presidential Scandals* (Hillside, NJ: Enslow 1990), p. 31.

Ibid.

New York World, May 26, 1884.

McFeely, p. 492.

Quinn-Musgrove and Kanter. p. 96.

Simpson, p. 74.

Brooks D. Simpson, *Ulysses S. Grant; Triumph Over Adversity, 1822–1865* (Boston, MA: Houghton Mifflin, 2000), p. 52.

Ibid., p. 53.

McFeely, p. 237.

CHAPTER 4

Carl Sferrazza Anthony, p. 308.

Sol Barzman, *The First Ladies*, p. 174.

William DeGregorio, *The Complete Book of U.S. Presidents*, p. 150.

See appendix for life expectancy charts for presidential children.

Carl Byker and David Mrazek, *Woodrow Wilson, A Passionate Man* (WGBH Educational Foundation and Community Television of Southern California, 2002).

George W. Bush, *A Charge to Keep* (New York: William Morrow, 1999), p. 14.

Lincoln address at New Salem, Illinois, March 9, 1832, Library of Congress.

H. Donald Winkler, *The Women in Lincoln's Life* (Nashville, TN.: Rutledge Press, 2001), p. xii.

Susan Edwards, *White House Kids* (New York: Avon, 1999), pp. 9–10.

Frank Donovan, *Women in Their Lives: The Dis-*

taff *Side of the Founding Fathers* (New York: Dodd, Mead & Co., 1966), p. 253.

David McCullough, p. 65.

Quinn-Musgrove and Kanter, p. 22.

Sol Barzman, p. 83.

Alyn Brodsky, *Grover Cleveland, a Study in Character* (New York: St. Martin's Press, 2000), p. 427.

Margaret Truman, *First Ladies*, p. 230.

"Bilious fever" was a "catch-all phrase designed to cover the ignorance of the attending physicians." Sol Barzman, p. 98.

Christine Sadler, *Children in the White House* (New York: Putnam, 1967), p. 128.

Sol Barzman, p. 224.

www.whitehouse.gov/history/firstladies/im25.html

From a letter to James Garfield from his wife, Lucretia, December 6, 1863. *www.americanpresidents.org/letter/20.asp*

Ibid.

Allan Peskin, *Garfield* (Kent, OH: Kent State University Press, 1978), p. 156.

From a letter to Lucretia Garfield from her husband, James Garfield, written on the same day that she was writing him. December 6, 1863. *www.americanpresidents.org/letter/20.asp*

Robert Sobel, *An American Enigma* (Washington, DC: Regnery, 1998), p. 8.

Almost all newspaper and biographical accounts show July 7, 1924, as the date of death for Calvin Coolidge, Jr., but Quinn-Musgrove and Kanter hold to an April 7, 1924, date even in their revised, updated book. Quinn-Musgrove and Kanter, p. 172.

Jean H. Baker, *Mary Todd Lincoln* (New York: Norton, 1987), p. 368.

Susan Eisenhower, *Mrs. Ike: Memories and Reflections on the Life of Mamie Eisenhower* (New York: Farrar, Straus and Giroux, 1996), p. 102.

Ibid.

Ibid., p. 111.

Freeman Cleaves, p. 247. In this case, as in the case of the Harrison son, Cleves is spelled without the "a." Whereas the author of this Harrison biography, unrelated to the Harrison family, spells it *with* an "a."

Dr. David A. Lewis and Darryl Hicks, *The Presidential Zero-Year Mystery* (Plainfield, NJ: Haven Books, 1980), p. 24.

John and Claire Whitcomb, *Real Life in the White House*, pp. 56–57.

James M. McPherson, *To the Best of My Ability: The American Presidents* (London: Dorling Kindersley, 2000), pp. 72–74; Rebecca Stefoff, *William Henry Harrison* (Ada, OK: Garrett Educational, 1990), pp. 109–113.

Freeman Cleaves, *Old Tippecanoe*, p. 91.

General Harrison to Carter Basset Harrison, November 27, 1794, Harrison Papers, I: 21–22, Library of Congress.

Ben F. Sager, *The Harrison Mansion*, p. 13.

Freeman Cleaves, p. 99.

Ibid., p. 101.

Ibid.

Ibid., p. 162.

Ibid., p. 163, kindly.

Most historic accounts place her date of death as 1845 but Jennifer Capps, curator for the President Benjamin Harrison House, has documentations showing that Anna lived to 1865, giving birth to twelve children, six of which are born after the 1845 date. DeGregorio, p. 139. Kane, Podell and Anzovin, p. 102.

For a time Jane's father served as president of Bowdoin College in Maine, thus many historians mistakenly refer to the family as from that state.

In 1843, Pierce took a leadership role in the Temperance Movement. Roy Franklin Nichols, *Franklin Pierce, Young Hickory of the Granite Hills* (Newtown, CT: American Political Biography Press, 1931), p. 123.

Sol Barzman. p. 134.

Ibid.

The Lincoln Library of Social Studies, p. 1121.

Roy Franklin Nichols, p. 203.

Sol Barzman, p. 135.

Ibid.

Quinn-Musgrove and Kanter, p. 78.

Roy Franklin Nichols, *Franklin Pierce, Young Hickory of the Granite Hills*, p. 224.

Sol Barzman, p. 135.

From a letter written by Jane's cousin on January 7, 1853, as reported in Sol Barzman, p. 135.

Ibid.

Roy Franklin Nichols, *Franklin Pierce, Young Hickory of the Granite Hills*, p. 225.

Watson, Robert, *The Presidents' Wives, Reassessing the Office of First Lady* (Boulder: Lynne Rienner, 2000), p. 60.

The first lady rarely attended church although

she insisted that her husband's staffers do so. Carl Sferrazza Anthony, p. 228.

Ibid.

Former first lady Barbara Bush and Franklin Pierce are fourth cousins, four times removed. They are both descended from Thomas Pierce and Elizabeth Cole (1618), who had two sons, James Pierce and Steven Pierce. Barbara is a descendant of James, and Franklin Pierce is a descendant of Steven.

Katherine Leiner, *First Children, Growing Up in the White House*, p. 26.

H. Donald Winkler, p. 11.

Ibid., p. 1.

Ibid.

H. Donald Winkler, p. 126.

Letter from Lincoln to wife Mary, April 16, 1848, Paul M. Angle and Earl Schenk Miers, eds., *The Living Lincoln* (New York: Barnes and Noble, 1992), p. 115.

Ibid.

Ibid., p. 142.

Perling cites Beveridge as a source, saying that the boys hid behind a "screening hedge." Perling, p. 130.

Ward Hill Lamon, *Recollections of Abraham Lincoln, 1847–1865* (Lincoln, NE: University of Nebraska Press, reprinted from the A. C. McClurg & Co 1895), p. 164.

Letter from Lincoln to Dr. A. G. Henry, an old friend, from Springfield, IL, July 4, 1860, Angle and Miers, p. 347.

Perling, p. 134. DeGregorio, however, states flatly that Tad had a cleft palate. William

DeGregorio, *The Complete Book of U.S. Presidents*, p. 227.

Katherine Leiner, *First Children, Growing Up in the White House*, p. 26.

Perling, p. 131. Carl Sandburg, Vol. I, p. 458.

Carl Sandburg, *Abraham Lincoln, The War Years, Volume I* (New York: Harcourt, Brace & World, 1939), p. 455.

Susan Edwards, *White House Kids*, p. 15.

Carl Sandburg, Vol. I, p. 456.

Susan Edwards, p. 15.

Quinn-Musgrove and Kanter, p. 84.

Carl Sandburg, Vol. I, p. 457.

Angle, Paul M. and Miers, Earl Schenk, eds., *The Living Lincoln* (New York: Barnes and Noble, 1992), p. 469.

Carl Sandburg, p. 458.

Katherine Leiner, p. 28.

Letter from Lincoln to wife Mary, August 8, 1863. Angle and Miers, eds., *The Living Lincoln* (New York: Barnes and Noble, 1992), p. 569.

Carl Sandburg, Vol. III, p. 527.

Katherine Leiner, p. 30. Jean H. Baker, Susan Edwards, and other writers, however, say that Tad was also at the White House when the assassination took place. Susan Edwards, p. 19. Jean H. Baker, p. 245.

Katherine Leiner, pp. 30–31.

From correspondence with Timothy P. Townsend, historian, Lincoln Home National Historic Site, August 2002.

Carl Sandburg, Vol. IV, p. 288.

Philip B. Kunhardt, Jr., Philip B. Kunhardt, III,

and Peter W. Kunhardt, *Lincoln* (New York: Knopf, 1992), p. 361.

Elizabeth Keckley, *Thirty Years a Slave, and Four Years in the White House* (New York: G.W. Carleton, 1868), p. 197.

Peter Collier, p. 143.

Looker, pp. 13–14.

Looker, pp. 146–147.

Looker, p. 33.

H. W. Brands, *TR, The Last Romantic* (New York: Basic Books, 1997), p. 796.

Ibid., p. 100.

Quentin Roosevelt in a letter to his girlfriend, Flora Whitney, May 1918.

Alice Roosevelt Longworth, *Crowded Hours: Reminiscences of Alice Roosevelt Longworth* (New York, London: Charles Scribner's Sons, 1933), p. 255.

H. Paul Jeffers, p. 88.

Captain Edward V. Rickenbacker, *Fighting the Flying Circus* (New York, Frederick A. Stokes, 1919), *www.richthofen.com/rickenbacker/rick20.htm*, pp. 2–3.

Rickenbacker, p. 3.

Theodore Roosevelt to Kermit Roosevelt, July 13, 1918.

H. Paul Jeffers, p. 106.

Edward J. Renehan, Jr. *The Lion's Pride: Theodore Roosevelt and His Family in War and Peace* (New York: Oxford Press, 1998) *www.worldwar1.com/dbc/roosev.htm*

David Grubin and Geoffrey C. Ward, *Theodore Roosevelt*, A PBS Video, WGBH Education Foundation, Boston, 1996.

Sol Barzman, p. 276.

Some historical accounts suggest that he took a solitary walk "in the misty dawn." "The Presidents," *The Saturday Evening Post* (Indianapolis: Curtis Publishing, 1989), p. 113.

Sol Barzman, p. 280.

Quinn-Musgrove and Kanter, p.149.

Ibid.

J. J. Perling, p. 300.

From an interview with Cyndy Bittinger, executive director, The Calvin Coolidge Memorial Foundation.

Quinn-Musgrove, Sandra and Kanter, Sanford, *America's Royalty* (Westport, CT: Greenwood Press, 1983), p. 150.

Robert Sobel, *Coolidge, an American Enigma*, p. 239.

Some historians (see Quinn-Musgrove and Kanter) have incorrectly reported that Calvin Coolidge, Jr., "stubbed" his toe.

Barzman, Sol. *The First Ladies* (New York: Cowles, 1970), p. 281.

Robert Sobel, p. 295.

Ibid.

Historians Quinn-Musgrove and Kanter mistakenly report his death in the spring, April 7, 1924. Quinn-Musgrove and Kanter, p. 172.

Robert Sobel, p. 296.

American President Website (*http://www.americanpresident.org/KoTrain/Courses/CC/CC_Family_Life.htm*)

Robert Sobel, p. 296.

John and Claire Whitcomb, pp. 285–286.

Robert Sobel, p. 298.

Louis I. Dublin, Alfred J. Lotka and Mortimer Spiegelman, *Length of Life* (New York: Ronald Press, 1948), pp. 66, 217, 222.

Bertrand Meyer, *Les Dames de L'Elysée* (Paris: Librairie Academique Perrin, 1987).

Calvin Coolidge, *Autobiography of Calvin Coolidge* (New York: Cosmopolitan, 1929), p. 190.

Grace quoted this passage from Philippians to a friend, Grace Coolidge, Letters, Coolidge Collection, Forbes Library, Northampton, Massachusetts.

Robert E. Gilbert, *The Mortal Presidency* (New York, Basic Books, 1992).

Jib Fowles, *Starstruck* (Washington: Smithsonian Institution Press, 1992), p. 238.

Mary Loftus, "The Other Side of Fame," *Psychology Today*, May/June, 1995, p. 48.

Jib Fowles, *Starstruck*, p. 238.

Mary Loftus, p. 48.

Geoffrey C. Ward, *Thomas Jefferson, A Film by Ken Burns* (Burbank, CA: PBS and AOL–Time Warner, 1996).

CHAPTER 5

Eleanor Wilson McAdoo, *The Woodrow Wilsons* (New York: Macmillan, 1937), p. 181.

Conversation with Steven Ford, May 23, 2002.

Philip B. Kunhardt, Jr., Philip B. Kunhardt, III, and Peter W. Kunhardt, *Echoes from the White House* (New York and Washington: A Four Score Production, with WNET and WETA, distributed by PBS, 2001).

Ibid.

Conversation with George W. Bush, December 21, 1998.

Mary Loftus, "The Other Side of Fame," *Psychology Today*, May–June 1995, Vol. 28, Issue 3, p. 48.

Washington Post, February 21, 1980.

Webb Garrison and Beth Wieder, *A Treasury of White House Tales* (New York: Knopf, 1992), p. 361.

New York Times, January 19, 1889, p. 1.

James Grant Wilson, *Presidents of the United States 1789–1914* (New York: Charles Scribner's and Sons, 1914), pp. 259–260.

Robert T. Lincoln to J. G. Holland, Chicago, June 6, 1865, Rufus Rockwell Wilson, ed., *Intimate Memories of Lincoln* (Elmira: Primavera Press, 1945), p. 499.

Peter Collier, p. 389.

Joseph Nathan Kane, Janet Podell, Steve Anzovin, *Facts About the Presidents*, p. 342. The seventh edition of this highly respected authority on presidents, published in 2001, misses Elliott's last marriage to Patricia Peabody Whitehead and Franklin, Jr.'s, last marriage to Linda McKay Stevenson Weicker.

Quinn-Musgrove and Kanter, pp. 179–189. A revised version of this book published in 1995 does not list James Roosevelt's last marriage to Mary Lena Winskill, which took place in 1969.

Doris Kearns Goodwin, *No Ordinary Time* (New York: Simon and Schuster, 1994), p. 178.

John T. McQuiston, "Franklin D. Roosevelt Jr. Is Dead; Ex-New York Congressman, 74," *New York Times*, August 18, 1988.

Michael Beschloss, "The Curse of the Famous Scion," *Newsweek*, August 14, 1995, p. 59.

Quinn-Musgrove and Kanter, p. 179.

Peter Collier, p. 158.

Peter Collier, Ibid. Attributed to John Boetigger, Jr., *A Love in Shadow* (New York: Norton, 1978), p. 53.

Joseph P. Lash, *Franklin and Eleanor* (New York: Norton, 1971), p. 300.

Ibid., p. 343.

Ibid., p. 301.

Anna Roosevelt, *Scamper, the Bunny Who Went to the White House* (New York: Macmillan, 1934).

"Anna Roosevelt Halsted, Only Daughter of FDR," *Wahington Post*, December 2, 1975.

Boettiger's departure overseas left Anna vulnerable to constant corporate intrigues as Hearst moved to take back editorial control of his own paper. Joseph P. Lash, *Franklin and Eleanor*, p. 699.

Doris Kearns Goodwin, *No Ordinary Time*, pp. 472–473. Although she was not designated by the White House as an "official White House hostess." Robert P. Watson, *The Presidents' Wives*, pp. 57–59.

Joseph P. Lash, *Franklin and Eleanor*, p. 721.

"Anna Roosevelt Halsted, Only Daughter of FDR," *Washington Post*, December 2, 1975.

"Anna Roosevelt dies at 69 in NY," Associated Press, December 2, 1975.

Quinn-Musgrove and Kanter and other historians mistakenly say that he was twenty-six years old. Perling suggests that he was "nearing twenty-six." Actually, he had just turned twenty-five on December 23, 1932. The inauguration was held on March 4, 1933. Quinn-Musgrove and Kanter, *America's Royalty*, p. 181. J. J. Perling, *Presidents' Sons*, p. 312.

There are different spellings for Miss Cushing's first name. Most accounts spell it "Betsy." Pulitzer Prize winner Doris Kearns Goodwin spells it "Betsey." Doris Kearns Goodwin, *No Ordinary Time*, p. 177. Joseph P. Lash, *Franklin and Eleanor*, p. 322.

Joseph P. Lash, *Franklin and Eleanor*, p. 322.

J. J. Perling, p. 312.

Ibid.

New York Times, September 3, 1933.

New York Times, September 13, 1933.

Boston Evening Transcript, September 21, 1933.

J. J. Perling, p. 313.

Quinn-Musgrove and Kanter, p. 181.

J. J. Perling, p. 313.

New York Times, July 13, 1935.

The Saturday Evening Post, July 2, 1938.

Time, July 4, 1938.

Philadelphia Public Ledger, July 2, 1938.

The Saturday Evening Post, July 2, 1938.

Collier's Weekly, August 20, 1938.

Quinn-Musgrove and Kanter suggest he was president, p. 182. Most accounts have him serving as vice president.

Jeffrey A. Perlman, "James Roosevelt, Son of F.D.R., Dies at 83." *Los Angeles Times*, August 14, 1991.

William DeGregorio, p. 481.

Dennis Hevesi, "Elliott Roosevelt, General and Author, Dies at 80," *New York Times*, October

28, 1990.

Jeffrey A. Perlman, "James Roosevelt, Son of F.D.R., Dies at 83."

Quinn-Musgrove and Kanter say he was eighty-five years and nine months at death, *America's Royalty*, p. 181.

Michael Beschloss, "The Curse of the Famous Scion," p. 59.

Joseph P. Lash, *Franklin and Eleanor*, p. 490.

Ibid.

Time, August 29, 1938.

New York Times reported three hundred missions, the Associated Press reported eighty-nine. Dennis Hevesi, "Elliott Roosevelt, General and Author, Dies at 80," *New York Times*, October 28, 1990. "Elliott Roosevelt, author, dies at 80," The Associated Press, as reported in the *Poughkeepsie Journal*, October 28, 1990.

"Elliott Roosevelt, author, dies at 80," The Associated Press, as reported in the *Poughkeepsie Journal*, October 28, 1990.

Dennis Hevesi, "Elliott Roosevelt, General and Author, Dies at 80," *New York Times*, October 28, 1990.

Newsweek, July 10 and July 24, 1944.

New York Herald Tribune, January 19, 1945.

Joseph P. Lash, *Eleanor: The Years Alone* (New York: Norton, 1972), p. 90.

Joseph P. Lash, *A World of Love: Eleanor Roosevelt and Her Friends* (Garden City, NY: Doubleday, 1984), p. 161.

Michael Beschloss, "The Curse of the Famous Scion," p. 59.

New York Times, March 25, 1935; April 4, 1935;

November 20, 1935; December 23, 1935.

Doris Kearns Goodwin, *No Ordinary Time*, p. 178.

Ibid.

John T. McQuiston, "Franklin D. Roosevelt Jr. Is Dead; Ex-New York Congressman, 74," *New York Times*, August 18, 1988.

Washington Star, April 28, 1981.

New York Times, April 30, 1933.

Joseph Lash, *Eleanor: The Years Alone* (New York: Norton, 1974), p. 182.

Joseph P. Lash, *Franklin and Eleanor*, p. 325.

Michael Beschloss, "The Curse of the Famous Scion," *Newsweek*, August 14, 1995, p. 59.

CHAPTER 6

Letter from Thomas Jefferson to Patsy, March 28, 1787, J. P. Boyd, editor, *The Papers of Thomas Jefferson*, Vol. 11 (Princeton, NJ: Princeton University Press).

Paul C. Nagel, *The Adams Women: Abigail and Louisa Adams, Their Sisters and Daughters* (New York and Oxford: Oxford University Press, 1987), p. 124.

Ibid.

Ibid.

Gordon Langley Hall, *Mr. Jefferson's Ladies* (Boston: Beacon Press, 1966), p. 12.

Sarah N. Randolph, *The Domestic Life of Thomas Jefferson* (1871; rpt. New York: Ungar, 1958), p. 63.

Ibid.

Ibid.

Ibid.

Elizabeth Langhorne, *Monticello: A Family Story* (Chapel Hill: Algonquin Books, 1987), p. 24.

Joseph J. Ellis, *American Sphinx: The Character of Thomas Jefferson* (New York: Alfred A. Knopf, 1996), p. 67. Ellis notes that "Jefferson did not seem to possess any sense of complicity in causing her pregnancies or any sense of warning as her health deteriorated after each new miscarriage or birth."

Hall, p. 66.

Ibid.

Kate Dickinson Sweetser, *Famous Girls of The White House* (New York: Thomas Y. Crowell Company, 1930), p. 58.

Hall, p. 81.

Sweetser, p. 67.

Claude G. Bowers, *The Young Jefferson*, 1743–1789 (Boston: Houghton Mifflin Company, 1945), p. 465.

Hall, pp. 93–94.

Ibid., p. 126. Sister d'Hinnisdal, who taught Christian doctrine, along with fifteen other nuns, was beheaded. The Abbess Mother Louise-Therese and Sister Camille fled in disguise, saving Patsy's friend, Madeleine de Soyecourt.

Claude G. Bowers, p. 498.

Langhorne, p. 49. Langhorne states, "Although there is family tradition to the contrary, it is now clear that Tom Randolph never saw his future bride in Paris, but went directly from Scotland to Virginia. He had left Edinburgh, in fact, without receiving a degree."

Hall, p. 93.

Hall, p. 124.

Fawn M. Brodie, *Thomas Jefferson: An Intimate History* (New York: W.W. Norton, 1974), p. 297.

Langhorne, p. 102.

Hall, p. 170. (Langhorne, p. 128, states Jack Eppes did not leave until Congress adjourned. His letters to Jefferson, however, are dated prior to March 26, the date Hall states Congress adjourned.)

Langhorne, p. 130.

Brodie, p. 380.

Bernard A. Weisberger, *America Afire: Jefferson, Adams and the Revolutionary Election of 1800* (New York: HarperCollins, 2000), p. 122. John Adams had earlier described Jefferson as wanting a reputation "as an humble, modest, meek man, wholly without ambition or vanity." But if the opportunity came for the presidency, he said, everyone would see that he is "as ambitious as Oliver Cromwell." But his letters to Patsy show otherwise.

*www.whitehouse.gov/history/firstladies/mj3/*html

Langhorne, p. 133.

Merrill D. Peterson, *Thomas Jefferson and the New Nation: A Biography* (New York: Oxford University Press, 1970), p. 925.

Edward Dumbauld, "Jefferson and Adams' English Garden Tour," in *Jefferson and the Arts: An Extended View*, ed. William Howard Adams (Washington, DC: National Gallery of Art, 1976), p. 149.

Ibid.

Hall, p. 89.

Thomas Jefferson to John Adams, November 7, 1819 (Ford, 12:134, 135).

Dos Passos, pp. 180–181.

Ellis, p. 139.

Hall, p. 172.

Langhorne, p. 91.

Ibid.

Thomas Mann Randolph to Thomas Jefferson, March 20, 1802 (Massachusetts Historical Society).

Bear, *Family Letters*, p. 223.

Thomas Jefferson to Martha Jefferson Randolph, February 5, 1801 (Bear, *Family Letters*, p. 195).

Hall, p. 146.

Langhorne, p. 209.

Ibid., p. 231.

Sweetser, p. 58.

Langhorne, p. 245.

Ibid.

Dos Passos, p. 307.

Hetty Carr to Dabney S. Carr, March 13, 1826 (Carr-Cary Papers, U. Va.).

Brodie, p. 465.

B. L. Rayner, Life of *Thomas Jefferson* (Online: edited by Eyler Robert Coates, Sr., 1997. Eyler Robert Coates, Sr.), Chapter 39, p. 7.

Ibid., p. 8.

Ibid., p. 7.

Ibid.

Ibid., p. 8.

Ibid., p. 7.

Hall, pp. 223–234.

Brodey, "Reminiscences of Isaac Jefferson," p. 480.

S. 16, In Senate of the United States, 22nd Congress, 1st Session, March 20, 1832.

Patsy's son, George Wythe Randolph, was to become the Confederacy's first secretary of war.

"Andrew Johnson's Obituary," *New York Times*, August 1, 1875, p. 1.

Hans L. Trefousse, *Andrew Johnson; A Biography* (New York: W.W. Norton, 1989), p. 73.

Ibid., p. 102.

Ibid.

Quinn-Musgrove and Kanter, *America's Royalty*, p. 99. Robert W. Winston, *Andrew Johnson, Plebian and Patriot* (New York: Henry Holt, 1928), p. 494.

Sol Barzman, p. 24, and Hans L. Trefousse, p. 168.

Hans L. Trefousse, p. 101.

Ibid.

Ibid., p. 168.

Ibid., p. 356.

Ibid., p. 229.

Robert W. Winston, *Andrew Johnson, Plebian and Patriot* (New York: Henry Holt, 1928), p. 494.

Ibid., p. 239.

Carl Sferrazza Anthony, p. 308.

Ibid., p. 364.

CHAPTER 7

Maureen Reagan, *http://womenshistory.about.com/library/qu/blqureag.htm*

Ishbel Ross, *Sons of Adam, Daughters of Eve: The Role of Women in American History* (New York: Harper & Row, 1969), p. 77.

Langhorne, p. 256. Martha Jefferson Randolph to Benjamin Franklin Randolph (Smith-Carter Papers, U. Va.). According to Langhorne: Incorrectly dated January 27, 1838. Correct to January 27, 1836, when Martha was still living and Lewis Randolph was in Arkansas, as referred to in the letter.

The first woman suffrage law in the United States was passed in the territory of Wyoming on December 10, 1869. The state of Colorado followed in 1893; Utah and Idaho in 1896; Washington in 1910; California in 1911; Arizona, Kansas, and Oregon in 1912; Illinois in 1913; Nevada and Montana in 1914.

www.brynmawr.edu/about/history.shtml

Sweetser, p. 264.

Millicent Carey McIntosh, "Helen Taft Manning . . . An Olympian Destiny," *Bryn Mawr Bulletin*, Summer, 1957.

Mary Gardiner, "Helen Taft Manning, A Resolution," Annual Meeting of the Alumnae Association of Bryn Mawr College, June 1, 1957.

Ishbel Ross, *An American Family: The Tafts — 1678 to 1964* (Cleveland and New York: The World Publishing Company, 1964), p. 321.

www.wilpf.org/history, Women's International League for Peace and Freedom, p. 1.

Doris Weatherford, *A History of the American Suffragist Movement* (Santa Barbara, CA; Denver, CO; and Oxford, England: The Moschovitis Group, Inc., 1998), pp. 195–196.

www.vassun.vssar.edu/-daniels/1905_1914.html

Sweetser, pp. 288–289.

Frances Wright Saunders, *First Lady Between Two*

Worlds: Ellen Axson Wilson (Chapel Hill and London: The University of North Carolina Press, 1985), pp. 170, 184–185.

Ibid., p. 224.

www.spartacus.schoolnet.co.uk/USAsuffrage.htm, p. 7.

Quinn-Musgrove and Kanter, p. 147.

Obituary, *New York Times*, March 14, 1901.

Quinn-Musgrove and Kanter, p. 129.

Ibid.

Interview with Ann Moore, librarian at President Benjamin Harrison Home Library.

Margaret Truman, *First Ladies: An Intimate Group Portrait of White House Wives* (New York: Fawcett Columbine, 1995), p. 52.

Spoken by actress Shelly Fabares. Jeff Wilson, Associated Press, "More than 1,000 attend Maureen Reagan's funeral." (*The Californian North County Times, NC Times.net*, 2001).

Ibid.

Ibid.

John McCain, "Eulogy Given by Senator John McCain at the Memorial Service for Maureen Reagan," *http://mccain.senate.gov/maureenspch.htm*, p. 3.

Ibid.

Maureen Reagan, *First Father, First Daughter: A Memoir* (Boston: Little, Brown and Company, 1989), p. 41.

Ibid.

Ibid., p. 42.

Ibid.

Ibid., p. 65.

Ibid., p. 64.

Ibid., p. 75.

Ibid., p. 98.

Ibid., p. 99.

Ibid.

Ibid., pp. 122–123.

Ibid., pp. 122–134. (All references to Maureen Reagan's spousal abuse come from this chapter.)

John Nichols, " 'Republican Feminist': Recalling a Better Reagan," *Common Dreams News Center, http://www.commondreams.org/views01/0809-03. htm,* p. 1.

John Gizzi, "Maureen Reagan, 1941–2001," Online Human Events, *The National Conservative Weekly,* August 13, 2001. *http:///www. humaneventsonline.com/articles/08-13-01/tgizzi. html,* p. 1.

"Daughter: Ronald Reagan's health deteriorating," January 24, 2000. *http://europe.cnn.com/ 2000/US/01/24/reagan.health.01,* p. 2.

John McCain, ibid.

For more information on malignant melanomas, please see *www.skincarephysicians.com/ melanomanet*

"Jane Wyman's Daughter, Maureen Reagan, 60, Dies of Cancer — August 8, 2001." *http://www. meredy.com/janewyman/maureen.htm,* p. 2.

Jeff Wilson, p. 2.

From 1935 till 1942, her school year was divided between Independence, Missouri and a private school in Washington, D.C., with Margaret attending a full semester in each school, for each year. Source, the Truman Library.

Margaret Truman, with Margaret Cousins, *Sou-*

venir: Margaret Truman's Own Story (New York: McGraw-Hill, 1956), p. 39.

Truman, *Souvenir*, p. 113.

Ibid., p. 278.

Margaret Truman, *Bess W. Truman* (New York: Macmillan Publishing Company, 1986), p. 365.

Paul Hume, "Postlude: Margaret Truman Sings Here Again with Light Program," *Washington Post*, December 6, 1950.

Truman, *Souvenir*, p. 279.

David Wise, *The Politics of Lying, Government Deception, Secrecy and Power* (New York: Random House, 1973), p. 314.

Barbara Heggie, "What Makes Margaret Sing?" *Woman's Home Companion*, January, 1951, p. 54.

Ibid.

Truman, *Souvenir*, p. 351.

Clifton E. Daniel died February 21, 2000 of complications from a stroke and heart disease.

Contemporary Authors Online. The Gale Group, 2001. Reproduced in Biography Resource Center. Farmington Hills, MI: The Gale Group, 2001, p. 3.

Contemporary Authors Online, p. 2.

www.amazon.com/exec/obidos/ASIN/04492127650/ref=ase_stopyourkilling/104-24

CHAPTER 8

Diary and Letters of Rutherford B. Hayes, Ohio Archeological and Historical Society, Vol. 4, p. 24, July 7, 1881.

Freeman Cleaves, *Old Tippecanoe*, p. 7.

Jane C. Walker, *John Tyler, A President of Many Firsts* (Blacksburg, VA: McDonald and Woodward, 2001), p. 4.

Kane, Podell, Anzovin, p. 500.

Ibid., p. 3.

Mary Loftus, "The Other Side of Fame," *Psychology Today*, May/June, 1995, p. 48.

Davis was rumored to have offered Taylor the post of Quartermaster General. *Richmond Dispatch*, October 26, 1862, p. 3.

The Texas Handbook, *www.angelfire.com/va3/valleywar/people/taylor*

www.taylor-barry-roots.com/civilwar/RichardTaylor

The Texas Handbook, ibid.

Sol Barzman, *The First Ladies* (New York: Cowles Book Company, 1970.) pp. 117, 118.

The Texas Handbook, ibid.

Ibid.

Ibid.

Ibid.

Ibid.

Ibid.

Champ Clark and the editors of Time-Life Books, *The Civil War: Decoying the Yanks* (Alexandria, VA: Time-Life Books, 1984), p. 116.

Richard Taylor, *Destruction and Reconstruction: Personal Experiences of the Late War*, Richard B. Harwell, ed. (New York: Longmans, Green and Company, 1955), pp. 49–50.

Ibid., p. 50.

Clark, ibid., p. 120.

Shelby Foote, *The Civil War, A Narrative, From Sumter to Perryville* (New York: Random

House, 1958), p. 428.

Taylor and most of his forces had arrived from Louisiana too late for the battle of Bull Run. The "Tigers" were already there. Douglas Southall Freeman, *Lee's Lieutenants*, Vol. I (New York: Scribner and Sons, 1942), p. 349.

Clark, p. 126.

Ibid.

Shelby Foote, ibid. p. 431.

Clark, p. 135.

Ibid.

The Texas Handbook, ibid.

T. Michael Parrish, p. 181.

Robert Tanner, *Stonewall in the Valley* (New York: Doubleday, 1976), p. 185.

Ibid., p. 128.

Richard Taylor, p. 54.

Jackson's famous orders were issued on May 13, 1862. Douglas Southall Freeman, p. 370.

Ibid., p. 133.

John S. Cooper, White House Heroes, Part II, *www.suite101.com/article.cfm/presidents__and__first_ladies*.

The Texas Handbook, ibid.

The American Civil War Overview, Chapter XII, The Trans-Mississippi: The Red River Campaign, *www.civilwarhome.com/redriver*.

www.toledo_bend.com/srala/area/mansfield.

The Texas Handbook, ibid.

Ibid.

Shelby Foote, *The Civil War, Red River to Appomattox*, p. 998.

Ibid.

Hudson Strode, ed., *Jefferson Davis Private Let-*

ters, 1823–1889 (New York: Harcourt, Brace & World, 1966), pp. 236–238, Varina Davis to Jefferson Davis, Georgia, February 2, 1866.

Shelby Foote, *The Civil War, Red River to Appomattox*, p. 998.

Ibid.

T. Michael Parrish, p. 479.

Douglas Southall Freeman, p. 349.

www.multied.com/bio/cwcgens/csaTaylor

The Texas Handbook, ibid.

William E. Barton, *President Lincoln*, as reported in J. J. Perling, p. 135.

Illinois State Journal, June 30, 1936.

Alice Miller, p. 106.

Congress of the United States, *U.S. Statutes at Large*, pp. 599–602. Library of Congress.

Dr. Kevin Leman, *The New Birth Order Book* (Grand Rapids, MI.: Fleming H. Revell, 1985).

J. J. Perling, p. 131.

Ibid., p. 134.

Donald Winkler, p. 187.

David Herbert Donald, *Lincoln* (New York: Simon and Schuster, 1995), p. 109.

Ibid., p. 428.

Donald Winkler, pp. 135, 136.

David Herbert Donald, ibid.

Ibid., 136.

This is not a universally accepted point. Michael Burlingame offers multiple sources suggesting that Mary could be quite strong in her discipline of Robert and that Lincoln also was tougher with his older son, before Eddie's death. Michael Burlingame, *The Inner World of Abraham Lincoln* (Chicago: University of Illinois Press, 1994) pp. 57–72.

Albert J. Beveridge, *Abraham Lincoln, Vol. I* (Boston: Houghton Mifflin, 1928), p. 506. For a further firsthand account of Lincoln's parenting read *Herndon's Lincoln*, originally published in 1888, now reprinted. William H. Herndon and Jesse William Weik, *Herndon's Lincoln* (Scituate, MA: Digital Scanning, 1999), Herndon Lincoln Publishing.

David Herbert Donald, p. 275. And yet some accounts have Lincoln erupting with anger at his first son. Michael Burlingame, p. 64.

J. J. Perling, p. 137.

Ibid., p. 138.

Ibid.

Carl Sandburg, Vol. III, p. 416.

Katherine Helm, *The True Story of Mary, Wife of Lincoln* (New York: Harper & Brothers, 1928), p. 227.

J. J. Perling, p. 139.

Burke Davis, *To Appomattox* (New York: Rhinehart, 1959), p. 381.

Philip B. Kunhardt, Jr., Philip B. Kunhardt, III, and Peter W. Kunhardt, *Lincoln* (New York: Knopf, 1992), p. 367.

John S. Cooper, ibid.

Ibid., p. 147.

J. J. Perling, p. 143.

Washington Evening Star, September 25, 1868.

Ibid., p. 148.

Abraham Lincoln Papers, Library of Congress. Gibson W. Harris to Abraham Lincoln, November 7, 1860.

Ishbel Ross, *The President's Wife: Mary Todd Lin-*

coln (New York, G.P. Putnam's Sons, 1973), p. 165.

Jean H. Baker, *Mary Todd Lincoln* (New York: Norton, 1987), p. 323.

Ibid., p. 323.

Ibid.

Chicago Inter Ocean, May 20–21, 1875.

Philip B. Kunhardt, Jr., Philip B. Kunhardt, III, and Peter W. Kunhardt, p. 397.

Julia Grant contended that she was unaware of Mary Lincoln's presence in Pau. Most historians find this far-fetched and suspect that it was payback for some past offense of Mrs. Lincoln to Julia and her husband.

Ibid., p. 149.

Ibid.

New York World, May 10, 1884.

S. L. Carson, p. 535. Sheldon Hochheiser, corporate historian at AT&T, discounts this story. Interview with Hochheiser, July 2002.

John S. Cooper, ibid.

Merrill D. Peterson, *Lincoln in American Memory* (New York: Oxford University Press, 1994), p. 258.

Illinois State Register, June 28, 1926.

H. Donald Winkler, p. 215.

Ward Hill Lamon, *Recollections of Abraham Lincoln 1847–1865* (Chicago: A.C. McClurg & Co., 1895), pp. 115–118.

John S. Cooper, ibid.

Ibid.

Ibid.

Ishbel Ross, *An American Family: The Tafts 1678–1964* (Cleveland & New York: The World Publishing Co., 1964), p. 299.

New York Herald Tribune, July 26, 1926.

Brooks D. Simpson, *Ulysses S. Grant; Triumph Over Adversity, 1822–1865* (Boston, New York: Houghton Mifflin, 2000), p. 84.

Ibid., p. 197.

DeGregorio, p. 282.

Ibid., p. 282.

Sardis Birchard had been a favorite uncle to Rutherford B. Hayes. Barzman, Sol. *The First Ladies* (New York: Cowles, 1970), p. 176.

John S. Cooper, ibid.

Ibid.

J. J. Perling, p. 191.

Harry Barnard, *Rutherford B. Hayes and His America* (New York: Bobbs-Merrill, 1954), p. 292.

Ibid.

Ibid., p. 367.

www.rbhayes.orgmssfidn/hayes_coll/wchayes/

J. J. Perling, ibid.

Lucy Hayes, *www2.worldbook.com*

John S. Cooper, ibid.

Ibid.

There is some historical debate over this incident. A bullet was fired into the dining room of the president-elect's home in Ohio, while the family was eating dinner. Some suggest that it might have been an errant shot, accidental or coincidental.

J. J. Perling, p. 194.

Ari Hoogenboom, *Rutherford B. Hayes, Warrior and President* (Lawrence, KS.: University of Kansas Press, 1995), p. 478.

John S. Cooper, ibid.
Ari Hoogenboom, p. 608.
John S. Cooper, ibid.
www.rbhayes.orgmssfidn/hayes_coll/wchayes/

CHAPTER 9

Ishbel Ross, *An American Family: The Tafts 1678–1964* (Cleveland and New York: The World Publishing Co., 1964), p. 402.

T. Michael Parrish, *Richard Taylor; Soldier, Prince of Dixie* (Chapel Hill, NC: University of North Carolina Press, 1992), p. 496.

H. Paul Jeffers, p. 11.

Ibid.

Ibid., p. 13.

Ibid., p. 27.

Ibid.

Ibid., p. 28.

Ibid., p. 33.

Peter Collier, p. 126.

H. W. Brands, editor, *The Selected Letters of Theodore Roosevelt* (New York: Cooper Square Press, 2001), p. 344.

H. Paul Jeffers, p. 49.

Ibid., p. 91.

Ibid.

Ibid., p. 104.

Ibid., p. 114.

Mrs. Theodore Roosevelt, Jr., *Day Before Yesterday: The Reminiscences of Mrs. Theodore Roosevelt, Jr.* (Garden City, NY: Doubleday, 1959), p. 118.

Peter Collier, p. 242.

Ibid., p. 331.

Mrs. Theodore Roosevelt, Jr., *Day Before Yesterday: The Reminiscences of Mrs. Theodore Roosevelt, Jr.* (Garden City, NY: Doubleday, 1959), p. 304.

Peter Collier, p. 391.

Ibid., p. 395.

H. Paul Jeffers, p. 214.

Peter Collier, p. 404.

Ibid., 408.

Ibid., 406.

H. Paul Jeffers, p. 174.

Mrs. Theodore Roosevelt, Jr., *Day Before Yesterday*, as reported in H. Paul Jeffers, p. 75.

Peter Collier, p. 418.

Quinn-Musgrove and Kanter suggest that Ted died in a comfortable bed in London, but most contemporary accounts confirm that he died in France with his troops. Quinn-Musgrove and Kanter, p. 153.

H. Paul Jeffers, p. 262.

George Patton also saw Ted Roosevelt as unnecessarily reckless. "Great courage, but no soldier," he once wrote. Edward J. Renehan, Jr., *www.worldwar1.com/dbc/roosev.ht* But perhaps Patton was shamed by an experience in North Africa where Ted had given him his own foxhole during a German strafing attack. Peter Collier, p. 419.

Ibid., p. 20.

Herman Hagedorn, *The Roosevelt Family of Sagamore Hill* (New York: Macmillan, 1954), p. 50.

H. Paul Jeffers, p. 264.

Ross, p. 188.

Ibid., p. 157.

Ibid., pp. 121–122.

Ibid., p. 182.

Ibid., p. 204.

Joseph B. Treaster, "Obituary of Charles P. Taft, Former Mayor of Cincinnati," *New York Times*, June 25, 1983.

Ishbel Ross, p. 125.

Ibid., p. 125.

Ibid., p. 131.

Woodrow Wilson, *War Messages*, 65th Congress, 1st Session, Senate Doc. No. 5, Serial No. 7264, Washington, D.C., 1917, pp. 3–8, passim.

Ross, p. 314.

Ibid., p. 378.

Ibid., p. 371.

Ibid., p. 378.

Clarence E. Wunderlin, Jr., *The Papers of Robert A. Taft, Volume 1, 1889–1938* (Kent: Kent State University Press, 1997), p. 271.

Historic World Leaders, Gale Research, 1994. Reproduced in *Biography Resource Center*. Farmington Hills, MI: The Gale Group, 2002. (*http://galenet.galegroup.com/servlet/BioRC*), p. 5.

John Fitzgerald Kennedy, *Profiles in Courage* (New York: Harper & Row, 1956), p. 211.

Stephen Goode, "Is Voter Crossover 1952, Déjà vu?" *Insight on the News*, March 13, 2000, p. 22, quoting Eric Foner, from his book *The Story of American Freedom*.

Ross, p. 369.

Historic World Leaders, p. 5.

Ross, p. 403.

Ibid., p. 404.

Carl Sferrazza Anthony, p. 310.

Ross, p. 301.

Ibid., p. 350.

Ibid., pp. 384–385.

Peggy Lane and Bob Weston, "Mr. Cincinnati Dead at 85," *Cincinnati Enquirer*, June 25, 1983.

Ross, p. 388.

Charles P. Taft, unpublished, undated manuscript.

Ibid., p. 8.

Laura Pulfer, "Drag the Kids to Chat with Charlie Taft," *Cincinnati Enquirer*, February 20, 2000, p. 16.

Peggy Lane and Bob Weston, "Mr. Cincinnati Dead at 85," *Cincinnati Enquirer*, June 25, 1983.

Seth C. Taft Interview, July 18, 2002, and Seth Taft, *Take On the World! Rules of the Road* (Euclid, OH: Williams Custom Publishing, 1999), pp. 10–11.

Ishbel Ross, p. 188.

Julie Nixon Eisenhower, *Special People*.

John S. D. Eisenhower, *Strictly Personal* (Garden City, NY: Doubleday, 1974), p. 1.

Ibid., p. 63.

Ibid., p. 97.

Ibid., p. 96.

Ibid., p. 78.

Ibid., p. 79.

Ibid.

Ibid., p. xii.
Ibid., p. 207.

CHAPTER 10

Washington Post, February 21, 1980.

www.rbhayes.org/mssfind/HAYES_COLL/ hayessccttr.htm

Quinn-Musgrove and Kanter, p. 48.

Peter Collier, p. 162.

Richard Willing, "Research downplays risk of cousin marriages," *USA Today*, April, 4, 2002, p. 3a.

The term first lady was not used until 1870.

Quinn-Musgrove and Kanter, p. 25.

The Washington Memorial was begun in 1848 and completed in 1884.

Marie Smith and Louise Durbin, *White House Brides* (Washington, DC: Acropolis Books, 1966), p. 23.

Ibid.

Wilbur Cross and Ann Novotny, *White House Weddings* (New York: David McKay Co., 1967), p. 26.

Marie Smith and Louise Durbin, p. 23.

William A. DeGregorio, p. 74. The press and most historians tend to portray Eliza as a snob. While admitting that she was outspoken, researchers at the James Monroe Museum and Memorial Library say that such portrayals are inaccurate. James Monroe Museum and Memorial Library, 908 Charles St., Fredericksburg, VA 22401.

Maria Hester Monroe was sent to an exclusive

French-run boarding school in Philadelphia from 1816–1819. Nellie Custis sent her own children to this school. Maria Hester was considered ambitious, well trained and artistic. She sang and played beautifully. There is a bound book of her sheet music dated from about 1818 at the James Monroe Museum and Memorial Library.

Sol Barzman, p. 44.

Correspondence with David Voelkel, assistant director and curator at the James Monroe Museum and Memorial Library. July 2002.

Smith and Durbin, p. 20.

Cross and Novotny, p. 25.

Smith and Durbin, p. 19. David Voelkel says that the press was looking for a reason to criticize the president, that the wedding was planned in the newly acceptable "New York style," where only family was present. Correspondence with David Voelkel, assistant director and curator at the James Monroe Museum and Memorial Library, July 2002.

William A. DeGregorio, p. 74.

Smith and Durbin, p. 25.

William A. DeGregorio, p. 74.

Correspondence with David Voelkel of the James Monroe Museum and Memorial Library, July 2002.

Smith and Durbin, p. 32.

Ibid., p. 31.

Cross and Novotny, p. 34.

Ibid., p. 36.

Ibid.

Smith and Durbin write that Lizzie Tyler was

twenty years old at her marriage. Cross and Novotny say she was nineteen. Actually, she was eighteen and would become nineteen the following July 11, 1823. Smith and Durbin, p. 55; Cross and Novotny, p. 69.

Smith and Durbin, p. 55.

Cross and Novotny, p. 70.

The Daniel Webster Papers, Library of Congress.

Smith and Durbin, p. 62.

Attributed to W. H. Woodward, Grant's biographer. Cross and Novotny, p. 85. As to her exact age at the wedding, some writers differ but family correspondence confirms that she was eighteen. McFeely says she was eighteen, as do Smith and Durbin. Cross and Novotny have her turning seventeen in July 1872, making her also eighteen at the time of her May marriage in 1874. McFeely, p. 400; Smith and Durbin, p. 18; Cross and Novotny, p. 85.

Jean Edward Smith says that Sartoris was "ten years her senior," which would make him twenty-seven. This is probably incorrect. Sartoris died at age forty-two in 1893. Smith, p. 574. Cross and Novotny, p. 97.

William McFeely, p. 401.

Cross and Novotny, p. 87.

New York Daily Graphic. Cross and Novotny, p. 84.

Jean Edward Smith, Grant (New York: Simon and Schuster, 2001), p. 573.

Cross and Novotny, p. 91.

New York Herald, May 22, 1874.

In a testimony to history's neglect of the biographies of presidential children, one encounters a smorgasbord of dates for Nellie's age. According to authors Wilbur Cross and Ann Novotny, Nellie Grant "was only twelve years old" when her father took office in 1869 (Cross and Novotny, p. 85). *Washington Post* writers Marie Smith and Louise Durbin describe her as "a promising beauty of fourteen when the Grants moved into the Executive Mansion" (Smith and Durbin, p. 85). Grant biographer, Jean Edward Smith, describes her as "only thirteen when Grant was inaugurated" (Jean Edward Smith, p. 573). Smith wins this particular contest; she was indeed thirteen.

Smith and Durbin, p. 86.

Ibid.

Jean Edward Smith, p. 573. Other authors say she made the voyage to Europe the year before. Cross and Novotny, p. 85.

Cross and Novotny, p. 86.

Jean Edward Smith, p. 574.

McFeely, p. 401.

Henry James to Alice James, May 19, 1879. Ed. Leon Edel. *Letters of Henry James* (Cambridge, MA: 1974–75), Vol. II, pp. 233–234.

Cross and Novotny, p. 97.

McFeely, p. 400.

Cross and Novotny, p. 138.

Ibid., p. 144.

Betty Boyd Caroli, *The Roosevelt Women*, p. 401.

Ibid., p. 402.

Ibid., p. 401.

Cross and Novotny, p. 141.

Carol Felsenthal, *Alice Roosevelt Longworth* (New York: G.P. Putnam's Sons, 1988), p. 101.

It was worth $25,000 at the time.
Cross and Novotny, p. 147.
Carol Felsenthal, p. 102.
Ibid., p. 103.
Carol Felsenthal, p. 102.
Alice's room is now used as the White House family dining room.
Differing accounts offer different numbers of the attending guests. One report says there were 680, Smith and Durbin, p. 120.
Ibid., p. 121.
Carol Felsenthal, p. 105.
Ibid., p. 106.
Cross and Novotny, p. 158.
Smith and Durbin, p. 123.
Ibid., p. 129.
Felsenthal, p. 108.
Ibid., p. 108.
Betty Boyd Caroli, *The Roosevelt Women*, p. 406.
Smith and Durbin, p. 124.
If Alice did indeed burn her husband's Stradivarius, she must have been very angry. Sources at the Theodore Roosevelt Association speculate that it is more likely that she sold it for the money.
New York Times, April 7, 1967, p. 37.
Eleanor Wilson McAdoo, *The Woodrow Wilsons* (New York: The Macmillan Company, 1937), p. 207.
Ibid., p. 221.
Ibid., p. 191.
Ibid., p. 217.
Cross and Novotny, p. 180.
Ishbel Ross, *First Lady Between Two Worlds*.

Ibid., p. 172.

Ibid., p. 186.

Ibid., p. 187.

Ibid., p. 188.

Ibid., p. 186.

Ibid., p. 171.

New York Times, January 16, 1933.

Quinn-Musgrove and Kanter, p. 167.

Typically, there are different versions of this with some accounts saying no lilies, only cherry and apple blossoms and flowering dogwood.

www.bioguide.congress.gov/scripts/biodisplay. pl?index=M000293

"Mrs. Eleanor Wilson McAdoo, President's Daughter, 77, Dies," *New York Times*, April 7, 1967, p. 37.

Elta Roberts to Margaret Woodrow Wilson, March 27, 1941, Library of Congress.

Ishbel Ross, *Power with Grace: The Life Story of Mrs. Woodrow Wilson* (New York: G.P. Putman's Sons, 1975), p. 302.

Bess Furman, *White House Profile: A Social History of the White House, Its Occupants and Its Festivities* (Indianapolis and New York: The Bobbs-Merrill Company, Inc., 1951), p. 289.

Frances Wright Saunders, Ellen Axson Wilson: *First Lady Between Two Worlds* (Chapel Hill and London: The University of North Carolina Press, 1985), p. 256.

Boyd Fisher, "Piggy Play," attached to letter, Boyd Fisher to Margaret Woodrow Wilson, December 28, 1913, University of California, Santa Barbara, Wilson-McAdoo Collection. Brnath Mss. 18.

Ibid.

Boyd Fisher to Margaret Woodrow Wilson, December 28, 1913. University of California, Santa Barbara, Wilson-McAdoo Collection. Brnath Mss. 18.

"Miss Wilson Belle At Greenwich Party," *New York Times*, February 15, 1914.

Frances Wright Saunders, p. 268.

"An Intimate, Chatty Glimpse of Miss Margaret Wilson," *Baltimore Sun*, undated, University of California, Santa Barbara, Wilson-MacAdoo Collection. Brnath Mss. 18.

Ibid.

Elizabeth Harbison Davis, *I Played Their Accompaniments* (New York, London: D. Appleton-Century Company, 1940), p. 133.

Ibid., p. 135.

Ibid., p. 136.

Bess Furman, p. 299.

Ishbel Ross, p. 254.

Ibid., p. 258.

"Wilson's Daughter Dies a Recluse at 57 in Religious Colony in India," *New York Times*, February 14, 1944.

"Freed by Mercy of Miss Wilson," *New York Times*, Tuesday, March 30, 1926, front page.

Judith Anodea, "Sri Aurobindo: 1872–1950," *http://www.gaiamind.org/Aurobindo.html*

Sri Ramakrishna, *The Gospel of Sri Ramakrishna*, translated by Swami Nikhilananda, edited by Joseph Campbell and Margaret Woodrow Wilson (New York: Ramakrishna-Vivekananda Center, 1942), p. viii.

Margaret Woodrow Wilson to Eleanor Wilson

McAdoo, undated, University of California, Santa Barbara, Wilson-McAdoo Collection. Brnath Mss. 18.

"Wilson's Daughter Dies a Recluse at 57 in Religious Colony in India," *New York Times*, February 14, 1944.

Margaret Woodrow Wilson to Eleanor Wilson McAdoo, undated, University of California, Santa Barbara, Wilson-McAdoo Collection. Brnath Mss. 18.

Ibid. Some writings refer to Margaret as "Dishta." This is probably due to a mistake in her obituary in the *New York Times*. The name is incorrect, as shown by Margaret's own writings.

Margaret Woodrow Wilson to Lois Kellogg Roth, undated letter from India, University of California, Santa Barbara, Wilson-McAdoo Collection. Brnath Mss. 18.

Risha Blackand, Library at the Sri Aurobindo Ashram, Pondicherry, India.

Lady Bird Johnson, *A White House Diary* (New York: Holt, Rinehart & Winston, 1970), p. 404.

Ibid., p. 405.

www.americanhi_story.si.edu/presidency/3a4.html

New York Times, December 7, 1967.

Lady Bird Johnson, p. 599.

Ibid., p. 600.

Life, October 30, 1992. p. 30.

www.americanhi_story.si.edu/presidency/3a4.html

"A Nader's Raider among the Nixons: For Tricia and Ed it's no secret." *Life*, January 22, 1971, Time, Inc., p. 21.

Sol Barzman, p. 353.

Ibid.

Julie Nixon Eisenhower, *Pat Nixon: The Untold Story* (New York: Simon and Schuster, 1986), pp. 255– 256.

"Behind the Main Event," *Life*, June 18, 1971, p. 41.

Ibid., p. 45.

Richard Nixon, *RN: The Memoirs of Richard Nixon* (New York: Grosset & Dunlap, 1978), pp. 507–508.

Eleanor Wilson, p. 183.

Sally Quinn, "The Canny Candor of Alice Longworth," p. d1.

"Vietnam Archive: Pentagon Study Traces 3 Decades of Growing U.S. Involvement," *New York Times*, June 13, 1971, p. 1.

CHAPTER 11

Betty Ford with Chris Chase, *The Times of My Life*, p. 167.

Maud Shaw, *White House Nannie: My Years with Caroline and John Kennedy, Jr.* (New York: New American Library, 1965, 1966), p. 101.

Benjamin C. Bradlee, *Conversations with Kennedy* (New York: W.W. Norton & Company, Inc., 1975), p. 160.

Ibid.

Susan Reed, *People*, November 28, 1983, v. 20 p. 142(4).

Ellen Alderman and Caroline Kennedy, *In Our Defense: The Bill of Rights in Action* (New York: William Morrow and Company, Inc., 1991); and *The Right to Privacy* (New York: Borzoi Books, Alfred A. Knopf, Inc., 1995).

Mark Fitzgerald, "NNA Convention Celebrates First Amendment Rights" (National Newspapers Association), *Editor & Publisher*, October 12, 1991, v. 124 n. 41 p. 19(2).

Ellen Alderman and Caroline Kennedy, jacket notes.

Spencer S. Hsu, "Campaigner Born, Wedded to Politics; Lynda Robb More Visible Than Ever." *Washington Post*, November 5, 2000, p. C8.

Jake Tapper, "Dead senator running?" *www. salon.com/news/feature/1999/11/17/robb/print. html*, p. 7.

Spencer S. Hsu, op. cit.

(Profile, Interview) "Luci in the sky: now firmly in control of her famous family's holding company, Luci Baines Johnson is flying high." *Texas Monthly*, 1998, March, 1998 v. 26 n. 3 p. 58(6).

People, July 25, 1994, v. 42, n. 4, p. 76.

"The president requests. . . ." *People*, Time, Inc., 1994, July 25, 1994 v. 42 n. 4 p. 76(5).

"Luci in the sky: now firmly in control of her famous family's holding company, Luci Baines Johnson is flying high." Texas Monthly (Texas Monthly, Inc., 1998) March 1998, v. 26 n. 3 p. 58(6).

Ibid.

Lewis L. Gould, *American First Ladies: Their Lives and Their Legacy* (New York and London: Garland Publishing, Inc., 1996), p. 500.

Faye Fiore and Geraldine Baum, "Column One: 2 Nixon Sisters, 1 Big Feud," *Los Angeles Times*, April 23, 2002. *www.latimes.com/news/la-042302sisters.story*, p. 3.

Gerald R. Ford, Inaugural Speech.

Ibid., pp. 255–256.

"A Nader's Raider among the Nixons: For Tricia and Ed it's no secret." *Life* magazine, January 22, 1971, Time, Inc., p. 21.

Faye Fiore and Geraldine Baum, "Column One: 2 Nixon Daughters, 1 Big Feud: The former president's daughters aren't speaking to each other in a dispute over the control of his library. The rift stalls talks on acquiring his papers and further threatens his legacy." *Los Angeles Times* (Los Angeles, CA: The Times Mirror Company; *Los Angeles Times* 2002). April 23, 2002, Start Page A.1.

Ibid.

Margaret Carlson, "Peace Is at Hand: The Nixon daughters, feuding over their father's library, finally patch things up." *Time* magazine, May 13, 2002 (Time, Inc., 2002), p. 53.

Julie Nixon Eisenhower, *Special People*.

Julie Nixon Eisenhower, *Pat Nixon: The Untold Story*, pp. 229–230.

Ibid., p. 250.

Julie Nixon Eisenhower, *Pat Nixon, The Untold Story* (New York: Simon and Schuster, 1986), p. 250.

Ibid., p. 251.

Ibid.

"Nixons Meet Over Library Dispute," August 7, 2002.

Martin Merzer and Allison Klein, Herald Staff Writers, "Nixon Pal Bebe Rebozo Dead at 85 Key Biscayne Banker Loyal to the End," *Miami Herald* (*The Miami Herald*, 1998), May

9, 1998, Section: Front, Edition: Final, Page: 1A.

Betty Ford with Chris Chase, *The Times of My Life* (New York: Harper & Row, Publishers and The Reader's Digest Association, Inc., 1978), p. 2.

Ibid., p. 147.

Ibid., pp. 75–76.

Ibid., p. 155.

Ibid., pp. 154–155.

Ibid., pp. 167–168.

Ibid., p. 161.

Cameron Crowe, "Why Jack Ford Still Lives with His Parents: A White House Portrait," 1976, *Rolling Stone*, July 29, 1976, Issue No. 218, p. 30.

Betty Ford with Chris Chase, *The Times of My Life*, p. 167.

Ibid., p. 113.

Ibid., p. 31.

"Fords of a feather: Gerald's son Jack gets (GOP) conventional." *People*, August 19, 1996, v. 46 n. 8 p. 63(1), Time, Inc., 1996.

Bill Thompson, "Belated recognition of Gerald Ford's courage." Knight-Ridder/Tribune News Service 2001, May 25, 2001, pK6364.

Gerald R. Ford, *A Time to Heal: The Autobiography of Gerald R. Ford* (New York: Harper & Row, 1979), p. 436.

Betty Ford with Chris Chase, p. 112.

Ibid., pp. 130–131.

Ibid., p. 161.

Ibid., p. 194.

Steven Ford was the subject of a paternity suit

which he and the family handled graciously, saying that they would assume responsibility. The ultimate finding determined that Steve was not the father.

Betty Ford with Chris Chase, p. 213.

Ibid., p. 110.

Ibid., p. 163.

Ibid., p. 158.

Ibid., p. 125.

Ibid., p. 153.

Ibid., p. 142.

Rosalynn Carter, *First Lady from Plains* (Boston: Houghton Mifflin Company, 1984), pp. 64–65.

Houston Post, December 15, 1980, p. 10.

Ibid., p. 340.

Ibid., p. 65.

Ibid., p. 66.

L. Eric Elie, "Chip Carter working on the fringe of politics," *Atlanta Journal–Constitution*, May 16, 1988, p. C-01.

Patricia J. Mays, "Former president's son following in dad's footsteps," "From Wall Street to Main Street . . .", *www.onlineathens.com/ stories/041899/new_ 0418990010.shtml*, p. 2.

Ibid.

Note: Quinn-Musgrove and Kanter say Caron's last name is Griffith, p. 188; *The Atlanta Journal–Constitution* called her Caron Morgan (Lillian Lee Kim, 5/5/98). *www.uftree.com/UFT/ WebPages/jholcomb/JECARTER/d0/i0000818.htm*, a website quoting an informal book written by Jimmy Carter for a family reunion, calls her Griffin.

Lillian Lee Kim, "Campaign aide, college student and grandson of a president, James Earl Carter IV is a politician in training." *Atlanta Journal–Constitution.* May 5, 1998, p. D01.

Rosalynn Carter, p. 182.

Ibid.

Rosalynn Carter, p. 64.

Kane, Podell and Anzovin., p. 450.

Interview with Michael Reagan, September 25, 2001.

Maureen Reagan, *First Father, First Daughter: A Memoir,* p. 50.

Michael Reagan, *Making Waves* (Nashville: Thomas Nelson Publishers, 1996), p. 245.

Michael Reagan, *The City on a Hill: Fulfilling Ronald Reagan's Vision for America* (Nashville: Thomas Nelson Publishers, 1997), p. 35.

Michael Reagan, *On the Outside Looking In* (New York: Zebra Books, Kensington Publishing Corp., 1988), p. 35.

Ibid., p. 265.

Ibid., p. 266.

Michael Reagan, *Making Waves,* p. 245.

Amy Blumenfeld and Richard Jerome, "When Dad Is President." *People,* June 18, 2001 (Time, Inc., 2001), p. 52+.

Patti Davis, *The Way I See It* (New York: G.P. Putnam's Sons, 1992), p. 13.

Ibid.

Ibid.

Patti Davis, "A Chelsea Warning: A president's daughter should stay out of the spotlight, says Patti Davis. She learned the hard way." *Rosie* magazine, September, 2002, pp. 68, 70.

Patti Davis, *The Way I See It,* p. 334.

Patti Davis, *Angels Don't Die: My Father's Gift of Faith* (New York: HarperCollins Publishers, 1995), Foreword.

Ibid., p. 5.

Patti Davis, *The Way I See It,* pp. 210–211.

Lou Cannon, *President Reagan: The Role of a Lifetime* (New York: Simon and Schuster, 1989), p. 229.

Gloria Borger, "A feuding first family," August 31, 1987 (*U.S. News & World Report,*1987), p. 22.

Richard Corliss, "Ron Reagan Show." (Television program reviews.) *Time,* August 26, 1991. (Time, Inc., 1991), p. 63.

Sam Donaldson, "Home front" book reviews. *Washington Monthly,* April 1986 (Washington Monthly Company, 1986), p. 57.

The George Bush Presidential Library, College Station, Texas.

Carl S. Anthony, p. 324.

Ibid.

Wayne Schafnit, so-called "wizard of the web pages," at the Canyonville Symposium, 1998.

Interview with Marvin Bush, 1988.

"The Graduate: With First Childhood and now Stanford behind her, Chelsea gets ready for life on her own." *People,* July 2, 2001 (Time, Inc., 2001), p. 52.

Mark Dagostino, "Insider," *People,* July 22, 2002 (Time, Inc., 2002), p. 41.

William DeGregorio, p. 757.

The George Bush Presidential Library, op. cit.

Ibid.

William DeGregorio, op. cit.

Ibid., p. 91.

CHAPTER 12

Kunhardt Productions, *The American President*, op. cit.

George W. Bush, *A Charge to Keep*, p. 182.

Elysa Gardner writes a fascinating article on the children of music artists where the same difficulties are experienced. Elysa Gardner, "Offspring of artists make their own music." *USA Today*, August 3, 2001, p. 6e.

J. J. Perling, p. 256.

H. Paul Jeffers, p. 152.

Hubert Humphrey III led in a statewide poll conducted by MPR, June 3, 1998.

S. L. Carson, "Presidential Children: Abandonment, Hysteria and Suicide," p. 538.

Carl Sferrazza Anthony, p. 312.

Neil Bush speech, 1998, Canyonville Symposium, Box 1100, Canyonville, Oregon.

Kunhardt Productions, *The American President*, op. cit.

Paul C. Nagel, *John Quincy Adams, A Public Life, A Private Life*, p. 278.

Ibid.

Kunhardt Productions, *The American President*, a PBS series.

J. J. Perling, *Presidents' Sons* (New York: Odyssey Press, 1947), p. 75.

Perling, p. 76.

Harrison to William Henry Harrison, Jr., November 7, 1828, Harrison Papers, 7:1145. The

Library of Congress.

H. Paul Jeffers, p. 94.

Peter Collier, p. 117.

Ibid., p. 62.

A spokesman for the Theodore Roosevelt Association insisted to the author that there was no family conspiratorial effort to keep this fact from the general public.

Carl Sferrazza Anthony, p. 311.

Forrest McDonald, *The Presidency of Thomas Jefferson* (Lawrence, Manhattan, Wichita: The University Press of Kansas, 1976), pp. 31–32.

H. Paul Jeffers, p. 174.

Carl Sferrazza Anthony, p. 309.

Ibid., p. 309.

Kunhardt Productions, *The American President*, op. cit.

Carl Sandburg, Vol. I, p. 458.

K. Pitzer, *Guiding Children*, Children, Youth & Family Consortium, January 1991. *www.cyfc.unm.edu/Documents/H/N/HN1053.html*

Doug Wead, *George Bush: Man of Integrity* (Eugene, OR: Harvest House, 1988), p. 117.

Carl Sferrazza Anthony, p. 89.

Ross, p. 204.

Michael Burlingame, *The Inner World of Abraham Lincoln* (Chicago: University of Illinois Press, 1994), p. 60.

K. Jack Bauer, p. 69.

Papers of William Henry Harrison, Library of Congress, Vol. 6. No. 1088.

Shepherd, Jack, *Cannibals of the Heart*, p. 188.

Angle and Miers, p. 94.

Michael Burlingame, p. 61.

Michael Reagan with Joe Hyam, *Michael Reagan: On the Outside Looking In* (New York: Zebra Books, 1988), pp. 82–83.

Ibid.

Perling, p. 77.

Quinn-Musgrove and Kanter, p. 43.

Quinn-Musgrove and Kanter, p. 13.

J. J. Perling, p. 6.

McCullough, David, *John Adams*, p. 251.

Ibid., p. 263.

McCullough, David, *John Adams*, p. 254.

Smith was eventually appointed by the Senate after then-President Adams's second attempt.

Quinn-Musgrove and Kanter declare flatly that he died from cirrhosis of the liver. Quinn-Musgrove and Kanter, p. 12.

Kunhardt Productions, *The American President*, op. cit.

John and Claire Whitcomb, *Real Life in the White House* (New York: Routledge, 2000), pp. 56–57; White House website (*http://www.whitehouse.gov/history/firstladies/ la6.html*).

Jeanne Elium and Don Elium, p. 6.

Carolyn Kleiner, "Breaking the Cycle," *U.S. News & World Report*, April 29, 2002, p. 49.

Bill Minutaglio, *First Son, George W. Bush* (New York: Times Books, 1999), p. 125.

George Herbert Walker, Jr. is the executive vice president of the New York Mets.

James Carney and John F. Dickerson, "A work in progress," *Time*, October 22, 2001, p. 40. Richard Benedetto, "Bush relays message from the heart." *USA Today*, June 21, 2002, p. 4a.

Paul C. Nagel, *John Quincy Adams, A Public Life, A Private Life,* p. 299.

Carl Sferrazza Anthony, p. 95.

"Bush Down Home," *Newsweek,* June 18, 2001, p. 9.

Doug Wead, *George Bush: Man of Integrity.*

"10 Days in September, Epilogue, With World's Eyes on Him, Bush Stresses Results," *Washington Post,* February 3, 2002, p. a15.

Gloria Borger, "Practicing the art of secrecy," *U.S. News & World Report,* March 18, 2001, p. 24.

Peggy Noonan, "Loose Lips, Pink Slips," *Wall Street Journal,* January 22, 2002.

Linda Kulman, "Who owns history?" *U.S. News & World Report,* April 29, 2002.

Stuart Taylor, "Before the Bar of History," *Newsweek,* December 10, 2001, p. 47.

U. S. News & World Report, February 25–March 4, 2002, double issue.

Ron Fournier, "Crises Transform Bush Presidency," Associated Press as reported in *Orlando Sentinel,* January 20, 2002, p. a7.

Jeffrey H. Birnbaum, "The Making of a President 2001," *Fortune,* November 12, 2001, p. 135.

"10 Days in September, Epilogue, With World's Eyes on Him, Bush Stresses Results," op. cit.

Robert G. Kaiser and David B. Ottaway, "Saudi Leader's Anger Revealed Shaky Ties," *Washington Post,* February 10, 2002, p. a10.

Bedard, Paul. "George 'McKinley' trades up to a 'Theodore' Bush," *U.S. News & World Report,* January 14, 2002, p. 4.

Time, December 31, 2001–January 7, 2002, double issue, p. 111.

Notebook, *Time*, January 2002.

"10 Days in September, Epilogue, There Is No Doubt in My Mind, Not One Doubt," *Washington Post*, February 3, 2002, p. a14.

Mortimer B. Zuckerman, "A man on a mission," *U.S. News & World Report*, March 18, 2002, p. 76.

E. J. Dionne, Jr., "Conservatism Recast, Why This President's Reach Could Be Monumental," *Washington Post*, January 27, 2002, p. b1.

Borger, Gloria, "Same old, same old." *U.S. News & World Report*, January 21, 2002, p. 31.

Fareed Zakaria, "Spend It Now, Mr. President," *Newsweek*, May 20, 2002, p. 38.

William M. Welch, "Bush: Stimulus plan mostly tax cuts," *USA Today*, October 5, 2001, p. 14a.

David Sanger, "Bush relishes reactions to his rallying cry," *New York Times*, as reported in the *International Herald Tribune*, February 18, 2002, p. 1.

Mortimer B. Zuckerman, op. cit.

John F. Dickerson, "Meet the President as the Cutup in Chief," *Time*, February 18, 2002, p. 4.

Glenna Whitley, "George & Laura, Love & Marriage," *Ladies Home Journal*, February 2002, p. 146.

Margaret Carlson, "A Pillow Away from the President," *Time*, December 31, 2001–January 7, 2002, double issue, p. 111.

"What a Difference a Year Makes," *People*, January 21, 2002, p. 84.

"The Secret Skill of Leaders." *U.S. News & World Report*, January 14, 2002, p. 8.

Jeffrey H. Birnbaum, p. 136.

George Bush, *All the Best, George Bush: My Life in Letters and Other Writing* (New York: Scribner, 1999), p. 325.

George Bush, op. cit., p. 353.

Author's interview with Marvin Bush, 1988.

Kunhardt Productions, *The American Presidency*.

George Bush, op. cit., pp. 347–348.

Ibid., p. 498.

Ibid., p. 571.

Ibid.

Bob Maddox, *A Preacher in the White House* (Nashville: Baptist Press, 1980).

EPILOGUE

Frances Wright Saunders, *First Lady Between Two Worlds*, p. 216.

William DeGregorio, p. 435.

Francis Russell, *The Shadow of Blooming Grove: Warren G. Harding in His Times* (New York and Toronto: McGraw-Hill, 1968), pp. 358 and 360.

Edward J. Renehan, op. cit.

Edward J. Renehan, Jr., *The Lion's Pride: Theodore Roosevelt and His Family in Peace and War* (New York: Oxford University Press, 1998), pp. 6 and 7.

Most sources indicate Jacky died of camp fever, a catchall term for illnesses contracted in crowded military conditions. Harrison Clark, *All Cloudless Glory: The Life of George Washington, From Youth to Yorktown* (Washington, DC: Regnery Publishing, Inc., 1995) indicates that he died of typhus.

John E. Ferling, *The First of Men: A Life of George Washington* (Knoxville: The University of Tennessee Press, 1988), p. 81.

Frank Donovan, *The Women in Their Lives: The Distaff Side of the Founding Fathers* (New York: Dodd, Mead & Company, 1966), pp. 124–125. Both Quinn-Musgrove and Kanter and J. J. Perling indicate that Patsy Custis died at age thirteen. Other sources, including John E. Ferling in *The First of Men: A Life of George Washignton*, provide information which they attribute to *The Diaries of George Washington*, and which indicate that she died at age seventeen.

John E. Ferling, *The First of Men: A Life of George Washington* (Knoxville: University of Tennessee Press, 1988), p. 344.

Lewis L. Gould, *American First Ladies: Their Lives and Their Legacy* (New York and London: Garland Publishing, Inc., 1996), p. 7.

J. J. Perling, p. 356. George Washington's Last Will and Testament states: "And whereas it has always been my intention, since my expectation of having issue has ceased, to consider the grandchildren of my wife in the same light as I do my own relations and to act a friendly part by them, more specially by the two whom we have reared from their earliest infancy, namely, Eleanor Parke Custis and George Washington Parke Custis . . . I give and bequeath to George Washington Parke Custis the Grandson of my wife and my ward, and to his heirs. . . ."

Seigel, Beatrice, *George and Martha Washignton at Home in New York* (New York: Macmillan Publishing Co., Four Winds Press, 1989), p. 31.

Ferling, pp. 511–512.

Ibid., p. 511.

Kane, Podell, Anzovin, p. 26., *The Adams Papers*, The Massachusetts Historical Society and an interview with Anne Decker Cecere.

David McCullough, p. 65.

Quinn-Musgrove and Kanter, p. 16.

Gordon Langley Hall, *Mr. Jefferson's Ladies* (Boston: Beacon Press, 1966), p. 84.

Ibid., p. 38.

Ibid., pp. 42–43.

Ken Burns, *Thomas Jefferson* (The American Lives Film Project, 1996, PBS. Distributed by Warner Home Video, Burbank, CA).

Gordon Langley Hall states that Lucy died October 13, 1874, p. 73. Quinn-Musgrove and Kanter state she died November 17, 1785, p. 22.

Hall, p. 73.

Robert Allen Rutland, *The Presidency of James Madison* (Lawrence, KS: University Press of Kansas, 1990), p. 194.

Donovan, p. 320.

Ibid., p. 321.

Ibid., p. 327.

Martha "Patsy" Jefferson Randolph's son, James Madison Randolph, was the first baby born in the White House, but he was the grandson of a president, not a son.

Quinn-Musgrove and Kanter, p. 29.

John S. Cooper, "Charles Francis Adams: Unsung Hero." *www.suite101.com/article. cfm/presidents_ and_first_ladies/40724*, p.3.

Cincinnati Daily Gazette, November 2, 1830. Quinn-Musgrove and Kanter put his date of death at 1832. Almost all other sources confirm the date of 1830. Quinn-Musgrove and Kanter, p. 46. Joseph Nathan Kane, Janet Podell, and Steven Anzovin, p. 102.

Interview with Jennifer Capps, curator for the President Benjamin Harrison House, Indianapolis, IN.

Different dates are given for his age at death. Quinn-Musgrove and Kanter write that he was thirty-four. Jennifer E. Capps, curator of the President Benjamin Harrison Home, puts his age at thirty-three. See Dorothy W. Bowers, *The Irwins and the Harrisons*, December 17, 1999.

Most historic accounts place her date of death as 1845 but Jennifer Capps, curator for the President Benjamin Harrison House, has documents showing that Anna lived to 1865, giving birth to twelve children, six of whom were born after the 1845 date. DeGregorio, p. 139. Kane, Podell and Anzovin, p. 102.

DeGregorio, p. 150.

Barzman, p. 89.

Ibid., p. 192.

Cross and Novotny, p. 67.

DeGregorio, p. 150.

Quinn-Musgrove and Kanter, p. 61.

Quinn-Musgrove and Kanter, p. 66.

www.multied.com/bio/cwcgens/csaTaylor

Quinn-Musgrove and Kanter favor the date of July 26; Fillmore's biographer says the date was July 27. Quinn-Musgrove and Kanter, p. 82, Robert Rayback, pp. 116–117.

Barzman, p. 127.

Roy Franklin Nichols, p. 124.

Ibid.

S. L. Carson, "Presidential Children: Abandonment, Hysteria and Suicide," p. 533.

New York Times, February 21, 1862.

In the most recent version of their work, Quinn-Musgrove and Kanter suggest that the death of Charles might have been a suicide, although the source they cite, Robert Winston, is in fact writing of the death of Robert Johnson, not older brother Charles. Quinn-Musgrove and Kanter, *America's Royalty*, p. 99. Robert W. Winston, *Andrew Johnson, Plebian and Patriot* (New York: Henry Holt, 1928), p. 494. See also Sol Barzman, p. 157, Hans L. Trefoussse, p. 168.

Robert W. Winston, *Andrew Johnson, Plebian and Patriot* (New York: Henry Holt, 1928), p. 494.

William McFeely, p. 521.

Harry Barnard, *Rutherford B. Hayes and His America.* p. 228.

Ibid.

Quinn and Kanter, p. 102.

Harry Barnard, *Rutherford B. Hayes and His America*, p. 229.

William DeGregorio, p. 280.

Ibid., p. 281.

"Abram Garfield Rites Are Set for Tomorrow," *Cleveland Plain Dealer*, October 17, 1958.

Thomas C. Reeves, *Gentleman Boss: The Life of Chester Alan Arthur* (New York: Alfred A. Knopf, 1975), p. 35.

Ibid., p. 275.

Ibid., p. 124.

Shelley Ross, *Fall From Grace* (New York: Ballantine, 1988), p. 123.

Alyn Brodsky, p. 91.

Ibid., p. 267.

Marion Cleveland Amen Obituary, *New York Times*, June 18, 1977.

Historians differ on whether or not he graduated. Sandra Quinn-Musgrove and Sanford Kanter imply that he did not. Quinn-Musgrove and Kanter, p. 137. William DeGregorio says yes. DeGregorio, p. 321.

William DeGregorio, p. 375.

Washington Post, February 21, 1980, p. D1

John S. Cooper, "White House Heroes," Part I, *www.suite101.com/article.cfm/4996/ 91157*, pp. 2, 3.

Kermit Roosevelt's suicide only became public knowledge in 1980. H. Paul Jeffers, *Theodore Roosevelt, Jr., The Life of a War Hero* (Novato, CA: Presidio, 2002), p. 228.

H. W. Brands, *TR, The Last Romantic*, p. 796.

Quinn-Musgrove and Kanter, p. 166.

Carl Sferrazza Anthony, *Florence Harding: The First Lady, the Jazz Age, and the Death of America's Most Scandalous President* (New York: William Morrow and Company, Inc., 1998), p. 112, death certificate.

Ibid., p. 557. Anthony's endnote 2 states that an affidavit of search in the probate court records of three counties showed "no record for a DeWolfe marriage as far back as 1831 and until 1969 . . ."

Ibid., pp. 26–29.

William DeGregorio, p. 435.

Francis Russell, *The Shadow of Blooming Grove: Warren G. Harding in His Times* (New York and Toronto: McGraw-Hill, 1968), pp. 358 and 360.

Carl Sferrazza Anthony, p. 531.

Francis Russell, p. 643.

Interviews with Andrea Blaesing and Elizabeth Ann Blaesing, April 18, 2002.

Quinn-Musgrove and Kanter state that his date of death was April 7, 1924. Quinn-Musgrove and Kanter, p. 172. This is incorrect, according to historians at Calvin Coolidge Memorial Foundation.

Some historians spell John's middle name "Aspinal," but the FDR Library confirms the "Aspinwall" spelling. *The Almanac of Famous People*, 6th Ed., Gale Research, 1998; J. J. Perling, p. 312.

Ellen Alderman and Caroline Kennedy, *In Our Defense: The Bill of Rights in Action* (New York: William Morrow and Company, Inc., 1991); and *The Right to Privacy* (New York: Borzoi

Books, Alfred A. Knopf, Inc., 1995).

Faye Fiore and Geraldine Baum, "Column One: 2 Nixon Daughters, 1 Big Feud: The former president's daughters aren't speaking to each other in a dispute over the control of his library. The rift stalls talks on acquiring his papers and further threatens his legacy." *Los Angeles Times* (Los Angeles, CA: The Times Mirror Company; *Los Angeles Times*, 2002), April 23, 2002, Start Page A1.

Ibid.

Margaret Carlson, "Peace Is at Hand: The Nixon daughters, feuding over their father's library, finally patch things up." *Time* magazine, May 13, 2002 (Time, Inc., 2002), p. 53.

Steve was the subject of a paternity suit, but its ultimate outcome showed that he was not the father of the child.

George Bush Presidential Library, College Station, Texas.